SOFTWARE ENGINEERING PROCESSES

Principles and Applications

Yingxu Wang, Prof., Ph.D.
Graham King, Prof., Ph.D.

Taylor & Francis
Taylor & Francis Group

Boca Raton   London   New York   Singapore

A CRC title, part of the Taylor & Francis imprint, a member of the
Taylor & Francis Group, the academic division of T&F Informa plc.

Library of Congress Cataloging-in-Publication Data

Wang, Yingxu
    Software engineering processes : principles and applications / Yingxu Wang and Graham King
      p. cm.
    Includes bibliographical references and index.
    ISBN 0-8493-2366-5 (alk. paper)
    1. Software engineering. I. King, G. A. II. Title.
QA76.758. W38 2000
005.1—dc21
                                             00-021371
                                              CIP

© 2000 by CRC Press LLC

No claim to original U.S. Government works
International Standard Book Number 0-8493-2366-5
Library of Congress Card Number 00-021371

0

To MY PARENTS   Y.W.
To MY WIFE AND DAUGHTERS   G.A.K.

" Deal with the difficult
while it is still easy.
Solve large problems
when they are still small.
Preventing large problems
by taking small steps
is easier than solving them.
By small actions
great things are accomplished."

– **Lao Tzu** (604-531 BC)

"Then there is a metatheoretic level where you study
the whole structure of a class of problems. This is the
point of view that we have inherited from logic and
computability theory."

– **Richard Karp** (Turing Award Winner, 1985)

Contents Summary

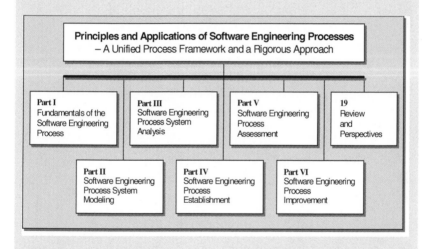

Principles and Applications of Software Engineering Processes
– A Unified Process Framework and a Rigorous Approach

Part I
Fundamentals of the
Software Engineering
Process

Part III
Software Engineering
Process System
Analysis

Part V
Software Engineering
Process
Assessment

19
Review
and
Perspectives

Part II
Software Engineering
Process System
Modeling

Part IV
Software Engineering
Process
Establishment

Part VI
Software Engineering
Process
Improvement

Table of Contents

Preface

S oftware engineering is a discipline of increasing importance in computing and informatics. The nature of problems in software engineering arise from the inherent complexity and diversity, the difficulty of establishing and stabilizing requirements, the changeability or malleability of software, the abstraction and intangibility of software products, the requirement of varying problem domain knowledge, the nondeterministic and polysolvability in design, the polyglotics and polymorphism in implementation, and the interactive dependency of software, hardware, and human being.

A new approach for dealing with the difficulties of large-scale software development emerged in the last decade. It sought to establish an appropriate software engineering process system. A software engineering process system is a set of empirical and best practices in software development, organization, and management which serves as an reference model for regulating the process activities in a software development organization.

Research into the software engineering process is a natural extension of scope from that of the software development methodologies necessary to meet the requirement for engineering large-scale software development. Conventional software development methodology studies cover methods, models, approaches, and phases of software development. The software engineering process, then, covers not only software development methodologies but also engineering methodologies and infrastructures for software corporation organization and project management.

As the scale of software increases continually and at an ever faster rate, greater complexity and professional practices become critical. Software development is no longer solely a black art or laboratory activity; instead, it has moved inexorably toward a key industrialized engineering process. In software engineering, the central role is no longer that of the programmers;

project managers and corporate management have critical roles to play. As programmers use programming technologies, software corporation managers seek organizational and strategic management methodologies, and project managers seek professional management and software quality assurance methodologies. These developments have resulted in a modern, expanded domain of software engineering which includes three important aspects: development methodology, organization and infrastructure, and management.

Understanding the need to examine the software engineering process follows naturally from the premise that has been found to be true in other engineering disciplines, that is, that better products result from better processes. For the expanded domain of software engineering, the existing methodologies that cover individual subdomains are becoming inadequate. Therefore, an overarching approach is sought for a suitable theoretical and practical infrastructure to accommodate all the modern software engineering practices and requirements. An interesting approach, which is capable of accommodating the complete domain of software engineering, has been recognized and termed the "software engineering process". Research into and adoption of the software engineering process paradigm will encompass all the approaches to software engineering.

To model the software engineering processes, a number of software process system models such as CMM, ISO 9001, BOOTSTRAP, ISO/IEC 15504 (SPICE) have been developed in the last decade. The variety and proliferation of software engineering process research and practices characterize the software engineering process as a young subdiscipline of software engineering that still needs integration and fundamental research. Studies in the software process reflect a current trend that shifts from controlling the quality of the final software product to the optimization of the processes that produce the software. It is also understood that the software engineering process, rather than the software products themselves, can be well established, stabilized, reused, and standardized.

A comprehensive and rigorous textbook is needed to address the unified and integrated principles, foundations, theories, frameworks, and best practices in software engineering process establishment, assessment, and improvement. This book is the first textbook intending to address both practical methodologies for process-based software engineering and the fundamental theories and philosophies behind them. This book covers broad areas of the new discipline of process-based software engineering such as software process foundations, modeling, analysis, establishment, assessment, and improvement.

The Aims of this Book

This book has emphasis on establishing a unified software engineering process framework integrating current process models, and developing a rigorous approach to process-based software engineering.

The aim is to investigate the philosophical, mathematical, and managerial foundations of software engineering; to establish a unified theoretical foundation for software engineering process modeling, analysis, establishment, assessment, and improvement; to explore the feature, orientation, interrelationship, and transformability of current process models; and to integrate the current process models and methodologies into a unified process framework–the software engineering process reference model (SEPRM).

Using a unified process framework, important current software process models are analyzed comparatively. The process frameworks and process capability determination methods of current models are formally described. As a means of introducing engineering rigor to process modeling, the algorithms of current process models are formally elicited. The ideas for mutual comparison between current models, the avoidance of ambiguity in application, and the simplification of manipulation for practitioners are addressed systematically.

The SEPRM is developed to show how to solve the problems of different process domains, orientations, structures, taxonomies, and methods. A set of process benchmarks has been derived that are based on a series of worldwide surveys of software engineering process practices. Based on the overarching SEPRM model and the unified process theory, this book demonstrates that for the first time, current process models can be integrated and their assessment results can be transformed from one to another. This has practical significance for those who are facing a requirement of multiple certifications, or to those who are pondering the implications of capability levels in different process models.

The Features of this Book

This book is characterized both as a comprehensive reference text for practitioners and as a *vade mecum* for students. The features of this book are that it:

- Investigates the philosophical, mathematical, and managerial foundations of software engineering

- Provides a unified software engineering process framework and an overarching software engineering process reference model (SEPRM)

- Develops a rigorous and practical approach to process-based software engineering

- Furnishes a detailed guide and case studies for practitioners in the industry

- Summarizes research findings, new methodologies, and applications in the discipline of software process engineering

Supplementary to the main body of text presented in this book, a number of reading aids is specially prepared for readers. A brief description of purposes is provided in front of each chapter, with a discussion of background of the chapter and its relationships to other parts and chapters of the book. A brief summary and a sidebar of knowledge structure are developed for each chapter which extract key knowledge and major achievements in each chapter. Annotated references are provided, helping readers to find related knowledge and/or alternative approaches in the literature, and to get familiar with the research and practices in the entire discipline of process-based software engineering.

The Structure of this Book

Software engineering process systems provide a fundamental infrastructure for organizing and implementing software engineering. The software engineering process discipline studies theories and foundations, modeling, analysis, establishment, assessment, improvement, and standardization of software processes. Viewing the knowledge structure of the software engineering process discipline as shown below, this book explores and investigates each topic systematically:

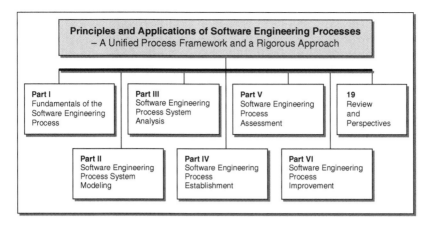

Part I – Fundamentals of the Software Engineering Process

The first part of this book investigates fundamentals of the software engineering process, and explores basic theories and empirical practices developed in this new discipline. A systematic and rigorous approach is taken in order to build a unified software engineering process framework.

The knowledge structure of this part, fundamentals of the software engineering process systems, is as follows:

- Chapter 1. Introduction
- Chapter 2. A Unified Framework of Software Engineering Process
- Chapter 3. Process Algebra
- Chapter 4. Process-Based Software Engineering

Based on the fundamental studies developed in this part, we will reach a key conclusion that software engineering is naturally a process system, and perhaps the most unique and complicated process system in all existing engineering disciplines.

Part II – Software Engineering Process System Modeling

Software engineering process system modeling explores a complete domain of software engineering processes, its architectures, and the fundamental framework. This part investigates current process models and contrasts them with the unified process framework developed in Part I. Comparative analyses of their interrelationships will be presented in Part III.

The knowledge structure of this part, software engineering process system modeling, is as follows:

- Chapter 5. The CMM Model
- Chapter 6. The ISO 9001 Model
- Chapter 7. The BOOTSTRAP Model
- Chapter 8. The ISO/IEC 15504 (SPICE) Model
- Chapter 9. The Software Engineering Process Reference Model: SEPRM

Part II adopts the unified process system framework developed in Part I as a fundamental common architecture in presenting the current process system models. A key conclusion of this part is that SEPRM is a superset paradigm of the current process models and the unified software engineering process framework. It is also demonstrated that the current process models can be fit within the unified framework of the software engineering process systems.

Part III – Software Engineering Process System Analysis

One of the most frequently-asked questions in the software industry is "what are the interrelationships between current process models?" In the previous part we presented formal views on individual process models. Part III explores the interrelationships between them via quantitative analysis, and investigates practical foundations of the software engineering process via benchmarking.

The knowledge structure of this part, software engineering process system analysis, is as follows:

- Chapter 10. Benchmarking the SEPRM Processes
- Chapter 11. Comparative Analysis of Current Process Models
- Chapter 12. Transformation of Capability Levels between Current Process Models

A rigorous and quantitative approach is adopted in order to analyze the characteristic attributes of process, the compatibility and correlation of process models, and the interrelationships and transformability of capability levels in different process models. Objective views on features and orientations of current process models are obtained from the analyses.

Part IV – Software Engineering Process Establishment

Software engineering process system establishment is the first important step in process-based software engineering because reliance is placed on both process assessment and improvement theories and practices. Working on the common foundation of a systematically established process system, this part explores methodologies and approaches to software engineering process system establishment such as process model reuse, tailoring, extension, and adaptation. The relationships of these methodologies with the theories and unified process framework developed in previous parts are discussed. Examples and case studies such as a parallel process model for software quality assurance, a minimum process model for software project management, a tailored CMM model, and an extension of ISO/IEC TR 15504 model are provided for demonstrating the applications of the process establishment methodologies.

The knowledge structure of this part, software engineering process establishment, is as follows:

- Chapter 13. Software Process Establishment Methodologies
- Chapter 14. An Extension of ISO/IEC TR 15504 Model

In this part we adopt a pragmatic view on software engineering process system establishment, assessment, and improvement. Systematic process establishment is recognized as the foundation for process assessment and improvement. A software engineering process system reference model, SEPRM, is viewed as the central infrastructure for process-based software engineering.

Part V – Software Engineering Process Assessment

Here we explore how the theories and algorithms of process assessment developed in Part I and Part II are applied in real world process system assessments. Three practical process assessment methodologies, the model-based, the benchmark-based, and the template-based, are developed. These assessment methodologies provide a step-by-step guide to carry out a process assessment, and show the applications of the unified software engineering process framework and SEPRM in the software industry.

The knowledge structure of this part, software engineering process assessment, is as follows:

- Chapter 15. Software Process Assessment Methodologies
- Chapter 16. Supporting Tools for Software Process Assessment

In this part process assessment is recognized as the basic measure for process improvement. Software process system assessment methodologies are presented in a phase-by-phase and step-by-step manner. Especially, a set of practical templates is developed to support an assessment according to the SEPRM reference model.

Part VI – Software Engineering Process Improvement

Part VI examines philosophies and generic approaches to software engineering process improvement. Three process improvement methodologies, the model-based, the benchmark-based, and the template-based, are developed. These improvement methodologies provide step-by-step guides on how to carry out a process improvement in accordance with the SEPRM process framework and methodologies. A set of case studies of real-world process improvement is provided, and key successful factors and benefits in process improvement are analyzed. Roles, prerequirements, and techniques of software process improvement that provide a useful guide for implementing process improvement according to the SEPRM reference model are described.

The knowledge structure of this part, software engineering process improvement, is as follows:

- Chapter 17. Software Process Improvement Methodologies
- Chapter 18. Case Studies in Software Process Improvement

These chapters recognize process improvement as a complicated, systematic, and highly professional activity in software engineering that requires theory and models, skilled technical and managerial staff, and motivated top management commitment. A system engineering perception on software process improvement is adopted rather than the all-too-prevalent philosophy of "fire-fighting". A new approach of benchmark-based process improvement is developed based on the philosophy that not all processes at Level 5 are the best and most economic solutions in process improvement. Instead, a software organization may play its hand so that its process capability is aimed at an optimizing profile which is better than that of its competitors in the same area.

In conclusion Chapter 19 presents a review and perspectives on the discipline of software engineering in general, and the software engineering process in particular.

The Audience for this Book

The readership of this book is intended to include graduate, senior-level undergraduate students, and teachers in software engineering or computer science; researchers and practitioners in software engineering; and software engineers and software project and organization managers in the software industry.

This book provides a comprehensive and rigorous text addressing unified and integrated principles, foundations, theories, frameworks, methodologies, best practices, alternative solutions, open issues for further research, and plentiful resources in software engineering process establishment, assessment, and improvement. Readers in the following categories will find the book adds value to their work and pursuits:

- **Software corporation executives** seeking strategic solutions in software engineering and wishing to avoid not seeing the forest for the trees

- **Software project managers** seeking cutting-edge technologies, best practices, and practical aids for improving process capabilities

- **Software engineers and practitioners** seeking empirical process repositories and classical process paradigms, and who want to optimize their roles in the software engineering process systems

- **Software engineering researchers** seeking state-of-the-art theories, approaches and methodologies, representative process paradigms, and open issues for further studies in software engineering and software engineering processes

- **Teachers and trainers** in software engineering seeking a systematic textbook on principles and applications of software engineering processes with a unified theoretical framework, comparative and critical analyses, a well-organized body of knowledge, in-depth comments, and questions and answers (in separate volumes)

- **Students and trainees** in software engineering seeking a systematic textbook providing academic views, clear knowledge structures, critical analyses, and plentiful annotated references

- **System analysts** seeking an insight into current process models and standards and their strengths and weaknesses; and wishing to mine a plentiful set of data surveyed in the software industry

- **Software process assessors** seeking theoretical and empirical guides, relationships and process capability transformation between current process models, as well as practical templates and supporting tools

- **Software tool developers** seeking an insight into process system framework structures, methodologies, algorithms, and interrelationships

This book is self-contained and only basic programming experience and software engineering concepts are required. This book is designed and expected to appeal to developers, scholars, and managers because software engineering methodologies and software quality issues are leading the agenda in the light of the information era.

Acknowledgments

This work was carried out in collaboration with the ISO/IEC JTC1/SC7, IEEE Technical Council on Software Engineering (TCSE) and Software Engineering Standard Committee (SESC), European Software Institute, the BSI Expert Panel ITS15-400 on Software Engineering, BCS, and IBM (Europe). The authors would like to acknowledge their support.

The authors sincerely thank our colleagues Ian Court, Margaret Ross, Geoff Staples, Alec Dorling, and Antony Bryant for many enjoyable discussions, debates, and proofreadings. We would like to acknowledge the inspiration from the work of C.A.R. Hoare, Watts Humphrey, Victor Basili, Barry Boehm, David L. Parnas, Jeff Kramer, Ian Sommerville, Manny Lehman, Wilhelm Schafer, Geoff Dromey, Ali Mili, Terry Rout, Mark Paulk, David Kitson, Khaled El Emam, Richard Messnarz, Pasi Kuvaja, Taz Duaghtrey, and Dilip Patel.

The authors would also like to thank the professional advice, practical assistance, or valuable help of Ron Powers, William Heyward, Dawn Mesa, Saba Zamir, Dawn Sullivan, Suzanne Lassandro, Jan-Crister Persson, Paula Kökeritz, Håkan Wickberg, Christine King, Huiling Yang, and Siyuan Wang.

Yingxu Wang
Graham King

Trademarks and Service Marks

BootCheck is a trademark of the BOOTSTRAP Institute

BOOTSTRAP is a service mark of the BOOTSTRAP Institute

CMM is a service mark of SEI

ISO 9000 is an international standard of ISO

ISO 9001 is an international standard of ISO

ISO/IEC 12207 is an international standard of ISO and IEC

ISO/IEC CD 15288 is a draft international standard of ISO and IEC

ISO/IEC TR 15504 is an international standard of ISO and IEC

PSP is a service mark of SEI

PULSE is a service mark of the PULSE Consortium

SEPRM (the unified Software Engineering Process Reference Model) is a service mark owned by the authors

TRILLIUM is a trademark of Northern Bell

TSP is a service mark of SEI

About the Authors

Yingxu Wang is Professor of Computer Science, and project manager with the Center for Software Engineering at IVF, Gothenburg, Sweden. He was a visiting professor in Computing Laboratory at Oxford University during 1995. He was awarded a PhD in software engineering by The Nottingham Trent University / Southampton Institute, UK.

Dr. Wang is a member of IEEE TCSE/SESC, ACM, and ISO/IEC JTC1/SC7, and is Chairman of the Computer Chapter of IEEE Sweden. He has accomplished a number of European, Swedish, and industry-funded research projects as manager and/or principal investigator, and has published over 100 papers in software engineering and computer science. He has won a dozen research achievement and academic teaching awards in the last 20 years. He can be reached at Yingxu.Wang@acm.org, Y.X.Wang@ieee.org, or http://msnhomepages.talkcity.com/CerfSt/DrYWang/ .

Graham King is Professor of Computer Systems Engineering at Southampton Institute, UK. He heads a research center which has a strong interest in all aspects of software engineering. He was awarded a PhD in architectures for signal processing by the Nottingham Trent University and has authored two previous books, and nearly 100 academic papers.

Dr. King is a member of the British Computer Society and the IEEE, and has been principal investigator for a number of research council and industry-funded projects. He can be reached at king_g@ieee.org.

PART I

FUNDAMENTALS OF THE SOFTWARE ENGINEERING PROCESS

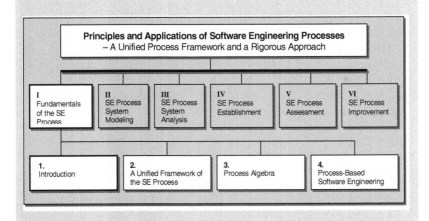

Principles and Applications of Software Engineering Processes
– A Unified Process Framework and a Rigorous Approach

I Fundamentals of the SE Process	II SE Process System Modeling	III SE Process System Analysis	IV SE Process Establishment	V SE Process Assessment	VI SE Process Improvement

1. Introduction	2. A Unified Framework of the SE Process	3. Process Algebra	4. Process-Based Software Engineering

The software engineering process is a set of sequential activities for software engineering organization, implementation, and management, which are functionally coherent and reusable. The first part of this book investigates fundamentals of the software engineering process and explores basic theories and empirical practices developed in this new discipline.

The knowledge structure of this part is as follows:

- Chapter 1. Introduction – The Nature of Software Engineering
- Chapter 2. A Unified Framework of the Software Engineering Process
- Chapter 3. Process Algebra
- Chapter 4. Process-Based Software Engineering

This part sets up the basic theories, a systematic and rigorous approach to the building of a unified software engineering process framework, and a set of defined and consistent terminology for the discipline of software engineering process and the practice of process-based software engineering.

Chapter 1 explores the philosophical, mathematical, and managerial foundations of software engineering. Chapter 2 establishes the theoretical foundations of process-based software engineering through investigating the generic software development organization model, process model, capability model, capability determination method, and process assessment/ improvement methods in software engineering. A formal process notation system, process algebra, is introduced in Chapter 3, followed by Chapter 4, which provides a generic view of methodologies of process-based software engineering.

The unified process theories and framework will be applied in the remaining parts of the book. The fundamental process theories will also be used as guidelines to organize the empirical best practices and processes that are found useful in the software industry.

Based on the fundamental studies developed in this part, we will reach a key conclusion that software engineering is perhaps the most unique discipline and the most complicated process system in almost all existing engineering disciplines.

Chapter 1

INTRODUCTION

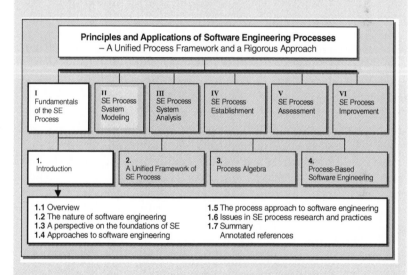

Principles and Applications of Software Engineering Processes
– A Unified Process Framework and a Rigorous Approach

I Fundamentals of the SE Process	II SE Process System Modeling	III SE Process System Analysis	IV SE Process Establishment	V SE Process Assessment	VI SE Process Improvement

1. Introduction	2. A Unified Framework of SE Process	3. Process Algebra	4. Process-Based Software Engineering

1.1 Overview
1.2 The nature of software engineering
1.3 A perspective on the foundations of SE
1.4 Approaches to software engineering

1.5 The process approach to software engineering
1.6 Issues in SE process research and practices
1.7 Summary
  Annotated references

1.1 Overview

Software engineering is an increasingly important discipline that studies large-scale software development methodologies and approaches. Recently, software engineering has shifted from a laboratory-oriented profession to a more industry-oriented process. This trend reflects the needs of the software industry moving toward integrating software development techniques with organization and management methodologies to form a process-based software engineering environment.

Historically, software engineering has focused on programming methodologies, programming languages, software development models, and tools. From the domain coverage point of view, these approaches have concentrated on purely technical aspects of software engineering. Areas now thought critical to software engineering – organizational and management infrastructures – have been largely ignored.

As software systems increase in scale, issues of complexity and professional practices become critical. Software development is no longer solely an academic or laboratory activity; instead, it has become a key industrialized process. In the software industry, the central role is no longer that of the programmers because project managers and corporate management also have critical roles to play. As programmers require programming technologies, the software corporation managers seek organization and strategic management methodologies, and the project managers seek management and software quality assurance methodologies. These needs have together formed the modern domain of software engineering which, to summarize, includes three important aspects: development methodology and infrastructure, organization, and management.

For this expanded domain of software engineering, the existing methodologies that cover individual subdomains are becoming inadequate. Therefore, an overarching approach is sought for a suitable theoretical and practical infrastructure in order to accommodate the full range of modern software engineering practices and requirements. An interesting approach, which is capable of subsuming most of these domains of software engineering, is the **process-based software engineering** methodology. Research into, and adoption of, the **software engineering process** approach may be made to encompass all the existing approaches to software engineering.

In defining a software engineering process system it is natural to think of a set of empirical practices in software development, organization, and management which comprises an abstract model of the entire set of activities within software development organizations. It is a case of standing back and seeing the bigger picture. Over and above the traditional aspects such as methods, models, approaches, and phases of software development, the software engineering process also covers engineering methodologies suitable for large-scale software development, organization, and management.

To model the software engineering processes, a number of software engineering process system models such as CMM, ISO 9001, BOOTSTRAP, and ISO/IEC TR 15504 (SPICE) have been developed in the last decade. Hereafter, a software engineering process system model will be shortly referred to as a **process model**. It is noteworthy that the term process model is different from the conventional **lifecycle model**. The latter consists of "phases" and is oriented on software development while the former consists of processes and covers all practices in large-scale software project organization, management, and development.

The variety and proliferation in software engineering process research and practices characterize the software engineering process an emerging discipline in software engineering that still needs integration and fundamental study. Studies in the software process reflect a current trend [Humphrey, 1995; Kugler and Rementeria, 1995; and Pfleeger, 1998] that shifts from controlling the quality of the final software product to the optimization of the processes that produce the software. It is also understood that, although almost all application software development are one-off projects, the software engineering process can be well-established, stabilized, reused, and standardized.

This book aims to investigate the philosophical, mathematical, and managerial foundations of software engineering. It intends to establish a unified theoretical foundation for software engineering process modeling, analysis, establishment, assessment, and improvement, and to explore the orientation, interrelationship, and transformability of current process models. It demonstrates one way forward in the drive to integrate the current process models and methodologies into a super reference model.

To achieve this, current software engineering process models are comparatively analyzed. Their process frameworks and process capability determination methods are rigorously described, and algorithms are formally elicited. This rigorous approach enables the mutual comparison between current process models, the avoidance of ambiguity in description, and the simplification of manipulation in applications.

A software engineering process reference model (SEPRM) is developed [Wang et al., 1996a/97a/98a/99e] for using as a vehicle with which to solve the problems of different process-domains, orientations, structures, frameworks and methods. A set of process benchmarks has been derived that is based on a series of worldwide surveys of software process practices [Wang et al., 1998a/99c], and these are used to support validation of the SEPRM model. Using the SEPRM approach, current process models can be integrated and their assessment results can be transformed from one to another for the first time.

In this chapter, the theoretical foundations of software engineering are explored. Then, existing approaches to software engineering in general and the process approach in particular are investigated. Based on the examination of the problems identified in software process research and practices, a systematic and algorithmic approach to software engineering process system modeling, analysis, establishment, assessment, and improvement is introduced.

1.2 The Nature of Software Engineering

The term software engineering was first reported in a European conference in 1968 [Naur and Randell, 1969; Bauer, 1976]. In this conference, Fritz Bauer introduced software engineering as:

> The establishment and use of sound engineering principles in order to obtain economical software that is reliable and works efficiently on real machines.

Since then, research on software engineering methodologies has been one of the major interests in computing science.

The nature of problems in software engineering has been addressed by Brooks (1975), McDermid (1991), and Wang et al. (1998b). A summary of fundamental characteristics of software engineering is listed below:

- Inherent complexity and diversity

- Difficulty of establishing and stabilizing requirements

- Changeability or malleability of software

- Abstraction and intangibility of software products

- Requirement of varying problem domain knowledge

- Nondeterministic and polysolvability in design

- Polyglotics and polymorphism in implementation

- Dependability of interactions between software, hardware, and human being

Along with the research and practices of software engineering, and the speedy development of the software industry, the definition of software engineering has further evolved. McDermid (1991) provided an extended definition of software engineering as follows:

> Software engineering is the science and art of specifying, designing, implementing and evolving – with economy, timeliness and elegance – programs, documentation and operating procedures whereby computers can be made useful to man.

This is representative of the second-generation definitions of software engineering.

Comparing the two definitions of software engineering, it can be seen that the former perceived software engineering as a **method** for **software** development while the latter implied that software engineering is both **science and art** for **programming**. Bearing in mind that the intention is to better represent trends and to recognize software engineering as an engineering discipline based on computer science while deemphasizing the uncontrollable and unrepeatable aspects of programming as an art, the authors [Wang et al., 1998b] offer a definition of software engineering as follows:

Definition 1.1 Software engineering is a discipline that adopts engineering approaches such as established methodologies, processes, tools, standards, organization methods, management methods, quality assurance systems, and the like to develop large-scale software with high productivity, low cost, controllable quality, and measurable development schedules.

In order to analyze the differences between the three generations of definition, a comparison of the implications and extensions of them is listed in Table 1.1. The table shows how the understanding of software engineering can be greatly improved by contrasting the perceived nature of software engineering as well as its means, aims, and attributes.

Table 1.1
Analysis of Representative Definitions of Software Engineering

No.	Nature	Means	Aims	Attributes of Aims
1	A method	Generic engineering Principles	Software	- economy - reliability - efficiency
2	The science and art	Life cycle methods: - specification - design - implementation - evolving	Program and document	- economy - timeliness - elegance
3	An engineering discipline	Engineering approaches: - methodologies - processes - tools - standards - organizational methods - management methods - quality assurance systems	Large scale software	- productivity - quality - cost - time

It is noteworthy that the perceived nature, means, and aims together with the attributes of their definitions have developed over time. The first-generation definition proposed software engineering as a method or approach to software development; the second-generation definition focused on scientific methods and art for programming; and the third-generation definition portrays software engineering as an engineering discipline for large-scale software development in an industrialized context.

1.3 A Perspective on the Foundations of Software Engineering

Having provided an improved understanding of the implications and extensions of software engineering as in Section 1.2, this section attempts to briefly investigate the foundations of software engineering from the perspectives of philosophy, theory and mathematics, and management science.

1.3.1 PHILOSOPHICAL FOUNDATIONS OF SOFTWARE ENGINEERING

Software engineering is a unique discipline that relies on special philosophical foundations at the top level. By contrasting the nature of software engineering with other engineering disciplines, it is clear that there are a number of interesting fundamental differences between them, as described below.

1.3.1.1 Virtualization vs. Realization

Given manufacturing engineering as an exemplar of conventional engineering, the common approach moves from abstract to concrete, and the final product is the physical realization of an abstract design. However, in software engineering, the approach is reversed. It moves from concrete to abstract. The final software product is the virtualization (coding) and invisible representation of an original design that expresses a real world problem. The only tangible part of a software product is its storage media or its run-time behaviors. As illustrated in Figure 1.1, this is probably the most unique and interesting feature of software engineering.

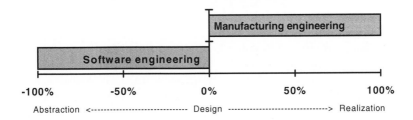

Figure 1.1 Difference between software engineering and other manufacturing engineering

1.3.1.2 Problem Domains: Infinite vs. Limited

The problem domain of software engineering encompasses almost all domains in the real world, from scientific problems and real-time control to word processing and games. It is infinitely larger when compared with the specific and limited problem domains of the other engineering disciplines. This stems from the notion of a computer as a universal machine, and is a feature fundamentally dominating the complexity in engineering implementation of large-scale software systems.

1.3.1.3 Design-Intensive vs. Repetitive-Production

As demonstrated in Figure 1.2, software development is a design-intensive process rather than a mass production process. In Figure 1.2 the design activities include specification, design, implementation, test, and maintenance; the production activities consist of duplication and package.

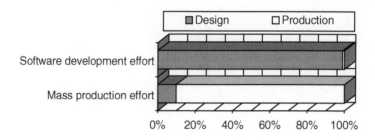

Figure 1.2 Effort distribution in software development and mass production

1.3.1.4 Process Standardization vs. Product Standardization

Directly related to the fact that software engineering is design intensive, it is recognized that the development of specific application software is characterized as mainly a one-off activity in design and production. This is because there are fewer standard software applications or products that can be mass produced save a few kinds of system software or general utilities.

Thus, for the design-intensive software development, the only element that can possibly be standardized and reused significantly are mainly the software engineering processes, not the final products themselves as in other manufacturing engineering disciplines.

1.3.1.5 Universal Logic Description vs. Domain-Specific Description

Software engineering adopts only a few fundamental logical structures, for example: sequence, condition, iteration, recursion, and concurrency. However, these provide a powerful descriptive and abstractive capability for dealing with the real-world problems.

By contrast, in other engineering disciplines, domain-and-application-specific notations have to be adopted that have limited descriptivity.

1.3.1.6 Software-Based Products vs. Physical Products

The creation as software of conventional physical products by the use of programmable and reconfigurable parts is a new and quiet industrial revolution. The 19th Century industrial revolutions were oriented on mass production by machinery and standardized process and components [Marshall, 1938]. The development of soft systems is a revolution that transforms the information processing and intelligent parts of the conventional physical products into software.

Based on the above discussion it might be argued that software engineering has become a discipline that is at the root of the knowledge structure of most engineering disciplines. The philosophical considerations explored in this subsection have attempted to clarify a set of fundamental characteristics of software engineering. These considerations also provide a basis for judging the soundness or unsoundness of specific technical solutions for software engineering, while not losing the sight of the woods for the trees.

1.3.2   THEORETICAL FOUNDATIONS OF SOFTWARE ENGINEERING

In theoretical computer science, the mathematical, logical, algebraic, and functional foundations of software engineering and programming methodologies have been studied. An outline structure of the theoretical and mathematical foundations of software engineering is described in Table 1.2.

Table 1.2
Structure of the Mathematical Foundations of Software Engineering

No.	System	Category	Branch
1	Applied mathematics		
1.1		Discrete mathematics	
1.1.1			Set theory
1.1.2			Mathematical logic
1.1.3			Functions
1.1.4			Relations
1.2		Advanced mathematics	
1.2.1			Abstract algebra
1.2.2			Process algebra
1.2.3			Category theory
1.2.4			Domain theory
1.3		Relevant mathematics	
1.3.1			Numerical methods

1.3.2			Probability theory
1.3.3			Graph theory
1.3.4			Queuing theory
1.3.5			Fuzzy logic
1.3.6			Statistics
2	**Theoretical computing**		
2.1		Classical theory	
2.1.1			Automata theory
2.1.2			Formal language theory
2.1.3			Computability theory
2.1.4			Algorithm complexity
2.1.5			Abstract data structures
2.2		Formal methods	
2.2.1			Algebraic specification
2.2.2			Process algebra (eg., CSP, CCS)
2.2.3			Model-oriented specification (eg., Z, VDM)
2.2.4			Refinement
2.2.5			Formal implementation
2.2.6			Verification and correction proof
2.2.7			Concurrent processing
3	**Relevant theories**		
3.1		Systems theory	
3.2		Information theory	
3.3		Measurement theory	
3.4		Cognitive theory	
3.5		Artificial intelligence	

In Table 1.2, the basic discrete mathematics (1.1) [Grassman and Tremblay, 1995] and classical theory of computing (2.1) [Hoare, 1969/89; Dijkstra, 1965/68/72; Knuth, 1974; Liskov and Zilles, 1974; Stoy, 1977; Gersting, 1982; Lewis and Papadimitriou, 1988; Bovet and Crescenzi, 1994] are assumed essential for software engineers. The formal methods (2.2) [Dijkstra, 1976; Gries, 1981; Hoare, 1985/95; Spivey, 1988; Dawes, 1991] are likely to influence the fundamental programming methods of the future, so that long term thinking engineers and managers will need to be aware of these topics. The relevant mathematics (1.3) [Hays, 1963; Waerden, 1969; Mathews, 1992; Grassman and Tremblay, 1995] and relevant theories (3) [Kolmogorov, 1933; Turing, 1936; MaCulloch and Pitts, 1943; Shannon, 1948; SSI, 1950, Ellis and Fred, 1962; Lindsay and Norman, 1972; Hartnett, 1977; Roberts, 1979; Kyburg, 1984; and Harvey, 1994] are optional for particular domain applications. The advanced mathematics (1.2) [Maclane, 1971; Hoare, 1985/86] are topics for long-term basic research in both software engineering and computer science.

1.3.3   MANAGERIAL FOUNDATIONS OF SOFTWARE ENGINEERING

Although the managerial foundations of software engineering have often been ignored in software engineering research and education, management sciences have, in fact, strongly influenced the formation of software engineering as a discipline. In tracing the history of software engineering, it has been found that many of the important concepts of software engineering, such as specification, requirement analysis, design, test, process, and quality, were borrowed or inspired by the methods and practices developed in management sciences and related engineering disciplines.

The managerial foundations of software engineering were cross-fertilized by the research in management science, systems theory, and quality system principles. A number of leading institutions, such as ISO TC176 and ASQ, are actively studying management theories and quality principles, as well as their application to software engineering. A brief structure of the management foundations of software engineering is summarized in Table 1.3.

Table 1.3
Structure of Managerial Foundations of Software Engineering

No.	Category	Subcategory
1	Basic theories	
1.1		Sociology
1.2		Anthropology
1.3		Semiotics
1.4		Linguistics
1.5		Psychology
2	Systems theory	
2.1		General systems theory
2.2		System design and analysis
2.3		System modeling and simulation
3	Management science	
3.1		Strategic planning
3.2		Operational theory
3.3		Decision theory
3.4		Organization methods
3.5		Management economics
4	Quality system principles	
4.1		Total quality management (TQM)
4.2		Business process reengineering
4.3		The Deming circle: Plan-Do-Check-Act (PDCA)

The fundamental theories of management are listed in Table 1.3(1). In this listing, sociology concerns organizational theory, anthropology addresses organizational culture, semiotics relates to the theories of communication and knowledge, linguistics studies language theory, and psychology concerns human behavior and learning.

As shown in Table 1.3(2), systems theory is used as a basis for management science and many other engineering disciplines. Systems theory was founded by Ludwig von Bertalanffy in the 1920s [SSI, 1950] in order to establish unified principles in both the natural and social sciences. Since then, books and articles on systems theory have proliferated [Ellis and Fred, 1962; Hall, 1967; Klir, 1972; Hartnett, 1977; Checkland and Peter, 1981]. Systems theory has provided interdisciplinary and strategic solutions that are qualitative and quantitative, organized and creative, theoretical and empirical, and pragmatic for a wide range of problems.

Management science, as shown in Table 1.3(3), is a scientific approach to solving system problems in the field of management. It includes operational theory [Fabrycky et al. 1984], decision theory [Keen and Morton, 1978; Steven, 1980], organization methods [Radnor, 1970; Kolb, 1970], strategic planning [Anthony, 1965; Khaden and Schultzki, 1983; William, 1991] and management economics [Richardson, 1966]. Management science provides management with a variety of decision aids and rules.

Three quality system principles, as listed in Table 1.3(4), have been developed during the 1970s and 1980s. The important quality management philosophies that are applicable to software engineering organization and management are TQM [Deming, 1982a/b/c; EFQM, 1993; Dunn and Richard, 1994], business process reengineering [Schein, 1961; Johansson et al., 1993; Thomas, 1994] and the Deming Circle [Deming, 1982a].

Studies of organization and management have, over time, covered methodologies for project management, project estimation, project planning, software quality assurance, configuration management, requirement/ contract management, document management, and human resource management. Table 1.4 provides a summary of the software engineering organization and management methodologies in practice.

The above review demonstrates that software engineering is a unique discipline with philosophical, mathematical, and managerial foundations based on interdisciplinary knowledge. Clearly it has borrowed from other disciplines and these discipline strands have combined to form the whole.

Table 1.4
Classification of Software Engineering
Organization and Management Methodologies

No.	Category	Typical Methods
1	Project management methods	Methods of metric-based, productivity-oriented, quality-oriented, schedule-driven, standard process models, benchmark analysis, checklist / milestones, etc.
2	Project estimation/ planning methods	Methods of KLOC metric, COCOMO model, the function-points, program evaluation and review technique (PERT), critical path method (CPM), Gantt chart, etc.
3	Software quality assurance methods	Methods of quality manual / policy, process review, process audit, peer review, inspection, defect prevention, subcontractor quality control, benchmark analysis, process tracking, etc.
4	Configuration management methods	Methods of version control, change control, version history record, software component library, reuse library, system file library, etc.
5	Requirement/contract management methods	Methods of system requirement management, software requirement management, standard contractual procedure, subcontractor management, purchasing management, etc.
6	Document management methods	Methods of document library, classification, access control, maintenance, distribution, etc.
7	Human resource management methods	Methods of position criteria, career development plan, training, experience exchange, domain knowledge development, etc.

1.4 Approaches to Software Engineering

As discussed in Section 1.4, software engineering is a discipline that has emerged from computer science and engineering and is based on inter-disciplinary theoretical and empirical methodologies. Initial approaches developed thus far have concentrated on technical aspects of software engineering such as programming methodologies, software development models, automated software engineering, and formal methods. While a cutting-edge approach, the software engineering process has been developed in the last decade for addressing the modern domain of software engineering. Each of these approaches will now be analyzed and examined.

1.4.1 PROGRAMMING METHODOLOGIES

A set of fundamental principles has been developed to cope with the complexity of problem specification and solution. Some of the important principles are abstraction, information hiding, functional decomposition, modularization, and reusability.

In tracing the history of programming methodologies, it can be seen that functional decomposition has been adopted in programming since the 1950s [McDermid, 1991]. In the 1970s the most significant progress in programming methodologies was structured programming [Hoare, 1972; Dijkstra, 1965/68/72] and abstract data types (ADTs) [Liskov and Zilles, 1974]. These methods are still useful in programming and software system design.

Since the 1980s object-oriented programming (OOP) [Stroustrup, 1986; Snyder, 1987] has been broadly adopted. Object-orientation technologies have inherited the merits of structured programming and ADTs, and have represented them in well-organized mechanisms such as encapsulation, inheritance, reusability, and polymorphism. The most powerful feature of OOP is the supporting of software reuse by inheriting code and structure information at object and system levels. It has been found that a built-in-test (BIT) method for OOP enables tests to be reused as that of code by extending the standard structures of object and object-oriented software to incorporate the BITs [Wang et al., 97c/98c/99b/d].

Along with the development of the Internet, and inspired by hardware engineering approaches, a new concept of programming, known as component-based programming, has been proposed. This approach is based on the "plug-in" and "add-on" software framework structure, and the broad availability of "commercial off-the-shelf (COTS)" software components.

1.4.2 SOFTWARE DEVELOPMENT MODELS

Programming methodologies have been mainly oriented on the conceptual and theoretical aspects of software engineering. A number of software development models have been introduced, among these are: the Waterfall [Royce 1970], Prototype [Curtis et al., 1987], Spiral [Boehm, 1988], the V [GMOD, 1992], Evolutionary [Lehman, 1985; Gilb, 1988; Gustavsson, 1989], and Incremental [Mills et al., 1980] models.

Supplementary to the above development models, a variety of detailed methods have been proposed for each phase of the development models. For instance, for just the software design phase, a number of design methods have been in existence, typically flowcharts, data flow diagrams, Nassi-Shneiderman charts, program description languages (PDLs), entity-relationship diagrams, Yourdon methods, and Jackson system development. Of course, some of these methods can also be used in other phases of software development.

The software development model approach attempts to provide a set of guidelines for the design and implementation of software at system and module levels. However, this approach has been focused on technical aspects of software development lifecycles. Detailed descriptions and applications of existing software development models may be referred to in classical software engineering books [McDermid, 1991; Pressman, 1992; Sommerville, 1996; and Pfleeger, 1998].

1.4.3 AUTOMATED SOFTWARE ENGINEERING

The programming methodologies and software development models described above provide theoretical and technical approaches for software design and implementation. In order to support the methodologies and models, an automated software engineering approach has been sought through the adoption of computer and system software as supporting tools.

The applications of artificial intelligence and knowledge-based techniques in software development have been a key focus in this approach. Two categories of software engineering tools, **computer-aided software engineering** (CASE) and the **unified modeling language** (UML) tools, have been built for automatic implementation of different software development phases. A review of a variety of software engineering support tools is listed in Table 1.5.

In recent years, the development of the UML tool set [Rumbaugh et al., 1998] has been one of the major achievements in automated software engineering. The UML tools enable many phases in software development to be fully or largely automated, such as in the phases of system design, software design, and code generation. Although reports of industry application experiences of UML in large-scale software development are still expected, encouraging progress towards automated software engineering is being made.

The main technical difficulties in automating software development are requirement acquisition and specification, application domain knowledge representation, and implementation correctness proof. As discussed in the philosophical considerations (a) and (b) in Section 1.3.1, all of these problems need further fundamental study. This has led to attention being paid to formal methods as described in the next section.

Table 1.5
Classification of Software Engineering Supporting Tools

No.	Category	Subcategory	Tool Coverage
1	System analysis tools		Requirement analysis, acquisition, specification, prototyping, modeling, interface generation, framework generation, etc.
2	Software development tools		
2.1		Requirement analysis/specification tools	Requirement analysis, domain knowledge representation, specification, etc.
2.2		Programming tools	Compilers, debuggers, code generators, reuse support systems, object-banks, programming environment, etc.
2.3		Testing tools	Module, integration, system, acceptance, prototype, object, and interface testing, etc.
2.4		Maintenance tools	Reverse engineering, re-engineering, reuse library, static analysis, dynamic analysis, etc.
3	CASE tools		UML, ClearCase, Analysts Toolkit, Automate+, Bachman Set, Excelerator, IEW, LBMS, Maestro, Oracle CASE, Select, System architect, Top CASE, Unix SCCS, Yourdon ADT, etc.

1.4.4 FORMAL METHODS

Formal methods are a set of mathematics and logic-based methodologies and theoretical principles for software development. The logical, algebraic, and functional foundations of programming have been studied in formal methods. A number of applications of formal methods in safety-critical system design and program correctness proof have been reported [Hayes, 1987; Schneider, 1989]. The category theory developed in pure mathematics science has been found useful for establishing a unified foundation of formal methods [Hoare, 1995].

As structured programming and object-oriented programming solved many problems in software development in the 1970s and 1980s, formal methods now attempt to dig deeply into the nature of programming and to provide new solutions for rigorous and correction-provable software development. A knowledge structure of the formal approach to software engineering has been described in Table 1.2 (Part 2.2). Although our knowledge about the nature of programming has been greatly improved by the studies of formal methods, only a few of them, such as Z and SDL, have been directly applied in real-world software engineering.

Along with the fast growth of the Internet and the Internet-based programming environment in the 1990s, there has been evidence that the software engineering agenda has been driven by the industry and users. Technical innovations in everyday software engineering practices have been a major force in industrialized software engineering progress in recent years, but many new gaps have been found that require theoretical study in the overall software engineering fabric.

Table 1.6
Domain Coverage of the Approaches to Software Engineering

No.	Approach	Description	Coverage of SE Problems		
			Technique	Organization	Management
1	Programming methodologies	- functional decomposition - structural programming - object-oriented programming - component-based programming	H	L	L
2	Software development models	- life cycle model - waterfall model - spiral model - rapid prototype model - other combined models	H	M	L
3	Automated software engineering	- CASE tools - UML tool - other tools	H	L	L
4	Formal methods	- CSP - SDL - Z - Clean room - other	H	L	L
5	Software engineering processes	- CMM - Trillium - BOOTSTRAP - ISO/IEC 15504 - SEPRM - other	H	H	H

Notes: H – High, M – Medium, L – low

1.4.5 THE SOFTWARE ENGINEERING PROCESS

The software engineering facets described in Sections 1.4.1 through 1.4.4 have mainly concentrated on the aspects of software engineering as summarized in Table 1.6. Important areas of software engineering such as the organization and management infrastructures have been left untouched. Further, the systems processes by which software is created are so far unaddressed. This draws attention to the emergence of a system process approach to software engineering.

The software engineering process approach concerns systematical, organizational, and managerial infrastructures of software engineering. It is necessary to expand the horizons of software engineering in this way because of the rapidly increasing complexity and scale demanded by software products. The need to improve software quality is also a driving force for managers.

In a view of domain coverage it is recognized that the conventional approaches, methodologies, and tools that cover individual subdomains of software engineering are inadequate. Thus, it makes sense to think in terms of an overarching set of approaches for a suitable theoretical and practical infrastructure that accommodates both new demands and improves on existing methodologies. An interesting way forward, which is capable of accommodating the full domain of modern software engineering, is that of the software engineering process.

1.5 The Process Approach to Software Engineering

The software process was originally studied as a software management method [Gilb, 1988; Humphrey, 1989], a quality assurance approach [Evans and Marciniak, 1987; ISO, 1991], or as a set of software development techniques [Curtis, 1987; Fayad, 1997a]. The reorientation of the software process to the software engineering process reflects recent trends in seeking an ideal means for organizing and describing the whole process framework of software engineering.

Two events in 1987, the development of CMM and of ISO 9000, marked the full emergence of the software engineering process as a new discipline. The software engineering process deals with foundations, modeling, establishment, assessment, improvement, and standardization of software processes. Generally, a process may be described as a set of linked activities that take an input and transform it to create an output. The software engineering process as a system is no different; it takes a software requirement as its input, while the software product is its output.

Definition 1.2 The software engineering process is a set of sequential practices that are functionally coherent and reusable for software engineering organization, implementation, and management. It is usually referred to as the **software process**, or simply the **process**.

Studies of the software process require an interdisciplinary theoretical and empirical basis. It is interesting to note that the term "software process" was inspired by management sciences [Eskiciogla and Davies, 1981; Bignell et al., 1985; Johansson et al., 1993]. Thus, the concept of a software process is more general than that of the conventional term "process" as developed in computer science where process is defined as "an execution of a subroutine [Brinch, 1973; Milenkovic, 1992]."

This section reviews the historical evolution of the process approach to software engineering, introduces the current process system models, and investigates problems identified in the process approach.

1.5.1 REVIEW OF HISTORY OF THE SOFTWARE ENGINEERING PROCESS

There are two main historical threads in tracing the emergence of the software engineering process approach. They are software engineering itself and management science. Research into the engineering processes and management principles in management sciences began in the 1960s [Simon, 1960; Schein, 1961; Ellis and Fred, 1962; Juran et al., 1962; Anthony, 1965; Richardson, 1966; Hall, 1967]. In the 1970s and 1980s, management science was well established in almost all branches as shown in Table 1.3 [Radnor, 1970; Grayson, 1973; Hartnett, 1977; Keen and Morton, 1978; Crosby, 1979; Brech, 1980; Juran and Gryna, 1980; Deming, 1982a/b/c; Khaden and Schultzki, 1983; Fabrycky et al., 1984; Leavitt, 1988]. Worthy of particular note are Crosby, Juran and Deming who developed the approach of quality conformity to requirements and specifications [Crosby, 1979; Juran, 1980; Deming, 1982a] and proposed a number of agendas that must be carried out in order to deliver total quality. These concepts have largely influenced software development processes and software quality assurance technology. In 1982, the **Deming Circle**, Plan-Do-Check-Act (PDCA), was proposed in management science studies [Deming, 1982a] and has drawn much interest in software process modeling and analysis. Then, a project designated ISO TC176 in 1987 to develop an international standard for quality systems [ISO 9000, 1991/93/94] that are applicable to a wide range of engineering systems including software engineering [ISO 9001, 1989/94] was implemented.

In the software engineering sector, research into the software engineering process can be traced to as early as 1965 in Weinwurm and Zagorski's work. However, interest in the software process was initiated in the 1970s after the so called "software crisis" [Naur and Randell, 1969; Baker, 1972; Brooks, 1975; Hoare, 1975]. The software process as a recognized branch of software engineering was formed in the 1980s following the work of Basili (1980), Aron (1983), Agresti (1986), Evans (1987), Boehm (1981/86/87), Gilb (1988), Humphrey (1987/88/89). These works led to the development of the capability maturity model (CMM) [Humphrey, 1987; Paulk et al., 1993a/b/c] and several other models, such as the IEEE Software Engineering Standards [IEEE, 1983] and British Standard BS 5750 [BSI, 1987] in the late 1980s. Since then the software engineering process has attracted much interest and recognition in software engineering research and practices.

1.5.2   CURRENT SOFTWARE ENGINEERING PROCESS METHODS AND MODELS

A number of software process models have been developed in the last decade such as TickIT [DTI, 1987; TickIT, 1987/92], ISO 9001 [ISO 9001, 1987/94], CMM [Paulk et al., 1993a/b/c/95a; Humphrey, 1987/88/89], BOOTSTRAP [BOOTSTRAP team, 1993], ISO/IEC 12207 [ISO/IEC 12207, 1995]; ISO/IEC TR 15504 (SPICE) [ISO/IEC 15504, 1997/98], and a number of regional and internal models [BSI, 1987; Trillium, 1992/94]. According to a recent worldwide survey [Wang et al., 1998a/99c], the ISO 9000 serial models are the most popular, followed by CMM and ISO/IEC TR 15504. Some regional, internal, and industry sector process models, such as Trillium, also share a significant part of application in the software industry. A previous survey of the distribution of the models in 1996 [Kugler and Rementeria, 1995] had shown a similar trend to that of the above distribution.

Based on the statistics and historical and theoretical significance, this book selects the four most used models for analysis. They are: CMM, ISO 9001, BOOTSTRAP, and ISO/IEC TR 15504 (SPICE), where SPICE is a synonym or the international project name of ISO/IEC TR 15504 during its development.

1.5.2.1 CMM

The SEI Capability Maturity Model (CMM) was initially developed as an assessment model for software engineering management capabilities [Humphrey, 1987/88]. As such it was expected that it would provide useful measures of organizations bidding or tendering for software contracts. It was soon found that the concept of "process" for software engineering has more utility than that of capability assessment, and that software development organizations may use the capability model for internal process improvement. As a result of this deeper understanding, new practices in process-based software engineering have been emerging in the last decade. This is to be considered as one of the important inspirations arising from CMM and related research.

CMM modeled 18 key practice areas and 150 key practices [Paulk et al., 1993a/b/c]. These key practices and key practice areas were grouped into a 5-level process capability scale known as the initial, repeatable, defined, managed, and optimizing levels. Detailed description of CMM will be provided in Chapter 5, but what is significant is the systematic breakdown of software engineering activities, and the analytical judgement that the model allows.

1.5.2.2 ISO 9001

From another angle of management science looking at software engineering, ISO 9001 (1989/94) and ISO 9000-3 (1991) were developed within the suite of ISO 9000 international standards for quality systems [ISO 9000, 1991/93/94]. ISO 9001 (Quality Systems – Model for Quality Assurance in Design, Development, Production, Installation, and Servicing) and ISO 9000-3 (Quality Management and Quality Assurance Standards Part 3 – Guidelines for the Application of ISO 9000 to the Development, Supply, and Maintenance of Software) are important parts of ISO 9000, and are designed for software engineering.

ISO 9001 modeled a basic set of requirements for establishing and maintaining a quality management and assurance system for software engineering. It identified 20 main topic areas and 177 management issues, and categorized them into three subsystems known as management, product management, and development management. Perhaps because of its simplicity, ISO 9001 has been the most popular process model that is adopted in the software industry [Mobil Europe, 1995; Wang et al., 1998a]. Detailed description of ISO 9001 will be provided in Chapter 6, but an important characteristic of ISO 9001 is the underlying notion of a threshold standard and pass/fail criteria.

1.5.2.3 BOOTSTRAP

BOOTSTRAP [BOOTSTRAP team, 1993; Koch, 1993; Haase et al., 1994; Kuvaja et al., 1994], released in 1993, was an extension of the CMM model that was customized to European ideas. A number of new technology processes and a flexible and precise rating method had been developed in BOOTSTRAP. In BOOTSTRAP, more technical and methodological process activities were tackled and, when an attempt was made add these process activities into the CMM capability model, a mixture of process and capability in a single dimension was produced. This was thought unhelpful and it began to be understood that there was a need to distinguish process (the software engineering activities) from capability (the measurement of the software engineering activities). The concept of a two-dimensional process model evolved from this work.

BOOTSTRAP modeled 3 process categories, 9 attributes, and 201 quality system attributes. These attributes are rated against 5 capability levels identical to that of CMM. However, intermediate process attributes were introduced to measure the differences between the defined capability levels. A main feature, then, is a more precise capability measure rounded to a quarter of a capability level. Detailed description of BOOTSTRAP will be provided in Chapter 7.

1.5.2.4 ISO/IEC TR 15504 (SPICE)

In 1992, the ISO/IEC JTC1 software engineering committee recognized a need to develop a new international standard for software process assessment and improvement [ISO/IEC 1992]. Then, after a six-year international collaborative project (SPICE) within the ISO/IEC JTC1/SC7/WG10, an ISO 15504 Technical Report suite was completed.

Inspired by BOOTSTRAP, ISO/IEC 15504 has recognized the value inherent in separating the "process" dimension from the "capability" dimension for a software engineering process model. As a result, a true two-dimensional process system model was developed for the first time. However, what is interesting is that in the ISO/IEC TR 15504 model, the activities for the process dimension and the attributes for the capability dimension at some points overlap. This means that there is still a need to further distinguish the process activities and the measurement attributes and indicators in the two dimensions.

ISO/IEC TR 15504 modeled 5 process categories, 35 processes, and 201 base practices. The processes are measured at 6 levels with 9 attributes. As a new 2-dimensional process model, the rating method of ISO/IEC 15504 is quite complicated. Detailed description of ISO/IEC 15504 will be provided in Chapter 8.

1.6 Issues in Software Engineering Process Research and Practices

As software engineering process study is at an early stage in its development, there are still debates concerning it. A number of criticisms have been raised about the process approach in general and CMM in particular. In a paper entitled "A Critical Look at Software Capability Evaluation," Bollinger and McGowan (1991) investigated the subjectivity and inaccuracy of the CMM process model and the process assessment methodology. Brodman and Johnson (1994) pointed out the need to tailor CMM for small software organizations, and the fact that there was no such mechanism available.

Further, a series of criticisms in a special column *in Communications of the ACM* was published recently entitled, "Software Development Process: the Necessary Evil?" [Fayad et al., 1997a] and "Process Assessment: Considered Wasteful" [Fayad, 1997b]. Although this column was mainly focused on CMM, it has triggered a lot of interesting discussion on both progress and problems inherent in the process approach and current process models.

1.6.1 PROBLEMS AND OPEN ISSUES IDENTIFIED

Generally, problems identified in the software engineering process debate may be traced to three root causes:

- Lack of formal description
- Chaotic interrelationships
- Deficiency of validation

This subsection describes the problems in the three categories. Solutions for these problems will be sought systematically throughout this book.

1.6.1.1 Problems in Process Modeling

Currently, it is seen as necessary to simplify the diversity of process models and to give legitimacy to modeling and analysis by creating a unified theory and integrated framework, and by introducing formal and algorithmic description.

(a) Basic requirements for process models

A variety of international, regional, and internal process models have been developed with various sizes, purposes, orientation, and structures. These models need to be summarized in terms of their methodologies, usage, and applications. More importantly, the following issues have to be tackled:

- What are the basic requirements for a process model?

- What should be essentially covered by a process model?

- What is the complete view of the software engineering process system?

These issues are investigated in Chapter 2.

(b) Classification of process models

The existing process models have been developed using various approaches such as checklists, independent models, derived models, empirical models, or descriptive models. Classifying the existing models from the viewpoints of model frameworks and methodologies is addressed in Chapter 2.

(c) Formal description of process models

Almost all existing process models are empirical-and-descriptive models. These models lack rigorous and formal description of model structure, process framework, adequacy rating scale, capability rating scale, and capability determination algorithm. Problems of ambiguity, instability, too much subjectivity, and inaccuracy in process assessment and application were identified in existing process models.

In Chapters 5 - 9, the frameworks of the major current models will be formally described. Their capability determination methods will be systematically elicited in order to create the algorithms for the current models. The formal approach will be demonstrated as being particularly useful for process designers, analysts, users, assessors, and tool developers, and will enable them to understand the current process system models.

1.6.1.2 Problems in Process Analysis

In analyzing current process models, one cannot avoid problems of different orientation, incompatibility, and nontransformability. This subsection briefly describes the problems in process system analysis. A detailed exploration is provided in Chapters 10 through 12.

(a) Orientation

The current process models exhibit different orientations in software process modeling. Divisions between current process models cause many problems in comparative analysis and modeling. In order to integrate the existing models and to create a complete view of the software engineering process, this book will develop a new reference model approach in which the process systems of current models are treated as subsets of a super reference model – the SEPRM [Wang et al., 1996a/97a/98a/99e]. This will be explored in Chapter 9.

(b) Compatibility

Ensuring system compatibility is a proven successful practice in the software and computer industry. However, the compatibility of the current process models and their assessment results are found to be quite limited. By treating the current process models as subsets of SEPRM in Chapters 10 – 12, the compatibility problem can be solved without the cost of changing the existing models.

(c) Transformability

Comparability and transformability between models are fundamental requirements for a mature scientific discipline. By relating the assessment results of process capability levels between the current process models, a software development organization can avoid being assessed several times as required by different process models at very high cost. However, transformability between the current process models has never been studied and it seems quite a hard problem for the conventional one-to-one mapping approach. By treating current models as subsets of SEPRM and by establishing quantitative transformability, the capability transformation problem will be solved in Chapter 12.

1.6.1.3 Problems in Model Validation

Current process models have only provided some informal discussions on rationales at the middle (process) level. The validation of a process system both at the highest (organization) and lowest (attribute) levels are conspicuous by their absence. At the top level, a least-complete set of fundamental process categories of a software development organization has to be identified and modeled. At the bottom level, the attributes of a complete set of process practices should be identified and benchmarked. These points are expanded as follows:

(a) Functional process organization in a software development organization

It is observed that some models organize processes at a number of fixed capability levels, some models group processes into different management topic areas, and some models categorize processes according to life-cycle practices. This poses the question: what is the best approach for modeling the software process system at the highest level? A structure of process systems with the organization, development, and management subsystems will be investigated in Chapter 2.

(b) Benchmark of process attributes

Quantitative analysis and benchmark of process attributes are other foundations needed to validate a model at the lowest level. Reports of benchmarks for the current models are rarely to be found in literature. Therefore, a series of worldwide surveys on a superset of processes has been conducted [Wang et al., 1998a/99c]. A set of benchmarks on process attributes, such as mean weighted importance and ratios of significance, practice, and effectiveness, have been derived to validate the SEPRM reference model, and to support the analysis of the current models. The benchmarks and their applications will be addressed in Chapter 10.

1.6.2 METHODS AND APPROACHES OF THIS WORK

There should be a systematic solution to the class of the problems identified in Section 1.6.1, and this would enable a unified software engineering process system framework. To achieve this it is necessary to adopt a new set of approaches, as shown in Table 1.7, which includes a comparison with conventional methods.

The rationales of the methods and approaches adopted or developed in this book are described below.

Table 1.7
Methods and Approaches to Software Engineering Process Modeling

Aspect	Methods Used in Existing Work	Methods Developed in This Book
Modeling	- empirical-and-descriptive modeling - natural language description	- formal-and-descriptive modeling - a formal and rigorous approach
Analysis	- one-to-one - qualitative - unidirectional mapping	- many-to-many - quantitative - bidirectional mapping
Model Coverage	- individual aspects and orientation - varying overlaps	- unified fundamental framework - overarching superset model
Model Validation	- post-industry trials	- studies of theoretical foundations - characterize BPAs by quantitative attribute benchmarking - pre-industry survey of practical foundations of practices and attributes

1.6.2.1 Methods in Process System Modeling

Potential modeling techniques for software engineering process systems can be empirical/formal, descriptive/prescriptive, and qualitative/quantitative. The current process system models such as ISO/IEC TR 15504, CMM, ISO 9001, and BOOTSTRAP are empirical-and-descriptive models. These models use natural language to describe the process system models, which creates redundancy, ambiguity, and difficulty in quantification. Instead of the descriptive "what to do" for a process model, a prescriptive approach may be taken to model "how to do" in a process system. However, this is not the main goal of system modeling because it diverges from the abstraction principles used in modeling a complicated process system.

A formal and algorithmic approach is adopted in this book. The rigorous approach is suitable for describing the methodologies of existing and new process system models because it offers less ambiguity, increases accuracy, and enables quantification and tool support.

1.6.2.2 Methods in Process System Analysis

Conventional analysis methods for the process systems are mainly one-to-one, qualitative, and unidirectional. The one-to-one approach is difficult to use in exploring the whole picture of the major process system models, and the complexity in pairwise analysis of n models is found to be of an explosive exponential order. The qualitative approach is carried out at high levels of a process system, which is quite subjective and sometimes leads to contradiction between different authors. The single directional mapping from one model to another describes only one side of a coin, because the mapping between models has been recognized as being asymmetric [Wang et al., 1997a/99e].

These are the reasons why a many-to-many, quantitative, and bidirectional approach is used to enable efficient, less subjective, and complete mapping and analysis of current process system models.

1.6.2.3 Methods for Process Model Integration

Existing process system models cover different areas of software engineering activities with varying orientation and overlaps. Generally, these models focus on different aspects of an entire software engineering process system domain. To incorporate the current process system models as member subsystems, a unified process system framework is needed. To achieve this, an overarching software process system reference model is developed in Chapter 9.

1.6.2.4 Methods for Process Model Validation

The validation of process models may be pre or postrelease. The postrelease option is less satisfactory. This is because lessons learned can only be internalized by changes to the model which, being late in the development cycle, will be costly. It is far better to validate the model prerelease, and to do this it is necessary to base the validation on quantitative methods and on large-scale surveys of the effectiveness of existing models.

1.7 Summary

In this chapter we have seen that the process approach to software engineering is a significant trend that has been recognized by both academics and the software industry.

Software engineering has been defined as a discipline that adopts engineering approaches to develop large-scale software with high productivity, low cost, controllable quality, and measurable development schedules.

Engineering approaches to large-scale software development have been identified as established methodologies, processes, tools, standards, organization methods, management methods, and quality assurance systems.

The software engineering process is a set of sequential practices, which are functionally coherent and reusable, for software engineering organization, implementation, and management. It is usually referred to as the software process, or simply the process.

For the newly expanded domain of software engineering, the existing methodologies covering individual subdomains are becoming inadequate. Therefore, an overarching approach is sought for a suitable theoretical and practical infrastructure capable of accommodating the full range of modern software engineering practices and requirements. The whole domain of software engineering is potentially covered by the process-based software engineering methodology. Research into, and adoption of, the software engineering process approach may be made to encompass all the existing approaches to software engineering.

The basic knowledge structure of this chapter is as follows:

Chapter 1. Introduction

- General
  - Purposes of this chapter
    - To investigate the nature and philosophical, mathematical, and managerial foundations of software engineering

    - To review existing approaches to software engineering

    - To explore the new approach of process-based software engineering and related issues in research and practices

- The nature of software engineering
  - Evolvement of definitions of software engineering
    - A programming method
    - A scientific branch and art
    - An engineering discipline

  - Fundamental characteristics of software engineering
    - The inherent complexity and diversity
    - The difficulty of establishing and stabilizing requirements
    - The changeability or malleability of software
    - The abstraction and intangibility of software products
    - The requirement of varying problem domain knowledge
    - The nondeterministic and polysolvability in design
    - The polyglotics and polymorphism in implementation
    - The dependability of interactions between software, hardware, and human being

- A perspective on the foundations of software engineering
  - Philosophical foundations of software engineering

  - Theoretical foundations of software engineering
    - Applied mathematics
    - Theoretical computing
    - Relevant theories

  - Managerial foundations of software engineering
    - Basic theories
    - System theory
    - Management science
    - Quality system principles

- Approaches to software engineering
  - Programming methodologies
  - Software development models
  - Automated software engineering
  - Formal methods
  - The software engineering process

- The process approach to software engineering
  - History and interdisciplinary background
  - Current software process models
    - CMM
    - ISO 9001
    - BOOTSTRAP
    - ISO/IEC TR 15504
    - SEPRM

- Issues in software engineering process research and practices
  - Problems identified
    - Problems in process modeling
    - Problems in process analysis
    - Problems in model validation

  - Methods and approaches of this work
    - Methods in process system modeling
    - Methods in process system analysis
    - Methods for process model integration
    - Methods for process model validation

The above sidebar is designed for review of the subject topics and their relations developed in this chapter.

With the understanding of the structure of theoretical foundations of software engineering and the identification of the problems in the process approach, it is necessary to develop a unifying process infrastructure through Part I to Part III in this book. The unified process framework will accommodate and integrate existing process models, and solve a large proportion of the problems identified so far in software engineering process research and practices. The unified theory and process framework will be applied in Parts IV to VI to derive practical methodologies of process system establishment, assessment, and improvement for practitioners.

The main aim of this book is to advocate a systematic and rigorous approach to process-based software engineering. It is expected that by this approach, existing chaotic problems in current process models can be solved, and a unifying process approach to software engineering can be established with fully investigated foundations and integrated methodologies.

It is also expected that this approach will help process system analysts and developers to mutually compare multimodels; practitioners to better understand existing models; assessors to easier manipulate current models with less ambiguity; and tool developers to accurately implement supporting tools.

Annotated References

The term software engineering was first advocated by Bauer in 1968 [Naur and Randell, 1969]. Many good textbooks on generic software engineering have been published in the 1990s. McDermid (1991) edited an academic reference book covering almost every aspect of software engineering and related science branches. Sommerville (1996) presented a more formal approach to software engineering. Pressman (1992) wrote a popular text for practitioners. Pfleeger (1998) published an easy reading text describing the latest development with informative resources.

Software engineering methodologies have evolved over the following orientations, and all the methodologies developed in the last three decades have shown effectiveness and broad usability:

- Programming methodologies: see Dijkstra, 1968/76; Knuth, 1974; Liskov and Zilles, 1974; Hoare, 1969/72/86; and Gries, 1981.

- Software development models: see Waterfall (Royce, 1970), Prototype (Curtis et al., 1987), Spiral (Boehm, 1988), V (GMOD, 1992), Evolutionary (Lehman, 1985; Gilb, 1988; Gustavsson, 1989), and Incremental (Mills et al., 1980).

- Case tools and automated software engineering: see Boehm et al., 1986; Wasserman, 1990; Bandinelli, 1992; Barghouti and Krishnamurthy, 1993; and Rumbaugh et al., 1998.

- Formal methods: see Dijkstra, 1976; Gries, 1981; Hoare, 1985/95; Milner, 1989; Hayes, 1987; Spivey, 1988; Dawes, 1991; and Bandinelli, 1992.

- Software processes: Weinwurm and Zagorski (1965) was recognized as the first article that discussed software process. Note that the process concept for software development was initiated earlier than the term "software engineering" [Bauer, 1968, in Naur and Randell, 1969]. For further development, see Basili, 1980; Aron, 1983; Agresti, 1986; Evans, 1987; Boehm, 1986/94; Humphrey, 1987/88/89/99; Gilb, 1988. On process-based software engineering, see Barghouti and Krishnamurthy, 1993; Garg and Jazayeri, 1995; Wang et al., 1997a/99c/e.

On computer science foundations for software engineering processes, see Dijkstra, 1965/68/72/76; Weinberg, 1971; Baker, 1972; Knuth, 1974; Liskov and Zilles, 1974; Brooks, 1975/87/95; Hoare, 1969/72/75/85/86/89/95; Stoy, 1977; Boehm, 1976/81/88; Gries, 1981; Gersting, 1982; Lewis and Papadimitriou, 1988; Spivey, 1988; Dawes, 1991; Harvey, 1994; and Bovet and Crescenzi, 1994.

On mathematical foundations for software engineering processes: see Hays, 1963; Waerden, 1969; Maclane, 1971; Hoare, 1986; Mathews, 1992; Grassman and Tremblay, 1995.

On managerial science foundations for software engineering processes, see:

- Systems theory (SSI, 1950)

- Operational theory (Fabrycky et al., 1984)

- Decision theory (Keen and Morton, 1978; Steven, 1980)

- Organization methods (Radnor et al., 1970; Kolb et al., 1970)

- Strategic planning (Anthony, 1965; Khaden and Schultzki, 1983; William, 1991)

- Management economics (Richardson, 1966)

- Quality system principles (Shewhart, 1939; Juran, 1962/80/88/89; Crosby, 1979; Deming, 1982a/b/86; Imai, 1986; Buckland et al., 1991).

A variety of software process models, international, regional, and internal, have been developed in the last decade. See TickIT [DTI, 1987, TickIT, 1987/92], ISO 9001 [ISO 9001, 1989/94], CMM [Paulk et al., 1991/93a/b/c/1995a; Humphrey, 1987/88/89], Trillium [Trillium, 1992/94], BOOTSTRAP [BOOTSTRAP team, 1993], ISO 12207 [ISO 12207, 1995], ISO/IEC TR 15504 (SPICE) [ISO/IEC 15504, 1992/93/96/97/98], and SEPRM [Wang et al., 1996a/97a/98a/99c/e].

Questions and Problems

1.1 What is the nature of software engineering? Is software engineering unique or special in relation to the other engineering disciplines?

1.2 Software engineering is dependent on interdisciplinary foundations. Can you identify any of these disciplines that software engineering is based on?

1.3 There is an argument that programming has no scientific foundations because both professionals and amateurs can write programs. Do you agree with this observation? Why?

1.4 What are the advantages of adopting a formal and algorithmic approach to process system modeling and description?

1.5 What are the advantages of adopting a formal and quantitative approach to process system analysis?

1.6 In Section 1.2 eight fundamental characteristics of software engineering were identified. Choose one of them and explain its impact on the engineering of software development.

1.7 Why it is considered that software engineering has shifted from a laboratory-oriented profession to an industry-oriented process?

1.8 Explain what the modern domain of software engineering is.

1.9 Software engineering methodologies have been evolved from programming methods, software development models, CASE tools, and formal methods to the software engineering process. Referring to Table 1.6, try to analyze the advantages and disadvantages of each approach to software engineering.

1.10 The software engineering process is considered as originating from two sources. Can you identify and briefly describe the sources of technologies that lead to the development of the software engineering process?

1.11 What is your reaction to the observation of the phenomenon that a variety of software engineering process models currently exist? Choose one of the following and explain:

(a) Complain that we already have enough models; no more are needed.
(b) Try to analyze their differences and similarity.
(c) Try to understand the usability of those process models.
(d) Demand standardization of process models.
(e) Support integration of process models.
(f) Explore innovative processes that have not been covered by current process models.

1.12 Analyze what software engineering can learn from the other engineering disciplines.

1.13 May software engineering methodologies and approaches be borrowed and applied to the other engineering disciplines? Can you provide an example?

Chapter 2

A UNIFIED FRAMEWORK OF THE SOFTWARE ENGINEERING PROCESS

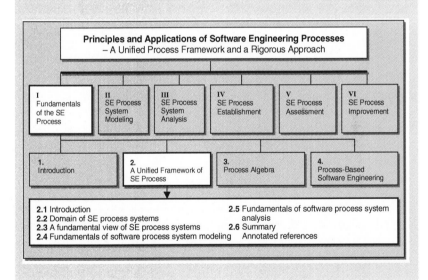

Principles and Applications of Software Engineering Processes
– A Unified Process Framework and a Rigorous Approach

I Fundamentals of the SE Process	II SE Process System Modeling	III SE Process System Analysis	IV SE Process Establishment	V SE Process Assessment	VI SE Process Improvement

1. Introduction	2. A Unified Framework of SE Process	3. Process Algebra	4. Process-Based Software Engineering

2.1 Introduction
2.2 Domain of SE process systems
2.3 A fundamental view of SE process systems
2.4 Fundamentals of software process system modeling

2.5 Fundamentals of software process system analysis
2.6 Summary
    Annotated references

This chapter intends to develop a unified framework of the software engineering process. The domain of software engineering processes is explored in order to gain a general view and a whole picture of the discipline. Fundamental methodologies and techniques in process system modeling and analysis are described, and an integrated theoretical and empirical foundation of process system paradigms is developed.

The objectives of this chapter are as follows:

- To develop a unified software engineering process framework

- To show fitness of current process models as subset paradigms of the unified process framework

- To pave the way for developing an integrated software engineering process reference model (SEPRM)

- To enable quantitative analysis of process characteristics of significance, practice, and effectiveness

2.1 Introduction

Organizing and implementing software engineering through software processes is a strategically important approach in the software industry [Humphrey, 1995; Pfleeger, 1998]. The concept of the software engineering process and the process approach to software engineering were addressed in Chapter 1. This chapter develops a unified framework for software engineering process systems, and investigates fundamental architectures and requirements for software engineering process modeling and analysis.

Modeling of an integrated software engineering process system starts from the analysis of the functionality of a generic software development organization, and by identifying its software engineering requirements.

A software development organization is defined as follows:

Definition 2.1 A **software development organization** is an independent organization, or a department or unit within an organization, which is responsible for development, maintenance, operation, and/or service of software or software-intensive systems.

A software engineering process system shall be elicited and abstracted systematically from the basic technical activities to the high-level administration practices in a software development organization. Building upon this, a fundamental structure of a generic process system may be derived.

The purpose of this chapter is to completely identify the software engineering process domain and its architecture. A unified framework of software engineering process systems will be developed which lays a theoretical and structural foundation for the remainder of the book. We will use this framework for formal description and analysis of current process models and methodologies, and for development of new process reference models.

Applying the unified process framework, unexpected gaps and omissions in current process models may be identified. Essential areas in process establishment, deployment, implementation, modeling, analysis, assessment and improvement may not have been covered by current process models, especially the lack of an abstract software development organization model, a complete process system model, and process benchmarks for characterizing the empirical attributes of the practices in processes.

2.2 Domain of Software Engineering Process Systems

The term "software engineering process system" was introduced by Definition 1.2 in Section 1.5. The term "domain" refers to the complete range of studies concerned by a system. This section investigates the domain of the software engineering process system, and the areas of interest in the discipline.

2.2.1 SOFTWARE PROCESS SYSTEM MODELING

According to systems theory, a software engineering process system is a dynamic, discrete, distributed, and nondeterministic system. In dealing with such a complicated system, a model of a software process system can be empirical or formal from the viewpoint of modeling techniques, and can be descriptive or prescriptive from the viewpoint of modeling purposes. Using the modeling techniques and purposes as defined below, software process models can be categorized and identified.

Definition 2.2 An empirical process model is a model that defines an organized and benchmarked software process system and best practices captured and elicited from the software industry.

Definition 2.3 A formal process model is a model that describes the structure and methodology of a software process system with an algorithmic approach or by an abstractive process description language.

Definition 2.4 A descriptive process model is a model that describes "what to do" according to a certain software process system.

Definition 2.5 A prescriptive process model is a model that describes "how to do" according to a certain software process system.

In practice there are four types of combinatory process models according to different modeling purposes and techniques as defined in Definitions 2.2 – 2.5. They are:

- (a) Empirical and descriptive
- (b) Empirical and prescriptive
- (c) Formal and descriptive
- (d) Formal and prescriptive

In accordance with these definitions, almost all current process system models fall into Category a, the empirical and descriptive models. Plenty of formal description languages designed for describing the software process have been reported [Saeki et al., 1991; Bandinelli, 1993; Finkelstein, 1994; Sutton and Osterweil, 1997], but there are still no complete formal process models. An empirical and prescriptive process model seems impractical because it would be superfluous and diverge from the principle of abstraction in system modeling. Based on the same rationale, we would not expect an emergence of a formal and prescriptive process model in the near future.

Current empirical-and-descriptive process models are designed to contribute answers for the following frequently asked questions in software engineering process system modeling and analysis:

- What are the best practices in software engineering?

- What are the successful experiences of the software development organizations in their processes?
- How is a software engineering process system established?
- How are the status and performance of an implemented process system controlled?
- How is an existing software engineering process system improved?

Improving current empirical-and-descriptive process system models for completeness and rigor requires a formal and descriptive process model with algorithmic and quantitative methodologies. These measures offer the best way to describe well-founded systems without ambiguity.

2.2.2 SOFTWARE PROCESS SYSTEM ESTABLISHMENT

Process system establishment is a precondition in a software development organization for implementing process-based software engineering. Although organizations that have experience in software development should have some sort of procedure – whether ad hoc or defined, informal or formal – the software engineering process as an infrastructural system needs to be formally and systematically established.

Definition 2.6 Software process establishment (SPE) is a systematic procedure to select and implement a process system by model tailoring, extension, and/or adaptation techniques.

Definition 2.6 indicates it usually might not be wise to develop an independent software engineering process system from scratch. It is better to refer to some existing and well-established process models or standards, then try to select the one that is most suitable to the organization's purposes and that could give more flexibility for future development. Because process system establishment is a costly organizational reengineering procedure, at the top of the agenda should be to investigate the usability and suitability of the candidate process models.

When a process system reference model is selected, the next step is to tailor and adapt the process model to make it fit with the organization's environment and culture. It is worth knowing that there is no process model that would fit a specific organization 100 percent. This is why there is a need to explore process system establishment methodologies.

2.2.3 SOFTWARE PROCESS SYSTEM ASSESSMENT

Process assessment enables software development organizations to find weaknesses and improvement opportunities in their process systems, and to provide would-be customers with assured confidence in their abilities and capabilities. Software process assessment is usually carried out in two steps: (a) process assessment, and (b) process capability determination.

The first step in process assessment is an on-site investigation and evaluation of the performance of a software organization's current process system. Software process assessment can be defined as follows:

Definition 2.7 Software process assessment (SPA) is a systematic procedure to investigate the existence, adequacy, and performance of an implemented process system against a model, standard, or benchmark.

The second step in process assessment is process capability determination. This can be carried out on-site or processed in the office after an assessment. The term "process capability determination" is defined as follows:

Definition 2.8 Process capability determination is a systematic procedure to derive a capability level for a process, project, and/or an organization based on the evidence of existence, adequacy, and performance of the required practices defined in a software engineering process system.

Although process capability determination is one of the important outcomes of a formal process assessment, it is not the main goal of assessment. The usual main goal of process assessment is to diagnose the current process system applied in an organization in order to improve it. However, a trend in which a software process capability level is used as a commercial weapon has evolved in order to win software contracts or to promote software products in the competitive software industry.

2.2.4 SOFTWARE PROCESS SYSTEM IMPROVEMENT

As described above, process assessment is the means for process improvement; process improvement is the final goal of process assessment. Software process improvement can be defined as follows:

Definition 2.9 Software process improvement (SPI) is a systematic procedure to improve the performance of an existing process system by changing the current processes or updating new processes in order to correct or avoid problems identified in the old process system by means of a process assessment.

Process improvement is thus a procedure that follows process assessment. The relationship between process assessment and improvement forms a repetitive Deming Circle, plan-do-check-act, until a software engineering process system is optimized in a given organization.

2.2.5   SOFTWARE PROCESS SYSTEM STANDARDIZATION

Standardization is an attempt to integrate, regulate, and optimize existing best practices and theories in research and in the industry. Considering that a variety of software process models have been developed by international, national, professional, and industrial institutions in the last decade, standardization is a timely strategic action in this discipline. Standards are often arrived, however, at as the result of trade-offs between cutting-edge development and existing ones that are widely accepted as good practices.

Some active international standardization bodies in areas of software engineering, software process, and software quality are The International Organization for Standardization (ISO), The International Electrotechnical Commission (IEC), and The Institute of Electrical and Electronics Engineers (IEEE). In the following we introduce these standardization bodies and related international standards on software engineering and software quality.

2.2.5.1 Software Engineering Process Standards

In 1987 a Software Engineering Subcommittee (SC7) was established by the ISO/IEC Joint Technical Committee-1 (JTC1) in order to recognize the importance and requirements for a set of software engineering standards. Since then, a dozen working groups (WGs) have been founded to cover specific software engineering areas such as:

- WG1: Open distributed processing (ODP) – Frameworks and components
- WG2: System software documentation
- WG3: Open distributed processing (ODP) – enterprise language
- WG4: Tools and environment
- WG5: Open distributed processing (ODP) – quality of service
- WG6: Evaluation and metrics

- WG7: Life cycle management
- WG8: Support of software life cycle processes
- WG9: Software integrity
- WG10: Software process assessment
- WG11: Software engineering data definition and representation
- WG12: Functional size measurements
- WG13: Software measurement framework
- WG14: Enhanced LOTOS

The list of JTC1/SC7 working groups is still expanding. As software engineering theory, methodologies, and practices evolve, we may expect more areas to be covered in software engineering standardization, such as system requirement definition, domain knowledge infrastructure, software architecture and frameworks, and software engineering notations.

A related standard developed in ISO/IEC JTC1/SC7 recently has been ISO/IEC 12207 (1995) – Software Life Cycle Processes. Others under development are ISO/IEC TR 15504 (1997/98) – Software Process Assessment, and ISO/IEC CD 15288 (1999) – System Life Cycle Processes.

A recent trend of ISO/IEC TR 15504 is to align its process dimension to ISO/IEC 12207. In addition, extension for ISO/IEC TR 15504 has been proposed to cover some system life cycle processes such as acquisition processes and broader system environment processes [Dorling and Wang et al., 1999a/b].

2.2.5.2 Software Quality Standards

Software quality system standardization is covered by the research inherent in the ISO Technical Committee 176 on quality management and quality assurance. ISO TC176 was initiated in 1979 with subcommittees working on generic quality systems and supporting technologies.

A major serial standard developed by ISO TC176 is ISO 9000 (1987/91/93/94). ISO 9000 was published in 1987 and revised in 1994. ISO 9000 has been recognized worldwide for establishing quality systems. It is designed for quality management and assurance, and specifies the basic requirements for development, production, installation, and service at system and product levels. Within ISO 9000, ISO 9001 (1989/1994) and ISO 9000-3 (1991) are applicable to software quality systems for certifying the processes, products, and services within a software development organization according to the ISO 9000 model.

Another related international software quality standard is ISO 9126 – Software Product Evaluation – Quality Characteristics and Guidelines for Their Use [ISO 9126 1991]. ISO 9126 extends principles of quality control to software and summarizes the major characteristics and attributes of software quality. An overview of ISO 9126 software quality model is shown in Table 2.1.

Table 2.1
ISO 9126 Software Quality Model

No.	Quality characteristics	Quality attribute
1	Functionality	
1.1		Suitability
1.2		Accuracy
1.3		Interoperability
1.4		Security
2	Reliability	
2.1		Maturity
2.2		Fault tolerance
2.3		Recoverability
3	Usability	
3.1		Understandability
3.2		Learnability
3.3		Operability
4	Efficiency	
4.1		Time behavior
4.2		Resource behavior
5	Maintainability	
5.1		Analyzability
5.2		Changeability
5.3		Stability
5.4		Testability
6	Portability	
6.1		Adaptability
6.2		Installability
6.3		Conformance
6.4		Replaceability

ISO 9126 adopted a philosophy of the black-box that represents the user's view of software products and systems. Recent investigations [Dromey, 1996; Pfleeger, 1998] argued that the ISO 9126 model has been focused only on the external attributes of software quality. Substantial internal attributes of software quality, such as of architecture, reuse description, coding styles, test completeness, run-time efficiency, resource usage efficiency, and exception handling, have not been modeled. Therefore, we consider that the internal quality attributes of software will be characterized by the software engineering process-oriented standards and models. This observation explores an interesting connection between software engineering process standardization and software product quality standardization described in this section.

2.3 A Fundamental View of Software Engineering Process Systems

This section identifies the professionals involved in a software development organization and their roles, interactions, and relationships. Meta subsystems of software engineering processes for regulating the professional roles' functionality and interactions will be derived in the context of a software development organization in the software industry.

2.3.1 A GENERIC MODEL OF SOFTWARE DEVELOPMENT ORGANIZATIONS

The professional roles in a software development organization could form a long list. Principally, as shown in Table 2.2, they are: senior manager, project manager, customer solution analyst, system analyst, system architect, software engineer, programmer, testing engineer, software quality assurance (SQA) engineer, maintenance engineer, customer supporting engineer, internal support staff, and so on.

Software engineering roles can be categorized into three functional parties: the developers, the managers, and the customers. Beginners in software engineering, such as students, tend to ignore the third party – customers – because in their learning context there are often no defined customers, or the programmers are virtual customers themselves. However, customers are a significant part of software engineering. This is the reason why almost programming models, from the waterfall and prototyping to spiral, have had defined roles for customers.

Table 2.2
Roles in Industrial-Oriented Software Engineering

No.	Category	Roles
1	Software engineering organization	
1.1		Software development organization manager
1.2		Organizational software engineering process designer
1.3		Software engineering environment and tools maintainer
1.4		Delivered systems manager
1.5		Maintenance engineer
1.6		System service evaluator
1.7		User problems and requirements analyst
1.8		User system solutions provider
1.9		User development coordinator
1.10		User testing coordinator
1.11		User technical supporter
1.12		Technical menus and help files author
1.13		Technical trainer
2	Software development	
2.1		Software engineering environment and tools manager
2.2		Software engineering methodology designer
2.3		System analyst
2.4		Domain engineer
2.5		Customer solution consultant
2.6		Requirements capture engineer
2.7		System architect
2.8		Algorithm developer
2.9		Programmer
2.10		Software testing engineer
2.11		System integration and configuration engineer
3	Software engineering project management	
3.1		Project manager
3.2		Project-level process designer
3.3		Project planning and estimation engineer
3.4		Project contract and requirements manager
3.5		System requirement specification analyst
3.6		Quality engineer
3.7		Project configuration and document manager
3.8		Project team coordinator

If one just concentrated on the functionality and interactions among the three parties, software engineering activities in an organization would still be informal and uncontrollable. To regulate the human activities and interactions within a software development organization, the environment of a software engineering process system should be based on the identification and modeling of the three parties' practices in a process context. As shown in Figure 2.1, three process subsystems, known as organization, development, and management, have been identified. The regulation of human activities in a process-based software engineering environment forms a generic high-level model of a software development organization.

Definition 2.10   A generic model of the software development organization is a high-level process model of an organization which is designed to regulate the functionality and interactions between the roles of developers, managers, and customers by a software engineering process system.

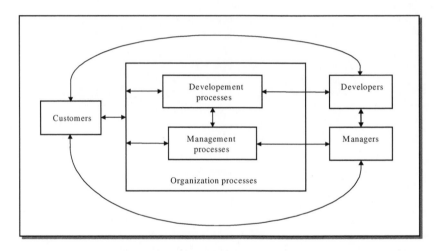

Figure 2.1 A generic high-level software development organization model

The generic software organization model depicted in Figure 2.1 identifies a least-complete set of process subsystems in a software development organization. The three process subsystems are considered complete and minimal to model a software engineering process system. It is complete because all the software engineering professionals and their roles identified in Table 2.2 can be fit in these processes; it is minimal because no subsystems can be merged into the others. The completeness, minimum property, and high-level abstraction of a software engineering model is essential to clarify the interrelationships and interactions between the main software engineering process streams, and is helpful for reducing the complexity of synchronization between process activities in the concurrent process subsystems in a software development organization.

In the generic software development organization model, as shown in Figure 2.1, the organization processes regulate the top-level activities that are generally practiced in a software development organization above project level. Beneath the organization process subsystem are the development process subsystem and corresponding management process subsystem that are interactive in parallel at project level. The former is the producer of software product and the object of the management processes; the latter is the supporter and controller of the development processes by means of schedule, quality, resources, and staff.

All professional roles, including the developers, managers, and customers, can fit in the generic process model as shown in Figure 2.1 and communicate with each other. In the following chapters, this generic model will be extracted into a comprehensive software engineering process model.

2.3.2 PROCESS SYSTEM ARCHITECTURE IN A SOFTWARE DEVELOPMENT ORGANIZATION

For modeling a process system, processes are elicited and integrated from the bottom, up. Processes in the development subsystem are first analyzed and then modeled. Corresponding to the development processes, the management processes are then deployed as measures to support and control the development processes. The third step is to design the organization processes, which are the top-level management processes oriented to the whole software development organization, and which are applicable to all software engineering projects within the organization.

It is generally considered that there would be a number of parallel development and management processes for individual projects within a software development organization. For the purpose of controlling a process system, software engineering processes are implemented and practiced top down, from the organization level to the project level. Therefore, the relationship between the organization, management, and development processes can be further refined as in Figure 2.2.

Figure 2.2 shows the common practices in organizing a software engineering process system. It is noteworthy that there is only one organization process subsystem in a software development organization, which will be based on the organization's process reference model (OPRM). At project level, a number of parallel development and management processes may exist based on the individual project's tailored process model (PTPM) and which are derived models of the OPRM reference model. In Figure 2.2 the process reference model, OPRM, is the key for empirical process-based software engineering. If an OPRM is well established in an organization, the PTPMs at project level can easily be derived.

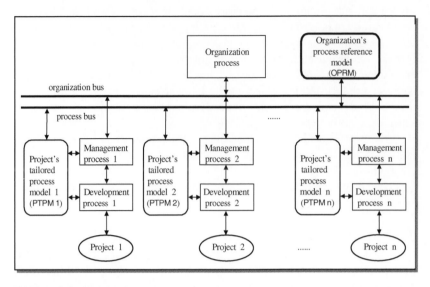

Figure 2.2 Process organization and implementation in a software development organization

Definition 2.11 A process reference model is an established, validated, and proven software engineering process model that consists of a comprehensive set of software processes and reflects the benchmarked best practices in the software industry.

At the top level, a software development organization may adopt an existing international standard or an established process model as its OPRM; or, it can develop a specific organization-oriented OPRM based on the existing models and the organization's own practices and experiences in software engineering. The OPRM plays a crucial rule in the regulation and standardization of an organization's software engineering practices.

At project level, the OPRM reference model could, and usually should, be tailored or adapted to a specific project according to the nature of the project, taking into account application domain, scope, complexity, schedule, experience of project team, reuse opportunities identified and/or resources availability, and so on. For a PTPM of an individual project, the management and development processes should be one-to-one designed and synchronized. Tailoring of a PTPM from a comprehensive OPRM makes the software project leaders' tasks dramatically easier. Using this approach, project organization and conduct can be performed well within an organization's unified software engineering process infrastructure.

2.4 Fundamentals of Software Process System Modeling

For objective, accurate, stable, nonambiguous and effective modeling, analysis, assessment, and improvement of a software engineering process system, the following fundamental aspects need to be investigated. They are the process model, the process assessment model, and the process improvement model as shown in Figure 2.3. This section describes a unified framework of the software engineering process system and its requirements in accordance with the structure provided in Figure 2.3.

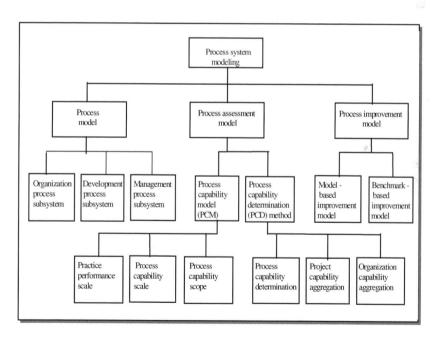

Figure 2.3 Fundamental structure of software process system modeling

2.4.1 PROCESS MODEL

A process model is a blueprint of how to organize, implement, conduct, and manage software engineering processes in an organization with an established, validated, and proven process system and good practices.

Definition 2.12 A process model is a model of a process system that describes process organization, categorization, hierarchy, interrelationship, and tailorability.

2.4.1.1 Taxonomy of Software Process Systems

A bottom up taxonomy of software process systems is: practice, process, process category, process subsystem, and process system. Terms in the process taxonomy are formally described as follows.

Definition 2.13 A practice is an activity or a state in a software engineering process that carries out a specific task of the process.

A practice is the minimum unit that can be modeled in a process system. In this book, a practice will henceforth be referred to as a base process activity (BPA).

Definition 2.14 A process is a set of sequential practices (or BPAs) which are functionally coherent and reusable for software project organization, implementation, and management.

Definition 2.15 A process category is a set of processes that are functionally coherent and reusable in an aspect of software engineering.

Definition 2.16 A process subsystem is a set of process categories that are functionally coherent and reusable in a main part of software engineering.

A process subsystem is the second-highest-level structure in a process system. As described in the generic model of software development organizations in Section 2.3, a least-complete set of process subsystems covers organization, development, and management in software engineering.

Definition 2.17 A process system is an entire set of structured software processes described by a process model.

Hierarchically, a process system can be divided into subsystems, categories, processes, and practices (BPAs) as defined in Definitions 2.13 – 2.16, respectively. The usage of a process taxonomy is to enable process system modeling and analyses to be carried out at the same level, and to avoid comparison of apples with pears among varying process models.

2.4.1.2 The Domain of a Process Model

Corresponding to the hierarchical structure of a process system described above, the domain of a process model can be introduced below.

Definition 2.18 A domain of a process model is a set of ranges of functional coverage that a process model specifies at different levels of the process taxonomy.

The domain of a process model determines what to describe and check, and what is important at different hierarchical levels in a software process system. For example, we can describe the domain of a process category as being the number of processes and the domain of a process as being the number of practices (BPAs).

At the highest level of the process taxonomy, the domain of a process system covers three process subsystems: organization, development, and management, as shown in Figure 2.1. The formal definitions of these subsystems are developed below.

Definition 2.19 Organization processes are processes that belong to a top-level administrative process subsystem, which are practiced above project level within a software development organization.

Definition 2.20 Development processes are processes that belong to a technical process subsystem, which regulate the development activities in software design, implementation, and maintenance.

Definition 2.21 Management processes are processes that belong to a supporting process subsystem, which control the development processes by means of resource, staff, schedule, and quality.

A comparison of the domains of current process models (refer to Chapters 5 – 9) in accordance with the taxonomy is shown in Table 2.3. It is noteworthy that current process models adopt different terms in each level of the process taxonomy. For instance, at the process level, CMM uses "key practice areas", and ISO 9001 prefers "main topic areas". Only ISO/IEC TR 15504 and SEPRM adopt the term "processes".

Table 2.3
Taxonomy and Domains of Current Software Process Systems

Domain level	CMM	Bootstrap	ISO/IEC TR 15504	ISO 9001	SEPRM
System	CMM	Bootstrap	ISO/IEC TR 15504	ISO 9001	SEPRM
Sub-system	-	Process areas [3]	-	Subsystems [3]	Subsystems [3]
Category	Process levels [5]	Process categories [9]	Process categories (PCs) [5]	-	Process categories [12]
Process	Key practice areas (KPAs) [18]	Processes [32]	Processes (PRs) [35]	Main topic areas (MTAs) [20]	Processes [51]
Practice	Key Practices (KPs) [150]	Quality system attributes (QSAs) [201]	Base practices (BPs) [201]	Management issues (MIs) [177]	Base process activities (BPAs) [444]

In Table 2.3, the numbers in the squared brackets indicate the sizes of domains at different hierarchical levels. For example, at the process level, the sizes of domain of CMM, ISO/IEC TR 15504, and SEPRM are 18, 35, and 51, respectively; at the practice level, their sizes of domain are 150, 201, and 444, respectively.

2.4.2 PROCESS ASSESSMENT MODEL

As shown in Figure 2.3, a process assessment model consists of a process capability model and a process capability determination method. The former is a yardstick for process capability measurement; the latter is a method describing how to use the yardstick in measuring a given process model.

2.4.2.1 Process Capability Model

A process capability model is the kernel of a process assessment model. It provides a set of scales for quantitatively evaluating a software development organization's capabilities at process, project, and entire organization levels. A process capability model can be defined as follows:

Definition 2.22 A process capability model (PCM) is a measurement scale of software process capability for quantitatively evaluating the existence, adequacy, effectiveness, and compatibility of a process.

Attempting to quantitatively measure a complicated software engineering process system is a hard problem. The following subsections introduce basic scales of practice performance and process capability in a process capability model, and analyze scopes of process capabilities at different hierarchical levels in a process model.

(a) Practice performance scale

As described in Definition 2.13 and the taxonomy of a process system (Table 2.3), the practice is the basic unit of a process system. The performance of a practice can be assessed using a number of confidential degrees for its existence, adequacy, and effectiveness in process. Typical practice performance scales adopted in current process models (refer to Chapters 5 – 9) are contrasted in Table 2.4.

Table 2.4
Modeling of Practice Performance Rating Scales

Model	Practice Performance Rating Scale			
CMM	Yes	No	Doesn't apply	don't know
BOOTSTRAP	Complete/extensive	largely satisfied	Partially satisfied	Absent/poor
ISO/IEC TR 15504	Fully achieved	largely achieved	Partially achieved	not achieved
ISO 9001	Satisfied	not satisfied		
SEPRM	Fully adequate	largely adequate	Partially adequate	not adequate

(b) Process capability scale

The process capability scale is commonly measured by a set of process capability levels (PCLs). Most of the current process models (refer to Chapters 5 – 9) adopt a five- or six-level scale as shown in Table 2.5, where Level 5 is at the top and Level 0 or 1 is at the bottom.

Table 2.5
Modeling of Process Capability Scales

Capability Level	CMM	BOOTSTRAP	ISO/IEC TR 15504	ISO 9001	SEPRM
0	-	-	Incomplete	Fail	Incomplete
1	Initial	Initial	Performed	-	Loose
2	Repeated	Repeated	Managed	-	Integrated
3	Defined	Defined	Established	-	Stable
4	Managed	Managed	Predictable	-	Effective
5	Optimizing	Optimizing	Optimizing	Pass	Refined

The terms used in describing process capability levels vary as shown in Table 2.5. However, these capability scales defined in current process models can be grouped into three categories:

- The pass/fail threshold scale such as that of ISO 9001

- The management-oriented scale such as those of CMM, BOOTSTRAP, and ISO/IEC TR 15504

- The process-oriented scale such as that of SEPRM

Detailed description of the three categories of process capability scales is provided below.

i. *Pass/fail threshold capability scale*

The pass/fail threshold capability scale is the simplest measurement of process capabilities and is practical in general areas. The disadvantages of this scale are:

- Lack of precise discrimination between the capability levels for all those software development organizations that have passed the threshold

- Not suitable for step-by-step process improvement

For example, the authors have found that the capability levels of the ISO 9001-registered software development organizations would be mainly located between the CMM levels two and three, with a few exceptionally higher [Wang et al., 1996c/97a]. Thus, application of this type of capability scale would not differentiate the capabilities of software development organizations that have passed the ISO 9001 capability threshold.

ii. *Management-oriented capability scale*

The capability scales of BOOTSTRAP and ISO/IEC TR 15504 are mainly inherited from the CMM [Humphrey, 1987/88/89; Paulk, 1991/93a/b/c]. This category of capability scales is relatively process management-capability-oriented. All three models have defined 0/1 ~ 5 scales for rating process capability levels. However, the different terms associated with respective capability levels are found not to be straightforward or literally independent.

For instance, it is difficult to answer the following questions without referring to Table 2.5:

- Which capability level would be lower and should be implemented earlier in a process system, the *defined* or the *repeated* processes?

- Would the *managed* processes need to be implemented in earlier stages, say, at least from Level 2, in order to establish a basis for the performance of the other capability levels?

The design of the ISO/IEC TR 15504 capability scale has considered the logical issues mentioned above to some extent. However, there is still an argument as to whether all the capability levels need to be *managed* rather than that only at Level 2 in ISO/IEC TR 15504 or at Level 4 in CMM and BOOTSTRAP. This argument leads to the development of a third category of capability scale, the process-oriented capability scale, as described below.

iii. *Process-oriented capability scale*

For measuring processes by straightforward process capability levels rather than the management levels of processes as discussed in Category ii, a third type of direct process-oriented capability scale has been developed [Wang et al., 1997a/99e]. The process-oriented capability scale measures a process' capability from the bottom up and defines levels of *incomplete, loose, integrated, stable, effective,* and *refined*. This scale is designed to avoid the contradiction found in the Categories i and ii capability scales. The direct process-oriented capability scale has been adopted in the SEPRM model (refer to Chapter 9) as shown in Table 2.5.

(c) Process capability scope

The process capability scales described above can be applied to measure software process practices and performances within different scopes, such as in the scopes of a process, a project or an organization. Generally, a larger scope of capability can be aggregated from the smaller scopes contained in it. The process capability scopes are defined from the bottom up as follows:

Definition 2.23 A process capability scope is an aggregation of all the performance ratings, such as existence, adequacy, and effectiveness, of the practices (BPAs) which belong to the process.

Definition 2.24 A project process capability scope is an aggregation of all process capability levels of processes conducted in a project.

Definition 2.25 An organization process capability scope is an aggregation of the process capability levels from a number of sampled projects carried out in a software development organization.

Definition 2.25 indicates that an organization's capability level is dependent on more than one project's capabilities carried out within the software development organization.

The capability scopes and their representations in current process models (refer to Chapters 5 – 9) are shown in Table 2.6.

2.4.2.2 The Process Capability Determination Method

The process capability determination method is a bridge connecting the process models with the process capability models as described in Sections 2.4.1 and 2.4.2.1. A definition of the process capability determination method is given below.

Table 2.6
Modeling of Process Capability Scopes

Capability scope	CMM	BOOTSTRAP	ISO/IEC TR 15504	ISO 9001	SEPRM
Practice	Performance Rating	Performance Rating	Performance Rating	Fulfillment	Performance Rating
Process	Performance Rating	Performance Rating	Capability level with attributes	Fulfillment	Capability level
Project	-	-	Process capability profile	-	Capability level + process capability profile
Organization	Capability Level	Capability level with quadruples	-	Pass/Fail	Capability level + process capability profile

Definition 2.26 A process capability determination (PCD) model is an operational model that specifies how to apply the process capability scales to measure a given process system described by a process model.

As described in Definitions 2.7 and 2.8, process assessment and capability determination are two linked procedures to evaluate process activities in practice, process, project, and organization scopes. In conventional, natural language-described process models, process capability determination has been found difficult to carry out accurately and reliably because the informal and empirical capability determination methods are too dependent on the subjective judgments of individual assessors at each level of aggregation of the process scopes.

For implementing quantitative, stable, and less subjective process assessment, this book develops a formal and algorithmic capability determination method. In the algorithmic approach, the assessor-dependent factor of process capability determination is limited to the lowest scope – the practice scope, while the higher-level capabilities are required to be derived according to a suite of rigorously described methods and a set of expressions as follows.

Although a manual data collection phase for rating the performance of a practice (the minimum element in process) cannot be avoided, a 4-level detailed rating scale is provided for assessors, as shown in Expression 2.1, to accurately derive their evaluation of the basic elements of a process. Experience shows (refer to Section 12.7) that a +/-10% variation in ratings between different assessors in the elementary practice scope will not result in significant differences in the higher scopes of process capability determination. This is one of the advantages of the algorithmic approach to process capability determination. This approach has been adopted in the SEPRM model and implemented in the SEPRM process assessment algorithm, which will be described in Chapter 9.

(a) Practice performance rating

Definition 2.27 Practice performance, *PP(i)*, is rated by the maximum adequacy degrees among fully (F, 90 – 100%), largely (L, 60 – 89%), partially (P, 25 – 59%), and not (N, 10 – 24%) achieved, i.e.:

$$PP(i) = max\ \{\ F \mid L \mid P \mid N\ \}$$
$$= max\ \{\ 5 \mid 3 \mid 1 \mid 0\ \} \tag{2.1}$$

where *i* is the index number of a practice.

In Expression 2.1, a set of numerical values is assigned for the fully (5), largely (3), partially (1), and not (0) adequacy of practice performance ratings. These values will be used in manually or automatically calculating process capability levels in later chapters.

Definition 2.28 Assume a process, *p*, consists of m_p practices. An average practice performance of the practices in a process, $\overline{PP}(p)$, can be derived by:

$$\overline{PP}(p) = \frac{1}{m_p} \sum_{i=1}^{m_p} PP(i) \tag{2.2}$$

(b) Process capability determination

Definition 2.29 A process' capability level, $PCL_{proc}(p)$, is an aggregation of the mean performance of m_p practices, $\overline{PP}(p)$, which belong to the process p, i.e.:

$$PCL_{proc}(p) = \overline{PP}(p)$$
$$= \frac{1}{m_p} \sum_{i=1}^{m_p} PP(i) \qquad (2.3)$$

Expression 2.3 is designed to provide a precise decimal process capability level between $0 - 5.0$.

(c) Project capability aggregation

Project capability can be aggregated from the PCLs of all processes conducted in a project.

Definition 2.30 A project's process capability level, $PCL_{proj}(j)$, is an aggregation of all capabilities of the k processes, $PCL_{proc}(p)$, conducted in project j, i.e.:

$$PCL_{proj}(j) = \frac{1}{k} \sum_{p=1}^{k} PCL_{proc}(p) \qquad (2.4)$$

A precise decimal project capability level between $0 - 5.0$ can be derived by Expression 2.4.

(d) Organization capability aggregation

Organization capability is an aggregation of all capabilities of a number of sampled projects assessed in a software development organization.

Definition 2.31 An organization's process capability level, PCL_{org}, is an aggregation of n projects' capability levels, $PCL_{proj}(p)$, sampled and assessed in a software development organization, *i.e.:*

$$PCL_{org} = \frac{1}{n} \sum_{p=1}^{n} PCL_{proj}(p) \qquad (2.5)$$

Expression 2.5 indicates that more than one projects' capabilities should be obtained to derive an organization's capability level. A recommended minimum number, n, is three. Expression 2.5 can be used to reflect the historical experience that a software organization has accumulated in various software development projects. A precise decimal organization capability level between $0 - 5.0$ can be derived by the expression.

2.4.3 PROCESS IMPROVEMENT MODEL

In Section 2.4.2 a set of quantitative measurements and method have been developed to help understand the baseline of a process system by process assessment. Based on awareness of the status and performance of a process system, improvement can be designed and carried out. This subsection describes alternative approaches that may be taken for software process improvement. A process improvement model can be defined as follows:

Definition 2.32 A process improvement model (PIM) is an operational model that provides guidance for improving a process system's capability by changing, updating, or enhancing existing processes based on the findings provided in a process assessment.

As shown in Figure 2.3, process improvement models can be classified into two categories: model-based and benchmark-based improvement.

(a) Model-based improvement

Definition 2.33   A model-based process improvement model is an operational model that describes process improvement methods based on model- or standard-based assessment results.

(b) Benchmark-based improvement

Definition 2.34 A benchmark-based process improvement model is an operational model that describes process improvement methods based on benchmark-based assessment results.

Detailed process improvement methodologies will be discussed in Chapter 4 and Part VI.

2.5 Fundamentals of Software Process System Analysis

Conventional analyses of software engineering process models and systems were mainly qualitative and one-to-one mapping. In moving towards more accurate, objective, and stable analysis, this section develops a set of quantitative methods for analyzing software process models and process attributes which are suitable for all one-to-one, one-to-many, and many-to-one analysis areas.

2.5.1 ANALYSIS OF SOFTWARE PROCESS MODELS

In software engineering process system analysis, it is necessary to consider the following issues:

- What is the core process concept represented in current process models?

- What are the common features modeled in current process models?

- What are their special orientations?

- What are the interrelationships between current process models?

- How can we measure the relationships between current process models?

Relations between multiprocess models can be described by terms of compatibility and correlation. By analyzing the degree of compatibility and the level and ratio of correlation, the orientation of current process models and the relationships between them can be clarified, and a fundamental knowledge structure can be elicited and established.

This subsection introduces definitions and describes quantitative methods for analyzing compatibility and correlation between process models. Applications of these methods and related analysis results will be addressed in Chapter 11.

2.5.1.1 Compatibility between Process Models

A major issue identified in software engineering process analysis and application is that of partial overlaps between the domains of current process models. A term compatibility between a set of process models, as illustrated in Figure 2.4, is introduced to describe the problem.

Definition 2.35 Compatibility between a set of process models is defined as the degree of the joint domain coverage, which is determined by the sets of BPAs of the models.

In the definition, the suggestion is that it is appropriate to analyze process system compatibility at the basic unit, BPA, level because analyses at higher levels can be fairly subjective and inaccurate.

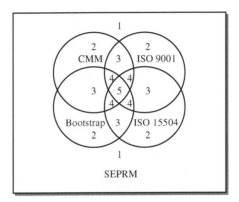

Figure 2.4 Compatibility between current process models

According to Definition 2.35, for k existing models, the compatibility degree, C_k, can be described at k levels. Referring to Figure 2.4, where $k=5$, the five compatibility levels can be specified by:

- C_1 : BPAs that are only defined in a specific model
- C_2 : Shared BPAs identified in two of the models
- C_3 : Shared BPAs identified in three of the models
- C_4 : Shared BPAs identified in four of the models, and
- C_5 : BPAs shared by all five models

Thus, the compatibility of a process model M to other k-1 models, c_k (M), can be determined by:

$$c_k(M) = \#\{BPA_i \mid BPA_i \in C_k\}, \quad k=1,2,...,5 \text{ and } i = 1 ... n$$

$$= \sum_{i=1}^{n} \{1 \mid BPA_i \in C_k\}, \quad k=1,2,...,5 \tag{2.6}$$

where n $(n=444)$ is the total number of BPAs identified in the entire joint domain of all models; # is a cardinal calculus for counting the numbers of elements in a set.

The BPAs with higher compatibility, such as those at C_5 and C_4, indicate the key practices in software engineering processes. The BPAs with C_1 and C_2 show the special orientation of a process model in some specific aspects. Applications of this subsection and detailed analysis will be provided in Chapter 10.

2.5.1.2 Correlation between Process Models

In this subsection, definitions of *relation* and *mapping* between a pair of process models are introduced respectively. Then a formal definition of *correlation* is derived.

(a) Relation

Definition 2.36 The domain of a process model, X, can be described as a relation, $R(X)$, according to relational algebra:

$$R(X) = R(x_1, x_2, ..., x_n) \tag{2.7}$$

where $x_1, x_2, ..., x_n$ is the n BPAs identified in model X.

(b) Mapping

Definition 2.37 For two process models, $R(X) = R(x_1, x_2, ..., x_n)$ and $S(Y) = S(y_1, y_2, ..., y_k)$, a mapping between them, $m(R, S)$, is defined as:

$$m(R, S) = \{x_i \mid x_i \in R \cap S \wedge 1 \le i \le n\} \tag{2.8}$$

and similarly,

$$m(S, R) = \{y_j \mid y_j \in S \cap R \wedge 1 \le j \le k\}$$

Note the number of elements in two mapped sets, $m(R, S)$ and $m(S, R)$, are identical but the sequences of the elements may be different. Thus, we consider that $m(R, S) \ne m(S, R)$ in a bidirectional mapping between two models.

(c) Correlation

The concept of mapping can be applied to explore correlation between a set of process models. Pairwise mappings of current process models have been reported in the literature and attracted much interest in the software industry [Koch, 1993; Paulk, et al. 1994/95b; Jarvinen, 1994; Kugler and Messnarz, 1994; Kitson, 1996]. The approaches of existing mappings were mainly conducted at high levels (such as at the process or process category levels), in single direction (e.g., from CMM to ISO/IEC TR 15504, or from ISO 9001 to CMM), and nonquantitative. Some of the mapping results were argued to be fairly subjective, and in some aspects were even contradictory.

For enabling quantitative, objective, and bidirectional mapping between current process models, a new approach – quantitative correlation analysis – needs to be developed. To achieve the aims of quantitative, objective, and bidirectional analysis, correlation analyses are suggested at the BPA level. As described in Definition 2.13, BPA (practice) is the fundamental element in a process for describing the base activities and the implication of a process. BPAs are usually specific and single actions in a process. A BPA's implication and extension are much clearer than that of a process or a process category. Analysis at the BPA level is also helpful to distinguish possible differences between the literal identical or similar processes while consisting of different BPAs underneath. Although working at the BPA level requires much more effort in analysis, it is fundamental for deriving less subjective and more accurate correlation pictures between current process models.

For modeling the correlation between two process models, an absolute and a relative measurement may be considered. The former represents a level of correlation, and the latter a ratio of correlation.

Definition 2.38 The correlation level between two process models is defined as the number of identical or equivalent BPAs identified in both domains of a pair of process models.

The correlation level between two process models R and S, $r(R, S)$, can be measured by applying the cardinal calculus # of set to, or by simply counting, the BPAs commonly identified in a pair of models, i.e.:

$$r(R, S) = \# \{ x_i \mid x_i \in m(R, S) \}$$

$$= \sum_{i=1}^{n} \{ 1 \mid x_i \in m(R, S) \}$$

$$= \sum_{i=1}^{n} \{ 1 \mid x_i \in R \cap S \} \qquad (2.9)$$

where n is the number of BPAs in R.

According to Definition 2.38, it is intuitive that $r(R, S) = r(S, R)$. This means that values of the correlation level between two models are symmetrical.

Definition 2.39 The correlation ratio of a process model R against a model S, $\rho(R,S)$, is a relative degree of identity or equivalency that model R compares to S.

The correlation ratio can be quantitatively calculated by:

$$\rho(R,S) = \frac{r(R,S)}{\#R}\%$$
$$= \frac{r(R,S)}{n}\% \tag{2.10}$$

where $\#R$ is the number of elements (BPAs), n, identified in model R.

Note that $\rho(R,S) \neq \rho(S,R)$ according to Definition 2.39. This means that the correlation ratio is dependent on both the correlation level and the size of the model that it is analyzing.

The correlation derived at the BPA level can be aggregated to process and system levels. The former deals with detailed mapping between processes of different models while the latter provides an overall view for correlation between a pair of process models.

2.5.2 ANALYSIS OF SOFTWARE PROCESS ATTRIBUTES

In Section 2.5.1 we described quantitative measurements for relations between software process models. This subsection seeks useful process attributes to quantitatively evaluate practical characteristics of software processes and practices of current process models.

In comparative analysis of current process models, it is found that a number of basic questions need to be raised for software engineering process modeling, such as:

- What are the criteria needed to include or drop a BPA in a process?

- How are a BPA and a process characterized?

- How is a process model valid at the fundamental BPA level?

To answer these questions, five process attributes are developed to serve as the criteria for BPA characterization, evaluation, and validation. The five process attributes are mean weighted importance; ratios of significance, of practice, and of effectiveness; and the characteristic value of the BPA. Practical values of the attributes for each BPA have been derived from worldwide surveys in the software industry [Wang et al., 1997a/98a/99c].

2.5.2.1 Mean Weighted Importance

Definition 2.40 Given the importance weight of a BPA, w_i, in a scale [0, 1, ..., 5], a statistical **mean weighted importance** of a BPA is defined as a mathematical average of the empirical weighting values obtained from the survey samples, i.e.:

$$W = \frac{\sum_{i=0}^{5} w_i * i}{n_W} \tag{2.11}$$

where n_W is the total number of samples in a survey.

2.5.2.2 Ratio of Significance

The importance weighting for a BPA, w_i, is defined within [0 ... 5]. The numbers of heavy ($3 \leq w_i \leq 5$) and light ($0 \leq w_i \leq 2$) weights for the significance of BPAs in the total samples n_W, n_w plus $n_{\overline{w}}$, are categorized by:

$$n_w = \#\{ w_i \mid w_i \geq 3 \wedge w_i \leq 5 \}$$

$$= \sum_{i=1}^{n_W} \{ 1 \mid w_i \geq 3 \wedge w_i \leq 5 \} \tag{2.12}$$

and

$$n_{\overline{w}} = \#\{ w_i \mid w_i \geq 0 \wedge w_i \leq 2 \}$$

$$= \sum_{i=1}^{n_W} \{ 1 \mid w_i \geq 0 \wedge w_i \leq 2 \} \tag{2.13}$$

respectively.

Definition 2.41 Based on Expressions 2.12 and 2.13, the **ratio of significance** of a BPA, r_w, which is heavily weighted in a set of survey samples can be defined as:

$$r_w = \frac{n_w}{n_w + n_{\overline{w}}} * 100\% \tag{2.14}$$

and similarly, the ratio of nonsignificance of a BPA, $r_{\overline{w}}$, is defined by:

$$r_{\overline{w}} = \frac{n_{\overline{w}}}{n_w + n_{\overline{w}}} * 100\%$$

$$= 1 - r_w \tag{2.15}$$

2.5.2.3 Ratio of Practice

Definition 2.42 Assuming that n_p and $n_{\overline{p}}$ are numbers of evaluation for characterizing a BPA practical or nonpractical, respectively, the ratio of practice for a BPA, r_p, is defined as:

$$r_p = \frac{n_p}{n_p + n_{\overline{p}}} * 100\% \tag{2.16}$$

and the ratio of nonpractice of a BPA, $r_{\overline{p}}$, is:

$$r_{\overline{p}} = \frac{n_{\overline{p}}}{n_p + n_{\overline{p}}} * 100\%$$

$$= 1 - r_p \tag{2.17}$$

2.5.2.4 Ratio of Effectiveness

Definition 2.43 Assuming that n_e and $n_{\overline{e}}$ are numbers of evaluation for characterizing a BPA effective or noneffective, respectively, the ratio of effectiveness for a BPA, r_e, is defined as:

$$r_e = \frac{n_e}{n_e + n_{\overline{e}}} * 100\% \tag{2.18}$$

and the ratio of noneffectiveness of a BPAs, $r_{\overline{e}}$, is:

$$r_{\bar{e}} = \frac{n_{\bar{e}}}{n_e + n_{\bar{e}}} * 100\%$$

$$= 1 - r_e \qquad (2.19)$$

2.5.2.5 Characteristic Value (Usage)

Practical characteristics of the BPAs, or usage, in a process system can be combinatorially represented by the last three attributes, the ratios of significance, practice, and effectiveness, as follows:

Definition 2.44 A characteristic value, or usage, of a BPA, φ, can be determined by a production of the ratios of significance (r_w), practice (r_p), and effectiveness (r_e), i.e.:

$$\varphi = (r_w * r_p * r_e) * 100\% \qquad (2.20)$$

The characteristic value φ provides a combined indication of a BPA's significance, practice, and effectiveness in process, or simply usage. The higher the value of φ, the more important and effective the BPA in practice, and vice versa. Therefore, φ can be used to index the importance and effectiveness of a BPA in practice.

The process system relations and process attributes developed in this section will be applied in the following chapters for describing and analyzing current software engineering process models, especially the SEPRM model.

2.6 Summary

In this chapter, a whole picture of the software engineering process domain and its architecture have been presented. Taking this view, a unified framework of software engineering process systems has been developed. Formal approaches have been introduced into software engineering process system modeling and analysis with the intention of avoiding ambiguity and improving accuracy in understanding and applying the existing and new process methodologies.

The basic knowledge structure of this chapter is as follows:

Chapter 2. A Unified Framework of the Software Engineering Process

- General
  - Purpose of this chapter
    - To develop a unified software engineering process framework
    - To show fitness of current process models as subset paradigms of the unified process framework
    - To pave the way for developing an integrated software engineering process reference model (SEPRM)
    - To enable quantitative analysis of process characteristics of significance, practice, and effectiveness

  - A discipline of the software engineering process
    - Foundations
    - Common features
    - Alternative approaches

- Domain of software engineering process systems
  - Modeling and analysis
    - Empirical vs. formal
    - Descriptive vs. prescriptive

  - Establishment
    - SPE
    - Selection of a process system reference model
    - Customization of the reference model

  - Assessment
    - SPA
    - Process capability determination

  - Improvement
    - SPI
    - Relations to SPA

  - Standardization
    - Software process – internal view of software artifacts
    - Software quality – external view of software artifacts

- A fundamental view of software engineering process systems
  - The generic model of software development organizations
  - The process system architecture
  - Basis concept: regulating software engineering roles and interactions via a process system
  - The role of a process system reference model
  - Derived process models at project level

- Architecture of software process system modeling
  - Process model
    - Taxonomy
    - Domain
    - Reference model
    - Project model
    - Comparison between current process systems

  - Process assessment model
    - Process capability model
      - Practice performance scale
      - Process capability scale
      - Process-oriented capability scale
        - Pass/fail threshold
        - Managerial process capability scale
        - Direct process capability scale
    - Process capability determination model
      - Rating scopes: process, project, organization
      - Rating methods
      - Approaches to measure process capability
        - Pass/fail threshold
        - Managerial process maturity level
        - Direct process capability level
    - Comparison between current process systems

  - Process improvement model
    - Assessment-based
    - Benchmark-based

- Approaches to software process system analysis
  - Process system relations
    - Compatibility
    - Correlation
    - Mapping

> – Process attributes
>   – Mean weighted importance
>   – Ratio of significance
>   – Ratio of practice
>   – Ratio of effectiveness
>   – Characteristic value (Usage)

A set of fundamental concepts has been developed in this chapter for software engineering process system modeling, analysis, and applications. Some of these, which set the stage for the remainder of this book, are as follows:

- A fundamental view of software engineering process systems

- Domain of software engineering process framework

- The generic model of software development organizations

- Process organization in software engineering

- Description and analysis of process relations between process systems

- Characterizing and analysis of process attributes

The process system framework developed in this chapter lays a foundation of software engineering process theory. The unified process framework will serve as a high-level conceptual model for the studies in the rest of this book.

Annotated References

Software engineering process system modeling deals with process framework modeling, process capability modeling, and process capability determination.

- On process framework modeling, Humphrey (1987/88/89) and Paulk et al. (1991/93a/b/c/95a) developed the first set of software processes that covered 18 key practice areas and 150 key practices. The BOOTSTRAP team (1993) and ISO/IEC TR 15504 (1997/1998) extended the process domain to 32 processes, 201 quality-system-attributes, 35 processes, and 201 base practices, respectively. In developing a comprehensive software engineering process reference model (SEPRM), Wang et al. (1996a/97a/98a/99c/e) developed a superset of process domain that covered 51 processes and 444 base process activities. A number of sub-domain process models were developed that covered specific process areas in software engineering; see Bate et al. (1993); Boehm and Bose (1994); Sommerville and Sawyer (1997); Humphrey (1996/97/98); and Jacobson et al. (1998).

- On process capability modeling, Humphrey (1987/88/89) and Paulk et al. (1991) developed the first capability maturity model and revealed that software engineering process can be measured by the process capability maturity levels. The BOOTSTRAP team (1993) and ISO/IEC TR 15504 (1997/1998) extended the capability level measurements to more precise rating scales with a set of capability attributes. In observing that the existing process capability measurement were mainly rated process management capability levels rather than the processes themselves, Wang et al. (1997a/b/99e) developed a direct process rating scale with a set of process capability levels: incomplete, loose, integrated, stable, effective, and refined.

- On process capability determination methodologies, conventional process models provided only operational guidance on how the capability rating scales may be used in process assessment and measurement [Paulk et al., 1991/93a/b/c/95a; ISO 9001, 1989/94; BOOTSTRAP team, 1993; ISO/IEC TR 15504, 1997/1998]. Wang et al. developed a set of formal and algorithmic process capability determination methods [Wang et al., 1997b/99e/h] and elicited the algorithms of current process models, which had been described by natural language.

Software engineering process system analysis explores framework structures, theories, orientations, domain coverage, usability, and characteristics of existing software process models. Conventional approaches were mainly focused on single directional, qualitative, and pairwise analysis between two models [Koch, 1993; Paulk et al., 1994/95b; Jarvinen, 1994; Kugler and Messnarz, 1994; Kitson, 1996]. Wang et al. (1997a/b/99e) developed a framework for systematically characterizing and quantitatively analyzing software engineering process systems with the following formal attributes:

– Compatibility
– Correlation

– Characteristic attributes of processes (mean weighted importance, ratios of significant/practice/effectiveness, and usage)
– Benchmarking of process characteristic attributes

Wang et al. (1997a/b) found that a software process and process system can be described by a relation using set theory, so that mapping between process systems becomes a problem of mapping of relational sets. Based on this formalization, it was further found [Wang et al., 1997a/b] that mappings between process systems were asymmetry, that is, for seeking the whole relational picture between a pair of process models, the mapping should be carried out bidirectionally.

Studies into formal description of process systems and various process description languages may be referred to Saeki et al. (1991), Bandinelli (1993), Finkelstein (1994), and Sutton and Osterweil (1997).

Questions and Problems

2.1 Software engineering process models can be categorized into empirical, formal, descriptive, and prescriptive models. What are the type(s) of current process models, such as CMM, ISO/IEC TR 15504? What are the type(s) of process models this book is aimed at developing?

2.2 Using your own words, describe what software process system modeling is.

2.3 Compare the concept of software process establishment (SPE), assessment (SPA), and improvement (SPI), and explain their inter-relationships.

2.4 Analyze the software quality attributes as described in Table 2.1 and explain what attributes are unique for software quality that are not required for conventional products.

2.5 Comparing conventional programmers with the roles of software engineering professions as described in Table 2.2, explain why an engineering approach to software development has been adopted in the industry.

2.6 Describe the generic approach to software engineering organization and implementation.

2.7 What are the roles of a software engineering process system reference model?

2.8 What is the taxonomy of software engineering process systems adopted in this book? What are the equivalent terms used in other major process models?

2.9 Compare and explain the software process capability scales modeled in current process models.

2.10 What is the classification of types of process capability scales? Explain the advantages and disadvantages of each type of process capability scale.

2.11 What is the compatibility between process models? How is process system compatibility measured?

2.12 What is mapping between process models? How is process system mapping carried out?

2.13 What is the correlation between process models? How are process system correlation levels and ratios measured?

2.14 Assuming a software engineer asks you why a process model includes a certain process but another doesn't, what is your explanation? What are your criteria to include or drop a process in a software engineering process model?

2.15 What kinds of process attributes can be modeled? How are the process attributes measured?

2.16 Do you think the current empirical researches have exhausted the search for useful processes and practices in software engineering modeling? Can you suggest any more?

2.17 Figure 2.3 presents a generic structure of the unified software engineering process system framework. Assuming a new process model consists of a questionnaire and ten processes, analyze what needs to be added in order to be a complete process system model.

Chapter 3

PROCESS ALGEBRA

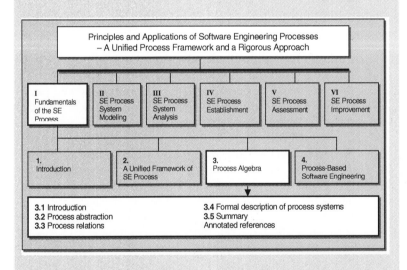

Principles and Applications of Software Engineering Processes
– A Unified Process Framework and a Rigorous Approach

| I Fundamentals of the SE Process | II SE Process System Modeling | III SE Process System Analysis | IV SE Process Establishment | V SE Process Assessment | VI SE Process Improvement |

1. Introduction

2. A Unified Framework of SE Process

3. Process Algebra

4. Process-Based Software Engineering

3.1 Introduction
3.2 Process abstraction
3.3 Process relations

3.4 Formal description of process systems
3.5 Summary
Annotated references

This chapter introduces notations and formal methods for description of software engineering processes and their relationships. A paradigm of process algebra, Communicating Sequential Processes (CSP), is adopted for process system description, modeling, and analysis.

The objectives of this chapter are as follows:

- To investigate formal methods for process description and modeling

- To study the approaches for process abstraction

- To introduce a paradigm of process algebra – CSP

- To demonstrate how process patterns, relationships, and interactions are formally described by process algebra

3.1 Introduction

Algebra is a form of mathematics that simplifies difficult problems by using symbols to represent constants, variables, and calculations. Algebra is also the basis for mathematical expression of abstract entities and their relations. Algebra enables complicated problems to be expressed and investigated in a formal and rigorous way.

If it is considered that numbers are the first degree of human abstraction in mathematics for representing real-world entities and their attributes, algebra, then, is the second degree of abstraction over numbers, which represent both real-world and abstract entities, attributes, and relations between unknown (variables) and known numbers (constants).

Boole (1815-1864) found that logic, the rules of thought, could be represented by binary algebra. This led to the establishment of a branch of modern algebra – **Boolean algebra**. Further, Hoare (1985) and Milner (1989) developed a way to represent computer communicating and concurrent processes by algebra, known as **process algebra**. In his book, *Communicating Sequential Processes* (CSP), Hoare wrote:

The great advantage of mathematics is that the rules are much simpler than those of a natural language, and the vocabulary is much smaller. Consequently, when presented with something unfamiliar, it is possible to work out a solution for yourself by logical deduction and invention rather than by consulting books or experts.

…

This is why mathematics, like programming, can be so enjoyable. … So one must learn to concentrate attention on the cold, dry text of the mathematical expressions and cultivate an appreciation for their elegant abstraction. In particular, some of the recursively defined algorithms have something of the breathtaking beauty of a fugue composed by J. S. Bach.

Process algebra is a set of formal notations and rules for describing algebraic relations of software processes. Process algebra developed by Hoare's CSP and Milner's CCS (the Calculus of Communicating Systems) provides a foundation and powerful tool for formally describing software engineering process and process systems.

This chapter introduces fundamentals of process algebra and extensions of CSP to real-time system description. In order to pave the way for the formal description of current process models in Part II, the emphasis will be put on how the CSP-like process algebra is applied in software engineering process system description and modeling.

3.2 Process Abstraction

Process abstraction and formal description are important in software engineering process modeling and analysis. This section introduces the concept of event, process, and a set of meta-processes. Algebraic expressions of the meta-processes are developed using CSP-like notations and syntax.

3.2.1 EVENT

Definition 3.1 An event, *e,* is any internal or external signal, message, variable, scheduling, conditional change, or timing that is specified in association with specific activities in a process.

Typical events in a system are a timing event, I/O event, system hardware/software event, process event, and interrupt event.

Definition 3.2 An event set, E, is the domain of events (or the alphabet as in CSP) that can be handled by a process P, i.e.:

$$E \triangleq \alpha P$$
$$= \{e_1, e_2, ..., e_n\} \qquad (3.1)$$

3.2.2 PROCESS

Definition 3.3 A generic process, P, is defined as a set of activities associated with a set of events E, i.e.:

$$e_i \rightarrow P, \ \text{if } e_i \in E \qquad (3.2)$$

Expression 3.2 shows that event e_i can trigger process P, or process P can handle event e_i, if e_i is defined in P's event set E.

3.2.3 META-PROCESSES

This subsection describes a set of meta-processes where "meta" means the elementary and primary processes in a system. Complex processes can be derived, as shown in the following sections, from the meta-processes by a set of process combinatory roles.

3.2.3.1 System Dispatch

Definition 3.4 System dispatch is a meta-process that acts at the top level of a process system for dispatching and/or executing a specific process according to system timing or a predefined event table.

A system dispatch process, *SYSTEM*, can be denoted by:

$$SYSTEM \triangleq \{ t_i \Rightarrow P_j \lor e_i \Rightarrow P_j \}, \ i,j = 1, 2, 3, ... \qquad (3.3)$$

where $t_i \Rightarrow P_j$ means a system timing t_i triggers a process P_j, and $e_i \Rightarrow P_j$ means an event e_i triggers the process P_j.

3.2.3.2 Assignment

Definition 3.5 Assignment is a meta-process that assigns a variable x with a constant value c, i.e.:

$$x := c \qquad (3.4)$$

3.2.3.3 Get System Time

Definition 3.6 Get system time is a meta-process that reads the system clock and assigns the current system time t_i to a system time variable t.

A get-system-time process, $@T$, can be denoted by:

$$@T \triangleq t := t_i \qquad (3.5)$$

3.2.3.4 Synchronization

Synchronization between processes can be classified into two types: time synchronization and event synchronization.

Definition 3.7 Time synchronization is a meta-process that holds a process's execution until moment t of the system clock.

A time synchronization process, *SYNC-T*, can be denoted by:

$$SYNC\text{-}T \triangleq @(t) \qquad (3.6)$$

Definition 3.8 Event synchronization is a meta-process that holds a process's execution until event e occurs.

An event synchronization process, *SYNC-E*, can be denoted by:

$$SYNC\text{-}E \triangleq @(e) \qquad (3.7)$$

3.2.3.5 Read and Write

Definition 3.9 Read is a meta-process that gets a message from a memory location or system port.

A read process, *READ*, which gets a message m from a memory or port location l can be denoted by:

$$READ \triangleq l \mathbin{?} m \qquad (3.8)$$

Definition 3.10 Write is a meta-process that puts a message into a memory location or system port.

A write process, *WRITE*, which puts a message m into a memory or port location l can be denoted by:

$$WRITE \triangleq l \: ! \: m \tag{3.9}$$

3.2.3.6 Input and Output

Definition 3.11 Input is a meta-process that receives a message from a system I/O channel which connects the system to other systems.

An input process, *IN*, which receives a message *m* from channel *c* can be denoted by:

$$IN \triangleq c \: ? \: m \tag{3.10}$$

Definition 3.12 Output is a meta-process that sends a message to a system I/O channel which connects the system to other systems.

An output process, *OUT*, which sends a message *m* to a channel *c* can be denoted by:

$$OUT \triangleq c \: ! \: m \tag{3.11}$$

3.2.3.7 Stop

Definition 3.13 Stop is a meta-process that terminates a system's operation. A stop process is denoted by *STOP*.

3.3 Process Relations

This section develops a set of relational operations for describing relationships between processes. The relational operators, such as of sequential, branch, parallel, iteration, interrupt, and recursion, define the rules to form combinatorial processes from simple and meta-processes.

3.3.1 SEQUENTIAL PROCESS

The sequential relation is the simplest relation between processes. This subsection discusses two types of sequential processes: serial and pipeline processes.

3.3.1.1 Serial

Definition 3.14 Serial is a process relation in which a number of processes are executed one by one.

A relational operator ";" is adopted to denote the serial relation between processes. Assuming two processes, P and Q, are serial, their relation can be expressed as follows:

$$P ; Q \qquad (3.12)$$

Expression 3.12 reads, "P followed by Q."

3.3.1.2 Pipeline

Definition 3.15 Pipeline is a process relation in which a number of processes are interconnected to each other, and a process takes the output of the other process(es) as its input.

A relational operator, », is adopted to denote the pipeline relation between processes. Assuming two processes, P and Q, are pipelined, their relation can be expressed as follows:

$$P » Q \qquad (3.13)$$

Expression 3.13 reads, "P output to Q."

3.3.2 BRANCH PROCESS

The branch relation describes the selection of processes based on a conditional event. This subsection discusses three types of branch processes: the event-driven choice, the deterministic choice, and the nondeterministic choice.

3.3.2.1 The Event-Driven Choice

Definition 3.16 The event-driven choice is a process relation in which the execution of a process is determined by the event corresponding to the process.

A relational operator, $|$, is adopted to denote an event-driven choice between processes. Assuming process P accepts event a as input, and Q accepts b, an event-driven choice can be expressed as follows:

$$(a \to P \mid b \to Q) \qquad\qquad (3.14)$$

Expression 3.14 reads, "a then P choice b then Q."

3.3.2.2 The Deterministic Choice

Definition 3.17 The deterministic choice is a process relation in which a set of processes are executed in an externally determinable order.

A relational operator, [], is adopted to denote the relation of deterministic choice between processes. Assuming two processes, P and Q, are related to each other by deterministic choice, their relation can be expressed as follows:

$$P \, [] \, Q \qquad\qquad (3.15)$$

Expression 3.15 reads, "P choice Q."

3.3.2.3 The Nondeterministic Choice

Definition 3.18 The nondeterministic choice is a process relation in which a set of processes are executed in a nondetermined or random order dependent on run-time conditions.

A relational operator, ⊓, is adopted to denote the relation of nondeterministic choice between processes. Nondeterministic choice is also known as "or". Assuming two processes, P and Q, are related to each other by nondeterministic choice, their relation can be expressed as follows:

$$P \sqcap Q \qquad\qquad (3.16)$$

Expression 3.16 reads, "P or Q," or "P nondeterministic choice Q."

3.3.3 PARALLEL PROCESS

Parallel describes the simultaneous and concurrent relation between processes. This subsection discusses three types of parallel processes: the synchronous parallel, the concurrency, and the interleave processes.

3.3.3.1 The Synchronous Parallel

Definition 3.19 The synchronous parallel is a process relation in which a set of processes are executed simultaneously according to a common timing system.

A relational operator, ‖, is adopted to denote a synchronous parallel relation between processes. Assuming two processes, P and Q, are synchronous parallel between each other, their relation can be expressed as follows:

$$P \parallel Q \tag{3.17}$$

Expression 3.17 reads, "P in parallel with Q."

3.3.3.2 Asynchronous Parallel – Concurrency

Definition 3.20 Concurrency is an asynchronous process relation in which a set of processes are executed simultaneously according to independent timing systems, and each such process is executed as a complete task.

A relational operator, ⫴, is adopted to denote a concurrent relation between processes. Assuming two processes, P and Q, are concurrent between each other, their relation can be expressed as follows:

$$P \between Q \tag{3.18}$$

Expression 3.18 reads, "P concurrent with Q."

3.3.3.3 Asynchronous Parallel – Interleave

Definition 3.21 Interleave is an asynchronous process relation in which a set of processes are executed simultaneously according to independent timing systems, and the execution of each such process would be interrupted by other processes.

A relational operator, ⫼, is adopted to denote an interleave relation between processes. Assuming two processes, P and Q, are interleave-related between each other, their relation can be expressed as follows:

$$P \mid\mid\mid Q \tag{3.19}$$

Expression 3.19 reads, "P interleave Q."

3.3.4 ITERATION PROCESS

The iteration relation describes the cyclic relation between processes. This subsection discusses two types of iterative processes: the repeat and the while-do processes.

3.3.4.1 Repeat

Definition 3.22 Repeat is a process relation in which a process is executed repeatedly for a certain times.

A relational operator, $(\ )^n$, is adopted to denote the repeat relation for iterated processes. Assume a process, P, is repeated for n times, the combinatorial process can be expressed as follows:

$$(P)^n \tag{3.20}$$

where $n \in \mathbb{N}$, $n \geq 0$, and P can be a simple process or a combinatorial process. Expression 3.20 reads, "repeat P for n times."

3.3.4.2 While-Do

Definition 3.23 While-Do is a process relation in which a process is executed repeatedly when a certain condition is true.

A relational operator, $*$, is adopted to denote the while-do relation for iterated processes. Assuming a process, P, is iterated until condition γ is not true, the while-do process can be expressed as follows:

$$\gamma * P \tag{3.21}$$

where P can be a simple process or a combinatorial process. Expression 3.21 reads, "while γ do P."

3.3.5 INTERRUPT PROCESS

The interrupt relation describes execution priority and control-taking-over between processes. This subsection discusses interrupt and interrupt return processes.

3.3.5.1 Interrupt

Definition 3.24 Interrupt is a process relation in which a running process is temporarily held before termination by another process that has higher priority, and the interrupted process will be resumed when the high priority process has been completed.

A relational operator, $\nearrow$, is adopted to denote the interrupt relation between processes, and between processes and the system. Assuming process P is interrupted by process Q, the interrupt relation can be expressed as follows:

$$P \nearrow Q \tag{3.22}$$

A special case of interrupt is between a process P and the system environment *SYSTEM*, i.e.:

$$P \nearrow SYSTEM \tag{3.23}$$

In such a case, process P is interrupted by the system dispatcher, *SYSTEM*, and will not automatically return from the interruption, except the system invokes P for a new mission.

Expressions 3.22 and 3.23 read, "P interrupted by Q," or "P interrupted by *SYSTEM*", respectively.

3.3.5.2 Interrupt Return

Definition 3.25 Interrupt return is a process relation in which an interrupted process resumes its running from the point of interruption.

A relational operator, $\searrow$, is adopted to denote an interrupt return between processes. Assuming the running condition of an interrupted process P is regained from process Q, the interrupt return relation can be expressed as follows:

$$Q \searrow P \tag{3.24}$$

Expression 3.24 reads, "Q interrupt returned to P."

3.3.6 RECURSION PROCESS

Recursive technology is frequently used in programming to simplify procedure structure. For example, a simple recursive procedure is given below.

Example 3.1 A recursive procedure.

```
ProcedureA (x: integer): integer;
   Var
        x, y: integer;
   begin
        while x <= 10 do
             begin
                  y := x + 2;
                  Print(x, y);
                  ProcedureA(y);
             end;
   end;
```

When given x=1 as the input to ProcedureA, the output of this recursive procedure is: 1, 3; 3, 5; 5, 7; 7, 9; 9, 11.

In software engineering process modeling, recursive processes can be represented in a similar way. For example, assume a simple everlasting clock, *CLOCK,* which does nothing but tick, i.e.

$$\alpha CLOCK \triangleq \{tick\} \tag{3.25}$$

behaves sequentially as follows:

$$CLOCK \triangleq tick \rightarrow tick \rightarrow tick \rightarrow... \tag{3.26}$$

Using recursive expression, the endless process *CLOCK* can be defined as simply as follows:

$$CLOCK \triangleq tick \rightarrow CLOCK \tag{3.27}$$

Expression 3.27 represents a *CLOCK* that first emits a single tick, then it works with the same behavior as that of the CLOCK defined in expression 3.26.

Definition 3.26 A process, *X,* that begins with a prefix, *x,* which belongs to its alphabet, αX, is said to be **guarded**, i.e.:

$$X = F(X) \triangleq x \rightarrow X \tag{3.28}$$

is a guarded process.

In the remainder of this chapter, we will use *F(X)* to refer to the guarded process *X*.

Definition 3.27 A generic recursive process, *P*, is defined as:

$$P \triangleq \mu X \bullet F(X) \tag{3.29}$$

where μX indicates a recursion of a local variable X that represents the given process *P;* and $F(X)$ is a guarded expression of process X.

Example 3.2 A generic recursive representation of *CLOCK* defined in Expression 3.27 can be given as follows:

$$CLOCK \triangleq \mu X \bullet F(X)$$
$$= \mu X \bullet (tick \rightarrow X)$$

A set of algebraic laws governing the relations of processes has been developed in CSP. These laws provide foundations for understanding and predicting algebraic properties and behaviors of combinatorial processes and process systems. Interested readers may refer to Hoare (1985).

3.4 Formal Description of Process Systems

In the previous sections the meta-processes and relations for building combinatorial processes have been described. This section explores the approach to formally describe software engineering process systems using process algebra.

3.4.1 ROLE OF PROCESS COMBINATION

So far, a set of 11 notations of process relations has been defined. A process relation set, *R*, can be summarized below:

$$R \triangleq \{;, », |, [], \sqcap, \|, [\!|, \|\!|, \mu X \bullet F(X), (\ )^n, \gamma^*P\} \tag{3.30}$$

Adopting the CSP-like process notations and process relations introduced in previous sections, a generic software engineering process, P, can be formally described as follows:

$$P \triangleq (\text{process } R_i \text{ process})^n, \quad R_i \in R \tag{3.31}$$

where R_i is a relation that belongs to the set of process relations described by Expression 3.30, and n is the number of iteration of the processes described in the brackets.

Example 3.3 Given $r = \parallel$, derive $P \triangleq (P_1 \, r \, P_2 \,)^2$ and explain the physical meaning of process P.

According to the definitions of process relations, the following expression of P can be obtained:

$$
\begin{aligned}
P \triangleq (P_1 \, r \, P_2 \,)^2 \\
= (P_1 \parallel P_2 \,)^2 \\
= (P_1 \parallel P_2 \,); (P_1 \parallel P_2 \,)
\end{aligned}
$$

The physical meaning of process P is to execute subprocesses P_1 and P_2 in parallel two times.

Note that in Expression 3.31 a process can be a combined process, so that flexible process expressions may be derived from this expression.

3.4.2 FORMAL DESCRIPTION OF SOFTWARE PROCESSES

Applying the extended CSP process algebra developed in this chapter, readers are able to describe a software engineering process model in a formal way. The formal description is useful for providing precise and accurate definitions of the structure and interrelationships of a process model, and to avoid any ambiguity inherent in the conventional natural language descriptions.

3.4.2.1 System Level Description

System level description provides a formal expression of the structure of a software engineering process system. Observing the example below, it can be seen that the process algebra is capable and flexible enough to describe a given process system.

Example 3.4 The CMM process model, *CMM-PM*, can be formally described as shown in Expression 3.32. Expression 3.32 shows that the high-level structure of the CMM model is sequential with five process capability levels ($CL_1 - CL_5$).

$$
\begin{aligned}
CMM\text{-}PM \triangleq \quad & CL_1 && // \; Initial \\
& ; CL_2 && // \; Repeated \\
& ; CL_3 && // \; Defined \\
& ; CL_4 && // \; Managed \\
& ; CL_5 && // \; Optimizing \quad\quad (3.32)
\end{aligned}
$$

It is noteworthy that, in the algebraic process expression, comments can be provided after // to include additional information or explanation.

An illustration of Expression 3.32 can be derived in Figure 3.1 using the process diagram. Obviously there is one-to-one correspondence between the algebraic process description and the visual illustration of process diagram.

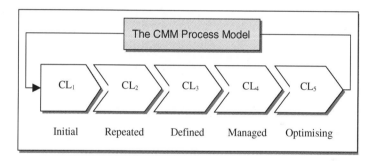

Figure 3.1 A process diagram of the structure of the CMM process model

3.4.2.2 Process Level Description

CSP-like process algebra can also be used to describe more detailed process configuration and more complicated process relations.

Example 3.5 The parallel feature between the development processes and management processes in software engineering has been identified in Chapter 2. A formal description of the parallel software development process model, PPM, using process algebra is as follows:

$$PPM \triangleq DP; \qquad \textit{// Development process category}$$
$$\qquad \| MP \qquad \textit{// Management process category}$$
$$= (DP_1 \| MP_1) \quad \textit{// Requirement analysis/requirement review}$$
$$; (DP_2 \| MP_2) \quad \textit{// Design/design review}$$
$$; (DP_3 \| MP_3) \quad \textit{// Coding/code review}$$
$$; (DP_4 \| MP_4) \quad \textit{// Module testing/module test review}$$
$$; (DP_5 \| MP_5) \quad \textit{// Integration and system test/integration and}$$
$$\qquad \textit{system test review}$$
$$; (DP_6 \| MP_6) \quad \textit{// Design/design review} \qquad (3.33)$$

A process diagram corresponding to Expression 3.33 is shown in Figure 3.2. It indicates how each development process is supported and monitored by a counterpart of the management processes. Detailed discussions of this PPM model will be provided in Chapter 13.

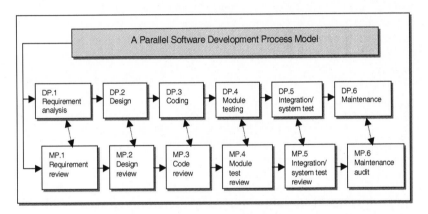

Figure 3.2 A process diagram of parallel software development processes

3.5 Summary

This chapter has introduced CSP as a paradigm of the process algebra. The capability of CSP has been extended to cover important real-time system behaviors such as system dispatching, timing, and interrupt. The extended CSP has been used to describe sample software engineering process models at system and process levels.

The basic knowledge structure of this chapter is as follows:

Chapter 3. Process Algebra

- General
  - Purposes of this chapter
    - To investigate formal methods for process description and modeling
    - To study the approaches for process abstraction
    - To introduce a paradigm of process algebra – CSP
    - To demonstrate how process patterns, relationships, and interactions are formally described by process algebra

  - Advantages of process algebra in formal description of software engineering process systems.

- Process abstraction
  - Basic concept
    - Event
    - Process
    - Meta-process

  - Meta-processes
    - System dispatcher: $SYSTEM \triangleq \{ t_i \Rightarrow P_j \vee e_i \Rightarrow P_j \}$
    - Assignment: $x := c$
    - Get system time: $@T \triangleq t := t_I$
    - Time synchronous: $SYNC\text{-}T \triangleq @(t)$
    - Event synchronous: $SYNC\text{-}E \triangleq @(e)$
    - Read: $READ \triangleq l\,?\,m$
    - Write: $WRITE \triangleq l\,!\,m$
    - Input: $IN \triangleq c\,?\,m$
    - Output: $OUT \triangleq c\,!\,m$
    - Stop: $STOP$

- Process relations
  - Serial: $P\,;\,Q$
  - Pipeline: $P \gg Q$
  - Event-driven choice: $(a \rightarrow P \mid b \rightarrow Q)$
  - Deterministic choice: $P\,[]\,Q$
  - Nondeterministic choice: $P \sqcap Q$
  - Synchronous parallel: $P \parallel Q$

> – Concurrency: $P \lfloor J\ Q$
> – Interleave: $P\ |||\ Q$
> – Repeat: $(P)^n$
> – While-do: $\gamma * P$
> – Interrupt: $P \nearrow Q$
> – Interrupt return: $Q \searrow P$
> – Recursion: $P \triangleq \mu X \bullet F(X)$
>
> - Formal description of software engineering processes
>   – Roles of process combination
> $$P \triangleq (\text{process}\ R\ \text{process})^n$$
> $$R \triangleq \{;, \gg, |, [], \sqcap, ||, \lfloor J, |||, \mu X \bullet F(X), (\ )^n, \gamma * P\}$$
>
>   – Formal description of software engineering processes
>   – Algebraic process expression
>   – Process diagram
>   – Applications

Major achievements and issues for further research suggested by this chapter are highlighted below:

- This chapter has extended the application of **process algebra** to describe software engineering process systems, and has explored its relationship to **process diagrams**.

- The CSP process algebra paradigm has been extended to timing, interrupt, read/write, I/O, etc., to make it suitable for real-time software engineering process system description.

- The advantages of the algebraic approach to process description are that the process algebra enables complicated problems to be expressed and investigated in a formal and rigorous way.

- Boole found that logic, the rules of thought, could be represented by algebra. Hoare and Milner developed a way to represent computer communication and concurrent processes by process algebra. This chapter has intended to introduce process algebra, particularly CSP, to the software engineering process description by extending CSP to cover real-time processes and their relations.

- Process abstraction and formal description is important in software engineering process modeling and analysis. A set of relational operators for describing relationships between processes, and roles to form combinatorial processes from simple and meta-processes, have been developed.

An extended CSP-like process algebra and process diagrams will be used to formally describe the structures and process configurations of current process models throughout the book, especially in Part II.

Annotated References

Algebra as a term was first introduced by Muhammad al-Khwarizmi (780 – 850), known as "al-jabr" in Hindu 1200 years ago. However, it can be traced to the ancient Egyptians more than 3500 years ago. In the 17th century, Rene Descartes (1596 – 1650) discovered that geometric structures could be converted into algebraic equations. Then, 200 years later, George Boole (1815 – 1864) found that logic, the rules of thought, can be represented by algebra. This is one of the foundations of modern computer science and software engineering.

In theoretical computing, Hoare (1985) and Milner (1989) developed a way to represent communicating processes by algebra. In the same period, SDL (CCITT Specification and Description Language) [CCITT, 1988] and LOTOS [ISO 8807, 1988; Yasumoto et al., 1994] were developed within ITU (former CCITT) and ISO, respectively. Reed and Roscoe (1986) partially extended CSP theory and application into real-time systems, known as the timed CSP (T-CSP). Spivey, Bowen, Hayes, etc. developed the Z notation [Spivey, 1988/90/92; Hayes, 1987; Bowen et al., 1998].

Osterweil (1987) asserted that "software processes are software too", and discussed enactability of software processes. Milner (1989) demonstrated that computer communication and concurrency processes can be described by CCS and Petri Nets. Curtis and his colleagues (1992) identified a series of objectives for software process modeling such as communication, improvement, management, automatic guidance, and automatic execution (enacting). Bandinelli and his colleagues (1992) perceived software process as real-time systems and used Petri Nets to describe the software processes.

Haeberer (1999) reviewed algebraic methodology and software technology in *Lecture Notes in Computer Science*, Vol. 1548.

Studies into formal description of process systems and various process description languages may be referred to Saeki et al. (1991), Bandinelli (1993), Finkelstein (1994), and Sutton and Osterweil (1997).

Questions and Problems

3.1 Explain what the advantages of algebraic expression of problems and relations between entities are.

3.2 What is process algebra? What are the existing paradigms of process algebra?

3.3 What is a meta-process? List the meta-processes and their expressions as defined in Section 3.2.

3.4 How many process relations are introduced in this chapter? List the process relations and the relational operators.

3.5 What are the differences between deterministic and nondeterministic choice?

3.6 Contrast the synchronous parallel, concurrency, and interleave process relations and explain what differentiates them from each other.

3.7 What is the usage of recursive processes? What is the generic expression of recursive processes in process algebra?

3.8 Assume $r = ;$, $P_1 = $ coding, and $P_2 = $ test. Describe $P \triangleq (P_1 \, r \, P_2)^1$, and explain the physical meaning of process P.

3.9 Assume $r_1 = ;$, $r_2 = \parallel$, $P_1 = $ design, $P_2 = $ coding, and $P_3 = $ test. Derive $P \triangleq (P_1 \, r_1 \, (P_2 \, r_2 \, P_3)^1)^1$.

3.10 Draw process diagrams for Ex.3.8 and Ex.3.9, respectively.

Chapter 4

PROCESS-BASED SOFTWARE ENGINEERING

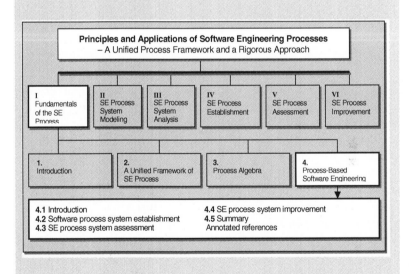

Principles and Applications of Software Engineering Processes
– A Unified Process Framework and a Rigorous Approach

| I Fundamentals of the SE Process | II SE Process System Modeling | III SE Process System Analysis | IV SE Process Establishment | V SE Process Assessment | VI SE Process Improvement |

| 1. Introduction | 2. A Unified Framework of SE Process | 3. Process Algebra | 4. Process-Based Software Engineering |

4.1 Introduction
4.2 Software process system establishment
4.3 SE process system assessment
4.4 SE process system improvement
4.5 Summary
Annotated references

This chapter describes important concepts of process-based software engineering. Key methodologies in process-based software engineering are introduced for process system establishment, assessment, and improvement.

The objectives of this chapter are as follows:

- To introduce the concept of process-based software engineering

- To describe basic process methodologies for software engineering

- To describe software process system establishment procedures and methods

- To describe software process system assessment methods and their classification

- To describe software process system improvement philosophies and methodologies

4.1 Introduction

In the literature of software engineering process research, it has been assumed that a process system already existed in software development organizations so a process assessment and improvement project could be carried out directly. However convenient this assumption is, it is not true that the majority of software organizations have formal, definable processes.

In reality, a process assessment project starts by the mapping of a software organization's existing processes to a process model that has been chosen for the assessment. The usual cases are that a software development organization has only some loose and informal practices, rather than a defined and coherent process system. Assessors have found that the following conversation is typical in the first phase of an assessment:

Assessor(s): Now, let's look at process X. What are your evidences of its performance?

Assessees: Sorry, we're afraid we don't have such a process.

Assessor(s):	Really? You've just completed project Y. If you have no process X, how could you get the software developed?
Assessees:	Well, yes. Of course we had certain practices for this. But, unfortunately, we don't have a defined process of the kind you are expecting.
Assessor(s):	... ?!

This scenario leads to the observation that rigorous process-based software engineering has to start from process establishment rather than process assessment in a software development organization. Therefore, the right order of events in creating software engineering process excellence in an organization is first, process establishment; second, process assessment; and then process improvement as shown in Figure 4.1.

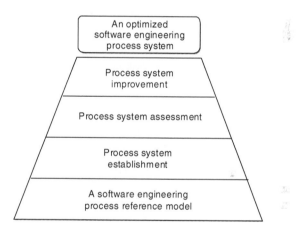

Figure 4.1 Process-based software engineering

With the fundamental architectures and requirements for software engineering process models described in Chapter 2, a software engineering process framework can be systematically established in the organization, development, and management areas at all levels.

4.2 Software Engineering Process System Establishment

Conventional theories and practices in process-based software engineering were mainly focused on software process system assessment and improvement. While an initial, fundamental step, process system establishment, was perhaps widely overlooked. This phenomenon might reflect an intention of the software industry that it was demanding instant effect from the process technology in software engineering.

However, considering that a large proportion of the software industry is still immature as shown in the scenario given in Section 4.1, an initial focus has to be put on software process system establishment. When a process system is established and experienced, improvement can be initiated effectively via process assessment and benchmarking.

A typical software process establishment (SPE) approach and a set of SPE methods identified so far are shown in Table 4.1. This subsection describes the procedure of SPE and introduces the main methodologies for SPE. Full development of the SPE methodologies will be explored in Part IV.

Table 4.1
Software Process System Establishment Procedure and Methods

No.	SPE Procedure	SPE Method
1	Select and reuse a process system reference model at organization level	Tailoring of a reference model
2	Derive a process model at project level	Extension of a reference model
3	Apply the derived project process model as a software engineering platform	Adaptation of a reference model

4.2.1 PROCEDURE TO DERIVE A SOFTWARE PROJECT PROCESS MODEL

This subsection explores the three basic steps, as shown in Table 4.1, for deriving a software project process model.

4.2.1.1 Select and Reuse a Process System Reference Model at Organization Level

The most efficient way for establishing a process system is to reuse a standard or well-accepted process model. As shown in Figure 2.2, in selecting an existing process model as an organization's reference model, one of the key issues is that the reference model should be reasonably comprehensive in order to enable an easy derivation of working process models at project level. The other key issue is that the reference model should able to serve many purposes in software engineering such as multi-type process assessment, improvement, training, and internal standardization. The third issue is the flexibility of the reference model, i.e., the selected reference model should allow incorporation of the host organization's experience and special needs into the reference model and derived models.

When an organization's process system is determined, the next step is to keep it as the organization's official and unified software engineering platform. Based on this, various process models should be derived for different projects.

4.2.1.2 Derive a Process Model at Project Level

After commencing a new project, the first thing that a project manager needs to do is to derive the project's process model. The project process model will serve as a blueprint for organizing all activities that are going to be enacted within the scope of the project, including technical, managerial, organizational, customer, and supporting activities.

A checklist of factors for consideration in deriving a project process model from the reference model is shown in Table 4.2. When all factors are weighted by high (H), Medium (M), or low (L), a rating for what kind of project process model is needed can be determined according to Expressions 4.1 and 4.2.

Assume that S_i is the ith weight for factor i and n is the number of total factors; the average score, S, or the level of requirement for a derived model is defined as:

$$S = 1/n \sum_{i=1}^{n} S_i \tag{4.1}$$

According to the average score S, the type of derived model determined by the weighted factors can be estimated as follows:

$$S \quad \begin{cases} > 3, & \text{the need is for a complete project process model} \\ = 3, & \text{the need is for a medium project process model} \\ < 3, & \text{the need is for a light project process model} \end{cases} \quad (4.2)$$

For instance, applying Expression 4.1 to the weights of the ten factors as shown in Table 4.2 results in an estimated average score $S = 3.6$. According to Expression 4.2, the project process model has to be a relatively complete model which covers more related process areas modeled in the reference model. This requirement provides a good representation of the nature of this project characterized in Table 4.2.

Table 4.2
Determining Type of Derived Process Models for a Project

No.	Project Factor	Weight H	Weight M	Weight L	Score
1	Importance	✔			S1 = 5
2	Difficulty			✔	S2 = 1
3	Complexity	✔			S3 = 5
4	Size		✔		S4 = 3
5	Domain knowledge requirement		✔		S5 = 3
6	Experience requirement	✔			S6 = 5
7	Special process needed			✔	S7 = 1
8	Schedule constraints		✔		S8 = 3
9	Budget constraints	✔			S9 = 5
10	Other process constraints	✔			S10 = 5
Total		**25**	**9**	**2**	**S = 3.6**

Note: H = High (5), M = Medium (3), L = Low (1).

Note the factors shown in Table 4.2 are examples for demonstrating how the type of project process model can be determined in a formal way. It is by no means exhaustive. Therefore, readers may add, delete, and/or modify the factors in order to make them suitable for their specific projects.

4.2.1.3 Apply the Derived Project Process Model

When a project process system model is derived, the next step is to accept, as a common platform, the process model at both project and individual levels and apply the project process model to all activities within the project scope. Guidance for how to perform the technical and managerial activities specified in a project process model is outside of the scope of this book; readers may refer to Humphrey (1995) and Pressman (1992).

It can be seen that the reference model approach to implement software engineering provides project managers with a means to consistently derive and organize a project process model. It also provides software engineers and others in a software project with a clear picture of their roles, interaction, and relationship to each other.

4.2.2 METHODS FOR DERIVING A SOFTWARE PROJECT PROCESS MODEL

In establishing a process model for a software project, three types of methodologies may be identified. They are process model tailoring, extension, and adaptation, ordered increasingly according to their technical difficulty in applications.

4.2.2.1 Process Model Tailoring

Definition 4.1 Tailoring is a model customization method for making a process model suitable for a specific software project by deleting unnecessary processes.

Model tailoring is the simplest method to derive a project process model from a comprehensive organizational process reference model. The only technique is to delete what is not needed in order to execute a specific software project based on one's understanding of both the reference model and the nature of the project.

4.2.2.2 Process Model Extension

Definition 4.2 Extension is a model customization method for making a process model suitable for a specific software project by adding additional processes.

Model extension requires a project manager capable of integrating new processes adopted from either process models or best practices repositories into the current project process model or organizational process reference model. When new processes are introduced, a validation phase is needed for monitoring their fitness and performance.

4.2.2.3 Process Model Adaptation

Definition 4.3 Adaptation is a model customization method for making a process model suitable for a specific software project by modifying, updating, and fine-tuning related processes.

Model adaptation is useful when a project manager is experienced in a process reference model and prepared to monitor the performance of adapted processes during a project life span.

All three approaches for process model derivation and establishment can be used individually or together to result in an excellent project process model for software engineering. Detailed process system establishment methodologies and related case studies will be provided in Part IV of this book.

4.3 Software Engineering Process System Assessment

If one cannot measure a process system, one cannot improve it. Therefore, software process assessment (SPA) is at the heart of process improvement. Various methodologies of SPA have been developed in the last decade. The SPA methodologies can be classified as shown in Table 4.3.

Table 4.3
Categorization of Software Process System Assessment Methods

No.	Category	SPA Method
1	From the viewpoint of reference system	
1.1		Model-based assessment
1.2		Standard-based assessment
1.3		Benchmark-based assessment
1.4		Integrated assessment (Model + Benchmark)
2	From the viewpoint of model structure	
2.1		Checklist-based assessment
2.2		1-D process-based assessment
2.3		2-D process-based assessment
3	From the viewpoint of assessor's party	
3.1		First-party assessment
3.2		Second-party assessment
3.3		Third-party assessment
3.4		Authorized assessment

This section describes the integrated SPA framework as shown in Table 4.3, and demonstrates that current process models, such as CMM, ISO 9001, BOOTSTRAP, ISO/IEC TR 15504, and SEPRM, can be perfectly fitted into this framework.

4.3.1 PROCESS ASSESSMENT METHODS FROM THE VIEWPOINT OF REFERENCE SYSTEMS

From the viewpoint of reference systems there are four types of assessment methods. They are: model-based, standard-based, benchmark-based, and integrated (model-and-benchmark-based) assessment.

4.3.1.1 Model-Based Assessment

Definition 4.4 Model-based assessment is an SPA method by which a software development organization is evaluated against a specific process and capability model, and according to a specific capability determination method provided in the model.

Model-based assessment is a kind of absolute assessment approach. Using this approach, a software development organization is evaluated against a fixed process framework and a defined capability scale. The assessment result reports a regressed capability level of a software development organization in the capability scale of the model. CMM (see Chapter 5) and BOOTSTRAP (see Chapter 7) are examples of model-based assessment methodologies.

4.3.1.2 Standard-Based Assessment

Definition 4.5 Standard-based assessment is an SPA method by which a software development organization is evaluated against a specific process and capability model defined by a standard, and according to a specific capability determination method provided in the standard.

Standard-based assessment is a special type of model-based assessment method. It also provides an absolute assessment approach by which a software development organization's process capability is rated against a defined capability scale. ISO/IEC TR 15504 (see Chapter 8) and partially ISO 9001 (see Chapter 6) are examples of standard-based assessment methodologies.

4.3.1.3 Benchmark-Based Assessment

Prior to defining benchmark-based assessment, it was necessary to introduce the concept of a software process benchmark. A benchmark of a software engineering process system can be described as follows:

Definition 4.6 A benchmark of a software process system is a set of statistical reference data that represents all processes' average performance in software engineering.

Based on the definition of a software process benchmark, a new type of SPA methodology can be developed.

Definition 4.7 Benchmark-based assessment is an SPA method by which a software development organization is evaluated against a set of benchmarks of software processes, and according to a specific capability determination method.

Benchmark-based assessment is a kind of relative assessment approach. By this approach a software development organization is evaluated against a set of benchmarks. Thus, the assessment result associated with a software development organization's capability level may be presented in three relative levels: below, equal, or above the benchmarks of each process.

IBM has developed a benchmark of a selected set of software practices in Europe [IBM, 1996] which contains 66 benchmarked practices. Having carried out a series of worldwide surveys, the authors have established a superset of benchmarks on 444 practices in 51 processes according to the SEPRM model (refer to Chapters 9, 10, and Appendix D) [Wang et al., 1998a/1999c]. Further work on benchmark based SPA has been reported by Wang et al. (1999f) on the establishment of a national software engineering practices benchmark, and a comparison between that national benchmark and the European benchmark.

4.3.1.4 Integrated Assessment

Definition 4.8 Integrated assessment is a kind of composite model- and benchmark-based SPA method in which a software development organization is evaluated against both benchmarked process model and a capability model, and according to a specific capability determination method provided in the model.

The integrated assessment method inherits the advantages of both absolute and relative SPA methods as described in this section. Using the integrated assessment method, a software development organization can be evaluated against both a benchmark and an absolute capability scale at the same time. The SEPRM model (see Chapter 9) is such an integrated SPA model.

Another advantage of the integrated assessment method is its ability for quantitative software process improvement. This feature will be described in Section 4.4.

4.3.2 PROCESS ASSESSMENT METHODS FROM THE VIEWPOINT OF MODEL STRUCTURES

From the viewpoint of model framework structures, there are three types of assessment methods. They are: checklist-based assessment, 1-D process-based assessment, and 2-D process-based assessment, as illustrated in Figure 4.2.

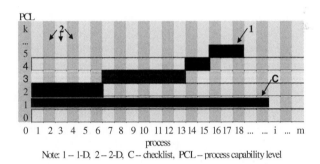

Note: 1 -- 1-D, 2 -- 2-D, C -- checklist, PCL -- process capability level

Figure 4.2 Process assessment methods according to different model structures

Figure 4.2 illustrates that a two-dimensional (2-D) process model allows all processes to be performed and rated at any process capability level. A one-dimensional (1-D) process model is a special case of 2-D models, where a group of processes are defined and rated at a certain capability level. For example, according to the 1-D process model, processes 7 – 13 in Figure 4.2 can only be performed, and therefore rated at level 3 and below. Similarly, the checklist-based process model is a simpler 1-D process model, where all processes are defined and rated at a single level with the same importance.

4.3.2.1 Checklist-Based Assessment

Definition 4.9 Checklist-based assessment is an SPA method that is based on a pass/fail checklist for each practice and process specified in a process model.

A checklist-based assessment model is the simplest assessment methodology. This kind of method is only suitable for SPA. It is not much help in step-by-step process improvement. The ISO 9001 model provides a checklist-based assessment method.

4.3.2.2 One-Dimension Process-Based Assessment

Definition 4.10 1-D process assessment is an SPA method that determines a software development organization's capability from a set of processes in a single process dimension.

The 1-D assessment is an extension of the checklist-based assessment. This type of model is suitable for process improvement in project or organization scopes while, at the same time, being relatively weak in detailed process scope simply because processes have been grouped and preallocated at specific capability levels as shown in Figure 4.2. CMM and BOOTSTRAP are examples of 1-D assessment models.

An issue present in such methods is that there are no widely accepted criteria prescribing how a set of software processes are grouped and mapped onto different capability levels. In principle, the processes defined in a model would be practiced at any capability level. That is, software processes in practice have no inherited capability levels; only the software development organization and the people who are implementing and performing the processes can be measured by capability levels.

4.3.2.3 Two-Dimension Process-Based Assessment

Definition 4.11 2-D process assessment is an SPA method that employs both process and capability dimensions in a process model, and derives processes' capability by evaluating the process model against the capability model.

The 2-D assessment method enables every process in the process dimension to be performed and evaluated against the capability dimension at all levels. This is a flexible approach to software process assessment although effort spent in a 2-D process assessment would be much higher than that of a 1-D or checklist assessment. This type of model is suitable for process improvement from process scope to project and organization scopes because it provides precise measurement for every process at all the capability levels. ISO/IEC TR 15504 (Chapter 8) and SEPRM (Chapter 9) are examples of 2-D assessment models.

Conventionally, 1-D methods were considered to have provided a process dimension in process assessment. By comparing this with the 2-D assessment methods described above and in Figure 4.2, it may be predicted that another kind of 1-D process assessment model which implements only the capability dimension while leaving the process dimension open for a software development organization or the process model providers to design and implement. This would provide a level of flexibility in software process assessment and standardization.

4.3.3 PROCESS ASSESSMENT METHODS FROM THE VIEWPOINT OF ASSESSOR REPRESENTATIVE

From the viewpoint of assessor's representative, there are four types of assessment methods. They are: first-party, second-party, third-party, and authorized assessment.

4.3.3.1 First-Party Assessment

Definition 4.12 First-party assessment is a kind of internal assessment that is conducted by a software development organization itself and applies an independent or internal SPA model or standard.

A first-party assessment is an important quantitative management method to help a software development organization to understand the current status, problems, strengths, weaknesses, trends, and effectiveness of its software engineering activities. A first-party assessment can be adopted to prepare for an authorized or other-parties assessment. It is also useful in a self-motivational software process improvement scheme.

4.3.3.2 Second-Party Assessment

Definition 4.13 Second-party assessment is a kind of independent assessment conducted by a primary party for evaluation of an associate party's software process capability against a specific SPA model or standard.

Examples of this kind of assessment can be a supplier assessment by a purchaser, or a subcontractor assessment by a main contractor. Supplier assessment may be carried out against an independent process standard or a mutually recognized process model. Subcontractor assessment may be carried out with the same process model or standard that the main contractor uses, either internal or independent.

4.3.3.3 Third-Party Assessment

Definition 4.14 Third-party assessment is a kind of independent assessment that employs assessor(s) from the third-party and uses independent process models or standards.

For example, a CMM-certified assessment is a third-party assessment leading to the recognition of a CMM software capability maturity level.

4.3.3.4 Authorized Assessment

Definition 4.15 Authorized assessment is a special kind of third-party assessment against an independent standard and leads to registration or certification by the standardization organization.

A conformance assessment for ISO 9001, for example, is an authorized assessment leading to a registration to ISO 9001 certification.

4.3.4 USAGE OF CURRENT PROCESS MODELS IN PROCESS ASSESSMENT

As a conclusion of the discussions on process assessment methodologies in this section, and by referring to the unified software engineering process assessment framework developed in Section 2.4, a summary of the features of current process models is listed in Table 4.4

In practice, one or combined process assessment models and methodologies may be adopted. Detailed process system assessment methodologies and case studies will be provided in Part V for exploring the model-based, benchmark-based, template-based, and tool-based software process assessments.

Table 4.4
Categorization of Current Models for Process Assessment

Method	CMM	Bootstrap	ISO 15504	ISO 9001	SEPRM
By system of reference	Model-Based	Model-based	Standard-based	Standard-based	Model-based, and Benchmark-based
By structure of model	1-D	1-D	2-D	1-D	2-D
By party of assessor	P1, P2, P3	P1, P2, P3	A, P1, P2, P3	A, P1, P2, P3	At, P1, P2, P3

Notes: A – authorized assessment, P1 – first-party assessment, P2 – second-party assessment, and P3 – third-party assessment; † Based on the capability transform function of SEPRM, a capability level of SEPRM can be quantitatively transferred into a correspondent ISO/IEC TR 15504 or ISO 9001 level (see Chapter 12).

4.4 Software Engineering Process System Improvement

Software engineering process system improvement is the goal of process assessment, acting on the issues found in an assessment and enhancing the processes that are proven effective in the process system. This section attempts to describe major philosophies in software process improvement (SPI) and alternative SPI methodologies.

4.4.1 SOFTWARE PROCESS IMPROVEMENT PHILOSOPHIES AND APPROACHES

There are various philosophies underpinning software process improvement. Key categories of SPI philosophy are as follows:

- Goal-oriented process improvement

- Operational process improvement

- Continuous process improvement

This subsection discusses the philosophies behind the process improvement methodologies. The usability of the SPI approaches and their relationships are also commented upon.

Definition 4.16 Goal-oriented process improvement is an SPI approach by which a process system's capability is improved by moving towards a predefined goal, usually a specific process capability level.

This approach is simple, and is the most widely adopted philosophy in software engineering. For example, ISO 9001 provides a pass/fail goal with a basic set of requirements for a software process system. CMM, ISO/IEC TR 15504, and SEPRM provide a 5/6-level capability scale which enables software development organizations to set more precise and quantitative improvement goals.

Definition 4.17 Operational process improvement is an SPI approach by which a process system's capability is improved by moving towards an optimum combined profile rather than a maximum capability level.

This is a realistic and pragmatic philosophy for process improvement. It is argued that in order to maintain sufficient competence, a software organization does not need to push all its software engineering processes to the highest level because it is not necessary and not economic. The philosophy provides alternative thinking to the idea "the higher the better for process capability" as is presented in the goal-oriented process improvement approach.

Using the operational improvement approach, an optimized process improvement strategy identifies a sufficient (the minimum required) and economic target process profile, which provides an organization with sufficient margins of competence in every process. It does not necessarily set them all at the highest level of a capability scale.

Definition 4.18 Continuous process improvement is an SPI approach by which a process system's capability is required to be improved all the time, and toward endless higher capability levels.

This is considered an oriental philosophy that accepts no top limits or discrete goals because "ideal" standards are continuously changing. It is this assumption that change is normal that is in tune with modern management theory. Continuous process improvement has been proven effective in engineering process optimization and quality assurance. Using this approach, SPI is a continuous, spiral-like procedure. The Deming Circle, plan-do-check-act, is a typical component of this philosophy.

In continuous process improvement there is no end for process optimization, and all processes are supposed to be improved all the time. There is argument that the goals for improvement are not explicitly stated in this philosophy. Therefore, when adopting continuous process improvement, top management should make clear the current goals, as well as the short, middle, and long-term ones.

Generally, goal-oriented methodologies will still constitute the mainstream in SPI. While 2-D process models provide more precise process assessment results, and the benchmark-based process models provide empirical indications of process attributes, operational process improvement, especially benchmark-based improvement, will gain wider application. Also, the continuous process improvement approach will provide a basis for sustainable long-term strategic planning.

4.4.2 SOFTWARE PROCESS SYSTEM IMPROVEMENT METHODOLOGIES

The above discussion on the philosophies for process improvement yields the basis of an investigation of possible software process improvement methodologies. As shown in Table 4.5, there are two basic SPI methods – assessment-based and benchmark-based process improvement. These have been introduced in Section 2.5.3. The former improves a process system from a given level in a defined scale to a next higher level; the latter provides improvement strategies by identifying gaps between a software development organization's process system and a set of established benchmarks. In addition, a combined approach may be adopted.

Table 4.5
Categorization of SPI Methods

No.	SPI Method	
1	Assessment-based improvement	
1.1		Model-based improvement
1.2		Standard-based improvement
2	Benchmark-based improvement	
3	Integrated (assessment-and-benchmark-based improvement	

In Table 4.5, it is shown that assessment-based process improvement can be further divided into model-based and standard-based process improvement. In addition, there is an integrated method that combines both assessment- and benchmark-based methods.

4.4.2.1 Model-Based Improvement

Definition 4.19 Model-based improvement is an SPI method by which a process system can be improved by basing its performance and capability profile on a model-based assessment.

Using this idea, the processes inherent in a software development organization are improved according to a process system model with step-by-step suggestions. CMM and BOOTSTRAP are examples of such a model-based process improvement methodology.

4.4.2.2 Standard-Based Improvement

Definition 4.20 Standard-based improvement is an SPI method in which a process system can be improved by basing its performance and capability profile on a standard-based assessment.

Using this approach, the processes inherent in a software development organization are improved according to a standardized process system model. ISO/IEC 15504 provides a standard-based improvement method. However, it is noteworthy that ISO 9001 is probably not suitable because it lacks a process improvement model and a step-by-step improvement mechanism as analyzed in Section 4.3.

4.4.2.3 Benchmark-Based Improvement

Definition 4.21 Benchmark-based improvement is an SPI method in which a process system can be improved by basing its performance and capability profile on a benchmark-based assessment.

Benchmark-based improvement is a kind of relative improvement approach. Using this approach, the processes inherent in a software development organization are improved according to a set of process benchmarks. As described in Section 4.3, benchmark-based process improvement is supported by the operational process improvement philosophy. It should provide an optimized and economical process improvement solution. SEPRM is the first benchmarked model for enabling benchmark-based process improvements [Wang et al., 1998a/99e].

4.4.2.4 Integrated Improvement

Definition 4.22 Integrated improvement is a combined model- and benchmark-based SPI method in which the process system can be improved by basing its performance and capability profile on an integrated model- and benchmark-based assessment.

The integrated process improvement method inherits the advantages of both absolute and relative SPI methods. Using the integrated improvement method, the processes of a software development organization are improved according to a benchmarked process system model. SEPRM is designed to support integrated model- and benchmark-based process improvement [Wang et al., 1999e].

4.4.3 USAGE OF CURRENT PROCESS MODELS IN PROCESS IMPROVEMENT

A summary of the usage of current process models for process improvement is listed in Table 4.6. Detailed process system improvement methodologies in software engineering and case studies will be addressed in Part VI.

Table 4.6
Categorization of Current Models for Software Process Improvement

Methodology	CMM	Bootstrap	ISO 15504	ISO 9001	SEPRM
Model-/standard-based improvement	✔	✔	✔	✔	✔
Benchmark-based improvement					✔
Integrated improvement					✔

4.5 Summary

This chapter has extended the unified process theory to cover methodologies for process-based software engineering such as process system establishment, assessment, and improvement.

The basic knowledge structure of this chapter is as follows:

Chapter 4. Process-Based Software Engineering

- General
  - Purposes of this chapter
    - To introduce the concept of process-based software engineering

    - To describe basic process methodologies for software engineering

    - To describe software process system establishment procedures and methods

    - To describe software process system assessment methods and their classification

    - To describe software process system improvement philosophies and methodologies

- Process system establishment
  - Procedure
    - To select a process reference model for the organization
    - To derive a process model for a project
    - To apply the derived project process model as a software engineering platform

  - Methods
    - Tailoring
    - Extension
    - Adaptation

- Process system assessment
  - Structures of process assessment model
    - Checklist process model
    - 1-D process model
    - 2-D process models
    - Relationships and features

  - Method of process system assessment
    - Model-based assessment
    - Benchmark-based assessment
    - Usage of current process models for system assessment

- Process system improvement
  - Approaches to process system improvement
    - Goal-oriented process improvement
    - Benchmark-based process improvement
    - Continuous process improvement

  - Method of process system improvement
    - Model-based improvement
    - Benchmark-based improvement
    - Usage of current process models for system Improvement

Major achievements and issues for further research suggested by this chapter are highlighted below:

- The differences between checklist, 1-D, and 2-D process models and their features

- The need for a focus on process system establishment

- Three philosophies for software process improvement

- Classification of software process assessment

A framework structure of process-based software engineering has been built in this chapter. Main concepts, definitions, and methodologies introduced in this chapter will be applied in the remainder of the book.

Extended descriptions and case studies for process-based software engineering will be provided in Parts IV – VI, which cover software process system establishment, assessment, and improvement, respectively.

Annotated References

Work leading to the wide acceptation of the concept and techniques of software process were developed by Weinwurm and Zagorski, 1965; Basili, 1980; Aron, 1983; Agresti, 1986; Evans, 1987; Boehm, 1986/94; Humphrey, 1987/88/89/95/99; Gilb, 1988; and Lehman, 1991.

The scope of software engineering process research was extended and methodologies were refined by Paulk and his colleagues, 1991/93c; ISO 9001, 1994; Dorling, 1993/95; Kuvaja et al., 1994; Rout, 1995; El Eman et al., 1997; ISO/IEC TR 15504, 1998; Wang et al., 1996a/97a/b/98a/b/99c/e/f; and Zahran, 1998.

On concept and approaches to process-based software engineering, see Barghouti and Krishnamurthy, 1993; Garg and Jazayeri, 1995; and Wang et al., 1996a/97a/b/99e. On empirical foundations of software process and survey report of benchmarks of software engineering processes and best practices, see Wang et al. (1998a/99c).

Questions and Problems

4.1 What are the roles of processes in software engineering?

4.2 What are the differences between the checklist, 1-D, and 2-D process models?

4.3 What are the advantages and disadvantages of the checklist, 1-D, and 2-D process models?

4.4 How did this chapter classify the methods of process system establishment?

4.5 Can you suggest any additional approach(es) for process system establishment based on the literature?

4.6 How did this chapter classify the methods of process system assessment?

4.7 Can you suggest any novel approach(es) for process system assessment based on the literature?

4.8 How did this chapter classify the methods of process system improvement?

4.9 Can you suggest any additional approach(es) for process system improvement based on the literature?

4.10 What are the purposes of a self-assessment for an organization's software process system?

4.11 What are the different philosophies behind software process improvement?

4.12 What is a benchmark of a software process system? What are the approaches to help you establish a benchmark for an empirical research topic?

4.13 If an organization asks you to provide a software process assessment with the aim of working toward a widely recognized certification, what process model would you choose? What is/are the reason(s) behind your choice?

4.14 What key methodologies should a software process improvement plan include for a newly established software development organization? What should be included for a well-established software organization that has many years of successful software development experience?

4.15 Assuming a software organization needs help for establishing a small part of the processes presented in a process model, what do you need to know in order to recommend the priority of processes that would be implemented in the organization?

PART II

SOFTWARE ENGINEERING PROCESS SYSTEM MODELING

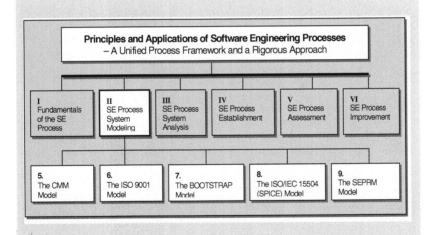

Software engineering process system modeling explores the complete domain of software engineering processes, architectures, and the underlying framework. This part investigates current process models, and contrasts them with the unified process framework developed in Part I.

The knowledge structure of this part is as follows:

- Chapter 5. The CMM Model
- Chapter 6. The ISO 9001 Model
- Chapter 7. The BOOTSTRAP Model
- Chapter 8. The ISO/IEC TR 15504 (SPICE) Model
- Chapter 9. The Software Engineering Process Reference Model: SEPRM

The philosophies implied in each process system model are as shown in Table II.1. It is obvious that historically and technically the current process models represent various design orientation and philosophical views of software engineering. Thus, an overarching process system model, the Software Engineering Process Reference Model (SEPRM), will be developed in order to integrate current process models according to the unified process framework developed in Part I.

Table II.1
Philosophies and Background Orientations of
Current Software Engineering Process Models

Chronology	Model	Philosophy or Background Orientation
1987	CMM	To present a software project contractor's perception on the organizational and managerial capacity of a software development organization.
1991	ISO 9001	To present a generic quality system perception on software development.
1993	BOOTSTRAP	To present a combined view of software lifecycle processes and quality system principles.
1998	ISO/IEC TR 15504 (SPICE)	To present a set of structured capability measurements for all software lifecycle processes, and for all parties such as software developers, acquirers, contractors, and customers.
1998	SEPRM	To present a comprehensive and integrated process system reference model, with sound foundations and process benchmark support, for process-based software engineering.

The current process models analyzed in this part (except SEPRM) were originally described using natural language. Neither formal descriptions nor quantitative algorithms were adopted. This part introduces a formal and algorithmic approach to the description of current process models for the first time, intended:

- To enable mutual comparison between multimodels

- To avoid ambiguity in application

- To simplify manipulation in assessment

- To support implementation of computer-aided software process assessment and improvement tools based on the formal models and algorithms

Using the unified process system framework developed in Part I as fundamental architecture, structures and methods of current software process models such as CMM, ISO 9001, BOOTSTRAP, and ISO/IEC TR 15504 are examined. Algorithms of these models are elicited and formalized. The usability of current process models for software engineering process system establishment, assessment, and improvement are analyzed. In order to present both sides of the coin for each model in this part, the features and limitations of these models in particular aspects of software engineering applications are discussed using the repository of empirical and theoretical studies.

SEPRM is developed as a superset of the paradigms found in current process models, and used to demonstrate the advantages of the unified process framework and what a complete picture of a software engineering process system may look like based on the improved understanding that results.

In this part it is also demonstrated that current process models can be fit very well within the unified process framework. To demonstrate this, a bit repetition is employed in order to unify the style of representations for all models.

Chapter 5

THE CMM MODEL

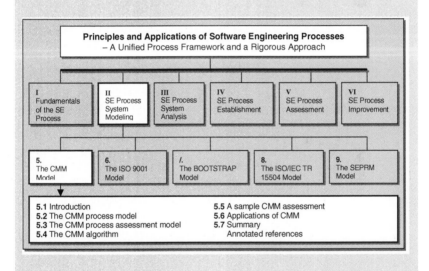

Principles and Applications of Software Engineering Processes
– A Unified Process Framework and a Rigorous Approach

I Fundamentals of the SE Process	II SE Process System Modeling	III SE Process System Analysis	IV SE Process Establishment	V SE Process Assessment	VI SE Process Improvement

5. The CMM Model	6. The ISO 9001 Model	7. The BOOTSTRAP Model	8. The ISO/IEC TR 15504 Model	9. The SEPRM Model

5.1 Introduction
5.2 The CMM process model
5.3 The CMM process assessment model
5.4 The CMM algorithm

5.5 A sample CMM assessment
5.6 Applications of CMM
5.7 Summary
   Annotated references

CMM was the first process methodology that tried to model software engineering process systems. This chapter describes the CMM model, including its process model, process capability model, and process capability determination methodology.

To avoid any ambiguity and redundancy in conventional natural language description of CMM, this chapter adopts a formal and algorithmic approach. A CMM algorithm will be elicited and a sample assessment will be provided in order to demonstrate how a CMM-based process assessment is carried out in practice. The usability of CMM is discussed on the basis of empirical experience in the software industry and research reports in the literature.

The objectives of this chapter are as follows:

- To review the history and background of CMM development

- To describe the CMM process model and taxonomy

- To describe the CMM capability model and capability determination methodology

- To develop an approach to formally describe the CMM process model, and to algorithmically describe the CMM process capability determination method

- To develop a CMM algorithm for software process assessment

- To explain how the CMM algorithm can be used in process assessment and how its algorithm complexity is estimated

- To demonstrate a case study of a practical CMM assessment by using the CMM algorithm

- To discuss the usability of CMM in process establishment, assessment, and improvement in software engineering

5.1 Introduction

The capability maturity model (CMM) [Paulk et al., 1991; Humphrey et al., 1987/88/89] was initially developed in the Software Engineering Institute (SEI) at Carnegie-Mellon University in 1987. The current version of CMM (Version 1.1) was released in 1993 [Paulk et al., 1993a/b/c/95a].

In order to understand the background of the development of CMM and its philosophy, it is helpful to review technical developments in the computer industry and market requirements in the 1980s through which a software industry was enabled and demanded.

Software vendors have existed since the first stored-program-controlled computer was invented in 1946, but an application explosion occurred with the advent of the microprocessor in the 1970s. After the invention of the first microprocessor by Intel in 1971, and the development of first-generation personal computers (PCs) by Apple in 1977, and by IBM in 1982 with MS-DOS, programming approaches have changed dramatically from a laboratory-based and machine-dependent activity to an individual-enabled and common-platform-based activity. That technical development created a chance to enable a software industry to emerge in the 1980s as an independent sector providing system and application software for the computer and other traditional industries, as well as for personal computing needs.

Along with the technical development, the major industrial sectors, such as telecommunications, banking, defense, and personal computing, had been the important customers of the emerging software industry. Since the software industry was still relatively young, it contained professionals and amateurs, experienced software development organizations and those newly established. Therefore, ways of distinguishing and selecting software providers had been a critical problem.

This requirement led to the development of the SEI method for assessing software project contractors [Humphrey, 1988/89] and the SEI capability maturity model (CMM) for software [Paulk et al., 1991/1993a/b/c]. A set of important concepts and successful experience, such as process, quality, and management techniques, have been introduced into software engineering from management science and engineering, especially from the work of Walter Shewhart (1939), Joseph Juran (1962/80/88/89), W. Edwards Deming (1982a/b, 1986), and Philip Crosby (1979), as reviewed in Chapter 2.

However, in addition to the initial goals of CMM for software engineering management capability modeling and software organization maturity measurement, researchers and the software industry soon realized that the concept of software process introduced in CMM is a universal model for organizing software engineering. This led to studies in process-based software engineering environment and the development of a number of new software process models.

This chapter provides a formal description of CMM in accordance with the unified process system framework developed in Part I. A framework and taxonomy of the CMM process model are introduced in Section 5.2. The CMM capability model and process capability determination method are described in Section 5.3. Based on this, a CMM process assessment algorithm is elicited, and an example of CMM assessment is provided in

Sections 5.4 and 5.5, respectively. Finally, the usability of CMM is discussed in Section 5.6.

5.2 The CMM Process Model

This section describes the CMM process taxonomy and framework. The terms and process structure of CMM are introduced using the original form of expression, and are contrasted with the unified software process system framework developed in Part I.

5.2.1 TAXONOMY OF THE CMM PROCESS MODEL

Referring to the generic process taxonomy defined in Chapter 2, the CMM process hierarchy and domains are listed in Table 5.1.

Table 5.1
Process Hierarchy and Domains of the CMM Process Model

Taxonomy	Subsystem	Category	Process	Practice
Process scope	-	Capability levels (CLs)	Key practice areas (KPAs)	Key practices (KPs)
Size of domain	-	5	18	150
Identification	-	CL[i]	KPA[i, k]	KP[i, k, j]

Table 5.1 defines the configuration of the CMM process model. As shown, the KPs and KPAs used in CMM are equivalent to the practices and processes, respectively, as defined in the unified process system framework.

In order to provide a formal identification for each entity defined at various levels of coverage known as process scopes, the indexing of CL, KPA, and KP are described using a naming convention as shown in Table 5.1. In the table, i is the number of CL, k the number of KPA at ith CL, and j the number of KP in kth KPA at CL_i.

5.2.2 FRAMEWORK OF THE CMM PROCESS MODEL

CMM models a software process system at 5 capability levels, in 18 key practice areas, and 150 key practices. A hierarchical structure of the CMM framework is shown in Table 5.2.

Table 5.2
The CMM Process Model

ID.	Level	Key Practice Area (KPA)	Identified KPs	Purpose of KPA
CL₁	Initial		0	–
CL₂	Repeated		62	
KPA₂.₁		Requirement management	3	To establish a common understanding between the customer and the software project of the customer's requirements that will be addressed by the software project.
KPA₂.₂		Software project planning	15	To establish reasonable plans for performing the software engineering and for managing the software project.
KPA₂.₃		Software project tracking and oversight	13	To establish adequate visibility into actual progress so that management can take effective actions when the software project's performance deviates significantly from the software plans.
KPA₂.₄		Software subcontract management	13	To select qualified software subcontractors and manage them effectively.
KPA₂.₅		Software quality assurance	8	To provide management with appropriate visibility into the process being used by the software project and of the products being built.
KPA₂.₆		Software configuration management	10	To establish and maintain the integrity of the products of the software project throughout the project's software life cycle.
CL₃	Defined		50	
KPA₃.₁		Organization process focus	7	To establish the organizational responsibility for software process activities that improve the organization's overall software process capability.
KPA₃.₂		Organization process definition	6	To develop and maintain a usable set of software process assets that improve process performance across the projects and provide a basis for cumulative, long-term benefits to the organization.
KPA₃.₃		Training program	6	To develop the skills and knowledge of individuals so that they can perform their roles effectively and efficiently.

KPA3.4		Integrated software management	11	To integrate the software engineering and management activities into a coherent, defined software process that is tailored from the organization's standard software process and related process assets, which are described in KPA 3.2.
KPA3.5		Software product engineering	10	To consistently perform a well-defined engineering process that integrates all the software engineering activities to produce correct, consistent software products effectively and efficiently.
KPA3.6		Intergroup coordination	7	To establish a means for the software engineering group to participate actively with the other engineering groups so that the project is better able to satisfy the customer's needs effectively and efficiently.
KPA3.7		Peer reviews	3	To remove defects from the software work products early and efficiently.
CL4	Managed		12	
KPA4.1		Quantitative process management	7	To control the process performance of the software project quantitatively.
KPA4.2		Software quality management	5	To develop a quantitative understanding of the project's software products and achieve specific quality goals.
CL5	Optimizing		26	
KPA5.1		Defect prevention	8	To identify the cause of defects and prevent them from recurring.
KPA5.2		Technology change management	8	To identify beneficial new technologies (i.e., tools, methods, and processes) and transfer them into the organization in an orderly manner, as is described in KPA5.3.
KPA5.3		Process change management	10	To continually improve the software processes used in the organization with the intent of improving software quality, increasing productivity, and decreasing the cycle time for product development.

In Table 5.2 the descriptions of purpose of each KPA are provided [Paulk et al., 1993a]. By referring to Table 5.2 readers may find that CMM processes mainly emphasize management issues of software engineering processes such as organization, software development management, project planning, project management processes, etc.

In Table 5.2, the number of defined KPs for each KPA is provided. The definitions of the KPs are listed in Appendix C where, in the column of CMM, a jth KP of KPA k at capability level i, *KP [i,k,j]*, is represented by:

$$KP[i,k,j] = KP_{i.k.j}$$
$$= BPA_{i'.k'.r'.j'} \tag{5.1}$$

where i', k', r', and j' are the index numbers of subsystem, category, process, and practice, respectively, as defined in the unified process system framework and SEPRM.

For example, in Appendix C, readers can identify KP[2,5,4] as:

$$KP[i,k,j] = KP[2,5,4]$$
$$= QSA_{2.5.4}$$
$$= BPA_{3.1.8.1}$$
$$= BPA_{244}$$
$$= \text{'Audit software development activities'}$$

5.2.3 FORMAL DESCRIPTION OF THE CMM PROCESS MODEL

By using the CSP-like process algebra introduced in Chapter 3, we are able to formally describe the CMM process model and its processes in this subsection. The formal description is useful for providing precise and accurate definitions of the structure and interrelationships of the CMM processes, and to avoid the ambiguity inherent in conventional natural language description. Following methods based on theory, the rigorous approach is also a necessary exercise for problem abstraction, which is important in software engineering.

5.2.3.1 The Structure of the CMM Process Model

A formal description of the high-level structure of the CMM process model, *CMM_PM*, is shown in Expression 5.2 and illustrated in Figure 5.1. Basically, this is a sequential process model at the system level.

$$
\begin{aligned}
CMM\_PM \triangleq\ & CL_1 && //\ \text{Initial} \\
& ;\, CL_2 && //\ \text{Repeated} \\
& ;\, CL_3 && //\ \text{Defined} \\
& ;\, CL_4 && //\ \text{Managed} \\
& ;\, CL_5 && //\ \text{Optimizing} \tag{5.2}
\end{aligned}
$$

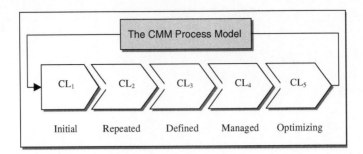

Figure 5.1 The CMM process model

In the CMM process model, all process capability levels except Level 1 can be extended to a number of parallel processes (KPAs) as shown in Expression 5.3. Further, each KPA can be extended to a number of KPs in a similar way.

$$CL_1 \triangleq \varnothing$$
$$CL_2 \triangleq KPA_{2.1} \parallel KPA_{2.2} \parallel KPA_{2.3} \parallel KPA_{2.4} \parallel KPA_{2.5} \parallel KPA_{2.6}$$
$$CL_3 \triangleq KPA_{3.1} \parallel KPA_{3.2} \parallel KPA_{3.3} \parallel KPA_{3.4} \parallel KPA_{3.5} \parallel KPA_{3.6} \parallel KPA_{3.7}$$
$$CL_4 \triangleq KPA_{4.1} \parallel KPA_{4.2}$$
$$CL_5 \triangleq KPA_{5.1} \parallel KPA_{5.2} \parallel KPA_{5.3} \tag{5.3}$$

There is no defined KPA or KP at Level 1 since this level is treated as the baseline for an initial software development organization according to CMM.

5.2.3.2 Definitions of CMM Processes

The CMM processes, known as KPAs at each capability level, can be formally defined by Expressions 5.4 – 5.7 and are illustrated in Figures 5.2 – 5.5.

$$
\begin{aligned}
CL_2 \triangleq \ & KPA_{2.1} && \text{// Requirement management} \\
& \parallel KPA_{2.2} && \text{// Software project planning} \\
& \parallel KPA_{2.3} && \text{// Software project tracking and oversight} \\
& \parallel KPA_{2.4} && \text{// Software subcontract management} \\
& \parallel KPA_{2.5} && \text{// Software quality assurance} \\
& \parallel KPA_{2.6} && \text{// Software configuration management} \quad (5.4)
\end{aligned}
$$

A process diagram corresponding to the six processes at CMM Level 2 as defined in Expression 5.4 is shown in Figure 5.2.

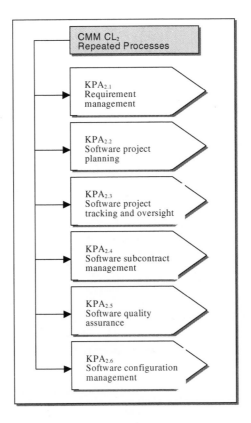

Figure 5.2 CMM Level 2 processes – the repeated KPAs

A process diagram corresponding to the seven processes at CMM level 3, as defined in Expression 5.5, is shown in Figure 5.3.

$$
\begin{array}{lll}
CL_3 \triangleq & KPA_{3.1} & \text{// Organization process focus} \\
& \| \ KPA_{3.2} & \text{// Organization process definition} \\
& \| \ KPA_{3.3} & \text{// Training program} \\
& \| \ KPA_{3.4} & \text{// Integrated software management} \\
& \| \ KPA_{3.5} & \text{// Software product engineering} \\
& \| \ KPA_{3.6} & \text{// Intergroup coordination} \\
& \| \ KPA_{3.7} & \text{// Peer reviews} \qquad\qquad (5.5)
\end{array}
$$

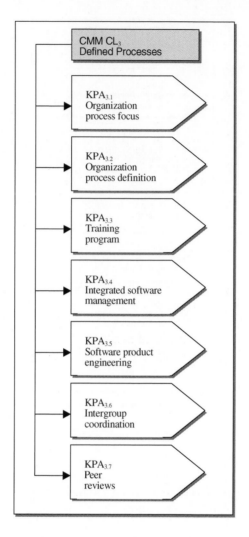

Figure 5.3 CMM Level 3 processes – the defined KPAs

A process diagram corresponding to the two processes at CMM Level 4, as defined in Expression 5.6, is shown in Figure 5.4.

$$CL_4 \triangleq KPA_{4.1} \qquad \text{// Quantitative process management}$$
$$\| KPA_{4.2} \qquad \text{// Software quality management} \qquad (5.6)$$

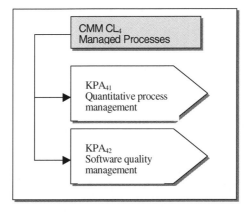

Figure 5.4 CMM Level 4 processes – the managed KPAs

A process diagram corresponding to the three processes at CMM Level 5, as defined in Expression 5.7, is shown in Figure 5.5.

$$
\begin{aligned}
CL_5 \triangleq\ &KPA_{5.1} && \text{// Defect prevention} \\
\|\ &KPA_{5.2} && \text{// Technology change management} \\
\|\ &KPA_{5.3} && \text{// Process change management}
\end{aligned} \tag{5.7}
$$

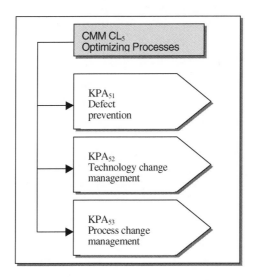

Figure 5.5 CMM Level 5 processes – the optimizing KPAs

Detailed practices of each KPA at KP level, which are documented in Appendix C, can be described in the same way as above. Extending the formal CMM process model onto KP level can be taken as an exercise for readers.

5.3 The CMM Process Assessment Model

The CMM process model has been systematically introduced in Section 5.2. This section explores the CMM process capability model and process capability determination method. Both of the above form the CMM process assessment model.

5.3.1 THE CMM PROCESS CAPABILITY MODEL

As introduced in Section 2.4.2, a process capability model is a yardstick for process assessment. This section describes the CMM process capability model, which includes a practice performance scale, a process capability scale, and a process capability scope definition.

5.3.1.1 Practice Performance Scale

A practice performance rating scale for the KPs in CMM is defined in Table 5.3. It employs a kind of *yes/no* evaluation for the KPs' existence and performance, with Option 2 adding some extent of tailorability for the domain of the specified KPs. In Table 5.3, the rating thresholds provide a set of quantitative measurements for rating a KP's performance with the scale.

Table 5.3
Practice Performance Scale of the KPs

Scale	Description	Rating threshold
4	Yes	≥ 80%
3	No	< 80%
2	Doesn't apply	-
1	Don't know	-

In Table 5.3, Scale 1 is usually treated as equivalent to 3 in assessment, because *"don't know"* implies no such practice in the assessed software development organization.

5.3.1.2 Process Capability Scale

CMM develops a five-level software process capability model as shown in Table 5.4 [Paulk et al., 1993a]. Each capability level is defined in the table with supplemental description of capability performance indicators in the last column.

Table 5.4
The CMM Process Capability Model

Capability level (CL[i])	Title	Description	Performance Indicator
CL[1]	Initial	At this level, the software process is characterized as ad hoc, and occasionally even chaotic. Few processes are defined, and success depends on individual effort.	Schedule and cost targets are typically overrun.
CL[2]	Repeated	At this level, basic project management processes are established to track cost, schedule, and functionality. The necessary process discipline is in place to repeat earlier successes on projects with similar applications.	Plans based on past performance are more realistic.
CL[3]	Defined	At this level, the software process for both management and engineering activities is documented, standardized, and integrated into a standard software process for the organization. All projects use an approved, tailored version of the organization's standard software process for developing and maintaining software.	Performance improves with well-defined processes.
CL[4]	Managed	At this level, detailed measures of the software process and product quality are collected. Both the software process and products are quantitatively understood and controlled.	Performance continues to improve based on quantitative understanding of process and product.
CL[5]	Optimizing	At this level, continuous process improvement is enabled by quantitative feedback from the process and from piloting innovative ideas and technologies	Performance continuously improves to increase process efficiency, eliminate costly rework, and allow development time to be shortened.

Based on the software process capability model, a CMM process capability scale is described in Table 5.5. For each capability level *i*, the number of identified KPs ($N_{KP}[i,j]$) and the minimum required number of KPs for satisfying an assessment ($P_{KP}[i,j]$) are listed, respectively.

Table 5.5
The CMM Process Capability Scale

Capability Level (CL[i])	Description	Identified KPs ($N_{KP}[i,j]$)	Pass Threshold ($P_{KP}[i,j]$)
CL[1]	Initial	$N_{KP1} = 0$	$P_{KP1} = 0$
CL[2]	Repeated	$N_{KP2} = 62$	$P_{KP2} = 50$
CL[3]	Defined	$N_{KP3} = 50$	$P_{KP3} = 40$
CL[4]	Managed	$N_{KP4} = 12$	$P_{KP4} = 10$
CL[5]	Optimizing	$N_{KP5} = 26$	$P_{KP4} = 21$
Total	5	150	121

Contrasting Tables 5.5 and 5.2, it may be observed that the capability levels are used for both capability scales as in the CMM capability model, and process group names as in the CMM process model. The overlap in the process and capability dimensions is a particular feature of a 1-D process system model.

5.3.1.3 Process Capability Scope

The CMM process capability scopes are shown in Table 5.6. Comparing Table 5.6 with Table 2.3 in Chapter 2, it is clear that CMM assesses process capability at the levels of KP, KPA, project, and organization scope from the bottom, up.

Table 5.6
Process Capability Scope of CMM

Capability Scope	Practice	Process	Project	Organization
CMM terms	KPs	KPAs / levels	Project	Organization
CMM methods	Performance rating	Performance rating	Capability level	Capability level

5.3.2   THE CMM PROCESS CAPABILITY DETERMINATION METHODOLOGY

Using the formal definitions of the CMM process model and process capability model developed in Sections 5.2 and 5.3.1, we can now consider how to apply the CMM capability model to the process model for the assessment of process capability at practice, process, project, and organization levels.

5.3.2.1 Practice Performance Rating Method

Let $r_{KP}[i,j]$ be a rating of performance of the jth KP at the ith capability level. Then $r_{KP}[i,j]$ can be rated according to the practice performance scale as defined in Table 5.3, i.e.:

$r_{KP}[i,j]$ = 4, if the KP's performance is at least 80% satisfied
　　　　 = 3, if the KP's performance is less than 80% satisfied
　　　　 = 2, if the KP does not apply in the assessment
　　　　 = 1, if the answer for the KP is "don't know" in assessment　　(5.8)

5.3.2.2 Process Capability Rating Method

The number of satisfied KPs at a level i, $SAT_{KP}[i]$, is assessed according to the following formula:

$$SAT_{KP}[i] = \#\{ KP[i,j] \mid Passed \}, \quad i = 1, 2, ..., 5$$
$$= \#\{ KP[i,j] \mid r_{KP}[i,j] = 4 \lor r_{KP}[i,j] = 2\}$$
$$= \sum_{j=1}^{N_{KPi}} \{ 1 \mid r_{KP}[i,j] = 4 \lor r_{KP}[i,j] = 2\} \quad (5.9)$$

where $\#$ is a cardinal calculus that counts the numbers of KPs that satisfy or that do not apply in the assessment, and N_{KPi} is the number of defined KPs at level i.

A pass threshold, $P_{KP}[i]$, for a capability level, i, in CMM is defined as:

$$P_{KP[i]} = N_{KP[i]} * 80\% \quad (5.10)$$

This means that 80% of the KPs defined at a level should be satisfied for fulfilling the requirements of process capability at this level, i.e.:

$$SAT_{KP}[i] \geq P_{KP[i]}$$
$$\geq N_{KP[i]} * 80\% \quad (5.11)$$

The pass thresholds at each capability level have been defined in Table 5.5 for reference.

The CMM capability levels and their related KPAs and KPs are predefined and fixed according to the CMM model. CMM evaluates the process capability from the bottom level (Level 1), and does not concern the practices at higher levels if a lower level is inadequate. Therefore, a software development organization cannot win a higher level until it has fulfilled the requirements for the level(s) lower than that.

5.3.2.3 Project Capability Determination Method

A CMM process capability level for a project p in a software development organization, $PCL_{proj}[p]$, can be defined as the maximum integer level, i, the software development organization achieved, i.e.:

$$PCL_{proj}[p] = max \{i \mid SAT_{KP}[i] \geq P_{KP}[i]\}, \quad i = 1,2, ..., 5 \qquad (5.12)$$

where $P_{KP}[i]$ is the pass threshold for Level i as defined in Table 5.5.

5.3.2.4 Organization Capability Determination Method

A CMM process capability level for an organization is defined as a mathematical mean of those of n assessed projects, i.e.:

$$PCL_{org} = \left\lfloor \frac{1}{n}\sum_{p=1}^{n} PCL_{proj}[p] \right\rfloor \qquad (5.13)$$

where $\lfloor x \rfloor$ means "round x to the nearest lower integer."

Expression 5.13 indicates that an established software organization and its successful experience in the project scope can be cumulatively taken into account when determining the organization's process capability level.

It is noteworthy that CMM has not suggested how many project assessment results are sufficient to derive the organization's process capability level. Generally, it is expected that $n \geq 3$ is a valid aggregation of an organization's process capability level based on the projects that are carried out in the organization.

5.4 The CMM Algorithm

So far we have explored the CMM process model, process capability model, and capability determination method. Using the models and method we are already able to manually assess and calculate a software project's or an organization's process capability in CMM.

In order to describe the CMM methodology precisely, and to enable mutual comparison and tool implementation, this section extends the CMM process capability determination methodology into a formal CMM algorithm.

5.4.1 DESCRIPTION OF THE CMM ALGORITHM

The CMM capability determination method as defined in Expressions 5.8 – 5.12 up to the scope of project can be formally described in the following algorithm. An organization's process capability level can be easily aggregated according to Expression 5.13, when multiple projects have been assessed.

Algorithm 5.1 The CMM process capability determination algorithm

Assume: $KP[i,j]$ - the jth KP defined at level i, $i = 1,2,3,4,5$
             N_{KPi} - number of KPs at level i
             $SAT_{KP}[i]$ - number of KPs satisfied at level i
             PCL - process capability level
             $PCL_{proj}[p]$ - process capability level of project p
Input: Sample indicators of KPs and KPAs' existence and performance
Output: $PCL_{proj}[p]$

Begin

   // Step 1: Initialization

   $N_{KP}[1] := 0;$ // Assign numbers of defined KPs at each level
   $N_{KP}[2] := 62;$
   $N_{KP}[3] := 50;$
   $N_{KP}[4] := 12;$
   $N_{KP}[5] := 26;$

   // Step 2: KP performance rating

   // 2.1 Assess KPs at Level 2
   level := 2;
   $SAT_{KP}[level] := 0;$
   for $j := 1$ to $N_{KP}[2]$ do
       begin
          // Rate performance of $KP[j]$ according to the practice
          // performance scale defined in Table 5.3
          if $(KP[level, j] = 4) \vee (KP[level, j] = 2)$

```
                then  // the KP is satisfied
                        SAT_KP[level] := SAT_KP[level] + 1;
                        // else, it is not satisfied, skip
        end;

// 2.2 Assess KPs at Level 3
level := 3;
SAT_KP[level]:=0;
for  j:=1 to N_KP[3] do
        begin
            // Rate performance of KP[j] according to Table 5.3
            if (KP[level, j] = 4) ∨ (KP[level, j] = 2)
                then  // the KP is satisfied
                        SAT_KP[level] := SAT_KP[level] + 1;
                        // else, it is not satisfied, skip
        end;

// 2.3 Assess KPs at Level 4
level := 4;
SAT_KP[level]:=0;
for  j:=1 to N_KP[4] do
        begin
            // Rate performance of KP[j] according to Table 5.3
            if (KP[level, j] = 4) ∨ (KP[level, j] = 2)
                then  // the KP is satisfied
                        SAT_KP[level] := SAT_KP[level]+ 1;
                        // else, it is not satisfied, skip
        end;

// 2.4 Assess KPs at Level 5
level := 5;
SAT_KP[level]:=0;
for  j:=1 to N_KP[5] do
        begin
            // Rate performance of KP[j] according to Table 5.3
            if (KP[level, j] = 4) ∨ (KP[level, j] = 2)
                then  // the KP is satisfied
                        SAT_KP[level] := SAT_KP[level]+ 1;
                        // else, it is not satisfied, skip
        end;

// Step 3: Process capability determination

if SAT_KP[2] < (N_KP[2] * 80%)          // According to Expression 5.11
    then // Initial
```

```
            PCL := 1
      else  if SAT_KP[3] < (N_KP[3] * 80%)
             then // Repeatable
                 PCL := 2
             else  if  SAT_KP[4] < (N_KP[4] * 80%)
                 then  // Defined
                     PCL :=3
                 else  if SAT_KP[5] < (N_KP[5] * 80%)
                     then  // Managed
                         PCL :=4
                     Else   // Optimizing
                         PCL :=5;
      PCL_proj[p] := PCL;          // According to Expression 5.12

End                                                              ∎
```

5.4.2 EXPLANATION OF THE CMM ALGORITHM

A CMM assessment according to Algorithm 5.1 is carried out in three steps:

- **Step 1:** Initialization

- **Step 2:** KP performance rating

- **Step 3:** Process capability determination

This subsection explains the main functions of Algorithm 5.1 for a CMM process assessment.

5.4.2.1 Initialization

This step is designed to specify the numbers of KPs defined in CMM. For obtaining a detailed configuration of KPs in the CMM process model, readers may refer to Table 5.2 and Appendix C.

5.4.2.2 KP Performance Rating

In this step, all KPs for each KPA at each capability level are rated according to Expressions 5.8 and 5.9, using the definitions of practice performance scale listed in Table 5.3.

The rating methods for all KPs at levels 2 – 5 are identical as shown in algorithm Steps 2.1 – 2.4, except that at each level the number of KPs, $N_{KP}[i]$, are different as initialized in Step 1. The basic function for KP rating at each level is to count the number of satisfied KPs by increasing $SAT_{KP}[level]$ by one if the examined KP is rated as 4 or 2 according to the rating scale in Table 5.3.

It is suggested that each KP at all levels should be rated, even when there is an early indication that a software project would only achieve a certain level lower than 5.

5.4.2.3 Project Process Capability Determination

This step derives the maximum aggregated process capability level for an assessed software project based on the KP ratings obtained in Step 2. The capability level of a project is determined by Expression 5.12, or by checking with Table 5.7 for the minimum required numbers of KPs level-by-level. This means that a project should satisfy all lower levels before it can satisfy a certain level i, $i = 1, 2, ..., 5$.

Table 5.7
The CMM Process Capability Scale

Capability Level (CL[i])	Description	Minimum Satisfied KPs	Maximum Satisfied KPs
CL_1	Initial	-	-
CL_2	Repeated	50	62
CL_3	Defined	90	112
CL_4	Managed	100	124
CL_5	Optimizing	121	150

5.4.3 ANALYSIS OF THE CMM ALGORITHM

The effort expended in conducting a CMM assessment depends on its algorithm complexity. By examining the complexity of an algorithm, the time spent in a CMM assessment can be estimated quite accurately.

Reviewing the CMM algorithm, it may be observed that the algorithm complexity of CMM, $c(CMM)$, is mainly determined by the number of KPs, N_{KP}, which need to be rated individually in a CMM assessment according to Algorithm 5.1, Step 2, i.e.:

$$c(CMM) = O(N_{KP})$$
$$= N_{KP}$$
$$= \sum_{i=1}^{5} N_{KP}[i] \qquad (5.14)$$

where $O(x)$ means in the order of number x; $N_{KP}[i]$ is the KPs at level i, $1 \le i \le 5$. The unit of the algorithm complexity is "times of KP ratings", or of practice ratings.

As given in CMM, $N_{KP}[1]=0$, $N_{KP}[2]=62$, $N_{KP}[3]=50$, $N_{KP}[4]=12$, and $N_{KP}[5]=16$. Thus, the total rating cost, or the algorithm complexity, for determining a capability level of project scope in CMM is:

$$c(CMM) = O(N_{KP})$$
$$= N_{KP}$$
$$= \sum_{i=1}^{5} N_{KP}[i]$$
$$= 0 + 62 + 50 + 12 + 16$$
$$= 150 \text{ [times of KP ratings]}$$

There is a certain range of rates between the algorithm complexity and the person-days needed for an assessment. Empirical data for relating the algorithm complexity to person-days expended in a CMM process assessment will be discussed in Chapter 12.

5.5 A Sample CMM Assessment

The capability rating framework and the capability determination algorithm of CMM have been formally described in Sections 5.3 and 5.4. This section demonstrates how to apply the CMM expressions and algorithm to quantitatively determine a sample software development organization's process capability level in CMM.

5.5.1 KP PERFORMANCE RATING IN CMM

A set of detailed ratings of the 150 KPs has been listed in Appendix C, where the raw data rating $\{4,3,2,1\}$ corresponds to the CMM KP rating scale $\{Y(4),Y(4),N(3),N(3)\}$. By referring to Table 5.3, a mapping between the rating scales of the raw data and the CMM KP is defined in Table 5.8.

Table 5.8
Mapping between Raw Data in Assessment onto CMM Rating Scale

Raw Data Rating Scale (in Appendix C)	CMM KP Rating Scale	Description in CMM
4	4	Yes
3	4	Yes
2	3	No
1	3	No

Processing the raw data of the KPs' performance ratings according to Table 5.8 and then applying Expression 5.8 allows the number of satisfied KPs at a level i, $SAT_{KP}[i]$, to be derived by:

$$SAT_{KP}[i] = \#\{ KP[i,j] \mid Passed \}$$
$$= \#\{ KP[i,j] \mid r_{KP}[i,j] = 4 \lor r_{KP}[i,j] = 2\}$$
$$= \sum_{j=1}^{N_{KPi}} \{ 1 \mid r_{KP}[i,j] = 4 \lor r_{KP}[i,j] = 2\}$$

For example, $KPA_{5.1}$, defect prevention, has eight KPs rated:

$$KPA_{5.1} = \{KP_{5.1.1}, KP_{5.1.2}, KP_{5.1.3}, KP_{5.1.4}, KP_{5.1.5}, KP_{5.1.6}, KP_{5.1.7}, KP_{5.1.8}\}$$
$$= \{2,2,4,4,4,4,4,2\},$$

respectively in Appendix C.

Mapping the raw data onto CMM scale according to Table 5.8, the KP ratings are as follows:

$$KPA[5,1] = \{N, N, Y, Y, Y, Y, Y, N\}$$
$$= \{3,3,4,4,4,4,4,3\}$$

Thus, according to Expression 5.8, the number of satisfied KPs for $KPA_{5.1}$ are:

$$SAT_{KP}[5] = \#\{ KP_{5.1.3}, KP_{5.1.4}, KP_{5.1.5}, KP_{5.1.6}, KP_{5.1.7}\}$$
$$= 5,$$

and the rest, $KP_{5.1.1}$, $KP_{5.1.2}$, $KP_{5.1.8}$, are those of unsatisfied KPs in $KPA_{5.1}$.

A summary of the 18 KPA capability ratings in CMM is listed in Table 5.9.

Table 5.9
Summary Assessment Record in CMM

CL_i	Key Practice Areas ($KPA[i,j]$)	Identified KPs ($N_{KP}[i,j]$)	Pass Threshold ($P_{KP}[i,j]$)	Assessment Result ($SAT_{KP}[i,j]$) 4 | 3 | 2 | 1 | 1				
CL_5	Optimizing	$N_{KP}[5]=26$	$P_{KP}[5]=21$	$SAT_{KP}[5] = 16$				
$KPA_{5.1}$	Defect prevention	8		5	3	0	0	0
$KPA_{5.2}$	Technology change management	8		4	4	0	0	0
$KPA_{5.3}$	Process change management	10		7	3	0	0	0
CL_4	Managed	$N_{KP}[4]=12$	$P_{KP}[4]=10$	$SAT_{KP}[4] = 7$				
$KPA_{4.1}$	Quantitative process management	7		3	4	0	0	0
$KPA_{4.2}$	Software quality management	5		4	1	1	0	0
CL_3	Defined	$N_{KP}[3]=50$	$P_{KP}[3]=40$	$SAT_{KP}[3] = 44$				
$KPA_{3.1}$	Organization process focus	7		5	2	0	0	0
$KPA_{3.2}$	Organization process definition	6		6	0	0	0	0
$KPA_{3.3}$	Training program	6		5	1	1	0	0
$KPA_{3.4}$	Integrated software management	11		11	0	0	0	0
$KPA_{3.5}$	Software product engineering	10		10	0	0	0	0
$KPA_{3.6}$	Intergroup coordination	7		4	3	0	0	0
$KPA_{3.7}$	Peer reviews	3		3	0	0	0	0
CL_2	Repeated	$N_{KP}[2]=62$	$P_{KP}[2]=50$	$SAT_{KP}[2] = 56$				
$KPA_{2.1}$	Requirement management	3		3	0	0	0	0
$KPA_{2.2}$	Software project planning	15		15	0	0	0	0
$KPA_{2.3}$	Software project tracking and oversight	13		10	3	0	0	0
$KPA_{2.4}$	Software subcontract management	13		10	3	0	0	0
$KPA_{2.5}$	Software quality assurance	8		8	0	0	0	0
$KPA_{2.6}$	Software configuration management	10		10	0	0	0	0
CL_1	Initial	$N_{KP}[1]=0$	$P_{KP}[1]=0$	$KP_{sat}[1] = 0$				

5.5.2 PROCESS CAPABILITY DETERMINATION IN CMM

Using the assessment result listed in Table 5.9, a process capability profile of the software development organization in CMM can be derived as shown in Figure 5.6.

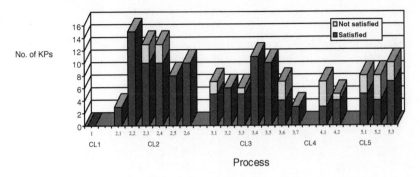

No. of KPs

Figure 5.6 Process capability profile of a software project in CMM

5.5.3 PROJECT CAPABILITY DETERMINATION IN CMM

The process capability level for a project p, $PCL_{\text{proj}}[p]$, in CMM has been defined as the maximum integer level, i, which a software project fulfilled as in Expression 5.12.

Applying Expression 5.12 to the ratings of the 18 KPAs and 150 BPs ratings summarized in Table 5.9, the capability level of the project can be determined. Considering that:

$$(SAT_{\text{KP}}[2] = 56) > (P_{\text{KP}}[2] = 50)$$

$$(SAT_{\text{KP}}[3] = 44) > (P_{\text{KP}}[3] = 40)$$

$$(SAT_{\text{KP}}[4] = \ 7) < (P_{\text{KP}}[4] = 10)$$

the capability level of the sample software project is calculated as:

$$PCL_{\text{proj}}[p] = max \ \{i \ | \ SAT_{\text{KP}}[i] \geq P_{\text{KP}}[i]\}, \quad i = 1, 2, ..., 5$$
$$= max \ \{3 \ | \ SAT_{\text{KP}}[3] \geq P_{\text{KP}}[3]\}$$
$$= 3$$

Thus, the project of the software development organization is assessed to be at Level 3, the defined process capability level, in CMM.

5.6 Applications of CMM

In the previous sections we have explored the CMM theory and methodology for process system modeling and assessment. This section analyzes the usability of CMM in software engineering process system establishment, assessment, and improvement. In order to present both sides of the coin, the limitations of CMM in some aspects of software engineering applications are discussed using the body of empirical and theoretical studies on CMM.

5.6.1 CMM FOR SOFTWARE PROCESS SYSTEM ESTABLISHMENT

In the CMM model, a capability level and its related KPAs and KPs are predefined and fixed. For process system establishment, CMM models process capability from the bottom level and would not concern the performances of processes at higher levels if those in the lower level were inadequate. The merits of this approach are straightforward and concentrate on limiting the focus.

However, this implies that CMM requires a software development organization to implement the processes modeled by the KPAs and KPs level-by-level. This would be suitable for a new software organization to plan and establish its process system step-by-step from Level 2 toward Level 5 while, for an established software organization, this approach may lead to its concentrating only on the KPAs at the current targeted level (and those lower than it) because the KPAs associated with the levels higher than the target may be ruled out by the organization to achieve the planned level.

Thus, fundamentally, the 1-D process model, like CMM, has inherited limitations in theory and application. An argument on the logic of the 1-D process model was whether we would recommend only a subset of a whole process system for an organization if all processes are considered essential for producing quality software? It is also found that, from a structural view, the modeled priority level of the KPAs in CMM and the practical priority in a software development organization would not be easily matched. For example, the defect prevention KPA with eight KPs in CMM are preallocated at Level 5 while a software development organization at lower levels may need to introduce these processes earlier in their practices. Therefore, practices in software engineering process establishment require the CMM approach to provide more flexibility and tailorability in order to allow only the process capability degrees, rather than a collection of KPA processes being divided into different levels. Using this approach, the CMM model may be made more adaptable to the various requirements of different software development organizations in practical software engineering process establishment.

5.6.2 CMM FOR SOFTWARE PROCESS SYSTEM ASSESSMENT

With regard to the unified software process system framework developed in Part I, CMM is suitable for the first-, second-, and third-party assessment for a software engineering process system in a software development organization.

The CMM 1-D process methodology is oriented to software process assessment at project level while it is relatively less focused on process and practice levels because a CMM assessment does not present the intermediate KPA level assessment result in the assessment outcomes.

According to the CMM methodology, a software development organization could not win a higher CMM level of recognition even if it has fulfilled the requirements for that level but lacks practices at the lower level(s). It seems that the CMM capability determination methodology needs to consider the higher level practices of software organizations and their impact on process assessment results in order to allow the process merits to be taken into account in an organization's final capability level.

5.6.3 CMM FOR SOFTWARE PROCESS SYSTEM IMPROVEMENT

The CMM model is applicable for stepwise process improvement according to a group of predefined processes associated with specific capability levels. In a CMM-based process improvement scheme, CMM evaluates an organization's process capability from the bottom, up. An organization's software engineering practices and merits at higher capability levels could not be taken into account if those at the lower level were inadequate.

This approach may lead an established software development organization to concentrate on limited KPAs at a targeted level (and those lower than it), and to postpone application of some existing higher level processes because those could not be reflected in the process improvement results according to the CMM approach. Based on these concerns, it seems that more flexibility needs to be introduced into the CMM process improvement approach. Thus, it would be perfect if CMM allows the organizations to determine their priority to improve which process(es) rather than a prescribed order for process improvement.

From the discussion in this section it may be understood that there is no perfect model for such a complicated software engineering process system. There is an argument that says perhaps the earlier a model is developed, the more imperfect the model would be. This is because the more applications a model has gained, the deeper the imperfections are found to be. These comments also apply to all other process models that will be presented in the following chapters.

Therefore, to be aware of and to use the advantages of a process model in practice while avoiding disadvantages is desirable. It is one of the important purposes of this book to improve process model integration and evolution in process-based software engineering research and practices.

5.7 Summary

This chapter has introduced a formal and rigorous approach into the description of CMM. CSP-like process algebra has been adopted for presenting the CMM process model, and mathematical and algorithmic methods have been applied for presenting the CMM process capability determination methodology. Using these formal techniques, CMM has been systematically described and analyzed by contrasting with the unified process system framework developed in Part I. An empirical case study has been provided for demonstrating the method and approach in conducting a CMM assessment.

The basic knowledge structure of this chapter is as follows:

Chapter 5. The CMM Model

- General
  - Purposes of this chapter
    - To review the history and background of CMM development

– To describe the CMM process model and taxonomy

– To describe the CMM capability model and capability determination methodology

– To formally describe the CMM process model, and to algorithmically describe the CMM process capability determination method

– To develop a CMM algorithm for software process assessment

– To explain how the CMM algorithm can be used in process assessment and how its algorithm complexity is estimated

– To demonstrate a case study of a practical CMM assessment by using the CMM algorithm

– To discuss the usability of CMM in process establishment, assessment, and improvement in software engineering

– Historical demand from/for the software industry
   – To model the software engineering process capability
   – To measure the maturity level of a software development organization
   – To provide a process framework for organizing and implementing software engineering

• The CMM process model
   – Taxonomy of the CMM process model
      – Process scopes
      – Size of domain of each scope

   – Framework of the CMM process model
      – Structure of the CMM process model
      – Definitions of KPAs in CMM

   – Formal description of the CMM process model
      – CMM abstract process patterns
      – CMM process diagrams
      – Interpretation and illustration of the process algebra expressions

• The CMM process assessment model

- The CMM process capability model
  - Configuration
    - 5 process capability levels (CLs)
    - 18 processes (KPAs)
    - 150 practices (KPs)
  - Definitions of the 5 process capability levels
  - The KP rating scale
  - The process rating scale

- The CMM process capability determination method
  - Formal description of CMM capability determination methodology
  - Meanings of expressions and their operations
  - Common features with the methodology developed in the unified process framework in Part I
  - Differences from the methodology developed in the unified process framework in Part I

- The CMM algorithm
  - Algorithm 5.1: CMM process assessment
  - Explanation of Algorithm 5.1
  - Relation between Algorithm 5.1 and the capability determination expressions in Section 5.3.2
  - The CMM algorithm complexity and the main factor affecting it

- A sample CMM process assessment
  - Understanding assessment data documented in Appendix C
  - Manual process assessment in CMM
  - Algorithm-based assessment in CMM
  - Interpretation of assessment results

- Usability of CMM
  - Merits and demerits in process system establishment
  - Merits and demerits in process system assessment
  - Merits and demerits in process system improvement

Major achievements and issues for further research suggested by this chapter are highlighted below:

- The design philosophy behind CMM is a software project contractor's perception on the organizational and managerial capacity of a software development organization. It has noted, however, that the interpretations of CMM have been shifted from the original second-party point of view to the third-party and first-party-oriented applications in the software industry.

- Despite the fact that programming had been a profession for almost half a century, it is a shock to realize that the software industry is still relatively young. The discipline of software engineering is still being built. Because of the formalism and systematism of CMM, the process-based approach is widely accepted by researchers in software engineering and practitioners in the software industry.

- Process algebra, introduced in Chapter 3, is found useful in software engineering process system modeling and analysis. This finding is also helpful to explain the foundations of software engineering and software engineering processes.

- CMM has developed a straightforward and stepwise software engineering process assessment and improvement methodology. It is relatively easy in application and has intensive adoption in the software industry worldwide.

- A CMM algorithm has been elicited in order to precisely and systematically interpret the CMM methodology, and to quantitatively compare the complexity of the CMM method with others.

- The 1-D process model, like CMM, has inherited limitations in theory and applications. There were structural arguments about whether CMM provided a process dimension or a capability dimension in process system modeling. There were also logical arguments about whether we would recommend only a subset of a whole process system for an organization if all processes were considered essential for producing quality software.

This chapter has established a basis for understanding and analyzing CMM as a paradigm of the unified software engineering process system framework. Relationships of CMM with other process system models will be discussed in Part III of this book. Applications of CMM in process-based software engineering and case studies will be provided in Parts IV – VI.

Annotated References

CMM (V.1.1) was developed by Paulk and his colleagues (1993a) with the supplement of a set of detailed key practices in Paulk et al. (1993b), and a questionnaire in Zubrow et al. (1994). Paulk et al. (1993c) describes the CMM V.1.1 and its features as more consistent in wording and easier to use. A summary of differences between Version 1.0 [Paulk et al. 1991] and Version 1.1 is also presented.

For more background and related work that led to the development of CMM, see Humphrey and his colleagues (1987/88/89). As described by Paulk et al. (1993c), the framework of CMM for software process was inspired by the principles of product quality in management science espoused by Walter Shewhart (1939), W. Edwards Deming (1982a/b/86), Joseph Juran (1962/80/88/89), and Philip Crosby (1979).

Applications and case studies of CMM were reported in Humphrey et al. (1991b), Kitson and Masters (1992), and Saiedian and Kuzara (1995). There are annual Software Engineering Process Group Conferences (SEPG) and annual conferences on Software Technology and Engineering Practice (STEP) sponsored by SEI.

For looking at relationships of CMM with other process models, see Paulk et al. (1994/95b), Kitson (1996), Wang et al. (1997a/b/99e), *and IEEE Software Process Newsletter*, No.4, Fall (1997).

Some critics of CMM may be referred to Bollinger and McGowan (1991), Brodman and Johnson (1994), and Fayad and Laitinen (1997a/b). Readers may also be interested in reading the counterpoint comments on Bollinger and McGowan's article by Humphrey and Curtis (1991a).

Questions and Problems

5.1 Explain the design philosophy behind the development of CMM.

5.2 Using your own words, briefly describe the structure of the CMM process model and its taxonomy.

5.3 Use process algebra to derive a formal CMM process model based on the process diagrams given in Figures 5.1 – 5.5. (Try not to copy Expressions 5.2 – 5.7 before you finish.)

5.4 Briefly describe the CMM process capability model and capability determination methodology using your own words.

5.5 Can you repeat the sample CMM assessment based on the data provided in Appendix C and derive the same capability level as that of the example shown in Section 5.5?

5.6 Try to conduct a CMM exercise assessment for a software project or organization with which you are familiar, according to the formal approach presented in this chapter.

5.7 Consider what the CMM capability level is if an organization has achieved all Level 5 and Level 4 processes (KPAs) but has a lack of Level 2 practices?

5.8 Are there any significant differences between an organization that is newly established and operating in ad hoc ways (at CMM Level 1) and an organization as described in Ex.5.7? What are the differences in their derived capability levels according to CMM methodology?

5.9 Most of the established software development organizations are currently considered to be located between CMM Level 2 and Level 3. Observing the CMM process model, do you think those organizations could produce reasonably good software? Why?

5.10 Try to organize a small software project with at least three persons. Then do a self-assessment for this project and report your capability level in CMM.

5.11 Try to write a CMM assessment report for Exs. 5.6 or 5.10 and describe the following:

- Purpose(s) of the CMM assessment
- The CMM model and methodology you adopted
- The input of the CMM assessment
- The procedure of the CMM assessment
- The output of the CMM assessment
- The effort you spend for the CMM assessment
- Experience you gained in the CMM assessment
- Conclusions

5.12 Try to write a CMM process improvement plan based on the assessment report developed in Ex.5.11. In the process improvement plan, describe the following:

- Purpose(s) of the CMM process improvement plan
- Brief introduction of the CMM assessment results
- Analyze the strengths of the organization's process capability according to CMM
- Analyze the weaknesses of the organization's process capability according to CMM
- Recommend a process improvement plan to address the process weaknesses or for moving to a higher CMM capability level
- Explain what is the benefit of implementing this process improvement plan and how well your plan will meet the organization's business goal
- Estimate the costs of this process improvement effort
- Predict the risks for executing the process improvement plan that you have suggested
- Conclusions

5.13 What is the usage of CMM in software engineering process establishment, assessment, and improvement?

Chapter 6

THE ISO 9001 MODEL

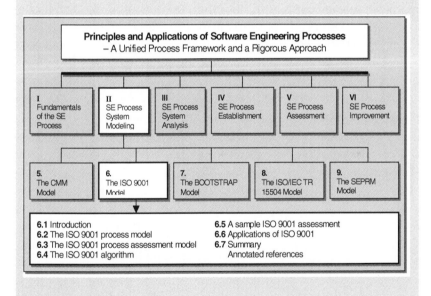

Principles and Applications of Software Engineering Processes
– A Unified Process Framework and a Rigorous Approach

| I Fundamentals of the SE Process | II SE Process System Modeling | III SE Process System Analysis | IV SE Process Establishment | V SE Process Assessment | VI SE Process Improvement |

| 5. The CMM Model | 6. The ISO 9001 Model | 7. The BOOTSTRAP Model | 8. The ISO/IEC TR 15504 Model | 9. The SEPRM Model |

6.1 Introduction
6.2 The ISO 9001 process model
6.3 The ISO 9001 process assessment model
6.4 The ISO 9001 algorithm

6.5 A sample ISO 9001 assessment
6.6 Applications of ISO 9001
6.7 Summary
    Annotated references

159

ISO 9001, a part of the ISO 9000 series of international standards for quality system management, is widely accepted for software engineering process system assessment and improvement. This chapter describes the ISO 9001 methodology by interpreting its process model, process capability model, and process capability determination methodology.

This chapter adopts a formal and algorithmic approach to describe ISO 9001. An ISO 9001 algorithm will be elicited and a sample assessment will be provided in order to demonstrate how an ISO 9001-based process assessment is carried out in practice. The usability of ISO 9001 is discussed on the basis of empirical experience in the software industry and research reports in the literature.

The objectives of this chapter are as follows:

- To review the history and background of ISO 9001 development

- To describe the ISO 9001 process model and taxonomy

- To describe the ISO 9001 capability model and capability determination methodology

- To formally describe the ISO 9001 process model, and to algorithmically describe the ISO 9001 process capability determination method

- To develop an ISO 9001 algorithm for software process assessment

- To explain how the ISO 9001 algorithm can be used in process assessment and how its algorithm complexity is estimated

- To demonstrate a case study of a practical ISO 9001 assessment by using the ISO 9001 algorithm

- To discuss the usability of ISO 9001 in process establishment, assessment, and improvement in software engineering

6.1 Introduction

In Chapter 5 we reviewed the background of CMM development by using the thread of the software project contractor's management requirements for a software development organization. In this chapter we will explore the background of ISO 9000 in general, and ISO 9001 in particular, with a thread of quality system principles.

Generic quality system principles in management science were considered to benefit from the contributions of Walter Shewhart (1939), Joseph Juran (1962/80/88/89), Philip Crosby (1979), W. Edwards Deming (1982a/b/86), and others. The fundamental quality system principles are:

- Statistical quality control

- Total quality management (TQM)

- Continuous improvement

In his work *Statistical Methods from the Viewpoint of Quality Control*, Shewhart (1939) established the statistical foundations of a generic quality control system. He developed the concept of "plan-do-check-act" iteration. The statistical quality control approach has largely influenced today's software process capability modeling and software metrics studies. As a proof of this, almost all major current process models require systematic data collection and recommend quantitative process improvement.

Deming's work (1982a/b/86) drew the attention of researchers and industrial practitioners to both quality and productivity. He proposed the approach to TQM. TQM is a management philosophy for achieving quality improvement by creating a quality culture and attitude throughout the entire organization's commitment and involvement. This approach has been widely accepted in the manufacturing industry, information systems [Buckland et al., 1991], and has been presented in the ISO 9000 standards.

Both statistical quality control and TQM have been extensively applied in the Japanese manufacturing industry. Based on these a *KAIZEN* method was developed in the 1980s in Japan (Imai, 1986; Huda and Preston, 1992). Imai (1986) proposed the term *KAIZEN* as the key to Japan's competitive success in its manufacturing industries. *KAIZEN* is actually two Chinese characters (*Gai-Shan*). *ZEN* means good, satisfactory, or perfect; *KAI* means change, update, or reform. Therefore, *KAI-ZEN* simply means to make better, while its internal philosophy implies gradual and continuous improvement and/or attaining perfection. This is perhaps the most influential philosophy that has been widely accepted as one of the important quality principles together with those of statistical quality control and TQM. All of these principles form the foundation of ISO 9000.

ISO 9000 [ISO 1991/93/94] is a set of international standards for quality systems. It is designed for quality management and assurance, and specifies the basic requirements for the development, production, installation, and servicing at system level and product level. ISO 9000 provides a management organization approach, a product management system, and a development management system based on quality system principles. ISO 9000 was first published in 1987 and revised in 1994.

Within the ISO 9000 suite, ISO 9001 [ISO 1989/94] and ISO 9000-3 [ISO, 1991] are applicable to the software process and quality systems for a software development organization. ISO 9001 aims to set minimum requirements for a general quality management system. The ISO 9001 model is generic, simple, and it has been accepted and supported worldwide. According to recent surveys [Wang et al., 1998a; Mobil Europe, 1995] the ISO 9001 model is still the most popular process system model in the software industry.

This chapter provides a formal description of ISO 9001 in accordance with the unified process system framework developed in Part I. A framework and taxonomy of the ISO 9001 process model are introduced in Section 6.2. The ISO 9001 capability model and process capability determination method are described in Section 6.3. Based on this, an ISO 9001 process assessment algorithm is elicited and an example of ISO 9001 assessment is provided in Sections 6.4 and 6.5, respectively. Finally, the usability of ISO 9001 is discussed in Section 6.6.

6.2 The ISO 9001 Process Model

This section describes the ISO 9001 process taxonomy and framework. The terms and process structure of ISO 9001 are introduced using the original form of expression, and are contrasted with the unified software process system framework developed in Part I.

6.2.1 TAXONOMY OF THE ISO 9001 PROCESS MODEL

Referring to the generic process taxonomy defined in Chapter 2, the ISO 9001 process hierarchy and domains are listed in Table 6.1.

Table 6.1
Process Hierarchy and Domains of the ISO 9001 Process Model

Taxonomy	Subsystem	Category	Process	Practice
Process level	Subsystems (SSs)	-	Main topic areas (MTAs)	Management issues (MIs)
Size of domain	3	-	20	177
Identification	SS[i]	-	MTA[i,k]	MI[i,k,j]

Table 6.1 defines the configuration of the ISO 9001 model. As shown in Table 6.1, the MIs and MTAs used in ISO 9001 are equivalent to the practices and processes, respectively, as defined in the unified process system framework.

In order to provide a formal identification for each entity defined at various levels of coverage known as process scopes, the indexing of SS, MTA, and MI are described using a naming convention as shown in Table 6.1. In the table, i is the number of SS; k, the number of MTA in ith SS; and j, the number of MI in kth MTA and ith SS.

6.2.2 FRAMEWORK OF THE ISO 9001 PROCESS MODEL

ISO 9001 models a software process system in 3 process subsystems, 20 main topic areas, and 177 management issues [ISO, 1994; Jenner, 1995]. A hierarchical structure of the ISO 9001 framework is shown in Table 6.2.

Table 6.2
The ISO 9001 Process Model

ID.	Subsystem (SS$_i$)	Main Topic Area (MTA[i,k])	Identified MIs (N$_{MI}$[i,k])
SS$_1$	Organization Management		53
MTA$_{1.1}$		Management responsibility	15
MTA$_{1.2}$		Quality system	7
MTA$_{1.3}$		Document and data control	8
MTA$_{1.4}$		Internal quality audits	6
MTA$_{1.5}$		Corrective and preventive action	6
MTA$_{1.6}$		Quality system records	7
MTA$_{1.7}$		Training	4
SS$_2$	Product Management		31
MTA$_{2.1}$		Product management	4

MTA$_{2.2}$		Control of customer-supplied product	4
MTA$_{2.3}$		Purchasing	8
MTA$_{2.4}$		Handling, storage, packaging, preservation, and delivery	9
MTA$_{2.5}$		Control of nonconforming product	6
SS$_3$	Development Management		93
MTA$_{3.1}$		Contract reviews	9
MTA$_{3.2}$		Process control	23
MTA$_{3.3}$		Design and development control	30
MTA$_{3.4}$		Inspection and testing	11
MTA$_{3.5}$		Inspection and test status	2
MTA$_{3.6}$		Control of inspection, measuring, and test equipment	12
MTA$_{3.7}$		Statistical techniques	2
MTA$_{3.8}$		Servicing and software maintenance	4
Total	3	20	177

In Table 6.2 the number of defined MIs for each MTA is provided. The definitions of the MIs are listed in Appendix C where, in the column of ISO 9001, a *j*th MI of MTA *k* in process subsystem *i*, MI*[i,k,j]*, is represented by:

$$MI[i,k,j] = MI_{i.k.j}$$
$$= BPA_{i'.k'.r'.j'} \qquad (6.1)$$

where *i'*, *k'*, *r'*, and *j'* are the index numbers of subsystem, category, process, and practice, respectively, as defined in the unified process system framework and SEPRM.

For example, in Appendix C, readers can identify MI[3,2,21] as:

$$MI[i,k,j] = MI[3,2,21]$$
$$= MI_{3.2.21}$$
$$= BPA_{3.1.8.1}$$
$$= BPA_{244}$$
$$= \text{"Audit software development activities"}$$

6.2.3 FORMAL DESCRIPTION OF THE ISO 9001 PROCESS MODEL

By using the CSP-like process algebra introduced in Chapter 3, we are able to formally describe the ISO 9001 process model and its processes in this subsection. The formal description is useful for providing precise and accurate definitions of the structure and interrelationships of the ISO 9001 processes, and to avoid ambiguity inherent in conventional natural language description.

6.2.3.1 The Structure of the ISO 9001 Process Model

A formal description of the structure of the ISO 9001 process model, *ISO9001_PM*, is shown in Expression 6.2 and illustrated in Figure 6.1. Basically, this is a parallel process model with three subsystems at the system level.

$$
\begin{array}{lll}
ISO9001\_PM \;\triangleq\; SS_1 & \text{// Organization management} & \\
\quad\quad\quad\quad\;\| \; SS_2 & \text{// Product management} & \\
\quad\quad\quad\quad\;\| \; SS_3 & \text{// Development management} & (6.2)
\end{array}
$$

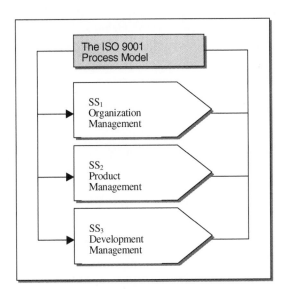

Figure 6.1 The ISO 9001 process model

In the ISO 9001 process model, each process subsystem can be extended to a number of parallel processes (MTAs) as shown in Expression 6.3. Further, each MTA can be extended to a number of MIs in a similar way.

$$SS_1 \triangleq MTA_{1.1} \parallel MTA_{1.2} \parallel MTA_{1.3} \parallel MTA_{1.4} \parallel MTA_{1.5} \parallel MTA_{1.6} \parallel MTA_{1.7}$$

$$SS_2 \triangleq MTA_{2.1} \parallel MTA_{2.2} \parallel MTA_{2.3} \parallel MTA_{2.4} \parallel MTA_{2.5}$$

$$SS_3 \triangleq MTA_{3.1} \parallel MTA_{3.2} \parallel MTA_{3.3} \parallel MTA_{3.4} \parallel MTA_{3.5}$$
$$\parallel MTA_{3.6} \parallel MTA_{3.7} \parallel MTA_{3.8} \tag{6.3}$$

6.2.3.2 Definitions of the ISO 9001 Processes

The ISO 9001 processes, known as MTAs, in each process subsystem can be formally defined by Expressions 6.4 – 6.6 and are illustrated in Figures 6.2 – 6.4.

$$
\begin{aligned}
SS_1 \triangleq \quad & MTA_{1.1} && \text{// Management responsibility} \\
\parallel \; & MTA_{1.2} && \text{// Quality system} \\
\parallel \; & MTA_{1.3} && \text{// Document and data control} \\
\parallel \; & MTA_{1.4} && \text{// Internal quality audits} \\
\parallel \; & MTA_{1.5} && \text{// Corrective and preventive action} \\
\parallel \; & MTA_{1.6} && \text{// Quality system records} \\
\parallel \; & MTA_{1.7} && \text{// Training} \tag{6.4}
\end{aligned}
$$

A process diagram corresponding to the seven processes of ISO 9001 subsystem SS_1, as defined in Expression 6.4, is shown in Figure 6.2.

A process diagram corresponding to the five processes of ISO 9001 subsystem SS_2, as defined in Expression 6.5, is shown in Figure 6.3.

$$
\begin{aligned}
SS_2 \triangleq \quad & MTA_{2.1} && \text{// Product management} \\
\parallel \; & MTA_{2.2} && \text{// Control of customer-supplied product} \\
\parallel \; & MTA_{2.3} && \text{// Purchasing} \\
\parallel \; & MTA_{2.4} && \text{// Handling, storage, packaging,} \\
& && \text{// preservation, and delivery} \\
\parallel \; & MTA_{2.5} && \text{// Control of nonconforming product} \tag{6.5}
\end{aligned}
$$

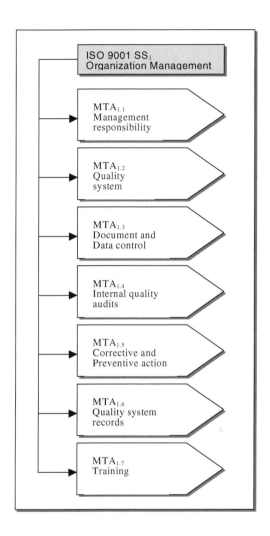

Figure 6.2 ISO 9001 Subsystem 1 processes – the organization management MTAs

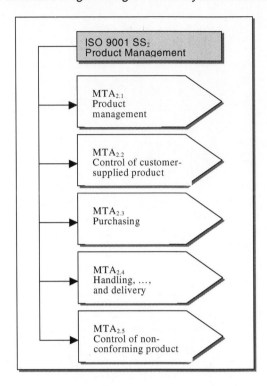

Figure 6.3 ISO 9001 Subsystem 2 processes – the product management MTAs

A process diagram corresponding to the eight processes of ISO 9001 subsystem SS_3, as defined in Expression 6.6, is shown in Figure 6.4.

$$SS_3 \triangleq MTA_{3.1} \qquad \text{// Contract review}$$

$$\| MTA_{3.2} \qquad \text{// Process control}$$

$$\| MTA_{3.3} \qquad \text{// Design and development control}$$

$$\| MTA_{3.4} \qquad \text{// Inspection and testing}$$

$$\| MTA_{3.5} \qquad \text{// Inspection and test status}$$

$$\| MTA_{3.6} \qquad \text{// Control of inspection, measuring, and}$$

$$\text{// test equipment}$$

$$\| MTA_{3.7} \qquad \text{// Statistical techniques}$$

$$\| MTA_{3.8} \qquad \text{// Servicing and software maintenance} \qquad (6.6)$$

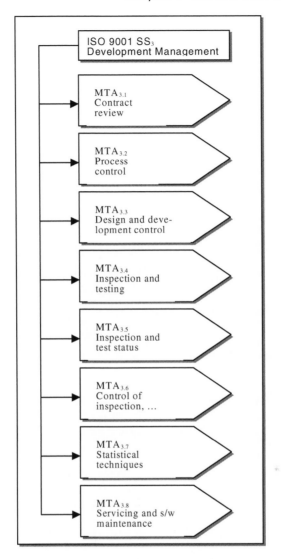

Figure 6.4 ISO 9001 Subsystem 3 processes – the development management MTAs

Detailed practices of each MTA at the MI level, which are documented in Appendix C, can be described in the same way as above. Extending of the formal ISO 9001 process model onto the MI level can be taken as an exercise for readers.

6.3 The ISO 9001 Process Assessment Model

The ISO 9001 process model was systematically introduced in Section 6.2. This section explores the ISO 9001 process capability model and process capability determination method. Both of the above form the ISO 9001 process assessment model.

6.3.1 THE ISO 9001 PROCESS CAPABILITY MODEL

In this section we intend to interpret the ISO 9001 model and methodology in accordance with the unified process system framework. We will elicit the ISO 9001 process capability model, which includes a practice performance scale, a process capability scale, and a process capability scope definition.

6.3.1.1 Practice Performance Scale

A practice performance rating scale for the MIs in ISO 9001 is defined in Table 6.3. It employs a kind of *yes/no* checklist for the MIs' existence and performance. The rating thresholds provide a set of quantitative measurements for rating a MI's performance with the scale.

Table 6.3
Practice Performance Scale of the MIs

Scale	Description	Rating threshold
1 (Y)	Satisfied	-
0 (N)	Not-satisfied	-

ISO 9001 requires that all 177 MIs have to be checked, without any option or tailorability. There is no rating threshold specified in the ISO 9001 model, so the assessors have room to determine if an MI has satisfied the requirements for ISO 9001 based on their experience and judgment.

6.3.1.2 Process Capability Scale

Using the practice performance scale of MIs defined in Section 6.3.1.1, an ISO 9001 process capability scale is described in Table 6.4. For each

MTA[i,k], the number of identified MIs ($N_{MI}[i,k]$) and the required number of MIs for satisfying an assessment ($P_{MI}[i,k]$) are listed respectively.

Table 6.4
The ISO 9001 Process Capability Scale

ID.	Subsystem (SS[i])	Main Topic Area (MTA[i,k])	Identified MIs ($N_{MI}[i,k]$)	Pass Threshold ($P_{MI}[i,k]$)
SS[1]	Organization Management		53	53
MTA$_{1.1}$		Management responsibility	15	15
MTA$_{1.2}$		Quality system	7	7
MTA$_{1.3}$		Document and data control	8	8
MTA$_{1.4}$		Internal quality audits	6	6
MTA$_{1.5}$		Corrective and preventive action	6	6
MTA$_{1.6}$		Quality system records	7	7
MTA$_{1.7}$		Training	4	4
SS[2]	Product Management		31	31
MTA$_{2.1}$		Product management	4	4
MTA$_{2.2}$		Control of customer-supplied product	4	4
MTA$_{2.3}$		Purchasing	8	8
MTA$_{2.4}$		Handling, storage, packaging, preservation, and delivery	9	9
MTA$_{2.5}$		Control of nonconforming product	6	6
SS[3]	Development Management		93	93
MTA$_{3.1}$		Contract reviews	9	9
MTA$_{3.2}$		Process control	23	23
MTA$_{3.3}$		Design and development control	30	30
MTA$_{3.4}$		Inspection and testing	11	11
MTA$_{3.5}$		Inspection and test status	2	2
MTA$_{3.6}$		Control of inspection, measuring, and test equipment	12	12
MTA$_{3.7}$		Statistical techniques	2	2
MTA$_{3.8}$		Servicing and software maintenance	4	4
Total	3	20	177	177

Observing Table 6.4, it may be found that the condition of an MTA's satisfaction at process level is that all MIs contained in it have to be satisfied. Therefore, the capability rating scale of ISO 9001 is relatively straightforward. It is a *go/no-go* checklist assessment based on the philosophy of providing an essential (minimum) set of requirements for quality management systems.

6.3.1.3 Process Capability Scope

The ISO 9001 process capability scopes are shown in Table 6.5. Comparing Table 6.5 with Table 2.3 in Chapter 2, it is clear that ISO 9001 assesses process capability at the levels of MI, MTA, and organization scope from the bottom, up.

Table 6.5
Process Capability Scope of ISO 9001

Capability Scope	Practice	Process	Project	Organization
ISO 9001 terms	MIs	MTAs	-	Organization
ISO 9001 methods	Fulfillment check	Fulfillment check	-	Pass/Fail

6.3.2 THE ISO 9001 PROCESS CAPABILITY DETERMINATION METHODOLOGY

Using the formal definitions of the ISO 9001 process model and process capability model developed in Sections 6.2 and 6.3.1, we can now consider how to apply the ISO 9001 capability model to the process model for the assessment of process capability at practice, process, and organization levels.

6.3.2.1 Practice Performance Rating Method

Let $r_{MI}[i,k,j]$ be a rating of performance of the jth MI in the kth process $(MTA[i,k])$ and ith process subsystem $(SS[i])$. Then $r_{MI}[i,k,j]$ can be rated according to the practice performance scale as defined in Table 6.3, i.e.:

$$r_{MI}[i,k,j] = 1 \quad \text{if the MI exists and its performance is satisfied}$$
$$= 0 \quad \text{otherwise} \tag{6.7}$$

6.3.2.2 Process Capability Rating Method

The number of satisfied MIs in a process subsystem (SS[i]), $SAT_{MI}[i]$, is assessed according to the following expression:

$$SAT_{MI}[i] = \#\{ MI[i,j] \mid Passed \}, \quad i = 1, 2, 3$$
$$= \#\{ MI[i,j] \mid r_{MI}[i,j] = 1 \}$$
$$= \sum_{j=1}^{N_{MI}} \{ 1 \mid r_{MI}[i,j] = 1 \} \tag{6.8}$$

where $r_{MI}[i,j]$ is a rating value of the jth MI's performance in SS[i] process subsystem based on the definition in Table 6.3, and N_{MIi} is the number of identified MIs in the process subsystem.

As described in Section 6.3.2.1, the pass threshold, $P_{MI}[i,j]$, for a process subsystem *SS[i]* in ISO 9001 is defined as:

$$P_{MI[i,j]} = N_{MI[I,j]} \tag{6.9}$$

This means that every MI defined in an MTA and an SS should fulfill the requirements of process capability at the MTA and SS levels, i.e.:

$$\begin{aligned} SAT_{MI}[i,j] &= P_{MI[i,j]} \\ &= N_{M[i,j]} \end{aligned} \tag{6.10}$$

The pass thresholds for each MTA and SS have been defined in Table 6.4 for reference.

6.3.2.3 Organization Capability Determination Method

As shown in Table 6.5, ISO 9001 has not defined a capability scope at project level. An ISO 9001 process capability level for a software development organization, PCL_{org}, can be determined by:

$$\begin{aligned} PCL_{org} &= pass, \quad if\ SAT_{MI} = P_{MI} \\ &= fail, \quad otherwise \end{aligned} \tag{6.11}$$

where SAT_{MI} is the total number of satisfied MIs in an ISO 9001 assessment, and P_{MI} is the total pass threshold for the assessed MIs defined in ISO 9001 ($P_{MI} = 177$).

6.4 The ISO 9001 Algorithm

So far, we have explored the ISO 9001 process model, process capability model, and capability determination method. Using the models and method we are already able to manually assess and calculate a software organization's process capability in ISO 9001.

In order to describe the ISO 9001 methodology precisely, and to enable mutual comparison and tool implementation, this section extends the ISO

9001 process capability determination methodology into a formal ISO 9001 algorithm.

6.4.1 DESCRIPTION OF THE ISO 9001 ALGORITHM

The ISO 9001 capability determination method as defined in Expressions 6.7 – 6.11 can be formally described in the following algorithm.

Algorithm 6.1 The ISO 9001 process capability determination algorithm

Assume: N_{MI} - Total number of MIs defined in ISO 9001
        SAT_{MI} - Number of satisfied MIs in assessment
        $MI[i,k,j]$ - The ith MI in MTA[i,k] of SS[i]
        $N_{MI}[i,k]$ - Number of defined MIs in MTA[i,k] of SS[i]
        $N_{MI}[i]$ - Number of defined MIs in SS[i]
        PCL_{org} - Process capability level of an organization
Input: Sample indicators of processes' existence and performance
Output: PCL_{org}

Begin

  // Step 1: Initialization

  $N_{MI}[1]:= 3;$ //Assign numbers of defined MTAs in each subsystem (SS)
  $N_{MI}[2] := 5;$
  $N_{MI}[3] := 8;$

  $N_{MI}[1,1]:=15;$ //Assign numbers of defined MIs in each process (MTA)
  $N_{MI}[1,2] := 7;$
  $N_{MI}[1,3] := 8;$
  $N_{MI}[1,4] := 6;$
  $N_{MI}[1,5] := 6;$
  $N_{MI}[1,6] := 7;$
  $N_{MI}[1,7] := 4;$

  $N_{MI}[2,1] := 4;$
  $N_{MI}[2,2] := 4;$
  $N_{MI}[2,3] := 8;$
  $N_{MI}[2,4] := 9;$
  $N_{MI}[2,5] := 6;$

  $N_{MI}[3,1] := 9;$

$N_{MI}[3,2] := 23;$
$N_{MI}[3,3] := 30;$
$N_{MI}[3,4] := 11;$
$N_{MI}[3,5] := 2;$
$N_{MI}[3,6] := 12;$
$N_{MI}[3,7] := 2;$
$N_{MI}[3,8] := 4;$

// Step 2: MI performance rating

$N_{MI} := 177;$
for $i := 1$ to 3 do   // Check 3 process subsystems
    for $k := 1$ to $N_{MI}[i]$ do   // Check all MTAs in a subsystem
        for $j := 1$ to $N_{MI}[i,k]$ do   // Check all MIs in an MTA
            begin
                // evaluate $MI[i,k,j]$ according to the rating scale
                // defined in Table 6.3
                if $MI[i,k,j]=1$
                    then // It is satisfied
                        $SAT_{MI} := SAT_{MI} + 1$ // increase number of
                                                   // satisfied MIs
                    // else, it is not satisfied, skip
            end;

// Step 2: Process capability determination

if $SAT_{MI} = N_{MI}$ // According to Expression 6.11
    then // The ISO 9001 assessment passed
        $PCL_{org} := $ 'passed';
    else // The ISO 9001 assessment failed
        $PCL_{org} := $ 'failed';

End   ∎

6.4.2 EXPLANATION OF THE ISO 9001 ALGORITHM

An ISO 9001 assessment according to Algorithm 6.1 is carried out in three steps:

- **Step 1:** Initialization

- **Step 2:** MI performance rating

- **Step 3:** Process capability determination

This subsection explains the main functions of Algorithm 6.1 for an ISO 9001 process assessment.

6.4.2.1 Initialization

This step is designed to specify the numbers of MIs defined in ISO 9001. For obtaining a detailed configuration of MIs in the ISO 9001 process model, readers may refer to Table 6.2 and Appendix C.

6.4.2.2 MI Performance Rating

In this step, all MIs for each MTA and then for each SS are rated according to Expressions 6.7 and 6.8 using the definitions of practice performance scale listed in Table 6.3.

The rating methods for all MIs at MTA level and SS level are identical as shown in the algorithm Step 2, except that for each MTA and SS the numbers of MIs, $N_{MI}[i,k]$ and $N_{MI}[i]$, are different as initialized in Step 1. The basic function for MI rating in the kernel of the iteration in Step 2 is to count the number of satisfied MIs by increasing SAT_{MI} by one if the examined MI is rated as 1 according to the rating scale in Table 6.3.

It is suggested that each MI for all MTAs and SSs should be rated, even when there is an early indication that a software organization would fail an assessment.

6.4.2.3 Organization Process Capability Determination

This step derives the maximum aggregated process capability level for an assessed software organization based on the MI ratings obtained in Step 2. The capability level of an organization is determined by Expression 6.11. This means that a software development organization should satisfy all 177 required MIs before it can pass an ISO 9001 assessment.

6.4.3 ANALYSIS OF THE ISO 9001 ALGORITHM

The effort expended in conducting an ISO 9001 assessment depends on its algorithm complexity. By examining the complexity of an algorithm, the time spent in an ISO 9001 assessment can be estimated quite accurately.

Reviewing the ISO 9001 algorithm in Subsection 6.4.1, it may be observed that the algorithm complexity of ISO 9001, *c(ISO9001)*, is mainly determined by the number of MIs, N_{MI}, that need to be rated individually in an ISO 9001 assessment according to Algorithm 6.1, Step 2, i.e.:

$$c(ISO9001) = O(N_{MI})$$
$$= N_{MI} \tag{6.12}$$

where the unit of the algorithm complexity is "times of MI ratings," or of practice ratings.

As given in ISO 9001, $N_{MI} = 177$. Thus the total rating cost, or the algorithm complexity, for determining a capability level for the project scope in ISO 9001 is:

$$c(ISO9001) = O(N_{MI})$$
$$= N_{MI}$$
$$= 177 \text{ [times of MI ratings]}$$

There is a certain range of rates between the algorithm complexity and the person-days needed for an assessment. Empirical data for relating the algorithm complexity to person-days expended in an ISO 9001 process assessment will be discussed in Chapter 12.

6.5 A Sample ISO 9001 Assessment

The capability rating framework and the capability determination algorithm of ISO 9001 were formally described in Sections 6.3 and 6.4. This section demonstrates how to apply the ISO 9001 expressions and algorithm to quantitatively determine a sample software development organization's process capability level in ISO 9001.

6.5.1   MI PERFORMANCE RATING IN ISO 9001

A set of detailed ratings of the 177 MIs have been listed in Appendix C, where the raw data rating {4,3,2,1} corresponds to the ISO 9001 MI rating scale {Y(1), Y(1), N(0), N(0)}. By referring to Table 6.3, a mapping between the rating scales of the raw data and the ISO 9001 MI is defined in Table 6.6.

Table 6.6
Mapping between Raw Data in Assessment onto
the ISO 9001 Rating Scale

Raw Data Rating Scale (in Appendix C)	ISO 9001 MI Rating Scale	Description in ISO 9001
4	1	Yes
3	1	Yes
2	0	No
1	0	No

Processing the raw data of the MIs' performance ratings according to Table 6.6 and then applying Expression 6.7 allows the number of satisfied MIs in the 20 MTAs, $SAT_{MI}[i,k]$, to be derived by:

$$
\begin{aligned}
SAT_{MI}[i,k] &= \#\{MI[i,k,j] \mid Passed\} \\
&= \#\{MI[i,k,j] \mid r_{MI}[i,k,j] = 1\} \\
&= \sum_{j=1}^{N_{MIi}} \{1 \mid r_{MI}[i,k,j] = 1\}
\end{aligned}
$$

For example, $MTA_{1.1}$, management responsibility, has 15 MIs rated:

$$
\begin{aligned}
MTA_{1.1} &= \{MI_{1.1.1}, MI_{1.1.2}, \ldots, MI_{1.1.15}\} \\
&= \{4,4, \ldots, 4\},
\end{aligned}
$$

respectively in Appendix C.

Mapping the raw data onto the ISO 9001 scale according to Table 6.6, the MI ratings are as follows:

$$
\begin{aligned}
MTA[1,1] &= \{Y, Y, \ldots, Y\} \\
&= \{1,1, \ldots, 1\}
\end{aligned}
$$

Thus, according to Expression 6.7, the number of satisfied MIs for MTA[1,1] is:

$$
\begin{aligned}
SAT_{MI}[1,1] &= \#\{MI_{1.1.1}, MI_{1.1.2}, \ldots, MI_{1.1.15}\} \\
&= 15
\end{aligned}
$$

A summary of the 20 MTA capability ratings in ISO 9001 is listed in Table 6.7.

Table 6.7
Summary Assessment Record in ISO 9001

No.	Subsystem (SS[i])	Main topic area (MTA[i,k])	Pass Threshold ($P_{MI}[i,k] = N_{MI}[i,k]$)	Assessment Result ($SAT_{MI}[i,k]$)
SS_1	Organization Management		53	53
$MTA_{1.1}$		Management responsibility	15	15
$MTA_{1.2}$		Quality system	7	7
$MTA_{1.3}$		Document and data control	8	8
$MTA_{1.4}$		Internal quality audits	6	6
$MTA_{1.5}$		Corrective and preventive action	6	6
$MTA_{1.6}$		Quality system records	7	7
$MTA_{1.7}$		Training	4	4
SS_2	Product Management		31	31
$MTA_{2.1}$		Product management	4	4
$MTA_{2.2}$		Control of customer-supplied product	4	4
$MTA_{2.3}$		Purchasing	8	8
$MTA_{2.4}$		Handling, storage, packaging, preservation, and delivery	9	9
$MTA_{2.5}$		Control of nonconforming product	6	6
SS_3	Development Management		93	93
$MTA_{3.1}$		Contract reviews	9	9
$MTA_{3.2}$		Process control	23	23
$MTA_{3.3}$		Design and development control	30	30
$MTA_{3.4}$		Inspection and testing	11	11
$MTA_{3.5}$		Inspection and test status	2	2
$MTA_{3.6}$		Control of inspection, measuring, and test equipment	12	12
$MTA_{3.7}$		Statistical techniques	2	2
$MTA_{3.8}$		Servicing and software maintenance	4	4
Total	3	20	177	177

6.5.2 PROCESS CAPABILITY DETERMINATION IN ISO 9001

Using the assessment result listed in Table 6.7, a process capability profile of the software development organization in ISO 9001 can be derived as shown in Figure 6.5.

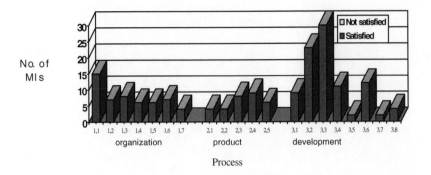

Figure 6.5 Process capability profile of a software organization in ISO 9001

6.5.3 ORGANIZATION CAPABILITY DETERMINATION IN ISO 9001

The process capability level of an organization, PCL_{org}, in ISO 9001 has been defined as complete fulfillment of the requirements of the 177 MIs as shown in Expression 6.11:

$$PCL_{org} = pass, \quad if \ SAT_{MI} = P_{MI}$$
$$= fail, \quad otherwise$$

Analyzing the rating record in Table 6.7, it can be seen that all of the 177 MIs have satisfied the requirements for an ISO 9001 assessment. Therefore, based on Expression 6.11, the assessment result is:

$$PCL_{org} = pass, \ since \ SAT_{MI} = P_{MI} = 177$$

The sample software development organization has passed the assessment of the ISO 9001 requirements.

6.6 Applications of ISO 9001

In the previous sections we explored the ISO 9001 theory and methodology for process system modeling and assessment. This section analyzes the usability of ISO 9001 in software engineering process system establishment, assessment, and improvement. In order to present both sides of the coin, the limitations of ISO 9001 in some aspects of software engineering applications are discussed using the body of empirical and theoretical studies on ISO 9001.

6.6.1 ISO 9001 FOR SOFTWARE PROCESS SYSTEM ESTABLISHMENT

ISO 9001 is a one-dimensional, checklist-based process assessment method used for the first-, second-, third-party, and authorized assessment of a software engineering process system in a software development organization.

The ISO 9000 framework was not originally designed for the software engineering environment. ISO 9001 is a modification and enhancement of an ISO 9000 model biased toward a software development organization. ISO 9001 treats software development processes in the same as any mass manufacturing system. However, as analyzed in Chapter 1, software development is a creative and design-intensive process rather than a repetitive manufacturing process. Thus, awareness of this limitation of ISO 9001 is helpful in ISO 9001-based process system establishment.

The capability rating scale in ISO 9001 is quite straightforward. It is a *go/no-go* assessment based on the philosophy of providing an essential (minimum) set of requirements for quality systems. Because ISO 9001 is the lightest weight process model among the current process models presented in this part of the book, it would be suitable for an organization initiating a software engineering process system from scratch. For a much more mature software development organization, it is recommended that a staged process model be chosen, and that there be an adoption of a continuous process improvement strategy in a long-term plan.

6.6.2 ISO 9001 FOR SOFTWARE PROCESS SYSTEM ASSESSMENT

For software process assessment, ISO 9001 provides the weakest process maturity requirements among all major process models, because it is designed as a minimum requirement checklist.

The ISO 9001 capability determination methodology for a software organization's quality system is a set of essential check points. All the 177 sample points should be satisfied for readiness for an ISO 9001 registration.

However, it is a minimum set of requirements and lacks a step-by-step capability determination system. All software development organizations above the threshold hold the same certification. Therefore, maturity differences may be lost among the ISO 9001 registered software development organizations. This might well affect the motivation of an organization in pursuing continuous process improvement as analyzed in the following subsection.

6.6.3 ISO 9001 FOR SOFTWARE PROCESS SYSTEM IMPROVEMENT

It may be understood via Algorithm 6.1 that the ISO 9001 methodology is suitable for basic process assessment. It is not suitable for process improvement because it lacks a process system that supports staged capability determination and improvement, and the important concept of continuous process improvement is not effectively reflected in the ISO 9001 approach.

6.7 Summary

This chapter introduced a formal and rigorous approach into the description of ISO 9001. CSP-like process algebra has been adopted for presenting the ISO 9001 process model, and mathematical and algorithmic methods have been applied for presenting the ISO 9001 process capability determination methodology. Using these formal techniques, ISO 9001 has been systematically described and analyzed by contrasting it with the unified process system framework developed in Part I. An empirical case study has been provided for demonstrating the method and approach in conducting an ISO 9001 assessment.

The basic knowledge structure of this chapter is as follows:

Chapter 6. The ISO 9001 Model

- General
  - Purposes of this chapter
    - To review the history and background of ISO 9001

development

– To describe the ISO 9001 process model and taxonomy

– To describe the ISO 9001 capability model and capability determination methodology

– To formally describe the ISO 9001 process model, and to algorithmically describe the ISO 9001 process capability determination method

– To develop an ISO 9001 algorithm for software process assessment

– To explain how the ISO 9001 algorithm can be used in process assessment and how its algorithm complexity is estimated

– To demonstrate a case study of a practical ISO 9001 assessment by using the ISO 9001 algorithm

– To discuss the usability of ISO 9001 in process establishment, assessment, and improvement in software engineering

– ISO 9001 philosophy and background
    – Quality system principles
        – Statistical quality control
        – TQM
        – Continuous improvement
    – Orientation to quality system management for a software development organization
    – Difference between software engineering and conventional mass manufacturing industry

• The ISO 9001 process model
    – Taxonomy of the ISO 9001 process model
        – Process scopes
        – Size of domain of each scope

    – Framework of the ISO 9001 process model
        – Structure of the ISO 9001 process model
        – Definitions of MTAs in ISO 9001

    – Formal description of ISO 9001 process model

- ISO 9001 abstract process patterns
- ISO 9001 process diagrams
- Interpretation and illustration of the process algebra expressions

- The ISO 9001 process assessment model
  - The ISO 9001 process capability model
    - Configuration
      - 3 process subsystems (SSs)
      - 20 processes (MTAs)
      - 177 practices (MIs)
    - MI rating scale
    - Process rating scale

  - The ISO 9001 process capability determination method
    - Formal description of ISO 9001 capability determination methodology
    - Meanings of expressions and their operation
    - Common features with the methodology developed in the unified process framework in Part I
    - Differences from the methodology developed in the unified process framework in Part I

- The ISO 9001 algorithm
  - Algorithm 6.1: ISO 9001 process assessment
  - Explanation of Algorithm 6.1
  - Relation between Algorithm 6.1 and the capability determination expressions in Section 6.3.2
  - The ISO 9001 algorithm complexity and the main factors that affect it

- A sample ISO 9001 process assessment
  - Understand assessment data documented in Appendix C
  - Manual process assessment in ISO 9001
  - Algorithm-based assessment in ISO 9001
  - Interpretation of assessment results

- Usability of ISO 9001
  - Merits and demerits in process system establishment
  - Merits and demerits in process system assessment
  - Merits and demerits in process system improvement

Major achievements and issues for further research suggested by this chapter are highlighted below:

- The design philosophy behind ISO 9001 is a generic quality system perception on software development. Although this philosophy has been proven successful in the conventional manufacturing industry, there is still a need for supporting evidence of its effectiveness and impact on the design-intensive software engineering and nonconventional software industries.

- As discussed in Section 1.3 on the foundations of software engineering, we are expecting further research on the common features and differences between conventional mass manufacturing and software development. It appears likely that software engineering will prove to be sufficiently unique as an engineering discipline in that it relies upon special foundations and applies a different philosophy.

- ISO 9001 has developed a straightforward checklist-based process methodology for a quality management system of a software development organization. Because of its simplicity, ISO 9001 has been widely accepted and applied in the software industry.

- An ISO 9001 algorithm has been elicited in order to precisely and systematically interpret the ISO 9001 methodology, and to quantitatively compare the complexity of the ISO 9001 method with others.

- ISO 9001 is the weakest process model among the current models for software engineering process system modeling, assessment, and improvement. It lacks a staged process capability framework for software engineering process assessment and improvement.

This chapter has established a basis for understanding and analyzing ISO 9001 as a paradigm of the unified software engineering process system framework. Relationships of ISO 9001 with other process system models will be discussed in Part III of this book. Applications of ISO 9001 in process-based software engineering and case studies will be provided in Parts IV – VI.

Annotated References

A structure of the ISO 9000 standards suite is as follows:

- ISO 9000:

  - ISO 9000-1 (1994): Quality Management and Quality Assurance Standards (Part 1) - Guidelines for Selection and Use.

  - ISO 9000-2 (1994): Quality Management and Quality Assurance Standards (Part 2) – Generic Guidelines for Application of ISO 9001, ISO 9002, and ISO 9003.

  - ISO 9000-3 (1991): Quality Management and Quality Assurance Standards (Part 3) – Guidelines to Apply ISO 9001 for Development, Supply, and Maintenance of Software.

  - ISO 9000-4 (1993): Quality Management and Quality System (Part 4) – Guidelines for Dependability Program Management.

- ISO 9001 (1994): Quality Systems – Model for Quality Assurance in Design, Development, Production, Installation, and Servicing.

- ISO 9002 (1994): Quality Systems – Model for Quality Assurance in Production, Installation, and Servicing.

- ISO 9003 (1994): Quality Systems – Model for Quality Assurance in Final Inspection and Test.

- ISO 9004:

  - ISO 9004-1 (1994): Quality Management and Quality System Elements (Part 1) – Guidelines.

  - ISO 9004-2 (1991): Quality Management and Quality System Elements (Part 2) – Guidelines for Services.

  - ISO 9004-4 (1993): Quality Management and Quality System Elements (Part 4) – Guidelines for Quality Improvement.

There are a number of derived versions of ISO 9000 standards adopted by national or regional standardization bodies, such as: ANSI/ASQC 9001 in the USA, EN29001 in Europe, BS/EN29001 in the UK, and AS/NZS 9001 in Australia and New Zealand. Some variation or extension of ISO 9000 standards also exist, such as IEEE 1298 (IEEE 1998) and TickIT (TickIT 1987/92).

In Jenner's work (1995), a set of 177 management issues (MIs) was identified in the ISO 9001 conformance checklist for assessors based on the ISO 9001 revised version in 1994.

For further details on quality system principles such as statistical quality control, TQM, and continuous improvement, read Shewhart (1939), Juran (1962/80/88/89), Crosby (1979), Deming (1982a/b, 1986), Imai (1986), Feigenbaum (1991), Feigenbaum (1991), and Buckland et al. (1991).

Wang et al. (1997a/b/99e) presented a series of comparative analyses of relationships and mutual mappings between the major process models including ISO 9001. According to Wang et al. (1996c), those organizations that can pass the threshold of ISO 9001 assessment are equivalent to CMM capability levels 2 – 3. Referring to Zubrow's statistics (1997), this implies that about 38% of those CMM-assessed organizations are technically at or above the ISO 9001 requirement level.

Seddon (1997) set out 10 arguments against ISO 9000. He argued that the command-and-control ethos that pervades the ISO 9000 way of thinking – an inflexible compliance to a rigid set of written rules – is precisely what most companies do not need. In its place, he showed how real quality can be achieved by viewing the organization as a system and focusing on continuous improvement as the best means to create higher quality products and services.

A number of related international standards on generic quality systems have been developed, such as ISO 8258 – Shewhart Control Charts (1991), ISO 10011 – Guidelines for Auditing Quality Systems (1988), and ISO 10013 – Guidelines for Developing Quality Manuals (ISO 1992).

Questions and Problems

6.1 Explain the design philosophy behind the development of ISO 9001.

6.2 Using your own words, briefly describe the structure of the ISO 9001 process model and its taxonomy.

6.3 Using process algebra, derive a formal ISO 9001 process model based on the process diagrams given in Figures 6.1 – 6.4. (Try not to copy Expressions 6.2 – 6.6 before you finish.)

6.4 Briefly describe the ISO 9001 process capability model and capability determination methodology using your own words.

6.5 Can you repeat the sample ISO 9001 assessment based on the data provided in Appendix C and derive the same capability level as that of the example shown in Section 6.5?

6.6 Try to conduct an ISO 9001 exercise assessment for an organization with which you are familiar according to the formal approach presented in this chapter.

6.7 Consider how to distinguish the following ISO 9001 registered software organizations' capability levels:

(a) Organization A is ISO 9001 registered and at CMM Level 4;
(b) Organization B is at CMM Level 2.

6.8 Are there any significant differences between an organization that is newly established based on the ISO 9001 quality system, and an organization that is experienced in software development but has just updated and reoriented its processes onto the ISO 9001 model? Could both of these organizations be registered for ISO 9001?

6.9 What are the possible different impacts of implementing the ISO 9001 requirements on small- and large-sized software development organizations?

6.10 Try to organize a small software project with at least three persons. Then, do a self-assessment for this project and report your capability level in ISO 9001.

6.11 Try to write an ISO 9001 assessment report for Exs. 6.6 or 6.10 and describe the following:

- Purpose(s) of the ISO 9001 assessment
- The ISO 9001 model and methodology you adopted
- The input of the ISO 9001 assessment
- The procedure of the ISO 9001 assessment
- The output of the ISO 9001 assessment
- The effort you spend for the ISO 9001 assessment

- Experience you gained in the ISO 9001 assessment
- Conclusions

6.12 Try to write an ISO 9001 process improvement plan based on the assessment report developed in Ex. 6.11. In the process improvement plan, describe the following:

- Purpose(s) of the ISO 9001 process improvement plan
- Brief introduction of the ISO 9001 assessment results
- Analyze strengths of the organization's process capability according to ISO 9001
- Analyze weaknesses of the organization's process capability according to ISO 9001
- Recommend a process improvement plan to address the process weaknesses or to pursue continuous process improvement
- Explain the benefit of implementing this process improvement plan and how well your plan will meet the organization's business goal
- Estimate the costs of this process improvement effort
- Predict the risks for executing the process improvement plan that you have suggested
- Conclusions

6.13 What is the usage of ISO 9001 in software engineering process establishment, assessment, and improvement?

Chapter 7

THE BOOTSTRAP MODEL

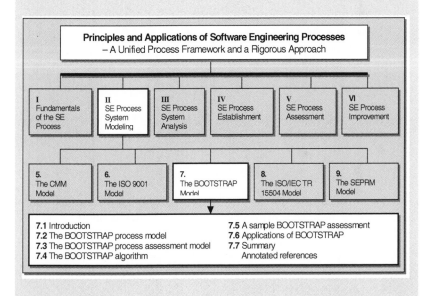

Principles and Applications of Software Engineering Processes – A Unified Process Framework and a Rigorous Approach					
I Fundamentals of the SE Process	II SE Process System Modeling	III SE Process System Analysis	IV SE Process Establishment	V SE Process Assessment	VI SE Process Improvement
5. The CMM Model	6. The ISO 9001 Model	7. The BOOTSTRAP Model	8. The ISO/IEC TR 15504 Model	9. The SEPRM Model	

7.1 Introduction
7.2 The BOOTSTRAP process model
7.3 The BOOTSTRAP process assessment model
7.4 The BOOTSTRAP algorithm

7.5 A sample BOOTSTRAP assessment
7.6 Applications of BOOTSTRAP
7.7 Summary
Annotated references

191

BOOTSTRAP is a European enhanced and adapted process methodology for software engineering process system assessment and improvement. This chapter describes the BOOTSTRAP model, including its process model, process capability model, and process capability determination methodology.

This chapter adopts a formal and algorithmic approach to describe BOOTSTRAP. A BOOTSTRAP algorithm will be elicited and a sample assessment will be provided in order to demonstrate how a BOOTSTRAP-based process assessment is carried out in practice. The usability of BOOTSTRAP is discussed on the basis of empirical experience in the software industry and research reports in the literature.

The objectives of this chapter are as follows:

- To review the history and background of BOOTSTRAP development

- To describe the BOOTSTRAP process model and taxonomy

- To describe the BOOTSTRAP capability model and capability determination methodology

- To formally describe the BOOTSTRAP process model and to algorithmically describe the BOOTSTRAP process capability determination method

- To develop a BOOTSTRAP algorithm for software process assessment

- To explain how the BOOTSTRAP algorithm can be used in process assessment and how its algorithm complexity is estimated

- To demonstrate a case study of a practical BOOTSTRAP assessment by using the BOOTSTRAP algorithm

- To discuss the usability of BOOTSTRAP in process establishment, assessment, and improvement in software engineering

7.1 Introduction

We have perceived in previous chapters that CMM and ISO 9001 presented the contractors' and quality managers' view, respectively, for a software engineering process system. The philosophy of BOOTSTRAP is to present the developers' technical view on software processes. With this view as a main thread in this chapter, we will explore the BOOTSTRAP methodology and usability.

BOOTSTRAP [Koch, 1993; Haase et al., 1994; and Kuvaja et al., 1994a] was developed in a research project sponsored by the European ESPRIT program during 1990 – 1993 [ESPRIT, 1991]. After completion of the project, a BOOTSTRAP Institute based in Finland was founded to maintain and apply the model. BOOTSTRAP has gained significant recognition in the European software industry. This chapter describes BOOTSTRAP V.2.3.

The BOOTSTRAP model has relatively great similarity to CMM. New features developed in the BOOTSTRAP model are that: (a) a process assessment result is represented by both a capability level and a process profile; (b) a refined process capability scale exists with quartiles between two levels; and (c) there is an improved practice rating scale with four adequate measurements. BOOTSTRAP identified and addressed the following features specific to the European software industry:

- A high degree of adaptation to international standards, such as those of ISO 9001, ESA PSS-05-0 (ESA 1991)

- Existence of a large portion of small- and medium-sized enterprises (SMEs), which could not afford a heavy overhead process approach

- Emphases on software process improvement via process assessment

This chapter provides a formal description of BOOTSTRAP in accordance with the unified process system framework developed in Part I. A framework and taxonomy of the BOOTSTRAP process model are introduced in Section 7.2. The BOOTSTRAP capability model and process capability determination method are described in Section 7.3. Based on this, a BOOTSTRAP process assessment algorithm is elicited and an example of BOOTSTRAP assessment is provided in Sections 7.4 and 7.5, respectively. Finally, the usability of BOOTSTRAP is discussed in Section 7.6.

7.2 The BOOTSTRAP Process Model

This section describes the BOOTSTRAP process taxonomy and framework. The terms and process structure of BOOTSTRAP are introduced using the original form of expression, and are contrasted with the unified software process system framework developed in Part I.

7.2.1 TAXONOMY OF THE BOOTSTRAP PROCESS MODEL

Referring to the generic process taxonomy defined in Chapter 2, the BOOTSTRAP process hierarchy and domains are listed in Table 7.1.

Table 7.1
Process Hierarchy and Domains of the BOOTSTRAP Process Model

Taxonomy	Subsystem	Category	Process	Practice
Process scope	Process areas (PAs)	Process categories (PCs)	Processes (PRs)	Quality system attributes (QSAs)
Size of domain	3	9	32	201
Identification	PA[i]	PC[i,k]	PR[i,k,r]	QSA[i,k,r,j]

Table 7.1 defines the configuration of the BOOTSTRAP model. As shown, the QSAs, PRs, PCs, and PAs used in BOOTSTRAP are equivalent to the practices, processes, category, and subsystem, respectively, as defined in the unified process system framework.

In order to provide a formal identification for each entity defined at various levels of coverage known as process scopes, the indexing of PA, PC, PR, and QSA are described using a naming convention as shown in Table 7.1. In the table, i is the number of PA; $k,$ the number of PC in ith PA; $r,$ the number of PR in kth PR and in ith PA; and $j,$ the number of QSA in rth PR, kth PC, and ith PA.

7.2.2 FRAMEWORK OF THE BOOTSTRAP PROCESS MODEL

The fundamental concept of BOOTSTRAP is a set of 201 QSAs. Based on this premise, BOOTSTRAP claims it is an attribute-based method for process assessment and improvement [Koch, 1993; Kuvaja et al., 1994a]. The QSAs of BOOTSTRAP are classified in two ways: functional and measurable technology [BOOTSTRAP Institute, 1994]. According to the functional classification, the QSAs are categorized into three process areas known as organization, methodology, and technology. According to the measurable classification, for process assessment, BOOTSTRAP specifies the QSAs at different capability levels similar to those of CMM.

From the functional organization point of view, BOOTSTRAP models a software process system in 3 process areas (PAs), 9 process categories (PCs), 32 processes (PRs), and 201 quality system attributes (QSAs). A hierarchical structure of the BOOTSTRAP framework is shown in Table 7.2.

Table 7.2
The BOOTSTRAP Process Model

ID.	PA	PC	PR	Description	No. of QSAs
1	PA₁			**Organization**	**21**
1.1		PC₁.₁		Quality system	14
1.1.1			PR₁.₁.₁	Quality system	14
1.2		PC₁.₂		Resource management	7
1.2.1			PR₁.₂.₁	Resource needs and work environment	3
1.2.2			PR₁.₂.₂	Personnel selection and training	4
2	PA₂			**Methodology**	**131**
2.1		PC₂.₁		Process-related functions	34
2.1.1			PR₂.₁.₁	Process description	11
2.1.2			PR₂.₁.₂	Process measurement	6
2.1.3			PR₂.₁.₃	Process control	17
2.2		PC₂.₂		Life cycle-independent functions	48
2.2.1			PR₂.₂.₁	Project management	11
2.2.2			PR₂.₂.₂	Quality management	11
2.2.3			PR₂.₂.₃	Risk avoidance and management	8
2.2.4			PR₂.₂.₄	Configuration and change management	11
2.2.5			PR₂.₂.₅	Subcontractor management	7
2.3		PC₂.₃		Life cycle functions	49
2.3.1			PR₂.₃.₁	Develop cycle model	1
2.3.2			PR₂.₃.₂	Special purpose systems	11
2.3.3			PR₂.₃.₃	User requirements	2
2.3.4			PR₂.₃.₄	Software requirements	3
2.3.5			PR₂.₃.₅	Architecture design	3
2.3.6			PR₂.₃.₆	Detailed design and implementation	8
2.3.7			PR₂.₃.₇	Testing	3
2.3.8			PR₂.₃.₈	Integration	2
2.3.9			PR₂.₃.₉	Acceptance testing and transfer	7
2.3.10			PR₂.₃.₁₀	Operation and maintenance	9
3	PA₃			**Technology**	**49**
3.1		PC₃.₁		Technology innovation	4
3.1.1			PR₃₁₁	Technology innovation	4
3.2		PC₃.₂		Technology for life cycle-independent functions	11
3.2.1			PR₃.₂.₁	Communication	2
3.2.2			PR₃.₂.₂	Project management	2
3.2.3			PR₃.₂.₃	Quality management	4

3.2.4		PR$_{3.2.4}$	Configuration and change management	3
3.3	PC$_{3.3}$		Technology for life cycle functions	29
3.3.1		PR$_{3.3.1}$	User requirements	2
3.3.2		PR$_{3.3.2}$	Software requirements	3
3.3.3		PR$_{3.3.3}$	Architecture design	2
3.3.4		PR$_{3.3.4}$	Detailed design and implementation	6
3.3.5		PR$_{3.3.5}$	Testing	3
3.3.6		PR$_{3.3.6}$	Integration	4
3.3.7		PR$_{3.3.7}$	Acceptance testing and transfer	3
3.3.8		PR$_{3.3.8}$	Operation and maintenance	6
3.4	PC$_{3.4}$		Tool integration	5
3.4.1		PR$_{3.4.1}$	Tool integration	5
Total	3 9 32			201

From Table 7.2 it may be observed that BOOTSTRAP processes are a combination of quality system techniques and software development lifecycle techniques. In BOOTSTRAP, the process area of technology is modeled as a counterpart of methodology, where the methodology processes refer to the procedures in applying the organization framework at project level while the technology processes define the implementation of methodologies with particular tools.

In Table 7.2, the number of defined QSAs for each process, in a process category and a process area, is provided. The definitions of the QSAs are listed in Appendix C where, in the column of BOOTSTRAP, a *j*th QSA of process *r* in process category *k* in process area *i* is represented by:

$$QSA[i,k,r,j] = QSA_{i.k.r.j}$$
$$= BPA_{i'.k'.r'.j'} \tag{7.1}$$

where *i'*, *k'*, *r'* and *j'*, are the index numbers of subsystem, category, process, and practice, respectively, as defined in the unified process system framework and SEPRM.

For example, in Appendix C, readers can identify QSA[2,1,3,3] as:

$$QSA[i,k,r,j] = QSA[2,1,3,3]$$
$$= QSA_{2.1.3.3}$$
$$= BPA_{3.1.8.1}$$
$$= BPA_{244}$$
$$= \text{"Audit software development activities"}$$

BOOTSTRAP has developed a functional framework for the QSAs as shown in Table 7.2. It is a technical advance on CMM that moves toward developing an independent process dimension in process system modeling. However, BOOTSTRAP has not fully separated the dimensions of process and its capability measurement because the capability levels, as described in the next section, are still dependent on a configuration of the same set of QSAs. This dependability between capability levels and a subset of practices (QSAs) characterizes that BOOTSTRAP is still a 1-D process system model. We will further discuss this feature in Section 7.3.

7.2.3 FORMAL DESCRIPTION OF THE BOOTSTRAP PROCESS MODEL

By using the CSP-like process algebra introduced in Chapter 3, we are able to formally describe the BOOTSTRAP process model and its processes in this subsection. The formal description of the BOOTSTRAP process model provides precise and accurate definitions of the structure and interrelationships of the BOOTSTRAP processes, and avoids ambiguity inherent in conventional natural language description.

7.2.3.1 The Structure of the BOOTSTRAP Process Model

A formal description of the structure of the BOOTSTRAP process model, *BOOTSTRAP-PM*, is shown in Expression 7.2 and illustrated in Figure 7.1. Basically, this is a parallel process model at the system level.

$$
\begin{aligned}
BOOTSTRAP\text{-}PM \triangleq\ &PA_1 && \text{// Organization} \\
&\|\ PA_2 && \text{// Methodology} \\
&\|\ PA_3 && \text{// Technology}
\end{aligned}
\tag{7.2}
$$

In the BOOTSTRAP process model, each process area can be extended to a number of parallel PCs as shown in Expression 7.3. Further, each PC can be extended to a number of QSAs in a similar way.

$$
\begin{aligned}
PA_1 &\triangleq PC_{1.1} \| PC_{1.2} \\
PA_2 &\triangleq PC_{2.1} \| PC_{2.2} \| PC_{2.3} \\
PA_3 &\triangleq PC_{3.1} \| PC_{3.2} \| PC_{3.3} \| PC_{3.4}
\end{aligned}
\tag{7.3}
$$

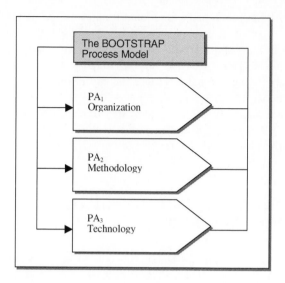

Figure 7.1 The BOOTSTRAP process model

7.2.3.2 Definitions of BOOTSTRAP Processes

The BOOTSTRAP processes, known as PRs, at each capability level can be formally defined by Expressions 7.4 – 7.6 and are illustrated in Figures 7.2 – 7.4.

$$
\begin{aligned}
PA_1 &\triangleq PC_{1.1} && \text{// Quality system} \\
&\parallel PC_{1.2} && \text{// Resource management} \\
&\triangleq PR_{1.1.1} && \text{// Quality system} \\
&\parallel (\ PR_{1.2.1} && \text{// Resource needs and work environment} \\
&\quad \parallel PR_{1.2.2} && \text{// Personnel selection and training} \\
&\quad)
\end{aligned}
\tag{7.4}
$$

A process diagram corresponding to the two process categories and three processes in BOOTSTRAP PA_1 as defined in Expression 7.4 is shown in Figure 7.2.

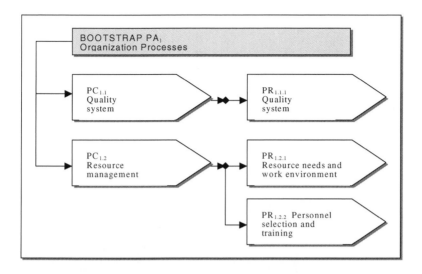

Figure 7.2 BOOTSTRAP process area-1 – the organization PRs

A process diagram corresponding to the three process categories and 18 processes in BOOTSTRAP PA$_2$, as defined in Expression 7.5, is shown in Figure 7.3.

$$PA_2 \triangleq \quad PC_{2.1} \qquad\qquad \text{// Process related functions}$$

$$\qquad \| \; PC_{2.2} \qquad\qquad \text{// Life cycle-independent functions}$$

$$\qquad \| \; PC_{2.3} \qquad\qquad \text{// Life cycle functions}$$

$$\triangleq \quad (PR_{2.1.1} \| \; PR_{2.1.2} \; \| \; PR_{2.1.3})$$

$$\| \; (PR_{2.2.1} \| \; PR_{2.2.2} \| \; PR_{2.2.3} \; \| \; PR_{2.2.4} \; \| \; PR_{2.2.5})$$

$$\| \; (PR_{2.3.1} \| \; PR_{2.3.2} \|$$

$$(PR_{2.3.3}; PR_{2.3.4}; PR_{2.3.5}; PR_{2.3.6}; PR_{2.3.7}; PR_{2.3.8};$$

$$PR_{2.3.9}; PR_{2.3.10}) \qquad\qquad\qquad\qquad (7.5)$$

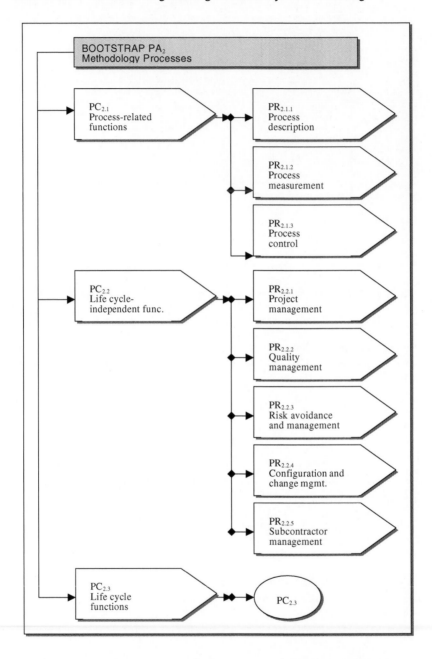

Figure 7.3 BOOTSTRAP process area-2 – the methodology processes

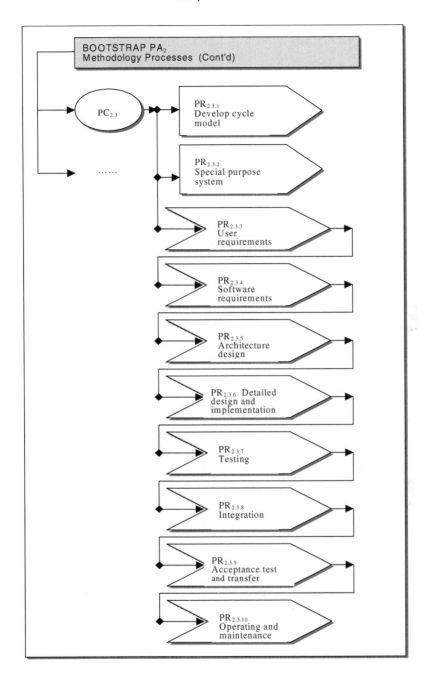

Figure 7.3 (Cont'd) BOOTSTRAP process area-2 – the methodology processes

A process diagram corresponding to the four process categories and 14 processes in BOOTSTRAP PA_3, as defined in Expression 7.6, is shown in Figure 7.4.

$$
\begin{aligned}
PA_3 \triangleq \ & PC_{3.1} && \text{// Technology innovation} \\
& \| \ PC_{3.2} && \text{// Tech. for life cycle-independent functions} \\
& \| \ PC_{3.3} && \text{// Technology for life cycle functions} \\
& \| \ PC_{3.4} && \text{// Tool integration} \\
\triangleq \ & PR_{3.1.1} \\
& \| \ (PR_{3.2.1} \| \ PR_{3.2.2} \| \ PR_{3.2.3} \ \| \ PR_{2.2.4}) \\
& \| \ (PR_{3.3.1} \| \ PR_{3.3.2} \| \ PR_{3.3.3} \| \ PR_{3.3.4} \| \ PR_{3.3.5} \ \| \ PR_{3.3.6} \\
& \qquad\quad \| \ PR_{3.3.7} \ \| \ PR_{3.3.8}) \\
& \| \ PR_{3.4.1}
\end{aligned}
\tag{7.6}
$$

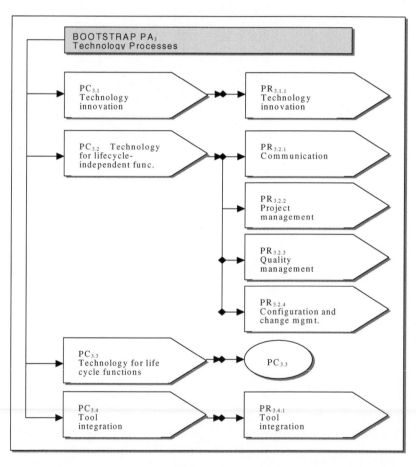

Figure 7.4 BOOTSTRAP process area-3 – the technology processes

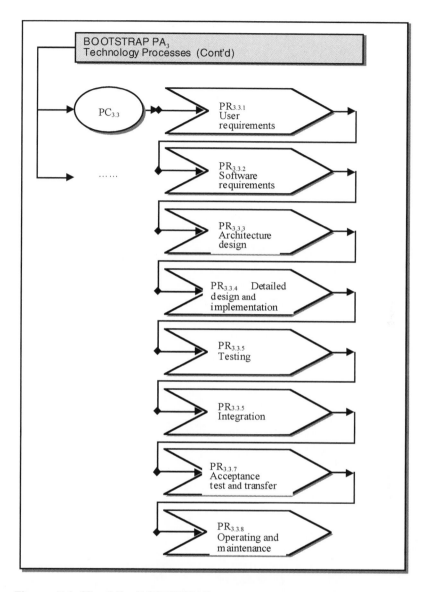

Figure 7.4 (Cont'd)   BOOTSTRAP process area-3 – the technology processes

Detailed practices of each PR at QSA level, which are documented in Appendix C, can be described in the same way as above. Extending the formal BOOTSTRAP process model onto the QSA level can be taken as an exercise for readers.

7.3 The BOOTSTRAP Process Assessment Model

The BOOTSTRAP process model was systematically introduced in Section 7.2. This section explores the BOOTSTRAP process capability model and process capability determination method. Both of the above form the BOOTSTRAP process assessment model.

7.3.1 THE BOOTSTRAP PROCESS CAPABILITY MODEL

This section describes the BOOTSTRAP process capability model, which includes a practice performance scale, a process capability scale, and a process capability scope definition.

7.3.1.1 Practice Performance Scale

A practice performance rating scale for the QSAs in BOOTSTRAP is defined in four (plus one) levels as described in Table 7.3. In Table 7.3, the rating thresholds provide a set of quantitative measurements for rating a QSA's performance with the scale.

Table 7.3
Practice Performance Scale of the QSAs

Scale	Description	Rating threshold
4	Complete / extensive	≥80%
3	Largely satisfied	66.7% - 79.9%
2	Partially satisfied	33.3% - 66.6%
1	Absent / poor	≤33.2%
0	Doesn't apply	-

The supplementary scale 0 in Table 7.3, *doesn't apply*, is designed to increase the tailorability and flexibility of the BOOTSTRAP process model. In BOOTSTRAP QSA rating, a score 0 is usually treated as equivalent to 4.

7.3.1.2 Process Capability Scale

As shown in Table 7.4, process capability in BOOTSTRAP [Koch, 1993; Haase, 1994; Kuvaja et al., 1994a/b] is determined by a five-level process capability scale, which is identical to that of CMM as defined in Table 5.4. A refinement of the capability scale in BOOTSTRAP is that quartiles are added to each capability level to enable further precise assessment of the process capability.

Table 7.4
The BOOTSTRAP Process Capability Model

Capability Level (CL[i])	Quartiles Between CLs	Description	Identified QSAs ($N_{QSA}[i]$)	Pass Threshold ($P_{QSA}[i]$)
CL[1]		Initial	$N_{QSA}[1] = 0$	$P_{QSA}[1] = 0$
CL[2]		Repeated	$N_{QSA}[2] = 40$	$P_{QSA}[2] = 32$
	CL2.1			
	CL2.2			
	CL2.3			
	CL2.4			
CL[3]		Defined	$N_{QSA}[3] = 81$	$P_{QSA}[3] = 65$
	CL3.1			
	CL3.2			
	CL3.3			
	CL3.4			
CL[4]		Managed	$N_{QSA}[4] = 27$	$P_{QSA}[4] = 22$
	CL4.1			
	CL4.2			
	CL4.3			
	CL4.4			
CL[5]		Optimizing	$N_{QSA}[5] = 53$	$P_{QSA}[5] = 53$
	CL5.1			
	CL5.2			
	CL5.3			
	CL5.4			
Total		5	201	162

In Table 7.4, the different distances (number of QSAs) between two adjacent levels indicate the various difficulties in capability improvement from the current level to the next higher level according to the model.

It may be observed from Table 7.4 that, for process assessment, BOOTSTRAP adopted the same approach to pre-assign the 201 QSAs into different capability levels. In Section 7.2.2 we have analyzed that BOOTSTRAP has not fully separated the dimensions of process and of its capability measurement because the capability levels are still dependent on different architectures of the same set of QSAs. Although BOOTSTRAP overlaps the process and capability dimensions at the practice (QSA) level, CMM overlaps the two dimensions at the process (KPA) level. This means that BOOTSTRAP pre-allocates and determines the process capability levels by different QSAs while CMM does the same by different KPAs. So in BOOTSTRAP we may say that a capability level is determined by a certain subset of its practices (QSAs); while that of CMM is determined by a certain subset of its processes (KPAs).

7.3.1.3 Process Capability Scope

The BOOTSTRAP process capability scope is shown in Table 7.5. Comparing Table 7.5 with Table 2.3 in Chapter 2, it is obvious that BOOTSTRAP assesses process capability at the levels of QSA, PR, project, and organization scope from the bottom, up.

Table 7.5
Process Capability Scope of BOOTSTRAP

Capability Scope	Practice	Process	Project	Organization
Bootstrap terms	QSAs	PRs / levels	Project	Organization
Bootstrap method	Performance rating	Performance rating	Capability level with quartiles	Capability level with quartiles

7.3.2 THE BOOTSTRAP PROCESS CAPABILITY DETERMINATION METHODOLOGY

Using the formal definition of the BOOTSTRAP process model and process capability model developed in Sections 7.2 and 7.3.1, we can now consider how to apply the BOOTSTRAP capability model to the process model for the assessment of process capability at practice, process, project, and organization levels.

7.3.2.1 Process Performance Rating Method

Let $r_{QSA}[i,j]$ be a rating of performance of the jth QSA at the ith process capability level. Then $r_{QSA}[i,j]$ can be rated according to the practice performance scale as defined in Table 7.3, i.e.:

$r_{QSA}[i,j] = 4,$ if the QSA's performance is at least 80% satisfied
$\qquad\quad = 3,$ if the QSA's performance adequacy is between 66.7-79.9%
$\qquad\quad = 2,$ if the QSA's performance adequacy is between 33.3-66.6%
$\qquad\quad = 1,$ if the QSA's performance adequacy is less than 33.2%
$\qquad\quad = 0,$ if the QSA doesn't apply in this assessment $\qquad$ (7.7)

7.3.2.2 Process Capability Rating Method

The number of satisfied QSAs at a level i, $SAT_{QSA}[i]$, is assessed according to the following expression:

$$
\begin{aligned}
SAT_{QSA}[i] &= \# \{ QSA[i,j] \mid \text{Passed} \} \\
&= \# \{ QSA[i,j] \mid r_{QSA}[i,j] \geq 3 \vee r_{QSA}[i,j] = 0 \} \\
&= \sum_{j=1}^{N_{QSAi}} \{ 1 \mid r_{QSA}[i,j] \geq 3 \vee r_{QSA}[i,j] = 0 \}
\end{aligned}
\tag{7.8}
$$

where N_{QSAi} is the number of defined QSAs at level i.

Expression 7.8 indicates that the number of the satisfied QSAs at a capability level can be obtained simply by counting the QSAs that satisfy or do not apply in the assessment.

A pass threshold, $P_{QSA}[i]$, for a capability level, i, in BOOTSTRAP is defined as:

$$
P_{QSA}[i] = N_{QSA}[i] * 80\%
\tag{7.9}
$$

This means that 80% of the QSAs defined at a level should be satisfied for fulfilling the requirements of process capability at this level, i.e.:

$$
\begin{aligned}
SAT_{QSA}[i] &\geq P_{QSA}[i] \\
&\geq N_{QSA}[i] * 80\%
\end{aligned}
\tag{7.10}
$$

The pass thresholds at each capability level have been defined in Table 7.4 for reference.

BOOTSTRAP capability levels and their related QSAs are predefined and fixed according to its methodology, as is the case for CMM. However, BOOTSTRAP allows an organization's practices at higher levels to be taken into account in the final capability determination. This feature will be explained in the next subsection.

7.3.2.3 Project Capability Determination Method

BOOTSTRAP adopts a dynamic capability scale for process assessment. BOOTSTRAP assesses a project's capability by taking account of the practices (QSAs) at all levels. The higher level practices within an organization which, at the level(s) higher than the maximum fulfilled capability level, are treated as merits in capability determination.

The total score for a project – the number of QSAs satisfied at all levels, N_{QSA} – is a sum of the QSAs satisfied at each level, i.e.:

$$N_{QSA} = \sum_{i=1}^{5} SAT_{QSA}[i] \qquad (7.11)$$

Thus, the process capability level of a project, *PCL*, is calculated by two items in BOOTSTRAP: a base score and an additional technical merit score gained by practices at higher levels as described below:

$$
\begin{aligned}
PCL &= Base + Additional \\
&= max \{ i \mid SAT'_{QSA}[i] \geq P'_{QSA}[i] \} + \\
&\quad (SAT'_{QSA}[5] - SAT'_{QSA}[i]) / \sum_{j=i+1}^{5} N_{QSA}[j] \qquad (7.12)
\end{aligned}
$$

where $SAT'_{QSA}[i]$ and $N'_{QSA}[i]$ represent the *i*th accumulated score and threshold up to level *i,* respectively. The latter can be derived based on the individual pass thresholds defined in Table 7.4 as $\{P'_{QSA}[1], P'_{QSA}[2], P'_{QSA}[3], P'_{QSA}[4], P'_{QSA}[5] \} = \{0, 32, 97, 119, 162\}$.

When a *PCL* obtained by Expression 7.12 is neither an integer nor a quartile, a quarterly rounded capability level, PCL_r , needs to be derived according to the following expression:

$$PCL_r = \lfloor PCL \rfloor_{\frac{1}{4}} \qquad (7.13)$$

where $\lfloor x \rfloor_{\frac{1}{4}}$ means round *x* to the nearest lower quarter. For example, $\lfloor 1.80 \rfloor_{\frac{1}{4}} = 1.75$, $\lfloor 3.23 \rfloor_{\frac{1}{4}} = 3.0$, and $\lfloor 4.5 \rfloor_{\frac{1}{4}} = 4.5$.

Thus, a project's capability level in BOOTSTRAP can be obtained by substituting Expression 7.12 into 7.13:

$$
\begin{aligned}
PCL_{proj}[p] &= PCL_r \\
&= \lfloor PCL \rfloor_{\frac{1}{4}} \\
&= \lfloor max \{ i \mid SAT'_{QSA}[i] \geq P'_{QSA}[i]\} + \\
&\quad (SAT'_{QSA}[5] - SAT'_{QSA}[i]) / \sum_{j=i+1}^{5} N_{QSA}[j] \rfloor_{\frac{1}{4}} \qquad (7.14)
\end{aligned}
$$

7.3.2.4 Organization Capability Determination Method

A BOOTSTRAP process capability level for an organization is defined as a quarterly rounded average of *n* assessed projects, i.e.:

$$PCL_{\text{org}} = \lfloor \tfrac{1}{n} \sum_{p=1}^{n} PCL_{\text{proj}}[p] \rfloor_{\frac{1}{4}} \qquad (7.15)$$

Expression 7.15 indicates that an established software organization and its successful experience in the project scope can be taken into account cumulatively when determining the organization's process capability level.

BOOTSTRAP does not suggest how many project assessments are sufficient to derive an organization's capability level. Generally, it is recommended that $n \geq 3$ for a valid aggregating of an organization's process capability level based on the projects carried out in the organization.

7.4 The BOOTSTRAP Algorithm

So far we have explored the BOOTSTRAP process model, process capability model, and capability determination method. Using the models and method we are already able to manually assess and calculate a software project's or an organization's process capability in BOOTSTRAP.

In order to describe the BOOTSTRAP methodology precisely, and to enable mutual comparison and tool implementation, this section extends the BOOTSTRAP process capability determination methodology into a formal BOOTSTRAP algorithm.

7.4.1 DESCRIPTION OF THE BOOTSTRAP ALGORITHM

The BOOTSTRAP capability determination method as defined in Expressions 7.7 - 7.14 up to the scope of project can be formally described in the following algorithm. An organization's process capability level can be aggregated according to Expression 7.15, when multiple projects have been assessed.

Algorithm 7.1 The BOOTSTRAP process capability determination algorithm

Assume: N_{QSAi} - number of QSAs at level i,

                                      $i = 1,2,3,4,5$

             $QSA[i, j]$ - the jth QSA at level i

             $SAT_{QSA}[I]$ - number of QSAs satisfied at level i

             $r_{QSA}[i, j]$ - rate of QSA j at level i

             N_{sat} - number of QSAs satisfied at all levels

             PCL - process capability level

             PCL_r - a rounded process capability level

             $PCL_{proj}[p]$ - process capability level of project p

Input: Sample indicators of BPA and processes' existence and performance

Output: $PCL_{proj}[p]$

Begin

    // Step 1: Initialization

    $N_{QSA}[1] := 0;$ // Assign number of defined QSAs at each level
    $N_{QSA}[2] := 40;$
    $N_{QSA}[3] := 81;$
    $N_{QSA}[4] := 27;$
    $N_{QSA}[5] := 53;$

    $P'_{QSA}[1] := 0;$ // Assign cumulated pass thresholds at each level
    $P'_{QSA}[2] := 32;$
    $P'_{QSA}[3] := 97;$
    $P'_{QSA}[4] := 119;$
    $P'_{QSA}[5] := 162;$

// Step 2: QSA performance rating

    // 2.1 Assess each QSA at every level
    for $i := 1$ to 5 do   // Assess all QSAs at each level
       begin
          for $j := 1$ to $N_{QSA}[i]$ do
             begin
                // Rate each $QSA[i, j]$ according to Expression 7.7 and
                // Table 7.3
                if ($r_{QSA}[i, j] \geq 3 \vee r_{QSA}[i, j] = 0$)

then $QSA[i, j]:=1$ // The QSA is satisfied
else $QSA[i, j]:=0;$
    end;

$$SAT'_{QSA}[\,i\,] := \sum_{j=1}^{N_{QSAi}} QSA[i, j];$$

end;

// 2.2 Count total satisfied number of *QSAs* at all levels

$$N_{sat} := \sum_{i=1}^{5} SAT'_{QSA}[i];$$

// Step 3: Process capability determination

if $(N_{sat} < P'_{QSA}[2])$
    then // Initial
        $PCL := 1 + (N_{sat} / (N_{QSA}[2]+N_{QSA}[3]+N_{QSA}[4]+N_{QSA}[5]))$
        // According to Expression 7.14
    else if $(N_{sat} < P'_{QSA}[3])$
        then // Repeatable
            $PCL := 2 + ((N_{sat} - SAT'_{QSA}[2]) /$
                    $(N_{QSA}[3]+N_{QSA}[4]+N_{QSA}[5]))$
        else   if $(N_{sat} < P'_{QSA}[4])$
            then // Defined
                $PCL := 3 + ((N_{sat} - SAT'_{QSA}[3]) /$
                        $(N_{QSA}[4]+N_{QSA}[5]))$
            else if $(N_{sat} < P'_{QSA}[5])$
                then // Managed
                    $PCL := 4 + ((N_{sat} - SAT'_{QSA}[4]) /$
                            $N_{QSA}[5]);$
                else // Optimized
                    $PCL := 5;$

$PCL_r = \lfloor PCL \rfloor_{\frac{1}{4}};$ // Rounded to the nearest lower quarter

                                // according to Expression 7.13

$PCL_{proj}[p] := PCL_r;$ // Expression 7.14

End   ■

7.4.2   EXPLANATION OF THE BOOTSTRAP ALGORITHM

A BOOTSTRAP assessment according to Algorithm 7.1 is carried out in three steps:

- **Step 1:** Initialization

- **Step 2:** QSA performance rating

- **Step 3:** Process capability determination

This subsection explains the main functions of Algorithm 7.1 for a BOOTSTRAP process assessment.

7.4.2.1 Initialization

This step is designed to specify the numbers of QSAs defined in BOOTSTRAP. For obtaining a detailed configuration of QSAs in the BOOTSTRAP process model, readers may refer to Table 7.2 and Appendix C.

7.4.2.2 QSA Performance Rating

In this step, all QSAs for each PR at each capability level are rated according to Expressions 7.7 and 7.8 using the definitions of the practice performance scale listed in Table 7.3.

The rating methods for all QSAs at Levels 2 – 5 are identical, as shown in algorithm Step 2.1, except that at each level i the number of QSAs, $N_{QSA}[i]$, are different as initialized in Step 1. The basic function for QSA rating at each level is to count the number of satisfied QSAs by increasing $SAT_{QSA}[level]$ by one if the examined QSA is rated as 4, 3, or 0 according to the rating scale in Table 7.3.

Step 2.2 counts the total number of satisfied SQAs at all levels in order to obtain N_{sat} or $SAT'_{QSA}[5]$ as defined in Expression 7.12.

According to the BOOTSTRAP algorithm, every QSA at all levels should be rated in order to derive the final process capability for a project, which would take the higher level(s) practices into account as additional merits.

7.4.2.3 Project Process Capability Determination

This step derives the maximum aggregated process capability level for an assessed software project based on the QSA ratings obtained in Step 2. The capability level of a project is determined by Expression 7.14.

7.4.3 ANALYSIS OF THE BOOTSTRAP ALGORITHM

The effort expended in conducting a BOOTSTRAP assessment depends on its algorithm complexity. By examining the complexity of an algorithm, the time spent in BOOTSTRAP assessment can be estimated quite accurately.

Reviewing the BOOTSTRAP algorithm in Subsection 7.4.1, it may be observed that the algorithm complexity of BOOTSTRAP, $c(BOOTSTRAP)$, is mainly determined by the number of QSAs, N_{QSA}, that need to be rated individually in a BOOTSTRAP assessment according to Algorithm 7.1, Step 2, i.e.:

$$
\begin{aligned}
c(BOOTSTRAP) &= O(N_{QSA}) \\
&= N_{QSA} \\
&= \sum_{i=1}^{5} N_{QSA}[i]
\end{aligned}
\tag{7.16}
$$

where $N_{QSA}[i]$ is the QSAs at level i, $1 \leq i \leq 5$. The unit of the algorithm complexity is "times of QSA ratings," or of practice ratings.

As given in BOOTSTRAP, $N_{QSA}[1]=0$, $N_{QSA}[2]=40$, $N_{QSA}[3]=81$, $N_{QSA}[4]=27$, *and* $N_{QSA}[5]=53$. Thus, the total rating cost, or the algorithm complexity, for determining a capability level of project scope in BOOTSTRAP is:

$$
\begin{aligned}
c(BOOTSTRAP) &= O(N_{QSA}) \\
&= N_{QSA} \\
&= \sum_{i=1}^{5} N_{QSA}[i] \\
&= 0 + 40 + 81 + 27 + 53 \\
&= 201 \ [\text{times of QSA ratings}]
\end{aligned}
$$

There is a certain range of rates between the algorithm complexity and the person-days needed for an assessment. Empirical data for relating the algorithm complexity to person-days expended in a BOOTSTRAP process assessment will be discussed in Chapter 12.

7.5 A Sample BOOTSTRAP Assessment

The capability rating framework and the capability determination algorithm of BOOTSTRAP have been formally described in Sections 7.3 and 7.4. This section demonstrates how to apply the BOOTSTRAP expressions and algorithm to quantitatively determine a sample software development organization's process capability level in BOOTSTRAP.

7.5.1 QSA PERFORMANCE RATING IN BOOTSTRAP

A set of detailed ratings of the 201 QSAs have been listed in Appendix C, where the raw data rating {4,3,2,1} corresponds to the BOOTSTRAP QSA rating scale {4,3,2,1}. By referring to Table 7.3, a mapping between the rating scales of the raw data and the BOOTSTRAP QSA is defined in Table 7.6.

Table 7.6
Mapping between Raw Data in Assessment onto BOOTSTRAP Rating Scale

Raw Data Rating Scale (in Appendix C)	BOOTSTRAP QSA Rating Scale	Description in BOOTSTRAP
4	4	Complete / extensive
3	3	Largely satisfied
2	2	Partially satisfied
1	1	Absent / poor

Processing the raw data of the QSAs performance ratings according to Table 7.6 and then applying Expression 7.8 allows the number of satisfied QSAs at a level i, $SAT_{QSA}[i]$, to be derived by:

$$
\begin{aligned}
SAT_{QSA}[i] &= \# \{ \; QSA[i,j] \mid \text{Passed} \; \} \\
&= \# \{ \; QSA[i,j] \mid r_{QSA}[i,j] \geq 3 \;\; \vee \;\; r_{QSA}[i,j] = 0 \} \\
&= \sum_{j=1}^{N_{SQAi}} \{ \; 1 \mid r_{QSA}[i,j] \geq 3 \;\; \vee \;\; r_{QSA}[i,j] = 0 \}
\end{aligned}
$$

For example, there are 40 QSAs at Level 2, CL_2, in BOOTSTRAP which are identified by a subscript "2" for the QSAs in Appendix C. Only five of the Level-2 QSAs, {$QSA_{2.1.3.13}$, $QSA_{2.2.4.4}$, $QSA_{2.2.4.11}$, $QSA_{2.3.1.10}$, $QSA_{2.3.1.29}$}, are rated unsatisfied (below 3) in Appendix C. Thus, according to Expression 7.8, the number of satisfied QSAs for CL_2 are:

$$SAT_{QSA}[2] = 40 - \#\{QSA_{2.1.3.13}, QSA_{2.2.4.4}, QSA_{2.2.4.11}, QSA_{2.3.1.10}, QSA_{2.3.1.29}\}$$
$$= 40 - 5$$
$$= 35$$

A summary of the ratings of the 201 QSAs at 5 capability levels in BOOTSTRAP is listed in Table 7.7. In the last two columns, $P'_{QSA}[i]$ and $SAT'_{QSA}[i]$ represent the ith accumulated threshold and the ith accumulated score at level i, respectively.

Table 7.7
Summary Assessment Record in BOOTSTRAP

Capability level (CL[i])	Description	Identified QSAs ($N_{QSA}[i]$)	Pass threshold ($P_{QSA}[i]$ | $P'_{QSA}[i]$)	Assessment result ($SAT_{QSA}[i]$ | $SAT'_{QSA}[i]$)
CL_5	Optimizing	53	43 | 162	19 | 134
CL_4	Managed	27	22 | 119	14 | 115
CL_3	Defined	81	65 | 97	66 | 101
CL_2	Repeated	40	32 | 32	35 | 35
CL_1	Initial	0	0 | 0	0 | 0

7.5.2 PROCESS CAPABILITY DETERMINATION IN BOOTSTRAP

Using the assessment result listed in Table 7.7, a process capability profile of the software development organization in BOOTSTRAP can be derived as shown in Figure 7.5. The data shown in the CL_i' columns are the accumulated scores up to Level i.

7.5.3 PROJECT CAPABILITY DETERMINATION IN BOOTSTRAP

The capability maturity level for a project p, $PCL_{proj}[p]$, in BOOTSTRAP has been defined as the maximum integer level, i, plus the quartile(s) a software development organization fulfilled as in Expression 7.14.

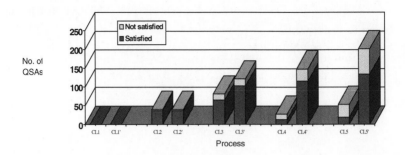

Figure 7.5 Process capability profile of a software organization in BOOTSTRAP

Applying Expression 7.14 to the ratings of the 201 QSAs at the five levels summarized in Table 7.7, the capability level of the software development organization can be determined. Considering that:

$$(SAT'_{QSA}[2] = 35) > (P'_{QSA}[2] = 32)$$
$$(SAT'_{QSA}[3] = 101) > (P'_{QSA}[3] = 97)$$
$$(SAT'_{QSA}[4] = 115) < (P'_{QSA}[4] = 119)$$
$$(SAT'_{QSA}[5] = 134) < (P'_{QSA}[4] = 162)$$

This indicates that the base score in BOOTSTRAP is 3. According to Expression 7.14, the capability level of the software development organization in BOOTSTRAP can be calculated as:

$$
\begin{aligned}
PCL_{proj}[p] &= PCL_r \\
&= \lfloor PCL \rfloor_{\frac{1}{4}} \\
&= \lfloor max\,\{\,i \mid SAT'_{QSA}[i] \geq P'_{QSA}[i]\} + \\
&\quad (SAT'_{QSA}[5] - SAT'_{QSA}[i]\,) / \sum_{j=i+1}^{5} N_{QSA}[j] \rfloor_{\frac{1}{4}} \\
&= \lfloor 3 + (134 - 101) / 80 \rfloor_{\frac{1}{4}} \\
&= \lfloor 3 + 0.41 \rfloor_{\frac{1}{4}} \\
&= 3.25
\end{aligned}
$$

The score shows that the project of the software development organization has fulfilled the capability Level 3, the defined process capability level, with a plus of one quartile above this level in BOOTSTRAP.

7.6 Applications of BOOTSTRAP

In the previous sections we explored the BOOTSTRAP theory and methodology for process system modeling and assessment. This section analyzes the usability of BOOTSTRAP in software engineering process system establishment, assessment, and improvement. In order to present both sides of the coin, the limitations of BOOTSTRAP in some aspects of software engineering applications are discussed using the body of empirical and theoretical studies on BOOTSTRAP.

7.6.1 BOOTSTRAP FOR SOFTWARE PROCESS SYSTEM ESTABLISHMENT

BOOTSTRAP was developed based on the inspiration and experience of CMM, ISO 9001, and other regional and internal models. The advantages of BOOTSTRAP methodology in process system modeling are as follows:

- Improved practice rating scale from simple "Yes/No" to four adequate scales.

- In addition to an aggregated process capability level, it presented assessment results as a process profile. This is considered the initial idea for 2-D process system modeling.

- Considered process – product correlation in a software development organization.

Some open issues identified in research and practices for BOOTSTRAP are as follows:

- Compared to the CMM model, the BOOTSTRAP process model lacks detailed description except for a generic questionnaire.

- As an adoption of a 1-D process model, BOOTSTRAP inherited the same difficulty of rationale for the preassignment of the practices (QSAs) into capability levels.

- Details of BOOTSTRAP methodology are based and documented on a number of internal reports. Researchers and practitioners outside were unable to independently apply and evaluate this methodology.

In Section 7.2.2 we discovered that BOOTSTRAP has not fully separated the dimensions of process and its capability measurement. This is because the capability levels are still dependent on a preassigned configuration of the same set of QSAs. However, it is interesting that BOOTSTRAP overlapped the process and capability dimensions at the practice (QSA) level while CMM overlapped the two dimensions at the process (KPA) levels. That is, BOOTSTRAP pre-allocates and determines the process capability levels by different QSAs while CMM does the same by different KPAs. So in BOOTSTRAP we may say that a capability level is determined by a certain subset of its practices (QSAs), while in CMM that is determined by a certain subset of its processes (KPAs).

Thus, fundamentally, BOOTSTRAP is still a 1-D process model, even though it introduced the process profile for interpreting the assessment results in a 2-D manner for the first time. Readers may refer to Section 5.6.1 for detailed analysis of the limitations and possible improvement approaches to 1-D process models.

7.6.2 BOOTSTRAP FOR SOFTWARE PROCESS SYSTEM ASSESSMENT

BOOTSTRAP is suitable for the first-, second-, and third-party assessment of a software engineering process system in a software development organization.

BOOTSTRAP assesses a project's capability by taking account of the practices (QSAs) at all levels. The higher level practices, which are at a level higher than the maximum fulfilled capability level, are treated as merits in capability calculation. This enables technical innovations (scores at higher levels) of a software development organization to be taken into account in the final capability determination. This is an improvement and an advantage over CMM in the methodology of capability determination.

In the BOOTSTRAP process capability model, a capability level and its related QSAs are predefined and fixed in the same way as that of CMM. In practical software engineering, the modeled priority level of the QSAs in BOOTSTRAP and the practical priority in a software development organization would be difficult to reconcile. Thus, a completely independent process dimension from the capability dimension is required in practice. This inspiration leads to development towards 2-D process system modeling methodologies, which will be introduced in the following chapters of this part.

7.6.3 BOOTSTRAP FOR SOFTWARE PROCESS SYSTEM IMPROVEMENT

BOOTSTRAP has put more emphasis on process improvement via process assessment. It is a basic philosophy and intends to assist understanding in a software organization and to find its strengths and weaknesses by process assessment. Then the target process profile is decided, and the process improvement plan can be set up. After a period of improvement according to the recommendation, another process assessment would be conducted in order to test the current status of the process system and to fine-tune the improvement activities.

However, because BOOTSTRAP has not provided a precisely defined and publicly available process model as discussed in the above subsection, the implementation and effectiveness of an improvement plan would be affected.

7.7 Summary

This chapter has introduced a formal and rigorous approach to the description of BOOTSTRAP. CSP-like process algebra has been adopted for presenting the BOOTSTRAP process model, and mathematical and algorithmic methods have been applied for presenting the BOOTSTRAP process capability determination methodology. Using these formal techniques, BOOTSTRAP has been systematically described and analyzed by contrasting with the unified process system framework developed in Part I. An empirical case study has been provided for demonstrating the method and approach in conducting a BOOTSTRAP assessment.

The basic knowledge structure of this chapter is as follows:

Chapter 7. The BOOTSTRAP Model

- General
  - Purposes of this chapter
    - To review the history and background of BOOTSTRAP development
    - To describe the BOOTSTRAP process model and

taxonomy

- To describe the BOOTSTRAP capability model and capability determination methodology

- To formally describe the BOOTSTRAP process model, and to algorithmically describe the BOOTSTRAP process capability determination method

- To develop a BOOTSTRAP algorithm for software process assessment

- To explain how the BOOTSTRAP algorithm can be used in process assessment and how its algorithm complexity is estimated

- To demonstrate a case study of a practical BOOTSTRAP assessment by using the BOOTSTRAP algorithm

- To discuss the usability of BOOTSTRAP in process establishment, assessment, and improvement in software engineering

- BOOTSTRAP philosophy and background
  - An enhanced and European-adapted CMM
  - A technical view of software development life cycles
  - An assessment-based process improvement approach
  - An integration of CMM with ISO 9001 quality system processes

- The BOOTSTRAP process model
  - Taxonomy of BOOTSTRAP process model
    - Process scopes
    - Size of domain of each scope

  - Framework of BOOTSTRAP process model
    - Structure of BOOTSTRAP process model
    - Definitions of QSAs in BOOTSTRAP

  - Formal description of BOOTSTRAP process model
    - BOOTSTRAP abstract process patterns
    - BOOTSTRAP process diagrams
    - Interpretation and illustration of the process algebra expressions

- The BOOTSTRAP process assessment model
  - BOOTSTRAP process capability model
    - Configuration
      - 3 process subsystems (SSs)
      - 9 process categories (PCs)
      - 32 processes (PRs)
      - 201 practices (QSAs)
    - QSA rating scale
    - Process rating scale

  - BOOTSTRAP process capability determination method
    - Formal description of BOOTSTRAP capability determination methodology
    - Meanings of expressions and their operation
    - Common features with the methodology developed in the unified process framework in Part I
    - Differences from the methodology developed in the unified process framework in Part I

- The BOOTSTRAP algorithm
  - Algorithm 7.1: BOOTSTRAP process assessment
  - Explanation of Algorithm 7.1
  - Relation between Algorithm 7.1 and the capability determination expressions in Section 7.3.2
  - The BOOTSTRAP algorithm complexity and the main factors affecting it

- A sample BOOTSTRAP process assessment
  - Understand assessment data documented in Appendix C
  - Manual process assessment in BOOTSTRAP
  - Algorithm-based assessment in BOOTSTRAP
  - Interpretation of assessment results

- Usability of BOOTSTRAP
  - Merits and demerits in process system establishment
  - Merits and demerits in process system assessment
  - Merits and demerits in process system improvement

Major achievements and issues for further research suggested by this chapter are highlighted below:

- The design philosophy behind BOOTSTRAP is to present a combined view of software life cycle processes and quality system principles. BOOTSTRAP's philosophy features in two approaches: (a) Adopting the quality system principles in modeling the organization process subsystem, and (b) Enhancing CMM processes by significant development process orientation.

- Major contributions of BOOTSTRAP are as follows:

  - A process assessment result is represented by both a capability level and a process profile.

  - A refined process capability scale with quartiles between two levels.

  - An improved practice rating scale from simple "Yes/No" to four adequate measurements.

  - An assessment-based software process improvement approach.

- Major open issues of BOOTSTRAP are as follows:

  - The BOOTSTRAP process model lacks a detailed description and definition. It is basically a hierarchical diagram and a generic questionnaire.

  - The BOOTSTRAP model has relatively greater similarity to CMM. The BOOTSTRAP capability model is almost identical with that of CMM.

  - BOOTSTRAP inherited the same difficulty for the pre-assignment of the practices (QSAs) into capability levels.

- A BOOTSTRAP algorithm has been elicited in order to precisely and systematically interpret the BOOTSTRAP methodology, and to quantitatively compare the complexity of the BOOTSTRAP method with the others.

- BOOTSTRAP's development, along with other models, has provided important theoretical and experimental preparation and inspiration for the development of the emerging international standard – ISO/IEC 15504 (SPICE) – for software process system modeling and assessment.

This chapter has established a basis for understanding and analyzing BOOTSTRAP as a paradigm of the unified software engineering process system framework. Relationships of BOOTSTRAP with other process system models will be discussed in Part III of this book. Applications of BOOTSTRAP in process-based software engineering and case studies will be provided in Parts IV – VI.

Annotated References

Koch (1993) highlighted two aspects of major interest: the idea behind BOOTSTRAP and perspectives on future improvement of the BOOTSTRAP methodology. Haase and his colleagues (1994) presented the technical aspects of BOOTSTRAP, two short case studies, and how the BOOTSTRAP method could be used to determine readiness for ISO 9001 certification. The BOOTSTRAP Team (1993), Huber (1993), and Kuvaja and Bicego (1994b) provided technical insight of BOOTSTRAP.

Kuvaja and his colleagues (1994a) provided a broader view of BOOTSTRAP on software process assessment and improvement. The background of BOOTSTRAP development and its relations with CMM and ISO 9001 was described in detail.

The BOOTSTRAP Institute (1994) released a Technical Report of the BOOTSTRAP Global Questionnaire (V.2.3). This report provided details of the BOOTSTRAP methodology. This questionnaire played an important role in implementing the BOOTSTRAP methodology, and in understanding the BOOTSTRAP methodology.

Wang et al. (1997a/b/99e) presented a series of comparative analyses of relationships and mutual mappings between major process models including BOOTSTRAP.

Questions and Problems

7.1 Explain the design philosophy behind the development of BOOTSTRAP.

7.2 Using your own words, briefly describe the structure of the BOOTSTRAP process model and its taxonomy.

7.3 Using process algebra, derive a formal BOOTSTRAP process model based on the process diagrams given in Figures 7.1 – 7.4. (Try not to copy Expressions 7.2 – 7.6 before you finish.)

7.4 Briefly describe the BOOTSTRAP process capability model and capability determination methodology using your own words.

7.5 Can you repeat the sample BOOTSTRAP assessment based on the data provided in Appendix C and derive the same capability level as that of the example shown in Section 7.5?

7.6 Try to conduct a BOOTSTRAP exercise assessment for an organization with which you are familiar, and according to the formal approach presented in this chapter.

7.7 Consider the BOOTSTRAP capability level of an organization that has achieved all Level 3 and Level 4 processes (PRs) but lacked Level 2 practices?

7.8 Are there any significant differences between an organization that is newly established and operating in ad hoc and an organization as described in Ex.7.7? What are the differences in their derived capability levels according to BOOTSTRAP methodology?

7.9 Most of the established software development organizations are currently considered to be located at BOOTSTRAP Level 2. Observing the BOOTSTRAP process model, do you think those organization could produce reasonably good software? Why?

7.10 Try to organize a small software project with at least three persons. Then do a self-assessment for this project and report your capability level in BOOTSTRAP.

7.11 Try to write a BOOTSTRAP assessment report for Exs. 7.6 or 7.10 and describe the following:

- Purpose(s) of the BOOTSTRAP assessment
- The BOOTSTRAP model and methodology you adopted
- The input of the BOOTSTRAP assessment
- The procedure of the BOOTSTRAP assessment
- The output of the BOOTSTRAP assessment

- The effort you spent for the BOOTSTRAP assessment
- Experience you gained in the BOOTSTRAP assessment
- Conclusions

7.12 Try to write a BOOTSTRAP process improvement plan based on the assessment report developed in Ex.7.11. In the process improvement plan, describe the following:

- Purpose(s) of the BOOTSTRAP process improvement plan
- Brief introduction of the BOOTSTRAP assessment results
- Analyze strengths of the organization's process capability according to BOOTSTRAP
- Analyze weaknesses of the organization's process capability according to BOOTSTRAP
- Recommend a process improvement plan to address the process weaknesses or to pursue continuous process improvement
- Explain the benefit of implementing this process improvement plan and how well your plan will meet the organization's business goal
- Estimate the costs of this process improvement effort
- Predict the risks for executing the process improvement plan that you have suggested
- Conclusions

7.13 What is the usage of BOOTSTRAP in software engineering process establishment, assessment, and improvement?

Chapter 8

THE ISO/IEC TR 15504 (SPICE) MODEL

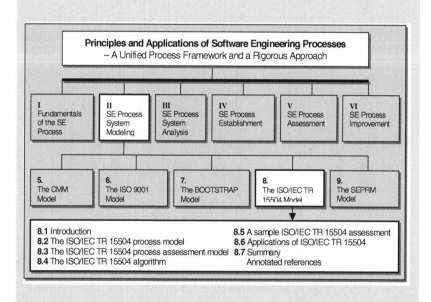

Principles and Applications of Software Engineering Processes
– A Unified Process Framework and a Rigorous Approach

| I Fundamentals of the SE Process | II SE Process System Modeling | III SE Process System Analysis | IV SE Process Establishment | V SE Process Assessment | VI SE Process Improvement |

| 5. The CMM Model | 6. The ISO 9001 Model | 7. The BOOTSTRAP Model | 8. The ISO/IEC TR 15504 Model | 9. The SEPRM Model |

8.1 Introduction
8.2 The ISO/IEC TR 15504 process model
8.3 The ISO/IEC TR 15504 process assessment model
8.4 The ISO/IEC TR 15504 algorithm

8.5 A sample ISO/IEC TR 15504 assessment
8.6 Applications of ISO/IEC TR 15504
8.7 Summary
Annotated references

ISO/IEC TR 15504 is an emerging international standard for software engineering process system assessment and improvement. SPICE, software process improvement and capability determination, is the name of the international project for the development of this standard. This chapter describes the ISO/IEC TR 15504 model, including its process model, process capability model, and process capability determination methodology.

This chapter adopts a formal and algorithmic approach to describe ISO/IEC TR 15504. An ISO/IEC TR 15504 algorithm will be elicited and a sample assessment will be provided in order to demonstrate how an ISO/IEC TR 15504-based process assessment is carried out in practice. The usability of ISO/IEC TR 15504 is discussed on the basis of empirical experience in the software industry and research reports in the literature.

The objectives of this chapter are as follows:

- To review the history and background of ISO/IEC TR 15504 development

- To describe the ISO/IEC TR 15504 process model and taxonomy

- To describe the ISO/IEC TR 15504 capability model and capability determination methodology

- To formally describe the ISO/IEC TR 15504 process model and to algorithmically describe the ISO/IEC TR 15504 process capability determination method

- To develop an ISO/IEC TR 15504 algorithm for software process assessment

- To explain how the ISO/IEC TR 15504 algorithm can be used in process assessment and how its algorithm complexity is estimated

- To demonstrate a case study of a practical ISO/IEC TR 15504 assessment by using the ISO/IEC TR 15504 algorithm

- To discuss the usability of ISO/IEC TR 15504 in process establishment, assessment, and improvement for software engineering

8.1 Introduction

The philosophy of ISO/IEC TR 15504 may be interpreted as aiming to develop a set of structured capability measurements for total software life cycle process evaluation. In this chapter we will formally describe the ISO/IEC TR 15504 model with this view.

ISO/IEC TR 15504 [ISO/IEC DTR 15504.1 – 15504.9, 1997; ISO/IEC TR 15504.1 – 15504.9, 1998] is being developed within the ISO/IEC JTC1/SC7 software engineering subcommittee with the intention of it being a future international software process assessment standard. The international project SPICE was initiated in 1991 [ISO/IEC JTC1/SC7, 1992/93a/b; Dorling, 1993/95]. An ISO/IEC 15004 technical report (TR) was released in 1998 [ISO/IEC TR 15504.1 – 15504.9, 1998] as a final step before publishing as an international standard. Now ISO/IEC TR 15504 is in the third phase of user trials.

ISO/IEC TR 15504 is a result of an international collaborative effort working towards developing an ISO software process assessment standard. ISO/IEC TR 15504 has incorporated experience and the improved understanding of software engineering processes gained in the development of CMM, BOOTSTRAP, ISO 9001, Trillium [Bell Canada, 1992/94], and other models.

ISO/IEC TR 15504 develops a 2-D process capability assessment model with a process and a process capability dimension based on the technology advances, and a more software engineering orientation. ISO/IEC TR 15504 assesses a software development organization at the process dimension against the process attributes at the capability dimension. The 2-D framework of ISO/IEC TR 15504 provides a refined process assessment approach and a process improvement platform for process-based software engineering.

This chapter provides a formal description of ISO/IEC TR 15504 in accordance with the unified process system framework developed in Part I. A framework and taxonomy of the ISO/IEC TR 15504 process model are introduced in Section 8.2. The ISO/IEC TR 15504 capability model and process capability determination method are described in Section 8.3. Based on this, an ISO/IEC TR 15504 process assessment algorithm is elicited and an example of ISO/IEC TR 15504 assessment is provided in Sections 8.4 and 8.5, respectively. Finally, the usability of ISO/IEC TR 15504 is discussed in Section 8.6.

8.2 The ISO/IEC TR 15504 Process Model

This section describes the ISO/IEC TR 15504 process taxonomy and framework. The terms and process structure of ISO/IEC TR 15504 are introduced using the original forms of expression, and are contrasted with the unified software process system framework developed in Part I.

8.2.1 TAXONOMY OF THE ISO/IEC TR 15504 PROCESS MODEL

Referring to the general process taxonomy defined in Chapter 2, the ISO/IEC TR 15504 process hierarchy and domains are listed in Table 8.1.

Table 8.1
Process Hierarchy and Domains of the ISO/IEC TR 15504 Process Model

Taxonomy	Subsystem	Category	Process	Practice
Process level	-	Process categories (PCs)	Processes (PRs)	Base practices (BPs)
Size of domain	-	5	35	201
Identification	-	PC[i]	PR[i,k]	BP[i,k,j]

Table 8.1 defines the configuration of the ISO/IEC TR 15504 process model. As shown, the BPs and PRs used in ISO/IEC TR 15504 are equivalent to the practices and processes, respectively, as defined in the unified process system framework.

In order to provide a formal identification for each entity defined at various levels of coverage known as process scopes, the indexing of PC, PR, and BP are described using a naming convention as shown in Table 8.1. In the table, i is the number of PC; k, the number of PR in ith PC; and j, the number of BP in kth PR of ith PC.

8.2.2 FRAMEWORK OF THE ISO/IEC TR 15504 PROCESS MODEL

ISO/IEC TR 15504 models a software process system in 5 process categories, 35 processes, and 201 base practices. A hierarchical structure of the ISO/IEC TR 15504 framework is shown in Table 8.2.

Table 8.2
The ISO/IEC TR 15504 Process Model

ID.	Process Category (PC[i])	Process (PR[i,k])	Identified BPs
CUS	Customer- supplier		39
CUS.1		Acquire software product	5
CUS.2		Establish contract	4
CUS.3		Identify customer needs	3
CUS.4		Perform joint audits and reviews	6
CUS.5		Package, deliver and install software	7

CUS.6		Support operation of software	7
CUS.7		Provide customer service	4
CUS.8		Assess customer satisfaction	3
ENG	Engineering		32
ENG.1		Develop system requirements	4
ENG.2		Develop software requirements	5
ENG.3		Develop software design	4
ENG.4		Implement software design	3
ENG.5		Integrate and test software	6
ENG.6		Integrate and test system	5
ENG.7		Maintain system and software	5
RRO	Project		50
PRO.1		Plan project life cycle	5
PRO.2		Establish project plan	10
PRO.3		Build project teams	4
PRO.4		Manage requirements	5
PRO.5		Manage quality	6
PRO.6		Manage risks	8
PRO.7		Manage resources and schedule	5
PRO.8		Manage subcontractors	7
SUP	Support		32
SUP.1		Develop documentation	5
SUP.2		Perform configuration management	8
SUP.3		Perform quality assurance	5
SUP.4		Perform problem resolution	6
SUP.5		Perform peer reviews	8
ORG	Organization		48
ORG.1		Engineer the business	6
ORG.2		Define the process	13
ORG.3		Improve the process	9
ORG.4		Perform training	4
ORG.5		Enable reuse	7
ORG.6		Provide software engineering environment	4
ORG.7		Provide work facilities	5
Total	5	35	201

In Table 8.2, the number of defined BPs for each PR is provided. The definitions of the BPs are listed in Appendix C, where, in the column of ISO/IEC TR 15504, a *j*th BP of process *k* in category *i*, *BP[i,k,j]*, is represented by:

$$BP[i,k,j] = BP_{i.k..j}$$
$$= BPA_{i'.k'.r.j'} \qquad (8.1)$$

where i', k', r', and j' are the index numbers of subsystem, category, process and practice, respectively, as defined in the unified process system framework and SEPRM.

For example, in Appendix C readers can identify BP[4,3,2] as:

$$BP[i,k,j] = BP[4,3,2]$$
$$= BP_{4.3.2}$$
$$= BPA_{3.1.8.1}$$
$$= BPA_{244}$$
$$= \text{"Audit software development activities"}$$

8.2.3 FORMAL DESCRIPTION OF THE ISO/IEC TR 15504 PROCESS MODEL

By using the CSP-like process algebra introduced in Chapter 3, we are able to formally describe the ISO/IEC TR 15504 process model and its processes in this subsection. The formal description is useful for providing precise and accurate definitions of the structure and interrelationships of the ISO/IEC TR 15504 processes, and avoiding the ambiguity inherent in conventional natural language description.

8.2.3.1 The Structure of the ISO/IEC TR 15504 Process Model

A formal description of the structure of the ISO/IEC TR 15504 process model, *ISO15504-PM*, is shown in Expression 8.2 and illustrated in Figure 8.1. Basically, this is a parallel process model of five process categories at the system level.

$$
\begin{aligned}
ISO15504\text{-}PM \ \triangleq \ & PC_1 && \text{// Customer-supplier processes} \\
& \| \ PC_2 && \text{// Engineering processes} \\
& \| \ PC_3 && \text{// Project processes} \\
& \| \ PC_4 && \text{// Support processes} \\
& \| \ PC_5 && \text{// Organization processes} && (8.2)
\end{aligned}
$$

In the ISO/IEC TR 15504 process model, each process category can be extended to a number of parallel PRs as shown in Expression 8.3. Further, each PR can be extended to a number of BPs in a similar way.

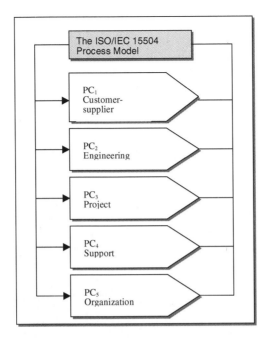

Figure 8.1 The ISO/IEC TR 15504 process model

$PC_1 \triangleq CUS_{1.1}||CUS_{1.2}||CUS_{1.3}||CUS_{1.4}||CUS_{1.5}||CUS_{1.6}||CUS_{1.7}||CUS_{1.8}$

$PC_2 \triangleq ENG_{2.1}||ENG_{2.2}||ENG_{2.3}||ENG_{2.4}||ENG_{2.5}||ENG_{2.6}||ENG_{2.7}$

$PC_3 \triangleq PRO_{3.1}||PRO_{3.2}||PRO_{3.3}||PRO_{3.4}||PRO_{3.5}||PRO_{3.6}||PRO_{3.7}||PRO_{3.8}$

$PC_4 \triangleq SUP_{4.1}||SUP_{4.2}||SUP_{4.3}||SUP_{4.4}||SUP_{4.5}$

$PC_5 \triangleq ORG_{5.1}||ORG_{5.2}||ORG_{5.3}||ORG_{5.4}||ORG_{5.5}||ORG_{5.6}||ORG_{5.7}$ (8.3)

8.2.3.2 Definitions of ISO/IEC TR 15504 Processes

The ISO/IEC TR 15504 processes, known as PRs, in each process category can be formally defined by Expressions 8.4 – 8.8, and are illustrated in Figures 8.2 – 8.6.

$$
\begin{array}{lll}
PC_1 \triangleq & CUS_{1.1} & \text{// Acquire software product} \\
& || \ CUS_{1.2} & \text{// Establish contract} \\
& || \ CUS_{1.3} & \text{// Identify customer needs} \\
& || \ CUS_{1.4} & \text{// Perform joint audits and reviews} \\
& || \ CUS_{1.5} & \text{// Package, deliver, and install software} \\
& || \ CUS_{1.6} & \text{// Support operation of software} \\
& || \ CUS_{1.7} & \text{// Provide customer service} \\
& || \ CUS_{1.8} & \text{// Assess customer satisfaction} \quad (8.4)
\end{array}
$$

A process diagram corresponding to the eight processes in the ISO/IEC TR 15504 customer-supplier (CUS) category, as defined in Expression 8.4, is shown in Figure 8.2.

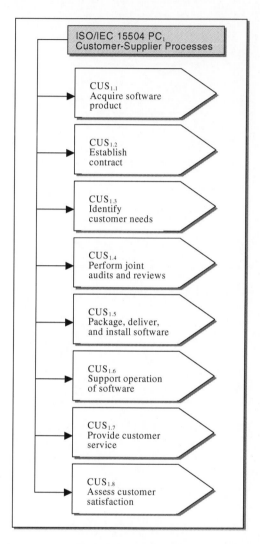

Figure 8.2 ISO/IEC TR 15504 process category 1 – the customer-supplier (CUS) processes

A process diagram corresponding to the seven serial processes in the ISO/IEC TR 15504 engineering (ENG) category, as defined in Expression 8.5, is shown in Figure 8.3.

$$
\begin{array}{lll}
PC_2 - & ENG_{2.1} & \text{// Develop system requirements} \\
& ; ENG_{2.2} & \text{// Develop software requirements} \\
& ; ENG_{2.3} & \text{// Develop software design} \\
& ; ENG_{2.4} & \text{// Implement software design} \\
& ; ENG_{2.5} & \text{// Integrate and test software} \\
& ; ENG_{2.6} & \text{// Integrate and test system} \\
& ; ENG_{2.7} & \text{// Maintain system and software} \quad (8.5)
\end{array}
$$

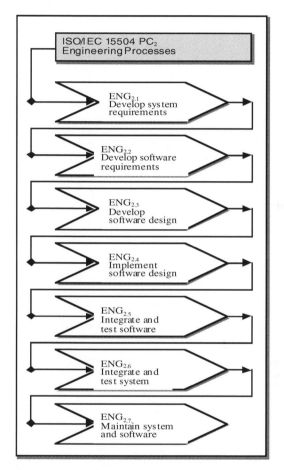

Figure 8.3 ISO/IEC TR 15504 process category 2 – the engineering (ENG) processes

A process diagram corresponding to the eight processes in the ISO/IEC TR 15504 project (PRO) category, as defined in Expression 8.6, is shown in Figure 8.4.

$$
\begin{array}{lll}
PC_3 \triangleq & PRO_{3.1} & \text{// Plan project life cycle} \\
& \| \ PRO_{3.2} & \text{// Establish project plan} \\
& \| \ PRO_{3.3} & \text{// Build project teams} \\
& \| \ PRO_{3.4} & \text{// Manage requirements} \\
& \| \ PRO_{3.5} & \text{// Manage quality} \\
& \| \ PRO_{3.6} & \text{// Manage risks} \\
& \| \ PRO_{3.7} & \text{// Manage resources and schedule} \\
& \| \ PRO_{3.8} & \text{// Manage subcontractors} \quad\quad (8.6)
\end{array}
$$

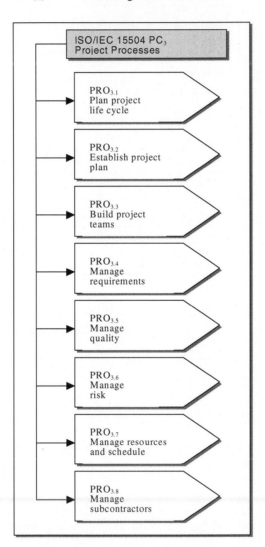

Figure 8.4 ISO/IEC TR 15504 process category 3 – the project (PRO) processes

A process diagram corresponding to the five processes in the ISO/IEC TR 15504 support (SUP) category, as defined in Expression 8.7, is shown in Figure 8.5.

$$PC_4 \triangleq SUP_{4.1} \qquad \text{// Develop documentation}$$
$$\| SUP_{4.2} \qquad \text{// Perform configuration management}$$
$$\| SUP_{4.3} \qquad \text{// Perform quality assurance}$$
$$\| SUP_{4.4} \qquad \text{// Perform problem resolution}$$
$$\| SUP_{4.5} \qquad \text{// Perform peer reviews} \qquad\qquad (8.7)$$

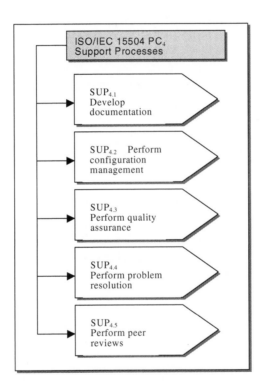

Figure 8.5 ISO/IEC TR 15504 process category 4 – the support (SUP) processes

A process diagram corresponding to the seven processes in the ISO/IEC TR 15504 organization (ORG) category, as defined in Expression 8.8, is shown in Figure 8.6.

$$PC_5 \triangleq ORG_{5.1} \qquad \text{// Engineer the business}$$

$\parallel ORG_{5.2}$	// Define the process
$\parallel ORG_{5.3}$	// Improve the process
$\parallel ORG_{5.4}$	// Perform training
$\parallel ORG_{5.5}$	// Enable reuse
$\parallel ORG_{5.6}$	// Provide software engineering environment
$\parallel ORG_{5.7}$	// Provide work facilities $\qquad\qquad$ (8.8)

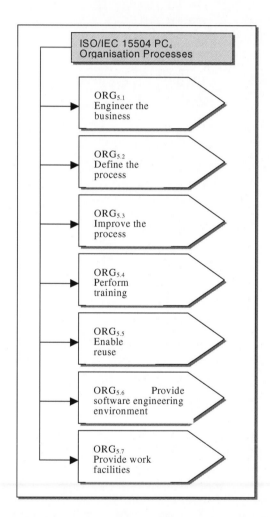

Figure 8.6 ISO/IEC TR 15504 process category 5 – the organization (ORG) processes

Detailed practices of each PR at BP level, which are documented in Appendix C, can be described in the same way as above. Extending the formal ISO/IEC TR 155504 process model onto the BP level can be taken as an exercise for readers.

8.3 The ISO/IEC TR 15504 Process Assessment Model

The ISO/IEC TR 15504 process model was systematically introduced in Section 8.2. This section explores the ISO/IEC TR 15504 process capability model and process capability determination method. Both of the above form the ISO/IEC TR 15504 process assessment model.

8.3.1 THE ISO/IEC TR 15504 PROCESS CAPABILITY MODEL

This section describes the ISO/IEC TR 15504 process capability model, which includes a practice performance scale, a process capability scale, and a process capability scope definition.

8.3.1.1 Practice Performance Scale

A practice performance rating scale for the BPs in ISO/IEC TR 15504 is defined in Table 8.3. Every BP is rated against each of the nine attributes as described in Table 8.4 by using this rating scale.

Table 8.3
Practice Performance Scale of the BPs

Scale	Description	Rating threshold
4 (F)	Fully achieved	86% - 100%
3 (L)	Largely achieved	51% - 85%
2 (P)	Partially achieved	16% - 50%
1 (N)	Not achieved	0% - 15%

8.3.1.2 Process Capability Scale

In the ISO/IEC TR 15504 capability dimension [ISO/IEC TR 15504-2 1998], a process capability scale is defined by capability levels with generic measurement aids known as process attributes. The process attributes are defined in ISO/IEC 15504-2 as below:

Definition 8.1: Process attributes are features of a process that can be evaluated on a scale of achievement which provides a measure of the capability of the process.

It is noteworthy that the process attributes are not intermediate capability levels as are those of the quartiles in BOOTSTRAP. The process attributes are designed as a set of generic measurements of process capability, or as extensions of the definitions of the capability levels.

The process capability scale of ISO/IEC TR 15504 is defined at six levels with nine process attributes as shown in Table 8.4. The ISO/IEC TR 15504 capability levels generally consist of two process attributes except Level 1 (one attribute) and Level 0 (no attribute).

Table 8.4
The ISO/IEC TR 15504 Process Capability Model

ID.	Capability Level (CL[i])	Process Attribute (PA$_{ij}$)	Description
CL[0]	Incomplete		There is general failure to attain the purpose of the process. There are little or no easily identifiable work products or outputs of the process.
CL[1]	Performed		The purpose of the process is generally achieved. The achievement may not be rigorously planned and tracked. Individuals within the organization recognize that an action should be performed, and there is general agreement that this action is performed as and when required. There are identifiable work products for the process, and these testify to the achievement of the purpose.
PA$_{11}$		Process performance	The extent to which the process achieves the process outcomes by transforming identifiable input work products to produce identifiable output work products.
CL[2]	Managed		The process delivers work products according to specified procedures and is planned and tracked. Work products conform to specified standards and requirements. The primary distinction from the Performed Level is that the performance of the process now delivers work products that fulfil expressed quality requirements within defined timescales and resource needs.

PA$_{21}$		Performance management	The extent to which the performance of the process is managed to produce work products that meet the defined objectives.
PA$_{22}$		Work product management	The extent to which the performance of the process is managed to produce work products that are appropriately documented, controlled, and verified.
CL[3]	Established		The process is performed and managed using a defined process based upon good software engineering principles. Individual implementations of the process use approved, tailored versions of standard, documented processes to achieve the process outcomes. The resources necessary to establish the process definition are also in place. The primary distinction from the Managed Level is that the process of the Established Level is using a defined process that is capable of achieving its process outcomes.
PA$_{31}$		Process definition	The extent to which the performance of the process uses a process definition based upon a standard process to achieve the process outcomes.
PA$_{32}$		Process resource	The extent to which the process draws upon suitable resources (for example, human resources and process infrastructure) that are appropriately allocated to deploy the defined process.
CL[4]	Predictable		The defined process is performed consistently in practice within defined control limits to achieve its defined process goals. Detailed measures of performance are collected and analyzed. This leads to a quantitative understanding of process capability and an improved ability to predict and manage performance. Performance is quantitatively managed. The quality of work products is quantitatively known. The primary distinction from the Established Level is that the defined process is now performed consistently within defined limits to achieve its process outcomes.
PA$_{41}$		Process measurement	The extent to which product and process goals and measures are used to ensure that performance of the process supports the achievement of the defined goals in support of the relevant business goals.
PA$_{42}$		Process resource	The extent to which the process is controlled through the collection, analysis, and use of product and process measures to correct, where necessary, the performance of the process to achieve the defined product and process goals.
CL[5]	Optimizing		Performance of the process is optimized to meet current and future business needs, and the process achieves repeatability in meeting its defined business goals. Quantitative process effectiveness and efficiency goals (targets) for performance are established based on the business goals of the organization. Continuous process monitoring against these goals is enabled by obtaining quantitative feedback, and improvement is achieved by analysis of the results. Optimizing a process involves

			piloting innovative ideas and technologies and changing noneffective processes to meet defined goals or objectives. The primary distinction from the Predictable Level is that the defined and standard processes now dynamically change and adapt to effectively meet current and future business goals.
PA$_{51}$		Process change	The extent to which changes to the definition, management, and performance of the process are controlled to achieve the relevant business goals of the organization.
PA$_{52}$		Continuous improvement	The extent to which changes to the process are identified and implemented to ensure continuous improvement in the fulfillment of the relevant business goals of the organization.

8.3.1.3 Process Capability Scope

The ISO/IEC TR 15504 process capability scopes are shown in Table 8.5. Comparing Table 8.5 with Table 2.3, it is clear that ISO/IEC TR 15504 assesses process capability at the levels of BP, process, and project scope, from the bottom, up against the process attributes and capability levels.

Table 8.5
Process Capability Scope of ISO/IEC TR 15504

Capability Scope	Practice	Process	Project	Organization
ISO/IEC TR 15504 terms	BPs	Processes	Project	-
ISO/IEC TR 15504 method	Performance rating	Capability level with attributes	Process capability profile	-

8.3.2 THE ISO/IEC TR 15504 PROCESS CAPABILITY DETERMINATION METHODOLOGY

Using the formal definitions of the ISO/IEC TR 15504 process model and process capability model developed in Sections 8.2 and 8.3.1, we can now consider how to apply the ISO/IEC TR 15504 capability model to the process model for the assessment of process capability at practice, process, and project levels.

8.3.2.1 Base Practice Performance Rating Method

Let $r_{BP}[PC,PR,s,i,j]$ be a rating of performance of the sth BP in process PR of process category PC against attribute j at capability level i. Then $r_{BP}[PC,PR,s,i,j]$ can be rated according to the practice performance scale as defined in Table 8.3, i.e.:

$$
\begin{aligned}
r_{BP}[PC,PR,s,i,j] &= 4, \text{ if the BP's performance is fully satisfied} \\
&= 3, \text{ if the BP's performance is largely satisfied} \\
&= 2, \text{ if the BP's performance is partially satisfied} \\
&= 1, \text{ if the BP's performance is not satisfied} \qquad (8.9)
\end{aligned}
$$

Expression 8.9 indicates that BP rating against an attribute is a selection from one of the attribute adequacy scales defined as *fully, largely, partially,* or *not adequate,* respectively.

8.3.2.2 Process Capability Rating Method

The process capability rating method of ISO/IEC TR 15504 is relatively complicated when compared to those of the other models. Process capability rating in ISO/IEC TR 15504 can be described as the following steps:

- Process performance adequacy rating

- Process attribute rating

- Process capability determination

(a) Process performance adequacy rating

Assuming that $PROC[PC,PR,i,j]$ is the adequacy of a process PR in the category PC against the jth attribute at the ith level, process performance adequacy can be determined by the following expression:

$$
\begin{aligned}
PROC[PC,PR,i,j] &= \{\rho_F[PC,PR,i,j], \rho_L[PC,PR,i,j], \\
&\quad \rho_P[PC,PR,i,j], \rho_N[PC,PR,i,j]\} \\
&= \{\rho_4[PC,PR,i,j], \rho_3[PC,PR,i,j], \\
&\quad \rho_2[PC,PR,i,j], \rho_1[PC,PR,i,j]\} \qquad (8.10)
\end{aligned}
$$

where $\rho_k[PC,PR,i,j]$, $k=4,3,2,1$, represents the corresponding summarized percentages of process performance adequacy among the rated *BPs*, $N_{BP}[PC,PR]$, contained in the process. The percentage of process performance adequacy against attribute j at capability level i is defined below:

$$\rho_F[PC,PR,i,j] = (n_F[PC,PR,i,j] \, / \, N_{BP}[PC,PR]) * 100\%, \quad k=4,3,2,1 \quad (8.11)$$

where $n_k[PC,PR,i,j]$ is the number of BPs at the same performance scale k, $k= 4,3,2,1$, as defined in Table 8.3, against attribute PA_{ij}.

(b) Process attribute rating

Using the distribution of process adequacy rated by Expression 8.11, a process's capability against the jth attribute at the ith level, $PA_{i,j}[PC,PR]$, can be calculated according to the following expression:

$$PA_{i,j}[PC,PR] = \Big\lfloor \sum_{k=1}^{4} \{k * \rho_k[PC,PR,i,j]\} \Big\rfloor \qquad (8.12)$$

where $\lfloor ... \rfloor$ means a downward rounding of the assessment result to an integer.

(c) Process capability determination

Process capability in ISO/IEC TR 15504, $PCL_{proc}[p]$, is defined as the maximum achievement of a process's maturity level, at which the attributes may be largely (L, 3) or fully (F, 4) achieved, and at all lower level(s) the attributes should be fully achieved, i.e.:

$$PCL_{proc}[p] = max \{i \mid PA_{i,j} \geq 3 \, \wedge \, PA_{i-1,j} = 4\} \qquad (8.13)$$

where i is a capability level, $i=1,2,....,5$; and j a process attribute, $j=1 \; or \; 2$ except that $j\equiv1$ at Level 1.

When several process instances are assessed for the same process, an aggregated process capability level can be derived. It is defined as a mathematical mean of the values of the process instances. When m process instances, $m > 1$, are assessed for process p, the capability level of the process can be derived in the following way:

$$PCL'_{proc}[p] = \Big\lfloor \frac{1}{m} \sum_{p=1}^{m} PCL_{proc}[p] \Big\rfloor \qquad (8.14)$$

where p is an index of the process instances.

The use of these expressions for ISO/IEC TR 15504 process assessment will be demonstrated in Section 8.5 with a real-world example.

8.3.2.3 Project Capability Determination Method

In the ISO/IEC TR 15504 model, assessment results at the level of project scope are usually represented in a form of **process profile**, which illustrates all processes vs. the capability levels by a 2-D chart.

To enable cross comparability and compatibility between the current process system models, a project's process capability level is defined as a mathematical mean of all the process capabilities of the k, $k=35$, processes defined in ISO/IEC TR 15504. That is, the capability level of a project j, $PCL_{proj}[j]$, is determined by:

$$PCL_{proj}[j] = \left\lfloor \frac{1}{k} \sum_{p=1}^{k} PCL_{proc}[p] \right\rfloor \qquad (8.15)$$

When the process capabilities are aggregated from m process instances, as described in Expression 8.14, a variation of Expression 8.15 can be derived as follows:

$$PCL_{proj}[j] = \left\lfloor \frac{1}{k} \sum_{p=1}^{k} PCL'_{proc}[p] \right\rfloor \qquad (8.16)$$

8.3.2.4 Organization Capability Determination Method

In the ISO/IEC TR 15504 model there is no defined capability level in the scope of an organization. The rationale for this is that a 2-D process profile is enough and might provide more details for presenting and characterizing the process capability of a software development organization. However, to ensure cross comparability and compatibility between the major process system models, a method for deriving an organization's capability level is provided as a supplement in this subsection.

According to the method developed in Section 2.4.2.2, an organization's process capability level, PCL_{org}, can be defined as a mathematical mean of those of n project's capabilities derived by Expression 8.15 or 8.16, i.e.:

$$PCL_{org} = \left\lfloor \frac{1}{n} \sum_{p=1}^{n} PCL_{proj}[p] \right\rfloor \qquad (8.17)$$

Expression 8.17 indicates that the historical experience, which a software development organization has accumulated in its practice of software development in various projects, can be reflected into the final determination of an organization's process capability. It is recommended that $n \geq 3$ for a valid aggregating of an organization's process capability level from those of the projects that have been carried out in the organization.

Review Sections 8.2 and 8.3; it can be seen that the ISO/IEC TR 15504 develops the first 2-D process system model with fully independent process and capability dimensions. The 2-D model completely separates a process system and its capability measurement. This approach enables all processes to perform at any of the process capability levels, and to be assessed against each capability level with related attributes.

8.4 The ISO/IEC TR 15504 Algorithm

So far we have explored the ISO/IEC TR 15504 process model, process capability model, and capability determination method. Using the models and method we are already able to manually assess and calculate a software project's or an organization's process capability in ISO/IEC TR 15504.

In order to describe the ISO/IEC TR 15504 methodology precisely, and to enable mutual comparison and tool implementation, this section extends the ISO/IEC TR 15504 process capability determination methodology into a formal ISO/IEC TR 15504 algorithm.

8.4.1 DESCRIPTION OF THE ISO/IEC TR 15504 ALGORITHM

The ISO/IEC TR 15504 process capability determination method as defined in Expressions 8.9 – 8.15 up to the scope of project can be formally described in the following algorithm. An organization's process capability level can be easily aggregated according to Expression 8.17 when multiple projects have been assessed.

Algorithm 8.1 The ISO/IEC TR 15504 process capability determination algorithm

Assume: $PA_{i,j}$ - The jth process attribute at Level i
$\qquad$ $N_{PR}[PC]$ - Number of processes in the category PC
$\qquad$ $N_{BP}[PC,PR]$ - Number of BPs in process $PC.PR$

$BP[PC,PR,s,i,j]$	- Adequacy of the sth BP in process $PC.PR$ against the jth attribute at level i
$n_k[PC,PR,I,j]$	- Number of fully/largely/partially/not adequate BPs of process $PC.PR$ against the jth attribute at Level i
$\rho_k[PC,PR,i,j]$	- Percentage of fully/largely/partially/not adequate BPs of process $PC.PR$ against attribute at Level i
$PA[PC,PR,i,j]$	- Capability level of process $PC.PR$ of the jth attribute at Level i
CL	- A capability level
$PCL_{proc}[PC,PR]$	- A capability level of process $PC.PR$
PCL_{proj}	- A capability level of a project

Input: Sample indicators of processes' existence and performance
Output: A process profile: $PCL_{proc}[PC,PR]$, and
         a project process capability level: PCL_{proj}

Begin

// **Step 1: Initialization**

// Assign numbers of processes in each category according to Table 8.2
$N_{PR}[1] := 8;$
$N_{PR}[2] := 7;$
$N_{PR}[3] := 8;$
$N_{PR}[4] := 5;$
$N_{PR}[5] := 7;$

// Assign numbers of defined BPs in each $PC.PR$ according to Table 8.2
$N_{PR}[CUS, 1] := 5;$
$N_{PR}[CUS, 2] := 4;$
$N_{PR}[CUS, 3] := 3;$
$N_{PR}[CUS, 4] := 6;$
$N_{PR}[CUS, 5] := 7;$
$N_{PR}[CUS, 6] := 7;$
$N_{PR}[CUS, 7] := 4;$
$N_{PR}[CUS, 8] := 3;$

$N_{BP}[ENG, 1] := 4;$
$N_{BP}[ENG, 2] := 5;$
$N_{BP}[ENG, 3] := 4;$
$N_{BP}[ENG, 4] := 3;$
$N_{BP}[ENG, 5] := 6;$

$N_{BP}[ENG, 6] := 5;$
$N_{BP}[ENG, 7] := 5;$

$N_{BP}[SUP, 1] := 5;$
$N_{BP}[SUP, 2] := 10;$
$N_{BP}[SUP, 3] := 4;$
$N_{BP}[SUP, 4] := 5;$
$N_{BP}[SUP, 5] := 6;$
$N_{BP}[SUP, 6] := 8;$
$N_{BP}[SUP, 7] := 5;$
$N_{BP}[SUP, 8] := 7;$

$N_{BP}[SUP, 1] := 5;$
$N_{BP}[SUP, 2] := 8;$
$N_{BP}[SUP, 3] := 5;$
$N_{BP}[SUP, 4] := 6;$
$N_{BP}[SUP, 5] := 8;$

$N_{BP}[ORG, 1] := 6;$
$N_{BP}[ORG, 2] := 13;$
$N_{BP}[ORG, 3] := 9;$
$N_{BP}[ORG, 4] := 4;$
$N_{BP}[ORG, 5] := 7;$
$N_{BP}[ORG, 6] := 4;$
$N_{BP}[ORG, 7] := 5;$

// Step 2: Process attribute rating

```
for PC:=1 to 5 do                    // the PCth process category
    for PR:=1 to N_BP[PC,PR] do  // the PC.PRth process
        begin
            for i:=1 to 5 do          // the ith capability level
                for j:=1 to 2 do      // the jth attribute at Level i
                    begin
                        if i=1 and j=2 then
                            skip;       // There is no defined attribute PA₁₂
                        n_F[PC,PR,i,j]:= 0;
                        n_L[PC,PR,i,j]:= 0;
                        n_P[PC,PR,i,j]:= 0;
                        n_N[PC,PR,i,j]:=0;
                        for s :=1 to N_BP[PC, PR] do
                            // Operation on each BP in the current
                            // process PC.PR
```

```
                    begin
                        // 2.1 Rate each BP in PC.PR for PAᵢⱼ
                        // (except PA₁₂) according to the
                        // performance rating scale in Table 8.3

                    case BP[PC,PR,s,i,j]
                            // Count numbers of BPs at each
                            // performance scale k, k=1,2,3,4
                            4: n_F[PC,PR,i,j]:= n_F[PC,PR,i,j]+1;
                            3: n_L[PC,PR,i,j]:= n_L[PC,PR,i,j]+1;
                            2: n_P[PC,PR,i,j]:= n_P[PC,PR,i,j]+1;
                            1: n_N[PC,PR,i,j]:= n_N[PC,PR,i,j]+1;
                            end;
                    end;


                        // 2.2 Derive process performance adequacy
                        // ratings according to Expression 8.11
                        ρ_F[PC,PR,i,j]:= n_F[PC,PR,i,j] / N_BP[PC, PR];
                        ρ_L[PC,PR,i,j]:= n_L[PC,PR,i,j] / N_BP[PC, PR];
                        ρ_P[PC,PR,i,j]:= n_P[PC,PR,i,j] / N_BP[PC, PR];
                        ρ_N[PC,PR,i,j]:= n_N[PC,PR,i,j] / N_BP[PC, PR];


                        // 2.3 Calculate process attribute ratings
                        // according to Expression 8.12
```
$$PA_{ij}[PC,PR]:= \lfloor \sum_{k=1}^{4} \{ k * \rho_k[PC,PR,i,j\} \rfloor;$$

```
                    End;
                end;

// Step 3: Process capability determination

for PC:=1 to 5 do
    for PR:=1 to N_RP[PC] do
        begin
            if (PA₁₁[PC,PR]= 4 ∧
            (PA₂₁[PC,PR]= 4  ∧ PA₂₂[PC,PR]= 4) ∧
            (PA₃₁[PC,PR]= 4  ∧ PA₃₂[PC,PR]= 4) ∧
            (PA₄₁[PC,PR]= 4  ∧ PA₄₂[PC,PR]= 4) ∧
            (PA₅₁[PC,PR] ≥ 3 ∧ PA₅₂[PC,PR] ≥ 3))
            then  // Optimizing
                    CL := 5
            else if (PA₁₁[PC,PR]= 4 ∧
```

$(PA_{21}[PC,PR] = 4 \wedge PA_{22}[PC,PR] = 4) \wedge$
$(PA_{31}[PC,PR] = 4 \wedge PA_{32}[PC,PR] = 4) \wedge$
$(PA_{41}[PC,PR] \geq 3 \wedge PA_{42}[PC,PR] \geq 3))$
then // Predictable
    $CL := 4$
else if $(PA_{11}[PC,PR] = 4 \wedge$
    $(PA_{21}[PC,PR] = 4 \wedge PA_{22}[PC,PR] = 4) \wedge$
    $(PA_{31}[PC,PR] \geq 3 \wedge PA_{32}[PC,PR] \geq 3))$
    then // Established
        $CL := 3$
    else if $(PA_{11}[PC,PR] = 4 \wedge$
        $(PA_{21}[PC,PR] \geq 3 \wedge PA_{22}[PC,PR] \geq 3))$
        then // Managed
            $CL := 2$
        else if $PA_{11}[PC,PR] \geq 3$
            then // Performed
                $CL := 1$
            else // Incomplete
                $CL := 0$

    // Save the capability level of process $PC.PR$ into
    // the process profile buffer
    $PCL_{proc}[PC,PR] := CL;$
  end;

// Step 4: Project capability determination

$k := 0;$
$CL := 0;$
for $PC := 1$ to 5 do
  for $PR := 1$ to $N_{PR}[PC]$ do
    begin
      $k := k+1;$
      $CL := CL + PCL_{proc}[PC,PR]$
    end;

// Derive the capability level of the project
$PCL_{proj} := int(CL / k);$ // to round the capability level to a lower integer

End   ■

8.4.2 EXPLANATION OF THE ISO/IEC TR 15504 ALGORITHM

An ISO/IEC TR 15504 assessment according to Algorithm 8.1 is carried out in four steps:

- **Step 1:** Initialization

- **Step 2:** Process attribute rating

- **Step 3:** Process capability determination

- **Step 4:** Project capability determination

This subsection explains the main functions of Algorithm 8.1 for an ISO/IEC TR 15504 process assessment.

8.4.2.1 Initialization

This step is designed to specify the number of BPs defined in ISO/IEC TR 15504. For obtaining a detailed configuration of BPs in the ISO/IEC TR 15504 process model, readers may refer to Table 8.2 and Appendix C.

8.4.2.2 Process Attribute Rating

This part of the algorithm can be divided into three substeps. The first substep is to rate all BPs in each process against nine attributes in a $201 * 9$ iteration. Then, the process performance adequacy ratings for each process are derived. Finally, the process attribute ratings are calculated for the 35 processes against the nine process attributes calculated in Step 2.3.

(a) Step 2.1: BP performance rating

In this substep, all 201 BPs in 35 processes are rated against PA_{ij}, i = 1,2, ...,5 and j = 1, 2 (except PA_{12}), according to the performance rating scale in Table 8.3. The rating method for a group of BPs in a PC.PR against a level attribute are identical as shown in algorithm Step 2.1, except that for different PRs the numbers of BPs, $N_{BP}[PC,PR,Level,Attribute]$, may vary as assigned in Step 1.

The basic function for BP rating for each process against an attribute is to count the number of BPs that have the same adequacy rating of k, $k=4,3,2,1$. After carrying out this substep, all 201 BPs should have been assigned one of the four performance ratings for each of the nine attributes.

(b) Step 2.2: Process performance adequacy rating

All process performance adequacy ratings are calculated in this substep according to Expression 8.11. By doing this, we get the distributions of 4 kinds of BP performance adequacy against each attribute. This is a preparation for deriving a process' attribute rating by the BPs belonging to it, as shown in the next substep.

(c) Step 2.3: Process attribute rating

All process attribute ratings are calculated in this step according to Expression 8.12. By this step, each process's capability against the nine attributes at the six capability levels is determined.

8.4.2.3 Process Capability Determination

This step determines the maximum aggregated process capability level for individual processes based on the attribute ratings obtained in Step 2. The final capability level is determined according to Expression 8.13. When completing this step, a process profile of all 35 processes is obtained.

8.4.2.4 Project Capability Determination

This step derives the process capability level of a project by calculating the mathematical mean of all processes' capabilities according to Expression 8.15. A process capability level for a project scope is an aggregation of the process profile derived in Step 3.

8.4.3 ANALYSIS OF THE ISO/IEC TR 15504 ALGORITHM

The effort expended in conducting an ISO/IEC TR 15504 assessment depends on its algorithm complexity. By examining the complexity of an algorithm, the time spent in an assessment can be estimated quite accurately.

Reviewing the ISO/IEC TR 15504 algorithm in Subsection 8.4.1, it may be observed that the algorithm complexity of ISO/IEC TR 15504, $c(ISO15504)$, is mainly determined by the number of BPs (N_{BP}) and PRs (N_{PR}) that need to be rated individually against the nine attributes according to Algorithm 8.1, Step 2, i.e.:

$$c(ISO15504) = O((N_{BP} + N_{PR}) * N_{PA})$$
$$= (N_{BP} + N_{PR}) * N_{PA} \tag{8.18}$$

where N_{BP} is the number of BPs, N_{PR} is the number of processes, and N_{PA} is the number of attributes. The unit of the algorithm complexity is "times of BP/PR ratings," or times of practice and process ratings.

As given in ISO/IEC TR 15504, $N_{BP}=201$, $N_{PR}=35$, and $N_{PA}=9$, the total rating cost, or the algorithm complexity, for determining a capability level in the project scope in ISO/IEC TR 15504 is:

$$
\begin{aligned}
c(ISO15504) &= O((N_{BP}+ N_{PR}) * N_{PA}) \\
&= (N_{BP}+ N_{PR}) * N_{PA} \\
&= (201 + 35) * 9 \\
&= 2124 \text{ [times of BP/PR ratings]}
\end{aligned}
$$

This data shows that ISO/IEC TR 15504 provides the most subtle and yet most complicated process assessment method among the current models. There is a certain range of factors between an algorithm's complexity and the person-days needed for an assessment. Empirical data for relating the algorithm complexity to person-days expended in an ISO/IEC TR 15504 process assessment will be discussed in Chapter 12.

8.5 A Sample ISO/IEC TR 15504 Assessment

The capability rating framework and the capability determination algorithm of ISO/IEC TR 15504 have been formally described in Sections 8.3 and 8.4. This section demonstrates how to apply the ISO/IEC TR 15504 expressions and algorithm to quantitatively determine a sample software development organization's process capability level in ISO/IEC TR 15504.

8.5.1 BP PERFORMANCE RATING IN ISO/IEC TR 15504

A set of detailed ratings of the 201BPs has been listed in Appendix C, where the raw rating data {4,3,2,1} is identical to the ISO/IEC TR 15504 BP rating scale {4(F),3(L),2(P),1(N)} as defined in Table 8.3.

A macro BP rating value as 4(F), 3(L), 2(P), or 1(N) can be mapped onto the detailed BP attribute ratings as shown in Table 8.6. Alternatively, the BP attribute ratings can be obtained by directly applying Table 8.3 for a BP against the nine attributes.

Table 8.6
Mapping between Macro BP Rating and BP Attribute Ratings

BP Attribute Rating	BP Macro Rating			
$(PA_{i,j})$	4 (F)	3 (L)	2 (P)	1 (N)
$PA_{5.2}$	4	2	1	1
$PA_{5.1}$	4	2	1	1
$PA_{4.2}$	4	3	2	1
$PA_{4.1}$	4	3	2	1
$PA_{3.2}$	4	4	3	1
$PA_{3.1}$	4	4	3	1
$PA_{2.2}$	4	4	4	1
$PA_{2.1}$	4	4	4	1
$PA_{1.1}$	4	4	4	1

Table 8.6 shows that in case a BP's macro rating value is BP =3(L), its attribute rating pattern is BP{$PA_{1.1}$, $PA_{2.1}$, $PA_{2.2}$, $PA_{3.1}$, $PA_{3.2}$, $PA_{4.1}$, $PA_{4.2}$, $PA_{5.1}$, $PA_{5.2}$} = BP{4, 4, 4, 4, 4, 3, 3, 2, 2}. When BP=2 (P), BP{$PA_{1.1}$, $PA_{2.1}$, $PA_{2.2}$, $PA_{3.1}$, $PA_{3.2}$, $PA_{4.1}$, $PA_{4.2}$, $PA_{5.1}$, $PA_{5.2}$} = BP{4, 4, 4, 3, 3, 2, 2, 1, 1}. Especially when BP=4 or BP=1, the BP attribute ratings are all 4 or 1, respectively.

8.5.2 PROCESS ATTRIBUTE RATING IN ISO/IEC TR 15504

With all BPs rated against the nine attributes as defined in Table 8.6, and by Expressions 8.9 and 8.11, a process consisting of these BPs can now be rated against the attributes as well.

For example, process ENG.1 in the ISO/IEC TR 15504 has four BPs identified as BP[PC.PR.s]: {BP[2.1.1], ..., BP[2.1.4]}. The macro rating values of these BPs are {4, 4, 3, 2} or {F, F, L, P}, respectively in Appendix C. By using the BP macro rating values, we can now show, via Table 8.7, how a process capability rating be derived.

Table 8.7
A Process Rating Example: ENG.1

Level	BP Performance Rating				Process Adequacy Rating	Process Attribute Rating
$(PA_{i,j})$	BP[ENG, 1,1] = 4 F	BP[ENG, 1,2] = 4 F	BP[ENG, 1,3] = 3 L	BP[ENG, 1,4] = 2 P	PROC [ENG,1,i,j]	$PA_{i,j}$[ENG, 1]
$PA_{5.2}$	4	4	2	1	$[\rho_4,\rho_3,\rho_2,\rho_1] =$ [50%,0,25%,25%]	$\lfloor 4*50\%+3*0+2*25\% +1*25\% \rfloor$ $= \lfloor 2.75 \rfloor = 2$ (P)
$PA_{5.1}$	4	4	2	1	[50%,0,25%,25%]	$\lfloor 2.75 \rfloor = 2$ (P)
$PA_{4.2}$	4	4	3	2	[50%,25%,25%,0]	$\lfloor 3.25 \rfloor = 3$ (L)
$PA_{4.1}$	4	4	3	2	[50%,25%,25%,0]	$\lfloor 3.25 \rfloor = 3$ (L)
$PA_{3.2}$	4	4	4	3	[75%,25%,0,0]	$\lfloor 3.75 \rfloor = 3$ (L)
$PA_{3.1}$	4	4	4	3	[75%,25%,0,0]	$\lfloor 3.75 \rfloor = 3$ (L)
$PA_{2.2}$	4	4	4	4	[100%,0,0,0]	$\lfloor 4.0 \rfloor = 4$ (F)
$PA_{2.1}$	4	4	4	4	[100%,0,0,0]	$\lfloor 4.0 \rfloor = 4$ (F)
$PA_{1.1}$	4	4	4	4	[100%,0,0,0]	$\lfloor 4.0 \rfloor = 4$ (F)
Methods	Table 8.6	Table 8.6	Table 8.6	Table 8.6	Expression 8.10	Expression 8.12

Referring to Algorithm 8.1, Table 8.7 shows three steps to derive a set of attribute ratings for a process as follows:

a. To obtain the BP attribute ratings according the method described in Table 8.6

b. To derive the process adequacy ratings by Expression 8.10

c. To calculate the process attribute ratings according to Expression 8.12

The above steps fully correspond to Steps 2.1 through 2.3 in Algorithm 8.1.

Similarly, all 35 processes of ISO/IEC TR 15504 in the five categories can be rated against the nine attributes as summarized below.

8.5.2.1 Customer-Supplier Process Category

The attribute ratings of the eight processes in the customer-supplier category (CUS.1 – CUS.8) are derived as in Table 8.8.

Table 8.8
Derived Process Attribute Ratings in the Customer-Supplier Category

$PA_{i,j}$	CUS.1	CUS.2	CUS.3	CUS.4	CUS.5	CUS.6	CUS.7	CUS.8
$PA_{5.2}$	2 (P)	2 (P)	3 (L)	1 (N)	3 (L)	2 (P)	1 (N)	1 (N)
$PA_{5.1}$	2 (P)	2 (P)	3 (L)	1 (N)	3 (L)	2 (P)	1 (N)	1 (N)
$PA_{4.2}$	2 (P)	3 (L)	4 (F)	2 (P)	4 (F)	3 (L)	2 (P)	3 (L)
$PA_{4.1}$	2 (P)	3 (L)	4 (F)	2 (P)	4 (F)	3 (L)	2 (P)	3 (L)
$PA_{3.2}$	2 (P)	3 (L)	4 (F)	2 (P)	4 (F)	3 (L)	2 (P)	3 (L)
$PA_{3.1}$	2 (P)	3 (L)	4 (F)	2 (P)	4 (F)	3 (L)	2 (P)	3 (L)
$PA_{2.2}$	4 (F)	4 (F)	4 (F)	3 (L)	4 (F)	4 (F)	4 (F)	4 (F)
$PA_{2.1}$	4 (F)	4 (F)	4 (F)	3 (L)	4 (F)	4 (F)	4 (F)	4 (F)
$PA_{1.1}$	4 (F)	4 (F)	4 (F)	3 (L)	4 (F)	4 (F)	4 (F)	4 (F)

8.5.2.2 Engineering Process Category

The attribute ratings of the seven processes in the engineering category
(ENG.1 – ENG.7) are derived as in Table 8.9.

Table 8.9
Derived Process Attribute Ratings in the Engineering Category

$PA_{i,j}$	ENG.1	ENG.2	ENG.3	ENG.4	ENG.5	ENG.6	ENG.7
$PA_{5.1}$	2 (P)	2 (P)	2 (P)	1 (N)	1 (N)	4 (F)	2 (P)
$PA_{5.2}$	2 (P)	2 (P)	2 (P)	1 (N)	1 (N)	4 (F)	2 (P)
$PA_{4.2}$	3 (L)	4 (F)	4 (F)	4 (F)	3 (L)	4 (F)	3 (L)
$PA_{4.1}$	3 (L)	4 (F)	4 (F)	4 (F)	3 (L)	4 (F)	3 (L)
$PA_{3.2}$	3 (L)	4 (F)	4 (F)	4 (F)	3 (L)	4 (F)	3 (L)
$PA_{3.1}$	3 (L)	4 (F)	4 (F)	4 (F)	3 (L)	4 (F)	3 (L)
$PA_{2.2}$	4 (F)	4 (F)	4 (F)	4 (F)	4 (F)	4 (F)	4 (F)
$PA_{2.1}$	4 (F)	4 (F)	4 (F)	4 (F)	4 (F)	4 (F)	4 (F)
$PA_{1.1}$	4 (F)	4 (F)	4 (F)	4 (F)	4 (F)	4 (F)	4 (F)

It is noteworthy that in Table 8.9 we have taken process ENG.1 as a detailed
example in Table 8.7 for demonstrating how these process attribute ratings
are derived.

8.5.2.3 Project Process category

The attribute ratings of the eight processes in the project category (PRO.1 –
PRO.8) are derived as in Table 8.10.

Table 8.10
Derived Process Attribute Ratings in the Project Category

PA$_{i,j}$	PRO.1	PRO.2	PRO.3	PRO.4	PRO.5	PRO.6	PRO.7	PRO.8
PA$_{5,2}$	3 (L)	3 (L)	1 (N)	1 (N)	2 (P)	1 (N)	2 (P)	2 (P)
PA$_{5,1}$	3 (L)	3 (L)	1 (N)	1 (N)	2 (P)	1 (N)	2 (P)	2 (P)
PA$_{4,2}$	4 (F)	3 (L)	2 (P)	3 (L)	4 (L)	2 (P)	4 (F)	3 (L)
PA$_{4,1}$	4 (F)	3 (L)	2 (P)	3 (L)	4 (L)	2 (P)	4 (F)	3 (L)
PA$_{3,2}$	4 (F)	3 (L)	2 (P)	3 (L)	4 (L)	2 (P)	4 (F)	3 (L)
PA$_{3,1}$	4 (F)	3 (L)	2 (P)	3 (L)	4 (L)	2 (P)	4 (F)	3 (L)
PA$_{2,2}$	4 (F)	4 (F)	4 (F)	4 (F)	4 (L)	3 (L)	4 (F)	4 (F)
PA$_{2,1}$	4 (F)	4 (F)	4 (F)	4 (F)	4 (L)	3 (L)	4 (F)	4 (F)
PA$_{1,1}$	4 (F)	4 (F)	4 (F)	4 (F)	4 (L)	3 (L)	4 (F)	4 (F)

8.5.2.4 Support Process Category

The attribute ratings of the five processes in the support category (SUP.1 – SUP.5) are derived as in Table 8.11.

Table 8.11
Derived Process Attribute Ratings in the Support Category

PA$_{i,j}$	SUP.1	SUP.2	SUP.3	SUP.4	SUP.5
PA$_{5,2}$	2 (P)	3 (L)	2 (P)	2 (P)	1 (N)
PA$_{5,1}$	2 (P)	3 (L)	2 (P)	2 (P)	1 (N)
PA$_{4,2}$	4 (F)	4 (F)	4 (F)	3 (L)	3 (L)
PA$_{4,1}$	4 (F)	4 (F)	4 (F)	3 (L)	3 (L)
PA$_{3,2}$	4 (F)	4 (F)	4 (F)	3 (L)	3 (L)
PA$_{3,1}$	4 (F)	4 (F)	4 (F)	3 (L)	3 (L)
PA$_{2,2}$	4 (F)	4 (F)	4 (F)	4 (F)	4 (F)
PA$_{2,1}$	4 (F)	4 (F)	4 (F)	4 (F)	4 (F)
PA$_{1,1}$	4 (F)	4 (F)	4 (F)	4 (F)	4 (F)

8.5.2.5 Organization Process Category

The attribute ratings of the seven processes in the organization category (ORG.1 – ORG.7) are derived as in Table 8.12.

Table 8.12
Derived Process Attribute Ratings in the Organization Category

PA$_{i,j}$	ORG.1	ORG.2	ORG.3	ORG.4	ORG.5	ORG.6	ORG.7
PA$_{5.2}$	2 (P)	1 (N)	1 (N)	3 (L)	1 (N)	3 (L)	2 (P)
PA$_{5.1}$	2 (P)	1 (N)	1 (N)	3 (L)	1 (N)	3 (L)	2 (P)
PA$_{4.2}$	3 (L)	3 (L)	2 (P)	4 (F)	2 (P)	3 (L)	3 (L)
PA$_{4.1}$	3 (L)	3 (L)	2 (P)	4 (F)	2 (P)	3 (L)	3 (L)
PA$_{3.2}$	3 (L)	3 (L)	2 (P)	4 (F)	2 (P)	3 (L)	3 (L)
PA$_{3.1}$	3 (L)	3 (L)	2 (P)	4 (F)	2 (P)	3 (L)	3 (L)
PA$_{2.2}$	3 (L)	3 (L)	3 (L)	4 (F)	3 (L)	4 (F)	4 (F)
PA$_{2.1}$	3 (L)	3 (L)	3 (L)	4 (F)	3 (L)	4 (F)	4 (F)
PA$_{1.1}$	3 (L)	3 (L)	3 (L)	4 (F)	3 (L)	4 (F)	4 (F)

8.5.3 PROCESS CAPABILITY DETERMINATION IN ISO/IEC TR 15504

When all process attribute ratings have been obtained as shown in Tables 8.8 through 8.12, the process capability levels of the 35 processes can then be derived individually according to Expression 8.13.

For example, process ENG.1 can be calculated as follows:

$$PCL_{proc}[ENG.1] = max \{ i \mid PA_{i,j} \geq 3 \ \wedge PA_{i-1,j} = 4 \}, \ j=1,2$$
$$= max \{3 \mid (PA_{3.1} = 3 \wedge PA_{3.2} = 3) \ \wedge$$
$$(PA_{2.1} = 4 \wedge PA_{2.2} = 4)\}$$
$$= 3$$

A derived process capability profile of all 35 processes in this ISO/IEC TR 15504 assessment is given in Figure 8.7.

8.5.4 PROJECT CAPABILITY DETERMINATION IN ISO/IEC TR 15504

Substituting the individual process capability levels shown in Figure 8.6 into Expression 8.15, the project capability of the sample software development organization can be aggregated as follows:

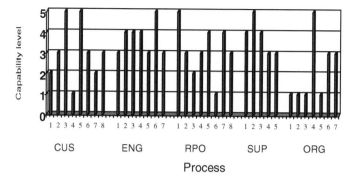

Figure 8.7 Process capability profile of a project in ISO/IEC TR 15504

$$PCL_{proj} \ [j] = \lfloor \tfrac{1}{k} \sum_{p=1}^{k} \ PCL_{proc}[p] \rfloor$$

$$= \lfloor 1 / 35 \sum_{p=1}^{35} \ PCL_{proc}[p] \rfloor$$

$$= \lfloor 1 / 35 * 109 \rfloor$$

$$= \lfloor 3.114 \rfloor$$

$$= 3$$

Thus, the sample project's process capability is determined to be Level 3, the established process capability level, in ISO/IEC TR 15504.

8.6 Applications of ISO/IEC TR 15504

In the previous sections we explored the ISO/IEC TR 15504 theory and methodology for process system modeling and assessment. This section analyzes the usability of ISO/IEC TR 15504 in software engineering process system establishment, assessment, and improvement. In order to present both sides of the coin, the limitations of ISO/IEC TR 15504 in some aspects of software engineering applications are discussed using the body of empirical and theoretical studies of ISO/IEC TR 15504.

8.6.1 ISO/IEC TR 15504 FOR SOFTWARE PROCESS SYSTEM ESTABLISHMENT

ISO/IEC TR 15504 develops the first 2-D process system model with fully independent process dimension and capability dimension. The 2-D model completely separates a process system and its capability measurement. This approach enables all processes to perform at any process capability level, and to be assessed against each capability level with related attributes. As a result, the processes and BPs have no longer been assigned a preallocated and fixed priority as in the 1-D process models.

From a structural view, the interrelationships of the ISO/IEC TR 15504 processes are relatively loosely defined. How the 5 process categories are synchronized within a software development organization is not addressed. It is also found that the domain of the ISO/IEC TR 15504 process model may need to be expanded significantly in order to provide a broad coverage and, thus, to increase compatibility with the existing process models.

8.6.2 ISO/IEC TR 15504 FOR SOFTWARE PROCESS SYSTEM ASSESSMENT

ISO/IEC TR 15504 develops a refined process capability scale with a set of nine generic process attributes at six capability levels. It presents a process assessment result by a 2-D process profile. In an assessment, ISO/IEC TR 15504 rates every process individually against the attributes, and from these the process profile and capability level are derived.

This approach can avoid the drawbacks of preassigning and grouping processes into different capability levels as is the case for CMM and BOOTSTRAP. This means any process can be and may be practiced at any capability level naturally, so that a software development organization is motivated to improve any process that has not yet achieved the expected capability level. Therefore, the ISO/IEC TR 15504 approach provides more flexibility and tailorability for a software development organization to prioritize its special needs in process improvement based on its specific circumstances.

However, in the ISO/IEC TR 15504 capability dimension, it is quite difficult to identify a set of generic process attributes that could be universally applicable for all the processes modeled in the process dimension. Therefore, it is found that some process attributes in the capability dimension are overlapped with certain processes in the process dimension. For instance, in some cases, the assessors have to use management and/or documentation attributes as a yardstick to measure the activities of management and/or documentation processes. This might well cause some logical confusion in practice.

The assessment complexity of ISO/IEC TR 15504 is quite high. Therefore, the cost of an ISO/IEC TR 15504 assessment would be much higher than those of the other process models.

It is noteworthy that ISO/IEC TR 15504 has not defined capability levels for the organization scope, nor aggregated project capability levels. This may cause some incompatibility in relating assessment results with other models.

8.6.3 ISO/IEC TR 15504 FOR SOFTWARE PROCESS SYSTEM IMPROVEMENT

ISO/IEC TR 15504 adopts the same assessment-based process improvement methodology as that of CMM and BOOTSTRAP. Based on the 2-D process framework and the representation of process capability in a 2-D process profile, a software engineering process system in an organization may be precisely analyzed and measured. This enables more effective process improvement according to the ISO/IEC TR 15504 model.

8.7 Summary

This chapter has introduced a formal and rigorous approach to the description of ISO/IEC TR 15504. CSP-like process algebra has been adopted for presenting the ISO/IEC TR 15504 process model, and mathematical and algorithmic methods have been applied for presenting the ISO/IEC TR 15504 process capability determination methodology. Using these formal techniques, ISO/IEC TR 15504 has been systematically described and analyzed by contrasting with the unified process system framework developed in Part I. An empirical case study has been provided for demonstrating the method and approach in conducting an ISO/IEC TR 15504 assessment.

The basic knowledge structure of this chapter is as follows:

Chapter 8. The ISO/IEC TR 15504 Model

- General
  - Purposes of this chapter
    - To review the history and background of ISO/IEC TR 15504 development

    - To describe the ISO/IEC TR 15504 process model and taxonomy

    - To describe the ISO/IEC TR 15504 capability model and capability determination methodology

    - To formally describe the ISO/IEC TR 15504 process model, and to algorithmically describe the ISO/IEC TR 15504 process capability determination method

    - To develop an ISO/IEC TR 15504 algorithm for software process assessment

    - To explain how the ISO/IEC TR 15504 algorithm can be used in process assessment and how its algorithm complexity is estimated

    - To demonstrate a case study of a practical ISO/IEC TR 15504 assessment by using the ISO/IEC TR 15504 algorithm

    - To discuss the usability of ISO/IEC TR 15504 in process establishment, assessment, and improvement in software engineering

  - ISO/IEC TR 15504 philosophy and background
    - Philosophy
      - An innovative international process system assessment model
      - A set of structured capability measurement for total software life cycle processes
    - Main sources of thoughts absorbed in ISO/IEC TR 15504
      - Process capability rating methodology: from CMM
      - The 2-D process assessment framework: inspired from BOOTSTRAP attribute-based profile representation for process capability
      - Process dimension: from ISO 12207, CMM,

BOOTSTRAP, Trillium, ISO 9001, etc.
– Process capability dimension: quality system
management principles as presented in ISO 9001 and
CMM

• The ISO/IEC TR 15504 process model
– Taxonomy of ISO/IEC TR 15504 process model
  – Process scopes
  – Size of domain of each scope

– Framework of ISO/IEC TR 15504 process model
  – Structure of ISO/IEC TR 15504 process model
  – Definitions of BPs in ISO/IEC TR 15504

– Formal description of ISO/IEC TR 15504 process model
  – ISO/IEC TR 15504 abstract process patterns
  – ISO/IEC TR 15504 process diagrams
  – Interpretation and illustration of the process algebra
    expressions

• The ISO/IEC TR 15504 process assessment model
– ISO/IEC TR 15504 process capability model
  – Configuration
    – 5 process categories (PCs)
    – 35 processes (PRs)
    – 201 practices (BPs)
  – BP rating scale
  – Process rating scale

– ISO/IEC TR 15504 process capability determination
  Methodology
    – Formal description of ISO/IEC TR 15504 capability
      determination method
    – Meanings of expressions and their operation
    – Common features with the methodology developed in the
      unified process framework in Part I
    – Differences from the methodology developed in the
      unified process framework in Part I

• The ISO/IEC TR 15504 algorithm
– Algorithm 8.1: ISO/IEC TR 15504 process assessment
– Explanation of Algorithm 8.1
– Relation between Algorithm 8.1 and the capability

> determination expressions defined in Section 8.3.2
> – The ISO/IEC TR 15504 algorithm complexity and the main factors affecting it
>
> • A sample ISO/IEC TR 15504 process assessment
>   – Understand assessment data documented in Appendix C
>   – Manual process assessment in ISO/IEC TR 15504
>   – Algorithm-based assessment in ISO/IEC TR 15504
>   – Interpretation of assessment results
>
> • Usability of ISO/IEC TR 15504
>   – Merits and demerits in process system establishment
>   – Merits and demerits in process system assessment
>   – Merits and demerits in process system improvement

Major achievements and issues for further research suggested by this chapter are highlighted below:

- The design philosophy behind ISO/IEC TR 15504 is to develop a set of structured capability measurements for all software lifecycle processes and for all parties, such as software developers, acquirers, contractors, and customers. As analyzed earlier, the software engineering process system seems to be one of the most complicated engineering systems. The search for useful and valid processes has much further to go, especially when considering that ISO/IEC TR 15504 has only identified 35 processes and 201 base practices in the model.

- Major contributions of ISO/IEC TR 15504 are as follows:

  - It is the first 2-D process system model with a fully independent process dimension and capability dimension. As a result, the processes and/or practices have no longer been assigned a pre-allocated and fixed priority.

  - A process assessment result is represented by a 2-D process profile.

  - There is a refined process capability scale with a set of nine generic process attributes at six capability levels.

  - A set of conformance criteria has been defined for enabling process models to be compared and to meet common requirements.

- Major open issues of ISO/IEC TR 15504 are perceived as follows:

  – It is found that the domain of the ISO/IEC TR 15504 processes may need to be expanded significantly in order to provide a broader coverage and to increase compatibility with the existing process models.

  – In ISO/IEC TR 15504 development and applications, there were difficulties in making the nine process attributes universally generic for all processes and BPs. As a result, it is often found that some of the attributes used as a rating scale were not suitable or applicable to some of the processes and BPs in assessment.

  – The capability dimension of ISO/IEC TR 15504 has grown relatively complicated. It also introduced some extent of overlaps with the process dimension. This indicates there is a need to further explore the roles and relationships of the two dimensions in process system modeling.

  – The assessment complexity of ISO/IEC TR 15504 is quite high with regard to the other process models. This means the cost of an ISO/IEC TR 15504 assessment would be much higher than that of the other process models.

- An ISO/IEC TR 15504 algorithm has been elicited in order to precisely and systematically interpret the ISO/IEC TR 15504 methodology, and to quantitatively compare the complexity of the ISO/IEC TR 15504 method with the others.

- Technically and historically, ISO/IEC TR 15504 has absorbed the basic capability rating scale from CMM; the software engineering process activities identified in ISO/IEC 12207, Trillium, and CMM; the attribute-based profile representation for process capability from BOOTSTRAP; and the general quality system management experience from ISO 9001.

This chapter has established a basis for understanding and analyzing ISO/IEC TR 15504 as a paradigm of the unified software engineering process system framework. Relationships of ISO/IEC TR 15504 with other process system models will be discussed in Part III of this book. Applications of ISO/IEC TR 15504 in process-based software engineering and case studies will be provided in Parts IV – VI.

Annotated References

An ISO/IEC standard development is usually divided into three phases:

- DTR – draft technical report
- TR – Technical report
- STD – Formal standard

ISO/IEC TR 15504 (Parts 1 – 9) were released in 1998. The DTR 15504 (Parts 1 – 9) V.2.0 were released in 1997. The material in this chapter relates to both TR and DTR 15504. Generally, the capability dimension of this chapter has been aligned to TR 15504, while the process dimension of this chapter is related to DTR 15504 for reasons of benchmarking data compatibility. The ISO 15504 algorithm was independently developed by the authors to be suitable for the latest version of ISO/IEC TR 15504.

Dorling (1993/95) reviewed the initiative and history of the SPICE project and the early development phases of ISO/IEC TR 15504. Official documents on the standard's requirements and specifications were in ISO/IEC JTC1/SC7 N944R (1992), N016R (1993b), and N017R (1993a). Route (1995) highlighted the technical issues in ISO/IEC TR 15504 development. Kitson (1996) related the ISO/IEC TR 15504 framework and ESI approach to software process assessment.

Wang et al. (1997a/b/99e) presented a series of comparative analyses of relationships and mutual mappings between major process models including ISO/IEC TR 15504. Wang et al. (1999g) reported a conformance analysis case study between a tailored CMM and ISO/IEC TR 15504.

For a more experienced report on ISO/IEC TR 15504, see SPICE Phase 2 Trial Report [SPICE Project, 1998]. For the latest development of ISO/IEC TR 15504 extensions for acquisition processes, see Dorling, Wang et al. (1999b). This extension is based on a European research project, PULSE.

Questions and Problems

8.1 Explain the design philosophy behind the development of ISO/IEC TR 15504.

8.2 Using your own words, briefly describe the structure of the ISO/IEC TR 15504 process model and its taxonomy.

8.3 Use process algebra to derive a formal ISO/IEC TR 15504 process model based on the process diagrams given in Figures 8.1 – 8.6. (Try not to copy Expressions 8.2 – 8.8 before you finish.)

8.4 Using your own words, briefly describe the ISO/IEC TR 15504 process capability model and capability determination methodology.

8.5 Can you repeat the sample ISO/IEC TR 15504 assessment based on the data provided in Appendix C and derive the same capability level as that of the example shown in Section 8.5?

8.6 Try to conduct an ISO/IEC TR 15504 exercise assessment for a software project with which you are familiar, and do so according to the formal approach presented in this chapter.

8.7 If a project's 35 processes have 20 processes at level 2, 10 at level 3, and 5 at level 4, what is its ISO/IEC TR 15504 capability level?

8.8 Based on Ex. 8.7, analyze the advantages and disadvantages of the capability level approach and process profile approach for presenting process capability.

8.9 Most of the established software development organizations are currently considered to be located between ISO/IEC TR 15504 Levels 1 and 3. Observe the ISO/IEC TR 15504 process model, do you think those organizations could produce reasonably good software? Why?

8.10 Try to organize a small software project with at least three persons. Then do a self-assessment for this project and report your capability level in ISO/IEC TR 15504.

8.11 Try to write an ISO/IEC TR 15504 assessment report for Ex. 8.6 or 8.10 and describe the following:

- Purpose(s) of the ISO/IEC TR 15504 assessment
- The ISO/IEC TR 15504 model and methodology you adopted
- The input of the ISO/IEC TR 15504 assessment
- The procedure of the ISO/IEC TR 15504 assessment
- The output of the ISO/IEC TR 15504 assessment
- The effort you spend for the ISO/IEC TR 15504 assessment
- Experience you gained in the ISO/IEC TR 15504 assessment
- Conclusions

8.12 Try to write an ISO/IEC TR 15504 process improvement plan based on the assessment report developed in Ex. 8.11. In the process improvement plan, describe the following:

- Purpose(s) of the ISO/IEC TR 15504 process improvement plan
- Brief introduction of the ISO/IEC TR 15504 assessment results
- Analyze strengths of the organization's process capability according to ISO/IEC TR 15504
- Analyze weaknesses of the organization's process capability according to ISO/IEC TR 15504
- Recommend a process improvement plan to address the process weaknesses or for moving to a higher ISO/IEC TR 15504 capability level
- Explain the benefit of implementing this process improvement plan and how well your plan will meet the organization's business goal
- Estimate the costs of this process improvement effort
- Predict the risks for executing the process improvement plan that you have suggested
- Conclusions

8.13 What is the usage of ISO/IEC TR 15504 in software engineering process establishment, assessment, and improvement?

Chapter 9

THE SOFTWARE ENGINEERING PROCESS REFERENCE MODEL: SEPRM

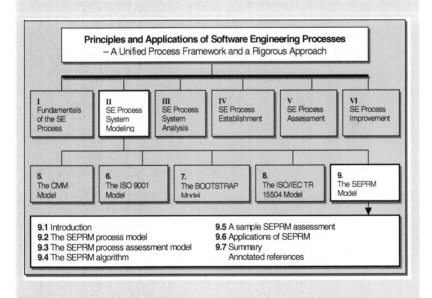

Principles and Applications of Software Engineering Processes
– A Unified Process Framework and a Rigorous Approach

I Fundamentals of the SE Process	II SE Process System Modeling	III SE Process System Analysis	IV SE Process Establishment	V SE Process Assessment	VI SE Process Improvement

5. The CMM Model	6. The ISO 9001 Model	7. The BOOTSTRAP Model	8. The ISO/IEC TR 15504 Model	9. The SEPRM Model

9.1 Introduction
9.2 The SEPRM process model
9.3 The SEPRM process assessment model
9.4 The SEPRM algorithm

9.5 A sample SEPRM assessment
9.6 Applications of SEPRM
9.7 Summary
Annotated references

In a coherent effort toward process model integration, unification, and formalization, the Software Engineering Process Reference Model (SEPRM) has been developed using a set of deeply investigated foundations and well-structured framework as described in Part I of this book. SEPRM provides an integrated and unified process system methodology for a software development organization. This chapter describes the SEPRM model, including its process model, process capability model, and process capability determination methodology.

A rigorous approach is adopted in the formal description of SEPRM. The process model of SEPRM is described by process algebra. The SEPRM capability determination method is described by an SEPRM algorithm. A sample assessment is provided in order to demonstrate how an SEPRM-based process assessment is carried out in practice. The usability of SEPRM is discussed and relations with the theoretical and empirical foundations throughout the book are summarized.

The objectives of this chapter are as follows:

- To review the history and background of SEPRM development

- To describe the SEPRM process model and taxonomy

- To describe the SEPRM capability model and capability determination methodology

- To formally describe the SEPRM process model and to algorithmically describe the SEPRM process capability determination method

- To develop an SEPRM algorithm for software process assessment

- To explain how the SEPRM algorithm might be used in process assessment and how its algorithm complexity is estimated

- To demonstrate a case study of a practical SEPRM assessment by using the SEPRM algorithm

- To discuss the usability of SEPRM in process establishment, assessment, and improvement in software engineering

9.1 Introduction

The philosophy of SEPRM is to provide a comprehensive and integrated process system reference model for process-based software engineering. SEPRM is a software engineering process system model that implements the full features of the unified process framework developed in Part I, and that integrates the advantages of the existing process models.

This chapter provides a formal description of SEPRM in accordance with the unified process system framework developed in Part I. The philosophy and rationales of SEPRM are reviewed in Section 9.1. A framework and taxonomy of the SEPRM process model are introduced in Section 9.2. The SEPRM capability model and process capability determination method are described in Section 9.3. Based on this, an SEPRM process assessment algorithm is developed and an example of SEPRM assessment is provided in Sections 9.4 and 9.5, respectively. Finally, the usability of SEPRM is discussed in Section 9.6.

9.1.1 OVERVIEW

As analyzed in Chapters 5 – 8 and contrasted in Appendix C, the current process models emphasize differing areas of an entire software process domain. Comparing current models with the unified process system framework developed in Part I, it is noteworthy that a number of essential areas in process deployment, establishment, modeling, analysis, assessment, and improvement have not been covered by the current models. The following major issues have been especially identified in research and practices:

- Lack of formalization in modeling and in description of algorithms in order to establish solid foundations for process-based software engineering.

- Lack of a super process model for completeness. The weak and sparse sample points on practices and processes may result in substantial distortion of an organization's process capability.

- Lack of quantitative benchmarks showing empirical attributes of processes, practices, and their selection criteria.

- Lack of consideration of compatibility and transformability.

There is a strong argument demanding a process system reference model that is designed to solve the above problems. A new software engineering process reference model (SEPRM) will now be explored on the basis of Part I where the foundations of the software process system have been investigated and the unified process system framework has been developed. The SEPRM model demonstrates a general view of what a complete process system model should contain in accordance with the unified process framework. SEPRM provides the means to integrate and unify the current process models, such as CMM, ISO 9001, BOOTSTRAP, and ISO/IEC 15504, by a well-founded process framework, a benchmarked superset of base process activities (BPAs), and a stable and mutually transformable capability determination algorithm.

The theoretical value of SEPRM is in the way it:

- Establishes a complete set of software engineering processes and attributes

- Develops a set of well-founded process model, process capability model, and process assessment model

- Introduces formal and quantitative methods into this area to enable objective and stable assessment

- Avoids preassignment and grouping of processes into different ranges of capability levels

- Avoids high operating complexity in process capability determination

- Offers a new approach to systematically and quantitatively compare and transform the process capability levels between existing process models

The practical value of SEPRM is to:

- Provide a comprehensive process reference model

- Develop a process capability determination methodology that is relatively lower in operating complexity and easier for application in process assessment and improvement

- Enable software development organizations to relate their capabilities to others using different process models

9.1.2 FOUNDATIONS OF THE SOFTWARE ENGINEERING PROCESS REFERENCE MODEL

Referring to the preparations in Part I, the philosophical, mathematical, and managerial foundations of software engineering were explored in Chapter 1. The theoretical foundations of the process approach to software engineering were developed in Chapter 2, which investigated the generic software development organization model, process model, capability model, capability determination method, and SPA/SPI methods in software engineering. The formal process notation system, process algebra, was introduced in Chapter 3, followed by Chapter 4 which provided a generic view of methodologies of process-based software engineering.

The empirical foundations of software engineering processes are summarized in Appendix D and will be analyzed in Chapter 10, which provides quantitative characteristics of the processes and BPAs identified in the software industry and in current process models.

In this chapter, SEPRM will be developed from the above theoretical and practical foundations, which incorporate an improved understanding of the nature of software engineering, the fundamental structure of software engineering process system, and the practical experience of the software industry. SEPRM is designed to provide a comprehensive software engineering process reference model, with sound foundations and empirical benchmark support, for software development organizations and software process system researchers.

9.1.3 PRACTICAL REQUIREMENTS FOR A SOFTWARE ENGINEERING PROCESS REFERENCE MODEL

In attempting a comparative analysis of the major existing process models, it is found that an intermediate reference model is quite useful for simplifying the many-to-many mapping into a many-to-one projection, and for reducing the complexity of mutual mapping of multiple models.

Existing work in one-to-one mapping among current process models is illustrated in Figure 9.1. Usually, conventional mappings are carried out at process level and are unidirectional. For more accurate mapping, it is necessary that the mapping be conducted at the BPA level. Terminology referring to the BPA differs from model to model, examples being: key practice (KP) in CMM, management issue (MI) in ISO 9001, quality system attribute (QSA) in BOOTSTRAP, and base practice (BP) in ISO/IEC 15504. As described in the unified process taxonomy in Chapter 2, all these elements of process are generally referred to as base process activities (BPAs) in SEPRM.

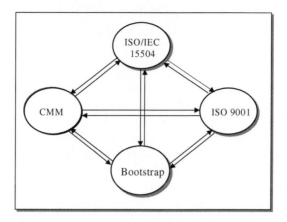

Figure 9.1 One-to-one mapping between current process models

Because of structural differences among the current process paradigms and variations among their BPA domains, the comparison of two models needs mapping twice, once in each direction. This has been described as the mapping asymmetry between process models [Wang et al., 1997a/b].

Generally, for n models, the complexity in mutually mapping each other, C_n, is in the order of n^2, i.e.:

$$C_n \triangleq O(n^2)$$
$$= n * (n-1) \qquad (9.1)$$

For example, for $n=4$ as shown in Figure 9.1, the mapping complexity is $C_n = n * (n-1) = 4*(4-1) = 12$.

However, where an intermediate reference model is adopted as shown in Figure 9.2, the complexity of mapping n models via the reference model, C_r, can be significantly reduced to:

$$C_r = O(n)$$
$$= n \qquad (9.2)$$

In the case of Figure 9.2, $C_r = n = 4$. Obviously the efficiency has increased by three times by the use of the reference model based approach. Generally, the larger the n, the more effective the reference model approach.

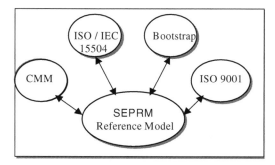

Figure 9.2 The role of a software process reference model

The other reason for requiring a reference model in mutually mapping and analyzing multiple models is that the fundamental BPAs defined in different process models result in a partial joint domain. Thus, some of the mappings at the BPA level would not exist, i.e., some mappings of BPAs would result in an empty set. However, with a reference model that defines a superset of BPAs to cover the entire process domain that all current models form, the mapping will never be empty. This reasoning emphasizes the utility of SEPRM in multiple model mapping.

In the rest of this chapter we formally describe and analyze the 2-D process framework and process capability determination method of SEPRM. Then, the SEPRM process capability determination algorithm is developed systematically. Applications of SEPRM in process domain analysis, process capability determination methodology analysis, and process capability transformation will be demonstrated in Part III.

9.2 The SEPRM Process Model

The SEPRM process model identifies a superset of processes and BPAs that cover the domains of current process models and new areas for software engineering environment and supporting tools. This section describes the taxonomy and framework of the SEPRM process model based on the unified process framework developed in Part I.

9.2.1 TAXONOMY OF THE SEPRM PROCESS MODEL

With reference to the process taxonomy defined in Chapter 2, the SEPRM process hierarchy and domains are listed in Table 9.1.

Table 9.1
Process Hierarchy and Domains of the SEPRM Process Model

Taxonomy	Subsystem	Category	Process	Practice
Process scope	Process subsystems (PS)	Process categories (PC)	Processes (PROC)	Base process activities (BPAs)
Size of domain	3	12	51	444
Identification	PS[i]	PC[i,k]	PROC[i,k,s]	BPA[i,k,s,j]

Table 9.1 defines the configuration of the SEPRM process model. As shown in Table 9.1, the BPAs, PROCs, PC, and PSs used in SEPRM are fully identical to the domain scopes as defined in the unified process system framework.

In order to provide a formal identification for each entity defined at various levels of coverage known as process scopes, the indexing of BPA, PROC, PC, and PS are described using a naming convention as shown in Table 9.1. In the table, i is the number of PS; k, the number of PC; s, the number of PROC; and j, the number of BPA.

9.2.2 FRAMEWORK OF THE SEPRM PROCESS MODEL

SEPRM models a software engineering process system in 3 process subsystems, 12 process categories, 51 processes, and 444 base process activities. A high-level hierarchical structure of the SEPRM framework is shown in Figure 9.3. According to the rationale for the unified process system framework described in Chapter 2, there are three independent process subsystems for software engineering known as organization, development, and management.

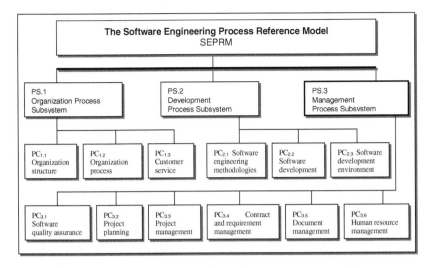

Figure 9.3 Hierarchical structure of SEPRM

The SEPRM framework described in Figure 9.3 can be extended to the process and BPA levels for showing the configuration of each process category and process. A detailed structure of the SEPRM framework, broken down to the process level, is shown in Table 9.2.

Table 9.2
The SEPRM Process Model

ID.	Subsystem	Category / Process	Identified BPAs
1	Organization		81
1.1		Organization structure processes	13
1.1.1		Organization definition	7
1.1.2		Project organization	6
1.2		Organization processes	26
1.2.1		Organization process definition	15
1.2.2		Organization process improvement	11
1.3		Customer service processes	39
1.3.1		Customer relations	13
1.3.2		Customer support	12
1.3.3		Software/system delivery	11
1.3.4		Service evaluation	6
2	Development		115
2.1		Software engineering methodology processes	23
2.1.1		Software engineering modeling	9

2.1.2		Reuse methodologies	7
2.1.3		Technology innovation	7
2.2		Software development processes	60
2.2.1		Development process definition	12
2.2.2		Requirement analysis	8
2.2.3		Design	9
2.2.4		Coding	8
2.2.5		Module testing	6
2.2.6		Integration and system testing	7
2.2.7		Maintenance	10
2.3		Software engineering infrastructure processes	32
2.3.1		Environment	7
2.3.2		Facilities	15
2.3.3		Development support tools	4
2.3.4		Management support tools	6
3	Management		248
3.1		Software quality assurance (SQA) processes	78
3.1.1		SQA process definition	17
3.1.2		Requirement review	5
3.1.3		Design review	4
3.1.4		Code review	3
3.1.5		Module testing audit	4
3.1.6		Integration and system testing audit	6
3.1.7		Maintenance audit	8
3.1.8		Audit and inspection	6
3.1.9		Peer review	10
3.1.10		Defect control	10
3.1.11		Subcontractor's quality control	5
3.2		Project planning processes	45
3.2.1		Project plan	20
3.2.2		Project estimation	7
3.2.3		Project risk avoidance	11
3.2.4		Project quality plan	7
3.3		Project management processes	55
3.3.1		Process management	8
3.3.2		Process tracking	15
3.3.3		Configuration management	8
3.3.4		Change control	9
3.3.5		Process review	8
3.3.6		Intergroup coordination	7
3.4		Contract and requirement management processes	42
3.4.1		Requirement management	12

3.4.2	Contract management	7
3.4.3	Subcontractor management	14
3.4.4	Purchasing management	9
3.5	Document management processes	17
3.5.1	Documentation	11
3.5.2	Process database/library	6
3.6	Human resource management processes	11
3.6.1	Staff selection and allocation	4
3.6.2	Training	7
Total	3	12 / 51	444

The configuration of the 444 BPAs in the SEPRM reference model is shown in Appendix C, in which the relationships between the defined BPAs and their counterparts in current process models are also mutually mapped. The BPAs of SEPRM in Appendix C can be referred to in two ways – a series number for easy indexing, and a category number for structured reference. The information shown in the columns of CMM, ISO 9001, BOOTSTRAP, and ISO/IEC 15504 are the identification numbers of the BPAs as defined in corresponding models.

In Table 9.2, the number of defined BPAs for each PROC is provided. The definitions of the BPAs are listed in Appendix C, where, in the column of "Cat. No.," a jth BPA in process s, category k, and subsystem i, $BPA[i,k,s,j]$, is represented by:

$$BPA[i,k,s,j] = BPA_{i.k.s.j} \qquad (9.3)$$

For example, in Appendix C, readers can identify BPA[3,1,8,1] as:

$$
\begin{aligned}
BPA[i,k,r,j] &= BPA[3,1,8,1] \\
&= BPA_{3.1.8.1} && \text{// The category number} \\
&= BPA_{244} && \text{// The index number} \\
&= \text{"Audit software development activities"}
\end{aligned}
$$

9.2.3 FORMAL DESCRIPTION OF THE SEPRM PROCESS MODEL

By using CSP-like process algebra as introduced in Chapter 3, we are able to formally describe the SEPRM process model and its processes in this subsection. This formal description is useful for providing precise and accurate definitions of the structure and interrelationships of the SEPRM processes, and to avoid the ambiguity inherent in natural language description.

9.2.3.1 The Structure of the SEPRM Process Model

A formal description of the structure of the SEPRM process model, *SEPRM-PM*, is shown in Expression 9.4 and illustrated in Figure 9.4. Obviously, SEPRM is a hybrid serial and parallel process system model, with the organization process subsystem at the top level, and the development and management process subsystems underneath.

$$
\begin{aligned}
SEPRM\text{-}PM \triangleq PS_1 \quad &// \text{Organization subsystem} \\
; (\quad PS_2 \quad &// \text{Development subsystem} \\
\parallel PS_3) \quad &// \text{Management subsystem} \quad (9.4)
\end{aligned}
$$

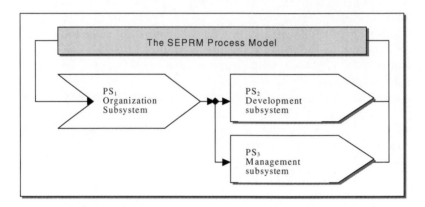

Figure 9.4 The SEPRM process model

In the SEPRM process model, each process subsystem can be extended downwards to a number of PCs, then to a number of PROCs as shown in Expressions 9.5 through 9.7. Further, each PROC can be extended to a number of BPAs in a similar way.

$$
\begin{aligned}
PS_1 \triangleq \quad PC_{1.1} \quad &// \text{Organization structure} \\
\parallel PC_{1.2} \quad &// \text{Organization process} \\
\parallel PC_{1.3} \quad &// \text{Customer services} \\
= \quad (PROC_{1.1.1} \parallel PROC_{1.1.2}) \quad & \\
\parallel (PROC_{1.2.1} \parallel PROC_{1.2.2}) \quad & \\
\parallel (PROC_{1.3.1} \parallel PROC_{1.3.2} \parallel PROC_{1.3.3} \parallel PROC_{1.3.4}) \quad &(9.5)
\end{aligned}
$$

$$PS_2 \triangleq PC_{2.1} \qquad // \text{ Software engineering methodologies}$$
$$\| PC_{2.2} \qquad // \text{ Software development}$$
$$\| PC_{2.3} \qquad // \text{ Software engineering infrastructure}$$
$$= (PROC_{2.1.1} \| PROC_{2.1.2} \| PROC_{2.1.3})$$
$$\| (PROC_{2.2.1}; PROC_{2.2.2}; PROC_{2.2.3}; PROC_{2.2.4}$$
$$; PROC_{2.2.5}; PROC_{2.2.6}; PROC_{2.2.7})$$
$$\| (PROC_{2.3.1} \| PROC_{2.3.2} \| PROC_{2.3.3} \| PROC_{2.3.4}) \quad (9.6)$$

$$PS_3 \triangleq PC_{3.1} \qquad // \text{ Software quality assurance}$$
$$\| PC_{3.2} \qquad // \text{ Project planning}$$
$$\| PC_{3.3} \qquad // \text{ Project management}$$
$$\| PC_{3.4} \qquad // \text{ Contract and requirement management}$$
$$\| PC_{3.5} \qquad // \text{ Document management}$$
$$\| PC_{3.6} \qquad // \text{ Human resource management}$$
$$= (PROC_{3.1.1} \| PROC_{3.1.2} \| PROC_{3.1.3} \| PROC_{3.1.4}$$
$$\| PROC_{3.1.5} \| PROC_{3.1.6} \| PROC_{3.1.7} \| PROC_{3.1.8}$$
$$\| PROC_{3.1.9} \| PROC_{3.1.10} \| PROC_{3.1.11})$$
$$\| (PROC_{3.2.1} \| PROC_{3.2.2} \| PROC_{3.2.3} \| PROC_{3.2.4})$$
$$\| (PROC_{3.3.1} \| PROC_{3.2.2} \| PROC_{3.3.3} \| PROC_{3.3.4}$$
$$\| PROC_{3.3.5} \| PROC_{3.3.6})$$
$$\| (PROC_{3.4.1} \| PROC_{3.4.2} \| PROC_{3.4.3} \| PROC_{3.4.4})$$
$$\| (PROC_{3.5.1} \| PROC_{3.5.2})$$
$$\| (PROC_{3.6.1} \| PROC_{3.6.2}) \quad (9.7)$$

9.2.3.2 Definitions of SEPRM Processes

The 12 SEPRM process categories, known as $PC_{1.1} - PC_{1.3}$, $PC_{2.1} - PC_{2.3}$, and $PC_{3.1} - PC_{3.6}$, can be formally defined by Expressions 9.8 – 9.19 and are illustrated in Figures 9.4 – 9.15.

$$PC_{1.1} \triangleq PROC_{1.1.1} \qquad // \text{ Organization definition}$$
$$\| PROC_{1.1.2} \qquad // \text{ Project organization} \quad (9.8)$$

A process diagram corresponding to the two processes in the SEPRM organization structure process category, as defined in Expression 9.8, is shown in Figure 9.5.

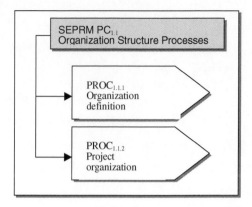

Figure 9.5 SEPRM process category 1.1 – the organization structure processes

A process diagram corresponding to the two processes in the SEPRM organization process category, as defined in Expression 9.9, is shown in Figure 9.6.

$$PC_{1.2} \triangleq PROC_{1.2.1} \quad // \text{ Organization process definition}$$
$$|| PROC_{1.2.2} \quad // \text{ Organization process improvement} \quad (9.9)$$

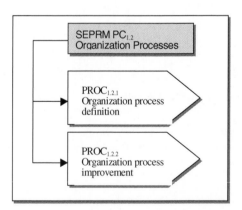

Figure 9.6 SEPRM process category 1.2 – the organization processes

A process diagram corresponding to the four processes in the SEPRM customer service process category, as defined in Expression 9.10, is shown in Figure 9.7.

$$PC_{1.3} \triangleq \quad PROC_{1.3.1} \qquad // \text{Customer relations}$$
$$\| PROC_{1.3.2} \qquad // \text{Customer support}$$
$$\| PROC_{1.3.3} \qquad // \text{Software and system delivery}$$
$$\| PROC_{1.3.4} \qquad // \text{Service evaluation} \qquad (9.10)$$

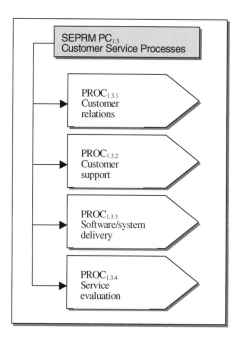

Figure 9.7 SEPRM process category 1.3 – the customer service processes

A process diagram corresponding to the three processes in the SEPRM software engineering methodology process category, as defined in Expression 9.11, is shown in Figure 9.8.

$$PC_{2.1} \triangleq \quad PROC_{2.1.1} \qquad // \text{Software engineering modeling}$$
$$\| PROC_{2.1.2} \qquad // \text{Reuse methodologies}$$
$$\| PROC_{2.1.3} \qquad // \text{Technology innovation} \qquad (9.11)$$

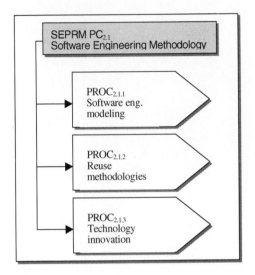

Figure 9.8 SEPRM process category 2.1 – the software engineering methodology processes

A process diagram corresponding to the seven processes in the SEPRM software development process category, as defined in Expression 9.12, is shown in Figure 9.9.

$$PC_{2.2} \triangleq PROC_{2.2.1} \quad // \text{Development process definition}$$

$$; PROC_{2.2.2} \quad // \text{Requirement analysis}$$

$$; PROC_{2.2.3} \quad // \text{Design}$$

$$; PROC_{2.2.4} \quad // \text{Coding}$$

$$; PROC_{2.2.5} \quad // \text{Module testing}$$

$$; PROC_{2.2.6} \quad // \text{Integration and system testing}$$

$$; PROC_{2.2.7} \quad // \text{Maintenance} \qquad (9.12)$$

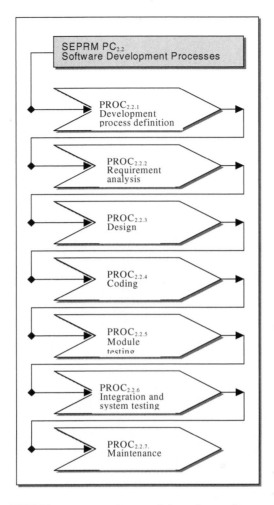

Figure 9.9 SEPRM process category 2.2 – the software development processes

A process diagram corresponding to the four processes in the SEPRM software engineering infrastructure process category, as defined in Expression 9.13, is shown in Figure 9.10.

$$
\begin{aligned}
PC_{2.3} \triangleq \ & PROC_{2.3.1} && // \text{Environment} \\
& \| \ PROC_{2.3.2} && // \text{Facilities} \\
& \| \ PROC_{2.3.3} && // \text{Development support tools} \\
& \| \ PROC_{2.3.4} && // \text{Management support tools} && (9.13)
\end{aligned}
$$

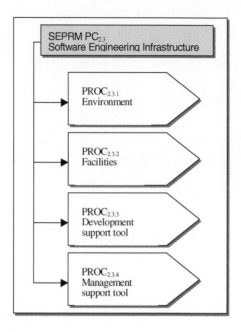

Figure 9.10 SEPRM process category 2.3 – the software engineering infrastructure processes

A process diagram corresponding to the 11 processes in the SEPRM software quality assurance process category, as defined in Expression 9.14, is shown in Figure 9.11.

$$PC_{3.1} \triangleq PROC_{3.1.1} \quad // \text{SQA procedure definition}$$

$\quad\quad\quad || PROC_{3.1.2} \quad$ // *Requirements review*

$\quad\quad\quad || PROC_{3.1.3} \quad$ // Design review

$\quad\quad\quad || PROC_{3.1.4} \quad$ // Code review

$\quad\quad\quad || PROC_{3.1.5} \quad$ // Module testing audit

$\quad\quad\quad || PROC_{3.1.6} \quad$ // Integration and system testing audit

$\quad\quad\quad || PROC_{3.1.7} \quad$ // Maintenance audit

$\quad\quad\quad || PROC_{3.1.8} \quad$ // Audit and inspection

$\quad\quad\quad || PROC_{3.1.9} \quad$ // Peer review

$\quad\quad\quad || PROC_{3.1.10} \quad$ // Defect control

$\quad\quad\quad || PROC_{3.1.11} \quad$ // Subcontractor's quality control $\quad$ (9.14)

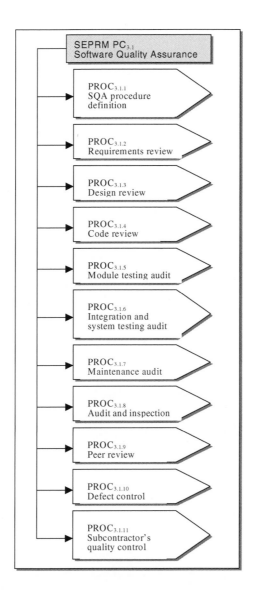

Figure 9.11 SEPRM process category 3.1 – the software quality assurance Processes

A process diagram corresponding to the four processes in the SEPRM project planning process category, as defined in Expression 9.15, is shown in Figure 9.12.

$$PC_{3.2} \triangleq PROC_{3.2.1} \qquad // \text{Project plan}$$
$$\parallel PROC_{3.2.2} \qquad // \text{Project estimation}$$
$$\parallel PROC_{3.2.3} \qquad // \text{Project risk avoidance}$$
$$\parallel PROC_{3.2.4} \qquad // \text{Project quality plan} \qquad (9.15)$$

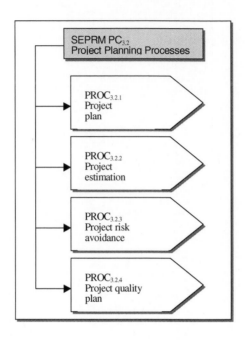

Figure 9.12 SEPRM process category 3.2 – the project planning processes

A process diagram corresponding to the six processes in the SEPRM project management process category, as defined in Expression 9.16, is shown in Figure 9.13.

$$PC_{3.3} \triangleq PROC_{3.3.1} \qquad // \text{Process management}$$
$$\parallel PROC_{3.3.2} \qquad // \text{Process tracking}$$
$$\parallel PROC_{3.3.3} \qquad // \text{Configuration management}$$
$$\parallel PROC_{3.3.4} \qquad // \text{Change control}$$
$$\parallel PROC_{3.3.5} \qquad // \text{Process review}$$
$$\parallel PROC_{3.3.6} \qquad // \text{Intergroup coordination} \qquad (9.16)$$

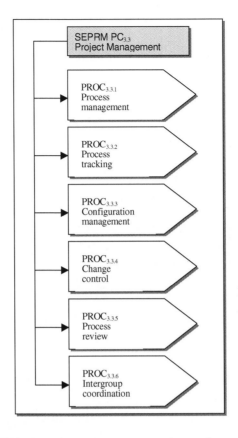

Figure 9.13 SEPRM process category 3.3 – the project management Processes

A process diagram corresponding to the four processes in the SEPRM contract and requirement management process category, as defined in Expression 9.17, is shown in Figure 9.14.

$$
\begin{array}{ll}
PC_{3.4} \triangleq PROC_{3.4.1} & // \text{Requirement management} \\
\| PROC_{3.4.2} & // \text{Contract management} \\
\| PROC_{3.4.3} & // \text{Subcontractor management} \\
\| PROC_{3.4.4} & // \text{Purchasing management} \quad (9.17)
\end{array}
$$

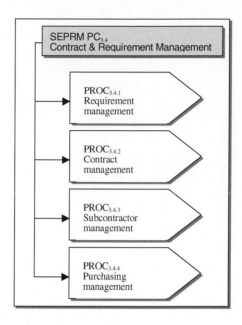

Figure 9.14 SEPRM process category 3.4 – the contract and requirement management processes

A process diagram corresponding to the two processes in the SEPRM document management process category, as defined in Expression 9.18, is shown in Figure 9.15.

$$PC_{3.5} \triangleq PROC_{3.5.1} \qquad // \text{Documentation}$$
$$|| PROC_{3.5.2} \qquad // \text{Process database/library} \qquad (9.18)$$

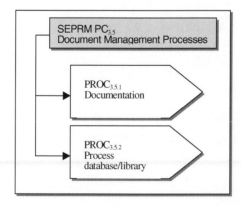

Figure 9.15 SEPRM process category 3.5 – the document management processes

A process diagram corresponding to the two processes in the SEPRM human resource management process category, as defined in Expression 9.19, is shown in Figure 9.16.

$$PC_{3.6} \triangleq PROC_{3.6.1} \qquad // \text{ Staff selection/allocation}$$
$$\| PROC_{3.6.2} \qquad // \text{ Training} \qquad (9.19)$$

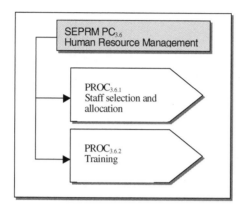

Figure 9.16 SEPRM process category 3.6 – the human resource management processes

Detailed practices of each PROC at BPA level, which are documented in Appendix C, can be described in the same way as above. Extending the formal SEPRM process model onto the BPA level can be taken as an exercise for readers.

9.3 The SEPRM Process Assessment Model

The SEPRM process model was systematically introduced in Section 9.2. This section explores the SEPRM process capability model and process capability determination method. Both of the above form the SEPRM process assessment model.

9.3.1 THE SEPRM PROCESS CAPABILITY MODEL

This section describes the SEPRM process capability model, which includes a practice performance scale, a process capability scale, and a process capability scope definition.

9.3.1.1 Practice Performance Scale

A practice performance rating scale for the BPAs in SEPRM is defined in Table 9.3. It employs a four-level scale for evaluating a BPA's existence and performance. The rating thresholds provide a set of quantitative measurements for rating a BPA's performance with the scale.

Table 9.3
Performance Rating Scale of the BPAs

Scale	Description	Rating Threshold
5 (F)	Fully adequate	90% - 100%
3 (L)	Largely adequate	60% - 89%
1 (P)	Partially adequate	25% - 59%
0 (N)	Not adequate	0 – 24%

9.3.1.2 Process Capability Scale

Referring to Chapter 2, there are three types of process capability scales: the pass-threshold-based, process-management-oriented, and process-oriented. The SEPRM process capability model is designed for directly rating and characterizing the performance of a process within context, rather than to indirectly evaluate the management maturity level for a process.

SEPRM develops a six-level software process capability model as shown in Table 9.4, with a set of defined criteria for rating the capability of a process. In Table 9.4, an index C[i,j] indicates a process capability criterion of *C [level, organization/project/individual]* in the organization, project, or individual context.

Table 9.4 shows that, in SEPRM, a process as an independent unit is assessed in the organization, project, and individual contexts against the six level process capability criteria. In order to relate the process capability criteria to the performance of BPAs in a process, there is another criterion for assessing a process: the average performance of the BPAs.

Table 9.4
The SEPRM Process Capability Model

Capability Level (CL[i])	Description	Process Capability Criteria		
		In Organization Context	**In Project Context**	**In Individual Context**
CL[0]	Incomplete	C[0,1] No process system reference model	C[0,2] No defined and repeatable process activities	C[0,3] Ad hoc
CL[1]	Loose	C[1,1] There are defined processes to some extent	C[1,2] Three are limited process activities defined and conducted	C[1,3] Varying
CL[2]	Integrated	C[2,1] There is a process system reference model established	C[2,2] There are relatively complete process activities defined and aligned to organization's process reference model	C[2,3] Generally process-based
CL[3]	Stable	C[3,1] There is a repeatable process system reference model	C[3,2] There are complete process activities derived from organization's process reference model	C[3,3] Repeatedly process-based
CL[4]	Effective	C[4,1] There is a proven process reference system model	C[4,2] - There are completed process activities derived from organization's process reference model - Performances of processes are monitored	C[4,3] Rigorously process-based
CL[5]	Refining	C[5,1] There is a proven and refined process system reference model	C[5,2] - There is a completed derived process model - Performances of processes are quantitatively monitored and fine-tuned	C[5,3] Rigorous and optimistic process-based

Thus, based on both the software process capability model and the BPA performance threshold, an SEPRM process capability scale is described in Table 9.5.

Table 9.5
The SEPRM Process Capability Scale

Capability Level (CL[i])	Description	Process Capability Criteria			BPA Average Performance Threshold
		Organization Context	Project Context	Individual Context	
CL[0]	Incomplete	C[0,1] Yes	C[0,2] Yes	C[0,3] Yes	C[0,4] 0 – 0.9
CL[1]	Loose	C[1,1] Achieved	C[1,2] Achieved	C[1,3] Achieved	C[1,4] 1.0 – 1.9
CL[2]	Integrated	C[2,1] Achieved	C[2,2] Achieved	C[2,3] Achieved	C[2,4] 2.0 – 2.9
CL[3]	Stable	C[3,1] Achieved	C[3,2] Achieved	C[3,3] Achieved	C[3,4] 3.0 – 3.9
CL[4]	Effective	C[4,1] Achieved	C[4,2] Achieved	C[4,3] Achieved	C[4,4] 4.0 – 4.5
CL[5]	Refining	C[5,1] Achieved	C[5,2] Achieved	C[5,3] Achieved	C[5,4] 4.6 -- 5.0

Table 9.5 shows there are four criteria that a process has to fulfill to reach a specific capability level. The first three are oriented to a process as whole; the last one is oriented to BPAs contained in a process. Therefore, the capability of a software development organization to operate a given process is determined by the maximum level i that a process achieved for fulfilling all four criteria for that level.

The SEPRM process assessment results are reported at the six levels plus a decimal value. This means it has the potential to distinguish the process capability at tenth-sublevels. This approach enables a software development organization to fine-tune its process system in continuous process improvement.

9.3.1.3 Process Capability Scope

The SEPRM process capability scopes are shown in Table 9.6. Comparing Table 9.6 with Table 2.3 in Chapter 2, it is clear that SEPRM assesses process capability at the levels of BPA, process, project, and organization scope from the bottom, up. The SEPRM capability model provides a complete implementation of the fundamental process framework developed in Chapter 2.

Table 9.6
Process Capability Scope of SEPRM

Capability Scope	Practice	Process	Project	Organization
SEPRM term	BPAs	Processes	Project	Organization
SEPRM method	Performance rating	Capability level	Capability level + process capability profile	Capability level + process capability profile

9.3.2 THE SEPRM PROCESS CAPABILITY DETERMINATION METHODOLOGY

Using the formal definitions of the SEPRM process model and process capability model developed in Sections 9.2 and 9.3.1, we can now consider how to apply the SEPRM capability model to the process model for the assessment of process capability at practice, process, project, and organization levels.

9.3.2.1 Practice Performance Rating Method

Let $r_{BPA}[i]$ be a rating of performance of the ith BPA in a process. Then $r_{BPA}[i]$ can be rated according to the practice performance scale as defined in Table 9.3, i.e.:

$$
\begin{aligned}
r_{BPA}[i] &= 5, \ \ \text{if the BP's performance is fully satisfied (or does not apply)} \\
&= 3, \ \ \text{if the BP's performance is largely satisfied} \\
&= 1, \ \ \text{if the BP's performance is partially satisfied} \\
&= 0, \ \ \text{if the BP's performance is not satisfied} \quad\quad (9.20)
\end{aligned}
$$

In Expression 9.20, one of the four numerical values is assigned for a BPA's performance. For providing flexibility and tailorability for the configuration of BPAs, the rating of a BPA can be skipped by assigning a value of 5 if the BPA does not apply in a project's or organization's context.

For a process, p, that consists of m_p BPAs, an average performance of the practices in the process, $\overline{PP}(p)$, can be derived by:

$$
\overline{PP}(p) = \frac{1}{m_p} \sum_{i=1}^{m_p} PP(i) \quad\quad (9.21)
$$

9.3.2.2 Process Capability Rating Method

According to the definitions in Table 9.5, the capability level of a process in SEPRM can be determined as two parts: the process criteria and the BPA criteria. The capability level of a process p, $PCL_{proc}(p)$, can be represented as follows:

$$PCL_{proc}(p) = min \{ PCL_c(p) + 0.9, \overline{PP}(p) \} \qquad (9.22)$$

where $PCL_c(p)$ represents the maximum achieved level of a process against the process criteria, $C[i,j]$, $i = 0, ..., 5$, $j=1,2, 3$, as defined in Table 9.5, i.e.:

$$PCL_c(p) = max \{ i \mid (C[i,j] = fulfilled) \wedge j=1,2,3\} \qquad (9.23)$$

Expression 9.22 requires a process to fulfill all four criteria at a level and those of the lower level(s) before it is considered to have achieved that capability level. Expression 9.22 selects the minimum value obtained either by the process criteria or BPA criteria. A compensation constant, 0.9, is added to the score of the process criteria in order to allow the BPA criteria to determine a precise decimal capability level.

In an assessment, assuming that the process criteria have been checked and achieved, the determination of a process's capability level in this case can be simplified by calculating only the BPA criteria, the BPA mean performance, $\overline{PP}(p)$, i.e.:

$$PCL_{proc}(p) = \overline{PP}(p)$$
$$= \frac{1}{m_p} \sum_{i=1}^{m_p} PP(i) \qquad (9.24)$$

9.3.2.3 Project Capability Determination Method

A project capability can be aggregated from the capabilities of all processes conducted within the project. Thus, a project's process capability level, $PCL_{proj}(j)$, is defined as a statistical average of all k process capabilities of project j, i.e.:

$$PCL_{proj}(j) = \frac{1}{k} \sum_{p=1}^{k} PCL_{proc}(p) \qquad (9.25)$$

A precise decimal project capability level between 0 - 5.0 can be derived by the expression.

9.3.2.4 Organization Capability Determination Method

An organization's capability is an aggregation of the capability levels of a number of sampled projects carried out in a software development organization.

An organization's process capability level, PCL_{org}, is a mathematical mean of those of n projects, $PCL_{\mathrm{proj}}(p)$, sampled in the software development organization, i.e.:

$$PCL_{\mathrm{org}} = \frac{1}{n} \sum_{p=1}^{n} PCL_{\mathrm{proj}}(p) \qquad (9.26)$$

Expression 9.26 indicates that more than one project's capabilities should be obtained to derive an organization's capability level. Generally, the more projects assessed, the more accurate the level derived. A recommended minimum number, n, as for all models, is three.

9.4 The SEPRM Algorithm

So far we have explored the SEPRM process model, process capability model, and capability determination method. Using the models and method we are already able to manually assess and calculate a software project's or an organization's process capability in SEPRM.

In order to describe the SEPRM methodology precisely, and to enable mutual comparison and tool implementation, this section extends the SEPRM process capability determination methodology into a formal SEPRM algorithm.

9.4.1 DESCRIPTION OF THE SEPRM ALGORITHM

The SEPRM process capability determination method as defined in Expressions 9.20 – 9.25 can be formally described in the following algorithm. An organization's process capability level can be easily aggregated according to Expression 9.26 when multiple projects have been assessed.

Algorithm 9.1 The SEPRM process capability determination
algorithm

Assume: $N_{PC}(SUBSYS)$ - Number of process categories in a
                                      process subsystem

        $N_{PROC}(SUBSYS,PC)$ - Number of processes in a category

        $N_{BPA}(SUBSYS,PC,PROC)$ - Number of BPAs in a process

        $BPA(SUBSYS,PC,PROC)$ - A BPA index

        CL - A capability level

        $PCL_{proc}(SUBSYS,PC,PROC)$ - A process capability level

        PCL_{proc} - Capability level of a project

Input: Sample indicators of BPA and processes existence
             and performance

Output: A process profile: $PCL_{proc}[SUBSYS,PC,PROC]$, and
             a project process capability level: PCL_{proj}

Begin

// Step 1: Initialization

    // Define numbers of process categories in each process subsystem
    // according to Table 9.2
    $N_{PC}[1] := 3;$
    $N_{PC}[2] := 3;$
    $N_{PC}[3] := 6;$

    // Define numbers of processes in each category according to Table 9.2
    $N_{proc}[1,1] := 2;$
    $N_{proc}[1,2] := 2;$
    $N_{proc}[1,3] := 4;$

    $N_{proc}[2,1] := 3;$
    $N_{proc}[2,2] := 7;$
    $N_{proc}[2,3] := 4;$

    $N_{proc}[3,1] := 11;$
    $N_{proc}[3,2] := 4;$
    $N_{proc}[3,3] := 6;$
    $N_{proc}[3,4] := 4;$
    $N_{proc}[3,5] := 2;$
    $N_{proc}[3,6] := 2;$

    // Define numbers of *BPAs* in each PROC according to Table 9.2

$N_{BPA} [1,1,1] := 7;$
$N_{BPA} [1,1,2] := 6;$
$N_{BPA} [1,2,1] := 15;$
$N_{BPA} [1,2,2] := 11;$
$N_{BPA} [1,3,1] := 13;$
$N_{BPA} [1,3,2] := 12;$
$N_{BPA} [1,3,3] := 11;$
$N_{BPA} [1,3,4] := 6;$

$N_{BPA} [2,1,1] := 9;$
$N_{BPA} [2,1,2] := 7;$
$N_{BPA} [2,1,3] := 7;$
$N_{BPA} [2,2,1] := 12;$
$N_{BPA} [2,2,2] := 8;$
$N_{BPA} [2,2,3] := 9;$
$N_{BPA} [2,2,4] := 8;$
$N_{BPA} [2,2,5] := 6;$
$N_{BPA} [2,2,6] := 7;$
$N_{BPA} [2,2,7] := 10;$
$N_{BPA} [2,3,1] := 7;$
$N_{BPA} [2,3,2] := 15;$
$N_{BPA} [2,3,3] := 4;$
$N_{BPA} [2,3,4] := 6;$

$N_{BPA} [3,1,1] := 17;$
$N_{BPA} [3,1,2] := 5;$
$N_{BPA} [3,1,3] := 4;$
$N_{BPA} [3,1,4] := 3;$
$N_{BPA} [3,1,5] := 4;$
$N_{BPA} [3,1,6] := 6;$
$N_{BPA} [3,1,7] := 8;$
$N_{BPA} [3,1,8] := 6;$
$N_{BPA} [3,1,9] := 10;$
$N_{BPA} [3,1,10] := 10;$
$N_{BPA} [3,1,11] := 5;$
$N_{BPA} [3,2,1] := 20;$
$N_{BPA} [3,2,2] := 7;$
$N_{BPA} [3,2,3] := 11;$
$N_{BPA} [3,2,4] := 7;$
$N_{BPA} [3,3,1] := 8;$
$N_{BPA} [3,3,1] := 15;$
$N_{BPA} [3,3,3] := 8;$
$N_{BPA} [3,3,4] := 9;$
$N_{BPA} [3,3,5] := 8;$

N_{BPA} *[3,3,6] := 7;*
N_{BPA} *[3,4,1] := 12;*
N_{BPA} *[3,4,1] := 7;*
N_{BPA} *[3,4,3] := 14;*
N_{BPA} *[3,4,4] := 9;*
N_{BPA} *[3,5,1] := 11;*
N_{BPA} *[3,5,2] := 6;*
N_{BPA} *[3,6,1] := 4;*
N_{BPA} *[3,6,2] := 7;*

// Step 2: Practice performance rating

```
for  SUBSYS := 1 to 3 do                    // the process subsystem index
    for  PC := 1 to N_PC(SUBSYS)  do    // the process category index
        for  PROC :=1 to N_proc(SUBSYS, PC) do   // the process index
            begin
                PP(SUBSYS, PC, PROC) := 0;

                for  BPA := 1 to N_BPA(SUBSYS, PC, PROC) do
                                    // The BPA index
                    begin
                        // Assess a BPA according to Expression 9.20,
                        // and record performance rating in
                        // BPA(SUBSYS, PC, PROC)
                        case BPA(SUBSYS, PC, PROC)
                            F:  // Fully adequate
                                PP(SUBSYS, PC, PROC) :=
                                    PP(SUBSYS, PC, PROC) + 5;
                            L:  // Largely adequate
                                PP(SUBSYS, PC, PROC) :=
                                    PP(SUBSYS, PC, PROC) + 3;
                            P:  // Partially adequate
                                PP(SUBSYS, PC, PROC) :=
                                    PP(SUBSYS, PC, PROC) + 1;
                            N:  // Not adequate
                                PP(SUBSYS, PC, PROC) :=
                                    PP(SUBSYS, PC, PROC) + 0;
                            NA: // Does not apply
                                PP(SUBSYS, PC, PROC) :=
                                    PP(SUBSYS, PC, PROC) + 5;
                    end;
            end;
end;
```

// Step 3: Process capability determination

for *SUBSYS := 1 to 3* do   // the process subsystem index
   for *PC := 1* to $N_{PC}(SUBSYS)$ do   // the process category index
      for *PROC :=1 to $N_{proc}(SUBSYS, PC)$* do   // the process index
         // 3.1 Assess each process against the six-level criteria
         // process criteria as defined in Table 9.5 and Exp. 9.23
         $CL_{PROC}(SUBSYS, PC, PROC) :=$
           max { i | (C[i,j] = fulfilled) ∧ j=1,2,3};

         // 3.2 Assess mean BPA performance according to
         // Expression 9.21
         $CL_{BPA}(SUBSYS, PC, PROC) := PP(SUBSYS, PC, PROC) /$
                              $N_{BPA}(SUBSYS,PC,PROC);$

         // 3.3 Determine process capability level according to
         // Expression 9.22
         $CL(SUBSYS, PC, PROC) :=$
           min {$CL_{PROC}(SUBSYS,PC,PROC)+0.9$,
            $CL_{BPA}(SUBSYS,PC,PROC)$};

         // 3.4 Save process capability profile
         $PCL_{proc}(SUBSYS,PC,PROC) := CL(SUBSYS,PC,PROC);$

// Step 4: Project capability determination

k := 51;   // Number of PROCs defined in SEPRM
CL := 0;
for *SUBSYS := 1 to 3* do   // the process subsystem index
   for PC *:= 1* to $N_{PC}(SUBSYS)$ do   // the process category index
      for *PROC :=1 to $N_{proc}(SUBSYS, PC)$* do   // the process index
         // Calculate cumulated process capability value
         $CL := CL + PCL_{proc}(SUBSYS, PC, PROC);$

// Derive capability level of the project
  $PCL_{proj} := CL / k;$ // Calculate project capability level according
                   // to Expression 9.25

End   ■

9.4.2 EXPLANATION OF THE SEPRM ALGORITHM

An SEPRM assessment according to Algorithm 9.1 is carried out in four steps:

- **Step 1:** Initialization

- **Step 2:** BPA performance rating

- **Step 3:** Process capability determination

- **Step 4:** Project capability determination

This subsection explains the main functions of Algorithm 9.1 for an SEPRM process assessment.

9.4.2.1 Initialization

This step is designed to specify the number of BPAs defined in SEPRM. For obtaining a detailed configuration of BPAs in the SEPRM process model, reference may be made to Table 9.2 and to Appendix C.

9.4.2.2 BPA Performance Rating

In this step, all BPAs for each process are rated according to Expression 9.20, using the definitions of practice performance scale in Table 9.3. The basic function of this step is to count the total values of the rated BPAs within individual processes.

9.4.2.3 Process Capability Determination

This step first derives the process capability ratings by both the process criteria and the BPA performance criteria according Expressions 9.23 and 9.21, respectively. Next, the capability level of the process is determined by taking the lower of the above results according to Expression 9.22. The qualitative score obtained according to the process criteria, as shown in algorithm Step 3.3, is compensated with 0.9 in order to allow the quantitative BPA score to determine the decimal capability level. In Step 3.4, a process capability profile of an SEPRM assessment is created.

9.4.2.4 Project Process Capability Determination

In the final step, using the aggregation inherent in Expression 9.25, the algorithm derives a process capability level for a software project based on all processes' capability levels derived in algorithm Step 3. The project capability level will be reported with the addition of the process capability profile.

9.4.3 ANALYSIS OF THE SEPRM ALGORITHM

SEPRM assesses each process against each of the six independent capability levels defined by their capability criteria. This approach can avoid the disadvantages of:

- Preassigning and grouping processes into different capability levels such as in CMM and BOOTSTRAP

- Operating too high a complexity in process capability determination such as in ISO/IEC TR 15504

- Requiring universal attributes that should be suitable for all processes, as in ISO/IEC TR 15504.

Reviewing the SEPRM algorithm in Subsection 9.4.1, it may be observed that the algorithm complexity of SEPRM, $c(SEPRM)$, is mainly determined by both the numbers of BPAs (N_{BPA}) and processes (N_{PROC}), which need to be rated individually in an SEPRM assessment according to Algorithm 9.1, Steps 2 and 3, i.e.:

$$c(SEPRM) = O\ (N_{BPA} + N_{PROC})$$
$$= N_{BPA} + 2*N_{PROC} \qquad (9.27)$$

where the unit of the algorithm complexity is "times of BPA/Process ratings."

As given in SEPRM, $N_{BPA}=444$, $N_{PROC}=51$. Thus the total rating cost, or the algorithm complexity, for determining a capability level of project scope in SEPRM is:

$$c(SEPRM) = O\ (N_{BPA} + N_{PROC})$$
$$= N_{BPA} + 2*N_{PROC}$$
$$= 444 + 2*51$$
$$= 546\ [\text{times of BPA/Process ratings}]$$

Interestingly, although the numbers of processes and BPAs of SEPRM have been almost doubled compared with those of ISO/IEC 15504, the algorithm complexity of SEPRM is still reasonably low. This means that SEPRM will be amenable to relatively easy usage by assessors and software development organizations.

There is a trade-off between an algorithm's complexity and the person-days needed for an assessment. Empirical data for relating the algorithm complexity to person-days expended in an SEPRM process assessment will be discussed in Chapter 12.

9.5 A Sample SEPRM Assessment

The capability rating framework and the capability determination algorithm of SEPRM were formally described in Sections 9.3 and 9.4. This section demonstrates how to apply the SEPRM expressions and algorithm to quantitatively determine a sample software development organization's process capability level in SEPRM [Wang at al., 1997d/99h].

9.5.1 BPA PERFORMANCE RATING IN SEPRM

A set of detailed ratings of the 444 BPAs have been listed in Appendix C, where the raw data rating {4, 3, 2, 1} corresponds to the SEPRM BPA rating scale {F(5), L(3), P(2), N(0)}. By referring to Table 9.3, a mapping between the rating scales of the raw data and the SEPRM BPA is defined in Table 9.7.

Table 9.7
Mapping between Raw Data in Assessment onto SEPRM Rating Scale

Raw Data Rating Scale (in Appendix C)	SEPRM BPA Rating Scale	Description in SEPRM
4	5 (F)	Fully adequate
3	3 (L)	Largely adequate
2	1 (P)	Partially adequate
1	0 (N)	Not adequate

Processing the raw data of the BPAs' performance ratings according to Table 9.7 and then applying Expressions 9.20 and 9.21 allows the average performance rating of the BPAs in a process to be derived.

For example, *PROC[1,1,1]*, organization definition, has seven BPAs rated F/F/F/L/F/N/F, respectively, in Appendix C. According to Expressions 9.20 – 9.21, the average rating of capability of the process can be quantitatively calculated below:

$$\overline{PP}(1,1,1) = \frac{1}{m_p} \sum_{i=1}^{m_p} PP(i) \qquad\qquad \text{(by Exp. 9.21)}$$

$$= 1/7 \sum_{i=1}^{7} PP(i) \qquad \text{(data from Appendix C)}$$

$$= \{F+F+F+L+F+N+F\}/\,7 \qquad \text{(data from Appendix C)}$$

$$= \{5+5+5+3+5+0+5\}/7 \qquad \text{(by Table 9.7 and Exp. 9.20)}$$

$$= 28/7$$

$$= 4.0$$

Similarly, all mean ratings of processes can be determined according to Expressions 9.20 – 9.21.

9.5.2 PROCESS CAPABILITY DETERMINATION IN SEPRM

The derived capability levels of the 51 processes according to the process criteria have been checked and shown to always be higher than those by BPA criteria. Therefore, according to Expression 9.24, the capability levels of all processes are directly determined by the average performance ratings of BPAs within the processes. For example, using the data derived above, the capability level of *PROC[1,1,1]* can be aggregated applying Expression 9.24 as follows:

$$PCL_{\text{proc}}[1,1,1] = \overline{PP}(p)$$

$$= \frac{1}{m_p} \sum_{i=1}^{m_p} PP(i)$$

$$= 4.0$$

A summary record of this SEPRM assessment is listed in Table 9.8. Based on the assessment record in Table 9.8, process capability profiles of the three process subsystems in SEPRM can be derived as shown in Figures 9.17 – 9.19.

Table 9.8
Summary Process Capability Rating Record in SEPRM

ID.	Subsystem	Category / Process	Process Capability Level
1	Organization		
1.1		Organization structure processes	
1.1.1		Organization definition	4.0
1.1.2		Project organization	3.3
1.2		Organization processes	
1.2.1		Organization process definition	3.1
1.2.2		Organization process improvement	2.2
1.3		Customer service processes	
1.3.1		Customer relations	3.0
1.3.2		Customer support	3.2
1.3.3		Software/system delivery	4.3
1.3.4		Service evaluation	4.0
2	Development		
2.1		Software engineering methodology processes	
2.1.1		Software engineering modeling	3.1
2.1.2		Reuse methodologies	2.6
2.1.3		Technology innovation	2.1
2.2		Software development processes	
2.2.1		Development process definition	4.5
2.2.2		Requirement analysis	3.4
2.2.3		Design	3.3
2.2.4		Coding	3.4
2.2.5		Module testing	3.3
2.2.6		Integration and system testing	3.1
2.2.7		Maintenance	2.9
2.3		Software engineering infrastructure processes	
2.3.1		Environment	3.0
2.3.2		Facilities	4.2
2.3.3		Development support tools	2.5
2.3.4		Management support tools	2.2
3	Management		
3.1		Software quality assurance (SQA) processes	
3.1.1		SQA process definition	4.1
3.1.2		Requirement review	4.2
3.1.3		Design review	3.0
3.1.4		Code review	2.7
3.1.5		Module testing audit	2.5

3.1.6	Integration and system testing audit	3.7
3.1.7	Maintenance audit	2.0
3.1.8	Audit and inspection	3.7
3.1.9	Peer review	3.2
3.1.10	Defect control	3.8
3.1.11	Subcontractor's quality control	4.2
3.2	Project planning processes	
3.2.1	Project plan	2.3
3.2.2	Project estimation	3.9
3.2.3	Project risk avoidance	2.4
3.2.4	Project quality plan	4.1
3.3	Project management processes	
3.3.1	Process management	2.4
3.3.2	Process tracking	3.7
3.3.3	Configuration management	4.5
3.3.4	Change control	2.8
3.3.5	Process review	3.4
3.3.6	Intergroup coordination	2.6
3.4	Contract and requirement management processes	
3.4.1	Requirement management	3.3
3.4.2	Contract management	4.4
3.4.3	Subcontractor management	3.4
3.4.4	Purchasing management	3.4
3.5	Document management processes	
3.5.1	Documentation	4.0
3.5.2	Process database/library	1.8
3.6	Human resource management processes	
3.6.1	Staff selection and allocation	4.5
3.6.2	Training	3.6

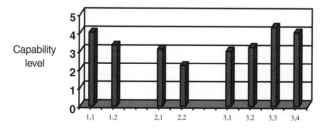

Organization process subsystem

Figure 9.17 Capability profile of organization process subsystem in SEPRM

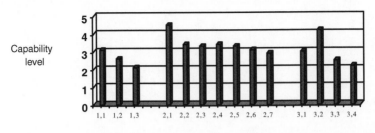

Development process subsystem

Figure 9.18 Capability profile of development process subsystem in SEPRM

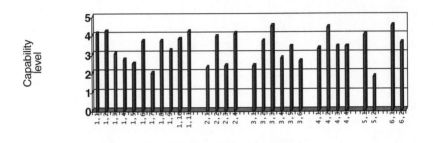

Management process subsystem

Figure 9.19 Capability profile of management process subsystem in SEPRM

9.5.3 PROJECT CAPABILITY DETERMINATION IN SEPRM

A process capability level for a project j, $PCL_{proj}[j]$, in SEPRM has been defined by Expression 9.25. Applying Expression 9.25 to the ratings of the 51 process ratings summarized in Table 9.8, the capability level of the project can be determined as:

$$PCL_{proj}(j) = \frac{1}{k} \sum_{p=1}^{k} PCL_{proc}(p) \qquad \text{(by Expression 9.25)}$$

$$= 1/51 \sum_{p=1}^{51} PCL_{proc}(p) \qquad \text{(data from Table 9.8)}$$

$$= 168.3 / 51 \qquad \text{(data from Table 9.8)}$$

$$= 3.3$$

Thus the software project's process capability assessed is to be at Level 3.3, corresponding to the stable process capability level in SEPRM.

9.6 Applications of SEPRM

In the previous sections we explored the theory behind SEPRM for process system modeling and assessment. This section analyzes the usability of SEPRM in software engineering process system establishment, assessment, and improvement.

9.6.1 SEPRM FOR SOFTWARE PROCESS SYSTEM ESTABLISHMENT

The philosophy of SEPRM is to provide a comprehensive and integrated software engineering process system reference model. SEPRM is a completely implemented paradigm of the unified process system framework established in Part I, and a systematic attempt to solve the issues we discussed in the previous chapters.

In comparative studies of existing process models we have gained an improved understanding of that software process system as a key for organization and implementing successful software engineering. The SEPRM has been developed from deeply investigated theoretical foundations and by industry benchmarking validation. The former was established in Part I, while the latter will be explored in Part III.

SEPRM is a complete 2-D software engineering process system model. Its process model is the most comprehensive, supported by a set of industry benchmarks. Its process capability model is independently operational with a unique process capability scale.

There were arguments as to whether there were enough process models already, and whether the search for modeling new processes and good practices for software engineering had been exhausted. Based on the discussions within Part I and Part II it may be concluded that software engineering is probably one of the most complicated engineering disciplines in the natural sciences and modern industry. Thus, there is a long way to go and SEPRM makes a valid contribution through its unique features and its superset function.

9.6.2 SEPRM FOR SOFTWARE PROCESS SYSTEM ASSESSMENT AND IMPROVEMENT

The conventional approach for process assessment and improvement is models and/or standards-based. With the support of a set of industry benchmarks, SEPRM enables a new approach to benchmark-based process assessment and improvement. In Part V of this book, after benchmarks of software engineering processes and practices are described in Chapter 10, we will demonstrate the new approach to process assessment and improvement.

Another interesting subject is whether and how the capability levels derived by current process models are related with each other. This is a frequently asked question in the software industry. The application of SEPRM in Part III will solve this problem, too.

9.7 Summary

This chapter introduced a formal and rigorous approach to the description of SEPRM. CSP-like process algebra was adopted for presenting the SEPRM process model, and mathematical and algorithmic methods were applied for presenting the SEPRM process capability determination methodology. Using these formal techniques, SEPRM has been systematically described and analyzed by contrasting with the unified process system framework developed in Part I. An empirical case study has been provided for demonstrating the method and approach in conducting an SEPRM assessment.

The basic knowledge structure of this chapter is as follows:

Chapter 9. The SEPRM Model

- General
    - Purposes of this chapter
        - To review the history and background of SEPRM development
        - To describe the SEPRM process model and taxonomy
        - To describe the SEPRM capability model and capability

determination methodology
- To formally describe the SEPRM process model and to algorithmically describe the SEPRM process capability determination method
- To develop an SEPRM algorithm for software process assessment
- To explain how the SEPRM algorithm can be used in process assessment and how its algorithm complexity is estimated
- To demonstrate a case study of a practical SEPRM assessment by using the SEPRM algorithm
- To discuss the usability of SEPRM in process establishment, assessment, and improvement in software engineering

- SEPRM philosophy and background
    - Oriented to explore the entire process domain of software engineering
    - Provides a comprehensive and integrated process reference system model with sound foundations and benchmarked data support
    - Inspired by all current process models and the work within ISO/IEC JTC1/SC7/WG10

- The SEPRM process model
  - Taxonomy of SEPRM process model
    - Process scopes
    - Size of domain of each scope

  - Framework of SEPRM process model
    - Structure of SEPRM process model
    - Definitions of BPAs in SEPRM

  - Formal description of SEPRM process model
    - SEPRM abstract process patterns
    - SEPRM process diagrams
    - Interpretation and illustration of the process algebra expressions

- The SEPRM process assessment model
  - SEPRM process capability model
    - Configuration
      - 3 process subsystems (PSs)

> - 6 process categories (PCs)
> - 51 processes (PROCs)
> - 444 practices (BPAs)
> - BPA rating scale
> - Process rating scale
>
> - SEPRM process capability determination method
>   - Formal description of SEPRM capability determination methodology
>   - Meanings of expressions and their operation
>   - Conformance with the methodology developed in the unified process framework in Part I
>
> - The SEPRM algorithm
>   - Algorithm 9.1: SEPRM process assessment
>   - Explanation of Algorithm 9.1
>   - Relation between Algorithm 9.1 and the capability determination expressions in Section 9.3.2
>   - The SEPRM algorithm complexity and the main factors affecting it
>
> - A sample SEPRM process assessment
>   - Understand assessment data documented in Appendix C
>   - Manual process assessment in SEPRM
>   - Algorithm-based assessment in SEPRM
>   - Interpretation of assessment results
>
> - Usability of SEPRM
>   - A comprehensive process system model identified 51 processes and 444 best practices in software engineering
>   - Model-based process assessment and improvement
>   - Benchmark-based process assessment and improvement
>   - Capability transformation between current process models

Major achievements and issues for further research suggested by this chapter are highlighted below:

- The design philosophy behind SEPRM is to provide a comprehensive and integrated process system reference model, with sound foundations and benchmarked data support, for process-based software engineering. SEPRM is a fully implemented paradigm of the unified process system framework established in Part I, and a systematic attempt to address the issues we discussed in the existing process models.

- The development of SEPRM was based on the great inspiration derived from existing process models and the research in empirical software engineering. From this we have gained improved understanding of the software process system as a key for organization and implementation of successful software engineering.

- Theoretical foundations of SEPRM have been established in Part I. Empirical foundations of SEPRM will be explored in Part III. SEPRM is a complete 2-D software engineering process system model. Its process model is the most comprehensive, which is supported by a set of industry benchmarks. Its process capability model is independently operational with a unique process capability scale.

- SEPRM enables a new approach to benchmark-based process assessment. We have introduced this concept in Chapter 2, and it will be demonstrated in PART III.

- SEPRM enables a derived process capability level to be transformed onto other process models; further, it allows, for the first time, the current process models to relate their capability levels among each other. This will be demonstrated in PART III.

This chapter has established a basis for understanding and analyzing SEPRM as a fully implemented paradigm of the unified software engineering process system framework. Relationships between SEPRM and other process system models will be discussed in Part III of this book. Applications of SEPRM in process-based software engineering and case studies will be provided in Parts IV – VI.

Annotated References

The first version of the SEPRM reference model framework was initially published in 1996 (Wang et al., 1996a). A series of investigations and supporting data benchmarking and validation was reported in (Wang et al., 1997a/b/d/98a/e/99c/e/f/h).

On theoretical foundations of software engineering processes, see:

- Formal methods and formal descriptions of software processes (Dijkstra, 1976; Gries, 1981; Hoare, 1985/95; Milner, 1989; Hayes, 1987; Spivey, 1988; Dawes, 1991; Saeki et al., 1991; Bandinelli, 1992/93; Finkelstein, 1994; and Sutton and Osterweil, 1997).

- Software process (Weinwurm and Zagorski, 1965; Basili, 1980; Aron, 1983; Agresti, 1986; Evans, 1987; Boehm, 1986/94; Gilb, 1988; and Humphrey, 1987/88/89/95/99).

- Process-based software engineering (Barghouti and Krishnamurthy, 1993; Garg and Jazayeri, 1995; Wang et al., 1996a/97a/b/99e), and empirical foundations of the software engineering process (Wang et al., 1998a/99c).

- Foundations of management science
  - Systems theory (SSI, 1950)
  - Operational theory (Fabrycky et al., 1984)
  - Decision theory (Keen and Morton, 1978; Steven, 1980)
  - Organization methods (Radnor et al., 1970; Kolb et al., 1970)
  - Strategic planning (Anthony, 1965, Khaden and Schultzki, 1983; and William, 1991)
  - Management economics (Richardson, 1966)
  - Quality system principles (Shewhart, 1939; Juran, 1962/80/88/89; Crosby, 1979; Deming, 1982a/b, 1986; Imai, 1986; and Buckland et al., 1991).

- Generic views of software engineering (McDermid, 1991; Pressman, 1992/98; Sommerville, 1996; and Pfleeger, 1998).

For comparative analyses of current process models, see Wang et al. (1997a/b/99e). On comparative assessments by using current process models, see Wang et al. (1999h). On benchmarking of software processes and practices, see Wang et al. (1998a/99c).

Questions and Problems

9.1 Explain the roles of a process reference model in process- based software engineering.

9.2 Assuming there are 10 process models, calculate the comparative analysis costs in the approaches of pairwise analysis and reference-model-based analysis, respectively.

9.3 Explain the design philosophy behind the development of SEPRM.

9.4 Using your own words, briefly describe the structure of the SEPRM process model and its taxonomy.

9.5 Use process algebra to derive a formal SEPRM process model based on the process diagrams given in Figures 9.4 – 9.16. (Try not to copy Expressions 9.4 – 9.19 before you finish.)

9.5 Briefly describe the SEPRM process capability model and capability determination methodology using your own words.

9.7 Can you repeat the sample SEPRM assessment based on the data provided in Appendix C and derive the same capability level as that of the example shown in Section 9.5?

9.8 Fill in Appendix C according to the SEPRM model by using the data that you collected in Exs. 5.6, 6.6, 7.6, and 8.6, and provide additional data for any BPAs uncovered.

9.9 Using the result of Ex. 9.8, try to derive your own process capability level in SEPRM according to the methodology presented in this chapter.

9.10 Try to conduct an SEPRM exercise assessment for a software project or organization with which you are familiar and according to the formal approach presented in this chapter.

9.11 Based on Exs 9.9 or 9.10, try to analyze how to improve the process capability by one level and which processes to give priority.

9.12 Try to compare the process profiles of yourself and one of your colleagues based on Ex.9.9, and report the significant differences and their meanings in SEPRM.

9.13 Most of the established software development organizations are currently considered to be located between SEPRM Levels 1 and 3. Observe the SEPRM process model, do you think those organizations could produce reasonably good software? Why?

9.14 Try to organize a small software project with at least three persons. Then do a self-assessment for this project and report your capability level in SEPRM.

9.15 Try to write an SEPRM assessment report for Exercise 9.10 or 9.14 and include the following:

- Purpose(s) of the SEPRM assessment
- The SEPRM model and methodology you adopted
- The input of the SEPRM assessment
- The procedure of the SEPRM assessment
- The output of the SEPRM assessment
- The effort you spend for the SEPRM assessment
- Experience you gained in the SEPRM assessment
- Conclusions

9.16 Try to write an SEPRM process improvement plan based on the assessment report developed in Ex. 9.15. In the process improvement plan, include the following:

- Purpose(s) of the SEPRM process improvement plan
- Brief introduction of the SEPRM assessment results
- Analyze strengths of the organization's process capability according to SEPRM
- Analyze weaknesses of the organization's process capability according to SEPRM
- Recommend a process improvement plan to address the process weaknesses or for moving to a higher SEPRM capability level

- Explain the benefit of implementing this process improvement plan and how well your plan will meet the organization's business goal
- Estimate the costs of this process improvement effort
- Predict the risks for executing the process improvement plan that you have suggested
- Conclusions

9.17 What is the usage of SEPRM in software engineering process establishment, assessment, and improvement?

PART III

SOFTWARE ENGINEERING PROCESS SYSTEM ANALYSIS

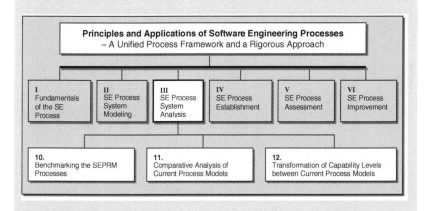

One of the most frequently-asked questions in the software industry seeks to identify the interrelationships between current process models. In Part II we presented formal views on individual process models. In Part III the intention is to explore the interrelationships between them via quantitative analysis, and to investigate the practical foundations of the software engineering process via benchmarking.

The knowledge structure of this part is as follows:

- Chapter 10. Benchmarking the SEPRM Processes

- Chapter 11. Comparative Analysis of Current Process Models

- Chapter 12. Transformation of Capability Levels between Current Process Models

Chapter 10 seeks to establish a set of characteristic attributes for software engineering processes via a series of worldwide industry surveys. A basic argument in the process modeling and analysis field was that the processes and the practices of current process models had been selected empirically, and their validation in practice and effectiveness was virtually absent in the literature. To deal with this issue, SEPRM is employed as an overarching process model with a superset of BPAs compatible with existing models such as CMM, ISO 9001, BOOTSTRAP, and ISO/IEC TR 15504. In total, 51 processes and 444 BPAs are quantitatively characterized with attributes of the mean weighted importance and the ratios of significance, of practice, and of effectiveness and usage.

Chapter 11 studies the interrelationships of current process models in the process dimension. The compatibility and correlation between current process models are quantitatively analyzed and contrasted in a rigorous way. The relational properties among current process models are mutually analyzed by taking the viewpoint of each with respect to each of the others. This chapter fulfills a prerequisite to explore process capability transformation in the following chapter.

Chapter 12 analyzes the interrelationships between the capability levels of current process models, and explores how a given capability level in one model may be related to another quantitatively. This goal is achieved through SEPRM as an overarching process model and transformable algorithm in process capability determination. Test cases are designed to analyze the robustness of current process models in process assessment and capability determination. Empirical data for estimation of assessment efforts by different process models are provided as references.

This part adopts a rigorous and quantitative approach in analyzing the characteristic attributes of process, the compatibility and correlation of process models, and the interrelationships and transformability of capability levels in different process models. Objective views on features, orientations, and relationships of current process models are obtained based on the analyses.

Chapter 10

BENCHMARKING THE SEPRM PROCESSES

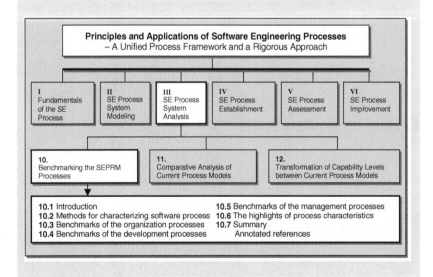

Principles and Applications of Software Engineering Processes
– A Unified Process Framework and a Rigorous Approach

| I Fundamentals of the SE Process | II SE Process System Modeling | III SE Process System Analysis | IV SE Process Establishment | V SE Process Assessment | VI SE Process Improvement |

10. Benchmarking the SEPRM Processes

11. Comparative Analysis of Current Process Models

12. Transformation of Capability Levels between Current Process Models

10.1 Introduction
10.2 Methods for characterizing software process
10.3 Benchmarks of the organization processes
10.4 Benchmarks of the development processes
10.5 Benchmarks of the management processes
10.6 The highlights of process characteristics
10.7 Summary
Annotated references

This chapter describes characteristic attributes of BPAs and characteristic curves of processes modeled in SEPRM using the findings from a series of worldwide surveys. A set of benchmarks for 444 BPAs and 51 processes will be derived in order to characterize the BPAs and processes by the quantitative attributes: mean weighted importance, and the ratios of significance, practice, and effectiveness. In doing this, the intention is to illustrate the general means by which any process model might be validated. Because of the complexity and the large number of issues to be looked at, SEPRM is used as a vehicle demonstrating all of the aspects that need to be covered when creating confidence in a model's worth and validity.

The objectives of this chapter are as follows:

- To establish a foundation of practice for the validation, calibration, and benchmarking of software process models

- To seek statistical criteria for selecting processes and BPAs in process system modeling

- To validate the BPAs and processes modeled in SEPRM

- To enable a new approach to benchmark-based process assessment and improvement

- To characterize a superset of processes and BPAs in order to provide reference points for existing process models and future new process models

10.1 Introduction

In Part I the theoretical foundations of the unified software engineering process framework were developed. This chapter attempts to establish the practical foundations of process models with a set of characteristic attributes of processes and BPAs supported by a series of industry surveys.

A basic argument in process modeling and analysis is that, for the most part, the processes and BPAs of current process models have been selected empirically, and that the validation of the BPAs in practice has not been carried out. To deal with this issue, the SEPRM is employed as an overarching process model with a superset of BPAs compatible with existing models such as CMM, ISO 9001, BOOTSTRAP, and ISO/IEC TR 15504. A series of surveys has been designed and carried out worldwide in order to seek practical evaluations of BPAs and processes in the software industry, and to quantitatively characterize them for software engineering process modeling and analysis [Wang et al., 1998a/99c].

In this chapter a superset of processes and BPAs will be characterized and validated. Detailed survey findings are documented in Appendix D. Benchmarks for the software engineering process system modeled by SEPRM will be derived. The 444 BPAs and 51 processes in the SEPRM model are thus supported by quantitative attributes. Via the mapping mechanism documented in Appendix C and described in Chapter 11, the processes and BPAs of the other process models can also be characterized indirectly by using these benchmarks.

The criteria for including processes and BPAs in a software engineering process model were developed in Chapter 2. Four attributes, the mean weighted importance and the ratios of significance, practice, and effectiveness, have been used to quantitatively characterize a BPA and a software process. This chapter establishes a set of benchmarks for these characteristic attributes of software processes.

By using the characteristic attribute criteria, the SEPRM model is validated by the supporting data, and its credibility is extended so that the SEPRM can be used as a benchmark-based as well as a model-based process assessment model. Applying the validated SEPRM software process, a software development organization can be assessed quantitatively, and process improvement opportunities can be identified and prioritized based on the significance and effectiveness of the BPAs.

In the remaining part of this chapter, Section 10.2 describes the methods for characterizing BPAs and processes, and for plotting and illustrating process benchmarks. Sections 10.3 through 10.5 report the facts of BPAs and characteristic curves of processes in the three process subsystems of SEPRM found in the worldwide surveys. Section 10.6 highlights the findings and characteristics of BPAs and processes in the derived benchmarks.

10.2 Methods for Characterizing Software Process

This section describes how to quantitatively characterize software engineering processes and BPAs by statistical data obtained from industry surveys. Attributes are used to characterize BPAs, and characteristic curves are used to describe processes.

10.2.1 CHARACTERIZING BPAs BY ATTRIBUTES

The SEPRM survey developed a set of multiple attribute questionnaires for all BPAs and processes, enabling information to be collected in a domain determined by a combination of attributes of significance, practice, and effectiveness in application.

The survey questionnaire listed the BPAs and asked an organization to give an importance weighting for each BPA (on a scale of 0 to 5), to state whether or not they applied the BPA in practice, and whether or not they thought it was effective in their processes.

Using the raw data, benchmarked attributes for each BPA were derived. Data analysis and processing methods of benchmarking are formally described in Section 2.5. For each BPA, the mean weighted importance; the ratios of significance, practice, and effectiveness; and the characteristic value in application were defined by Definitions 2.40 – 2.44 and Expressions 2.11 – 2.20.

Quantitative analysis results form a set of benchmarks for the attributes of the BPAs. The benchmarks are listed in Appendix D that show, for each BPA, the mean importance weighting (W), the percentage of organizations rating the BPA highly (i.e., weighting ≥ 3) significant (r_w), the percentage of organizations that applied the BPA (r_p) in practice, and the percentage that rated it as effective (r_e) in process. The final column φ, the characteristic value, uses a combination of these three percentages to provide an integrated indication of the BPA's usage. The higher the value of φ, the more important and effective the BPA in practice, and vice versa. Therefore, φ can be used to index the importance and effectiveness of a BPA in practice.

10.2.2 BENCHMARKING SOFTWARE PROCESSES BY CHARACTERISTIC CURVES

In searching for a way to interpret the industry survey data for process benchmarking, it was found that the software engineering processes can be described by a set of characteristic curves. Based on the benchmarked curves, the most or least significant, practical, and effective BPA in each process can be determined. The gaps between the practice curve and the significant, effective curves, which indicate where are the process improvement opportunities exist, can also be identified. Further, if a software development organization plots its data onto the characteristic curves of a process, the organization's strengths and weaknesses with regard to the software industry average practices in software engineering are evident. Thus, process improvement priorities and aims for gaining a competitive position among peers can be identified quantitatively.

10.2.3 PLOT AND ILLUSTRATION OF PROCESS BENCHMARKS

Detailed characteristic curves of processes will be plotted and illustrated in the following sections using the data documented in Appendix D. In Appendix D there are two index numbers, the series number (No.), and the category number (CatNo.) for each BPA. The category number, CatNo, consists of four digits for indexing a BPA as follows:

$$CatNo. \triangleq Subsys.Category.Process.Practice \qquad (10.1)$$

For instance, $BPA_{1.1.1.1}$ means the first practice located in Subsystem 1, Category 1, and Process 1 – "define organization structure."

The conventions used in plot and illustration of the characteristic curves of processes are explained as follows:

- The square-plotted curve represents the ratio of significance (r_w).

- The triangle-plotted curve represents the ratio of practice (r_p).

- The cross-plotted curve represents the ratio of effectiveness (r_e).

- The diamond-plotted curve represents the mean weighted importance of significance (W). W is scaled $0 - 5$, while it is multiplied by 10 for plotting in proper scale.

- In each process characteristic curve, the last two indexes of a *CatNo, Process.Practice*, will be provided for referring a BPA to the definition and benchmark in Appendix D.

The same plotting and identification convention applies to all following sections for characterizing a set of 444 BPAs in 3 subsystems, 12 categories, and 51 processes as modeled in SEPRM.

10.3 Benchmarks of the Organization Processes

The structure of the software engineering organization process subsystem of SEPRM is modeled as shown in Table 10.1. Detailed benchmarks for the organization process subsystems are listed in Appendix D.

Table 10.1
Structure of the Organization Process Subsystem

CatNo	Process Category	Process	BPA
1.1	Organization structure	2	13
1.1.1		Organization definition	7
1.1.2		Project organization	6
1.2	Organization process	2	26
1.2.1		Organization process definition	15
1.2.2		Organization process improvement	11
1.3	Customer services	4	42
1.3.1		Customer relations	13
1.3.2		Customer support	12
1.3.3		Software and system delivery	11
1.3.4		Service evaluation	6
Total	3	8	81

10.3.1 BENCHMARKS OF THE ORGANIZATION STRUCTURE PROCESS CATEGORY

This subsection demonstrates the derived benchmarks of the organization structure process category based on the data listed in Appendix D, BPA No. 1 – 13.

10.3.1.1 The Organization Definition Process

Characteristic curves of the organization definition process are derived in Figure 10.1. The BPAs 1.1 – 1.7 are defined in Appendix D, CatNo 1.1.1.1 – 1.1.1.7.

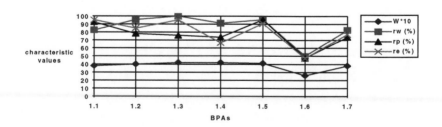

Figure 10.1 Characteristic curves of the organization definition process

10.3.1.2 The Project Organization Process

Characteristic curves of the project organization process are derived in Figure 10.2. The BPAs 2.1 – 2.6 are defined in Appendix D, CatNo 1.1.2.1 – 1.1.2.6.

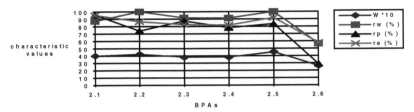

Figure 10.2 Characteristic curves of the project organization process

10.3.2 BENCHMARKS OF THE ORGANIZATION PROCESS CATEGORY

This subsection demonstrates the derived benchmarks of the organization process category based on the data listed in Appendix D, BPA No.14 – 39.

10.3.2.1 The Organization Process Definition

Characteristic curves of the organization process definition are derived in Figure 10.3. The BPAs 1.1 – 1.15 are defined in Appendix D, CatNo 1.2.1.1 – 1.2.1.15.

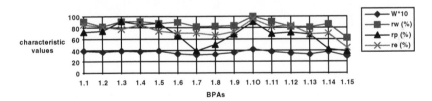

Figure 10.3 Characteristic curves of the organization process definition

10.3.2.2 The Organization Process Improvement

Characteristic curves of the organization process improvement are derived in Figure 10.4. The BPAs 2.1 – 2.11 are defined in Appendix D, CatNo 1.2.2.1 – 1.2.2.11.

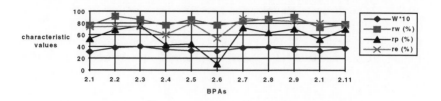

Figure 10.4 Characteristic curves of the organization process improvement

10.3.3 BENCHMARKS OF THE CUSTOMER SERVICE PROCESS CATEGORY

This subsection demonstrates the derived benchmarks of the customer service process category based on the data listed in Appendix D, BPA No. 40 – 81.

10.3.3.1 The Customer Relations Process

Characteristic curves of the customer relations process are derived in Figure 10.5. The BPAs 1.1 – 1.13 are defined in Appendix D, CatNo 1.3.1.1 – 1.3.1.13.

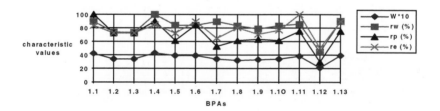

Figure 10.5 Characteristic curves of the customer relations process

10.3.3.2 The Customer Support Process

Characteristic curves of the customer support process are derived in Figure 10.6. The BPAs 2.1 – 2.12 are defined in Appendix D, CatNo 1.3.2.1 – 1.3.2.12.

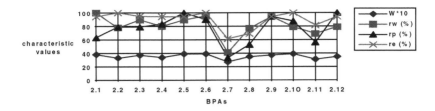

Figure 10.6 Characteristic curves of the customer support process

10.3.3.3 The Software/System Delivery Process

Characteristic curves of the software/system delivery process are derived in Figure 10.7. The BPAs 3.1 – 3.11 are defined in Appendix D, CatNo 1.3.3.1 – 1.3.3.11.

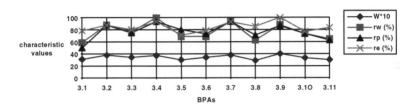

Figure 10.7 Characteristic curves of the software/system delivery process

10.3.3.4 The Service Evaluation Process

Characteristic curves of the service evaluation process are derived in Figure 10.8. The BPAs 4.1 – 4.6 are defined in Appendix D, CatNo 1.3.4.1 – 1.3.4.6.

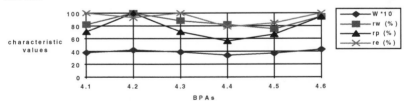

Figure 10.8 Characteristic curves of the service evaluation process

10.3.4 GENERAL CHARACTERISTICS OF THE ORGANIZATION PROCESS SUBSYSTEM

A general view of characteristics of the 81 BPAs in the 3 organization categories and 8 processes is shown in Table 10.2 and Figure 10.9.

Table 10.2
Statistical Characteristics of the Organization Process Subsystem

BPA Characteristics	Weight	No. of BPAs	Relative Number of BPAs (%)
Mean weighted importance (W)	5	0	0
	4	14	17.3
	3	62	76.5
	2	5	6.2
	1	0	0
	0	0	0
Ratio of significance (r_w)	E	24	29.6
	V	46	56.8
	F	9	11.1
	N	2	2.5
Ratio of practice (r_p)	E	15	18.5
	V	34	42.0
	F	22	27.2
	N	10	12.3
Ratio of effectiveness (r_e)	E	23	28.4
	V	46	56.8
	F	10	12.3
	N	2	2.5

Note: E - Extremely ($\geq 90\%$), V - very (70-89%), F - fairly (50-69%), and N - not ($<50\%$)

- For the mean weighted importance of BPAs in the software organization processes, 93.8% of the BPAs are heavily weighted, with 76.5% at weight scale 3.0 – 3.99 and 17.3% at weight scale 4.0 – 4.99. There are only 6.2% BPAs perceived to be not very important.

- For the ratio of significance of BPAs, 29.6% of the BPAs are weighted extremely significant, 56.8% are very significant, 11.1% are fairly significant, and only 2.5% are not significant.

- For the ratio of practice of BPAs, 18.5% BPAs have extremely high application rate, 42.0% BPAs have very high application rate, and 27.2% have fairly high application rate. But it is noteworthy that there are 12.3% BPAs which were perceived to be unused.

- For the ratio of effectiveness of BPAs, 28.4% of the BPAs are weighted extremely effective, 56.8% are very effective, and 12.3% are fairly effective. Only 2.5% BPAs in the set are found not effective.

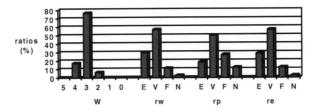

Figure 10.9 Overview of characteristics of the organization processes

10.4 Benchmarks of the Development Processes

The structure of the software development process subsystem of SEPRM is modeled as shown in Table 10.3. Detailed benchmarks for the development process subsystems are listed in Appendix D.

Table 10.3
Structure of the Software Development Process Subsystem

CatNo	Process Category	Process	BPA
2.1	Software engineering methodologies	3	23
2.1.1		Software engineering modeling	9
2.1.2		Reuse methodologies	7
2.1.3		Technology innovation	7
2.2	Software development processes	7	60
2.2.1		Development process definition	12
2.2.2		Requirement analysis	8
2.2.3		Design	9
2.2.4		Coding	8
2.2.5		Module testing	6
2.2.6		Integration and system testing	7
2.2.7		Maintenance	10
2.3	Software development	4	32

	environment		
2.3.1		Environment	7
2.3.2		Facilities	15
2.3.3		Development support tools	4
2.3.4		Management support tools	6
Total	3	14	115

10.4.1 BENCHMARKS OF THE SOFTWARE ENGINEERING METHODOLOGY PROCESS CATEGORY

This subsection demonstrates the derived benchmarks of the software engineering methodology process category based on the data listed in Appendix D, BPA No. 82 – 104.

10.4.1.1 The Software Engineering Modeling Process

Characteristic curves of the software engineering modeling process are derived in Figure 10.10. The BPAs 1.1 – 1.9 are defined in Appendix D, CatNo 2.1.1.1 – 2.1.1.9.

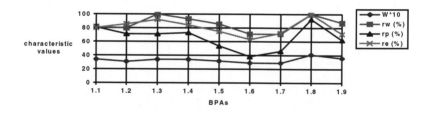

Figure 10.10 Characteristic curves of the software engineering modeling process

10.4.1.2 The Reuse Methodologies Process

Characteristic curves of the reuse methodologies process are derived in Figure 10.11. The BPAs 2.1 – 2.7 are defined in Appendix D, CatNo 2.1.2.1 – 2.1.2.7.

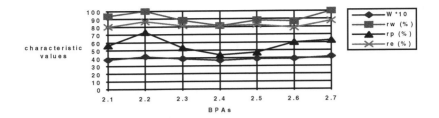

Figure 10.11 Characteristic curves of the reuse methodologies process

9.4.1.3 The Technology Innovation Process

Characteristic curves of the technology innovation process are derived in Figure 10.12. The BPAs 3.1 – 3.7 are defined in Appendix D, CatNo 2.1.3.1 – 2.1.3.7.

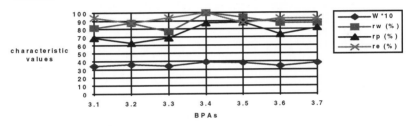

Figure 10.12 Characteristic curves of the technology innovation process

10.4.2 BENCHMARKS OF THE SOFTWARE DEVELOPMENT PROCESS CATEGORY

This subsection demonstrates the derived benchmarks of the software development process category based on the data listed in Appendix D, BPA No. 105 – 164.

10.4.2.1 The Development Process Definition

Characteristic curves of the development process definition are derived in Figure 10.13. The BPAs 1.1 – 1.12 are defined in Appendix D, CatNo 2.2.1.1 – 2.2.1.12.

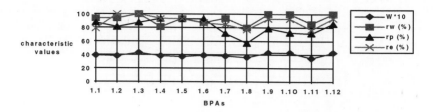

Figure 10.13 Characteristic curves of the development definition process

10.4.2.2 The Requirement Analysis Process

Characteristic curves of the requirement analysis process are derived in Figure 10.14. The BPAs 2.1 – 2.8 are defined in Appendix D, CatNo 2.2.2.1 – 2.2.2.8.

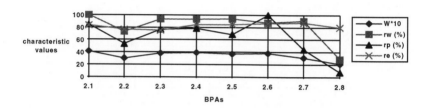

Figure 10.14 Characteristic curves of the requirement analysis process

10.4.2.3 The Design Process

Characteristic curves of the design process are derived in Figure 10.15. The BPAs 3.1 – 3.9 are defined in Appendix D, CatNo 2.2.3.1 – 2.2.3.9.

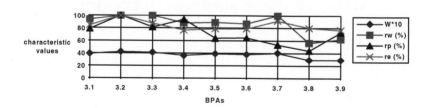

Figure 10.15 Characteristic curves of the design process

10.4.2.4 The Coding Process

Characteristic curves of the coding process are derived in Figure 10.16. The BPAs 4.1 – 4.8 are defined in Appendix D, CatNo 2.2.4.1 – 2.2.4.8.

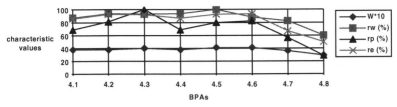

Figure 10.16 Characteristic curves of the coding process

10.4.2.5 The Module Testing Process

Characteristic curves of the module testing process are derived in Figure 10.17. The BPAs 5.1 – 5.6 are defined in Appendix D, CatNo 2.2.5.1 – 2.2.5.6.

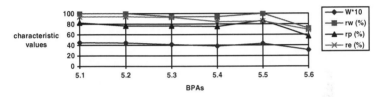

Figure 10.17 Characteristic curves of the module testing process

10.4.2.6 The Integration and System Testing Process

Characteristic curves of the integration and system testing process are derived in Figure 10.18. The BPAs 6.1 – 6.7 are defined in Appendix D, CatNo 2.2.6.1 – 2.2.6.7.

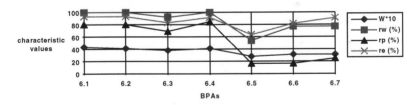

Figure 10.18 Characteristic curves of the integration and system testing process

10.4.2.7 The Maintenance Process

Characteristic curves of the maintenance process are derived in Figure 10.19. The BPAs 7.1 – 7.10 are defined in Appendix D, CatNo 2.2.7.1 – 2.2.7.10.

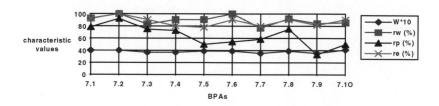

Figure 10.19 Characteristic curves of the maintenance process

10.4.3 BENCHMARKS OF THE SOFTWARE DEVELOPMENT ENVIRONMENT PROCESS CATEGORY

This subsection demonstrates the derived benchmarks of the software development environment process category based on the data listed in Appendix D, BPA No. 165 – 196.

10.4.3.1 The Environment Process

Characteristic curves of the environment process are derived in Figure 10.20. The BPAs 1.1 – 1.7 are defined in Appendix D, CatNo 2.3.1.1 – 2.3.1.7.

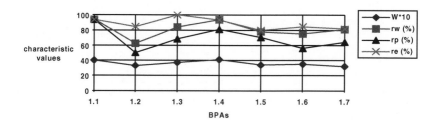

Figure 10.20 Characteristic curves of the environment process

10.4.3.2 The Facilities Process

Characteristic curves of the facilities process are derived in Figure 10.21. The BPAs 2.1 – 2.15 are defined in Appendix D, CatNo 2.3.2.1 – 2.3.2.15.

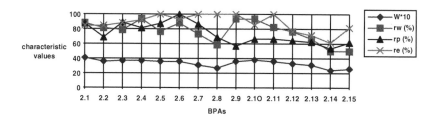

Figure 10.21 Characteristic curves of the facilities process

10.4.3.3 The Development Support Tools Process

Characteristic curves of the development support tools process are derived in Figure 10.22. The BPAs 3.1 – 3.4 are defined in Appendix D, CatNo 2.3.3.1 – 2.3.3.4.

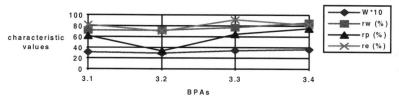

Figure 10.22 Characteristic curves of the development support tools process

10.4.3.4 The Management Support Tools Process

Characteristic curves of the management support tools process are derived in Figure 10.23. The BPAs 4.1 – 4.6 are defined in Appendix D, CatNo 2.3.4.1 – 2.3.4.6.

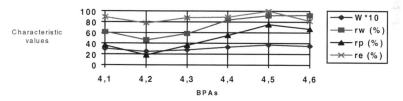

Figure 10.23 Characteristic curves of the management support tools process

10.4.4 GENERAL CHARACTERISTICS OF THE DEVELOPMENT PROCESS SUBSYSTEM

A general view of benchmarks of the 115 BPAs in the 3 development categories and 14 processes is shown in Table 10.4 and Figure 10.2.

Table 10.4
Statistical Characteristics of the Development Process Subsystem

BPA Characteristics	Weight	No. of BPAs	Relative Number of BPAs (%)
Mean weighted importance (W)	5	0	0
	4	27	23.5
	3	75	65.2
	2	13	11.3
	1	0	0
	0	0	0
Ratio of significance (r$_w$)	E	51	44.3
	V	51	44.3
	F	11	9.7
	N	2	1.7
Ratio of practice (r$_p$)	E	11	9.6
	V	47	40.9
	F	41	35.6
	N	16	13.9
Ratio of effectiveness (r$_e$)	E	45	39.1
	V	64	55.7
	F	6	5.2
	N	0	0

Note: E - Extremely (≥90%), V - very (70-89%), F - fairly (50-69%), and N - not (<50%)

- For the mean weighted importance of BPAs in the software development processes, 88.7% of the BPAs are heavily weighted with 65.2% at weight scale 3.0 – 3.99 and 23.5% at weight scale 4.0 – 4.99. Only 11.3% BPAs were perceived to be not very important.

- For the ratio of significance of BPAs, 44.3% of the BPAs are weighted extremely significant, 44.3% are very significant, 9.6% are fairly significant, and only 1.7% are not significant.

- For the ratio of practice of BPAs, 9.6% BPAs have extremely high application rate, 40.9% BPAs have very high application rate, and 35.6% have fairly high application rate. There are 13.9% BPAs perceived to be unused.

- For the ratio of effectiveness of BPAs, 39.1% of the BPAs are weighted extremely effective, 55.7% are very effective, and 5.2% are fairly effective. No BPA in the set is found not effective.

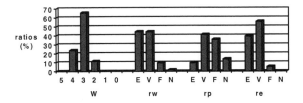

Figure 10.24 Overview of survey findings on the development processes

10.5 Benchmarks of the Management Processes

The structure of the software engineering management process subsystem of SEPRM is modeled as shown in Table 10.5. Detailed benchmarks for the management process subsystem are listed in Appendix D.

Table 10.5
Structure of the Software Engineering Management Process Subsystem

Category No.	Process Category	Process	BPA
3.1	Software quality assurance	11	78
3.1.1		SQA procedure definition	17
3.1.2		Requirements review	5
3.1.3		Design review	4
3.1.4		Code review	3
3.1.5		Module and integration testing	5
3.1.6		Acceptance testing	5
3.1.7		Maintenance audit	8
3.1.8		Internal audit and inspection	6
3.1.9		Peer reviews	10
3.1.10		Defect control	10
3.1.11		Subcontractor's quality control	5
3.2	Project planning	4	45
3.2.1		Project plan	20
3.2.2		Project estimation	7

3.2.3		Project risk avoidance	11
3.2.4		Project quality plan	7
3.3	Project management 6		55
3.3.1		Process management	8
3.3.2		Process tracking	15
3.3.3		Configuration management	8
3.3.4		Change control	9
3.3.5		Process review	8
3.3.6		Intergroup coordination	7
3.4	Contract and requirement management 4		42
3.4.1		Requirement management	12
3.4.2		Contract management	7
3.4.3		Subcontractor management	14
3.4.4		Purchasing management	9
3.5	Document management 2		17
3.5.1		Documentation	11
3.5.2		Process database/library	6
3.6	Human resource management 2		11
3.6.1		Staff selection/allocation	4
3.6.2		Training	7
Total	6	29	248

10.5.1 BENCHMARKS OF THE SOFTWARE QUALITY ASSURANCE PROCESS CATEGORY

This subsection demonstrates the derived benchmarks of the software quality assurance process category based on the data listed in Appendix D, BPA No. 197 – 274.

10.5.1.1 The SQA Procedure Definition Process

Characteristic curves of the SQA procedure definition process are derived in Figure 10.25. The BPAs 1.1 – 1.17 are defined in Appendix D, CatNo 3.1.1.1 – 3.1.1.17.

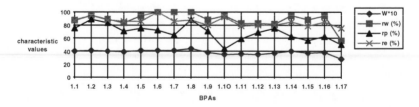

Figure 10.25 Characteristic curves of the SQA procedure definition process

10.5.1.2 The Requirement Review Process

Characteristic curves of the requirement review process are derived in Figure 10.26. The BPAs 2.1 – 2.5 are defined in Appendix D, CatNo 3.1.2.1 – 3.1.2.5.

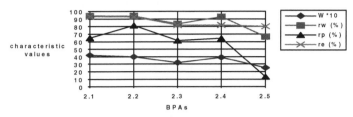

Figure 10.26 Characteristic curves of the requirement review process

10.5.1.3 The Design Review Process

Characteristic curves of the design review process are derived in Figure 10.27. The BPAs 3.1 – 3.4 are defined in Appendix D, CatNo 3.1.3.1 – 3.1.3.4.

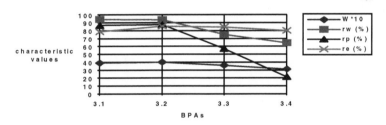

Figure 10.27 Characteristic curves of the design review process

10.5.1.4 The Code Review Process

Characteristic curves of the code review process are derived in Figure 10.28. The BPAs 4.1 – 4.3 are defined in Appendix D, CatNo 3.1.4.1 – 3.1.4.3.

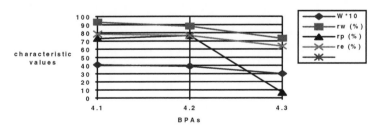

Figure 10.28 Characteristic curves of the code review process

10.5.1.5 The Module Testing Audit Process

Characteristic curves of the module testing audit process are derived in Figure 10.29. The BPAs 5.1 – 5.4 are defined in Appendix D, CatNo 3.1.5.1 – 3.1.5.4.

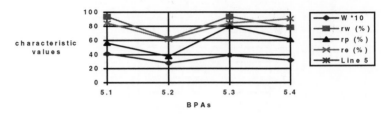

Figure 10.29 Characteristic curves of the module testing audit process

10.5.1.6 The Integration and System Testing Audit Process

Characteristic curves of the integration and system testing audit process are illustrated in Figure 10.30. The BPAs 6.1 – 6.6 are defined in Appendix D, CatNo 3.1.6.1 – 3.1.6.6.

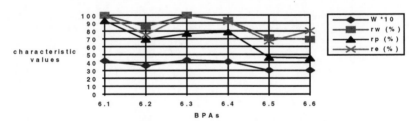

Figure 10.30 Characteristic curves of the integration and system testing process

10.5.1.7 The Maintenance Audit Process

Characteristic curves of the maintenance audit process are derived in Figure 10.31. The BPAs 7.1 – 7.8 are defined in Appendix D, CatNo 3.1.7.1 – 3.1.7.8.

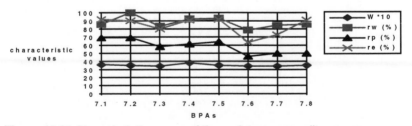

Figure 10.31 Characteristic curves of the maintenance audit process

10.5.1.8 The Audit and Inspection Process

Characteristic curves of the audit and inspection process are derived in Figure 10.32. The BPAs 8.1 – 8.6 are defined in Appendix D, CatNo 3.1.8.1 – 3.1.8.6.

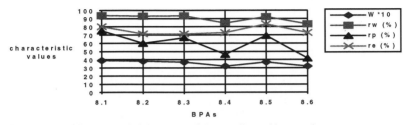

Figure 10.32 Characteristic curves of the audit and inspection process

10.5.1.9 The Peer Review Process

Characteristic curves of the peer review process are derived in Figure 10.33. The BPAs 9.1 – 9.10 are defined in Appendix D, CatNo 3.1.9.1 – 3.1.9.10.

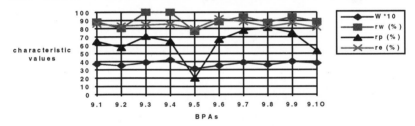

Figure 10.33 Characteristic curves of the peer review process

10.5.1.10 The Defect Control Process

Characteristic curves of the defect control process are derived in Figure 10.34. The BPAs 10.1 – 10.10 are defined in Appendix D, CatNo 3.1.10.1 – 3.1.10.10.

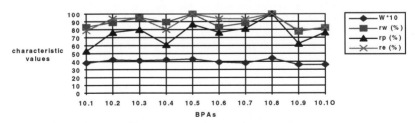

Figure 10.34 Characteristic curves of the defect control process

10.5.1.11 The Subcontractor's Quality Control Process

Characteristic curves of the subcontractor's quality control process are derived in Figure 10.35. The BPAs 11.1 – 11.5 are defined in Appendix D, CatNo 3.1.11.1 – 3.1.11.5.

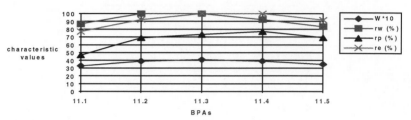

Figure 10.35 Characteristic curves of the subcontractor's quality control process

10.5.2 BENCHMARKS OF THE PROJECT PLANNING PROCESS CATEGORY

This subsection demonstrates the derived benchmarks of the project planning process category based on the data listed in Appendix D, BPA No. 275 – 319.

10.5.2.1 The General Project Plan Process

Characteristic curves of the general project plan process are derived in Figure 10.36. The BPAs 1.1 – 1.20 are defined in Appendix D, CatNo 3.2.1.1 – 3.2.1.20.

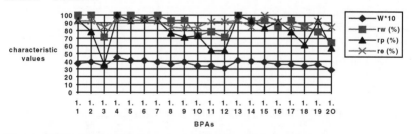

Figure 10.36 Characteristic curves of the general plan process

10.5.2.2 The Project Estimation Process

Characteristic curves of the project estimation process are derived in Figure 10.37. The BPAs 2.1 – 2.7 are defined in Appendix D, CatNo 3.2.2.1 – 3.2.2.7.

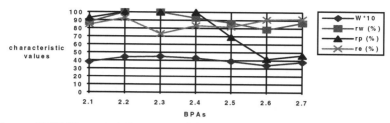

Figure 10.37 Characteristic curves of the project estimation process

10.5.2.3 The Project Risk Avoidance Process

Characteristic curves of the project risk avoidance process are derived in Figure 10.38. The BPAs 3.1 – 3.11 are defined in Appendix D, CatNo 3.2.3.1 – 3.2.3.11.

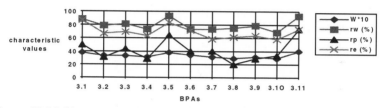

Figure 10.38 Characteristic curves of the project risk avoidance process

10.5.2.4 The Project Quality Plan Process

Characteristic curves of the project quality plan process are derived in Figure 10.39. The BPAs 4.1 – 4.7 are defined in Appendix D, CatNo 3.2.4.1 – 3.2.4.7.

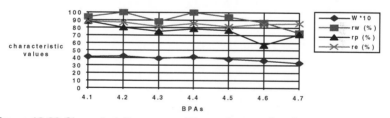

Figure 10.39 Characteristic curves of the project quality plan process

10.5.3 BENCHMARKS OF THE PROJECT MANAGEMENT PROCESS CATEGORY

This subsection demonstrates the derived benchmarks of the project management process category based on the data listed in Appendix D, BPA No. 320 – 347.

10.5.3.1 Process Management

Characteristic curves of the process-management process are derived in Figure 10.40. The BPAs 1.1 – 1.8 are defined in Appendix D, CatNo 3.3.1.1 – 3.3.1.8.

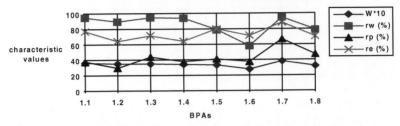

Figure 10.40 Characteristic curves of the process-management process

10.5.3.2 Process Tracking

Characteristic curves of the process-tracking process are derived in Figure 10.41. The BPAs 2.1 – 2.15 are defined in Appendix D, CatNo 3.3.2.1. – 3.3.2.15.

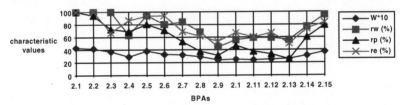

Figure 10.41 Characteristic curves of the process-tracking process

10.5.3.3 The Configuration Management Process

Characteristic curves of the configuration management process are derived in Figure 10.42. The BPAs 3.1 – 3.8 are defined in Appendix D, CatNo 3.3.3.1 – 3.3.3.8.

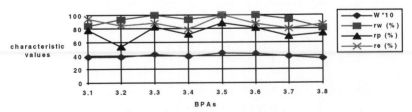

Figure 10.42 Characteristic curves of the configuration management process

10.5.3.4 The Change Control Process

Characteristic curves of the change control process are illustrated in Figure 10.43. The BPAs 4.1 – 4.9 are defined in Appendix D, CatNo 3.3.4.1 – 3.3.4.9.

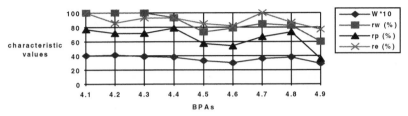

Figure 10.43 Characteristic curves of the change control process

10.5.3.5 Process Review

Characteristic curves of the process review process are derived in Figure 10.44. The BPAs 5.1 – 5.8 are defined in Appendix D, CatNo 3.3.5.1. – 3.3.5.8.

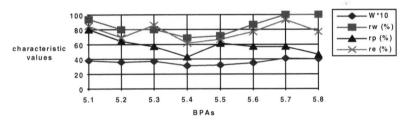

Figure 10.44 Characteristic curves of the process review process

10.5.3.6 The Intergroup Coordination Process

Characteristic curves of the intergroup coordination process are derived in Figure 10.45. The BPAs 6.1 – 6.7 are defined in Appendix D, CatNo 3.3.6.1. – 3.3.6.7.

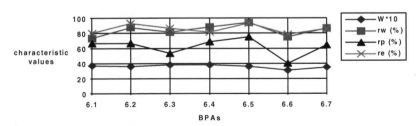

Figure 10.45 Characteristic curves of the intergroup coordination process

10.5.4 BENCHMARKS OF THE CONTRACT AND REQUIREMENT MANAGEMENT PROCESS CATEGORY

This subsection demonstrates the derived benchmarks of the contract and requirement management process category based on the data listed in Appendix D, BPA No. 375 – 416.

10.5.4.1 The Requirement Management Process

Characteristic curves of the requirement management process are derived in Figure 10.46. The BPAs 1.1 – 1.12 are defined in Appendix D, CatNo 3.4.1.1 – 3.4.1.12.

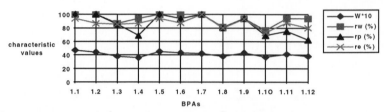

Figure 10.46 Characteristic curves of the requirement management process

10.5.4.2 The Contract Management Process

Characteristic curves of the contract management process are derived in Figure 10.47. The BPAs 2.1 – 2.7 are defined in Appendix D, CatNo 3.4.2.1 – 3.4.2.7.

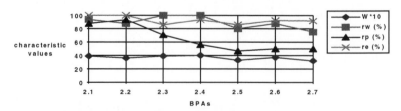

Figure 10.47 Characteristic curves of the contract management process

10.5.4.3 The Subcontractor Management Process

Characteristic curves of the subcontractor management process are derived in Figure 10.48. The BPAs 3.1 – 3.14 are defined in Appendix D, CatNo 3.4.3.1 – 3.4.3.14.

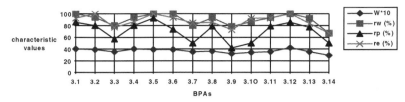

Figure 10.48 Characteristic curves of the subcontractor management process

10.5.4.4 The Purchasing Management Process

Characteristic curves of the purchasing management process are derived in Figure 10.49. The BPAs 4.1 – 4.9 are defined in Appendix D, CatNo 3.4.4.1 – 3.4.4.9.

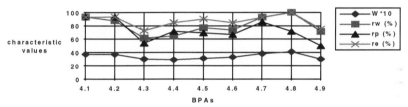

Figure 10.49 Characteristic curves of the purchasing management process

10.5.5 BENCHMARKS OF THE DOCUMENT MANAGEMENT PROCESS CATEGORY

This subsection demonstrates the derived benchmarks of the document management process category based on the data listed in Appendix D, BPA No. 417 – 433.

10.5.5.1 The Documentation Process

Characteristic curves of the documentation process are derived in Figure 10.50. The BPAs 1.1 – 1.11 are defined in Appendix D, CatNo 3.5.1.1 – 3.5.1.11.

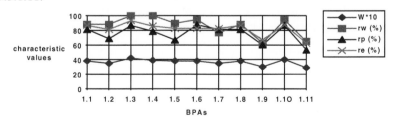

Figure 10.50 Characteristic curves of the documentation process

10.5.5.2 The Process Database/Library

Characteristic curves of the process database/library are derived in Figure 10.51. The BPAs 2.1 – 2.6 are defined in Appendix D, CatNo 3.5.2.1 – 3.5.2.6.

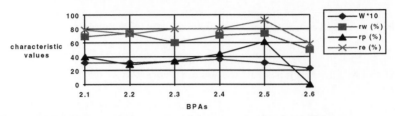

Figure 10.51 Characteristic curves of the process database/library

10.5.6 BENCHMARKS OF THE HUMAN RESOURCE MANAGEMENT PROCESS CATEGORY

This subsection demonstrates the derived benchmarks of the human resource management process category based on the data listed in Appendix D, BPA No. 434 – 444.

10.5.6.1 The Staff Selection and Allocation Process

Characteristic curves of the staff selection and allocation process are derived in Figure 10.52. The BPAs 1.1 – 1.4 are defined in Appendix D, CatNo 3.6.1.1 – 3.6.1.4.

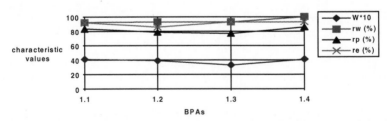

Figure 10.52 Characteristic curves of the staff selection and allocation process

10.5.6.2 The Training Process

Characteristic curves of the training process are derived in Figure 10.53. The BPAs 2.1 – 2.7 are defined in Appendix D, CatNo 3.6.2.1 – 3.6.2.7.

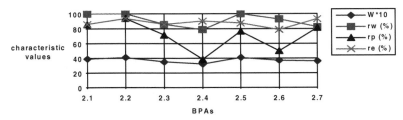

Figure 10.53 Characteristic curves of the training process

10.5.7 GENERAL CHARACTERISTICS OF THE MANAGEMENT PROCESS SUBSYSTEM

A general view of benchmarks of the 248 BPAs in the 6 management categories and 29 processes is shown in Table 10.6 and Figure 10.3.

Table 10.6
Statistical Characteristics of the Management Process Subsystem

BPA Characteristics	Weight	No. of BPAs	Relative Number of BPAs (%)
Mean weighted importance (W)	5	0	0
	4	64	25.8
	3	165	66.5
	2	19	7.7
	1	0	0
	0	0	0
Ratio of significance (r_w)	E	116	46.8
	V	107	43.1
	F	24	9.7
	N	1	0.4
Ratio of practice (r_p)	E	28	11.3
	V	91	36.7
	F	81	32.7
	N	48	19.3
Ratio of effectiveness (r_e)	E	82	33.1
	V	138	55.6
	F	28	11.3
	N	0	0

Note: E - Extremely (≥90%), V - very (70-89%), F - fairly (50-69%), and N - not (<50%)

- For the mean weighted importance of BPAs in software management processes, 92.3% of the BPAs are heavily weighted with 66.5% at weight scale 3.0 – 3.99 and 25.8% at weight scale 4.0 – 4.99. There are 7.7% BPAs perceived to be not very important.

- For the ratio of significance of BPAs in software management processes, 46.8% of the BPAs are weighted extremely significant, 43.1% are very significant, 9.7% are fairly significant, and only 0.4% are not significant.

- For the ratio of practice of BPAs in software management processes, 11.3% BPAs have extremely high application rate, 36.7% BPAs have very high application rate, and 32.7% have fairly high application rate. There are 19.4% BPAs perceived to be unused.

- For the ratio of effectiveness of BPAs in software management processes, 33.1% of the BPAs are weighted extremely effective, 55.6% are very effective, and 11.3% are fairly effective. No BPAs in the set are found not effective.

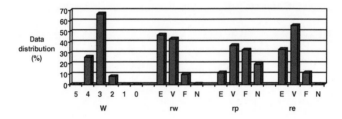

Figure 10.54 Overview of survey findings on the management processes

10.6 The Highlights of Process Characteristics

In Sections 10.3 – 10.5 the SEPRM benchmarks and characteristic curves of the 51 processes in 3 process subsystems were derived. These benchmarks enable readers to analyze which is the most or least significant, practical, and effective BPA in each process, and to identify the gaps between the practice curve and the significant and effective curves to point to process improvement opportunities. The process benchmarks provide a set of statistical references for analyzing a software development organization's strengths and weaknesses, and for identifying process improvement priorities and aims for gaining a competitive position among peers.

In this section a set of general views of the BPA attributes and process characteristics will be summarized. Then, the most/least outstanding processes as rated by the software industry in terms significance, practice, and effectiveness, as well as their combinations, will be identified.

General statistical characteristics of the BPAs modeled in SEPRM are summarized in Table 10.7 and illustrated in Figure 10.4.

Table 10.7
General Statistical Characteristics of the SEPRM Processes

BPA Characteristics	Weight	No. of BPAs	Relative Number of BPAs (%)
Mean weighted importance (W)	5	0	0
	4	105	23.7
	3	302	68.0
	2	37	8.3
	1	0	0
	0	0	0
Ratio of significance (r_w)	E	191	43.0
	V	204	45.9
	F	44	10.0
	N	5	1.1
Ratio of practice (r_p)	E	54	12.2
	V	172	38.7
	F	144	32.4
	N	74	16.7
Ratio of effectiveness (r_e)	E	150	33.8
	V	248	55.8
	F	44	9.9
	N	2	0.5

Note: E - Extremely (≥90%), V - very (70-89%), F - fairly (50-69%), and N - not (<50%)

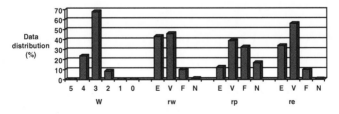

Figure 10.55 General view of BPA attributes modeled in SEPRM

According to the survey findings, process implementation and improvement priorities can be identified based on the statistical fact that almost all of the BPAs are evaluated effective, but 16.7% have not been practiced.

In addition to the general findings described above, the following subsections highlight the outstanding processes in terms of most/least significant, practical, effective, and useful.

10.6.1 THE MOST/LEAST SIGNIFICANT PROCESSES

Analyzing the ratio of significance for the BPAs in SEPRM, 43.0% of the BPAs are weighted extremely significant, 45.9% are very significant, 9.9% are fairly significant, and only 1.1% are not significant.

According to the survey data, more than 88% of the BPAs are highly significant. Therefore, at the process level, almost all of the 51 SEPRM processes are significant. While looking for details, the top 10 processes rated most or least significant are shown in Table 10.8. The most significant processes should be given priority in process establishment and improvement. The least significant processes are rated by relative scores, and, thus, by no means should they be considered "not useful" in a process system.

Table 10.8
Top Ten Most/Least Significant Processes

Sequence	Top 10	Bottom 10
1	3.6.1 Staff selection and allocation	3.5.2 Process database/library
2	3.4.1 Requirement management	2.3.4 Management support tools
3	3.3.3 Configuration management	3.3.2 Process tracking
4	2.2.5 Module testing	2.3.3 Development support tools
5	3.1.11 Subcontractor's quality control	1.3.3 Software/system delivery
6	2.2.1 Development process definition	2.3.2 Facilities
7	3.6.2 Training	3.2.3 Project risk avoidance
8	3.2.4 Project quality plan	3.4.4 Purchasing management
9	2.1.2 Reuse methodologies	1.3.2 Customer support
10	3.2.2 Project estimation	2.3.1 Environment

10.6.2 THE MOST/LEAST PRACTICAL PROCESSES

Looking at the ratio of practice for the BPAs in SEPRM, 12.2% BPAs have extremely high application rate, 38.7% BPAs have very high application rate, and 32.4% have fairly high application rate. It is noteworthy that there are 16.7% BPAs perceived to be relatively unused.

According to the survey data, 50.9% of the BPAs are very frequently applied, while 16.7% are less frequently used. The top 10 processes that are rated most or least practical are shown in Table 10.9. The most practical processes should be given priority in process establishment and improvement. The least practical processes can be interpreted, to some extent, as those that were applied relatively the least in the software industry.

Table 10.9
Top Ten Most/Least Practical Processes

Sequence	Top 10	Bottom 10
1	3.4.1 Requirement management	3.5.2 Process database/library
2	3.6.1 Staff selection and allocation	3.2.3 Project risk avoidance
3	2.2.1 Development process definition	3.3.1 Process management
4	3.2.1 Project plan	2.3.4 Management support tools
5	3.2.2 Project estimation	3.1.4 Code review
6	1.3.3 Software/system delivery	2.2.6 Integration and system testing
7	1.1.1 Organization definition	1.2.2 Organization process improvement
8	1.3.2 Customer support	2.1.2 Reuse methodologies
9	1.3.4 Service evaluation	3.1.2 Requirement review
10	2.1.3 Technology innovation	3.3.5 Process review

10.6.3 THE MOST/LEAST EFFECTIVE PROCESSES

For the ratio of effectiveness of the BPAs in SEPRM, 33.8% of the BPAs are weighted extremely effective, 55.8% are very effective, and 9.9% are fairly effective. Only 0.5% BPAs in the set are found not effective.

According to the survey data, nearly 90% of the BPAs are highly effective. The top 10 processes that are rated most or least effective are shown in Table 10.10. The most effective processes should be given priority in process establishment and improvement. The least effective processes indicate they are relatively less effective, but not necessarily of no use.

Table 10.10
Top Ten Most/Least Effective Processes

Sequence	Top 10	Bottom 10
1	3.4.2 Contract management	3.2.3 Project risk avoidance
2	1.3.4 Service evaluation	3.1.4 Code review
3	2.1.3 Technology innovation	3.3.1 Process management
4	3.1.11 Subcontractor's quality control	3.3.2 Process tracking
5	3.6.1 Staff selection and allocation	1.2.1 Organization process definition
6	1.3.2 Customer support	1.2.2 Organization process improvement

7	3.2.1 Project plan	3.1.8 Internal audit
8	3.1.10 Defect control	3.3.5 Process review
9	2.2.1 Development process definition	3.5.2 Process database/library
10	3.3.4 Change control	1.3.1 Customer relations

10.6.4 THE MOST/LEAST USEFUL PROCESSES

Because of the different magnitudes according to Expression 2.20, there is no comparability between the ratio of the combined characteristic value (or usage) of BPAs in SEPRM and the ratios of the others as described in previous subsections. Looking at the relative values of the characteristic attributes, the top 10 processes that are rated most or least useful are shown in Table 10.11.

Table 10.11
Top Ten Most/Least Useful (Combined Characteristics) Processes

Sequence	Top 10	Bottom 10
1	3.4.1 Requirement management	3.2.3 Project risk avoidance
2	3.6.1 Staff selection and allocation	3.3.1 Process management
3	3.2.1 Project plan	2.3.4 Management support tools
4	1.3.4 Service evaluation	3.1.4 Code review
5	2.2.5 Module testing	1.2.2 Organization process improvement
6	2.2.1 Development process definition	2.3.3 Development support tools
7	2.1.3 Technology innovation	3.3.5 Process review
8	3.1.10 Defect control	3.3.2 Process tracking
9	3.3.3 Configuration management	3.1.8 Internal audit
10	3.2.2 Project estimation	3.1.5 Module testing audit

10.7 Summary

This chapter has characterized the BPAs and processes modeled in SEPRM by industry surveys and benchmarking. Such surveys are important and yet very difficult and costly research methods for collecting data on complicated system modeling and validation. The worldwide survey on BPAs validating the SEPRM software engineering process model has resulted in the following objectives being achieved:

- The BPAs in the software engineering processes have been quantitatively characterized by attributes of the mean weighted importance and the ratios of significance, practice, and effectiveness.

- A set of benchmarks and characteristics of the attributes for all 444 BPAs has been obtained which can be used by any process owners, researchers, and practitioners for process establishment and improvement.

- A new approach to benchmark-based process assessment and improvement has been enabled. This will be described in Part V and Part VI.

- Characteristic curves for each process have been derived for showing the distribution and trends of the BPAs within a process.

The analyses in this chapter have been based on the data documented in Appendix D. Mining this wealth of data, readers may find new facts and additional statistically significant regulations in process-based software engineering.

The basic knowledge structure of this chapter is as follows:

Chapter 10. Benchmarking the SEPRM Processes

- General
  - Objectives of this chapter
    - To establish a foundation of practice for validation, calibration and benchmarking of software process models
    - To seek statistical criteria for selecting processes and BPAs in process system modeling
    - To validate the BPAs and processes modeled in SEPRM
    - To enable a new approach to benchmark-based process assessment and improvement
    - To characterize a superset of processes and BPAs in order to provide reference points for existing process models and future new process models

  - Methods adopted in this chapter
    - Quantitative characteristic attributes
    - Industry surveys and SEPRM-based process reference

models
- Statistical analysis and benchmarking of process characteristics
- Survey data visualization by process characteristic curves

- Relationship between this chapter and the process analysis methods developed in Section 2.5

- Methods for characterizing software processes
  - BPA: Characteristic attributes
    - Mean weighted importance
    - Ratio of significance
    - Ratio of practice
    - Ratio of effectiveness
    - The combined characteristic value (usage)

  - Process: Characteristic curves
    - Four types of process characteristic curves
    - Interpreting a process characteristic curve

  - Interpreting the benchmarking data documented in Appendix D
    - Structure
    - BPA and process indexing
    - Plotting a process characteristic curve

- Benchmarks of SEPRM processes
  - The organization process subsystem
    - Configuration
      - 3 process categories
      - 8 processes
      - 81 BPAs
    - What can be found in the process characteristic curves
    - General statistic characteristics of this process subsystem

  - The development process subsystem
    - Configuration
      - 3 process categories
      - 14 processes
      - 115 BPAs
    - What can be found in the process characteristic curves
    - General statistic characteristics of this process subsystem

- The management process subsystem
  - Configuration
    - 6 process categories
    - 29 processes
    - 248 BPAs
  - What can be found in the process characteristic curves
  - General statistic characteristics of this process subsystem

- Derived benchmarks of process characteristics
  - Analysis of process characteristics
    - Top 10 most/least significant processes
    - Top 10 most/least practical processes
    - Top 10 most/least effective processes
    - Top 10 most/least useful processes

  - Applications of the process benchmarks
    - Plot an organization's data onto the process characteristic curves
    - Contrast and analyze process features
      - Gaps to the benchmarked characteristic curves
      - Strengths
      - Weaknesses
      - Process improvement opportunities

Major achievements and issues for further research suggested by this chapter are highlighted below:

- The methods used are theoretically transformable to any software process model. The findings for the process characteristic attributes are applicable to ISO/IEC TR 15504, CMM, ISO 9001, BOOTSTRAP, or any new process models.

- A new approach to benchmark-based process assessment and improvement has been enabled which will be shown as an important alternative to the conventional model-based process assessment and improvement methodologies.

- It is interesting to find in the survey that all BPAs modeled in SEPRM have been proven useful and effective in process. The vast majority of BPAs have been evaluated and found significant, practical, and effective. Only 1.1% and 0.5% of the BPAs have been perceived as not practical in practice or not effective.

- According to Table 10.7, although almost all BPAs modeled in SEPRM have been rated significant and effective, there were 16.7% that are not currently common practice in the software industry. These relatively unused practices could bear investigation, and would indicate improvement opportunities.

- Benchmarking and characterizing BPAs and processes have been found useful in a wide range of applications in both process establishment and improvement. For process establishment, the implementation priority can be put on the BPAs with higher ratios of significance and effectiveness. For process improvement, the priority can be put on the BPAs that have the largest gaps between the current practices and the ratio of significance.

Benchmarking and characterizing the processes and BPAs are considered fundamental in software engineering process modeling and analysis. The benchmarks are useful for modeling and feature-identifying fundamental software process activities, for evaluating a software organization's current practice gaps to the benchmarks, and for identifying process improvement opportunities for an organization's software system. Comparing the benchmarks with current practices in an organization enables recommendations to be given as to which specific areas need to have processes established first, and which areas should have the highest priority for process improvement.

Applications of the benchmarks of software engineering processes in process establishment, assessment, and improvement will be provided in Part IV through Part VI.

Annotated References

Software engineering process benchmarking is a new topic in research. A European software practice benchmark was developed and maintained by IBM (1986). A SPICE benchmark database was under development during SPICE Trials Phase III [SPICE Project, 1998]. A Swedish national software engineering process benchmark was developed during 1997 – 1998 and reported in Wang et al. (1999f).

Dutta, Kulandaiswamy, and Wassenhove (1998) reported their work on benchmarking European software management best practices. Wang et al. (1998a/99c/f) conducted benchmarking of the practices and processes modeled in current process models based on a series of worldwide industry surveys and statistical analyses.

On related quantitative analysis, Kitson and Masters (1992) reported SEI software process assessment results during 1987-1991. Zubrow (1997) analyzed a large number of organizations that had undergone CMM assessment before 1997, and this was updated recently in SEI (1999).

Questions and Problems

10.1 Benchmarking is a useful quantitative research method for characterizing complicated systems. Explain the five purposes of process benchmarking.

10.2 List the five attributes for characterizing processes and BPAs, and explain their definitions and expressions.

10.3 Conduct a simulated benchmarking survey of one of the SEPRM development processes, as listed in Appendix D, within your project team or class. Then, report your benchmarked findings on the process you choose and provide analysis.

10.4 Compare your benchmarking results obtained in Problem 10.3 with the SEPRM benchmarks by plotting your data onto the related characteristic curves. Analyze your team's process performance, strengths, and weaknesses.

10.5 Conduct a simulated benchmarking survey of one of the SEPRM organization processes within your project team or class, and plot your results onto the related characteristic curves. Analyze your team's process performance, strengths, and weaknesses.

10.6 Repeat Problem 10.5 for a SEPRM management process.

10.7 If you are a process manager in a software development organization, the top management expects you to produce a process establishment and improvement proposal. What can you propose based on the process benchmarks developed in this chapter?

10.8 If you are a process model developer, how do you determine the inclusion or elimination of a candidate process or BPA with the support of the process benchmarks developed in this chapter?

10.9 Observing the top most/least significant processes as listed in Table 10.8, what can be found from the statistical results?

10.10 Observing the top most/least practical processes as listed in Table 10.9, what can you discover from the statistical results?

10.11 Observing the top most/least effective processes as listed in Table 10.10, what can be found from the statistical results?

10.12 Observing the top most/least useful processes as listed in Table 10.11, what can be gleaned from the statistical results?

Chapter 11

COMPARATIVE ANALYSIS
OF CURRENT
PROCESS MODELS

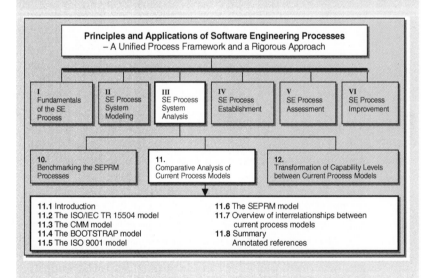

This chapter analyzes the interrelationships between the process domains of current process models. In the analysis attention is paid to both equivalency and any special orientation of current process models.

The objectives of this chapter are as follows:

- To analyze the relationships between current process models by using one-to-one, one-to-many, and/or many-to-one mappings

- To investigate compatibility and correlation between current process models

- To explore features and special orientation of current process models so that suitable or combined process models can be chosen for a specific software development organization

- To enable the development of process capability transformations between current process models which will be covered in the next chapter

11.1 Introduction

One of the most frequently asked questions in the software industry is "what are the coverages and interrelationships of current process models?" In Chapters 5 – 9 we presented formal views of individual process models. This chapter analyzes the interrelationships between the process domains of these models. The definitions and methods developed in Section 2.5.1 will be used to measure the interrelationships.

The compatibility and correlation between current process models, such as ISO/IEC TR 15504, CMM, BOOTSTRAP, ISO 9001, and SEPRM, are quantitatively analyzed and contrasted in this chapter. First, formal definitions of the compatibility and correlation between the models are described. Then, relational properties are mutually analyzed from the viewpoint of each of the five process models and the others. In doing so, each model is mapped onto the other four at system and BPA levels. To gain a complete view of the compatibility and correlation of a specific model with others, it is recommended that readers take a bidirectional comparison of the results provided in this chapter.

11.1.1 DOMAINS OF BPAs OF CURRENT PROCESS MODELS

The power and completeness of a process model is determined by both its process domain and its capability determination methodology. The process domain defined in SEPRM consists of 444 BPAs, a superset of those identified in the other four models. The BPAs are equivalently known as the 201 base practices (BPs) in ISO/IEC TR 15504, the 150 key practices (KPs) in CMM, the 201 quality system attributes (QSAs) in BOOTSTRAP, and the 177 management issues (MIs) in ISO 9001.

Appendix C documents detailed mappings between current process models at the BPA level. It is noteworthy that the mappings indicate various relationships between the BPAs identified in current models, such as one-to-one, one-to-many, and many-to-one relationships. Analyses in the following sections will be based on the mappings and configurations of the BPAs defined in current models.

11.1.2 COMPATIBILITY BETWEEN CURRENT PROCESS MODELS

In Section 2.5.1, Definition 2.35, compatibility between a number of process models is defined as the degree of joint domain coverage, which is determined by the sets of BPAs of the process models. The partially overlapped process domains and compatibility of current process models are illustrated in Figure 2.4.

For the five process models considered as shown in Figure 2.4, compatibility degree, C_k, can be described at five levels as follows:

- C_1 : BPAs that are only defined in a specific model

- C_2 : Shared BPAs identified in two of the models

- C_3 : Shared BPAs identified in three of the models

- C_4 : Shared BPAs identified in four of the models, and

- C_5 : BPAs shared by all five models

With the above definitions, compatibility can be quantitatively measured and analyzed according to Expression 2.6.

11.1.3 CORRELATION BETWEEN CURRENT PROCESS MODELS

In Section 2.5.1, correlation between current process models is described by the correlation level and ratio as given in Definitions 2.38 and 2.39. The correlation level between a pair of models is the number of identical or equivalent BPAs in the domains of the models. The correlation ratio of a model R against a model S is a relative degree of identity or equivalency that R compares to S.

Analysis of correlation is based on the concept and technique of mapping BPAs between different process models. As described in Section 2.5.1, mapping is defined as finding identical or equivalent BPAs in a pair of process models. When a mapping is carried out between two process models R and S, the correlation level $r(R, S)$ and ratio $\rho(R, S)$ can be calculated according to Expressions 2.9 and 2.10, respectively.

This chapter quantitatively analyzes the compatibility and correlation between the current process models based on the method developed in Section 2.5. In the following sections, individual process models are analyzed. Then, a summary of process configuration, compatibility, and correlation of current process models is provided based on each one-to-many analyzes.

11.2 The ISO/IEC TR 15504 Model

This section analyzes compatibility and correlation of ISO/IEC TR 15504 with the other four models, i.e., CMM, BOOTSTRAP, ISO 9001, and SEPRM. Process domain and BP configuration of ISO/IEC TR 15504 are contrasted with current process models.

11.2.1 COMPATIBILITY OF ISO/IEC TR 15504 TO OTHER MODELS

Applying Expression 2.6 to Appendix C, the compatibility of ISO/IEC TR 15504 to CMM, BOOTSTRAP, ISO 9001, and SEPRM is derived as shown in Table 11.1. An illustration of ISO/IEC TR 15504's compatibility to the other process models is provided in Figure 11.1.

Table 11.1
Compatibility Degree of ISO/IEC TR 15504 to Other Process Models

Compatibility	Category 1 Customer-Supplier	Category 2 Engineering	Category 3 Project	Category 4 Support	Category 5 Organization	C_k (ISO 15504)
C_1 (ISO15504)	0	0	0	0	0	0
C_2 (ISO15504)	29	15	18	12	28	102
C_3 (ISO15504)	9	12	20	8	11	60
C_4 (ISO15504)	1	5	12	9	5	32
C_5 (ISO15504)	0	0	0	3	4	7

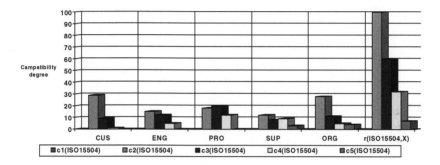

Figure 11.1 Compatibility of ISO/IEC TR 15504 with other models

Figure 11.1 shows that there is no BP in ISO/IEC TR 15504 with compatibility level 1, or no BP is only defined by the model itself. Generally, about half of the process domains of ISO/IEC TR 15504 have compatibility level 2 ($C_2(ISO15504)=102$), meaning that those 102 BPs can only be found in ISO/IEC TR 15504 and one of the other models, particularly SEPRM. The BPs with compatibility level 3 in ISO/IEC TR 15504 are relatively high ($C_3(ISO15504)=60$). Those BPs are mainly compatible to CMM and SEPRM. The BPs with compatibility level 4 in ISO/IEC TR 15504 are $C_4(ISO15504)=32$.

The seven BPs with the highest compatibility ($C_5(ISO15504)=7$) are those equivalent BPAs listed below:

- BPA No.18 – Document standard processes

- BPA No.31 – Identify improvement opportunities (Note this BPA was counted twice in the many-to-one mapping from ISO/IEC TR 15504 to SEPRM)

- BPA No.244 – Audit software development activities

- BPA No.343 – Establish configuration management library

- BPA No.347 – Control change requests

- BPA No.442 – Conduct technical training

The above BPAs with compatibility level 5 are located mainly within the management processes.

11.2.2 CORRELATION OF ISO/IEC TR 15504 WITH OTHER MODELS

System level correlation between ISO/IEC TR 15504 and CMM, BOOTSTRAP, ISO 9001, and SEPRM is listed in Table 11.2, where the symbol "X" represents one of the other four models correspondingly. Expressions 2.9 and 2.10 are used for deriving the values of correlation levels and ratios from the data documented in Appendix C. The same expressions apply to the following sections.

Table 11.2
Correlation: ISO/IEC TR 15504 vs. SEPRM, CMM, BOOTSTRAP, and ISO 9001

Correlation	Category 1 Customer-Supplier	Category 2 Enginee-ring	Category 3 Project	Category 4 Support	Category 5 Organiza-tion	r(ISO15504, X)	ρ(ISO15504, X)
SEPRM	39	32	50	32	48	201	45.3%
CMM	0	6	23	17	18	64	42.7%
Bootstrap	3	19	14	9	14	59	29.4%
ISO 9001	13	2	20	14	10	59	32.8%

The correlation data shown in Table 11.2 are illustrated in Figure 11.2. Generally, Figure 11.2 shows that ISO/IEC TR 15504 has the highest correlation with SEPRM, followed closely by CMM; its correlation to BOOTSTRAP and ISO 9001 are both at the 1/3 level. Detailed one-to-many relationships between ISO/IEC TR 15004 and the other four process models are analyzed below.

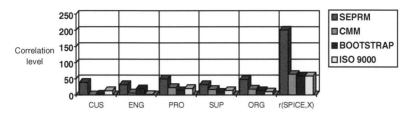

Figure 11.2 Correlation: ISO/IEC TR 15504 vs. SEPRM, CMM, BOOTSTRAP, and ISO 9001

11.2.2.1 ISO/IEC TR 15504 vs. SEPRM

The correlation level between ISO/IEC TR 15504 and SEPRM is *r(ISO15504, SEPRM)* = *201,* and the correlation ratio is ρ*(ISO15504, SEPRM)* = *45.3%.* Specifically, in the customer-supplier category, ISO15504 – SEPRM is the most correlative pair. Among the four pairs of correlation, ISO15504 – SEPRM is the most correlative in the categories of project and organization and is the least correlative in the categories of engineering and support.

11.2.2.2 ISO/IEC TR 15504 vs. CMM

The correlation level between ISO/IEC TR 15504 and CMM is *r(ISO15504, CMM)* = *64* and the correlation ratio is ρ*(ISO15504, CMM)* = *42.7%.* Specifically, among the four pairs of correlation, ISO15504 – CMM is the most correlative in the categories of project and organization and is the least correlative in the categories of customer – support and engineering.

11.2.2.3 ISO/IEC TR 15504 vs. BOOTSTRAP

The correlation level between ISO/IEC TR 15504 and BOOTSTRAP is *r(ISO15504, BOOTSTRAP)* = *59,* and the correlation ratio is ρ*(ISO15504, BOOTSTRAP)* = *29.4%.* Specifically, among the four pairs of correlation, ISO15504 – BOOTSTRAP is the most correlative in the process category of engineering and is the least correlative in the category of customer – supplier.

11.2.2.4 ISO/IEC TR 15504 vs. ISO 9001

The correlation level between ISO/IEC TR 15504 and ISO 9001 is *r(ISO15504, ISO 9001)* = *59,* and the correlation ratio is *p(ISO15504, ISO 9001)* = *32.8%.* Specifically, among the four pairs of correlation,

ISO15504 – ISO9001 is the most correlative in the category of project and is the least correlative in the category of engineering.

Mappings from the viewpoints of the other models to ISO/IEC TR 15504 can be found in Sections 11.3 through 11.6, respectively. Detailed distribution of the ISO/IEC TR 15504 correlation with SEPRM, CMM, BOOTSTRAP, and ISO 9001 at the BP level can be referenced in Appendix C.

11.3 The CMM Model

This section analyzes compatibility and correlation of CMM with the other four models, i.e., ISO/IEC TR 15504, BOOTSTRAP, ISO 9001, and SEPRM. Process domain and KP configuration of CMM are contrasted with current process models.

11.3.1 COMPATIBILITY OF CMM TO OTHER MODELS

Applying Expression 2.6 to Appendix C, the compatibility of CMM to ISO/IEC TR 15504, BOOTSTRAP, ISO 9001, and SEPRM is derived as shown in Table 11.3. An illustration of CMM's compatibility to the other process models is provided in Figure 11.3.

Table 11.3
Compatibility Degree of CMM to Other Process Models

Compatibility	Level 1 Initial	Level 2 Repeated	Level 3 Defined	Level 4 Managed	Level 5 Optimized	C_k(CMM)
C_1 (CMM)	0	0	0	0	0	0
C_2 (CMM)	0	14	22	8	9	53
C_3 (CMM)	0	24	18	0	13	55
C_4 (CMM)	0	21	7	4	3	35
C_5 (CMM)	0	3	3	0	1	7

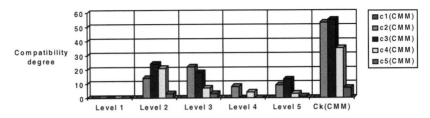

Figure 11.3 Compatibility of CMM with other models

Figure 11.3 shows that there is no KP in CMM with compatibility level 1, or no KP that is defined by the model only. Generally, about 1/3 of the process domain of CMM is at compatibility level 2 ($C_2(CMM)=53$), meaning that those 53 BPs can only be found in CMM and one of the other models, especially in SEPRM. The KPs with compatibility level 3 in CMM are $C_3(CMM)=55$, which indicates 1/3 of the KPs in CMM have a better compatibility relative to other models. The KPs with compatibility level 4 in CMM are $C_4(CMM)=35$. The seven KPs with the highest compatibility ($C_5(CMM)=7$) are those equivalent BPAs listed in Section 11.2.1 (with BPA No. 31 mapped twice).

11.3.2 CORRELATION OF CMM WITH OTHER MODELS

System level correlation between CMM and ISO/IEC TR 15504, BOOTSTRAP, ISO 9001, and SEPRM is listed in Table 11.4, where the symbol "X" represents one of the other four models.

Table 11.4
Correlation: CMM vs. SEPRM, ISO/IEC TR 15504, BOOTSTRAP, and ISO 9001

Correlation	Level 1 Initial	Level 2 Repeated	Level 3 Defined	Level 4 Managed	Level 5 Optimizing	r(CMM, X)	ρ(CMM, X)
SEPRM	0	62	50	12	26	150	33.8%
ISO/IEC TR 15504	0	34	18	3	9	64	31.8%
Bootstrap	0	18	19	2	10	49	24.4%
ISO 9001	0	29	8	7	7	51	28.8%

The correlation data shown in Table 11.4 are illustrated in Figure 11.4. Generally, Figure 11.4 shows that CMM has the highest correlation with

SEPRM, followed by ISO/IEC TR 15504; its correlation to BOOTSTRAP and ISO 9001 are relatively low. Detailed one-to-many relationships between CMM and the other four process models are analyzed below.

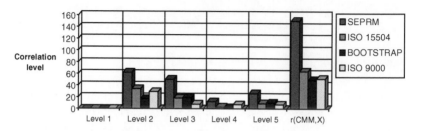

Figure 11.4 Correlation: CMM vs. SEPRM, ISO/IEC TR 15504, BOOTSTRAP, and ISO 9001

11.3.2.1 CMM vs. SEPRM

The correlation level between CMM and SEPRM is $r(CMM, SEPRM) = 150$, and the correlation ratio is $\rho(CMM, SEPRM) = 33.8\%$. Specifically, among the four pairs of correlation, CMM – SEPRM is the most correlative at capability levels 2 and 3 and is the least correlative at capability level 4. There is no correlation at capability level 1 because no KP has been defined at that level.

11.3.2.2 CMM vs. ISO/IEC TR 15504

The correlation level between CMM and ISO/IEC TR 15504 is $r(CMM, ISO15504) = 64$, and the correlation ratio is $\rho(CMM, ISO15504) = 31.8\%$. Specifically, among the four pairs of correlation, CMM – ISO15504 is the most correlative at level 2 and is the least correlative at level 4.

11.3.2.3 CMM vs. BOOTSTRAP

The correlation level between CMM and BOOTSTRAP is $r(CMM, BOOTSTRAP) = 49$, and the correctional ratio is $\rho(CMM, BOOTSTRAP) = 24.4\%$. Specifically, among the four pairs of correlation, CMM – BOOTSTRAP is the most correlative at level 3 and is the least correlative at level 4.

11.3.2.4 CMM vs. ISO 9001

The correlation level between CMM and ISO 9001 is $r(CMM, ISO9001) = 51$, and the correlation ratio is $\rho(CMM, ISO9001) = 28.8\%$. Specifically, among the four pairs of correlation, CMM – ISO9001 is the most correlative at level 2 and is the least correlative at levels 4 and 5.

Mappings from the viewpoints of the other models to CMM can be found in Sections 11.2, and 11.4 to 11.6, respectively. Detailed distribution of the CMM correlation with SEPRM, ISO/IEC TR 15504, BOOTSTRAP, and ISO 9001 at the KP level can be referenced in Appendix C.

11.4 The BOOTSTRAP Model

This section analyzes compatibility and correlation of BOOTSTRAP with the other four models, i.e., ISO/IEC TR 15504, CMM, ISO 9001, and SEPRM. Process domain and QSA configuration of BOOTSTRAP are contrasted with current process models.

11.4.1 COMPATIBILITY OF BOOTSTRAP TO OTHER MODELS

Applying Expression 2.6 to Appendix C, the compatibility of BOOTSTRAP to ISO/IEC TR 15504, CMM, ISO 9001, and SEPRM is derived as shown in Table 11.5. An illustration of BOOTSTRAP's compatibility to the other process models is provided in Figure 11.5.

Table 11.5
Compatibility Degree of BOOTSTRAP to Other Process Models

Compatibility	Subsystem 1 Organization	Subsystem 2 Methodology	Subsystem 3 Technology	C_k(BOOTSTRAP)
C_1(BOOTSTRAP)	0	0	0	0
C_2(BOOTSTRAP)	7	52	43	102
C_3(BOOTSTRAP)	8	55	5	68
C_4(BOOTSTRAP)	4	20	1	25
C_5(BOOTSTRAP)	2	4	0	6

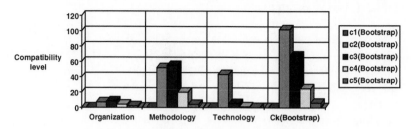

Figure 11.5 Compatibility of BOOTSTRAP with other models

Figure 11.5 shows that there is no QSA in BOOTSTRAP with compatibility level 1, or no QSAs that are only defined by the model itself. Generally, about 1/3 of the process domain of BOOTSTRAP is compatibility level 2 ($C_2(BOOTSTRAP)=102$), meaning that those 102 QSAs can only be found in BOOTSTRAP and one of the other models, especially in SEPRM. The QSAs with compatibility level 3 in BOOTSTRAP are relatively high ($C_3(BOOTSTRAP)= 68$). These QSAs are mainly compatible to SEPRM and ISO 9001. The QSAs with compatibility level 4 in BOOTSTRAP are $C_4(BOOTSTRAP)=25$. The six QSAs with the highest compatibility ($C_5(BOOTSTRAP)=6$) are those equivalent BPAs listed in Section 11.2.1.

11.4.2 CORRELATION OF BOOTSTRAP WITH OTHER MODELS

System level correlation between BOOTSTRAP and ISO/IEC TR 15504, CMM, ISO 9001, are SEPRM is listed in Table 11.6, where the symbol "X" represents one of the other four models.

Table 11.6
Correlation: BOOTSTRAP vs. SEPRM, ISO/IEC TR 15504, CMM, and ISO 9001

Correlation	Subsystem 1 Organization	Subsystem 2 Methodology	Subsystem 3 Technology	r(BOOTSTRAP, X)	ρ(BOOTSTRAP, X)
SEPRM	21	131	49	201	45.3%
ISO/IEC TR 15504	8	49	2	59	29.4%
CMM	6	41	2	49	32.7%
ISO 9001	11	58	6	75	42.4%

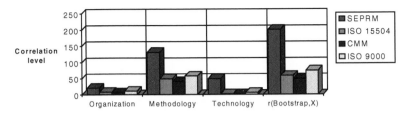

Figure 11.6 Correlation: BOOTSTRAP vs. SEPRM, ISO/IEC TR 15504, CMM, and ISO 9001

The correlation data shown in Table 11.6 are illustrated in Figure 11.6. Generally, Figure 11.6 shows that BOOTSTRAP has the highest correlation with SEPRM, followed by ISO 9001; its correlation to ISO/IEC TR 15504 and CMM are relatively low. Detailed one-to-many relationships between BOOTSTRAP and the other four process models are analyzed below.

11.4.2.1 BOOTSTRAP vs. SEPRM

The correlation level between BOOTSTRAP and SEPRM is $r(BOOTSTRAP, SEPRM) = 201$, and the correlation ratio is $\rho(BOOTSTRAP, SEPRM) = 45.3\%$. Specifically, among the four pairs of correlation, BOOTSTRAP – SEPRM is the most correlative in the methodology subsystem and is the least correlative in the organization subsystem.

11.4.2.2 BOOTSTRAP vs. ISO/IEC TR 15504

The correlation level between BOOTSTRAP and ISO/IEC TR 15504 is $r(BOOTSTRAP, ISO15504) = 59$, and the correlation ratio is $\rho(BOOTSTRAP, ISO15504) = 29.4\%$. Specifically, among the four pairs of correlation, BOOTSTRAP – ISO15504 is the most correlative in the methodology subsystem and is the least correlative in the subsystem of technology.

11.4.2.3 BOOTSTRAP vs. CMM

The correlation level between BOOTSTRAP and CMM is $r(BOOTSTRAP, CMM) = 49$, and the correlation ratio is $\rho(BOOTSTRAP, CMM) = 32.7\%$. Specifically, among the four pairs of correlation, BOOTSTRAP – CMM is the most correlative in the methodology subsystem and is the least correlative in the technology subsystem.

11.4.2.4   BOOTSTRAP vs. ISO 9001

The correlation level between BOOTSTRAP and ISO 9001 is $r(BOOTSTRAP, ISO9001) = 75$, and the correlation ratio is $\rho(BOOTSTRAP, ISO9001) = 42.4\%$. Specifically, among the four pairs of correlation, BOOTSTRAP – ISO9001 is the most correlative in the methodology subsystem and the least correlative in the technology subsystem.

Mappings from the viewpoints of the other models to BOOTSTRAP can be found in Sections 11.2 – 11.3 and 11.5 – 11.6, respectively. Detailed distribution of the BOOTSTRAP correlation with SEPRM, ISO/IEC TR 15504, CMM, and ISO 9001 at the QSA level can be referenced in Appendix C.

11.5 The ISO 9001 Model

This section analyzes compatibility and correlation of ISO 9001 with the other four models, i.e., ISO/IEC TR 15504, CMM, BOOTSTRAP, and SEPRM. Process domain and MI configuration of ISO 9001 are contrasted with current process models.

11.5.1 COMPATIBILITY OF ISO 9001 TO THE OTHER MODELS

Applying Expression 2.6 to Appendix C, the compatibility of ISO 9001 to ISO/IEC TR 15504, CMM, BOOTSTRAP, and SEPRM is derived as shown in Table 11.7. An illustration of ISO 9001's compatibility to the other process models is provided in Figure 11.7.

Table 11.7
Compatibility Degree of ISO 9001 to Other Degree Models

Compatibility	Subsystem 1 Organization Management	Subsystem 2 Product Management	Subsystem 3 Document Management	C_k(ISO9001)
C_1(ISO9001)	0	0	0	0
C_2(ISO9001)	15	10	50	75
C_3(ISO9001)	20	16	29	65
C_4(ISO9001)	16	3	12	31
C_5(ISO9001)	2	1	3	6

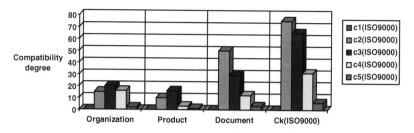

Figure 11.7 Compatibility of ISO 9001 with other models

Figure 11.7 shows that there is no MI in ISO 9001 with compatibility level 1, or no MI that is only defined by the model itself. Generally, about three quarters of the process domain of ISO 9001 have lower compatibility ($C_2(ISO9001)=75$ and $C_3(ISO9001)=65$), indicating ISO 9001 is relatively difficult to map onto other models except SEPRM. The MIs with compatibility level 4 in ISO 9001 are $C_4(ISO9001)=31$. The six MIs with the highest compatibility ($C_5(ISO9001)=6$) are those equivalent BPAs listed in Section 11.2.1.

11.5.2 CORRELATION OF ISO 9001 WITH OTHER MODELS

System level correlation between ISO 9001 and ISO/IEC TR 15504, CMM, BOOTSTRAP, and SEPRM is listed in Table 11.8, where the symbol "X" represents one of the other four models.

Table 11.8
Correlation: ISO 9001 vs. SEPRM, ISO/IEC TR 15504, CMM, and BOOTSTRAP

Correlation	Subsystem 1 Organization Management	Subsystem 2 Product Management	Subsystem 3 Document Management	r(ISO9001, X)	ρ(ISO9001, X)
SEPRM	53	31	93	177	39.9%
ISO/IEC TR 15504	23	12	23	58	28.9%
CMM	22	11	18	51	34.0%
Bootstrap	27	7	41	75	37.3%

The correlation data shown in Table 11.8 are illustrated in Figure 11.8. Generally, Figure 11.8 shows that ISO 9001 has the highest correlation with SEPRM, followed by BOOTSTRAP; its correlation to ISO/IEC TR 15504 and CMM are relatively low. Detailed one-to-many relationships between ISO 9001 and other four process models are analyzed below.

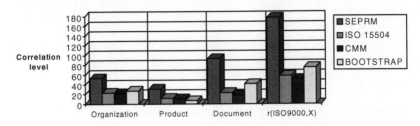

Figure 11.8 Correlation: ISO 9001 vs. SEPRM, ISO/IEC TR 15504, CMM, and BOOTSTRAP

11.5.2.1 ISO 9001 vs. SEPRM

The correlation level between ISO 9001 and SEPRM is *r(ISO9001, SEPRM)* = *177*, and the correlation ratio is ρ*(ISO9001, SEPRM)* = *39.9%*. Specifically, among the four pairs of correlation, ISO9001 – SEPRM is the most correlative in the document management subsystem and is the least correlative in the product management subsystem.

11.5.2.2 ISO 9001 vs. ISO/IEC TR 15504

The correlation level between ISO 9001 and ISO/IEC TR 15504 is *r(ISO9001, ISO15504)* = *58*, and the correlation ratio is ρ*(ISO9001, ISO15504)* = *28.9%*. Specifically, among the four pairs of correlation, ISO9001 – ISO15504 is the most correlative in the organization and development management subsystems and is the least correlative in the product management subsystem.

11.5.2.3 ISO 9001 vs. CMM

The correlation level between ISO 9001 and CMM is *r(ISO9001, CMM)* = *51*, and the correlation ratio is ρ*(ISO9001, CMM)* = *34.0 %*. Among the four pairs of the correlation, ISO9001 – CMM is most correlative in the organization management subsystem and is least correlative in the product management subsystem.

11.5.2.4 ISO 9001 vs. BOOTSTRAP

The correlation level between ISO 9001 and BOOTSTRAP is *r(ISO9001, BOOTSTRAP)* = *75* and the correlation ratio is ρ*(ISO9001, BOOTSTRAP)*

= *37.3 %.* Among the four pairs of the correlation, ISO9001 - BOOTSTRAP is most correlative in the document management subsystem and is least correlative in the product management subsystem.

Mappings from the viewpoints of the other models to ISO 9001 can be found in Sections 11.2 – 11.4 and 11.6. Detailed distribution of ISO 9001 correlation with SEPRM, ISO/IEC TR 15504, CMM, and BOOTSTRAP at the MI level can be referenced in Appendix C.

11.6 The SEPRM Model

This section analyzes compatibility and correlation of SEPRM with the other four models, i.e., ISO/IEC TR 15504, CMM, BOOTSTRAP, and ISO 9001. Process domain and BPA configuration of SEPRM are contrasted with current process models.

11.6.1 COMPATIBILITY OF SEPRM TO OTHER MODELS

According to the statistics by Wang et al. (1996a/b/97a/b), there are 729 equivalent BPAs individually identified in ISO/IEC TR 15504, CMM, BOOTSTRAP, and ISO 9001. By filtering the overlaps and redundancy in them, there are 407 independent BPAs elicited from the four models. These BPAs are the main collection of the SEPRM model. In the SEPRM process domain, there are 37 BPAs (8%) that are newly identified in the SEPRM model, such as the processes for evaluating different software development methodology models, the adoption of tools for software development, test, maintenance, organization and management, and the establishment of the database/library of software reuse, documentation, benchmark, etc.

Applying Expression 2.6 to Appendix C, the compatibility of SEPRM to ISO/IEC TR 15504, CMM, BOOTSTRAP, and ISO 9001 is derived as shown in Table 11.9. An illustration of SEPRM's compatibility to the other process models is provided in Figure 11.9.

Table 11.9
Compatibility Degree of SEPRM to Other Process Models

Compatibility	Subsystem 1 Organization	Subsystem 2 Development	Subsystem 3 Management	C_k(SEPRM)
C_1 (SEPRM)	1	17	19	37
C_2 (SEPRM)	56	70	143	269
C_3 (SEPRM)	20	22	58	100
C_4 (SEPRM)	2	6	24	32
C_5 (SEPRM)	2	0	4	6

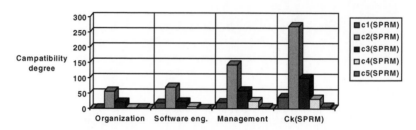

Figure 11.9 Compatibility of SEPRM with other models

Figure 11.9 shows that the 37 BPAs with level 1 compatibility, which are newly identified in the SEPRM model, are mainly distributed in the development and management subsystems as shown in Appendix C. Generally, about a half of the process domain of SEPRM is at compatibility level 2 ($C_2(SEPRM)=269$), meaning that those 269 BPAs can only be found in SEPRM and one of the other models; it also means that without SEPRM the compatibility between the other four models could be fairly low. The BPAs in SEPRM with a compatibility level higher than 3 are $C_3(SEPRM)=55$, $C_4(SEPRM)=35$, and $C_5(SEPRM)=6$, respectively, which indicates approximately 1/4 of the SEPRM BPAs have a better compatibility with other process models. Particularly, there are six BPAs with the highest compatibility ($C_5(SEPRM)=6$), which have been shown in Section 11.2.1.

11.6.2 CORRELATION OF SEPRM WITH OTHER MODELS

System level correlation between SEPRM and ISO/IEC TR 15504, CMM, BOOTSTRAP, and ISO 9001 are listed in Table 11.10, where the symbol "X" represents one of the other four models where appropriate.

Table 11.10
Correlation: SEPRM vs. ISO/IEC TR 15504, CMM, BOOTSTRAP,
and ISO 9001

Correlation	Subsystem 1 Organization	Subsystem 2 Development	Subsystem 3 Management	r(SEPRM, X)	ρ(SEPRM, X)
ISO/IEC TR 15504	61	47	93	201	100%
CMM	21	20	109	150	100%
Bootstrap	23	64	114	201	100%
ISO 9001	25	44	108	177	100%

The correlation data shown in Table 11.10 are illustrated in Figure 11.10. Generally, Figure 11.10 shows that SEPRM is 100% correlated to all ISO/IEC TR 15504, CMM, BOOTSTRAP, and ISO 9001, but not vice versa according to Definition 2.39. These four models can be completely mapped onto the SEPRM model as different subsets, although correlation in one-to-one mappings between the four models has been low as has been analyzed in previous sections. Detailed one-to-many relationships between SEPRM and the other four process models are analyzed below.

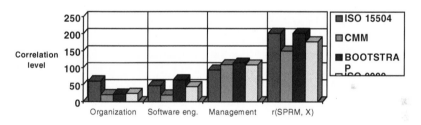

Figure 11.10 Correlation: SEPRM vs. ISO/IEC TR 15504, CMM, BOOTSTRAP, and ISO 9001

11.6.2.1 SEPRM vs. ISO/IEC TR 15504

The correlation level between SEPRM and ISO/IEC TR 15504 is *r(SEPRM, ISO15504) = 201*, and the correlation ratio is ρ*(SEPRM, ISO15504) = 100%*. Specifically, in the organization subsystem, SEPRM – ISO15504 is the most correlative pair. In the development subsystem, correlation of SEPRM – ISO15504 is relatively low. In the management subsystem, SEPRM – ISO15504 is the least correlative.

11.6.2.2 SEPRM vs. CMM

The correlation level between SEPRM and CMM is *r(SEPRM, CMM) = 150*, and the correlation ratio is ρ*(SEPRM, CMM) = 100%*. Specifically, in the organization subsystem, SEPRM – CMM is the least correlative pair. In the development subsystem, SEPRM – CMM is also the least correlative. In the management subsystem, correlation of SEPRM – CMM is relatively high.

11.6.2.3 SEPRM vs. BOOTSTRAP

The correlation level between SEPRM and BOOTSTRAP is *r(SEPRM, BOOTSTRAP) = 201,* and the correlation ratio is ρ*(SEPRM, BOOTSTRAP) = 100%*. Specifically, in the organization subsystem, correlation of SEPRM – BOOTSTRAP is relatively low. In the development subsystem, SEPRM – BOOTSTRAP is the most correlative. In the management subsystem, SEPRM – BOOTSTRAP is also the most correlative.

11.6.2.4 SEPRM vs. ISO 9001

The correlation level between SEPRM and ISO 9001 is *r(SEPRM, ISO9001) = 177,* and the correlation ratio is ρ*(SEPRM, ISO9001) = 100%*. Specifically, in the organization management subsystems, correlation of SEPRM – ISO9001 is relatively high; in the development subsystem, correlation of SEPRM – ISO9001 is relatively low.

Mappings from the viewpoints of the other models to SEPRM can be found in Sections 11.2 – 11.5, respectively. Detailed distribution of the SEPRM correlation with ISO/IEC TR 15504, CMM, BOOTSTRAP and ISO 9001 at the BPA level can be referenced in Appendix C.

11.7 An overview of Interrelationships between Current Process Models

In Sections 11.2 through 11.6 we analyzed the compatibility and correlation between current process models by the approach of one-to-many mapping. This section summarizes the findings on configuration orientation, compatibility, and correlation of current process models, and provides a many-to-many perception on interrelationships between current process models.

11.7.1 CONFIGURATION ORIENTATION OF CURRENT PROCESS MODELS

As described in the unified software engineering process framework in Part I, the BPA is the fundamental element in modeling a software process. By observing the configurations of BPAs in current process models, orientation and emphasis of these models can be explored quantitatively and objectively.

With regard to the structure of the unified process framework developed in Part I, configurations of the identified BPAs modeled in current process models in the organization, development, and management subsystems are contrasted in Figure 11.11. The various patterns of configurations of the BPAs indicate different orientations and focuses of current process models. It is obvious that SEPRM provides a superset of BPAs in all the three process subsystems.

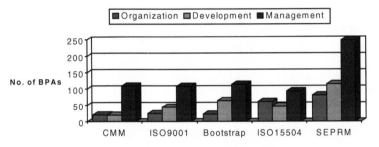

Figure 11.11 Configurations of current process models

Relative BPA configurations of current process models in the organization, development, and management process subsystems can be derived as shown in Figure 11.12, according to the distributions of percentages of BPAs within individual models. It is interesting to note that:

- CMM is the most management-oriented process model.

- BOOTSTRAP is the most technical-oriented process model.

- ISO/IEC TR 15504 is the most organization-oriented process model.

An average relative distribution of the BPAs in the three process systems, as shown in the SEPRM reference model, is approximately as follows:

$$Organization : Development : Management = 2 : 3 : 5 \qquad (11.1)$$

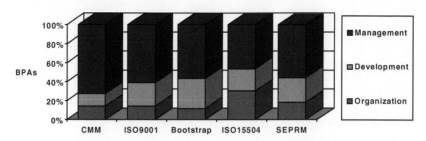

Figure 11.12 Orientation of current software process models

Expression 11.1 provides a reference ratio of process and BPA configurations in the three software engineering process subsystems. This expression indicates that for implementing process-based software engineering in large-scale software development, the deployment of effort and resources in organization, development, and management might be considered as 20% : 30% : 50%. It is noteworthy that conventional software development has been concentrated purely on the technical processes, while large-scale software development requires substantial resources and effort be put on organization infrastructures, management measures, and software quality assurance in software engineering.

11.7.2 COMPATIBILITY BETWEEN CURRENT PROCESS MODELS

The compatibility between current process models is summarized in Table 11.11, where the symbol "X" represents one of the other process models. The data in Table 11.11 provide a complete view on the distributions of compatibility degrees and relative compatibility (in the brackets) of current process models.

The relative compatibility of the five process models is contrasted in Figure 11.13. In the whole process domains as covered by the BPAs of current process models, there are six BPAs (1.4%) having the highest level of compatibility, and 37 BPAs (8.3%) are with compatibility level 1, meaning that they are only identified in SEPRM. The most common compatibility level is level 2 (60.6%) with more than a half of the BPAs (269) identified in both SEPRM and one of the other four models. The rest, nearly 1/3 of the total BPAs (132), are located at compatibility levels 3 (22.5%) and 4 (7.2%), respectively.

Table 11.11
Compatibility Levels between Current Process Models

Compatibility	SEPRM	ISO/IEC TR 15504	CMM	BOOTSTRAP	ISO 9001
$C_1(X)$	37 (8.3%)	0	0	0	0
$C_2(X)$	269 (60.6%)	102 (50.7%)	53 (35.3%)	102 (50.7%)	75 (42.4%)
$C_3(X)$	100 (22.5%)	60 (29.9%)	55 (36.7%)	68 (33.8%)	65 (36.7%)
$C_4(X)$	32 (7.2%)	32 (15.9%)	35 (23.3%)	25 (12.5%)	31 (17.5%)
$C_5(X)$	6 (1.4%)	7 (3.5%)	7 (4.7%)	6 (3.0%)	6 (3.4%)
Total	444	201	150	201	177

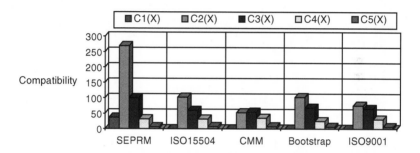

Figure 11.13 Compatibility distribution between current process models

The above view indicates that the process domains of ISO/IEC TR 15504, CMM, BOOTSTRAP, and ISO 9001 are relatively incompatible. Therefore, conventional one-to-one mappings between them would be very difficult and inaccurate. If the SEPRM reference model is adopted as an intermediate model, the comparative analysis between current process models is enabled on a sound foundation.

11.7.3 CORRELATION BETWEEN CURRENT PROCESS MODELS

It has been found theoretically and practically that the mappings between a pair of process models are asymmetrical [Wang et al., 1996b/97a]. Therefore, bidirectional mappings have been conducted in analyzing correlation between current process models at both system and BPA levels.

The correlation levels and ratios between current process models are summarized in Table 11.12. Table 11.12 shows, for example, that ISO/IEC TR 15504 and CMM have 64 shared BPAs, the correlation ratio of ISO/IEC TR 15504 to CMM is 42.7% while that of CMM versus ISO/IEC TR 15504 is 31.8%. This fact demonstrates the asymmetrical feature of correlation in process model mapping.

Considering the four major process models except SEPRM, the highest correlation ratio is 42.7% with ISO/IEC TR 15504 versus CMM; the lowest correlation ratio is 28.8% between CMM versus ISO 9001. The average correlation ratio among the four process models is about one-third without SEPRM.

Table 11.12
Correlation between Current Process Models

r(R, C) (ρ(R, C))	ISO/IEC TR 15504	CMM	BOOTSTRAP	ISO 9001	SEPRM
ISO/IEC TR 15504	201 (100%)	64 (42.7%)	59 (29.4%)	58 (32.8%)	201 (45.3%)
CMM	64 (31.8%)	150 (100%)	49 (24.4%)	51 (28.8%)	150 (33.8%)
BOOTSTRAP	59 (29.4%)	49 (32.7%)	201 (100%)	75 (42.4%)	201 (45.3)
ISO 9001	58 (28.9%)	51 (34.0%)	75 (37.3%)	177 (100%)	177 (39.9%)
SEPRM	201 (100%)	150 (100%)	201 (100%)	177 (100%)	444 (100%)

R – a related model at the *Rth* row;   C – a related model in the *Cth* column

Based on the data summarized in Table 11.12, a correlation profile between current process models is derived in Figure 11.14. The figure shows that, on average among the four current models, correlation between one and another is at the level of around one-third. However, as a superset of the four models, SEPRM has achieved the highest correlation with all the other models. This inherent characteristic forms the foundation for mutually transforming the capability levels between current process models via SEPRM in the next chapter.

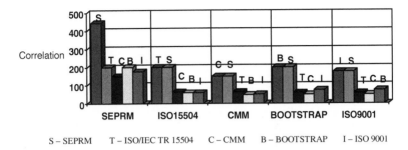

Figure 11.14 Correlation profile between current process models

11.8 Summary

This chapter has presented an objective view of the interrelationships between current process paradigms. SEPRM has been shown as a super model, developed according to the unified process framework and theory, which possesses higher compatibility and correlation with the existing process models.

The analyses of this chapter have been based on the data documented in Appendix C. Mining this set of data, readers may find new facts and additional statistically significant regulations in process-based software engineering.

The basic knowledge structure of this chapter is as follows:

Chapter 11. Comparative Analysis of Current Process Models

- General
  - Purposes of this chapter
    - To analyze the relationships between current process models by using one-to-one, one-to-many, and/or many-to-one mappings
    - To investigate compatibility and correlation between current process models
    - To explore features and special orientation of current

process models so that suitable or combined process models can be chosen for a specific software development organization

– To enable the development of process capability transformations between current process models which will be covered in the next chapter.

– Analyzing methods
- – Configuration: Bidirectional mapping of BPAs
- – Compatibility
  - $c_k (M) = \#\{BPA_i \mid BPA_i \in C_k \}, \; k=1,2,...,5$
    and $i = 1 ... n$

$$= \sum_{i=1}^{n} \{ 1 \mid BPA_i \in C_k \}, \; k=1,2,...,5 \qquad (2.6)$$

- – Correlation
  - $r(R, S) = \# \{ x_i \mid x_i \in m(R, S)\}$ $\qquad\qquad (2.9)$
  - $\rho(R,S) = \dfrac{r(R,S)}{\#R} \%$ $\qquad\qquad (2.10)$

- The ISO/IEC TR 15504 process model
  - – Background philosophy
    To present a set of structured capability measurements for all software lifecycle processes, and for all parties such as software developers, acquirers, contractors, and customers

  - – Configuration orientation
    Organization : Development : Management = 30.3% : 23.4% : 46.3%

  - – Compatibility
    - $C_1 (ISO15504) = 0$
    - $C_2 (ISO15504) = 23.0\%$
    - $C_3 (ISO15504) = 13.5\%$
    - $C_4 (ISO15504) = 7.2\%$
    - $C_5 (ISO15504) = 1.6\%$

  - – Correlation
    - – To SEPRM: 45.3%
    - – To CMM: 42.7%
    - – To BOOTSTRAP: 29.4%
    - – To ISO 9001:   32.8%

- The CMM process model
  - Background philosophy

    To present a software project contractor's perception of the organizational and managerial capacity of a software development organization

  - Configuration orientation

    Organization : Development : Management =
    14.0% : 13.3% : 72.7%

  - Compatibility
    - C_1 (CMM) = 0
    - C_2 (CMM) = 11.9%
    - C_3 (CMM) = 12.4%
    - C_4 (CMM) = 7.9%
    - C_5 (CMM) = 1.6%

  - Correlation
    - To SEPRM: 33.8%
    - To ISO/IEC TR 15504: 31.8%
    - To BOOTSTRAP: 24.4%
    - To ISO 9001:   28.8%

- The BOOTSTRAP process model
  - Background philosophy

    To present a combined view of software life cycle processes and quality system principles

  - Configuration orientation:

    Organization : Development : Management =
    11.5% : 31.8% : 56.7%

  - Compatibility
    - C_1 (BOOTSTRAP) = 0
    - C_2 (BOOTSTRAP) = 23.0%
    - C_3 (BOOTSTRAP) = 15.3%
    - C_4 (BOOTSTRAP) = 5.6%
    - C_5 (BOOTSTRAP) = 1.4%

  - Correlation
    - To SEPRM: 45.3%
    - To ISO/IEC TR 15504: 29.4%

        – To CMM: 32.7%
        – To ISO 9001:   42.4%

- The ISO 9001 process model
  - Background philosophy
    - To present a generic quality system perception of software Development

  - Configuration orientation
    - *Organization : Development : Management =*
      14.1% : 24.9% : 61.0%

  - Compatibility
    - C_1 (ISO 9001) = 0
    - C_2 (ISO 9001) = 16.9%
    - C_3 (ISO 9001) = 14.6%
    - C_4 (ISO 9001) = 7.0%
    - C_5 (ISO 9001) = 1.4%

  - Correlation
    - To SEPRM: 39.9%
    - To ISO/IEC TR 15504: 28.9%
    - To CMM: 34.0%
    - To BOOTSTRAP: 37.3%

- The SEPRM process model
  - Background philosophy
    - To present a comprehensive and integrated process system Reference model, with sound foundations and benchmarked Data support, for process-based software engineering

  - Configuration orientation
    - *Organization : Development : Management =*
      18.2% : 25.9% : 55.9%

  - Compatibility
    - C_1 (SEPRM) = 8.3%
    - C_2 (SEPRM) = 60.6%
    - C_3 (SEPRM) = 22.5%
    - C_4 (SEPRM) = 7.2%
    - C_5 (SEPRM) = 1.4%

- Correlation
  - To ISO/IEC TR 15504: 100%
  - To CMM: 100%
  - To BOOTSTRAP: 100%
  - To ISO 9001: 100%

- Summary of interrelationships between current process models
  - Average configuration orientation

    Organization : Development : Management = 2 : 3 : 5 (11.1)
  - Compatibility: Table 11.11
  - Correlation: Table 11.12

Major achievements and issues for further research suggested by this chapter are highlighted below:

- This chapter has developed a rigorous approach to analyzing the interrelationships among the process domains of current process paradigms. Quantitative and objective analysis results have been provided for revealing the interrelationships of current process models.

- The problems of what and how we measure in analyzing the interrelationships among the process domains of current process models have been solved. Compatibility and correlation, developed in Section 2.5.1, have been taken to quantitatively measure the interrelationships among current process models.

- As described in the unified software engineering process framework, BPA is the fundamental element in modeling a process system. By observing and analyzing the configurations of BPAs in current process models, the orientation and emphasis of these models can be explored quantitatively and objectively.

- For implementing process-based software engineering in large-scale software development, the deployment of effort and resources in organization, development, and management processes is derived as 20% : 30% : 50%. Although conventional software development has been concentrated purely on the technical processes, large-scale software development requires much more resources and effort for organizational infrastructures, management measures, and quality assurance in software engineering.

- It is found that the most common compatibility level between current process models is at level 2 (61%) with more than a half of the BPAs (269) identified in both SEPRM and one of the other four models. This indicates that the process domains of ISO/IEC TR 15504, CMM, BOOTSTRAP, and ISO 9001 are relatively incompatible. Therefore, conventional one-to-one mapping between them has encountered difficulties. If the SEPRM reference model is adopted as an intermediate model, comparative analysis between the current process models is enabled on a sound foundation.

- The correlation profile developed in Section 11.7.3 shows that, on average among the four major process models except SEPRM, correlation between one and another is at the level of around 30%. However, as a superset of the four models, SEPRM has achieved the highest correlation with all the other models. This inherent characteristic forms the foundation for mutually transforming the capability levels between current process models via SEPRM.

To enable further development of process capability transformations between current process models, it is a prerequisite to quantitatively analyze the compatibility and correlation between the process paradigms. Formal description of individual process models can be referred to as follows: Chapter 5 (CMM), Chapter 6 (ISO 9001), Chapter 7 (BOOTSTRAP), Chapter 8 (ISO/IEC TR 15504), and Chapter 9 (SEPRM), respectively. Comparative analysis of process capability measurements and relationships of capability levels between current process models will be developed in the next chapter.

Annotated Reference

A number of pairwise analyses of interrelationships between current process models have been reported. Paulk et al. (1994/95b) revealed the relationships between CMM and SPICE, and between CMM and ISO 9001. Kitson (1996) related the SPICE framework with the ESI approach to software process assessment. Koch (1993) and Jarvinen (1994) reported the background and relationship between BOOTSTRAP and CMM. Kugler and Messnarz (1994) described the relationships between BOOTSTRAP and ISO

9001. Wang et al. (1999g) reported a conformance analysis case study between a tailored CMM and ISO/IEC TR 15504.

Bidirectional, quantitative, many-to-many analyses between current process models were found necessary. Wang et al. (1997a/b/99e/g) presented a series of comparative analyses of relationships between current process models: ISO/IEC TR 15504, CMM, ISO 9001, BOOTSTRAP, and SEPRM.

Wang et al. (1997a/b/99e) developed a framework for systematically characterizing and quantitatively analyzing software engineering process systems with a set of metrics such as compatibility, correlation, characteristic attributes of processes, and benchmarking of these characteristic attributes.

Questions and Problems

11.1 In Chapters 5 – 9 we explored the philosophies behind each of current process models. To demonstrate that you understand the ethos, make a summary and comparison of these philosophies.

11.2 Referring to Figure 11.1 and Table 11.1, what are the highest and lowest compatibility levels between ISO/IEC TR 15504 and the other current process models?

11.3 Observing Figure 11.2 and Table 11.2, what are the most and least correlative models of ISO/IEC TR 15504?

11.4 Referring to Figure 11.3 and Table 11.3, what are the highest and lowest compatibility levels between CMM and the other current process models?

11.5 Observing Figure 11.4 and Table 11.4, what are the most and least correlative models of CMM?

11.6 Referring to Figure 11.5 and Table 11.5, what are the highest and lowest compatibility levels between BOOTSTRAP and the other current process models?

11.7 Observing Figure 11.6 and Table 11.6, what are the most and least correlative models of BOOTSTRAP?

11.8 Referring to Figure 11.7 and Table 11.7, what are the highest and lowest compatibility levels between ISO 9001 and the other current process models?

11.9 Observing Figure 11.8 and Table 11.8, what are the most and least correlative models of ISO 9001?

11.10 Referring to Figure 11.9 and Table 11.9, what are the highest and lowest compatibility levels between SEPRM and the other current process models?

11.11 Observing Figure 11.10 and Table 11.10, what are the most and least correlative models of SEPRM, and what are the advantages of SEPRM as a superset process model?

11.12 The correlation levels and ratios between current process models have been summarized in Table 11.12. Explain Table 11.12 using your own words.

Chapter 12

TRANSFORMATION OF CAPABILITY LEVELS BETWEEN CURRENT PROCESS MODELS

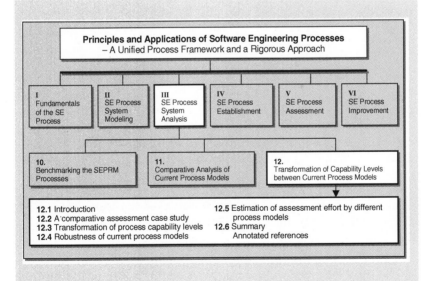

Principles and Applications of Software Engineering Processes
– A Unified Process Framework and a Rigorous Approach

| I Fundamentals of the SE Process | II SE Process System Modeling | III SE Process System Analysis | IV SE Process Establishment | V SE Process Assessment | VI SE Process Improvement |

10. Benchmarking the SEPRM Processes

11. Comparative Analysis of Current Process Models

12. Transformation of Capability Levels between Current Process Models

12.1 Introduction
12.2 A comparative assessment case study
12.3 Transformation of process capability levels
12.4 Robustness of current process models
12.5 Estimation of assessment effort by different process models
12.6 Summary
Annotated references

This chapter analyzes the interrelationships between the capability scales of current process models, and investigates how a given capability level in one model may be related to another. The stability of assessment results in current process models is tested by three specially designed cases. Empirical data on the time expended in process assessments using current process models are derived and related to the unit of person-hours for estimating the costs in process assessment.

The objectives of this chapter are as follows:

- To find out the interrelationships between the capability scales of current process models

- To seek an approach for transforming the capability levels between current process models

- To explore the stability of assessment for current process models

- To investigate the time and effort expended in process assessments using current process models

12.1 Introduction

The interrelationships between the process domains of current process models were explored in Chapter 11. This chapter analyzes the interrelationships between the capability domains of current process models, and explores how a given capability level in one model be quantitatively related to another. In the end of this chapter, the relationships of current process models in both of the process and capability dimensions will be clarified. This method also enables a software development organization to avoid being assessed several times against various process models that would be costly and time-consuming.

In the software industry and in software engineering research, it has long been expected that the ideal of a comparative assessment result, which applies all the current process models to the same software development organization, could be achieved. As a result, the interrelationship and transformability of the capability levels in different models need to be explored. With the establishment of the unified process framework and the development of the algorithms of current process models presented in this book, it is now possible to implement the ideal.

Through a comparative process assessment case study project for a sample software development organization using the CMM, ISO 9001, BOOTSTRAP, ISO/IEC TR 15504 (SPICE), and SEPRM methodologies, the possibility and approach for transformability are explored. This leads to the development of a method for transforming the capability levels between current process models.

A case study on comparative process assessment will be reviewed in Section 12.2. Then, a method for process capability transformation among current process models will be developed in Section 12.3. Using the capability transformation method, the robustness of assessment results and the costs of assessment efforts of current process models will be analyzed in Sections 12.4 and 12.5, respectively.

12.2 A Comparative Assessment Case Study

In Appendix C the raw data of process performance collected from the sample software development organization have been documented in the column labeled "rating" against the BPAs defined in SEPRM. Individual assessment results according to different models have been described in the sample assessment sections of Chapters 5 through 9, respectively. This section reviews and contrasts the assessment results as a preparation for the discussion of capability transformation between current process models.

12.2.1 THE SEPRM ASSESSMENT RESULT

An SEPRM process assessment was carried out in Section 9.5. In order to comparatively analyze the results of case studies in current process models, a set of the process capability profiles of the organization, development, and management subsystems are reproduced in Figures 12.1 – 12.3.

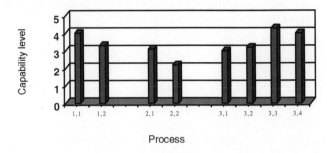

Figure 12.1 Capability profile of organization process subsystem assessed in SEPRM

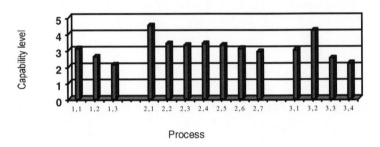

Figure 12.2 Capability profile of development process subsystem in SEPRM

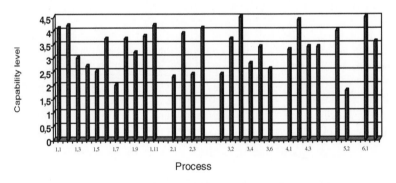

Figure 12.3 Capability profile of management process subsystem in SEPRM

With the individual process capability level as shown in Figures 12.1 to 12.3, the software development organization's capability level is determined to be Level 3.5, the stable process capability level, according to the SEPRM algorithm developed in Chapter 9.

12.2.2 THE ISO/IEC TR 15504 ASSESSMENT RESULT

An ISO/IEC 15504 process assessment was carried out in Section 8.5. The process capability profile of the 35 processes in the 5 process categories is reproduced in Figure 12.4.

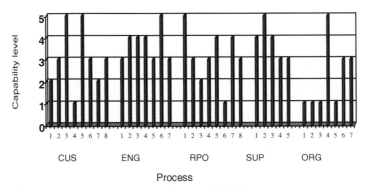

Figure 12.4 A process capability profile in ISO/IEC 15504

With the individual process capability level as shown in Figure 12.4, the software development organization's capability level is determined to be Level 3, the established process capability level, according to the ISO/IEC 15504 algorithm developed in Chapter 8.

12.2.3 THE CMM ASSESSMENT RESULT

A CMM process assessment was carried out in Section 5.5. The process capability profile of the 18 key process areas (KPAs) is reproduced in Figure 12.5.

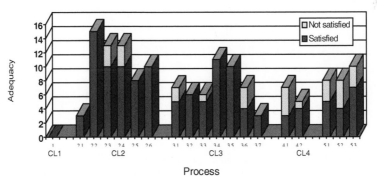

Figure 12.5 A process capability profile in CMM

With the individual process adequacy distribution as shown in Figure 12.5, the software development organization's capability level is determined to be Level 3, the defined process capability level, according to the CMM algorithm developed in Chapter 5.

12.2.4 THE BOOTSTRAP ASSESSMENT RESULT

A BOOTSTRAP process assessment was carried out in Section 7.5. The process capability profile of the 32 processes in the 5 process levels is reproduced in Figure 12.6.

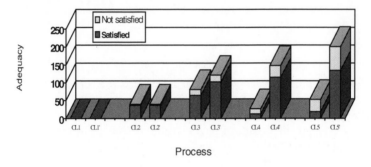

Figure 12.6 A process capability profile in BOOTSTRAP

With the individual process adequacy distribution as shown in Figure 12.6, the software development organization's capability level is determined to be Level 3.25, the defined process capability level, according to the BOOTSTRAP algorithm developed in Chapter 7.

12.2.5 THE ISO 9001 ASSESSMENT RESULT

An ISO 9001 process assessment was carried out in Section 6.5. The process capability profile of the 20 main topic areas (MTAs) is reproduced in Figure 12.7.

With the individual process adequacy distribution as shown in Figure 12.7, the software development organization's capability level is determined to be passed according to the ISO 9001 algorithm developed in Chapter 6.

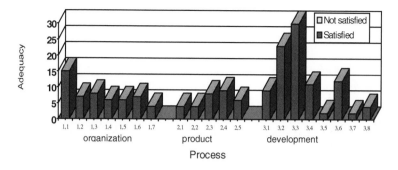

Figure 12.7 A process capability profile in ISO 9001

By using the assessment results provided in this section, the following sections discuss some interesting subjects in process-based software engineering, such as process capability transformation, robustness of assessment results, and assessment time estimation for current process models.

12.3 Transformation of Process Capability Levels

In Part I and Part II of this book, a formal and algorithmic capability determination approach was developed for software engineering process assessment based on the unified process framework and process assessment algorithms. In this formal approach, assessor-dependent factors in process assessment are limited to the lowest level – the practice (BPA) scope; the higher level capabilities, such as in the scopes of process and project, should be derived according to a set of rigorously described methods and related formulae. The assessment results may thus be objective, accurate, and stable.

The raw rating data of BPA performance have been documented in Appendix C for all BPAs defined in SEPRM. Because the SEPRM process model is a superset of those of the other existing models, a single set of BPA rating data enables multiple model-oriented process assessments based on the mapping mechanism provided in Appendix C.

By using the superset of BPA ratings, process capability levels in ISO/IEC 15504, CMM, BOOTSTRAP, ISO 9001, and SEPRM can be derived according to a set of algorithms. As a result, comparative and transformable assessment results for the same software development organization against the major process models are obtained.

In this approach the capability levels of a software development organization can be mutually transformed for the first time between the current models via SEPRM. This means that by providing the original raw rating data in the practice scope and supplementing the additional BPAs in SEPRM, a capability level in a known model among the five can now be transformed into any of the other four models quantitatively and objectively.

For instance, as demonstrated in Section 12.2, using the same set of BPA rating data listed in Appendix C, process capability levels of the same organization in each of current process models have been derived as summarized in Table 12.1.

Table 12.1
Transformation of Assessment Results between Current Process Models

Model	Assessed Capability Level	Description of Process
SEPRM	3.3	Stable
ISO/IEC 15504	3	Established
CMM	3	Defined
BOOTSTRAP	3.25	Defined
ISO 9001	Passed	Passed

Table 12.1 shows how the capability levels of the sample organization can be related and transformed among SEPRM, ISO/IEC 15504, CMM, BOOTSTRAP, and ISO 9001. The finding is that the assessments by current process models are comparable and the relationships between them are definite for a given software development organization. Therefore, this approach provides a practical way for mutually transforming the capability levels among the major software process models.

The case studies summarized in Table 12.1 are by no means suggestive of a fixed interrelationship of the capability levels between different process models for different software development organizations. They simply demonstrate how the capability levels can be mutually transformed, case by case, based on a unified superset of BPAs defined in SEPRM and the individual algorithms. Thus, an ISO 9001-passed software development organization could be related at CMM Level 2, ISO/IEC 15504 Level 4, BOOTSTRAP Level 2.75, SEPRM Level 3.2, or others, depending on the specific set of BPA rating data of the case.

What is significant is that there is a determinable interrelationship between the capability levels of current process models for any given case. Thus, any software development organization can apply this method to its own process data in order to transform a known process capability level in a model to the others quantitatively and objectively.

12.4 Robustness of Current Process Models

In order to test the stability or robustness of process assessment by current process models, the following method may be utilized. The idea is to shift the raw assessment data +/-10% randomly. This is intended to simulate the assessors' varying judgement differences upon performance of individual BPAs in an assessment. The testing results of robustness of current process models are shown in Table 12.2.

Table 12.2
Robustness of Assessment Results by Different Models

Model	Case B	Case C	Case A
	By −10% rated data	By original assessment data	By +10% rated data
SEPRM	3.2	3.3	3.4
ISO/IEC 15504	2	3	3
CMM	2	3	3
BOOTSTRAP	3.0	3.25	4.0
ISO 9001	Passed	Passed	Passed

Observing the testing results shown in Table 12.2, two worst cases (A and B) and a normal case (C) in process assessments for investigating the robustness of current process models are analyzed in the following subsections.

12.4.1 CASE A – BIASED OVERRATING

Case A, as shown in Table 12.2, is a worst case of a biased overrating of the real process performance. When an assessor intends to give higher ratings for BPAs at +10% level, the final assessment results of all models except BOOTSTRAP are quite stable.

12.4.2 CASE B – BIASED UNDERRATING

In another worst case (Case B) as shown in Table 12.2, the assessor may underrate the real process performance by bias. When an assessor intends to give lower ratings for BPAs at -10% level, the final assessment results of SEPRM and BOOTSTRAP have been kept stable, but the ISO/IEC 15504 and CMM results have been decreased from Level 3 to Level 2.

It is noteworthy that, in such a case, ISO 9001 might result in the largest instability, which can vary from "passed" to "failed" outcomes when a small part of BPAs are given lower ratings.

12.4.3 CASE C – A NORMAL CASE

In a normal case as shown in Table 12.2, the variety of the assessor's rating for BPAs would be kept at the average level that approaches the accurate value. That is, although some of the BPAs may be rated for higher or lower values in an assessment, the errors of the final assessment results, in the average case, will not be worse than those of the above Cases A and B.

This case indicates that, while an individual BPA would be over- or underrated randomly in real assessment, the average rating errors tend to offset statistically in an assessment as a whole. Based on this observation, we may infer that the final assessment results can still keep the tropism when the random rating errors exceed the ±10% ranges.

In analyzing Table 12.2, it can also be found that SEPRM possesses the highest robustness in both the worst Cases A and B. This feature demonstrates the merits of the SEPRM algorithm and its basis of the unified software engineering process framework.

12.5 Estimation of Assessment Effort for Different Process Models

Analyzing the algorithms of current process models established from Chapters 5 to 9, the theoretical effort expended in an assessment is determined exactly by the algorithm complexities of different process models. That is, the more complex an algorithm is, the more effort will need to be expended in an assessment. This parallel provides the basis of assessment effort estimation.

The algorithm complexities of the five process models in process capability determination are summarized in Table 12.3. The numbers show the assessment complexities in terms practice performance ratings or process capability level ratings. For detailed discussions readers may refer to related chapters in Part II.

Table 12.3
Operating Complexities of the Current Software Process Models

Capability Scope	CMM	BOOTSTRAP	ISO/IEC 15504	ISO 9001	SEPRM
Practice	150	201	201	177	444
Process	18	9	35	18	51
Project	150	201	(201+35)*9=2124	177	444+2*51 = 546
Organization	150*n	201 * n	2124 * n	177 * n	546 * n

Note: n – number of projects

In order to estimate the time expended in conducting an assessment using different process models, a relationship between the algorithm complexity and an average unit time spent on a BPA's rating have been investigated. According to the ISO/IEC 15504 trial data and the report related to other process models [SPICE Project, 1998; Wang et al., 1999e/h], an average rate of unit time for the BPA rating can be calibrated as 3.0 minutes per BPA. Using this as a reference rate and the data shown in Table 12.3, the time expended for BPA and process rating in different models is derived as follows:

- SEPRM   27.2   (person-hrs)

- ISO/IEC TR 15504   106.2   (person-hrs)

- CMM   7.5   (person-hrs)

- ISO 9001   9.0   (person-hrs)

- BOOTSTRAP   10.2   (person-hrs)

In summary, the operating complexities of current software engineering process assessment models, in person-hours, are shown in Figure 12.8.

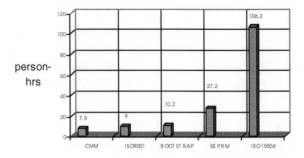

Figure 12.8 Operating complexities of current process models

It is noteworthy that overheads for assessment input preparation and report generation, as well as assessor's productivity and assessees' involvement, should also be taken into account. In practice, those overheads could be significantly high in relation to the above regular assessment effort [Wang et al., 1998f/99h].

12.6 Summary

This chapter has demonstrated that one of the important functions of SEPRM is to enable capability level transformation between current process models. Test cases have been designed to analyze the robustness of current process models in process assessment and capability determination. Empirical data for estimation of assessment efforts by different process models have been provided as references.

The basic knowledge structure of this chapter is as follows:

Chapter 12. Transformation of Capability Levels between
            Current Process Models

- General
  - Purposes of this chapter

      - To find out the interrelationships between the capability
        scales of current process models

- To seek an approach for transforming the capability levels between current process models

- To explore the stability of assessment for current process models

- To investigate the time and effort expended in process assessments using current process models

- A comparative assessment case study
  - Comparative assessments
    - For the same organization and the same process system
    - Apply multiple process models and algorithms

  - Understand the comparative assessment case study
    - Data as listed in Appendix C
    - Assessment results
      - Process profiles
      - Process capability levels

  - Refer to Chapters 5 through 9 in Part II for details

- Transformation of process capability levels
  - Concept of process capability transformation
    - Relate process capability levels between current process models
    - From a given process level in a certain model, derive equivalent process capability levels in the other models

  - Method for process capability transformation
    - Create a superset of BPAs which covers the domain of current process models
    - Establish multiple algorithms for current process models

  - Understand the case presented in Section 12.3

- Robustness of current process models
  - The nature of BPA ratings by assessors as human beings
    - Random errors of overrating or underrating
    - Statistical offset of the errors in average
  - Concept of robustness of process models
  - Understand the case presented in Section 12.4

- Estimation of assessment effort by different process models
  - The algorithm complexity of current process models
  - The calibration of the empirical reference rate of unit-time for a BPA rating
  - The time expended in assessments by current process models
  - Average time for an assessment by current process models: 32.4 person-hours

Major achievements and issues for further research suggested by this chapter are highlighted below:

- This chapter has addressed two important issues in software engineering process modeling and analysis – how to quantitatively analyze the interrelationship of process capability levels between current process models, and how to relate a given capability level in a process model to the others

- The process capability levels assessed by the five process models have been found quite correlative. Therefore, the capability levels can be mutually transformed between each other

- The stability or robustness of current process models has been tested by three specially designed cases. The test results have shown that there can be confidence in the robustness of current process models, especially SEPRM, which has the greatest robustness in both the worst cases, A and B. This feature has demonstrated the merits of the SEPRM algorithm and its sound basis created by the unified software engineering process framework

- In an attempt to estimate the costs of a process assessment, the algorithm complexities of current process models have been calibrated to the unit of person-hours based on empirical data. As a result, reference costs on the time expended in assessments by the five process models have been derived

- The process capability transformation method developed in this chapter has enabled the process capability level of a software development organization to be transformed, for the first time, between current process models. This means that by providing the original raw rating data of all BPAs, a capability level in a given model among the five can now be transformed into any of the other models quantitatively and objectively. In this approach, a software development organization may avoid being assessed several times against various process models that are costly and time-consuming

- The average time expended in assessment with current process models, except overhead in assessment preparation and report generation, is 32.4 (person-hrs), varying in a range from minimum 7.5 (person-hrs) in CMM to 106.2 (person-hrs) in ISO/IEC TR 15504

- Software development organizations can now assess their software engineering process practices according to the SEPRM reference model. Then, related process capability levels and process profiles to the major existing process models can be derived by transformations via SEPRM.

This chapter has extended the applications of the SEPRM reference model from software engineering process assessment and improvement to process capability transformation. Interrelationships of the process dimensions between SEPRM and the other process models were analyzed in Chapter 11. Applications of SEPRM in process-based software engineering and case studies will be provided in Parts IV – VI.

Annotated References

Process capability transformation is a new topic in research. Koch (1993) and Kuvaja et al. (1994a) related BOOTSTRAP capability maturity levels with those of CMM. Dorling and Wang et al. (1999a/b) reported capability level mapping between PULSE and ISO/IEC TR 15504.

Wang et al. (1997a/b/99e/g) carried out a series of comparative analyses of relationships and many-to-many mappings between current process models. Based on these works, Wang et al. (1997d/99h) reported comparative assessments and capability transformation between current process models.

Questions and Problems

12.1 Why do both practitioners and researchers expect a mechanism to transform process capability levels between current process models?

12.2 When assessing a software development organization according to SEPRM, using the mapping mechanism of SEPRM as shown in Appendix C, you can obtain the capability levels in the other models by recalculation according to their algorithms. Try to transform the SEPRM capability level of the project you assessed in Ex.9.10 into that of CMM and report your findings.

12.3 Section 12.4 demonstrated that the robustness of assessment results according to current process models is reasonably good. Try to compare your own assessment result of a SEPRM process with those of your colleagues in the same project, and analyze what the errors could be in an assessment for a single process.

12.4 This chapter has related the assessment efforts with the algorithm complexities of current process models. This approach provides a solid foundation for assessment cost estimation. Referring to Section 12.5, as well as Chapters 8 and 9, explain why SEPRM consists of the largest sets of BPAs and processes but ISO/IEC TR 15504 requires the highest assessment cost.

12.5 What are the overheads of process assessment costs? Could they significantly influence the total costs of a process assessment?

12.6 Software process assessments were considered a subjective procedure because all activities were judged by human beings. The quantitative and algorithmic approach developed in this book provides a new way toward objective assessment. However, one level of the assessment still requires assessors' personal judgment. What is this level?

PART IV

SOFTWARE ENGINEERING PROCESS ESTABLISHMENT

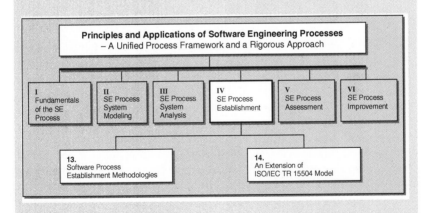

Principles and Applications of Software Engineering Processes
– A Unified Process Framework and a Rigorous Approach

| I Fundamentals of the SE Process | II SE Process System Modeling | III SE Process System Analysis | IV SE Process Establishment | V SE Process Assessment | VI SE Process Improvement |

13. Software Process Establishment Methodologies

14. An Extension of ISO/IEC TR 15504 Model

In the first three parts of this book, a unified process system framework and theory has been established. Using this unified process theory, current process models have been formally described and examined, and their relationships have been comparatively analyzed. A super SEPRM process system reference model has been developed for integrating current process models into a coherent framework.

In the second half of this book, the focus will be on how the unified theory and SEPRM may be applied in a real-world environment. Practical methodologies and guidelines will be developed for software engineering process establishment, assessment, and improvement through Parts IV – VI.

Software engineering process system establishment is the first important step in process-based software engineering because both process assessment and improvement theories and practices rely on working with the common foundation of a systematically established process system. Part IV of this book explores methodologies and approaches to software engineering process system establishment such as the reuse, tailoring, extension, and adaptation of process models. Relationships of these methodologies with the theories and unified process framework developed in previous parts are discussed. Examples and case studies, such as a parallel process model for software quality assurance, a minimum process model for software project management, a tailored CMM model, and an extension of ISO/IEC TR 15504 model, are provided for demonstrating the applications of the process establishment methodologies.

The knowledge structure of this part is as follows:

- Chapter 13. Software Process Establishment Methodologies
- Chapter 14. An Extension of ISO/IEC TR 15504 Model

Chapter 13 examines existing and new approaches to software process establishment. This chapter develops practical methodologies for software process establishment by reuse, tailoring, extension, and adaptation of process models. Process establishment technologies provide support and guidelines for building a process system at organization, project, team, or individual levels. The process establishment methodologies enable top management, project managers, and team leaders to describe their process structure and functional requirements in the easiest way. Three derived process models, a parallel process model for software quality assurance with one-to-one matching and synchronization between development and management processes, a minimum process model for software project management, and a tailored CMM, are explored.

Chapter 14 describes a complete paradigm of process establishment – the establishment of the PULSE software acquisition process model – as a compatible plug-in process module for ISO/IEC TR 15504. PULSE extends ISO/IEC TR 15504 to cover software and IT system acquisition process areas. As an extended compatible process model for ISO/IEC TR 15504, the

PULSE process capability levels have been designed to be transformable into certain ISO/IEC TR 15504 capability levels. The mapping of capability and attributes between the two models have been implemented to enable the PULSE assessment results to be related to that of the ISO/IEC TR 15504 model.

In this part, a pragmatic view of software engineering process system establishment, assessment, and improvement is adopted. Systematic process establishment is recognized as the foundation for process assessment and improvement. A software engineering process system reference model, such as SEPRM, is viewed as the central infrastructure for process system establishment.

Chapter 13

SOFTWARE PROCESS ESTABLISHMENT METHODOLOGIES

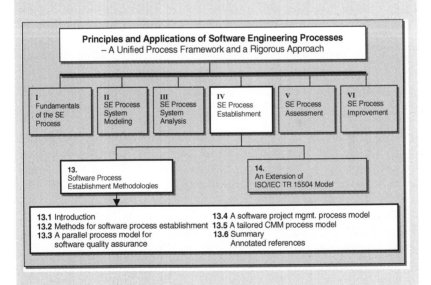

Principles and Applications of Software Engineering Processes
– A Unified Process Framework and a Rigorous Approach

| I
Fundamentals of the SE Process | II
SE Process System Modeling | III
SE Process System Analysis | IV
SE Process Establishment | V
SE Process Assessment | VI
SE Process Improvement |

13.
Software Process
Establishment Methodologies

14.
An Extension of
ISO/IEC TR 15504 Model

13.1 Introduction
13.2 Methods for software process establishment
13.3 A parallel process model for
    software quality assurance
13.4 A software project mgmt. process model
13.5 A tailored CMM process model
13.6 Summary
    Annotated references

This chapter describes principles and methodologies for software process system establishment and implementation. Examples and case studies in derived software process models are demonstrated.

The objectives of this chapter are as follows:

- To provide practical guidance on how to establish software engineering process systems at organization, project, and team levels

- To develop a set of useful methodologies for software process establishment and implementation

- To demonstrate a parallel process model for software quality assurance, which is a lightweight project process model tailored from SEPRM

- To demonstrate a process model for software project management, which is a medium-weight project process model tailored from SEPRM

- To demonstrate a case study on how CMM may be customized for small software development organizations

13.1 Introduction

In Chapter 4 a generic procedure for deriving a software project process model was introduced, and a number of methods for establishing software engineering process systems were explored. This chapter looks in further detail at software process establishment, and discusses applications and case studies of these methodologies.

From the viewpoint of scope or coverage of software process implementation, a software engineering process model can be classified as complete, medium, or light. Usually, a complete process model is established and applied in a whole organization as a reference. A medium- or light-weighted process model can be derived from the reference model for a specific software project according to its nature and requirements. In this chapter, reuse methods for software engineering process systems, and approaches to process system tailoring, adaptation, and extension are described. Both a minimum process model and a management model at project level are presented, deriving from the SEPRM process reference model. A tailored CMM model is explored which shows how CMM may be customized for use in small software development organizations.

Process establishment technologies provide support and guidelines for building a process system at organization, project, team, or individual levels. The process establishment methodologies enable top management, project managers, and team leaders to describe their process structure and functional requirements in the easiest way.

In the following sections, methodologies for software engineering process establishment are described in Section 13.2. Then, two derived process models from the SEPRM process reference model are explored as case studies in process establishment: (a) a parallel process model for software quality assurance in Section 13.3, and (b) a process model for software project management in Section 13.4. Finally, Section 13.5 describes a tailored CMM model and explores how CMM is customized for small software development organizations.

13.2 Methods for Software Engineering Process Establishment

The overall procedure for establishing a software engineering process system, as shown in Figure 13.1, was previously introduced in Section 4.2. This section develops four types of process system establishment methodologies for reuse, tailoring, extension, and adaptation of process models.

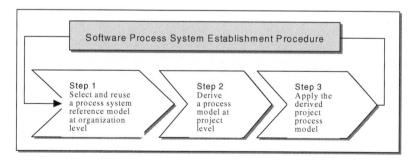

Figure 13.1 Procedure for establishing a software engineering process system

13.2.1 PROCESS MODEL REUSE

The software engineering process was defined in Definition 2.14 as a set of sequential activities, which are functionally coherent and reusable, for software project organization, implementation, and management. This subsection describes the concept of process reuse and the method for implementing process reuse.

Software development is a design-intensive process rather than a mass production process. The development of specific application software is characterized as mainly a one-off activity in design and production. Thus, in the design-intensive software development, that which can possibly be regulated, reused, and standardized are mainly the software engineering processes rather than the products themselves, as in other manufacturing engineering disciplines. Therefore, the software engineering processes – a set of regular activities in software engineering which are based on the best practices in the software industry – are highly reusable in software development organizations.

Conventional software reuse methods have been concentrated on code reuse. Some advances have been made in software test reuse by built-in tests [Wang et al., 1998c/1999b/d]. This section intends to extend the range of software reuse from code and test to the process. Reuse of established process systems, rather than redevelopment of processes from scratch within an organization, is a proven, efficient, and effective approach to process-based software engineering.

A fundamental approach to software engineering process reuse is to establish a standard software process reference system at organization level, and require all software projects within the organization to reuse the reference processes, tempering complementing with tailorability and adaptability. A comprehensive process reference model at organizational level and a tailorable mechanism of the reference model at project level are key techniques for the establishment and reuse of a process system.

This approach reflects an improved understanding in the software industry that higher quality software is produced by a well-defined and stable software engineering process system. The SEPRM process reference model, which defines a superset of processes and best practices, supports and provides for a basis for the software engineering process reuse. Empirically deriving a software engineering process model by tailoring a comprehensive process model makes software project leaders' tasks dramatically easier. Using this approach, a large-scale software project can be well organized and controlled by a unified, regular, and reusable software engineering process system within a software development organization.

For controlling a process system in a software development organization, processes should be implemented and practiced top-down from the organization level to the project level, as shown in Figure 2.2. This is a fundamental view to successful reuse of a software engineering process system. An organization's process reference model plays a central role in process model reuse because an individual project's tailored process model is derived from the reference model.

A process reference model is a generic and comprehensive model. It contains a superset of processes and reflects the best practices in the software industry. SEPRM is designed as a generic reusable process system reference model based on the unified process framework. Adoption and reuse of a software process reference model, such as SEPRM, as a software organization's process reference model at organizational and project levels are shortcuts to organizing successful software projects in a software development organization.

13.2.2 PROCESS MODEL TAILORING

Process tailoring, as defined in Chapter 4, is a model customization method for making a process model suitable for a specific software project by deleting the unnecessary processes. This means that process tailoring may be thought of as simply ticking the processes needed in a process reference model and crossing off all others that are not needed or not prioritized. If there is a need to append new processes, or to reconfigure the processes, the techniques are referred to another type of process customization method known as process adaptation. Process adaptation methods will be discussed in Section 13.2.4.

At the project level, a process reference model can be tailored according to factors related to the nature of the project, such as application domain, scope, complexity, schedule, experience of project team, reuse opportunities identified, and/or resources availability, and so on.

Process model tailoring is scenario-oriented. Assuming a software development organization is relatively mature in organization and technical processes but lacks of management and quality assurance processes, the comprehensive SEPRM process framework would be tailored as shown in Figure 13.2. At the lower levels, processes and BPAs contained in the selected process categories can also be tailored.

Two derived process models arrived at by process tailoring techniques for software quality assurance and software project management will be developed in Sections 13.3 and 13.4.

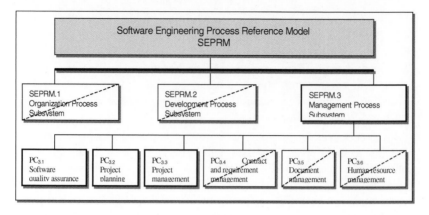

Figure 13.2 A scenario for tailoring SEPRM for project management

13.2.3 PROCESS MODEL EXTENSION

According to the unified software engineering process framework developed in Part I, a software process system consists of a process model, an assessment model, and an improvement model. Further, the assessment model can be divided into a process capability model and a capability determination method.

Corresponding to the above process model taxonomy, extension of an existing process system model can be achieved with many different emphases as shown in Table 13.1. In practice, extensions of process system models have mainly been reported on the process domains.

Table 13.1
Extension of a Process System Model

No.	Category	Aspects	Extension
1	Process model		New processes at BPA, process, and/or category levels
2	Assessment model		
2.1		Capability model	New capability rating scales and process capability levels
2.2		Capability determination method	New algorithms or capability mappings
3	Improvement model		New process improvement methods or measures

A trend in process system extension is to adopt a technology known as "plug-ins." A plug-in is an extended process module that can be easily plugged into a host process system model. A plug-in process module should usually have an identical structure and syntax as those of the host process model.

A paradigm of process extension, PULSE, will be described in the next chapter. PULSE extends ISO/IEC TR 15504 to covering software and IT system acquisition processes.

13.2.4 PROCESS MODEL ADAPTATION

Process model adaptation, as described in Section 4.2, is one of the most demanding or professional techniques in software engineering process system establishment and improvement. As in the case of process model tailoring, process model adaptation is also scenario-oriented. Process model adaptation requires not only good skills and experience, but also deep understanding of an organization's and project's environment.

Process model adaptation may be implemented via one of the following techniques or by a combination of them:

- Combining multiple processes

- Splitting a process into independent ones

- Changing the BPAs of a process

- Integrating multiple process system models

- Creating new processes for meeting special requirements and/or purposes

Successful implementation of process model adaptation also requires quantitative measurement and benchmarks. To achieve this, process assessment and improvement experiments may be needed for the final establishment of an adapted process system. A case study on process improvement via process system adaptation may be referred to in the discussion in Section 18.3.

13.3 A Parallel Process Model for Software Quality Assurance

This section develops a minimum process model for software quality assurance. Seven pairs of concurrent development processes and management processes are modeled by tailoring the SEPRM process reference model. This parallel process model provides a minimum and essential process model for software quality assurance (SQA).

13.3.1 SOFTWARE ENGINEERING MODELS VS. SOFTWARE DEVELOPMENT MODELS

Before establishing the parallel process model for software engineering, it is helpful to discuss the difference between the concepts of software engineering models and software development models.

Conventional software development models have been mainly oriented to software technical life cycles such as the Waterfall, Prototyping, Spiral, V, Incremental, and Evolutionary models. However, software engineering models are dominated by processes which identify and model the sequential or concurrent behaviors and interactions between the organization, development, and management activities in software engineering. Therefore, a fundamental concept is that the software engineering process models are at a higher level than those of the software development models as shown in Figure 13.3.

From another viewpoint, it may be interpreted that software development models are oriented to programmers while the software engineering process models are oriented to software corporation and project managers and software engineers.

The parallel process model (PPM) is a lightweight software engineering model that provides a minimum and core set of software engineering processes for software quality assurance. The parallelism implied in the PPM represents the key idea for process-based software engineering.

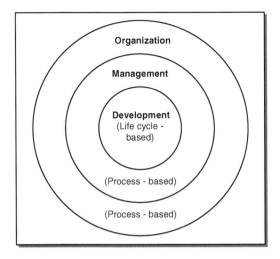

Figure 13.3 Software engineering process models vs. software development life cycle models

13.3.2 STRUCTURE OF THE PPM MODEL

In observing the SEPRM process reference model as shown in Section 9.2.2, it is noteworthy that the concurrent processes of software development (Processes 2.2.1 – 2.2.7) and of management (Processes 3.1.1 – 3.1.7) in a software development organization can be represented in parallel. The parallel structure reflects that each development process is supported and controlled by a corresponding management or quality assurance process. Thus, by tailoring the SEPRM model, a parallel process model (PPM) for SQA can be derived as shown in Figure 13.4.

The PPM models seven development processes (DP_1-DP_7) and seven counterpart SQA processes (MP_1 - MP_7). The parallel structure of the PPM ensures each development process is supported and controlled by a corresponding quality assurance and management process. Seven SQA processes are deployed with 47 BPAs to control the quality and correctness of the related development processes and their work products.

The parallelism between the 2×7 development and management processes as shown in Figure 13.4 indicates an important concept of software quality assurance in the PPM. The PPM is useful for modeling both technical and managerial aspects of software engineering, and it shows how regulated and structured activities can be established for SQA.

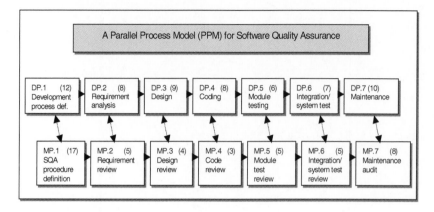

Note: DP$_i$ – development process i, MP$_i$ – management process i,
(n) – number of BPAs identified in a process

Figure 13.4 A parallel process model for SQA

13.3.3 IMPLEMENTATION OF THE PPM MODEL

According to the surveys of BPAs toward software engineering process excellence as described in Chapter 10, the PPM approach is widely adopted in practice. PPM can be used for maintaining a project's quality standard, and for assigning and deploying the roles of SQA engineer(s) in a software project.

The following subsections contrast the common practices of parallel development and SQA processes, and show interactions between the parallel processes. A set of 47 SQA measures in 7 processes are identified and applied to the 60 software development activities.

13.3.3.1 Parallel Process 1: Development Process Definition vs. SQA Process Definition

Table 13.2 contrasts the BPAs in Parallel Process 1 – development process and SQA process definitions. The BPA numbers shown in the table are the serial numbers as used in SEPRM and listed in Appendix D (The same applies to Tables 13.2 through 13.8). The characteristic curves of these processes have been shown in Figures 10.13 and 10.25.

Table 13.2
Structure of the Parallel Process 1

No.	BPAs in the Development Process	No.	BPAs in the QSA Process
105	Evaluate software development methodologies	197	Define SQA procedure
106	Model software process	198	Define project s/w engineering standards
107	Describe activities and responsibilities	199	Document SQA system
108	Establish task sequences	200	Issue quality manual
109	Identify process relationships	201	Distribute quality policy
110	Document process activities	202	Report SQA results
111	Identify control point of project	203	Assess process quality
112	Maintain consistency across all processes	204	Take correct actions
113	Develop software according to defined process	205	Assign independent reviewers
114	Derive project process by tailoring organization's standard process	206	Define extent of inspection
115	Approval processes and equipment	207	Conduct SQA for each process
116	Identify special requirements in developing special system: real-time/ safety-critical/etc	208	Assign qualified person(s) to special process
		209	Document quality records
		210	Review SQA system suitability
		211	Decisional role of SQA in processes
		212	Decisional role of SQA in final products
		213	Adopt SQA tools

13.3.3.2   Parallel Process 2: Requirement Analysis vs. Requirement Review

Table 13.3 contrasts the BPAs in Parallel Process 2 - requirement analysis and requirement review. The characteristic curves of these processes have been shown in Figures 10.14 and 10.26.

Table 13.3
Structure of the Parallel Process 2

No.	BPAs in the Development Process	No.	BPAs in the QSA Process
117	Analyze requirement according to defined process	214	Specification verification
118	Specify formal requirements	215	Formal review requirements
119	Define requirements feasibility/testability	216	Review statutory requirements
120	Prevent ambiguities in specification	217	Customer accepts specifications

No.			
121	Interpret/clarify requirements	218	Adopt specification verification tools
122	Specify acceptance criteria		
123	Allocate requirements for processes		
124	Adopt requirements acquisition tools		

13.3.3.3   Parallel Process 3: Design vs. Design Review

Table 13.4 contrasts the BPAs in Parallel Process 3 - software design and design review. The characteristic curves of these processes have been shown in Figures 10.15 and 10.27.

Table 13.4
Structure of the Parallel Process 3

No.	BPAs in the Development Process	No.	BPAs in the QSA Process
125	Design system according to defined process	219	Define design review procedure
126	Design software architecture	220	Document design review
127	Design module interfaces	221	Verify prototypes
128	Develop detailed design	222	Measure design review coverage
129	Establish document traceability		
130	Specify final design		
131	Define design change procedure		
132	Adopt architectural design tools		
133	Adopt module design tools		

13.3.3.4   Parallel Process 4: Coding vs. Code Review

Table 13.5 contrasts the BPAs in Parallel Process 4 - coding and code review. The characteristic curves of these processes have been shown in Figures 10.16 and 10.28.

Table 13.5
Structure of the Parallel Process 4

No.	BPAs in the Development Process	No.	BPAs in the QSA Process
134	Code according to defined process	223	Conduct code walk-through
135	Choose proper programming language(s)	224	Conduct code review
136	Develop software modules	225	Measure code review coverage
137	Develop unit verification procedures		
138	Verify software modules		
139	Document coding standards		
140	Define coding styles		
141	Adopt coding support/auto-generation tools		

13.3.3.5 Parallel Process 5: Module Testing vs. Module Testing Audit

Table 13.6 contrasts the BPAs in Parallel Process 5 - module testing and module testing audit. The characteristic curves of these processes have been shown in Figures 10.17 and 10.29.

Table 13.6
Structure of the Parallel Process 5

No.	BPAs in the Development Process	No.	BPAs in the QSA Process
142	Testing according to defined process	226	Measure test coverage
143	Determine test strategy	227	Estimate remaining error distribution
144	Specify test methods	228	Review test results
145	Generate test	229	Static/dynamic module test analysis
146	Conduct testing		
147	Adopt module testing tools		

13.3.3.6 Parallel Process 6: Integration and System Testing vs. System Testing Audit

Table 13.7 contrasts the BPAs in Parallel Process 6 – integration/system testing and system testing audit. The characteristic curves of these processes have been shown in Figures 10.18 and 10.30.

Table 13.7
Structure of the Parallel Process 6

No.	BPAs in the Development Process	No.	BPAs in the QSA Process
148	Integration test according to defined process	230	Identify nonconforming software/functions
149	Acceptance test according to defined process	231	Define inspection procedure
150	System tests generation	232	Inspection against requirements
151	Test integrated system	233	Document inspection/test results
152	Adopt software integration tools	234	Static/dynamic integration test analysis
153	Adopt module cross-reference tools	235	Static/dynamic acceptance test analysis
154	Adopt system acceptance testing tools		

13.3.3.7 Parallel Process 7: Maintenance vs. Maintenance Audit

Table 13.8 contrasts the BPAs in Parallel Process 7 - maintenance and maintenance audit. The characteristic curves of these processes have been shown in Figures 10.18 and 10.31.

Table 13.8
Structure of the Parallel Process 7

No.	BPAs in the Development Process	No.	BPAs in the QSA Process
155	Determine maintenance requirements	236	Reinspect repaired products
156	Analyze user problems and enhancements	237	Audit nonconformance records
157	Determine modifications for next upgrade	238	Audit nonconformance treatment
158	Implement/test modifications	239	Audit consistency with specification
159	Update user system	240	Audit consistency of system documents
160	Maintenance consistency with specifications	241	Audit consistency of system configuration
161	Maintain nonconforming products	242	Audit user satisfaction of maintenance
162	Record nonconformance treatment	243	Review regression testing results
163	Adopt regression testing tools		
164	Conduct regression testing		

The PPM model described above is a core set of parallel process activities for SQA as modeled in SEPRM. The PPM also serves as a formalization of the best practices in the software industry.

13.4 A Software Project Management Process Model

When a new software project is initiated, top management will require a project manager to conduct the project according to a given process reference model. The project manager may tailor and adapt the specified reference model of the organization to the specific project. This section demonstrates a derived software project management process model by using SEPRM as the reference model.

13.4.1 A DERIVED PROCESS MODEL FOR SOFTWARE PROJECT MANAGEMENT

As illustrated in Figure 13.2, tailoring SEPRM by focusing on the project management processes, a software project management process model (PMPM) can be derived as shown in Figure 13.5. In this case the PMPM consists of 4 project planning processes with 45 BPAs, and 6 project management processes with 55 BPAs.

13.4.2 PROJECT PLANNING PROCESSES

As shown in Figure 13.5, four processes, such as general project plan, project estimation, project risk avoidance, and a project quality plan, can be established in the project planning process category. What follows is a description of the purposes, characteristic values, and implementation priorities of these processes in project planning.

13.4.2.1 Project Plan Process

In creating a project plan it may be prudent to think about how such a plan might be put together. The general project plan process is designed to define the procedure for establishing a project plan and for specifying its scope. The process consists of 20 BPAs as shown in Table 13.9 with their benchmarks. Related characteristic curves of this process were shown in Figure 10.36.

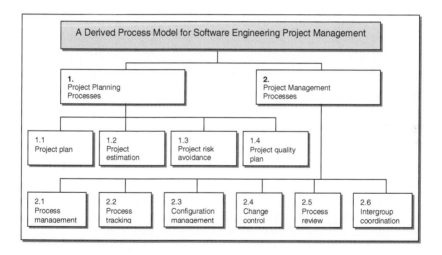

Figure 13.5 The PMPM software engineering project management process model

In Table 13.9, as well as in the following tables in this section, the serial number and category number are reference numbers of BPAs in SEPRM as shown in Chapter 9 and Appendix D. Naturally, the BPAs of the process can be tailored for a specific project if required.

Table 13.9
Benchmarks of Project Plan Process

No.	Cat. No.	BPAs	W [0 .. 5]	r_w (%)	r_p (%)	r_e (%)	φ (%)
275	3.2.1.1	Assign project proposal team	3.7	100	92.9	92.3	85.7
276	3.2.1.2	Design project process structure	3.9	100	78.6	92.3	72.5
277	3.2.1.3	Determine reuse strategy	3.4	71.4	35.7	84.6	21.6
278	3.2.1.4	Establish project schedule	4.5	100	100	93.3	93.3
279	3.2.1.5	Establish project commitments	4.1	100	92.9	92.9	86.2
280	3.2.1.6	Document project plans	4.1	93.8	93.8	93.3	82.0
281	3.2.1.7	Conduct progress management reviews	3.9	100	92.9	92.3	85.7
282	3.2.1.8	Conduct progress technical reviews	3.6	92.9	76.9	84.6	60.4
283	3.2.1.9	Management commitments in planning	3.9	93.3	71.4	83.3	55.6
284	3.2.1.10	Determine release strategy	3.4	73.3	73.3	84.6	45.5
285	3.2.1.11	Plan change control	3.4	78.6	53.8	91.7	38.8
286	3.2.1.12	Defined plan change procedure	3.1	71.4	53.8	91.7	35.3
287	3.2.1.13	Plan development	4.1	100	100	92.9	92.9
288	3.2.1.14	Plan testing	4.0	92.9	92.3	84.6	72.5
289	3.2.1.15	Plan system integration	3.9	92.9	83.3	100	77.4
290	3.2.1.16	Plan process management	3.6	85.7	91.7	91.7	72.0
291	3.2.1.17	Plan maintenance	3.6	93.3	78.6	85.7	62.9
292	3.2.1.18	Plan review and authorization	3.4	85.7	61.5	83.3	44.0
293	3.2.1.19	Assign development task	3.6	78.6	92.3	92.3	66.9
294	3.2.1.20	Adopt project/process planning tools	2.9	64.3	57.1	84.6	31.1

According to the characteristic values (φ) shown in Table 13.9, the implementation priority in process establishment may be to emphasize the most significant and useful BPAs, such as BPA_{278} – Establish project schedule, and BPA_{287} – Plan development. Similarly, less interest can be shown in the least significant and effective BPAs such as BPA_{277} – Determine reuse strategy.

Where tables accompany the section is the following text, i.e., 13.4.2.2 to 13.4.3.6. Readers are encouraged to evaluate the values attached to each BPA and decide which are the key issues in each case.

13.4.2.2 Project Estimation Process

The project estimation process is designed to establish a procedure for estimating project size, schedule, costs, and resources required. Project estimation has always been one of the most difficult activities. Experience is an essential criterion but it also helps considerably to have a framework or template for the process.

This process consists of seven BPAs as shown in Table 13.10 with their benchmarks. The BPAs of the process can be tailored for a specific project if required. Related characteristic curves of this process can be referred to in Figure 10.37.

Table 13.10
Benchmarks of Project Estimation Process

No.	Cat. No.	BPAs	W [0 .. 5]	r_w (%)	r_p (%)	r_e (%)	φ (%)
295	3.2.2.1	Estimate project costs	3.8	87.5	92.9	84.6	68.8
296	3.2.2.2	Estimate project time	4.4	100	100	92.9	92.9
297	3.2.2.3	Estimate resources requirement	4.5	100	100	73.3	73.3
298	3.2.2.4	Estimate staff requirement	4.3	92.9	100	83.3	77.4
299	3.2.2.5	Estimate software size	3.9	86.7	69.2	81.8	49.1
300	3.2.2.6	Estimate software complexity	3.4	78.6	41.7	90.9	29.8
301	3.2.2.7	Estimate critical resources	3.8	86.7	46.2	91.7	36.7

The values placed on each aspect considered in Table 13.10 demonstrate that time and staff are key issues in project estimation.

13.4.2.3 Project Risk Avoidance Process

The project risk avoidance process is designed to identify and quantify risks involved in a software project. This process consists of 11 BPAs as shown in Table 13.11 with their benchmarks. The BPAs of the process can be tailored for specific project if required. Related characteristic curves of this process can be referred to in Figure 10.38.

Table 13.11
Benchmarks of Project Risk Avoidance Process

No.	Cat. No.	BPAs	W [0 .. 5]	r_w (%)	r_p (%)	r_e (%)	φ (%)
302	3.2.3.1	Identify project risks	3.8	88.2	50.0	86.7	38.2
303	3.2.3.2	Establish risk management scope	3.3	78.6	30.8	66.7	16.1
304	3.2.3.3	Identify unstable specification-related risks	3.3	81.3	43.8	69.2	24.6
305	3.2.3.4	Identify process change-related risks	3.1	73.3	28.6	63.6	13.3
306	3.2.3.5	Identify market-related risks	3.8	93.3	64.3	83.3	50.0
307	3.2.3.6	Analyze and prioritize risks	3.4	73.3	40.0	71.4	21.0
308	3.2.3.7	Develop mitigation strategies	3.1	73.3	40.0	58.3	17.1
309	3.2.3.8	Define risk metrics for probability/impact	2.9	75.0	20.0	61.5	9.2

310	3.2.3.9	Implement mitigation strategies	3.1	78.6	28.6	63.6	14.3
311	3.2.3.10	Assess risk mitigation activities	2.9	68.6	33.3	58.3	13.4
312	3.2.3.11	Take corrective actions for identified risks	4.0	93.3	73.3	73.3	50.2

According to the characteristic values (φ) shown in Table 13.11, the implementation priority in process establishment may be put on the most significant and useful BPAs, such as BPA_{312} – Take correct actions for identified risk, and BPA_{306} – Identify market-related risks. Relatively, the least significant and useful BPAs in this process are BPA_{309} – Define risk metrics for probability/impact.

13.4.2.4 Project Quality Plan Process

The project quality plan process is designed to plan project quality assurance mechanism, goals, metrics, and measurements. This process consists of seven BPAs as shown in Table 13.12 with their benchmarks. The BPAs of the process can be tailored for a specific project if required. Related characteristic curves of this process can be referred to in Figure 10.39.

Table 13.12
Benchmarks of Project Quality Plan Process

No.	Cat. No.	BPAs	W [0 .. 5]	r_w (%)	r_p (%)	r_e (%)	φ (%)
313	3.2.4.1	Plan SQA	4.1	94.1	88.2	88.2	73.3
314	3.2.4.2	Establish quality goals	4.2	100	80.0	86.7	69.3
315	3.2.4.3	Define quality quantitative metrics	3.9	88.2	75.0	81.3	53.8
316	3.2.4.4	Identify quality activities	4.1	100	78.6	85.7	67.3
317	3.2.4.5	Track project quality goals	3.8	94.1	76.5	81.3	58.5
318	3.2.4.6	SQA team participate in project planning	3.6	86.7	57.1	84.6	41.9
319	3.2.4.7	Plan maintenance	3.3	73.3	71.4	85.7	44.9

13.4.3 PROJECT MANAGEMENT PROCESS

As shown in Figure 13.5, six processes, such as process management, process tracking, configuration management, change control, process review, and intergroup coordination, can be established in the project management process category. This subsection describes the purposes, characteristic values, and implementation priorities of these processes in project management.

13.4.3.1 Process Management

The process management process is designed to establish the collecting, documentation, and analysis of process data. This process consists of eight BPAs as shown in Table 13.13 with their benchmarks. The BPAs of the process can be tailored for a specific project if required. Related characteristic curves of this process can be referred to in Figure 10.40.

Table 13.13
Benchmarks of Process Management

No.	Cat. No.	BPAs	W [0 .. 5]	r_w (%)	r_p (%)	r_e (%)	φ (%)
320	3.3.1.1	Plan quantitative process management	3.6	94.7	37.5	76.9	27.3
321	3.3.1.2	Conduct quantitative process management	3.5	89.5	29.4	64.3	16.9
322	3.3.1.3	Collect data for quantitative analysis	3.5	94.7	43.8	71.4	29.6
323	3.3.1.4	Control defined process quantitatively	3.4	94.1	37.5	64.3	22.7
324	3.3.1.5	Document quantitative analysis results	3.3	78.9	41.2	80.0	26.0
325	3.3.1.6	Benchmark organization's baseline of process capability	2.8	57.9	37.5	71.4	15.5
326	3.3.1.7	Manage project by defined process	3.8	94.7	66.7	88.2	55.7
327	3.3.1.8	Adopt project/process management tools	3.2	78.9	47.1	70.6	26.2

13.4.3.2 Process Tracking

The process tracking process is designed to establish project process monitoring mechanisms such as schedule, quality, costs, and resources. This process consists of 15 BPAs as shown in Table 13.14 with their benchmarks. The BPAs of this process can be tailored for a specific project if required. Related characteristic curves of this process can be referred to in Figure 10.41.

Table 13.14
Benchmarks of Process Tacking

No.	Cat. No.	BPAs	W [0 .. 5]	r_w (%)	r_p (%)	r_e (%)	φ (%)
328	3.3.2.1	Track project progress	4.3	100	100	100	100
329	3.3.2.2	Track development schedule	4.2	100	94.1	100	94.1
330	3.3.2.3	Track process quality	3.7	100	72.2	66.7	48.1
331	3.3.2.4	Track software size	2.9	63.2	68.8	86.7	37.6
332	3.3.2.5	Track project cost	3.8	94.4	80.0	93.3	70.5
333	3.3.2.6	Track critical resources and performance	3.3	80.0	70.6	94.1	53.1

334	3.3.2.7	Track project risks	3.2	84.2	52.9	68.8	30.7
335	3.3.2.8	Track process productivity	2.9	68.4	37.5	61.5	15.8
336	3.3.2.9	Track system memory utilization	2.4	44.4	31.3	53.3	7.4
337	3.3.2.10	Track system throughput	2.5	55.6	46.7	66.7	17.3
338	3.3.2.11	Track system I/O channel capabilities	2.4	58.8	37.5	60.0	13.2
339	3.3.2.12	Track system networking	2.5	58.8	33.3	66.7	13.1
340	3.3.2.13	Adopt process tracking tools	2.6	55.6	25.0	50.0	6.9
341	3.3.2.14	Document project tracking data	3.1	76.5	60.0	73.3	33.6
342	3.3.2.15	Identify and handle process deviation	3.7	95.2	78.9	83.3	62.7

13.4.3.3 Configuration Management Process

The configuration management process is designed to establish a software configuration monitoring mechanism such as configuration system definition, maintenance, and work products identification. This process consists of eight BPAs as shown in Table 13.15 with their benchmarks. The BPAs of the process can be tailored for a specific project if required. Related characteristic curves of this process can be referred to in Figure 10.42.

Table 13.15
Benchmarks of Configuration Management Process

No.	Cat. No.	BPAs	W [0 .. 5]	r_w (%)	r_p (%)	r_e (%)	φ (%)
343	3.3.3.1	Establish configuration management library	3.8	84.2	77.8	94.4	61.9
344	3.3.3.2	Adopt configuration management tools	3.8	93.3	53.3	84.6	42.1
345	3.3.3.3	Identify product's configuration	4.2	100	82.4	88.2	72.7
346	3.3.3.4	Maintain configuration item descriptions	3.9	93.3	71.4	78.6	52.4
347	3.3.3.5	Control change requests	4.4	100	88.2	100	88.2
348	3.3.3.6	Release control	4.3	100	81.3	87.5	71.1
349	3.3.3.7	Maintain configuration item history	3.9	94.1	68.8	80.0	51.8
350	3.3.3.8	Report configuration status	3.6	81.3	73.3	86.7	51.6

13.4.3.4 Change Control Process

The change control process is designed to establish a change prediction, request, and management procedure. This process consists of nine BPAs as shown in Table 13.16 with their benchmarks. The BPAs of the process can be tailored for a specific project if required. Related characteristic curves of this process can be referred to in Figure 10.43.

Table 13.16
Benchmarks of Change Control Process

No.	Cat. No.	BPAs	W [0 .. 5]	r_w (%)	r_p (%)	r_e (%)	φ (%)
351	3.3.4.1	Establish change requests/approval system	4.0	100	76.9	100	76.9
352	3.3.4.2	Control requirement change	4.1	100	71.4	85.7	61.2
353	3.3.4.3	Control design change	3.9	100	71.4	92.9	66.3
354	3.3.4.4	Control code change	3.8	93.3	78.6	92.9	68.1
355	3.3.4.5	Control test data change	3.3	73.3	57.1	84.6	35.5
356	3.3.4.6	Control environment change	3.0	78.6	53.8	81.8	34.6
357	3.3.4.7	Control schedule change	3.6	84.6	66.7	100	56.4
358	3.3.4.8	Control configuration change	3.8	82.4	73.3	86.7	52.3
359	3.3.4.9	Adopt change control tools	2.9	60.0	35.7	76.9	16.5

13.4.3.5 Process Review

The process review process is designed to establish a formal process monitoring and review procedure with defined checking points and requirements. This process consists of eight BPAs as shown in Table 13.17 with their benchmarks. The BPAs of the process can be tailored for a specific project if required. Related characteristic curves of this process can be referred to in Figure 10.44.

Table 13.17
Benchmarks of Process Review

No.	Cat. No.	BPAs	W [0 .. 5]	r_w (%)	r_p (%)	r_e (%)	φ (%)
360	3.3.5.1	Review processes at milestones	3.8	93.8	80.0	84.6	63.5
361	3.3.5.2	Document project review data	3.6	80.0	64.3	69.2	35.6
362	3.3.5.3	Revise project process	3.7	80.0	57.1	85.7	39.2
363	3.3.5.4	Conduct statistical analysis of process	3.1	68.8	42.9	61.5	18.1
364	3.3.5.5	Gather process data	3.2	71.4	61.5	66.7	29.3
365	3.3.5.6	Compare actual/forecast errors	3.5	86.7	57.1	76.9	38.1
366	3.3.5.7	Compare actual/forecast schedule	4.1	100	57.1	92.9	53.1
367	3.3.5.8	Compare actual/forecast resources	4.0	100	46.2	76.9	35.5

13.4.3.6 Intergroup Coordination Process

The intergroup coordination process is designed to establish a cross team working environment for software development and management. This process consists of seven BPAs as shown in Table 13.18 with their benchmarks. The BPAs of the process can be tailored for a specific project if required. Related characteristic curves of this process can be referred to in Figure 10.45.

Table 13.18
Benchmarks of Intergroup Coordination Process

No.	Cat. No.	BPAs	W [0 .. 5]	r$_w$ (%)	r$_p$ (%)	r$_e$ (%)	φ (%)
368	3.3.6.1	Define interface between project groups	3.7	73.3	66.7	80.0	39.1
369	3.3.6.2	Plan intergroup activities	3.6	87.5	66.7	92.9	54.2
370	3.3.6.3	Identify intergroup critical dependencies	3.8	81.3	53.3	86.7	37.6
371	3.3.6.4	Handle intergroup issues	3.8	88.2	68.8	81.3	49.3
372	3.3.6.5	Technical/management representatives coordination	3.6	94.1	75.0	93.3	65.9
373	3.3.6.6	Review last process' output	3.1	75.0	40.0	78.6	23.6
374	3.3.6.7	Conduct intergroup representatives review	3.5	86.7	64.3	85.7	47.8

The project management process model and the parallel SQA process model may be used together to form a medium-weighted project process model, which covers the essential technical and managerial processes of software engineering at project or team levels.

13.5 A Tailored CMM Process Model

When a comprehensive process model is adopted, tailoring of the selected model to make it more suitable to organizational needs is always needed. The question is, how is it done?

This section describes a tailored CMM model (T-CMM) by Logos International and the tailoring methods used. T-CMM is a CMM-derived process model for small businesses, organizations, and projects. T-CMM was derived based on the work in Broadman and Johnson (1995/97) and has been recognized by SEI, the originator of CMM.

13.5.1   MOTIVATION FOR T-CMM

The motivation for a tailored CMM was based on the Logos experience with nearly 200 small organizations in software process improvement. Logos discovered that these small organizations and projects were encountering difficulties applying the CMM to their software process improvement effort because the CMM largely reflects the practices of large software organizations [Broadman and Johnson, 1994]. As a result, software organizations that are small or have small projects were experiencing vast difficulty in implementing process improvement programs based on the CMM and, thus, had not progressed very far on the software process maturity scale.

The tailoring, according to Broadman and Johnson (1995/97), has been focused on improving CMM's usability on:

- Documentation overload

- Layered management

- Scope of reviews overkill

- Limited resources

- High training costs

- Unrelated practices

13.5.2 METHOD FOR TAILORING CMM

The strategy for the tailoring was to produce a tailored CMM that met the demands of small organizations while maintaining the intent, structure, and key process areas (KPAs) of the CMM model as described in Chapter 5. Thus, only the CMM key practices (KPs) at the bottom level of the process taxonomy were tailored and adapted for usability.

The main points in tailoring the CMM model were as follows:

- Clarification of existing practices

- Underlining the clear issues

- Introduction of alternative practices

- Alignment of practices with the structures and resources of small organizations and small projects

13.5.3 THE T-CMM PROCESS AND CAPABILITY MODELS

Despite the fact that 82% of the CMM KPs were modified in the tailoring process, the changes that were introduced did not radically change its structure, especially at the KPA level and above. Therefore, the process taxonomy and structure of the T-CMM are identical to those of CMM as shown in Section 5.2. Also, the capability model and assessment method are the same as those of CMM as described in Section 5.3.

13.5.4 RELATIONSHIPS BETWEEN T-CMM AND ISO/IEC TR 15504

Mutual mappings between T-CMM and ISO/IEC TR 15504 have been carried out by Wang et al. (1999g). The conformance analysis of T-CMM with ISO/IEC TR 15504 was based on the comparison and contrast of their process and capability models, as well as their rating methods and rating results. Because of the different process organizations in T-CMM and ISO/IEC TR 15504, there are one-to-one, one-to-many, and many-to-one correlations between the two models. It has been found that all T-CMM KPAs are covered by the ISO/IEC TR 15504 processes, while, in the reverse sense, not all ISO/IEC TR 15504 processes are matched in T-CMM.

Overall, the compliance relationship between T-CMM and ISO/IEC TR 15504 is summarized below:

- The process models of T-CMM and ISO/IEC TR 15504 are highly correlative, especially at the KPA/process level. However, they do represent an exception case which contradicts the ISO/IEC TR 15504 requirement that "every process should can be evaluated in any capability levels [ISO/IEC 15504-2 1998]" since T-CMM KPAs are assigned to separate levels.

- The capability models between T-CMM and ISO/IEC TR 15504 are highly correlative. A minor difference in the capability models is that ISO/IEC 15504 has nine generic attributes for all processes while T-CMM has five common features for grouped KPAs.

- The rating method of T-CMM is a subset of ISO/IEC 15504 as shown in Figure 13.6. In Figure 13.6, the T-CMM capability areas of the 18 KPAs are marked by dark color. As a subset of the ISO/IEC TR 15504 capability domain, the T-CMM rating method is in conformance with ISO/IEC TR 15504.

- The rating results of T-CMM and ISO/IEC TR 15504 have highly equivalent meaning. The only difference is that ISO/IEC TR 15504 results in a capability profile of a set of processes while the T-CMM represents a single process capability level for a project or organization. A supplementary method for filling this gap was developed in Section 8.3.2.4, which provides an aggregated capability level at organization level from the ISO/IEC TR 15504 process capability profile.

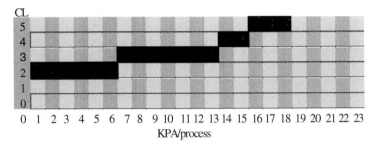

Figure 13.6 Domain of capability levels between T-CMM and ISO/IEC TR 15504

The above analysis provides a perspective on the compliance between the T-CMM and ISO/IEC TR 15504 models. The general finding is that, although there are minor and historical differences, T-CMM is over 72% compliant with ISO/IEC 15504 in process and capability dimensions, and in their capability rating methods and results [Wang et al., 1999g].

13.6 Summary

Software process system establishment is the first important step in process-based software engineering. This chapter has developed the methodologies and approaches to software process establishment. Three derived process models, the parallel process model for software quality assurance, the minimum process model for software project management, and T-CMM, have been explored.

The basic knowledge structure of this chapter is as follows:

Chapter 13. Software Process Establishment Methodologies

- General
  - Purposes of this chapter

    - To provide practical guidance on how to establish software engineering process systems at organization, project, and team levels

    - To develop a set of useful methodologies for software process establishment and implementation

    - To demonstrate a parallel process model for software quality assurance, which is a lightweight project process model tailored from SEPRM

    - To demonstrate a process model for software project management, which is a medium-weight project process model tailored from SEPRM

    - To demonstrate a case study on how CMM may be customized for small software development organizations

  - Process model classification from the viewpoint of model scope
    - A complete process model
    - A medium (partially tailored) process model
    - A lightweight (largely tailored) process model

  - Procedure for establishing a process system
    - Step 1: Select and reuse a process system reference model at organization level
    - Step 2: Derive a process model at project level
    - Step 3: Apply the derived project process model

- Process system establishment methodologies
  - Process model reuse
  - Process model tailoring
  - Process model extension
    - Extension of process model
    - Extension of assessment model
    - Extension of improvement model
  - Process model adaptation

        – Combine multiple processes
        – Split a process into independent ones
        – Change BPAs of a process
        – Integrate multiple process system models
        – Create new process for special requirements and purposes

- A parallel process model for SQA
  - Structure of PPM (Figure 13.4)

  - Process-based software engineering models vs. life cycle-based software development models

  - Process parallelism between the development and SQA processes

  - Major SQA techniques
    - Review
      - Self-review
      - Peer review
      - Joint review
    - Inspection
    - Audit
    - Testing

- A minimum process model for software project management
  - Structure of PMPM (Figure 13.5)

  - Project planning processes
    - Purposes
    - BPA configuration
    - BPA benchmarks
    - Identify implementation priority in process establishment

  - Project management processes
    - Purposes
    - BPA configuration
    - BPA benchmarks
    - Identify implementation priority in process establishment

- A Tailored CMM (T-CMM)
  - Motivation for T-CMM

  - Methods for tailoring CMM
    - Clarification of existing practices

– Underlining the clear issues
– Introduction of alternative practices
– Alignment of practices with structures and resources of
   small organizations and small projects

– Structure of T-CMM
   – Process model
      – KPAs unchanged
      – KP configuration: tailored
      – Process capability model: unchanged

– T-CMM vs. ISO/IEC TR 15504
   – Process models
   – Capability models
   – Capability determination methods and algorithms
   – Assessment results

Major achievements and issues for further research suggested by this chapter
are highlighted below:

- In this chapter, systematic software process establishment has been
  recognized as the foundation for process assessment and
  improvement. A software engineering process system reference
  model at organization level has been viewed as the central
  infrastructure for process-based software engineering.

- Process establishment technologies provide support and guidelines
  for readers to build a process system at organization, project, team,
  and individual levels. The process establishment methodologies
  enable top management, project managers, and team leaders to
  describe their process structure and functional requirements in the
  easiest way.

- The scope of process systems establishment has been classified into
  three categories: the complete, medium, and lightweight process
  system models. Usually, a complete process model is established and
  applied in a whole organization as a process system reference
  model. A medium or lightweight process model is derived from the
  reference model for a specific software project according to its
  nature and requirements.

- Conventional software reuse methods have been concentrated on code reuse. Extension of the range of software reuse from code to the process has been explored in this chapter. Reuse of established process systems, rather than redevelopment of them from scratch within a software organization, has been shown an effective and efficient approach to process-based software engineering.

- A fundamental approach to software engineering process reuse is to establish a standard software process reference system at organization level, and require all software projects within the organization to reuse the reference processes, complementing by tailorability and adaptability. A comprehensive process reference model at organizational level and a tailorable mechanism of the reference model at project level are key techniques for the establishment and reuse of a software engineering process system.

- At the project level, a process reference model can be tailored according to the nature of the project by considering the project's application domain, scope, complexity, schedule, experience of project team, reuse opportunities identified, and/or resources availability, etc.

- According to the unified software engineering process framework developed in Part I, a process system consists of a process model, an assessment model, and an improvement model. Further, the assessment model can be divided into a process capability model and a capability determination method. Corresponding to the above process model taxonomy, extension of an existing process system model can be done in related aspects.

- Process model adaptation is the most professional techniques in software engineering process system establishment and improvement. Process adaptation is scenario-oriented. Process adaptation requires not only good skills and experience, but also deep understanding of an organization's and project's environment.

- The parallelism between the 2×7 development and quality assurance processes shows an important concept of software quality assurance in the PPM. The PPM represents a minimum requirement for establishing regulated and structured activities for SQA.

- Conventional software development models have been oriented only to the technical aspects of software engineering while the PPM, as a simple paradigm of the software engineering process models, is oriented to both technical and managerial aspects of large-scale software development.

- When a new software project is initiated, top management may require the project manager to conduct the project according to a tailored SEPRM model. The project management may also adapt a derived model to a specific project by considering the nature of the project and any constraints existing.

This chapter has developed four practical methodologies for software process establishment, such as process model reuse, tailoring, extension, and adaptation. Applications of the process establishment methodologies have been demonstrated in deriving and implementing three process models. A complete process model extension paradigm for enhancing ISO/IEC TR 15504 will be described in Chapter 14.

Annotated References

For generic process establishment and implementation methodologies, readers may refer to Lehman (1991), Krasner et al. (1992), Feiler and Humphrey (1993), Kitson (1996), and ISO/IEC TR 15271 (1998), as well as Proceedings of the International Conference on the Software Process – ICSP1 (1991) to ICSP5 (1998).

For specific process establishment methodologies, such as process reuse, tailoring, extension, and adaptation, readers may refer to the SPIRE Project (1998), Curtis et al. (1988), Wang et al. (1997a/1998a/1999j), Cromer and Horch (1999), ISO/IEC TR 15504-10 (1999), and Dorling and Wang et al. (1999a/b).

For other related process paradigms, readers may refer to: ISO/IEC 12207 (1995), Information Technology – Software Life Cycle Processes; ISO/IEC TR 15271 (1998), Information Technology – Guide for ISO/IEC 12207; and ISO Draft Report 15288 (1999), Information Technology – Life Cycle Management – System Life Cycle Processes.

The Tailored CMM was developed by LOGOS International and presented in Broadman and Johnson (1995), as well as Johnson and

Broadman (1997). The initiation of this work is based on their findings on CMM's usability in the software industry as described in Brodman and Johnson (1994).

In a collaborated effort, Wang, Dorling, Broadman, and Johnson (1999g) carried out a case study on conformance analysis between the T-CMM and ISO/IEC TR 15504. This work is based on the conformance requirements defined in ISO/IEC TR 15504-2 that cover model purpose, scope, elements and indicators, mapping, and capability translation.

Questions and Problems

13.1 Why is process system establishment considered an important precondition of software process assessment and improvement?

13.2 In reviewing the classification of software process system establishment methodologies, what can you add to this classification?

13.3 Software engineering process reuse, above code, framework, and test reuse, is considered the highest level reuse in software development. Explain the concept of process reuse and its impact on software development.

13.4 Contrasting the process establishment methodologies of tailoring, extension, and adaptation, explain their usage in software engineering process system establishment.

13.5 Comparing the life cycle-based software development models and the process-based software engineering models, explain their differences and relationships.

13.6 The parallel process model (PPM) for software quality assurance as provided in Section 13.3 is derived from SEPRM. Explain what process establishment method is used for deriving the model and the usage of this model.

13.7 The software project management process model (PMPM) as provided in Section 13.4 is derived from SEPRM. Explain what process establishment method is used for deriving the model, and the usage of this model.

13.8 Why do small software organizations and small software projects need a tailored CMM?

13.9 Explain the steps taken in tailoring the CMM process model.

13.10 What is the relationship between T-CMM and ISO/IEC TR 15504?

Chapter 14

AN EXTENSION OF ISO/IEC TR 15504 MODEL

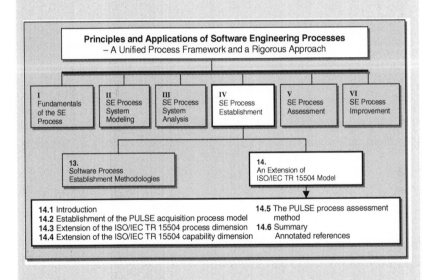

Principles and Applications of Software Engineering Processes
– A Unified Process Framework and a Rigorous Approach

| I Fundamentals of the SE Process | II SE Process System Modeling | III SE Process System Analysis | IV SE Process Establishment | V SE Process Assessment | VI SE Process Improvement |

13. Software Process Establishment Methodologies

14. An Extension of ISO/IEC TR 15504 Model

14.1 Introduction
14.2 Establishment of the PULSE acquisition process model
14.3 Extension of the ISO/IEC TR 15504 process dimension
14.4 Extension of the ISO/IEC TR 15504 capability dimension
14.5 The PULSE process assessment method
14.6 Summary
Annotated references

449

This chapter describes a paradigm of software engineering process system establishment, PULSE, which is an extended model and methodology of ISO/IEC TR 15504 for conducting software acquisition process assessments.

The objectives of this chapter are as follows:

- To demonstrate a complete example of process model establishment

- To offer an approach for extending an existing process standard or model

- To define an approach to develop plug-in process modules for a main process reference model

- To demonstrate how an organization's process reference model is extended or adapted to covering new processes for special needs

14.1 Introduction

In Chapters 4 and 13 the generic methodologies in process establishment, such as process system reuse, process model tailoring, adaptation, and extension, were explored. This chapter describes a paradigm of process establishment – the establishment of the PULSE software acquisition process model – as a compatible plug-in process module for ISO/IEC TR 15504 in order to extend its coverage to the software and IT system acquisition process area.

The main aim of the ISO/IEC 15504 (SPICE) project was to provide an assessment framework by which an organization may establish and subsequently improve its process capabilities in the supply, acquisition, development, operation, evolution, and support of software. A proposed amendment has been accepted recently by ISO/IEC JTC1/SC7/WG10 which revises the ISO/IEC TR 15504 model by separating the customer-supplier process category into independent acquirer and supplier process categories, and to extend it with an acquisition process model [ISO/IEC JTC1/SC7/WG10, 1999; Dorling and Wang et al., 1999b]. The PULSE acquisition process model, which is partially founded by a European Commission research project through the SPRITE-S2 Program, has been adopted for the extension in order to provide a sound foundation for acquisition process assessment in a broad application area of software and IT system procurement.

The PULSE methodology features a tool-based process assessment method, a template-based assessment data collection method, and a prototype for assessment report generation. Industry trials have shown the usefulness and impact of the PULSE model and related assessment results on improving the software and IT system acquisition processes in a wide range of industry sectors.

The PULSE project seeks to improve the software acquisition processes of organizations involved in the acquisition of software and IT systems. The project combines two approaches as shown below:

- By defining and verifying a formal methodology for identifying and assessing the processes used by such organizations for software and system acquisition

- By identifying a set of organizational actions that improve the ways in which acquisitions are managed, and the measurement of the success of the software and system acquisition team

The PULSE project provides a broad set of processes to assist organizations in improving the way that they acquire software and IT systems. The PULSE methodology covers:

- A software and system acquisition process reference model

- A software and system acquisition process assessment model

- A software and system acquisition process assessment method

- A software and system acquisition process assessment tool

The PULSE software and system acquisition process assessment methodology are designed to comply with the general requirements for an extended compatible model as defined in ISO/IEC TR 15504-2 (1998), and for performing 15504-compliant assessments as defined in ISO/IEC TR 15504-3 (1998).

14.2 Establishment of the PULSE Acquisition Process Model

This section describes the PULSE software and system acquisition process model, including its process reference model, assessment model, and assessment method. The context and interrelationships of the various components in the PULSE methodology are illustrated in Figure 14.1.

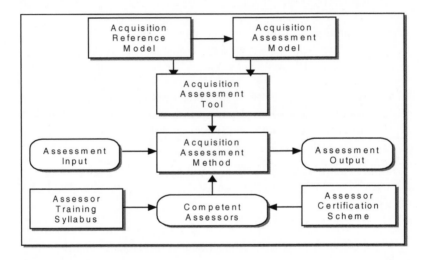

Figure14.1 Structure of the PULSE software and system acquisition process model

14.2.1 THE PULSE PROCESS REFERENCE MODEL

The acquisition process reference model of PULSE is developed in order to form the basis for software and system acquisition process assessment. The reference model defines, at a high level, the fundamental objectives that are essential to good software and system acquisition.

The PULSE process reference model is a generic model – this means it may be applied in a large population of acquisition types from standalone to total systems, from small to progressive acquisitions, and from new to enhancements or modifications of existing systems.

This reference model is applicable to any organization wishing to establish and subsequently improve its capabilities in the acquisition of software products and system. The model does not presume particular organizational structures, management philosophies, life cycle models, technologies, or methodologies.

The architecture of this reference model organizes the processes to help acquisition departments understand and use them for continuous improvement of the management of acquisition processes. Used with team and organizational focus, it offers a sound and principled way to manage, improve, and increase the capability of an organization to acquire the right systems the right way.

14.2.2 THE PULSE PROCESS ASSESSMENT MODEL

For acquisition process assessment, an assessor uses a more detailed PULSE assessment model compatible with the above reference model, containing a comprehensive set of indicators of process performance and process capability, to make judgment about the capability of the processes. This may be achieved in a particular context of acquisition, permitting judgment of the comprehensiveness of the acquisition processes and their acquisition capabilities.

14.2.3 THE PULSE PROCESS ASSESSMENT METHOD

The PULSE process assessment method describes how an assessment shall be performed in a step-by-step manner with the support of an assessment tool. The assessment method is designed to incorporate the phases, processes, and activities of an assessment, and to regulate the format and contents of the output produced. As shown in Figure 14.1, the assessment method plays a central role in a PULSE acquisition process assessment.

The architecture of the PULSE model is made up of two dimensions:

- The process dimension, which is characterized by process purpose statements that are the essential measurable objectives of a process

- The process capability dimension, which is characterized by a series of process attributes, applicable to any process, which represent the measurable characteristics necessary to manage a process and improve its capability to perform

The following sections describe the PULSE extensions to the process dimension and capability dimension of ISO/IEC TR 15504. The inter-relationship between the PULSE and ISO/IEC TR 15504 models will be addressed.

14.3 Extension of the ISO/IEC TR 15504 Process Dimension

In the process dimension, PULSE groups 25 processes and 16 subprocesses into four life cycle process categories according to the types of activity they address, where a subprocess is a coherent part of a process that defines a set of independent activities and functions in the theme of a process. A structure of the PULSE process dimension is described in Table 14.1.

Table 14.1
PULSE Process Structure

Symbol	Category	Process	Subprocess
ACQ	Acquisition		
ACQ.1		Acquisition needs	
ACQ.1.1			Acquisition policy
ACQ.1.2			Acquisition strategy
ACQ.1.3			Benefits analysis
ACQ.2		Requirements definition	
ACQ.2.1			Technical requirements
ACQ.2.2			Contract requirements
ACQ.2.3			Financial requirements
ACQ.2.4			Project requirements
ACQ.3		Contract award	
ACQ.3.1			Invitation to tender
ACQ.3.2			Tender evaluation
ACQ.3.3			Contract negotiation
ACQ.4		Contract performance	

ACQ.4.1			Supplier monitoring
ACQ.4.2			Acquisition acceptance
ACQ.4.3			Contract closure
SUP	Support		
SUP.1		Documentation	
SUP.2		Configuration management	
SUP.3		Quality assurance	
SUP.4		Verification	
SUP.5		Validation	
SUP.6		Joint review	
SUP.7		Audit	
SUP.8		Problem resolution	
MAN	Management		
MAN.1		Management	
MAN.2		Project management	
MAN.3		Quality management	
MAN.4		Risk management	
ORG	Organization		
ORG.1		Organizational alignment	
ORG.2		Improvement	
ORG.2.1			Process establishment
ORG.2.2			Process assessment
ORG.2.3			Process improvement
ORG.3		Human resource management	
ORG.4		Infrastructure	
ORG.5		Measurement	
ORG.6		Reuse	
ORG.7		Financial management	
ORG.8		Manage supplier relationships	
ORG.9		Manage user relationships	

14.3.1 THE ACQUISITION PROCESS CATEGORY

The acquisition process category consists of 4 processes and 13 subprocesses that directly impact the acquirer and is generally driven by the acquirer, such as the acquisition needs, requirements definition, contract award, and contract performance processes.

The acquisition process category expands on the Acquirer-Supplier basic process CUS.1 and component processes CUS.1.1 through CUS.1.4 in ISO/IEC TR 15504-2 (1998).

14.3.2 THE SUPPORT PROCESS CATEGORY

The support process category consists of eight processes that may be employed by any of the other processes (including other supporting processes) at various points in the acquisition life cycle.

The support process category is identical to that of ISO/IEC TR 15504 - 2 (1998), with modification of wording to apply to acquisition processes as necessary.

14.3.3 THE MANAGEMENT PROCESS CATEGORY

The management process category consists of processes that contain practices of a generic nature that may be used by anyone who manages any type of project or process within an acquisition life cycle.

The management process category is identical to that of ISO/IEC TR 15504-2 (1998), with necessary modification or rewording to apply to acquisition processes.

14.3.4 THE ORGANIZATION PROCESS CATEGORY

The organization process category consists of processes that establish the business goals of the organization and develop process, product, and resource assets which, when used by the projects in the organization, will help the organization achieve its business goals.

The organization process category extended its counterpart in ISO/IEC TR 15504-2 with three new processes ORG.7 – financial management, ORG.8 – manage supplier relationships, and ORG.9 – manage user relationships, as shown in Table 14.1.

14.3.5 DEFINITION OF THE ACQUISITION PROCESSES

The PULSE process dimension provides a structural view of types of activities. Each process in the PULSE model is described in terms of a purpose statement. These statements comprise the unique functional objectives of the process when instantiated in a particular environment. The purpose statement includes additional material identifying the outcomes of successful implementation of the process. Satisfying the purpose of a process represents the first step in building process capability.

As mentioned above, the PULSE model provides ISO/IEC TR 15504 a set of new acquisition processes. A detailed description of the extended processes is as follows:

14.3.5.1 ACQ.1 – Acquisition Needs Process

The purpose of the acquisition needs process is to establish the basis for obtaining a solution that best satisfies the needs expressed by the acquirer. For the acquirer, a common objective is to minimize the risks, costs, and efforts in pursuit of the best solutions for acquisition.

As a result of successful implementation of the process:

- Acquisition needs will be established.

- An acquisition policy will be established.

- An acquisition strategy will be developed providing the basis for planning all aspects of the acquisition.

- A cost-benefit analysis will be performed.

ACQ.1.1 Acquisition policy

The purpose of the acquisition policy process is to establish the common high level goals, basis for acquisition needs, and the methods to be deployed in the conduct of an acquisition.

As a result of successful implementation of the process:

- The concept or the need to deploy a common acquisition policy will be established.

- The systematic basis of or preference for technology, process, methods, vendors, standards, and legally enforceable regulations to optimize the acquisition will be established.

- The concept or need to ensure adequate resources for managing the acquisition, including the contractual, technical, financial, and project management skills of the acquirer will be established.

- The concept or need to define the standards of quality for deliverables acceptable to the stated and implied needs of the acquirer will be established.

- The concept or need to establish an effective and productive relationship with the supplier and other affected groups will be established.

ACQ.1.2 Acquisition strategy

The purpose of the acquisition strategy process is to ensure the products to be acquired will comply with the mission, goals, and objectives of the business, and to provide the basis for planning all aspects of the acquisition project. This process involves a combination of business infrastructure (budgetary, financial investment), acquisition methods (off-the-shelf, customized), and common policies (acquisition strategies, schedule determination).
As a result of successful implementation of the process:

- A planned approach for the acquisition that meets the acquisition policy and user/acquirer business needs will be developed.

- Specific goals (financial, contract, project, technical) and objectives for different or alternative approaches will be identified.

- The various ways in which solutions could meet the acquirers needs and expectations will be identified.

- The business risks, financial, technical, and resource implications for differing or alternative approaches or solutions will be identified.

ACQ.1.3 Benefits analysis

The purpose of the benefits analysis process is to establish the continuing relevance and benefit of the acquisition in meeting the evolving and changing needs of the acquirer's requirements and business needs.
As a result of successful implementation of the process:

- The critical success factors for the acquisition will be identified.

- Alignment of benefits of the acquisition to business objectives will be analyzed.

- Capital and life cycle analysis of benefits deriving from the investment in the acquisition will be performed.

14.3.5.2 ACQ.2 – Requirements Definition Process

The purpose of the requirements definition process is to establish the requirements of the system to be acquired. Successful implementation will gather, define, and track current and evolving acquisition needs and requirements throughout the life of the contract to establish successive acquisition requirement baselines.

As a result of successful implementation of the process:

- The different perspectives (e.g., financial, contractual, technical, project) of acquisition requirements that meet the needs of the acquirer will be defined.

- The requirements will be revised to remain consistent with acquisition.

- The requirements and potential solutions will be communicated to the affected groups.

- New or changed requirements will be incorporated into the requirements baseline.

ACQ.2.1   Technical requirements

The purpose of the technical requirements process is to establish the product and the technical requirements of the acquisition. This involves the elicitation of functional and nonfunctional requirements that consider the deployment life cycle of the products to establish a technical requirement baseline. Successful elicitation of technical requirements will gather and define current and evolving acquisition needs.

As a result of successful implementation of the process:

- The requirements will be defined and developed to match the needs and expectations of the acquirer.

- The requirements and potential solutions will be communicated to all affected groups.

- A mechanism will be established to incorporate changed or new requirements into the established baseline.

- A mechanism for identifying and managing the impact of changing technology to the technical requirements will be defined.

- The requirements will be compliant with the relevant statutory and regulatory requirements.

- The requirements will include compliance with the relevant national and international standards.

ACQ.2.2   Contract requirements

The purpose of the contract requirements process is to establish the specification and basis of contractual agreement between the acquirer and a prospective supplier. Contract requirements will be defined which clearly specify the awarding aspects – expectations, liabilities, legal, and other issues, and which comply with national and international laws of contract.

As a result of successful implementation of the process:

- A contractual approach will be defined which is compliant with relevant national, international, and regulatory laws, guidance, and policies.
- An agreement (contractual) terms and conditions will be defined to describe how the supplier will meet the needs and expectations.

- Acceptance criteria and mechanisms for handling of breaches of the fulfillment of the contract will be established.

- The rights of the acquirer to assume, modify, or evaluate, directly or indirectly, Intellectual Property Rights will be established.

- Warranties and service level agreements will be provided for where applicable.

- Provision for the suppliers to deliver other requirements (e.g., quality plan, escrow arrangements, etc.) will be defined.

- Recognized criteria for proprietary, regulatory, and other product liability issues will be established.

ACQ.2.3   Financial requirements

The purpose of the financial requirements process is to specify the requirements to prepare the infrastructure for an effective financial management of the acquisition project.

As a result of successful implementation of the process:

- Financial management, risks, and costs to the acquirer will be established.

- Financial terms for costs and payments governing the acquisition will be defined and recorded.

- Financial aspects of the contract awarding process will be traceable to the outcome.

- Requests for financing will be used to prepare budgets for project activities subject to authorized budgetary controls.

- Cost reporting with the supplier will be established against agreed cost estimation model(s).

- Payments will be managed in accordance with a defined procedure that interrelates to contract data and achievement from project management.

ACQ.2.4   Project requirements

The purpose of the project requirements process is to specify the requirements to ensure the acquisition projects are performed with adequate planning, staffing, directing, organizing, and controlling of project tasks and activities.

As a result of successful implementation of the process:

- Consistency between financial, technical, contract, and project requirements baselines will be established.

- Requirements for the organizational, management, controlling, and reporting aspects of a project will be defined.

- Requirements for a project's adequate staffing by a competent team (e.g., legal, contractual, technical, project competent resources) with clear responsibilities and goals will be defined.

- The needs for exchanging information between all affected parties will be established.

- Requirements for the completion and acceptance of interim work products and release of payments will be established.

- Risks associated with the project life cycle and with suppliers will be identified.

- Requirements for ownership of interactions and relationships with suppliers will be defined.

14.3.5.3 ACQ.3 – Contract Award Process

The purpose of the contract award process is to facilitate the achievement of a binding contract or agreement between the acquirer and the supplier. The process includes the qualification and selection of suppliers or evaluation of products, followed by a period of consultation and negotiation leading to contract award.

As a result of successful implementation of the process:

- Tender documentation will be prepared.

- Potential suppliers will be qualified.

- Invitations to tender will be issued.

- Tenders will be evaluated.

- A contract will be negotiated and awarded to a supplier.

ACQ.3.1   Invitation to tender

The purpose of the invitation to tender process is to prepare and issue the necessary documentation for tendering. The documentation will include, but not be limited to, the contract, project, finance, and technical requirements to be provided for use in the invitation to tender (ITT)/call for proposals (CFP).

As a result of successful implementation of the process:

- Rules will be defined for tender invitation and tender evaluation which comply with the acquisition policy and strategy.

- The baseline technical and nontechnical requirements will be established to accompany the ITT.

- The agreement (contractual) terms of reference and conditions for ITT will be established.

- The financial terms of reference for costs and payments for ITT will be defined.

- The project terms of reference for ITT will be defined.

- The technical terms of reference for ITT will be defined.

- An ITT will be prepared and issued in accordance with acquisition policies, and which complies with relevant national, international, and regulatory laws, requirements, and policies.

ACQ.3.2   Tender evaluation

The purpose of the tender evaluation process is to evaluate tendered solutions, associated off-the-shelf (OTS) products, and suppliers of tendered solutions in order to enter into contract negotiations.

As a result of successful implementation of the process:

- Criteria will be established for qualifying suppliers.

- Supplier capability determination will be performed as necessary.

- Criteria will be established for qualifying OTS products where these are offered as (part of) a tendered solution.

- OTS products will be evaluated as necessary against a defined plan to determine the degree of fit with the acquirers needs and expectations.

- The tendered solutions will be evaluated against the ITT requirements.

- The supplier(s) of the successful tendered solution(s) will be invited to enter into contract negotiation.

ACQ.3.3   Contract negotiation

The purpose of the contract negotiation process is to negotiate and approve a contract that clearly and unambiguously specifies the expectations, responsibilities, work products/deliverables, and liabilities of both the supplier and the acquirer.

As a result of successful implementation of the process:

- A contract will be negotiated, reviewed, approved, and awarded to a supplier.

- Mechanisms for monitoring the capability and performance of the supplier and for mitigation of identified risks will be reviewed and considered for inclusion in the contract conditions.

- Tenders will be notified of the result of tender selection.

14.3.5.4 ACQ.4 – Contract Performance Process

The purpose of the contract performance process is to ensure successful execution and performance of the contract using efficient and effective management controls. The process ensures activities performed are in accordance with contractual obligations. Clearly defined roles and points of interactions are defined between the acquirer and supplier, and the relationships between all affected groups are optimized to maximize the performance of contract fulfillment.

As a result of successful implementation of this process:

- A structure for exchanging information on progress and risks between the supplier and acquirer will be defined and executed.

- The performance of the supplier will be monitored throughout the contract.

- Customer acceptance will be performed.

- Contract closure will be performed.

ACQ.4.1   Supplier monitoring

The purpose of the supplier monitoring process is to monitor and facilitate the integration of the supplier's activities in the conduct of the acquisition project in accordance with the relevant requirements and management approaches.

As a result of successful implementation of the process:

- Joint activities will be conducted between the acquirer and the supplier as needed.

- Information and data on progress will be exchanged regularly with the supplier.

- Performance of the supplier will be monitored against agreed requirements.

- Problems will be recorded and tracked to resolution.

ACQ.4.2 Acquisition acceptance

The purpose of the acquisition acceptance process is to approve and accept the constituted product based on the acceptance criteria. The process will involve a planned and integrated approach that reduces duplication of activities between supplier and acquirer.

As a result of successful implementation of the process:

- Validation and/or verification will be performed against a planned and documented acceptance strategy.

- Acceptance will be performed based on the acquisition strategy and conducted according to agreed requirements.

- The delivered product will be evaluated against agreed requirements.

ACQ.4.3 Contract closure

The purpose of the acquisition closure process is to ensure comprehensive information pertaining to the execution and finalization of the project is collected and coordinated across all affected groups.

As a result of successful implementation of the process:

- Finalization of payments and scheduling of future payments will be agreed.

- Securing or return of confidential information provided by the supplier and acquirer will be confirmed.

- Exchange of acquisition information results among affected groups will be effected.

- Results of contract, project, technical, and financial aspects of the project will be assessed against original requirements and/or objectives.

- The performance of all affected groups will be reviewed.

- Relevant project information will be archived in a manner accessible for future acquisitions and improvements.

14.4 Extension of the ISO/IEC TR 15504 Capability Dimension

This section describes the PULSE process capability model and its extension to ISO/IEC TR 15504. New attributes have been introduced to make the capability dimension suitable for the software and system acquisition processes.

14.4.1 THE PULSE PROCESS CAPABILITY MODEL

A set of nine attributes has been identified for evaluating each process activity described in the PULSE process model as shown in Table 14.2. The attributes focus on important aspects of process performance and the level of process capability supplemented by a number of evaluation aids.

Table 14.2
The PULSE Process Capability Model

Symbol	Attribute	Focus	Evaluation Aids
Level 0	Incomplete	-	-
Level 1	Performed		
AT1	Performed	Is the task performed?	• Is the scope of work defined? • Are identifiable work products associated with a task produced?
Level 2	Managed		
AT21	Planned and tracked	Is the task planned and tracked?	• Are the objectives of the task identified? • Are key activities and milestones of the task defined? • Are resources and responsibility for performing the task assigned? • Is progress of the task monitored according to a defined plan?
AT22	Product integrity	Are the documents produced by the task appropriately managed, configured, and under change control?	• Are requirements for the documents (e.g., specifications, plans, code) defined? • Are dependencies among the documents identified? • Are documents appropriately identified? • Are configuration and changes to the

			documents defined and controlled? • Are the documents verified and adjusted to meet the defined requirements?
Level 3	**Defined**		
AT31	Documented	Is the task defined and documented?	• Is a description and requirement for the task documented? • Is the task documented and under configuration and change control? • Is appropriate guidance for execution of the task defined? • Is the task performed in accordance with its definition?
AT32	Quality achieved	Are suitable validation, verification, review, and auditing activities implemented?	• Are roles and responsibilities of quality activities for the task assigned? • Are quality activities carried out according to defined activities within the documented task and for any applied quality system? • Are records maintained to demonstrate quality achievement?
Level 4	**Established**		
AT41	Usage	Is the usage of the task proven, accepted, and stable?	• Does the defined task have proven coverage and tailorability? • Does the defined task have proven performance and capability? • Is the defined task accepted by those who are impacted by it? • Is the defined task stable?
AT42	Skills	Is the task performed by staff with appropriate skills, competence, and training?	• Are requisite knowledge, skills, and competence identified for responsible staff? • Is a strategy established towards developing competent staff for the task? • Is the scope and aim of training defined and planned?
Level 5	**Optimized**		
AT51	Measured	Is the performance and capability of the task quantitatively measured?	• Is efficiency of the task monitored and evaluated? • Is effectiveness of the task quantitatively analyzed? • Are the results of reviews, audits, and evaluations analyzed to identify trends and root causes of problems?
AT52	Improved	Does the task have an optimum environment and optimum operational satisfaction?	• Is the environment in which the task is performed regularly reviewed for potential improvements? • Is the defined task refined with experience? • Are best practices and new technologies regularly evaluated with a view to incorporating into the defined task? • Are potential improvement actions identified, prioritized, planned, and implemented?

The PULSE process attribute rating scales are defined as shown in Table 14.3.

Table 14.3
PULSE Attribute Rating Scale

Symbol	Description	Rating
F	Fully achieved	86% to 100%
L	Largely achieved	51% to 85%
P	Partially achieved	16% to 50%
N	Not achieved	0% to 15%

14.4.2 CAPABILITY TRANSFORMATION BETWEEN PULSE AND ISO/IEC TR 15504

A mapping between the PULSE capability model and ISO/IEC TR 15504 reference model is described in Table 14.4. This table provides a general view of the equivalency of capability levels between PULSE and ISO/IEC TR 15504.

Based on the mutual mappings between PULSE and ISO/IEC TR 15504, the PULSE process capability levels can be transformed into ISO/IEC TR 15504. A transformation algorithm has been implemented in the PULSE assessment tool to automatically relate the PULSE process capability levels onto ISO/IEC TR 15504.

14.5 The PULSE Process Assessment Method

This section describes the PULSE process assessment method and usage of the assessment model and reference model in PULSE assessment. A PULSE assessment is conducted in a number of phases, each of which contains a number of assessment processes and activities.

Table 14.4
Mapping between Capability Levels and Attributes of
PULSE and ISO/IEC TR 15504 Models

PULSE Capability Model		Mapping	ISO/IEC TR 15504 Reference Model	
CL/PA	PA		PA	CL/PA
CL0-Incomplete		◄──►		CL0-Incomplete
CL1-Performed				CL1-Performed
PA1.1	Performed	◄──►	Process performance	PA1.1
CL2-Managed				CL2-Managed
PA2.1	Planned and tracked	◄──►	Performance management	PA2.1
PA2.2	Document, configuration, and change control	◄──►	Work product management	PA2.2
CL3-Defined				CL3-Established
PA3.1	Process definition	◄──►	Process definition	PA3.1
PA3.2	Quality achievement		Process resource	PA3.2
CL4-Established				CL4-Predictable
PA4.1	Stability		Process measurement	PA4.1
PA4.2	Skills, competencies, and training		Process control	PA4.2
CL5-Optimized				CL5-Optimizing
PA5.1	Technical infrastructure	◄──►	Process change	PA5.1
PA5.2	Efficiency / effectiveness	◄──►	Continuous improvement	PA5.2

Note: ◄──► Major correlation; ── Minor correlation.

A structural view of the PULSE assessment method is shown in Table 14.5. It describes the structure of the assessment method and general approach of a PULSE assessment.

Table 14.5
Structure of PULSE Assessment Method

Phase	Process	Action
Assessment Input		
	Assessment input definition	
		Define assessment purpose
		Define acquisition requirement
		Define assessment scope

Assessment		
	Assessment preparation	
		Appoint assessment team
		Prepare assessment confidentiality agreement
		Plan schedule and resources
		Determine assessment reference model, assessment model, and tool
		Map organizational unit processes
		Define processes to be assessed and target capability levels
		Develop assessment brief
	Data collection, validation, and rating	
	Derive ratings and capability profile	
	Strengths and weakness analysis	
	Improvement opportunities analysis	
Assessment output		
	Assessment report	

A PULSE assessment is carried out using the support of a software tool [Dorling, Wang, and Steinmann, 1998]. The records of a performed PULSE assessment consist of filled-in templates and data files produced from an assessment software tool which contains ratings, evidence, notes, and the various generated process capability profiles.

14.6 Summary

In this chapter PULSE has been introduced as a paradigm of process model extension and establishment. PULSE is a plug-in process model for extending the emerging international standard ISO/IEC 15504 to cover the software and IT system acquisition processes. A systematic methodology, including the software acquisition process reference model, assessment model, assessment method, and assessment tool, has been developed in the PULSE project.

The relationship between PULSE and ISO/IEC TR 15504 has been explored. As an extended compatible assessment model for ISO/IEC TR 15504, the PULSE process capability levels have been designed to be transformable to certain ISO/IEC TR 15504 capability levels. The mapping of capabilities and attributes between the two models have been implemented to enable the PULSE assessment results to be related to those of the ISO/IEC TR 15504 model.

The basic knowledge structure of this chapter is as follows:

Chapter 14. An Extension of ISO/IEC 15504 Model

- General
  - Purposes of this chapter

    - To demonstrate a complete example of process model establishment

    - To offer an approach for extending an existing process standard or model

    - To define an approach to develop plug-in process modules for a main process reference model

    - To demonstrate how an organization's process reference model is extended or adapted to covering new processes for special needs

- Establishment of the PULSE acquisition process model
  - Structure of PULSE process model
    - Process reference model (oriented to ISO/IEC TR 15504)
    - Assessment model
    - Assessment method
    - Assessment tool

  - Relationship between PULSE and ISO/IEC TR 15504
    - Process dimension
    - Capability dimension

  - Approach to extend an existing model/standard
    - Compatibility and conformance
    - Plug-in process modules
    - Transformable capability levels

- Extension of ISO/IEC TR 15504 process dimension
  - The acquisition process category
    - ACQ.1: Acquisition needs
    - ACQ.2: Requirements definition

– ACQ.3: Contract award
– ACQ.4: Contract performance

– The organization process category
  – ORG.7: Financial management
  – ORG.8: Manage supplier relationships
  – ORG.9: Manage user relationships

- Extension of ISO/IEC TR 15504 capability dimension
  – Same process capability levels
  – Newly defined process attributes
    – Defined focuses for each attribute
    – Defined evaluation aids for each attribute
  – Capability transformation between PULSE and ISO/IEC TR 15504 (Table 14.4)

- PULSE process assessment method
  – Structure of PULSE assessment method (Table 14.5)
  – Assessment input phase
    – 1 process
    – 3 activities
  – Assessment phase
    – 5 processes
    – 7 activities
  – Assessment output phase
    – 1 process

Major achievements and issues for further research in this chapter are highlighted below:

- This chapter has described a paradigm of process establishment of the PULSE software acquisition process model. PULSE has been accepted as a compatible plug-in process module for ISO/IEC TR 15504 to extend its coverage to software and IT system acquisition process areas.

- The PULSE methodology is featured by a tool-based process assessment method, a template-based assessment data collection method, and a prototype for assessment report generation. Industry trials have shown the usefulness and impact of the PULSE model and related assessment results on improving the software and IT system acquisition processes in a wide range of industry sectors.

- Reviewing the experience gained in the extension project and process models conformance analyses with ISO/IEC TR 15504, the authors observed that as a software process system assessment standard, it would be more flexible if the future ISO/IEC 15504 concentrates on an enhanced capability dimension and process capability determination methodology. While for the process dimension, the standard would provide only a plug-in mechanism, a process schema and a set of compliant criteria for adopting different process modules may be developed by any qualified software processes providers

This chapter has shown the applications of the generic process establishment methodologies developed in Chapters 4 and 13 by the development of the PULSE software and system acquisition process model. The acceptance of the PULSE model as a formal extension of ISO/IEC TR 15504 has proven the feasibility of the approach taken in this part.

Annotated References

The extension of ISO/IEC TR 15504 reference model for acquirer processes based on the PULSE model is formally documented as ISO/IEC TR 15504 Part 10 (ISO/IEC JTC1/SC7/WG10 1999). For further details, see Dorling and Wang et al. (1999b), or http://www.iese.fhg.de/SPICE/.

The PULSE document suite includes the following technical reports as the main part:

- D1.1 – IT acquisition process reference model for process and process capability, 1998

- D2.1 – IT acquisition process assessment model, 1998

- D3.1 – IT acquisition process assessment method, 1998

- D4.1 – IT acquisition process assessment tool, 1998

- D6.1 – IT acquisition process assessor training curriculum, 1998

- D6.2 – PULSE assessor certification scheme, 1998

Questions and Problems

14.1 Explain what the motivation is to extend the ISO/IEC TR 15504 process model.

14.2 What is the structure of the PULSE process paradigm and the relationships between PULSE and ISO/ITC TR 15504?

14.3 To what extent has PULSE extended the coverage of ISO/IEC TR 15504 process model?

14.4 Compare and explain the similarity and differences between the capability dimensions of PULSE and ISO/IEC TR 15504.

14.5 Explain what the PULSE process capability determination methodology is.

14.6 Try to conduct a PULSE process assessment for the ACQ.2 – requirement definition process which includes four sub-processes of technical, contract, financial, and project requirements. Report the process capability levels of these processes in your sample organization.

PART V

SOFTWARE ENGINEERING PROCESS ASSESSMENT

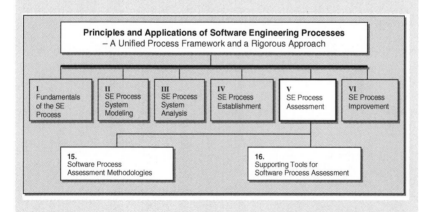

Principles and Applications of Software Engineering Processes
– A Unified Process Framework and a Rigorous Approach

I Fundamentals of the SE Process	II SE Process System Modeling	III SE Process System Analysis	IV SE Process Establishment	V SE Process Assessment	VI SE Process Improvement

15.
Software Process Assessment Methodologies

16.
Supporting Tools for Software Process Assessment

Classification of software process assessment methodologies was discussed in Part I, and theories and algorithms of current process models were described in Parts II and III. This part explores how the theories and algorithms of process assessment are applied in real-world process system assessments on the basis of established process systems as described in Part IV.

The rationale for conducting a software process assessment may vary. Some of the main reasons for performing a process assessment may be drawn from one or many of the following:

- To diagnose process system status and problems

- To find the baseline of a process system in a software development organization

- To enable process improvement for higher levels

- To evaluate the performance of a newly established process system

- To prove correctness and the satisfactory functioning of newly updated and implemented processes

- To evaluate the capability of internal project teams

- To look for a process capability certificate or conformance registration

- To show competence or qualification for contracting a software project

- To use as a case study in software engineering research

Three practical process assessment methodologies, such as the model-based, the benchmark-based, and the template-based, will be developed in this part. These assessment methodologies provide a step-by-step guide to carrying out a process assessment. They also demonstrate the applications of the unified software engineering process framework and SEPRM in the software industry.

The knowledge structure of this part is as follows:

- Chapter 15. Software Process Assessment Methodologies

- Chapter 16. Supporting Tools for Software Process Assessment

Chapter 15 examines existing and new approaches to software process assessment. This chapter develops two practical assessment methodologies, the model-based, and the benchmark-based process assessment. The former is a goal-oriented and absolute process assessment methodology while the latter is a new approach to operational and relative process assessment.

Chapter 16 explores a variety of software engineering process assessment supporting technologies and tools, and describes the implementation and applications of the generic process assessment methodologies developed in Chapter 15. A classification of process assessment tools and the basic requirements for the tools' implementation are explored. A set of practical templates has been developed for supporting template-based process assessment according to the SEPRM process reference model. Applications of the template-based and software-based assessment tools are demonstrated.

In this part, process assessment is recognized as the basic measure for process improvement. This part bridges the SEPRM theory and algorithm developed in Part I and Part II with practical process assessment applications in the software industry.

Chapter 15

SOFTWARE PROCESS ASSESSMENT METHODOLOGIES

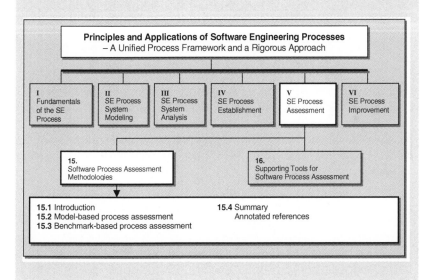

Principles and Applications of Software Engineering Processes
– A Unified Process Framework and a Rigorous Approach

| I Fundamentals of the SE Process | II SE Process System Modeling | III SE Process System Analysis | IV SE Process Establishment | V SE Process Assessment | VI SE Process Improvement |

15. Software Process Assessment Methodologies

16. Supporting Tools for Software Process Assessment

15.1 Introduction
15.2 Model-based process assessment
15.3 Benchmark-based process assessment

15.4 Summary
Annotated references

This chapter derives practical guidelines on how to apply and implement the software process assessment models, theories, and algorithms developed so far. A mode-based and a benchmark-based software process assessment methodology are provided on the basis of the SEPRM reference model.

The objectives of this chapter are as follows:

- To review the scale and practices involved in software process assessment in the worldwide software industry

- To explore a model-based software process assessment methodology

- To develop a benchmark-based software process assessment methodology

- To demonstrate how the generic SEPRM process assessment methodology and benchmarks might be applied in the software industry

15.1 Introduction

The classification of software process assessment methodologies was discussed in Part I, and theories and algorithms of current process models were described in Chapters 5 – 9. This chapter shows how to apply the theories and algorithms in real-world process assessment by developing two practical options: the model-based and the benchmark-based process assessment methodologies.

Before addressing these assessment methodologies, a review of the worldwide practices on process assessment in the software industry may reveal an overall picture of software process engineering in the industry. According to the statistics in the literature of software engineering process assessment and improvement [SPICE project, 1998; Mobil Europe, 1996; SEI, 1999; Curtis, 1992; and Zubrow, 1997], the magnitude of scales of software process assessments in major process models is estimated as shown in Table 15.1.

In Table 15.1, according to the Mobil Survey report (1995) conducted by John Symonds, until the end of 1995, up to 127,389 ISO 9000/9001 registrations had been awarded in 99 countries worldwide. There was a sharp increase of 32,163 registrations and 13 new countries during March to December 1995. One of the highlighted findings is that three-quarters of the ISO 9000/9001-certified companies are located in Europe, with nearly half of them in the UK.

Table 15.1
Numbers of Software Process Assessments in Major Process Models

No.	Model	Magnitude
1	ISO 9000/9001	127K / 42K
2	CMM (including self-assessments)	1K
3	ISO/IEC 15504 (Trials)	0.4K
4	Other (including internal models)	10K

Within the registered organizations, 33.1% of them were ISO 9001 (or software) oriented. This figure indicates that at least 42,165 software organizations in the world have passed the ISO 9001 assessment.

The data shown above presents a general view of the popularity of software process assessment and improvement in the software industry. By summarizing the large-scale industry practices, and on the basis of the unified process framework and SEPRM, more practical, coherent, and integrated software process assessment methodologies can be developed.

The following sections describe a model-based process assessment methodology with formalized operations, and develop a new methodology for benchmark-based process assessment.

15.2 Model-Based Process Assessment

This section explores a generic model-based software engineering process assessment method based on SEPRM. The SEPRM-based process assessment method consists of 3 phases and 12 processes. A structural view of the SEPRM-based process assessment method is shown in Table 15.2, where the output work product(s) of each process are specified by the related template(s) as shown in Appendix E.

Table 15.2
Structure of SEPRM Assessment Method

No.	Phase	Process	Work Product
1	Assessment Preparation		
1.1		Define assessment purpose	Template 1
1.2		Define assessment scope	Template 2
1.3		Appoint assessment team	Template 3
1.4		Prepare assessment confidentiality agreement	Template 4
1.5		Plan schedule and resources	Template 5
1.6		Map organization's processes onto the SEPRM reference model	Template 6
1.7		Specify processes to be assessed and target capability levels	Template 6
2	Assessment		
2.1		Develop assessment brief	Template 7
2.2		Data collection, validation, and rating	Template 8
2.3		Derive process ratings and capability profile	Template 8
2.4		Strengths and weakness analysis	Template 8
3	Assessment output		
3.1		Assessment report	Templates 1 – 8

In the following sections, each assessment process shown in Table 15.2 is described in terms of purpose, input/output work products, the method employed, and templates used. Additional notes are provided where relevant.

15.2.1 SEPRM ASSESSMENT PREPARATION PHASE

The assessment preparation phase includes seven processes as shown in Table 15.2. The processes of this phase are required prior to the assessment phase, and the output of the assessment preparation phase should be agreed to by the sponsor and the lead assessor.

15.2.1.1 Define Assessment Purpose

The purpose of this process is to define and describe the initiative, motivation, expectation, and aims of an SEPRM process assessment.

The method for defining assessment purpose and the input/output work products are shown in Table 15.3. A sample output of this process may be referenced in Table 16.3 and Template 1 in Appendix E.

Table 15.3
Define Assessment Purpose

Input	Method	Output
• Initial requirement and agreement; • Identification of sponsor, organization, department, project, and product; • Brief description of existing processes; • Brief description of assessment motivation and aims.	• Specify name of organization to be assessed; • Specify unit of organization to be assessed; • Specify project(s) to be assessed; • Identify sponsor of an assessment; • Specify aims of assessment; • Specify assessment classification; • Describe provisional date for the assessment; • Specify any special needs for the assessment.	Template 1: Assessment purpose

15.2.1.2 Define Assessment Scope

The purpose of this process is to define and describe the scope of the organizational unit and processes to be assessed, the constraints of the assessment, required outputs from the assessment, and the assessees and their roles and specialties.

The method for defining assessment scope and the input/output work products are shown in Table 15.4. A sample output of this process may be referenced in Table 16.4 and Template 2 in Appendix E.

Table 15.4
Define Assessment Scope

Input	Method	Output
• Initial requirement and agreement; • Assessment purpose (Template 1); • Process reference model (SEPRM).	• Describe existing processes and/or practices and their identities in assessee's terms and roughly classify them into related SEPRM process category; • Specify which processes among the existing processes identified above are required to be assessed; • Specify any constraints of the assessment in terms of resources, budget, and/or critical milestones; • Describe the expected output of the assessment, such as process attribute ratings, process capability profile, process strengths and weaknesses analysis report, potential process	Template 2: Assessment scope

> improvement opportunities, executive summary of assessment results, and/or other recommendations;
>
> - Identify assessees and their roles and specialties in process.

15.2.1.3 Appoint Assessment Team

The purpose of this process is to define the assessment team and assign responsibilities for their roles in assessment.

The method for appointing the assessment team and the input/output work products are shown in Table 15.5. A sample output of this process may be referenced in Table 16.5 and Template 3 in Appendix E.

Table 15.5
Appoint Assessment Team

Input	Method	Output
• Assessment purpose (Template 1); • Assessment scope (Template 2).	• Specify sponsor of the assessment; • Specify the lead assessor; • Specify assessor(s) in the team and assign responsibilities; • Specify additional team member(s), e.g., management and technical representatives of the organization to be assessed, etc.	Template 3: Assessment team and responsibilities

15.2.1.4 Prepare Assessment Confidentiality Agreement

The purpose of this process is to prepare and sign a confidentiality agreement regarding the assessment to be performed. If an assessment to be performed is an internal self-assessment, such a confidentiality agreement may not be necessary.

The method for preparing an assessment confidentiality agreement and the input/output work products are shown in Table 15.6. A sample output of this process may be referenced in Table 16.6 and Template 4 in Appendix E.

Table 15.6
Prepare Assessment Confidentiality Agreement

Input	Method	Output
• Assessment purpose (Template 1); • Assessment scope (Template 2); • Assessment team and responsibilities (Template 3).	An assessment confidentiality agreement as based on the outlines in Template 4 will be completed and signed based on the information of Templates 1 – 3 and the initial correspondence between the lead assessor and the sponsor.	Template 4: Assessment confidentiality agreement

15.2.1.5 Plan Schedule and Resources

The purpose of this process is to plan a schedule for the assessment and allocate resources for each phase of assessment.

The method for planning schedule and resources and the input/output work products are shown in Table 15.7. A sample output of this process may be referenced in Table 16.7 and Template 5 in Appendix E.

Table 15.7
Plan Schedule and Resources

Input	Method	Output
• Assessment purpose (Template 1); • Assessment scope (Template 2); • Assessment team and responsibilities (Template 3); • Assessment confidentiality agreement (Template 4).	A plan for the assessment schedule, responsibilities, and resources will be specified based on Template 5, which will cover all assessment phases and processes.	Template 5: Assessment schedule and resources

15.2.1.6 Map Organization's Processes onto the SEPRM Reference Model

The purpose of this process is to map the processes of the organization to be assessed onto the processes defined in the SEPRM process reference model.

The method for mapping the on-site processes onto SEPRM and the input/output work products are shown in Table 15.8. A sample output of this process may be referenced in Table 16.8 and Template 6 in Appendix E.

Table 15.8
Map Organization's Processes onto the SEPRM Reference Model

Input	Method	Output
• Assessment purpose (Template 1); • Assessment scope (Template 2); • Assessment team and responsibilities (Template 3); • Assessment confidentiality agreement (Template 4); • Assessment schedule and resources (Template 5).	• A detailed mapping between the SEPRM processes reference model and their correspondence to the existing processes in the organization as described in Template 2 will be determined; • The mapping of processes will be documented in the related columns of Template 6.	Template 6: (Part 1) Processes to be assessed and target capability levels

15.2.1.7 Specify Processes to be Assessed and Target Capability Levels

The purpose of this process is to select the processes to be assessed, and to define the target capability levels that the organization expects.

The method for specifying processes to be assessed and their target capability levels and related input/output work products are shown in Table 15.9. A sample output of this process may be referenced in Table 16.8 and Template 6 in Appendix E.

Table 15.9
Specify Process to be Assessed and Target Capability Levels

Input	Method	Output
• Assessment purpose (Template 1); • Assessment scope (Template 2); • Assessment team and responsibilities (Template 3); • Assessment confidentiality agreement (Template 4); • Assessment schedule and resources (Template 5); • Mapped processes (Part 1 of Template 6).	• All or part of the SEPRM processes suitable for the organization to be assessed will be selected for an assessment; • The expectation of target process capability levels for each process selected for assessment will be defined in consultation with the sponsor (and the organizational unit to be assessed); • Complete Template 6 by indicating processes selected for assessment and the target process capability levels according to the sponsor's expectation.	Template 6: (Part 2) Processes to be assessed and target process capability levels

15.2.2 SEPRM ASSESSMENT PHASE

The main phase of an SEPRM assessment includes four processes, which are: development of assessment brief; data collection, validation, and rating; derivation of process capability profile; and strengths and weaknesses analysis.

Data required for evaluating the processes within the scope of the assessment must be collected in a systematic and ordered manner, applying, at minimum, the following:

- The strategy and techniques for the selection, collection, analysis of data, and justification of the ratings will be explicitly identified and must be demonstrable.

- Each process identified in the assessment scope will be assessed on the basis of objective evidence.

- The objective evidence gathered for each process assessed will be sufficient to meet the assessment purpose and scope.

- Objective evidence that supports the assessors' judgment of process ratings will be recorded and maintained to provide the basis for verification of the ratings.

15.2.2.1 Develop Assessment Brief

The purpose of this process is to develop an assessment brief which summarizes the tasks, plan, aims, agreements, and approach of the assessment.

The method for outlining an assessment brief and the input/output work products are shown in Table 15.10. A sample output of this process may be referenced in Table 16.9 and Template 7 in Appendix E.

Table 15.10
Develop Assessment Brief

Input	Method	Output
• Assessment purpose (Template 1); • Assessment scope (Template 2); • Assessment team and responsibilities (Template 3); • Assessment confidentiality agreement (Template 4); • Assessment schedule and resources (Template 5); • Processes to be assessed and target capability levels (Template 6); • The SEPRM process reference model.	• Specify the items listed in Template 7 based on the output work products as documented in the completed Templates 1 – 6; • A briefing to the organization to be assessed will be made, using the completed Templates 1 – 7.	Template 7: Assessment brief

15.2.2.2 Data Collection, Validation, and Rating

The purpose of this process is to collect and record data to support evidence of process existence and performance, and to provide validated process attribute ratings. Raw data that indicate process existence and performance are investigated and collected for the selected processes as described in Template 6, and against the process rating scale as defined in SEPRM.

The method for data collection, validation, rating, and the input/output work products are shown in Table 15.11. The output of this process forms part of Table 16.10 and Template 8 in Appendix E.

Table 15.11
Data Collection, Validation, and Rating Process

Input	Method	Output
• Assessment purpose (Template 1);	• Each process and practice will be rated according to the SEPRM rating scale and algorithm;	• Intermediate assessment records.
• Assessment scope (Template 2);	• For deciding the rating for a process, related best practice and I/O work products will be used as indicators to support judgment of rating;	
• Assessment team and responsibilities (Template 3);	• Assessment rating will be performed by roundtable meeting and negotiation of process capability between assessors and assessees;	
• Assessment schedule and resources (Template 5);	• References to objective evidence and additional notes will be recorded;	
• Processes to be assessed and target capability levels (Template 6);	• Validation of ratings for process is achieved by roundtable rechecking between the assessors and assessees;	
• The SEPRM process reference model.	• The lead assessor will be responsible to ensure that the validated data sufficiently covers the assessment scope.	

15.2.2.3 Derive Process Ratings and Capability Profile

The purpose of this process is to derive process capability levels and profile according to SEPRM and its algorithm as developed in Chapter 9.

The method for rating processes, deriving process profile, and the input/output work products are shown in Table 15.12. A sample output of this process may be referenced in Figures 16.1 – 16.3.

Table 15.12
Derive Process Ratings and Capability Profile

Input	Method	Output
• Processes to be assessed and target capability levels (Template 6);	• This process will be performed by an assessment support tool or manually according to the SEPRM algorithm;	• Template 8: (Part 1) Assessed process capability levels;
• Additional assessment record;	• The derived process capability levels and profile will be documented in Template 8 (Part 1);	
• Validated ratings (The intermediate assessment records);	• A briefing of the assessment results will be provided for the assessed organization, and feedback from the organization will be considered in developing the final assessment report.	• Process capability profile.
• The SEPRM process reference model.		

15.2.2.4 Strengths and Weaknesses Analysis

The purpose of this process is to develop a quantitative report of process strengths and weaknesses. This is a task of significance for those organizations for which improvement is a key area.

The method for analyzing strengths and weaknesses definition, and the input/output work products, are shown in Table 15.13. A sample output of this process may be referenced in Table 16.10 and Template 8 in Appendix E.

Table 15.13
Strengths and weaknesses Analysis

Input	Method	Output
• Processes to be assessed and target capability levels (Template 6); • Process capability profiles as derived in Table 15.12; • The SEPRM process reference model.	• Fill in the values of the assessed level (AL) as derived by the assessment tool, and the target level (TL) as recorded in Template 6; • Calculate AL-TL for each process/component-process; • The resultant values provide an indicator that an assessed process may have relative strength if the value is plus or relative weakness if the value is minus; • The degree of strengths and weakness is in proportion to the value derived for a process.	Template 8: (Part 2) Process strengths and weaknesses analysis.

15.2.3 SEPRM ASSESSMENT OUTPUT PHASE

The assessment output phase is designed to report the results of an assessment as shown in Table 15.2. There is only one process in this phase – assessment input. The activities after this process, such as to propose an action plan for addressing the problems found in the assessment and for identifying process improvement opportunities, will be discussed in Chapters 16 and 17.

The purpose of the report process is to provide a formal assessment report according to the input, output, and analysis of the assessment. The method for reporting assessment results and the input/output work products are shown in Table 15.14.

Table 15.14
Assessment Report

Input	Method	Output

• Assessment purpose (Template 1);
 	
• Assessment scope (Template 2);
 	
• Assessment team and responsibilities (Template 3);
 	
• Assessment confidentiality agreement (Template 4);
 	
• Assessment schedule and resources (Template 5);
 	
• Processes to be assessed and target capability levels (Template 6);
 	
• Assessment brief (Template 7);
 	
• Process strengths and weaknesses analysis (Template 8);
 	
• Process capability profile(s);
 	
• The SEPRM process reference model.
	• Assembling of completed Templates 1 – 8;
	
	• In an executive summary section, elicit general findings, analysis, and candidate actions from the following parts of the report, and highlight them with brief descriptions;
	
	• In a conclusion section:
	  - Highlight overall findings from the data provided in Templates 1 – 8.
	  - Describe strengths and weaknesses of assessed processes;
	  - Propose any actions for future improvement;
	
	• Provide assessment report for sponsor review;
	
	• Provide presentation of assessment results to the organization assessed.
		Assessment report

The assessment report, particularly the analysis of strengths and weaknesses of the organization's process system, will be used in the light of the organization's needs to process improvement. We will describe the methodology of assessment-based process improvement in Part VI.

The sponsor of the assessment should report the assessment results to top management of the organization. The results and succeeding process improvement activities should also be made known to all departments and staff to whom they are relevant.

15.3 Benchmark-Based Process Assessment

The model-based software process assessment methodology described in the previous section provides a generic approach to practical software process assessment. This section intends to develop a new approach to benchmark-based process assessment and to demonstrate its applications.

15.3.1 A NEW APPROACH TO BENCHMARK-BASED SOFTWARE PROCESS ASSESSMENT

The term software process benchmark was given in Definition 4.6. Software process benchmarking is one of the important methodologies in software process engineering. Benchmarking is useful in both process assessment and improvement.

By contrasting the philosophy and features of benchmark-based process assessment with those of the model-based assessment, obtainers are given in Table 15.15.

Table 15.15
Contrast of Philosophy and Features of
Process Assessment Methodologies

Subject	Process-based Assessment	Benchmark-based Assessment
Philosophy	The higher the better	The smaller the advantage, the better
Assessment results	Absolute process capability levels	Relative process capability gaps
Target process capability levels	Set to absolute higher levels	Set to marginally higher than benchmarks
Usage	Support for virtue aims in competition	Support for adaptive aims in competition
Advantage	Widely practiced and experienced	A refined methodology
Drawback	Target capability level might overshoot and not be feasible	Depend on available benchmarks

Obviously, the implementation of a benchmark-based process assessment is dependent on the availability of established process benchmarks. To enable this methodology, process benchmarks are required to indicate the current levels of process capabilities in each of the individual business sectors in the software industry.

There are a few small-scale process benchmarks, such as the European process benchmarks developed by IBM [IBM, 1996] and the Swedish national software engineering process benchmarks [Wang et al., 1999f]. These process benchmarks have been covered for a small set of processes. The development of the SEPRM benchmarks as described in Chapter 10 provides a superset of 51 software engineering process benchmarks characterized by process attributes.

For instance, the IBM benchmark on software engineering practices in Europe contains benchmarks for 69 practices in 7 processes as shown in Figure 15.1. A comparison between the European and the Swedish benchmarks is also illustrated in Figure 15.1. It is interesting to find that the Swedish national benchmarks are quite close to the European ones. The average difference of all processes is only –0.6%. This means that the software engineering practices in the Swedish software industry have generally reached the European best practice level.

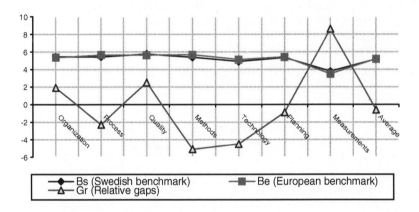

Figure 15.1 Comparison between the European and a national benchmark of software engineering processes

Magnified gaps between the two benchmarks are shown by the G_r curve. As shown in Fig.15.1, G_r indicates that, from the perspective of the European benchmarks, the organization, quality, and measurements practices of the Swedish software development organizations have exceeded the European benchmark; however, the process, methods, technology, and planning practices are below the European benchmarks.

15.3.2 SEPRM BENCHMARKS OF SOFTWARE ENGINEERING PROCESSES

A comprehensive set of process benchmarks for the SEPRM software engineering processes was established in Chapter 10. The SEPRM software engineering process benchmarks, in the form of process profile translated from the characteristic curves of φ, are shown in Figures 15.2 –15.4. In these figures, the capability levels of all 51 processes modeled in SEPRM are benchmarked in the organization, development, and management process subsystems.

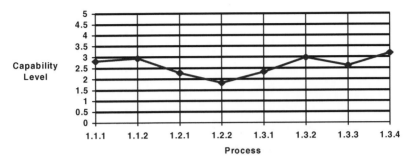

Figure 15.2 SEPRM capability benchmarks of organization processes

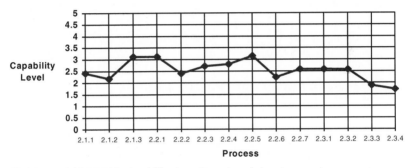

Figure 15.3 SEPRM capability benchmarks of development processes

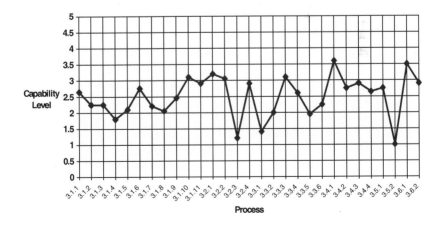

Figure 15.4 SEPRM capability benchmarks of management processes

When a specific process system profile is obtained and plotted onto the SEPRM benchmarked curves, an organization's process capability can be assessed against the benchmarks by gap analysis.

15.3.3 BENCHMARK-BASED ASSESSMENT METHOD

A formal procedure for a benchmark-based process assessment may be carried out in four steps:

- Adopt a benchmarked process model

- Conduct a baseline assessment

- Plot process capability profile onto the benchmarks

- Identify gaps between the process profile and the benchmarks

The following describes how the above procedures are conducted in an SEPRM benchmark-based assessment.

15.3.3.1 Adopt a Benchmarked Process Model

As described in Chapters 9 and 10, the SEPRM is the only benchmarked software engineering process assessment model. SEPRM supports both model-based and benchmark-based software process assessment, and provides a comprehensive set of processes and best practices in the reference model. Therefore, in the following subsections, when a benchmark-based process assessment is mentioned, it implies that SEPRM and its benchmarks are used in the assessment.

15.3.3.2 Conduct a Baseline Assessment

For conducting a baseline assessment, a process capability profile of the assessed organization will be derived according to the adopted process model. The method of this step is similar to those of the Phase 1 (Assessment preparation) and Phase 2 (Assessment) processes of the model-based assessment as described in Section 15.2, except process 2.4, strengths and weaknesses analysis, which will be replaced by following subsections.

15.3.3.3 Plot Process Capability Profile onto the Benchmarks

When an organization's process capability profile is derived, the key differences between the model-based and benchmark-based assessments are on selection of target capability levels and related analysis methods. Model-based assessment usually specifies an absolute higher capability level as the target capability level, while the benchmark-based assessment adopts a set of relative and dynamic target capability levels, the benchmarks, in analysis.

For instance, an organization's assessed capability levels of the 14 SEPRM development processes obtained in Subsection 15.3.3.2 can be plotted against the benchmarks as shown in Figure 15.5. With the support of the benchmarked curve, analysis of the assessment results is simplified as for gap identification.

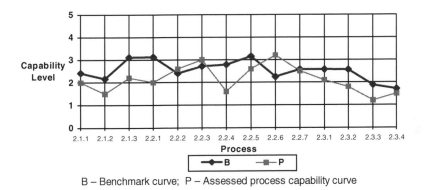

B – Benchmark curve; P – Assessed process capability curve

Figure 15.5 Plotted process capability profile against SEPRM benchmarks

The organization and management processes modeled in SEPRM can be plotted in the same way, by using the benchmarks provided in Figures 15.2 and 15.4, respectively.

15.3.3.4 Identify Gaps between a Process Profile and the Benchmarks

The gaps between a plotted process profile (P) and the benchmarks (B) can be analyzed based on Figure 15.5. Using the above figure, magnified gaps (G) between the current process capability levels and the benchmarks can be derived as shown in Figure 15.6. Figure 15.6 indicates that the larger the gaps below the average, the weaker the process capability shows.

An integrated process assessment approach based on both model and benchmark can be adopted to use the advantages of both methods to their maximum. The development of SEPRM has enabled the integrated process assessment methodology as a combination of both approaches described in Sections 15.2 and 15.3.

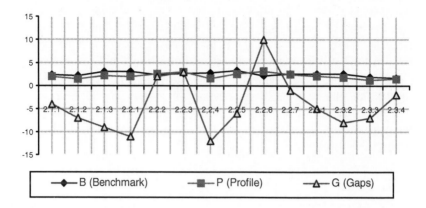

Figure 15.6 Capability gap analysis in a benchmark-based assessment

15.4 Summary

This chapter has developed two types of practical software process assessment methodologies: the model-based and the benchmark-based process assessment. These methodologies have provided step-by-step guidance to software process assessment, and have shown how to apply and implement the methodologies and theories developed in the unified software engineering process framework and SEPRM in the software industry.

The basic knowledge structure of this chapter is as follows:

Chapter 15. Software Process Assessment Methodologies

- General
  - Purpose(s) of this chapter
    - To review the scale and practices involved in software process assessment in the worldwide software industry

    - To explore a model-based software process assessment methodology

- To develop a benchmark-based software process assessment methodology

- To demonstrate how the generic SEPRM process assessment methodology and benchmarks might be applied in the software industry

- Review of process assessment practices and scale in the software industry

- Model-based process assessment methodology
  - The input-method-output (IMO) pattern for defining software process assessment method

  - Procedure
    - Assessment preparation phase
      - Define assessment purpose
      - Define assessment scope
      - Appoint assessment team
      - Prepare assessment confidentiality agreement
      - Plan schedule and resources
      - Map organization's processes onto the SEPRM reference model
      - Specify processes to be assessed and target capability levels

    - Assessment phase
      - Develop assessment brief
      - Data collection, validation, and rating
      - Derive process ratings and capability profile
      - Strengths and weakness analysis

    - Assessment output phase
      - Assessment report

  - Related input of each process
  - Related output templates of each process

- Benchmark-based process assessment methodology
  - The SEPRM process capability benchmarks

  - Benchmark-based assessment method
    - Adopt a benchmarked process model

– Conduct a baseline assessment
– Plot process profile onto the benchmark
– Identify gaps between the process profile and the benchmarks

– Contrast benchmark-based assessment with that of model-based
  – Philosophies
  – Assessment results
  – Target process capability levels
  – Usage
  – Advantages and drawbacks

• An integrated model- and benchmark-based process assessment
  – Use common assessment steps
  – Apply different methods for analyzing a resulted process profile
    – Absolute capability level analysis
    – Benchmark-oriented analysis

Major achievements and issues suggested by this chapter for further research are highlighted below:

• This chapter has provided a worldwide perception of software process assessment in the software industry.

• Two generic and practical process assessment methodologies, the model-based and benchmark-based process assessment methodologies, have been developed using SEPRM.

• An Input-Method-Output (IMO) pattern for defining software process assessment has been developed.

• A set of SEPRM software engineering process capability benchmarks has been provided.

• It has been predicted that more process benchmarks of current process models are to be expected in the future.

This chapter has explored two practical software process assessment methodologies based on the SEPRM reference model. Applications of the process assessment methodologies with supporting tools will be demonstrated in Chapter 16. Corresponding to the model-based and benchmark-based assessment methodologies, related process improvement methodologies will be developed in Part VI of this book.

Annotated References

This chapter has presented a set of generic software process assessment methodologies based on SEPRM and the latest developments in this area.

For CMM-specific assessment methods, see Paulk et al. (1993a/c/1995a) and Chapter 5 of this book.

For ISO/IEC TR 15504-specific assessment methods, see ISO/IEC TR 15504-3 (1998), Dorling (1993), Rout (1995), Kitson (1996), and Chapter 8 of this book.

For BOOTSTRAP-specific assessment methods, see Koch (1993), Haase et al. (1994), Kuvaja et al. (1994), BOOTSTRAP team (1993), and Chapter 7 of this book.

For background information of development of the SEPRM software engineering process benchmark, see Wang et al. (1996a/98a/99e).

There is a European software practice benchmark developed and maintained by IBM (1986). A Swedish national software engineering process benchmark was developed during 1997 – 1998 and reported by Wang et al. (1999f). A SPICE benchmark database was under development during SPICE Trials Phase III. For further details see SPICE Project (1998).

Questions and Problems

15.1 What are the relationships between the algorithmic, formal methodology developed in Chapter 9 and the practical methodologies developed in Section 15.2?

15.2 Taking your own organization or project as an example, try to conduct a model-based process assessment according to SEPRM and the methodology presented in Section 15.2.

15.3 Taking your own organization or project as an example, try to conduct a benchmark-based process assessment according to SEPRM and the methodology presented in Section 15.3.

15.4 A process assessment report can be developed by assembling all the templates provided in Section 15.2, and by providing additional analysis and comments. Draft an assessment report using the results you would have produced in Ex. 15.2.

15.5 Compare the efforts spent in developing the assessment reports in Ex.15.4 and Ex.9.15, and explain the practical advantages of the template-based process assessment approach developed in Section 15.2.

15.6 Using the results of a benchmark-based process assessment as produced in Ex.15.3, try to draft an assessment report for addressing the process strengths and weaknesses that you have assessed.

15.7 An integrated approach to process assessment can be developed by using both the model-based and benchmark-based methodologies presented in this chapter. Consider how you may incorporate the advantages of the model-based and benchmark-based assessment methods into an integrated process assessment.

15.8 By comparing the model-based and benchmark-based assessment methodologies, explain which method can help you understand a software process system and provide you more ideas for improving it.

Chapter 16

SUPPORTING TOOLS FOR SOFTWARE PROCESS ASSESSMENT

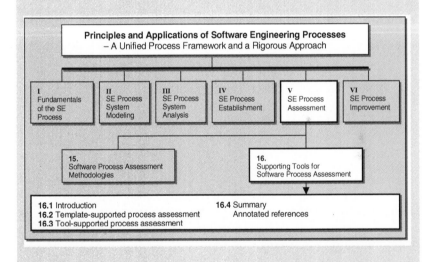

Principles and Applications of Software Engineering Processes
– A Unified Process Framework and a Rigorous Approach

I Fundamentals of the SE Process	II SE Process System Modeling	III SE Process System Analysis	IV SE Process Establishment	V SE Process Assessment	VI SE Process Improvement

15.
Software Process Assessment
Methodologies

16.
Supporting Tools for
Software Process Assessment

16.1 Introduction
16.2 Template-supported process assessment
16.3 Tool-supported process assessment

16.4 Summary
Annotated references

501

This chapter describes software engineering process assessment supporting technologies and tools. A classification of process assessment tools and the basic requirements for tools' implementation are explored. A set of practical process assessment templates is developed based on the SEPRM reference model.

The objectives of this chapter are as follows:

- To review software process assessment supporting technologies and tools

- To demonstrate how the generic assessment methodologies described in Chapter 15 are implemented and supported by assessment tools

- To develop a template-supported software process assessment method based on the SEPRM reference model

- To explore a tool-supported software process assessment method and the basic requirements for assessment tools

- To provide an insight into the practical methods used by assessors enabling those being assessed or those seeking to implement self-assessment to understand and reproduce a process assessment

16.1 Introduction

In Chapter 15 a set of practical process assessment methodologies was developed. This chapter describes a variety of software process assessment supporting tools, and shows how the assessment methodologies are implemented and supported.

In recent years, a number of software process assessment tools have been developed for supporting assessment data collection, storage, processing, and process capability rating and determination. A classification of software process assessment tools is shown in Table 16.1.

According to reports from the SPICE Project (1998) and Zubrow (1997), assessors have mainly used the nonstructured, paper-based tools such as checklist, questionnaire, and/or spreadsheet in software process assessment.

Two types of process assessment support tools have emerged, template-based paper working tools and integrated software tools.

Table 16.1
Classification of Process Assessment Supporting Tools

Category	Technology	Features Supported	
		Assessment	Capability Determination
Nonstructured paper-based tool			
	Checklist	√	
	Questionnaire	√	
	Spreadsheet	√	
Structured paper-based tool			
	Templates	√	
Software tool			
	Assessment data collection tool	√	
	Capability determination tool		√
	Integrated assessment tool	√	√

In addition to the process assessment tools, there are a number of experimental process simulation and enactment tools or environments. These tools are designed for automatically executing some of the software engineering processes in a way analogous with operating systems for executing software routines and procedures. Research in this area has attempted to apply CASE and AI technologies to the software engineering process system. Interested readers may refer to Hansen (1996), Gruhn (1998), Derniame et al. (1999), and Donzelli and Iazeolla (1999). Difficulties have been identified as those of human factors and management roles in the software engineering processes, and these would be among the fundamental differences between software routines and software engineering processes.

In the following sections, the template-based and software-tool-based process assessment methodologies will be explored with emphases on assessment data collection and process capability determination.

16.2 Template-Supported Process Assessment

Process assessment templates are a set of structured forms for regulating and guiding the activities during a software process assessment. Template-supported assessment is a practical and easy approach to software process assessment. A set of SEPRM-based templates as paper-working tools for supporting software process assessment has been developed as listed in Table 16.2. This section describes the design and layout of the templates and samples of completed templates in an assessment. Working templates ready for use for an SEPRM process assessment are documented in Appendix E.

Table 16.2
A Set of Templates for Process Assessment

No.	Template	Usage
1	Assessment purpose	To define purpose(s) of an assessment
2	Assessment scope	To define assessment scope, expected output, and constraints
3	Assessment team and responsibilities	To describe the assessment team, roles, and responsibilities
4	Assessment confidentiality agreement	To outline a format of an assessment confidentiality agreement
5	Assessment schedule and resources	To specify the schedule, milestones, and resources needed in an assessment
6	Processes to be assessed and target capability levels	To specify all processes to be assessed and their expected capability levels
7	Assessment brief	To outline a briefing report of an assessment for the organization and project to be assessed
8	Assessment results and process strengths and weaknesses analysis	To analyze status of processes based on the process profile obtained in an assessment

16.2.1   TEMPLATE 1 – ASSESSMENT PURPOSE

Template 1 is designed to define assessment purpose(s) as shown in Table 16.3. Template 1 is used for recording background information of the assessed organization and project, aims of assessment, type of assessment and duration, and special needs, if any. Its application in the context of assessment can be referenced in Table 15.3.

Table 16.3
Template 1 – Assessment Purpose

ID#: SEPRM98006   Date: - / - / -

No.	Subject	Remarks
1	Organization to be assessed	Specify name of organization
	Organization X	

2	Department to be assessed	Specify unit of organization
	IT Department	

3	Project(s) to be assessed	Specify project name(s)
	Embedded software A	

4	Sponsor of the assessment	Identify sponsor of the assessment
	S.S.S.	

5	Aims for assessment	Specify aims of assessment
5.1	Process establishment	
5.2	Process capability assessment	√
5.3	Process improvement	
5.4	Other (to be specified)	To trial the SEPRM process model and methodology

6	Assessment classification	Specify type of assessment
6.1	Assessment conformance to a certain model/standard	√
6.2	Independent (third-party) assessment	√
6.3	Second-party assessment	
6.4	Self-assessment	
6.5	Couched self-assessment	
6.6	Other (to be specified)	

7	Provisional date for assessment	Describe provisional date for the assessment
	- / - / -	

8	Special need(s) for assessment	Specify any special needs for the assessment
	Digital OHP	
	Availability of project manager	

16.2.2 TEMPLATE 2 – ASSESSMENT SCOPE

Template 2 is designed to define the assessment scope as shown in Table 16.4. Template 2 is used for recording existing processes in the organization, processes to be assessed, constraints of assessment, required assessment output, and description of assessees. Its application in the context of assessment can be referenced in Table 15.4.

Table 16.4
Template 2 – Assessment Scope

ID#: SEPRM98006   Date: - / - / -

No.	Subject	Remarks
1	Project to be assessed	
	Embedded software A	
2	Processes to be assessed in SEPRM	All SEPRM processes are to be assessed.
2.1	Organization process subsystem	
2.1.1	Organization structure process category	
2.1.1.1	Organization definition	√
2.1.1.2	Project organization	√
2.1.2	Organization process category	
2.1.2.1	Organization process definition	√
2.1.2.2	Organization process improvement	√
2.1.3	Customer service process category	
2.1.3.1	Customer relations	√
2.1.3.2	Customer support	√
2.1.3.3	Software/system delivery	√
2.1.3.4	Service evaluation	√
2.2	Development process subsystem	
2.2.1	Software engineering methodology process category	
2.2.1.1	Software engineering modeling	√
2.2.1.2	Reuse methodologies	√
2.2.1.3	Technology innovation	√
2.2.2	Software development process category	
2.2.2.1	Development process definition	√
2.2.2.2	Requirement analysis	√
2.2.2.3	Design	√
2.2.2.4	Coding	√
2.2.2.5	Module testing	√
2.2.2.6	Integration and system testing	√
2.2.2.7	Maintenance	√
2.2.3	Software development environment process category	
2.2.3.1	Environment	√
2.2.3.2	Facilities	√
2.2.3.3	Development support tools	√
2.2.3.4	Management support tools	√
2.3	Management process subsystem	
2.3.1	Software quality assurance (SQA) process category	

2.3.1.1	SQA process definition	√
2.3.1.2	Requirement review	√
2.3.1.3	Design review	√
2.3.1.4	Code review	√
2.3.1.5	Module testing audit	√
2.3.1.6	Integration and system testing audit	√
2.3.1.7	Maintenance audit	√
2.3.1.8	Audit and inspection	√
2.3.1.9	Peer review	√
2.3.1.10	Defect control	√
2.3.1.11	Subcontractor's quality control	√
2.3.2	Project planning process category	
2.3.2.1	Project plan	√
2.3.2.2	Project estimation	√
2.3.2.3	Project risk avoidance	√
2.3.2.4	Project quality plan	√
2.3.3	Project management process category	
2.3.3.1	Process management	√
2.3.3.2	Process tracking	√
2.3.3.3	Configuration management	√
2.3.3.4	Change control	√
2.3.3.5	Process review	√
2.3.3.6	Intergroup coordination	√
2.3.4	Contract and requirement management process category	
2.3.4.1	Requirement management	√
2.3.4.2	Contract management	√
2.3.4.3	Subcontractor management	√
2.3.4.4	Purchasing management	√
2.3.5	Document management process category	
2.3.5.1	Documentation	√
2.3.5.2	Process database/library	√
2.3.6	Human resource management process category	
2.3.6.1	Staff selection and allocation	√
2.3.6.2	Training	√
3	**Constraints of assessment**	For instance, resources, budget, and critical milestones
	Resources availability	
	Time limit for 5 day	
	Assessment expectation: capability level 3	
4	**Assessment output requirements**	Tick and describe additional output of assessment

4.1	Project process capability level	√
4.2	Process capability profile	√
4.3	Process strengths and weaknesses analysis report	√
4.4	Potential process improvement opportunities	√
4.5	Executive summary of assessment results	√
5	Background factors which may affect performance	
	At CMM level 2	
	ISO 9001 registered	

16.2.3 TEMPLATE 3 – ASSESSMENT TEAM AND RESPONSIBILITIES

Template 3 is designed to define the assessment team and its responsibilities as shown in Table 16.5. Template 3 is used for specifying the sponsor of the assessment, assessment team leader, assessors, and others such as unit management and technical representatives. Its application in the context of assessment can be referenced in Table 15.5.

Table 16.5
Template 3 – Assessment Team and Responsibilities

ID#: SEPRM98006   **Date:** *- / - / -*

No.	Role [Name]	Responsibility
1	Sponsor	Tick specific assessment supporting responsibilities for sponsor
	S.S.S.	- prepare assessment agreement - select unit representative(s) - organize assessment supporting activities - review assessment report - report to higher management
2	Lead Assessor	Assessment team leader
	A.A.A.	- prepare assessment agreement with sponsor - select assessor(s) with sponsor - develop assessment brief - organize assessment activities - review assessment report - present assessment report
3	Assessors	Responsibilities
3.1	Assessor 1	
	B.B.B.	- support questions - note taking - report writing

4	Others	
4.1	Project Management Representative	
	C.C.C.	Project leader
	D.D.D.	Quality assurance engineer
4.2	Project Technical Representative	
	E.E.E.	System analyst
	F.F.F.	Software engineer
	G.G.G.	Test engineer

16.2.4 TEMPLATE 4 – ASSESSMENT CONFIDENTIALITY AGREEMENT

Template 4 is designed to define the format of an assessment confidentiality agreement as shown in Table 16.6. Template 4 is used for specifying the purpose and scope of an assessment, mutual agreement on confidentiality, parties involved in the assessment, and signatures and date. Its application in the context of assessment can be referred to Table 15.6.

Table 16.6
Template 4 – Assessment Confidentiality Agreement

Assessment Confidentiality Agreement

ID#: SEPRM98006   **Date: - / - / -**

1. Scope and purpose of this document

This document has been agreed to provide mutual confidentiality to all parties involved in the assessment to be conducted at Organization X during < -/-/- > to < -/-/- >.

2. Parties to the agreement

The parties in this agreement will be Organization X (herein referred to as "Party A") and Organization Y (herein referred to as "Party B").

3. Confidentiality

Throughout the course of the assessment, and all times thereafter, the parties are hereby bound to observe complete confidentiality as to all matters concerning the affairs of each other; and all details relating to the assessment, now and in the future. None of the parties (including any associated companies or subsidiaries) will disclose information regarding the outcome of the assessment or engage in publicity pertaining to the other party without prior agreement from the other party.

All parties hereby confirm their acceptance.

Signed for and on behalf of Party A   Signed for and on behalf of Party B

Signature ....   Signature ....…..................

Full name   S.S.S   Full name   A.A.A

(print) ....   (print) ....

Position   Project manager   Position   Lead assessor

Address   ....   Address   ....

                ....

...........….................

                ....

....

Date   - / - / -   Date   - / - / -

Place   ....…........   Place   ....…..............

This agreement on confidentiality would not be necessary for a self-assessment or a cross-department internal assessment.

16.2.5 TEMPLATE 5 – ASSESSMENT SCHEDULE AND RESOURCES

Template 5 is designed to define the assessment schedule and resources as shown in Table 16.7. Template 5 is used for specifying the milestones of an assessment such as subject, responsible person(s), resources, and planned and completed dates. Its application in the context of assessment can be referenced in Table 15.7.

Table 16.7
Template 5 – Assessment Schedule and Resources

ID#: SEPRM98006   Date: - / - / -

No.	Subject	Responsibility	Resource	Planed date	Completed date
1	Initiation of an assessment	Lead assessor/sponsor	Paperwork		
2	Sponsor commitment	Sponsor	Paperwork		
3	Define assessment purpose	Lead assessor/sponsor	Paperwork		
4	Define assessment scope	Lead assessor/sponsor	Paperwork		
5	Sponsor approval of assessment input	Lead assessor/sponsor	Paperwork		
6	Appoint assessment team	Lead assessor/sponsor	Qualified assessors		
7	Prepare assessment confidentiality agreement	Lead assessor/sponsor	Paperwork		
8	Plan schedule and resources	Lead assessor/sponsor	Paperwork		
9	Determine assessment reference model, assessment model, and tool	Assessors	Paperwork		
10	Map customer's processes to SEPRM model	Assessors	Paperwork		
11	Define processes to be assessed and target capability levels	Assessors/ Sponsor	Paperwork		
12	Develop assessment brief	Lead assessor	PC, MS Word, and PowerPoint		
13	Organizational unit briefing	Lead assessor/sponsor	Assessment brief, PC, and PowerPoint		
14	Data collection	Assessors/ Assessees	PC and SEPRM tool		
15	Data validation	Assessors/ Assessees	PC and SEPRM tool		
16	Capability rating and analysis	Assessors/ Assessees	PC and SEPRM tool		
17	Briefing initial assessment results	Assessors/ Sponsor/ assessees	PC and SEPRM tool		
18	Process strengths and weaknesses analysis	Assessors	Paperwork		
19	Process improvement opportunity analysis	Assessors	Paperwork		

20 Develop assessment report	Lead assessor/sponsor	PC, MS Word, and completed templates		
21 Review and presentation of assessment report	Lead assessor/sponsor/ Assessees	PC, MS Word, and PowerPoint		
22 Action plan for process improvement	Sponsor/ Competent assessor/ Assessees	Paperwork		
23 Other (to be specified)				

16.2.6 TEMPLATE 6 – PROCESSES TO BE ASSESSED AND TARGET CAPABILITY LEVELS

Template 6 is designed to describe the processes to be assessed as shown in Table 16.8. Template 6 is used for mapping the existing processes at the organization onto the standard SEPRM processes, and specifying which processes will be assessed and what their target (expected) capability levels are. Its application in the context of assessment can be referenced in Tables 15.8 and 15.9.

Table 16.8
Template 6 – Processes to be Assessed and Target Capability Levels

ID#: SEPRM98006 Date: - / - / -

No.	Process	Selection in Assessment	Target Capability Level	Corresponding Processes On Site
1	Organization subsystem			
1.1	Organization structure category			
1.1.1	Organization definition	√	3	
1.1.2	Project organization	√	3	
1.2	Organization process category			
1.2.1	Organization process definition	√	3	
1.2.2	Organization process improvement	√	3	
1.3	Customer service category			
1.3.1	Customer relations	√	3	
1.3.2	Customer support	√	3	
1.3.3	Software/system delivery	√	3	
1.3.4	Service evaluation	√	3	
2	Development			
2.1	Software engineering methodology category			

2.1.1	Software engineering modeling	√	3
2.1.2	Reuse methodologies	√	3
2.1.3	Technology innovation	√	3
2.2	**Software development category**		
2.2.1	Development process definition	√	3
2.2.2	Requirement analysis	√	3
2.2.3	Design	√	3
2.2.4	Coding	√	3
2.2.5	Module testing	√	3
2.2.6	Integration and system testing	√	3
2.2.7	Maintenance	√	3
2.3	**Software development environment category**		
2.3.1	Environment	√	3
2.3.2	Facilities	√	3
2.3.3	Development support tools	√	3
2.3.4	Management support tools	√	3
3	**Management**		
3.1	**Software quality assurance category**		
3.1.1	SQA process definition	√	3
3.1.2	Requirement review	√	3
3.1.3	Design review	√	3
3.1.4	Code review	√	3
3.1.5	Module testing audit	√	3
3.1.6	Integration and system testing audit	√	3
3.1.7	Maintenance audit	√	3
3.1.8	Internal audit	√	3
3.1.9	Peer review	√	3
3.1.10	Defect control	√	3
3.1.11	Subcontractor's quality control	√	3
3.2	**Project planning category**		
3.2.1	Project plan	√	3
3.2.2	Project estimation	√	3
3.2.3	Project risk avoidance	√	3
3.2.4	Project quality plan	√	3
3.3	**Project management category**		
3.3.1	Process management	√	3
3.3.2	Process tracking	√	3
3.3.3	Configuration management	√	3
3.3.4	Change control	√	3
3.3.5	Process review	√	3
3.3.6	Intergroup coordination	√	3
3.4	**Contract and requirement management category**		
3.4.1	Requirement management	√	3
3.4.2	Contract management	√	3

3.4.3	Subcontractor management	√	3
3.4.4	Purchasing management	√	3
3.5	**Document management category**		
3.5.1	Documentation	√	3
3.5.2	Process database/library	√	3
3.6	**Human resource management category**		
3.6.1	Staff selection and allocation	√	3
3.6.2	Training	√	3

16.2.7 TEMPLATE 7 – ASSESSMENT BRIEF

Template 7 is designed to outline an assessment brief as shown in Table 16.9. It is used for introducing the assessees for the assessment organization as well as defining the purposes, procedures, and methods of the assessment. Template 7 specifies what will be addressed in an assessment brief, which may include all information defined in previous templates as well as the assessment approach and process models on which the assessment is based. Table 16.9 is configured as a summary of the previous templates. Its application in the context of assessment can be referenced in Table 15.9.

Table 16.9
Template 7 – Assessment Brief

ID#: SEPRM98006   Date: - / - / -

No.	Item	Remark
1	Organization	Refer to Table 16.3
	Organization X	Template 1
2	Department to be assessed	Refer to Table 16. 3
	IT Department	Template 1
3	Project(s)	Refer to Table 16. 3
	Embedded software A	Template 1
4	Sponsor	Refer to Table 16.3
	S.S.S	Template 1
5	Purpose of assessment	Refer to Table 16.3
	Independent (third-party) assessment;	Template 1
	To trial the SEPRM process model and methodology	

6	Scope of assessment	Refer to Table 16.4
	All 51 SEPRM processes	Template 2
7	Constraints of assessment	Refer to Table 16.4
	Resources availability	Template 2
	Time limit for 5 day	
	Assessment expectation: capability level 3	
8	Assessment team	Refer to Table 16. 5
	Sponsor: S.S.S.	Template 3
	Lead assessor: A.A.A.	
	Assessor: B.B.B.	
	Management representative: C.C.C., D.D.D.	
	Technical representative: E.E.E., F.F.F., G.G.G.	
9	Resources needed	Estimate amount of effort required and type of resource
	Refer to Table 16.7 (Template 5)	
10	Key milestones	Key milestones No. 1 – 22
	Refer to Table 16.7 (Template 5)	
11	Summary of process to be assessed and target capability level(s)	Refer to Table 16.8
	All 51 SEPRM processes	Template 6
	Target capability level: 3.0	
12	Assessment approach	Describe method and approach adopted for the assessment
	The assessment will be conducted according to the assessment method defined in Chapter 9.	Refer to SEPRM reference model and algorithm
	The assessment approach includes:	
	- Use of SEPRM process reference model	
	- Teamwork of assessors, sponsor, and assessees	
13	Other	To be specified by assessors

16.2.8 TEMPLATE 8 – PROCESS STRENGTHS AND WEAKNESSES ANALYSIS

The output of an assessment includes a process capability profile and a process strengths and weaknesses analysis. A set of process capability profiles of the organization according to SEPRM is shown in Figures 16.1 – 16.3.

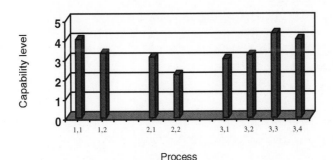

Figure 16.1 Capability profile of organization process subsystem assessed in SEPRM

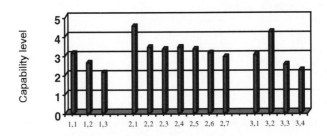

Figure 16.2 Capability profile of development process subsystem in SEPRM

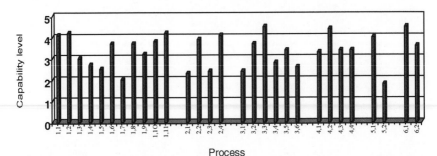

Figure 16.3 Capability profile of management process subsystem in SEPRM

Based on the process profiles, and taking into account the specific needs and objectives of the organization, the overall strengths and weaknesses of the organization can be identified by using Template 8.

Template 8 is designed to analyze process strengths and weaknesses as shown in Table 16.10. Template 8 is used for recording the assessed process levels, target process levels, and strength/weakness indications found in the assessment. Its application in context of assessment can be referenced in Table 15.10.

Table 16.10
Template 8 – Process Strengths and Weaknesses Analysis

ID#: SEPRM98006   **Date: - / - / -**

No.	Process	Assessed Level [AL]	Targeted Level [TL]	Strengths(+)/ Weaknesses (-) [AL-TL]
1	Organization			
1.1	Organization structure category			
1.1.1	Organization definition	4.0	3	1.0
1.1.2	Project organization	3.3	3	0.3
1.2	Organization process category			
1.2.1	Organization process definition	3.1	3	0.1
1.2.2	Organization process improvement	2.2	3	-0.8
1.3	Customer service category			
1.3.1	Customer relations	3.0	3	0
1.3.2	Customer support	3.2	3	0.2
1.3.3	Software and system delivery	4.3	3	1.3
1.3.4	Service evaluation	4.0	3	1.0
2	Development			
2.1	Software engineering methodology category			
2.1.1	Software engineering modeling	3.1	3	0.1
2.1.2	Reuse methodologies	2.6	3	-0.4
2.1.3	Technology innovation	2.1	3	-0.9
2.2	Software development category			
2.2.1	Development process definition	4.5	3	1.5
2.2.2	Requirement analysis	3.4	3	0.4
2.2.3	Design	3.3	3	0.3
2.2.4	Coding	3.4	3	0.4
2.2.5	Module testing	3.3	3	0.3
2.2.6	Integration and system testing	3.1	3	0.1
2.2.7	Maintenance	2.9	3	-0.1
2.3	Software development environment category			
2.3.1	Environment	3.0	3	0

2.3.2	Facilities	4.2	3	1.2
2.3.3	Development support tools	2.5	3	-0.5
2.3.4	Management support tools	2.2	3	-0.8
3	Management			
3.1	Software quality assurance category			
3.1.1	SQA process definition	4.1	3	1.1
3.1.2	Requirement review	4.2	3	1.2
3.1.3	Design review	3.0	3	0
3.1.4	Code review	2.7	3	-0.3
3.1.5	Module testing audit	2.5	3	-0.5
3.1.6	Integration and system testing audit	3.7	3	0.7
3.1.7	Maintenance audit	2.0	3	-1.0
3.1.8	Audit and inspection	3.7	3	0.7
3.1.9	Peer review	3.2	3	0.2
3.1.10	Defect control	3.8	3	0.8
3.1.11	Subcontractor's quality control	4.2	3	1.2
3.2	Project planning category			
3.2.1	Project plan	2.3	3	-0.7
3.2.2	Project estimation	3.9	3	0.9
3.2.3	Project risk avoidance	2.4	3	-0.6
3.2.4	Project quality plan	4.1	3	1.1
3.3	Project management category			
3.3.1	Process management	2.4	3	-0.6
3.3.2	Process tracking	3.7	3	0.7
3.3.3	Configuration management	4.5	3	1.5
3.3.4	Change control	2.8	3	-0.2
3.3.5	Process review	3.4	3	0.4
3.3.6	Intergroup coordination	2.6	3	-0.4
3.4	Contract and requirement management category			
3.4.1	Requirement management	3.3	3	0.3
3.4.2	Contract management	4.4	3	1.4
3.4.3	Subcontractor management	3.4	3	0.4
3.4.4	Purchasing management	3.4	3	0.4
3.5	Document management category			
3.5.1	Documentation	4.0	3	1.0
3.5.2	Process database/library	1.8	3	-1.2
3.6	Human resource management category			
3.6.1	Staff selection and allocation	4.5	3	1.5
3.6.2	Training	3.6	3	0.6

The assessment results listed in Table 16.10 show clearly the process strengths and weakness of the organization. The relative strengths of the organization are highlighted, in descending magnitude, as follows:

- Organization processes
  - Software and system delivery
  - Organization definition
  - Service evaluation

- Development processes
  - Development process definition
  - Facilities
  - Requirement analysis
  - Coding

- Management processes
  - Configuration management
  - Staff selection and allocation
  - Contract management
  - Requirement review
  - Subcontractor's quality control

The relative weaknesses of the organization are highlighted, in descending magnitude, as follows:

- Organization processes
  - Organization process improvement

- Development processes
  - Technology innovation
  - Management support tools
  - Development support tools
  - Reuse methodologies
  - Maintenance

- Management processes
  - Process database/library
  - Maintenance audit
  - Project plan
  - Project risk avoidance
  - Process management
  - Module testing audit
  - Intergroup coordination
  - Code review
  - Change control

The weaknesses identified in the process system as shown above indicate potential process improvement opportunities. The methodologies for process improvement will be explored in Part VI with case studies.

16.3 Tool-Supported Process Assessment

A number of software tools have been developed in recent years for supporting process assessment. This section introduces a variety of process assessment tools and describes their assessment supporting functions.

16.3.1 OVERVIEW OF PROCESS ASSESSMENT TOOLS

In this subsection, we introduce six typical process assessment tools that provide a wide range of functionality in software process assessment. Models or methods that the tools have adopted and the usage of the tools are briefly described. For further details about the tools described in this section, see the web sites provided in the annotated references.

16.3.1.1 SPICE 1-2-1

SPICE 1-2-1 is an ISO/IEC TR 15504-based software process assessment tool developed by IVF and HM&S. It supports self-assessment, assessment data collection and storage, process capability determination, and assessment results illustration and comparison.

16.3.1.2 PULSE

PULSE is an extended process model of ISO/IEC TR 15504 as described in Chapter 14. The PULSE assessment tool is developed by the PULSE Consortium partially supported by the EC SPRITE S2 program. The tool is designed to support IT system acquisition by defining a formal methodology for identifying and assessing the acquisition processes, and by identifying a set of organizational actions that improve the ways in which acquisitions are managed and measurement is made of the success of an IT acquisition organization.

The PULSE tool consists of two parts: *assessment* and *analysis*. The "assessment" functions cover the assessment aids for all 41 processes (component processes). Up to nine process attributes are assigned to each of these processes, to which the user can assign a score from 0 to 100%, respectively, or use a scale of N (not achieved), P (partially achieved), L (largely achieved) or F (fully achieved). Then, process capability levels and a visual process profile can be generated by the tool.

The "analysis" functions provide users with a number of charts for illustrating assessment results based on various criteria and the chosen form of display. This allows immediate, quantitative statements to be made concerning the strengths and weaknesses of whole organizations.

16.3.1.3 BootCheck

BootCheck is a BOOTSTRAP-based software process assessment tool developed by the BOOTSTRAP Institute and the European Software Institute. BootCheck supports assessment data collection, process capability determination, and assessment report generation. Its data collection adopts a questionnaire-driven approach.

Using BootCheck, a process assessment is conducted in the following four steps:

- Assessment preparation

- Evaluate processes and base practices

- Derive process profile

- Generate assessment report

The assessment results by BootCheck can be used to support a BOOTSTRAP-based process improvement program, particularly, for baselining an organization's process status, for seeking ISO 9001 registration, and for stepwise process improvement.

16.3.1.4 The SEAL Process Assessment Tool

The SEAL Process Assessment Tool was developed by the Software Engineering Applications Laboratory at University of the Witwatersrand,

South Africa, during 1995 to 1996. The SEAL tool supports ISO/IEC TR 15504-based assessment. It provides functions such as assessment data collection, process capability determination, ISO 9001 mapping, and process improvement assistant.

16.3.1.5 S:PRIME

S:PRIME is a CMM-based software process assessment tool developed by the Applied Software Engineering Center in Montreal, Canada. It can be used to identify and prioritize process improvement by providing risk mitigation and an action plan.

Based on a taxonomy-oriented risk identification method and CMM, the S:PRIME method is designed to meet the process metrology needs of small- and medium-size projects and organizations in software development and maintenance. A set of seven risk categories can be diagnosed by S:PRIME as follows:

- Contractual requirements

- Design and production

- Development environment

- Development processes

- Management

- Personnel

- External constraints

The S:PRIME tool uses two complementary questionnaires adapted to the context of a project or an organization to identify process-related risks and potential areas. Based on the identified risks, a remedial action plan can be produced by the tool.

16.3.1.6 Japanese Process Assessment Support Tools

A Process Assessment Support System and Modeling Framework was developed by Osaka University and the Nara Institute of Science and Technology in Japan [Matsushita et al., 1999]. It is a hypertext-supported SPICE software process assessment tool.

Omto et al. (1995) reported another process assessment tool known as the Software Process Assessment Support System (SPATS). It is a generic Windows-based software process assessment tool.

The development of software process assessment tools is a new and highly desirable potential area in software process assessment and improvement. More reports covering comparative evaluation and industry application experiences of using the existing and emerging assessment tools are expected.

16.3.2 FUNCTIONS OF TOOLS FOR SUPPORTING ASSESSMENT

A number of basic assessment support facilities, such as process explanation, assessment focus, evaluation aids, rating scale, and a notepad for recording evidence and findings, are provided to support the model-based assessment activities described in Chapter 15. This section describes the functions of tools in both the process and capability dimensions.

16.3.2.1 Process Dimension

For an example of the process dimension of the assessment tools, we look at the SPICE 1-2-1 process screenshot as shown in Figure 16.4. Assume we are assessing the ISO/IEC TR 15504 process ENG.1.3 – software design process. The process definition is displayed in the right-hand side tab, with the purpose of the process and the focus of the process for assessment. Additional assessment aids and what evidences the assessors need to look for may also be implemented in a pop-up menu.

16.3.2.2 Process Capability Dimension

A screenshot of the SPICE 1-2-1 capability dimension is shown in Figure 16.5. Rating scales for scoring the nine process attributes defined in ISO/IEC TR 15504 is shown on the left-hand side on the screen. The process attributes are explained in the right-hand side tabs, indicating required practices for achieving a process attribute that it is currently rating.

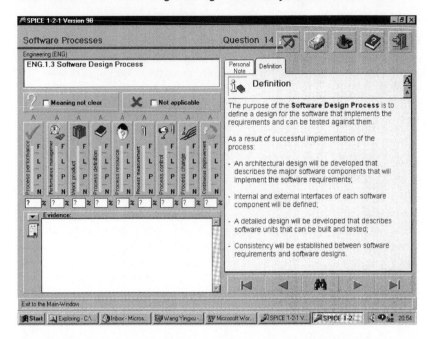

Figure 16.4 The process dimension facilities of an assessment tool

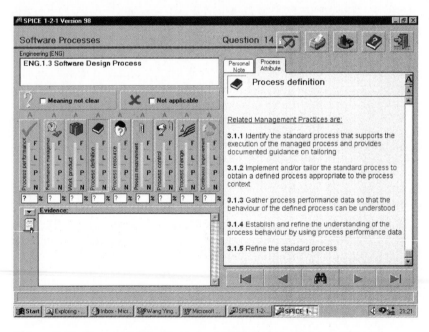

Figure 16.5 The capability dimension facilities of an assessment tool

Using the scales, a process can be rated against each of the attributes by "*F*ully/Largely/*P*artially/*N*ot achieved" or by a continued "0 – 100%" rating. During an assessment, the assessor can shift freely between the process dimension and the capability dimension in looking for the definition of a process and its focuses, and/or in considering the requirements and rating for a specific process attribute.

When all processes selected have been assessed, a process capability profile can be produced, and an assessment report for the assessment can be generated which includes illustrations of the assessment results and analysis of the process profile of the assessed organization.

The supporting functions of other model-based process assessment tools would be similar to those of the above example, while the implementation technology and platform that the tool is based on can be variable.

16.3.3 FUNCTIONS OF TOOLS FOR PROCESS CAPABILITY DETERMINATION

The kernel of a process assessment tool is the process capability determination algorithm. An algorithm determines the correctness and robustness of a software tool. In Chapters 5 – 9 we developed a set of algorithms for current process models with formal descriptions. Understanding and applying those algorithms will help build good software process assessment and improvement tools in the future.

16.4 Summary

This chapter has described the software process assessment supporting technologies and tools. Classification of process assessment tools has been explored. A set of practical process assessment templates has been developed based on the SEPRM reference model. The basic requirements for tools' implementation have been investigated.

The basic knowledge structure of this chapter is as follows:

Chapter 16. Supporting Tools for Software Process Assessment

- General
  - Purposes of this chapter
    - To review software process assessment supporting technologies and tools

    - To demonstrate how the generic assessment methodologies described in Chapter 15 are implemented and supported by assessment tools

    - To develop a template-supported software process assessment method based on the SEPRM reference model

    - To explore a tool-supported software process assessment method and the basic requirements for assessment tools

    - To provide an insight into the practical methods used by assessors to enable those being assessed or those seeking to implement self-assessment to understand and reproduce a process assessment

  - Classification of process assessment tools
    - Paper-based tools
    - Template-based tools
    - Software tools

- Template-supported process assessment
  - Templates for process assessment
    - Assessment purpose
    - Assessment scope
    - Assessment team and responsibilities
    - Assessment confidentiality agreement
    - Assessment schedule and resources
    - Processes to be assessed and target capability levels
    - Assessment brief
    - Assessment results and process strengths and weaknesses analysis

  - Understand the completed templates in the sample assessment

- Tool-supported process assessment
  - Basic requirements for assessment tools

- Process dimension
  - Process definition
  - Process explanation
  - Assessment focus

- Capability dimension
  - Rating scale
  - Rating explanation
  - Evaluation aids
  - A notepad

- A defined capability determination algorithm
  (Refer to Chapters 5 – 9)

- Features of existing process assessment tools

- Research in software process assessment simulation and
  enacting tools and environments

  - For automatically executing some selected software
    engineering processes

  - Compare these tools with operating systems for
    executing software routines and procedures

  - Identify issues in software process enacting: human
    factor simulation, management activities, and project
    parameters estimation

Major achievements and issues for further research suggested by this chapter
are highlighted below:

- This chapter has developed a classification of process assessment
  tools, and identified a set of basic requirements for them.

- A set of generic templates has been developed for supporting
  template-based process assessment according to the SEPRM process
  reference model.

- The basic requirements for a model-based process assessment tool
  have been identified in this chapter. Windows-based and web-based

technologies will be the main approaches to implement the software process assessment tools.

- The kernel of a process assessment tool is the process capability determination algorithm. A set of algorithms for current process models was developed in Part II of this book.

- A number of software tools have been developed in recent years for supporting process assessment. It is predicted that more and more process modeling, assessment, and improvement tools will emerge in process-based software engineering. More comparative evaluation reports and industry application experience about the existing software process assessment and improvement tools are also expected.

- Some experimental process simulation and enacting tools or environments have been developed to automatically execute some selected software engineering processes. However, difficulties have been identified for these tools as to simulation of human factors and management activities in the software engineering processes.

This chapter has demonstrated the implementation and applications of the generic process assessment methodologies developed in Chapter 15. For formal description of process models and algorithms, readers may refer to Chapters 5 – 9. Process improvement methodologies and case studies will be described in Chapters 17 – 18 in Part VI of this book.

Annotated References

For further details of the process assessment support tools described in this chapter, see the following web sites:

- SPICE 1-2-1: `http://www.ivf.se/cse/`

- PULSE: `http://www.ivf.se/cse/`   or
              `http://msnhomepages.talkcity.com/CerfSt/`
                   `DrYWang/`

- BootCheck: `http://www.bootstrap-institute.com/`

- SEAL: `http://www.seal.ac.za/`

- S:PRIME: `http://www.crim.ca/.cgla/english/`
                    `sprime.html`

For topics on software process simulation and enacting environments, interested readers may refer to Hansen (1996), Gruhn (1998), Derniame et al. (1999), and Donzelli and Iazeolla (1999).

Questions and Problems

16.1 What is the classification of support tools for process assessment and their usage in supporting software process assessment?

16.2 The template-based process assessment tool developed in this chapter provided a practical step-by-step support for software process assessment. Explain what the relationship is between the template tool and software tools.

16.3 Try to conduct a template-based software process assessment for your project by filling in each of the eight templates as provided in Appendix E.

16.4 Analyze the process strengths and weaknesses assessed as shown in Table 16.10, and explain what improvement opportunities you can identify from the strengths/weaknesses analysis.

16.5 Analyze the functions of existing process assessment tools as provided in Section 16.3 explain which tool you prefer to choose for a software process assessment, and why.

16.6 Describe the basic requirements for a software process assessment tool.

16.7 What are the purposes of software process simulation and enactment? What issues affect the implementation of software engineering process enactment and simulation?

PART VI

SOFTWARE ENGINEERING PROCESS IMPROVEMENT

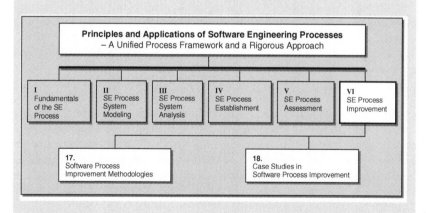

Principles and Applications of Software Engineering Processes
– A Unified Process Framework and a Rigorous Approach

| I
Fundamentals of the SE Process | II
SE Process System Modeling | III
SE Process System Analysis | IV
SE Process Establishment | V
SE Process Assessment | VI
SE Process Improvement |

17.
Software Process Improvement Methodologies

18.
Case Studies in Software Process Improvement

This part examines philosophies and generic approaches to software engineering process improvement. Three alternative improvement methodologies reflecting the technologies used in assessment as described in Part V are explored. These methodologies provide step-by-step guides to carry out a process improvement in accordance with the SEPRM process framework and methodologies. A set of case studies of real-world process improvement is provided, and key successful factors and benefits of process improvement are analyzed. Roles, prerequirements, and techniques of software process improvement are described that intend to provide a useful guide for implementing process improvement according to the SEPRM reference model.

The knowledge structure of this part is as follows:

- Chapter 17. Software Process Improvement Methodologies
- Chapter 18. Case Studies in Software Process Improvement

Chapter 17 presents a system engineering perception of software process improvement rather than the conventional philosophy of "fire-fighting" oriented process improvement. This chapter develops a set of rules and a generic approach to software process improvement. Three practical methodologies for process improvement, based on the SEPRM reference model, are explored. They are: model-based, benchmark-based, and template-based software process improvement.

Chapter 18 demonstrates how the software process improvement methodologies developed in Chapter 17 are applied in the software industry individually or in combination. Commonly recognized success factors and benefits of process improvement and their measurements are described. Three case studies are reported in order to show the practical approaches, experience, and lessons learned in process improvement in the software industry.

In this part, process improvement is recognized as a complicated, systematic, and highly professional activity in software engineering that requires theory and models, skilled technical and managerial staff, and motivated top management commitment. A system engineering perception on software process improvement is adopted. A new approach to benchmark-based process improvement provides that, instead of aiming for all Level 5, a software organization may simply try to have a better profile than the competition in the same area of interest.

By observing the industry case studies in software process improvement, readers may recognize that in the real environment, practical strategy in software process engineering is to view in the large and to implement in the small. The former means that if there is no strategic vision of a complete picture of the software engineering process system, the direction of improvement would be wrong. The latter indicates that software process improvement is naturally a graduated step-by-step program of accretion that incrementally improves the situation. If an improvement action plan is too ambitious or too fast, it would be unlikely succeed quite as planned due to inherent organizational resistance to changes, the human habit of inertia, and learning curves.

Chapter 17

SOFTWARE PROCESS IMPROVEMENT METHODOLOGIES

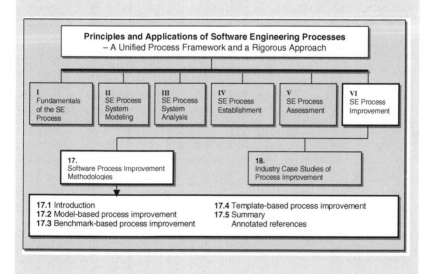

Principles and Applications of Software Engineering Processes
– A Unified Process Framework and a Rigorous Approach

| I Fundamentals of the SE Process | II SE Process System Modeling | III SE Process System Analysis | IV SE Process Establishment | V SE Process Assessment | VI SE Process Improvement |

17. Software Process Improvement Methodologies

18. Industry Case Studies of Process Improvement

17.1 Introduction
17.2 Model-based process improvement
17.3 Benchmark-based process improvement
17.4 Template-based process improvement
17.5 Summary
Annotated references

This chapter explores generic and practical software process improvement approaches. Methodologies of model-based, benchmark-based, and template-based software process improvement will be developed using the SEPRM software engineering process reference model.

The objectives of this chapter are as follows:

- To explore philosophies, rules, and generic approaches to software process improvement

- To explore a model-based software process improvement methodology

- To develop a benchmark-based software process improvement methodology

- To develop a template-based software process improvement methodology

- To demonstrate how the SEPRM process model and benchmarks are applied in process improvement

17.1 Introduction

In Chapter 4 the philosophies and generic approaches to software engineering process improvement were described. This chapter develops practical methodologies for software process improvement.

Software process improvement is a complicated, systematic, and highly professional activity in software engineering that requires theory and models, skilled technical and managerial staff, and motivated top management commitment. Software process improvement can only be based on established software processes, otherwise, effects will be virtual if the process system is not defined and established.

A set of basic rules that dominate software process improvement [Wang and King, 1999j] is as follows:

Rule 1: Software process improvement is complicated system engineering.

A process improvement program has to be thoroughly planned. There will be little achievement if an organization attempts to improve only a part of the many identified necessary processes in order to improve the whole process system and its performance.

Rule 2: Software process improvement itself is a goal-driven and continuous process.

It is goal-driven because process improvement should have predetermined goals and predesigned approaches to achieve these goals. It is a continuous process because the track of software process improvement is spiral-like and endless. During a software process improvement program, the goals may aim at higher levels, organizational requirements may be dynamic, and implement complicity may increase. Therefore, there is no absolute end for a process improvement.

Rule 3: Software process improvement is an experimental process.

Empirical process improvement recommendations should be treated as hypotheses. The impact and effectiveness of process improvement activities should be monitored and checked by periodical process review and/or assessments.

Rule 4: Software process improvement is risk-prone.

With regard directly to Rule 3, it can be seen that risks are naturally attached to any process improvement activities. Therefore, one should always be aware of and prepared for process change risks and potential impacts on other processes by an improvement activity. Also, as a corollary, risks for not implementing a required improvement for the identified problems should be estimated.

Rule 5: Software process improvement is a time varying system.

Process improvement operates in a dynamic environment with varying application domains and fast-changing technical platforms. This means there is no specific model that can be completely copied, and no specific methodology that can always be followed. Therefore, model and methodology adaptation is always required in process improvement.

Rule 6: Software process improvement is a random system dominated by human factors.

Further to Rule 5, process improvement is carried out by human beings. The main effective human factors in software engineering are flexibility and goal-orientation.

A basic assumption is that a skilled software engineer as an individual is an intelligent unit in a software engineering team and process who would automatically adjust activities to an optimizing goal in the system.

It is noteworthy that process improvement solutions for an identified problem would be manifold; implementation for a recommended solution would be achieved by multiple approaches; and time and efforts spent on implementation of an approach would vary greatly for different individuals or teams. All these varying human factors should be taken into account in a plan of process improvement.

Rule 7: Software process improvement has preconditions.

Process improvement requires formally defined, established, and experienced process systems. Process improvement on processes that are not systematically established has been proven wasteful.

Rule 8: Process improvement is based on process system reengineering.

The basic approach to software process improvement is by process reorganization and reengineering. Reengineering can be carried out by: (a) enhancing a process, (b) changing a process, (c) adapting a process, (d) canceling a process, and (e) reorganizing a process system.

Rule 9: Software process improvement achievement is cumulative.

Fortunately, having taken into account all the abovementioned technical, organizational, and cultural costs, the benefits of process improvement achievement can be cumulative, provided an organization continuously pursues software process improvement in a systematic and consistent way.

A generic procedure for software process improvement can be described in six steps as follows:

1) Examine the needs for process improvement.

2) Conduct a baseline assessment.

3) Identify process improvement opportunities.

4) Implement recommended improvement.

5) Review process improvement achievement.

6) Sustain improvement gains.

In the following sections, the generic process improvement procedures are explained and implemented through three different techniques:

- Model-based process improvement.

- Benchmark-based process improvement.

- Template-based process improvement

17.2 Model-Based Process Improvement

This section describes a method of model-based process improvement following the six generic steps as described in Section 17.1.

17.2.1 EXAMINING THE NEEDS FOR PROCESS IMPROVEMENT

A software process improvement program starts with the recognition of the organization's needs. Typical motivations for process improvement can be classified as follows:

- Organizational competitiveness

- Market requirements

- Contractual requirements

- International or regional regulation requirements

- Business benefits

Business benefits can be further identified and measured in terms of:

- Return on investment (ROI)

- Increment of productivity

- Reduction in time to market

- Gains in pretest defect detection

- Reduction of postrelease defects

- Reduction of rework rate

- Reduction of customer problems/complaints

To enable successful software process improvement, the following pre-requirements have to be fulfilled:

- Top-down management commitment

- Bottom-up motivation and involvement

- A dedicated process improvement team including both technical and managerial roles

- Sufficient resources such as budgets, time, and expertise

- Preparation for continuous process improvement and reinforcement

- Preparation for extensive training in new processes and implementation techniques for all levels of staff

When the real needs are identified, motivation is understood, and pre-requirements are fulfilled, a process improvement program can be progressed further to the following steps.

17.2.2 CONDUCTING A BASELINE PROCESS ASSESSMENT

A baseline process assessment is a diagnostic process assessment for probing current status and performance of a process system. The purposes of a baseline assessment are:

- To systematically examine the status of a process system

- To pinpoint the weak areas of a software process system

- To identify the process(es) that may be causal to the problems reported

- To identify the process(es) that would contribute significantly to meet the organization's business goals

By conducting a baseline assessment, the strengths and weaknesses of an organization's software process system will be understood. This enables the improvement areas to be identified in the next step.

17.2.3 IDENTIFYING PROCESS IMPROVEMENT OPPORTUNITIES

The purposes of this step are to identify weak process areas based on the process assessment results in order to determine improvement aims and priorities, and to establish an improvement action plan.

17.2.3.1 Identifying Weak Processes

Weak areas of a process system may be identified by looking for the following indicators:

- Processes that are required but not established or not performed

- Processes that lack some of the base process activities (BPAs)

- Processes that have not reached the required capability levels

- Processes that possess more higher capability levels than necessary; these may indicate a waste of energy

17.2.3.2 Determining Improvement Aims and Priorities

Corresponding to the types of weaknesses identified in a process system described above, the aims of improvement can be determined according to the following strategies:

- Process(es) to be newly established

- Process(es) to be completely performed

- Processes to be enhanced

- Process(es) to be balanced

- Process(es) to be changed

- Process(es) to be reorganized

Then, the priorities of improvement can be decided upon according to the processes' degree of weakness or gaps in the required capability levels.

Targets for improvement should be quantified for each priority area. These may be target values for process effectiveness, target process capability profiles, or combinations of the two.

17.2.3.3 Deriving an Improvement Action Plan

When the weaknesses of processes are identified and improvement aims and priorities are determined, a process improvement action plan can be made. A software process improvement action plan may consist of the following items:

- Actions, purposes, and priority

- Schedule and milestones of actions

- Responsibilities for actions

- Approaches to improvement

- Success criteria

- Risks and avoidance measures

In the process improvement action plan, it is important to ensure that key roles are clearly identified, appropriate milestones and review points are established, adequate resources are allocated, and risks associated with the plan are predicted and prepared.

17.2.4 IMPLEMENTING RECOMMENDED IMPROVEMENTS

Process improvement can be achieved by the following techniques:

- Enhancing inadequate processes

- Replacing ineffective processes

- Introducing new processes

- Reengineering process systems and interfaces

A process improvement program needs to be closely monitored according to the improvement plan in order to ensure tasks progress as expected, implementation is correct, and achievement is made. If any problems are encountered, causes should be analyzed and the action plan adjusted.

Clearly, implementation of process improvement often requires organizational architectural and/or cultural changes. Therefore, it is crucial to foster open communication and teamwork, to announce process system updatings, and to conduct training for the updated software process system.

Detailed records should be kept for use to both confirm the improvements and to improve the procedure of process improvement. In the case that unseen problems are experienced, a return to the original processes should be enabled.

17.2.5 REVIEWING PROCESS IMPROVEMENT ACHIEVEMENT

The purpose of this step is to confirm whether the planned improvement goals and target capability levels have been achieved.

Measurements of process effectiveness should be used to confirm achievement of process effectiveness targets. The possibility of undesirable side-effects should be investigated.

A new process assessment can be employed to review the improvement achievement. The review assessment can be either a self-assessment or a third-party assessment. Though the review assessment may focus on the affected processes in the improvement program, the whole process system should be assessed in order to find the impacts of improvement on other processes, or any possible side-effects or new imbalance of process capability.

17.2.6 SUSTAINING IMPROVEMENT GAINS

The purposes of this step are to make permanent deployment of improvement processes, and to sustain gains obtained in the improvement.

For a successful process improvement with proven effect, new or enhanced processes can now be deployed across all areas or projects in the organization where they are applicable. At the same time, the organization's process system reference model needs to be revised, and the updated reference model should be made known to all project managers and related staff.

Process improvement is a continuous pursuit; therefore, regular reviews of performance of the enhanced process system are required. Whenever necessary, a new round of the assessment or improvement program may be called and conducted.

17.3 Benchmark-Based Process Improvement

The model-based process improvement described in the previous section can be categorized as an absolute improvement approach with a philosophy of "the higher (the process capability level) the better." This section presents a new philosophy of relative process improvement, and develops a method for benchmark-based process improvement according to a philosophy of "the smaller the advantage, the better." The generic procedure of process improvement described in Sections 17.1 and 17.2 is still applicable in this section, but differences will be highlighted.

17.3.1 A NEW PHILOSOPHY OF RELATIVE PROCESS IMPROVEMENT

There is a well-known Chinese story of King Qi's horse racing about 1600 years ago. King Qi had the best horses in his kingdom. He liked horse racing very much and he expected to win every time. However, on one occasion he lost to Ji Tian, a wizard of that time.

The horses were categorized in three classes, i.e., for the King: K_1, K_2, and K_3; and for Tian: T_1, T_2, and T_3. In the first match, they determined the results as follows: $K_1 - T_1$, $K_2 - T_2$, and $K_3 - T_3$. Not surprisingly, the King won, as shown in Figure 17.1, because he had the best horses in each class.

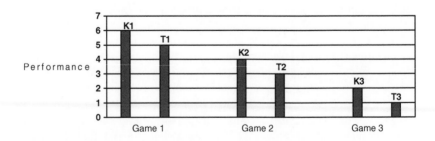

Figure 17.1 Example of benchmark-based decision making (1)

However, in the second match, the wizard changed his strategy. Tian used his third-class horse (T_3) against King Qi's first-class (K_1), and, of course, this allowed the King to win the first race. Then, in the following two races, Tian used his first- (T_1) and second- (K_2) class horses against the King's second- (K_2) and third- (K_3) class horses, respectively. Tian won the second three- race set and, for the first time in the history of the kingdom, defeated the King, as shown in Figure 17.2.

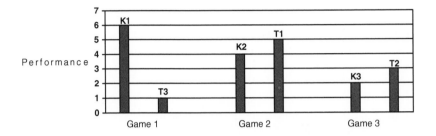

Figure 17.2 Example of benchmark-based decision making (2)

This story provides a useful operational strategy in decision-making for process improvement. That is, for software process improvement, an organization does not necessarily have to get all of its processes to the highest level to be competitive because it may not be the best, most feasible, and most economical solution for the organization. Instead, the best solution is just to have a marginal advantage over competitors in each process.

This inspires a new approach to software engineering process improvement – the smaller the advantage, the better. This concept revolves around the idea that just enough effort is all that is needed. In the light of this philosophy, a new method of benchmark-based process improvement is developed in the following subsections.

17.3.2 METHOD FOR BENCHMARK-BASED PROCESS IMPROVEMENT

The method of benchmark-based process improvement is an extension of the method of benchmark-based process assessment developed in Section 15.3. A benchmark-based process improvement can also be carried out in six steps as described in the generic improvement procedure.

With regard to the model-based process improvement methodology, the features of a benchmark-based process improvement are as follows:

- The philosophy for a benchmark-based process improvement is to "fill the gaps" rather than "the higher the better," which is common in model-based process improvement.

- The improvement opportunities are identified using gaps analysis between the plotted process profile and the benchmarks.

- The improvement priorities are determined by quantifying the magnitude of gaps between the plotted process profile and the benchmarks.

- The improvement achievement is evaluated by checking if the gaps have reduced, and if the process capabilities have been enhanced marginally above the process benchmarks.

A case for demonstrating an organization's baseline and improved capability profiles in a benchmark-based process improvement is shown in Figure 17.3. Figure 17.3 shows that the baseline process capability profile (P) of an organization has been improved to an adaptive process profile (R) that is marginally above and moves along with the benchmarked curves (B).

Note in Figure 17.3 that only the development process benchmarks and profiles are shown. Adopting the SEPRM benchmarks provided in Figures 15.2 and 15.4, the organization and management process subsystems improvement can be carried out in the same way.

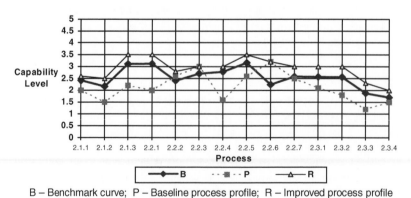

B – Benchmark curve; P – Baseline process profile; R – Improved process profile

Figure 17.3 SEPRM benchmark-based process improvement

17.4 Template-Based Process Improvement

This section describes another method of template-based process improvement. It is an extension of the template-based process assessment method developed in Section 16.2, and is designed to provide formal support for the model-based process improvement method presented in Section 17.2. The six-step generic procedure for conducting a software process improvement is also applicable for template-based process improvement.

In a template-based process assessment, the assessed process profile, and the overall strengths and weaknesses of a process system, have been obtained in Section 16.2 from Template 1 through Template 8. Using this analysis of the process profile and assessment findings, potential areas for improvement and priorities can be identified following the method provided in Table 17.1.

Table 17.1
Improvement Opportunities Analysis

Input	Method	Output
• Processes to be assessed and target capability levels (Template 6);	• Analysis of process improvement opportunities will be conducted according to the generic procedures as provided in Section 17.1;	Template 9: Process improvement opportunities analysis.
• Process capability profile as derived in the assessment;	• Identify improvement priorities of each process by evaluating the gap to the target capability level. The improvement priority will be described as high [H], medium [M], low [L], or No [N];	
• Process strengths and weaknesses analysis (Template 8);		
• The SEPRM process reference model.	• Analyze and describe impacts, and potential risks that may arise in an improvement activity.	

A template of improvement opportunities analysis (see Template 9 in Appendix E) is designed to support the method described above. For instance, taking the output of the assessment case presented in Section 15.2 as input for the template-based process improvement produces a working template is shown in Table 17.2.

In Table 17.2 the criteria adopted for classifying the improvement priority, *IP*, can be formally derived by the following Expression:

$$
\begin{aligned}
IP \; &= H, &&\textit{Weakness} > 1 \textit{ capability level;}\\
&= M, &&\textit{Weakness within 1 capability level;}\\
&= L, &&\textit{Strength} < 0.3 \textit{ capability level, which would} &&(17.1)\\
& && \quad \textit{be sensitive when capability turbulent;}\\
&= N, &&\textit{The rest, which have no improvement requirement with}\\
& && \quad \textit{regard to the specified target capability level.}
\end{aligned}
$$

Different thresholds would be defined in Expression 17.1 for a specific process improvement case.

Table 17.2
Template 9 – Process Improvement Opportunities Analysis

ID#: SEPRM98006   Date: - / - / -

No.	Process	Strengths(+)/ Weaknesses (-) [AL-TL]	Improvement Priority (IP)	Remarks and Risks
1	Organization			
1.1	Organization structure category			
1.1.1	Organization definition	1.0	N	
1.1.2	Project organization	0.3	N	
1.2	Organization process category			
1.2.1	Organization process definition	0.1	L	
1.2.2	Organization process improvement	-0.8	M	
1.3	Customer service category			
1.3.1	Customer relations	0	L	
1.3.2	Customer support	0.2	L	
1.3.3	Software and system delivery	1.3	N	
1.3.4	Service evaluation	1.0	N	
2	Development			
2.1	Software engineering methodology category			
2.1.1	Software engineering modeling	0.1	L	
2.1.2	Reuse methodologies	-0.4	M	
2.1.3	Technology innovation	-0.9	M	
2.2	Software development category			
2.2.1	Development process definition	1.5	N	
2.2.2	Requirement analysis	0.4	N	
2.2.3	Design	0.3	N	
2.2.4	Coding	0.4	N	
2.2.5	Module testing	0.3	N	
2.2.6	Integration and system testing	0.1	L	
2.2.7	Maintenance	-0.1	M	

2.3	Software engineering infrastructure category			
2.3.1	Environment	0	L	
2.3.2	Facilities	1.2	N	
2.3.3	Development support tools	-0.5	M	
2.3.4	Management support tools	-0.8	M	
3	Management			
3.1	Software quality assurance category			
3.1.1	SQA process definition	1.1	N	
3.1.2	Requirement review	1.2	N	
3.1.3	Design review	0	L	
3.1.4	Code review	-0.3	M	
3.1.5	Module testing audit	-0.5	M	
3.1.6	Integration and system testing audit	0.7	N	
3.1.7	Maintenance audit	-1.0	H	
3.1.8	Audit and inspection	0.7	N	
3.1.9	Peer review	0.2	L	
3.1.10	Defect control	0.8	N	
3.1.11	Subcontractor's quality control	1.2	N	
3.2	Project planning category			
3.2.1	Project plan	-0.7	M	
3.2.2	Project estimation	0.9	N	
3.2.3	Project risk avoidance	-0.6	M	
3.2.4	Project quality plan	1.1	N	
3.3	Project management category			
3.3.1	Process management	-0.6	M	
3.3.2	Process tracking	0.7	N	
3.3.3	Configuration management	1.5	N	
3.3.4	Change control	-0.2	M	
3.3.5	Process review	0.4	N	
3.3.6	Intergroup coordination	-0.4	M	
3.4	Contract and requirement management category			
3.4.1	Requirement management	0.3	N	
3.4.2	Contract management	1.4	N	
3.4.3	Subcontractor management	0.4	N	
3.4.4	Purchasing management	0.4	N	
3.5	Document management category			
3.5.1	Documentation	1.0	N	
3.5.2	Process database/library	-1.2	H	
3.6	Human resource management category			
3.6.1	Staff selection and allocation	1.5	N	
3.6.2	Training	0.6	N	

Table 17.2 indicates that the processes that have the highest priority for improvement in this case are maintenance audit and process database/library, followed by the medium priority processes:

- Technology innovation
- Organization process improvement
- Management support tools
- Project plan
- Project risk avoidance
- Process management
- Development support tools
- Module testing audit
- Reuse methodologies
- Intergroup coordination
- Code review
- Change control
- Maintenance

The other steps in a template-based process improvement are similar to those of the model-based process improvement. A detailed description of model-based process improvement may be referenced in Section 17.2. Case studies of real-world process improvement will be provided in Chapter 18.

17.5 Summary

This chapter has explored generic software process improvement approaches. Practical methodologies for model-based, benchmark-based, and template-based software process improvement have been provided using the SEPRM software engineering process reference model.

The basic knowledge structure of this chapter is as follows:

Chapter 17. Software Process Improvement Methodologies

- General

  − Purposes of this chapter
    - To explore philosophies, rules, and generic approaches to software process improvement

    - To explore a model-based software process improvement methodology

    - To develop a benchmark-based software process improvement methodology

    - To develop a template-based software process improvement methodology

    - To demonstrate how the SEPRM process model and benchmarks are applied in process improvement

  − Generic software process improvement procedure
    1) Examine the needs for process improvement

    2) Conduct a baseline assessment

    3) Identify process improvement opportunities

    4) Implement recommended improvement

    5) Review process improvement achievement

    6) Sustain improvement gains

- Basic rules of software process improvement
  − Rule 1: Process improvement is complicated system engineering

  − Rule 2: Process improvement itself is a goal-driven and continuous process

  − Rule 3: Process improvement is an experimental process

  − Rule 4: Process improvement is risk-prone

  − Rule 5: Process improvement is a time-varying system

  − Rule 6: Process improvement is a random system dominated by human factors

  - Rule 7: Process improvement has preconditions

  - Rule 8: Process improvement is based on process system reengineering

  - Rule 9: Process improvement achievement is cumulative

- Model-based process improvement methodology
  - Philosophy of absolute relative process improvement: "the higher the better"

  - How to implement the six-step generic approach in model-based process improvement?

  - Motivations to software process improvement:
    - Organizational competitiveness
    - Market requirements
    - Contractual requirements
    - International or regional regulation requirements
    - Business benefits

  - Prerequirements for software process improvement:
    - Top-down management commitment
    - Bottom-up motivation and involvement
    - A dedicated process improvement team
    - Sufficient resources
    - Prepared for continuous process improvement
    - Prepared for extensive training for new processes

  - Software process improvement technologies:
    - Enhancing inadequate processes
    - Replacing ineffective processes
    - Introducing new processes
    - Reengineering process system and interfaces between processes

- Benchmark-based process improvement methodology
  - Philosophy of relative process improvement: "the smaller the advantage, the better," or "to fill the gaps"

  - How to implement the six-step improvement in benchmark-based improvement

  - Differences between benchmark-based and model-based software process improvement:

  – Philosophy
  – Improvement opportunities identification
  – Improvement priorities determination
  – Improvement achievement evaluation

- Template-based process improvement methodology
  – A support tool for model-based software process improvement

  – Criteria for determining improvement priorities
    (Expression 17.1)

  – Template and how to work out it (Template 9)

  – How to interpret a completed improvement template?
    (Table 17.2)

Major achievements and issues for further research suggested by this chapter are highlighted below:

- This chapter has presented a system engineering perception on software process improvement. This is different from the conventional philosophy of "fire-fighting"-oriented process improvement.

- A set of basic rules has been provided for understanding the nature of process improvement.

- A six-step generic procedure for software process improvement has been developed which is suitable for implementing process improvement according to any established process models, particularly the SEPRM reference model.

- Motivations, prerequirements, purposes, weakness indicators, and techniques of software process improvement have been described in this chapter that provide a set of useful guidelines for implementing process improvement according to the SEPRM reference model.

- Based on the generic process improvement procedure, three practical methodologies for conducting software process improvement – model-based, benchmark-based, and template-based improvement – have been developed.

Applications of the process improvement methodologies in the software industry will be demonstrated by case studies in Chapter 18.

Annotated References

Software process improvement concepts and methodologies were largely inspired by the work in management science, particularly in quality system principles and enterprise reengineering research. Shewhart (1939) developed the concept of the "plan-do-check-act" iteration. Later, this concept was extensively applied in the Japanese manufacturing industry known as the "KAIZEN method" [Imai 1986], and was extended and interpreted by Deming (1982b/86) and known as the "Deming cycle."

On generic software process improvement literature, readers may refer to Humphrey (1988), Paulk and his colleagues (1993a), Curtis (1992), Basili (1993), Peterson and Radice (1994), and Wang et al. (1997a/98a/99e/h).

On model-based software process improvement, see Paulk and his colleagues (1995), Kuvaja and his colleagues (1994), Herbsleb (1994), El Eman and his colleagues (1993), ISO/IEC TR 15504 – 7 (1998), and the SPICE Project (1998).

On benchmark-based software process improvement, see IBM (1996) and Wang et al. (1998a/1999d/e). The work on SEPRM benchmark-based software process improvement was reported in [Wang et al., 1999e/j]. For template-based process improvement technology, see Wang et al. (1998f).

Basili and his colleagues (1994), Pfleeger and Rombach (1994), and Solingen and Berghout (1999) developed a "Goal/Question Metric Method" for software process improvement. For more articles on this technology, see Perry, Staudenmayer, and Votta (1994), Khoshgoftaar and Oman (1994), and Fenton and Pfleeger (1996).

Questions and Problems

17.1 Referring to the SPI Rules 1 and 7, analyze what the preconditions of software process improvement are.

17.2 Referring to the SPI Rule 6, explain what key human factors may influence the effect of software process improvement.

17.3   What is the generic procedure for implementing software process improvement in a software development organization?

17.4   By contrasting the model-based and benchmark-based process improvement options, summarize the common and different aspects.

17.5   Identify the improvement areas and their priorities using the model-based assessment results obtained in Ex.15.2.

17.6   Identify the improvement areas and their priorities using the benchmark-based assessment results obtained in Ex.15.3.

17.7   Using the analysis results of Ex.17.5, develop a model-based process improvement action plan according to SEPRM and the methodology presented in Sections 17.2 and 17.4.

17.8   Using the analysis results of Ex.17.6, develop a benchmark-based process improvement action plan according to SEPRM and the methodology presented in Section 17.3.

17.9   In Section 17.1 nine rules for software process improvement were presented. Explain which rule(s) you think most significant. Can you add any additional rules by your reading of this book?

17.10   Software process improvement can be conducted at organization, project (team), and/or individual levels. What level do you think the improvement priority should be given to? Why?

Chapter 18

CASE STUDIES IN SOFTWARE PROCESS IMPROVEMENT

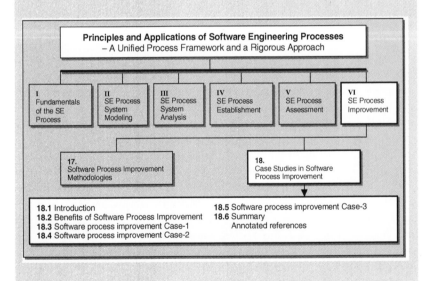

Principles and Applications of Software Engineering Processes
− A Unified Process Framework and a Rigorous Approach

| I Fundamentals of the SE Process | II SE Process System Modeling | III SE Process System Analysis | IV SE Process Establishment | V SE Process Assessment | VI SE Process Improvement |

17.
Software Process Improvement Methodologies

18.
Case Studies in Software Process Improvement

18.1 Introduction
18.2 Benefits of Software Process Improvement
18.3 Software process improvement Case-1
18.4 Software process improvement Case-2

18.5 Software process improvement Case-3
18.6 Summary
  Annotated references

This chapter demonstrates empirical software process improvement approaches by means of real-world case studies in the software industry.

The objectives of this chapter are as follows:

- To review a broad picture of software process improvement in the software industry

- To investigate the benefits and common goals of software process improvement in industry

- To explore a generic approach to assessment model-based software process improvement

- To demonstrate process improvement by the adaptation and integration of external and internal standards and models

18.1 Introduction

In Chapter 17 practical technologies of software process improvement were explored. These technologies can be applied in software development organizations individually or collectively. This chapter describes benefits accruing from process improvement and its measurement, and demonstrates three industry case studies on empirical process improvement.

Software process improvement has gained wide acceptance in the software industry. A worldwide software process improvement network (SPIN) was formed in the last decade. According to Curtis (1992) and Koch (1993), distributions of the CMM capability levels of 332 software development organizations in the USA, Japan, and Europe up to 1992/93 are shown in Table 18.1. The average data shown in Table 18.1 indicate that nearly 90% of the organizations were at CMM Level 1, and no organization was graded at Levels 4 and 5 as of 1992/93.

Comparing the data with Zubrow's survey in 1997, which has also been shown in Table 18.1, it can be found that, for those software development organizations that underwent CMM assessment before 1997, 27.3% improved from Level 1, and especially 2% have achieved Level 4 or 5. This was significant because more than a quarter of the software organizations were improved in a period of five years.

Table 18.1
Trends in Software Process Improvement in the Software Industry

Year	Sample Size	Region	CMM Capability Levels				
			Level 1	Level 2	Level 3	Level 4	Level 5
1992 (Curtis)	113	USA	86.0%	13.0%	1.0%	0	0
1992 (Curtis)	196	Japan	96.0%	3.0%	1.0%	0	0
1993 (Koch)	23	Europe	47.9%	52.1%	0	0	0
Average	332	Global	89.3%	9.8%	0.9%	0	0
1997 (Zubrow)	-	Global	62.0%	36.0%		2.0%	
Improvement in 5 (4) years	1997		-27.3%	25.3%		2.0%	

According to Wang et al. (1996c), CMM Levels 2 – 3 are equivalent to those organizations that would pass the threshold of ISO 9001 assessment. This implies that about 38% (as in 1997) and 10.7% (as in 1992/93) of those CMM-assessed organizations are technically at or above the ISO 9001 pass level.

In the following sections, we will discuss the benefits of software process improvement and how they are measured. We will present empirical process improvement experience and approaches by case studies in the software industry in Sections 18.3 through 18.5.

18.2 Benefits of Software Process Improvement

Before presenting the case studies in software process improvement, we discuss what might be expected in process improvement benefits, and how they are measured both quantitatively and qualitatively.

18.2.1 MEASUREMENTS FOR BENEFITS OF SOFTWARE PROCESS IMPROVEMENT

seven areas in software process improvement – budget, cycle time, development cost, maintenance cost, quality, innovation, and customer satisfaction – have been identified for assessing industry expectation for process improvement [Wang et al., 1999f]. Figure 18.1 shows the numbers of the software organizations that rate the importance of each area as "none/low/medium/high/very high," respectively. The rightmost bar in each area shows a weighted total value of significance of an area in process improvement.

As shown in Figure 18.1, the aspects of software process improvement considered most important are development budget, customer satisfaction, and quality, while relatively less important areas are development and maintenance costs.

According to the above work and the description in Section 17.2.1, a set of metrics of software process improvement benefits can be derived as shown in Table 18.2. There are seven quantitative and seven qualitative benefits identified, respectively. Detailed discussions on the benefit measurement metrics of process improvement will be provided in the following subsections.

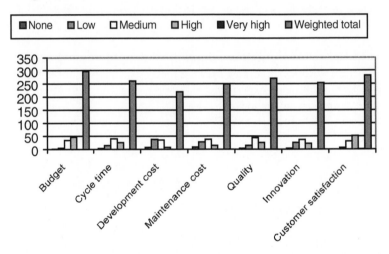

Figure 18.1 Areas of importance in software process improvement for the software industry

Table 18.2
Metrics of Benefit of Software Process Improvement

No.	Quantitative Measurement	Qualitative Measurement
1	Return on investment (ROI)	Organization efficiency
2	Increment of productivity	Project management efficiency
3	Reduction in time to market	Organization competitiveness
4	Gain of pretest defect detection	Individual competitiveness
5	Reduction of postrelease defects	Organization image
6	Reduction of rework rate	Establishment of business goal for pursuing improvement
7	Reduction of customer problems/complaints	Customer satisfaction

A number of leverages of software process improvement for business success have been identified in Messnarz and Tully (1999). They are financial, operating, production, marketing, and human leverages, which indicate that software process improvement is effective to almost all areas in a software development organization.

18.2.2 STATISTICS DATA ON BENEFITS OF SOFTWARE PROCESS IMPROVEMENT

Herbsleb (1994) reported a number of cases that benefit from CMM-based software process improvement, such as:

- *Hewlett Packard* has dropped its software defect rate from 0.4 defect/KLOC to 0.11 defect/KLOC.

- *Texas Instruments* has reduced the find-fix time for defects from 8 hours each to 11 minutes.

- *Schlumberger* has improved its planning slippage from 50% to 5%.

- *Raytheon* has gained $7.80 avoidance of rework costs for every $1.00 invested in process improvement.

In a European project on business benefits of software engineering best practices, the ESSI Office (1996) reported the following achievements in software process improvement in Europe by surveying more than 200 software companies and projects since 1993:

- *Engineering I&I S.P.A.*, a large Italian software house, has improved its project estimation accuracy by reducing by 60% the average estimation errors.

- *PROFit S.A.*, a medium-sized Spanish software house, has obtained a six-fold productivity gain in software reengineering and maintenance by efficient migration of applications.

- *CLAAS KGaA*, a German manufacturer acquiring embedded software, has gained millions of ECU boost to sales by specification and software management rethinking.

- *ENEL S.P.A.*, a large Italian electricity supplier, has gained up to an 18% cost reduction by formal specification method.

- *Datamat S.P.A.*, a large Italian systems integration company, has gained a competitive edge in turnkey software projects by the introduction of configuration management.

- *B&K Measurements A/S*, a Danish embedded software company, has gained a 75% reduction in the number of error reports by introducing systematic unit testing procedures and software quality assurance processes.

Based on the achievements listed above, ESSI has concluded that "the good news was that all these companies reported clear business benefits in software process improvement."

More sophisticated data on the benefits of software process improvement reported by Herbsleb (1994) at ESI is given in Table 18.3. Table 18.3 shows that return on investment in software process improvement is quite high in the financial context. In technical terms, this means software process improvement is a worthwhile pursuit for the software industry.

Table 18.3
Benefits of Software Process Improvement

No.	Parameter	Range	Median
1	Return on investment (ROI)	4.0 – 8.8	5.0
2	Productivity gain per year	9% – 67%	35%
3	Reduction in time to market	15% – 23%	19%
4	Pretest defect detection gain per year	6% – 25%	22%
5	Yearly reduction of postrelease defects	10% – 94%	39%

From Table 18.3 it is also found that the most outstanding benefit of process improvement is in software quality (reduction of defects), followed by productivity increment and design quality (pretest defect detection) improvement.

18.2.3 INDUSTRY COMMENTS ON SOFTWARE PROCESS IMPROVEMENT

The quantitative measurement of benefits in software process improvement having been demonstrated, now the qualitative benefits of process improvement as listed in Table 18.2 may be reviewed.

Although the qualitative benefits may be independent of direct financial gains, they, to some extent, are widely considered more beneficial in the software industry, and generate long-term impacts on the architecture and efficiency of a software development organization.

In a national benchmarking survey on software engineering practices [Wang et al., 1999f], almost all software development organizations that participated believe that software process improvement is important for the organizations' future success. In evaluating the responses, the following three themes emerged:

- Software process improvement is essential for the future success of a software development organization (T1).

- By applying software process improvement, an organization can significantly increase timeliness of project schedules and thereby reduce costs (T2).

- The organization is aware of software process improvement benefits, however it lacks the knowledge and skills to kick off the improvement activities (T3).

Statistical weightings on the themes are shown in Figure 18.2.

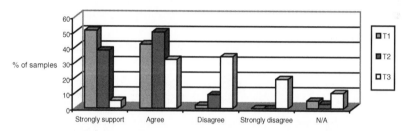

Figure 18.2 Views on software process improvement

Figure 18.2 indicates that almost all software organizations participating in the survey view software process improvement as an important basis for their software development projects. Most of the organizations believe that, via software process improvement and with adoption of the best practices and processes in software engineering, their ability to compete has been enhanced to the international standard.

Similarly and interestingly, Coch (1993) reported a set of positive user responses on BOOTSTRAP assessment and improvement in Europe. Some of them are quite generic, representing the view of the software industry on software process improvement and are as cited below:

- They point to fundamental software engineering problems and to good approaches for improvements.

- They enforce the capability for improvement by constructive suggestions, for instance, through action plans.

- They motivate individuals' thoughts about their own working methods and environment, and thereby stimulate new ideas on how to improve.

- They give a good picture of our software development practices in a very short time.

- They received a high degree of acceptance.

- They touch essential points of daily work.

- They should be prepared every two years in order to constantly follow organizational upgrades.

In the following sections we will describe three real-world process improvement cases in the software industry to show the generic approaches to and the valuable lessons learned from software process improvement.

18.3 Software Process Improvement Case-1

This case study describes Cromer and Horch's work (1999) on software process improvement in a small and dynamic software development company, *Organization A,* with varied project types and multiple successful approaches to software development.

18.3.1 BACKGROUND

Organization A is a small software company with fewer than 75 software developers operating on a multinational business base and a multicultural experience base. It has a diversity of project types ranging from real-time embedded software, hardware/software integrated systems, database manipulation software, and modeling and simulation software to management information systems. It has adopted multiple development approaches from international, national, IEEE, and in-house process standards, and has applied multiple processes in software engineering.

18.3.2 APPROACH TO PROCESS IMPROVEMENT

The organization successfully registered for ISO 9001 and achieved CMM Level 3 in recent years. An integrated and applicable organization's process standard has been set up to support the applications of both CMM and ISO 9001 process models.

The initiative of the process improvement program in Organization A was motivated by all typical internal and external business needs: customer satisfaction, software quality, company reputation, and better profit.

The task of pursuing process integration and improvement stumbled over unforeseen obstacles such as gaps in knowledge, overlaps of different models, and existence of project-specific approaches. When selecting suitable process models for the organization, it was realized there were many standards and many choices.

Eventually, a suitable solution was adopted in order to integrate the organization's internal processes with ISO 9001 procedures and CMM key process areas up to Level 3. To achieve the strategic goal, the team carried out the following crucial activities:

- Identified costs for process improvement

- Obtained management cognizance and commitment

- Obtained staff support

- Secured a budget

Then, the team addressed the plethora of standards to find a map for process improvement. They surveyed process standards sources, categorized standards as broad application or project-specific, and categorized process requirements by varying processes.

Adaptation and integration of process standards were designed for the establishment of a process system for the entire organization. Subsets of broad applicable standards were selected and adapted for all projects. Project-specific standards and processes were selected and adapted for distinct project requirements. All selected standards were codified into an integrated organizational process system with project-specific extensions or replacements.

With the establishment of the organization's process standards, progress was monitored. First, the team applied the integrated process standard to various types of software projects. Then, they measured the results of process performance. With the feedback and measurement, the team modified and updated the process standards as metrics and experience dictated.

So far, the process improvement team in Organization A has applicable industry standards identified, in-house standards codified, and project categories well defined. The applications of the organizational standard process to projects are underway. As a result, ISO 9001 registration has been accomplished, and CMM Level 3 has been achieved.

In the next phase process of improvement, the goals of the organization are to apply standard-effectiveness metrics to projects and manage projects based on process metrics.

18.3.3 LESSONS LEARNED

In this successful software process improvement program, Cromer and Horch reported that Organization A has learned:

- To choose good directions such as ISO 9001 and CMM as well as project team involvement in task planning

- To accept that errors have been made such as underestimated diversity of projects, overestimated staff readiness for changes, potential alternative routes of pursuing CMM in concert with project and standards categorization, and seeking CMM assessment before ISO 9001 registration

- To suggest company-wide and cross-section communications in order to enable everyone to have his or her position heard and to consent to the overall decision

In conclusion of their pursuit of software process improvement, they found "there is no viable (acceptable) alternative in today's marketplace."

18.4 Software Process Improvement Case-2

This section describes a case study in software process improvement in *Organization B*, a software component and system acquirer, by using the extended ISO/IEC TR 15504 model on software acquisition processes.

18.4.1 BACKGROUND

The PULSE process model, an extension of ISO/IEC TR 15504 as described in Chapter 14, was adopted in Organization B to improve its software acquisition processes.

18.4.2 APPROACH TO PROCESS IMPROVEMENT

In Chapter 17 we established the generic approach to model-based process improvement. This case study demonstrates how the generic improvement methodology is applied to bring an organization's process system capability to a targeted level.

18.4.2.1 Examining the Needs for Process Improvement

Organization B has experienced a number of problems in its software acquisition projects, especially on requirement specification and change management, deliverables acceptance, and risk management. Projects were frequently delayed due to the late discovery of problems and the high rate of reworks.

A process improvement plan was set to improve the acquisition, management, and organization processes to capability level 2 in order to solve the current problems.

18.4.2.2 Conducting a Baseline Assessment

To systematically examine the status and performance, and to analyze the strengths and weaknesses of the organization's process system, a baseline assessment was conducted.

The organization has aligned its processes to the extended ISO/IEC TR 15504 software and system acquisition process model as described in Chapter 14. According to the extended process model, the assessment scope was tailored and assessment results were derived as shown in Figure 18.3.

Process ID.	Process/ Subprocess	CL1 Performed	CL2 Managed	CL3 Defined	CL4 Established	CL5 Optimized
ACQ	Acquisition					
ACQ.1.1	Acquisition policy	■	■	■		
ACQ.1.2	Acquisition strategy					
ACQ.1.3	Benefits analysis					
ACQ.2.1	Technical requirements	■	■			
ACQ.2.2	Contract requirements	■	■			
ACQ.2.3	Financial requirements	■	■			
ACQ.2.4	Project requirements	■				
ACQ.3.1	Invitation to tender	■				
ACQ.3.2	Tender evaluation	■				
ACQ.3.3	Contract negotiation	■				
ACQ.4.1	Supplier monitoring	▪				
ACQ.4.2	Acquisition acceptance	■				
ACQ.4.3	Contract closure					
SUP	Support					
SUP.1	Documentation					
SUP.2	Configuration mgmt.					
SUP.3	Quality assurance					
SUP.4	Verification					
SUP.5	Validation					
SUP.6	Joint review					
SUP.7	Audit					
SUP.8	Problem resolution					
MAN	Management					
MAN.1	Management					
MAN.2	Project management	■				
MAN.3	Quality management	■				
MAN.4	Risk management	▪				
ORG	Organization					
ORG.1	Organizational alignment					
ORG.2	Improvement					
ORG.2.1	Process establishment					
ORG.2.2	Process assessment					
ORG.2.3	Process improvement					
ORG.3	Human resource mgmt.					
ORG.4	Infrastructure					
ORG.5	Measurement					
ORG.6	Reuse					
ORG.7	Financial management					
ORG.8	Manage supplier relationship	■				
ORG.9	Manage user relationship					

Figure 18.3 Assessed process profile of Organization B

18.4.2.3 Identifying Process Improvement Opportunities

According to the baseline assessment, a process profile and process strengths and weaknesses of the organization were derived as shown in Table 18.4. The findings of this assessment showed that the relative strengths of the organization's practices were the processes of ACQ1.1 – acquisition policy; ACQ2.1 – technical requirement; ACQ2.2 – contract requirement; and ACQ2.3 – financial requirement. The weakest processes were ACQ4.1 – supplier monitoring and MAN.4 – risk management.

Table 18.4
Process Strengths/Weaknesses Analysis and Improvement Opportunities

Process	Assessed Process	Assessed Level (AL)	Target Level (TL)	Strengths(+)/ Weaknesses(-) [AL-TL]	Improvement Priority [H I M I L]
ACQ	Acquisition processes				
ACQ.1.1	Acquisition policy	3	2	1	L
ACQ.2.1	Technical requirement	2	2	0	L
ACQ.2.2	Contract requirement	2	2	0	L
ACQ.2.3	Financial requirement	2	2	0	L
ACQ.2.4	Project requirement	1	2	-1	M
ACQ.3.1	Invitation to tender	1	2	-1	M
ACQ.3.2	Tender evaluation	1	2	-1	M
ACQ.3.3	Contract negotiation	1	2	-1	M
ACQ.4.1	Supplier monitoring	0	2	-2	H
ACQ.4.2	Acquisition acceptance	1	2	-1	M
MAN	Management processes				
MAN.2	Project management	1	2	-1	M
MAN.3	Quality management	1	2	-1	M
MAN.4	Risk management	0	2	-2	H
ORG	Organization processes				
ORG.8	Manage supplier Relationships	1	2	-1	M

They analyzed the gaps between the weak processes identified above and determined the target capability levels, improvement opportunities, and priorities. The following key areas were recommended as the highest priority for process improvement in the organization:

- The supplier monitoring process within the acquisition category

- The risk management process within the management process category

18.4.2.4 Implementing Recommended Improvement

The processes that would provide the highest benefit for improvement within the organization had been identified as the processes of supplier monitoring and risk management, followed by project requirement, invitation to tender, tender evaluation, contract negotiation, acquisition acceptance, project management, quality management, and manage supplier relationships.

According to the recommendations, adoption and improvement of the two high- and eight medium-prioritized processes were emphasized in all projects within the organization, and their performance was closely monitored at project and organization levels.

18.4.2.5 Reviewing Process Improvement Achievement

After a year of improvement in Organization B, a review assessment was carried out to confirm progress in process improvement. The results of the review assessment, as shown in Figure 18.4, indicated that the organization had successfully achieved the target of capability level 2.

With the defined processes in place, especially the enhancement of the technical requirements, supplier monitoring, and risk management processes, Organization B was able to solve the problems of requirement clarification and change negotiation with the developers in a much earlier phase. By improving the supplier monitoring process, the organization could find problems before a system was delivered. By adoption of the risk management process the organization has learned how to prevent rework and project delays from taking place.

With this updated status of process system as a new baseline, a higher-level process capability was targeted. Then, a similar iteration of process improvement as described in Sections 18.4.2.1 through 18.4.2.5 was begun for continuous process improvement.

18.4.3 LESSONS LEARNED

The most important thing learned in this case study is that software engineering processes are fundamental to the smooth running and success of a growing company.

Process ID.	Process/ Subprocess	CL1 Performed	CL2 Managed	CL3 Defined	CL4 Established	CL5 Optimized
ACQ	Acquisition					
ACQ.1.1	Acquisition policy	■	■	■		
ACQ.1.2	Acquisition strategy					
ACQ.1.3	Benefits analysis					
ACQ.2.1	Technical requirements	■	■	■	■	
ACQ.2.2	Contract requirements	■	■			
ACQ.2.3	Financial requirements	■	■			
ACQ.2.4	Project requirements	■	■			
ACQ.3.1	Invitation to tender	■	■			
ACQ.3.2	Tender evaluation	■	■			
ACQ.3.3	Contract negotiation	■	■			
ACQ.4.1	Supplier monitoring	■	■			
ACQ.4.2	Acquisition acceptance	■	■			
ACQ.4.3	Contract closure					
SUP	Support					
SUP.1	Documentation					
SUP.2	Configuration mgmt.					
SUP.3	Quality assurance					
SUP.4	Verification					
SUP.5	Validation					
SUP.6	Joint review					
SUP.7	Audit					
SUP.8	Problem resolution					
MAN	Management					
MAN.1	Management					
MAN.2	Project management	■	■	■		
MAN.3	Quality management	■	■			
MAN.4	Risk management	■	■			
ORG	Organization					
ORG.1	Organizational alignment					
ORG.2	Improvement					
ORG.2.1	Process establishment					
ORG.2.2	Process assessment					
ORG.2.3	Process improvement					
ORG.3	Human resource mgmt.					
ORG.4	Infrastructure					
ORG.5	Measurement					
ORG.6	Reuse					
ORG.7	Financial management					
ORG.8	Manage supplier relationship	■	■			
ORG.9	Manage user relationship					

Figure 18.4 Improved process profile obtained by a review assessment

Software requirements in particular are critical elements of software acquisition, and having an efficient, consistent, and cost-effective means of handling these is of paramount importance.

Close monitoring of entire development processes against functional requirements, quality criteria, and schedules enabled a software system acquirer to find problems earlier and to avoid risks of project delay and intensive postdelivery maintenance.

18.5 Software Process Improvement Case-3

This section describes a case study in software process improvement in *Organization C*, an embedded software developer, by using the ISO/IEC TR 15504 process model.

18.5.1 BACKGROUND

Organization C is an established software developer providing embedded software for laboratory instrument systems. This case study reports ISO/IEC TR 15504-based process improvement experience gained in a pilot software process improvement project carried out in the organization.

18.5.2 APPROACH TO PROCESS IMPROVEMENT

In Chapter 17 we established the generic approach to model-based process improvement. This case study demonstrates how the generic improvement methodology is applied in the software industry for addressing identified problems in an organization's software engineering process system. The ISO/IEC TR 15504 process model was adopted in the organization to implement systematic process improvement.

18.5.2.1 Examining the Needs for Process Improvement

In Organization C's practice, there was not a complete software engineering process system. For software development there was no formal testing process; instead, software was tested by peer programmers acting as users.

For software project management there were no defined software quality assurance processes; instead, a customer problems report and maintenance team had been established as fire fighters.

As a result, the more systems they developed and sold, the worse the maintenance situations. This was a crucial problem that had been troubling the management and quality assurance engineers in Organization C.

To satisfy customers' demands and to keep the market share of the software systems developed in Organization C, all the managers and developers realized that a formal software engineering process system was urgently needed. The need for establishing software requirement specification, software testing and software quality assurance (SQA) processes were especially emphasized.

A preliminary process improvement plan was set up to concentrate on defect reduction as a major goal of the organization.

18.5.2.2 Conducting a Baseline Assessment

As a starting point of the improvement program, it was decided to undertake a baseline process assessment to get a better picture of the current situation. An assessment team was appointed which included an experienced software process assessor (the mentor), a software quality assurance engineer, and representatives of software engineers and managers. The assessees included all technical, managerial, and support staff who had a role in the sampled projects.

The purpose of the baseline assessment was to pinpoint the status of current software processes and practices, and to identify the processes that contributed significantly to the inclusion of defects in the software products. The assessment scope was decided as all the ISO/IEC TR 15504 engineering processes (ENG.1 – ENG.7) and seven of the eight project processes (PRO.1 – PRO.7) as shown in Table 18.5.

All project staff were briefed about the purposes of the assessment, the ISO/IEC TR 15504 process model, mapping of the organization's processes onto the ISO/IEC TR 15504 processes, and a plan of the assessment.

Table 18.5
Assessment Scope of the ISO/IEC TR 15504 Processes

ID.	Process Category	Process	Selected
CUS	Customer- supplier		
CUS.1		Acquire software product	
CUS.2		Establish contract	
CUS.3		Identify customer needs	

CUS.4		Perform joint audits and reviews	
CUS.5		Package, deliver, and install software	
CUS.6		Support operation of software	
CUS.7		Provide customer service	
CUS.8		Assess customer satisfaction	
ENG	Engineering		
ENG.1		Develop system requirements	√
ENG.2		Develop software requirements	√
ENG.3		Develop software design	√
ENG.4		Implement software design	√
ENG.5		Integrate and test software	√
ENG.6		Integrate and test system	√
ENG.7		Maintain system and software	√
RRO	Project		
PRO.1		Plan project life cycle	√
PRO.2		Establish project plan	√
PRO.3		Build project teams	√
PRO.4		Manage requirements	√
PRO.5		Manage quality	√
PRO.6		Manage risks	√
PRO.7		Manage resources and schedules	√
PRO.8		Manage subcontractors	N/A
SUP	Support		
SUP.1		Develop documentation	
SUP.2		Perform configuration management	
SUP.3		Perform quality assurance	
SUP.4		Perform problem resolution	
SUP.5		Perform peer reviews	
ORG	Organization		
ORG.1		Engineer the business	
ORG.2		Define the process	
ORG.3		Improve the process	
ORG.4		Perform training	
ORG.5		Enable reuse	
ORG.6		Provide software engineering environment	
ORG.7		Provide work facilities	

After a two-week assessment according to the method and algorithm defined in Chapter 8 as well as the assessment approach described in Section 15.2, an assessment report was finally produced with a process profile as shown in Figure 18.5.

18.5.2.3 Identifying Process Improvement Opportunities

Process improvement opportunities could be one of the following: (a) enhancing inadequate processes, (b) replacing ineffective processes, or (c) introducing new processes.

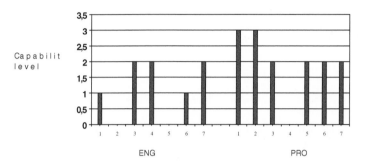

Figure 18.5 Process profile produced by the baseline assessment

Analyzing the assessment results as shown in Figure 18.5, it has been found that software was being developed without a clear understanding of requirements, so that the software engineers spent a lot of time going back and making corrections once they understood the requirements. A conclusion was that last-minute changes had the potential to introduce defects into the software. In addition, system test activities were not performed in a systematic way.

Detailed analysis showed that there was a satisfactory situation in the area of project management because most of the processes were at capability level two, and some at capability level 3 with no significant weaknesses except PRO.4 – management requirements. Software design and maintenance processes seemed to be satisfactory: ENG.3, ENG.4, and ENG.7 were all at level 2.

The problem areas appeared to be related to requirement definition and management (ENG.1, ENG.2, and PRO.4) and system testing (ENG.5 and ENG.6).

The assessment team decided to address these weak processes as keys for the improvement program. The team recommended that Organization C target the five prioritized processes at ISO/IEC TR 15504 capability level 2.

18.5.2.4 Implementing Recommended Improvement

The pinpointed process strengths and weaknesses and identified improvement areas were documented in a process improvement action plan, which included:

- Establishment of an organizational mechanism to monitor the implementation of the improvement program

- Detailed procedure and schedule for achieving the improvement

- Definition of criteria of achievement of the process improvement

- Resources required for the process improvement

- The main actions for improving the weak processes were recommended:

  - The introduction of a systematic approach to the collection and analysis of customer needs

  - The definition of a clearer interface between staff supporting the customer and staff developing software products

  - The introduction of a systematic approach to system and acceptance testing

  - The introduction of formal reviews to be held on completion of each of these processes

  - The launch of a training program for all staff involved in software development, management, and support

The team made an interim presentation to senior management about the improvement action plan that was well-received. Management approved the updated process improvement program, including the action plan, schedule, budget, and resources. Thus, process improvement activities were formally started at Organization C according to the action plan.

18.5.2.5 Reviewing Process Improvement Achievement

After acting throughout a completed project life cycle as planned in the process improvement program, a review assessment was carried out to confirm the improvement and benefits. An improved process profile was obtained by the review assessment as shown in Figure 18.6. The new process profile indicated that almost all processes had achieved the targeted capability levels except PRO.4.

The changes introduced in the process improvement program were carefully reviewed and documented. Those processes and practices that had proven benefits were distributed to all units to be used as references to plan their own improvement projects.

A new phase of process improvement was planned based on the review assessment. It was another iteration of the procedures as described thus far.

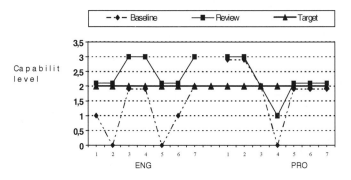

Figure 18.6 Model-based software process improvement

18.5.2.6 Sustaining Improvement Gains

A permanent process engineering team was appointed to monitor process improvement progress. Practical and effective processes were regulated at organizational and project levels. Advanced technology and new best practices were introduced into the process systems. Regular meetings were called to review process status and performance, identify problems occurring, find solutions for problems, and improve processes for preventing the causes of problems. Regular assessments of processes were conducted to reinforce the software engineering process system within Organization C, and to set new goals in continuous process improvement.

18.5.3 LESSONS LEARNED

With this process improvement case study the following important experiences were gained:

- The process improvement pattern, "baseline-assessment – action of improvement – review-assessment," adopted in this case study provides a practical and effective approach to process improvement.

- Process improvement should be set as one of the important business goals at the organizational level.

- Senior management initiative and involvement are among the keys to success.

- Sufficient resources for process improvement, including budget, qualified improvement team and consultant, and suitable process model and improvement approach, need to be made available.

- Provision of intensive training of staff is one of the most crucial activities for the adoption and effective operation of new processes in process improvement.

18.6 Summary

This chapter has reviewed the scale and trends of worldwide software process improvement in the software industry, and explored direct and indirect benefits as well as commonly recognized success factors in software process improvement. Three case studies were reported in order to show the practical approaches to process improvement in the software industry, and to summarize the experience and lessons learned.

The basic knowledge structure of this chapter is as follows:

Chapter 18. Case Studies in Software Process Improvement

- General
  - Purposes of this chapter
    - To review a broad picture of software process improvement in the software industry

    - To investigate the benefits and common goals of software process improvement in industry

    - To explore a generic approach to assessment model-based

software process improvement

- To demonstrate process improvement by the adaptation and integration of external and internal standards and models

- Benefits of software process improvement
  - Quantitative measurement
  - Qualitative measurement
  - Key success factors in software process improvement
  - Main barriers to software process improvement

- Software process improvement Case-1
  - Organization type: multiple application software developer
  - Main approach: improvement by establishing integrated internal process standards based on CMM, ISO 9001, and in-house process models
  - Key lessons learned: adaptation of software process standards and models to organizational needs

- Software process improvement Case-2
  - Organization type: software components and systems acquirer
  - Main approach: extended ISO/IEC TR 15504 model- and assessment-based process improvement
  - Key lessons learned: software process are fundamental to the smooth running and success of a software company

- Software process improvement Case-3
  - Organization type: an embedded software developer
  - Main approach: ISO/IEC TR 15504 model- and assessment-based process improvement
  - Key lessons learned: a pattern for process improvement: baseline-assessment, action of improvement, and review-assessment

- A generic software process improvement approach
  - Examine the needs for process improvement
  - Conduct a baseline assessment
  - Identify process improvement opportunities
  - Implement recommended improvement
  - Review process improvement achievement
  - Sustain improvement gains

Major achievements and issues for further research suggested by this chapter are highlighted below:

- Observing the industry case studies in software process improvement, it is learned that in the real-world environment, practical strategy in software process engineering is to view in the large and to implement in the small. The former indicates that if there is no strategic vision of the complete picture of a software engineering process system, the direction of improvement would be wrong. The latter shows that software process improvement is naturally a graduated and step-by-step pursuing program. If an improvement action plan is too ambitious and too fast, it would not likely be achieved as planned.

- The most significant benefits of process improvement in software engineering have been commonly recognized as follows:

  - Improvement of organization competitiveness

  - Improvement of software quality

  - Increment of software productivity

  - Reduction of time to market

- Some commonly recognized success factors in software process improvement are as follows:

  - Senior management involvement

  - Defined, well-received improvement goals

  - Established organizational roles and responsibilities for process improvement

  - Adaptation of international standards and established process models

  - Planed resources for process establishment and improvement

  - Staff training for adoption of new processes in a software engineering process system

  - Sustained improvement achievement by regulation of software process system, organization's quality policy, and staff training

  - Pursuit of continuous process improvement

- Some commonly recognized barriers and counterproductive practices in software process improvement are as follows:

  - Lack of senior management support

  - Lack of resources and qualified software process engineers

  - Lack of knowledge of software engineering process systems and best practices

  - Staff nonawareness of process improvement goals and procedures

  - Starting process improvement before a defined process system has been established in an organization

  - Pursuit of overly ambitious improvement goals in one step

  - Pursuit of one-off improvement or certification rather than continuous process improvement

- The new approach to benchmark-based process improvement provides an interesting research and experiment subject in software process engineering.

This chapter has shown an encouraging picture of software engineering process establishment, application, and improvement in the industry. Considering that more and more software development organizations have adopted software process systems as the key architectural framework for implementing and improving software engineering, we may expect more and more software organizations to seek to improve in the same ways.

Annotated References

The European Systems and Software Initiative (ESSI) was launched by the European Commission in 1993, and aimed at promoting the adoption of software best practices in European software development organizations. ESSI has sponsored a number of programs for software assessment and improvement projects and an experience repository. For details see: http://www.cordis.lu/esprit/src/stessi.htm.

Within ESSI programs, a VASIE process improvement experiments (PIEs) repository, maintained by the European Software Institute, is available at http://www.esi.se/VASIE. A number of case studies drawn from ESSI PIEs project process improvement experiences is documented at http://www.cordis.lu/espit/src/stessi.htm. The SPIRE project process improvement case studies are reported at http://www.cse.dcu.ir/spire.

In Curtis' (1992) and Zubrow's (1997) studies, a large number of organizations that have undergone CMM assessment before 1997 have been surveyed. The distributions of capability levels and motivations for process improvement have been revealed. Goldenson and Herbsleb (1995) carried out a follow-up survey on 61 CMM-assessed organizations and reported a number of factors that may affect process improvement success.

The SPICE Project (1998) and Herbsleb et al. (1994) have also studied the benefits of software process improvement with a set of statistics data. Messnarz and Tully (1999) identified the financial, operating, production, marketing and human leverages of software process improvement for business success.

Humphrey, Snyder, and Willis (1991b) reported a success story of software process improvement at Hughes Aircraft. Fitzgerald and O'Kane (1999) studied a software process improvement effort over time and revealed how Motorola's Cellular Infrastructure Group progressed to CMM Level 4, and what the critical success factors are in software process improvement.

Cromer and Horch (1999) reported their path to process standardization and improvement in the IEEE 4th International Software Engineering Standards Symposium. In the same proceedings, Wang et al. (1999f) reported the establishment of a national benchmark of software engineering practices, and the positive attitude and comments of the Swedish software industries on software process improvement.

There were arguments on the benefits of software process improvement. Jones (1996) reported a negative record with cases that had not obtained tangible benefits accruing. Based mainly on the CMM model, Fayad and Laitinen (1997) considered process assessment to be wasteful. Seddon (1997) listed a number of side-effects of ISO 9000.

Questions and Problems

18.1 According to the SEPRM process framework as described in Table 9.2, log your project effort distribution in each of the software engineering process and process categories. Try to record the effort (time and/or budget) you spend according to Table 9.2 and report the average ratio of effort of your project(s) in forms of:

<organization>% : <development>% : <management>%

18.2 According to the average ratio of effort distribution of your organization as derived in Ex.18.1, you may deploy your project team and assign software engineering roles on a sound basis. Assuming an average ratio of effort distribution is: <organization>% : <development>% : <management>% = 1 : 6 : 3, try to configure a putative software project team and assign the roles of the staff in it.

18.3 Describe what you can learn from process improvement Case Study One presented in Section 18.3.

18.4 Describe what you can learn from process improvement Case Study Two presented in Section 18.4.

18.5 Describe what you can learn from process improvement Case Study Three presented in Section 18.5.

18.6 In Section 18.2 the metrics of benefits of process improvement have been provided. Explain which of the top three quantitative and qualitative measurements you would apply in your software improvement project.

Chapter 19

REVIEW
AND
PERSPECTIVES

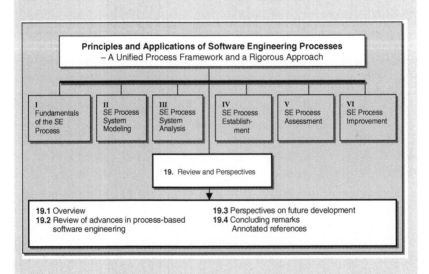

Principles and Applications of Software Engineering Processes
– A Unified Process Framework and a Rigorous Approach

| I
Fundamentals of the SE Process | II
SE Process System Modeling | III
SE Process System Analysis | IV
SE Process Establish-ment | V
SE Process Assessment | VI
SE Process Improvement |

19. Review and Perspectives

19.1 Overview
19.2 Review of advances in process-based software engineering

19.3 Perspectives on future development
19.4 Concluding remarks
Annotated references

585

19.1 Overview

Within the modern domain of software engineering, professional roles have extended from conventional programmers to a dramatically long list. As shown in Table 2.2, there are 13 software engineering organizational roles, 11 software development roles, and 8 managerial roles that have been identified in the software industry. They are typically listed as: senior manager, project manager, customer solution analyst, system analyst, system architect, software engineer, programmer, testing engineer, software quality assurance (SQA) engineer, maintenance engineer, customer supporting engineer, internal supporting staff, etc.

Using a rough estimation of the current scale of the global software industry, readers may recognize the tremendous development speed of the industry. Two decades ago, programmers and software professionals were mainly academics and researchers working in universities, research institutions and industry laboratories. In 1999, as reported by Jones (1999), there were 2,383,500 software development and software engineering professionals in the USA. In Asia, Bagchi (1999) reported that India's 338 universities and 48 engineering colleges produce 67,785 programmers who join the software industry every year. This implies that in the last decade India has graduated more than 0.67 million software engineers. Japan's and China's output of software engineers is considered about two to three times of that of India. Putting these data together and assuming an even distribution among the regions of North America, Europe, and Asia-Pacific, it is estimated conservatively, that there are more than 6 million software engineering professionals in the software industry all over the world.

Observing the amazingly fast development of the software industry, readers may make a comparison between the software industry today and the telecommunication industry half a century ago. After Alexander Graham Bell (1847 – 1922) invented the telephone in 1876, there was a peak for demand of telephony in many countries during the 1930s and the 1940s. Because telephone switching was carried out manually on exchange boards, an operator could not manage more than a couple dozen lines at that time. Therefore, people had predicted that to fulfil the demand of a telephonic society, almost all housewives would have to work at the exchange offices eventually. Inventions and development of the electromagnetic relay and then computer-controlled automatic switching systems met the demand.

Now the software industry has found that software development is brain-power-intensive. Furthermore, every application is not routine and repetitive work, so that software engineering and automation are not good bedfellows for implementation. By observing the nature of software development, many thought there would be no "silver bullet" [Brooks, 1975/87/95] and, inevitably, the software industry is and will continue to expand exponentially.

However, an optimistic aspect of software engineering as shown in this book is that there is an element of repeatability in software development – the software engineering process – that can be identified more and more precisely and be reused and even automated more and more via software engineering. Thus, it is the principle aim of process-based software engineering to identify precisely what are the repeatable and reusable processes in large-scale software development, and to support, regulate and automate as many processes as possible while leaving as little as possible for mental-intensive work. This book has attempted to document the basic research and industry best practices towards this fundamental aim of the discipline of process-based software engineering.

In the rest of this chapter, a brief review of progress and important findings of this book in process-based software engineering are provided in Section 19.2. Perspectives on future development in this discipline are provided in Section 19.3. These are followed by a summary and closing remarks.

19.2 Review of Advances in Process-Based Software Engineering

This book has addressed the fundamental theories, methodologies, and applications of the new discipline of process-based software engineering. The authors have investigated the philosophical, mathematical, and managerial foundations in order to establish a unified software engineering process framework, to develop a rigorous and practical approach to process-based software engineering, and to furnish a detailed guide and case studies for practitioners in the industry.

The proliferation of research into the software engineering process in the last decade has formed a new discipline. However, it may be argued that the characteristics of a mature discipline are that there is a theoretical framework and a rigorous, formal, and quantitative methodology. This work has intended to review the progress and summarize the experience of research, practices, and standardization in the software engineering process discipline, and to help the young discipline further evolve away from chaos and toward order in its foundations and, from largely empirical methods, toward formalization. This implies a move from the qualitative to quantitative in approach and in measurement.

In this book a variety of theories in process establishment, assessment, and improvement have been unified, and fundamental architectures and requirements for software engineering process modeling and analysis have been clarified. The unified framework developed in this book has attempted to lay a coherent theoretical and structural foundation for software process modeling and analysis. This framework and SEPRM have been validated by a set of process benchmarks and the successful mutual transformation of capability levels between current process models.

The delivered subjects and important progress in this book are summarized in Table 19.1.

Table 19.1
Review of the Work Developed in This Book

Chapter	Subject Area	Key Progress or Problems Solved
Part I	Fundamentals of the Software Engineering Process	
1	Introduction	• Investigated the nature and philosophical, mathematical, and managerial foundations of software engineering • Reviewed existing approaches to software engineering • Explored the new approach of process-based software engineering and related issues in research and practices
2	A unified framework of software engineering process	• Developed a unified software engineering process framework • Showed fitness of current process models as subset paradigms of the unified process framework • Paved the way for developing an integrated software engineering process reference model (SEPRM) • Enabled quantitative analysis of process characteristics of significance, practice, and effectiveness
3	Process algebra	• Investigated formal methods for process description and modeling • Studied the approaches for process abstraction • Introduced a paradigm of process algebra – CSP • Demonstrated how process patterns, relationships, and interactions are formally described by process algebra
4	Process-based software engineering	• Introduced the concept of process-based software engineering • Described basic process methodologies for software engineering

		• Described software process system establishment procedures and methods • Described software process system assessment methods and their classification • Described software process system improvement philosophies and methodologies
Part II	**Software Engineering Process System Modeling**	
5	The CMM model	• Reviewed the history and background of CMM development • Described the CMM process model and taxonomy • Described the CMM capability model and capability determination methodology • Developed an approach to formally describe the CMM process model, and to algorithmically describe the CMM process capability determination method • Developed a CMM algorithm for software process assessment • Explained how the CMM algorithm can be used in process assessment and how its algorithm complexity is estimated • Demonstrated a case study of a practical CMM assessment by using the CMM algorithm • Discussed the usability of CMM in process establishment, assessment, and improvement in software engineering
6	The ISO 9001 model	• Reviewed the history and background of ISO 9001 development • Described the ISO 9001 process model and taxonomy • Described the ISO 9001 capability model and capability determination methodology • Developed an approach to formally describe the ISO 9001 process model, and to algorithmically describe the ISO 9001 process capability determination method • Developed an ISO 9001 algorithm for software process assessment • Explained how the ISO 9001 algorithm can be used in process assessment and how its algorithm complexity is estimated • Demonstrated a case study of a practical ISO 9001 assessment by using the ISO 9001 algorithm • Discussed the usability of ISO 9001 in process establishment, assessment, and improvement in software engineering
7	The BOOTSTRAP model	• Reviewed the history and background of BOOTSTRAP development • Described the BOOTSTRAP process model and taxonomy • Described the BOOTSTRAP capability model and capability determination methodology • Developed an approach to formally describe the BOOTSTRAP process model, and to algorithmically describe the BOOTSTRAP process capability determination method

		• Developed a BOOTSTRAP algorithm for software process assessment • Explained how the BOOTSTRAP algorithm can be used in process assessment and how its algorithm complexity is estimated • Demonstrated a case study of a practical BOOTSTRAP assessment by using the BOOTSTRAP algorithm • Discussed the usability of BOOTSTRAP in process establishment, assessment, and improvement in software engineering
8	The ISO/IEC TR 15504 model	• Reviewed the history and background of ISO/IEC TR 15504 development • Described the ISO/IEC TR 15504 process model and taxonomy • Described the ISO/IEC TR 15504 capability model and capability determination methodology • Developed an approach to formally describe the ISO/IEC TR 15504 process model and to algorithmically describe the ISO/IEC TR 15504 process capability determination method • Developed an ISO/IEC TR 15504 algorithm for software process assessment • Explained how the ISO/IEC TR 15504 algorithm can be used in process assessment and how its algorithm complexity is estimated • Demonstrated a case study of a practical ISO/IEC TR 15504 assessment by using the ISO/IEC TR 15504 algorithm • Discussed the usability of ISO/IEC TR 15504 in process establishment, assessment, and improvement for software engineering
9	The SEPRM model	• Reviewed the history and background of SEPRM development • Described the SEPRM process model and taxonomy • Described the SEPRM capability model and capability determination methodology • Developed an approach to formally describe the SEPRM process model and to algorithmically describe the SEPRM process capability determination method • Developed an SEPRM algorithm for software process assessment • Explained how the SEPRM algorithm can be used in process assessment and how its algorithm complexity is estimated • Demonstrated a case study of a practical SEPRM assessment by using the SEPRM algorithm • Discussed the usability of SEPRM in process establishment, assessment, and improvement in software engineering
Part III	Software Engineering Process Establishment	
10	Benchmarking the SEPRM processes	• Established a foundation of practice for the validation, calibration and benchmarking of software process models

		• Sought statistical criteria for selecting processes and BPAs in process system modeling • Validated the BPAs and processes modeled in SEPRM • Enabled a new approach to benchmark-based process assessment and improvement • Characterized a superset of processes and BPAs in order to provide reference points for existing process models and future new process models
11	Comparative analysis of current process models	• Analyzed the relationships between current process models by using one-to-one, one-to-many, and/or many-to-one mappings • Investigated compatibility and correlation between current process models • Explored features and special orientation of current process models so that suitable or combined process models can be chosen for a specific software development organization • Enabled the development of process capability transformations between current process models
12	Transformation of capability levels between current process models	• Found out the interrelationships between the capability scales of current process models • Sought an approach for transforming the capability levels between current process models • Explored the stability of assessment for current process models • Investigated the time and effort expended in process assessments using current process models
Part IV	Software Engineering Process Establishment	
13	Software process establishment methodologies	• Provided practical guidance on how to establish software engineering process systems at organization, project, and team levels • Developed a set of useful methodologies for software process establishment and implementation • Demonstrated a parallel process model for software quality assurance which is a lightweight project process model tailored from SEPRM • Demonstrated a process model for software project management which is a medium-weight project process model tailored from SEPRM • Demonstrated a case study on how CMM may be customized for small software development organizations
14	An extension of ISO/IEC TR 15504 model	• Demonstrated a complete example of process model establishment • Offered an approach for extending an existing process standard or model • Defined an approach to develop plug-in process modules for a main process reference model • Demonstrated how an organization's process reference model is extended or adapted to cover new processes for special needs
Part V	Software Engineering	

	Process Assessment	
15	Software process assessment methodologies	• Reviewed the scale and practices involved in software process assessment in the worldwide software industry • Explored a model-based software process assessment methodology • Developed a benchmark-based software process assessment methodology • Demonstrated how the generic SEPRM process assessment methodology and benchmarks might be applied in the software industry
16	Supporting tools for software process assessment	• Reviewed software process assessment supporting technologies and tools • Demonstrated how the generic assessment methodologies described in Chapter 15 are implemented and supported by assessment tools • Developed a template-supported software process assessment method based on the SEPRM reference model • Explored a tool-supported software process assessment method and the basic requirements for assessment tools • Provided an insight into the practical methods used by assessors to enable those being assessed or those seeking to implement self-assessment to understand and reproduce a process assessment
Part VI	Software Engineering Process Improvement	
17	Software process improvement methodologies	• Explored philosophies, rules, and generic approaches to software process improvement • Explored a model-based software process improvement methodology • Developed a benchmark-based software process improvement methodology • Developed a template-based software process improvement methodology • Demonstrated how the SEPRM process model and benchmarks are applied in process improvement
18	Case studies in software process improvement	• Reviewed a broad picture of software process improvement in the software industry • Investigated the benefits and common goals of software process improvement in industry • Explored a generic approach to assessment model-based software process improvement • Demonstrated process improvement by the adaptation and integration of external and internal standards and models
19	Review and Perspectives	• Reviewed research and practices in the discipline of software engineering and software engineering process • Reviewed advances in this work toward a well-founded software engineering process system discipline • Provided perspectives on future development

This work has been part of the international effort for building a well-founded discipline of process-based software engineering. The integrated theories, methods, models, frameworks, and benchmarks of software engineering processes developed in this book have been found in a wide range of applications in software engineering.

19.3 Perspectives on Future Development

An idiom says that one can "gain new knowledge by reviewing the past." In this section the authors intend to present perspectives on future development in the discipline of process-based software engineering. The authors attempt to predict the trends in software engineering research, standardization, and the software industry. Some areas for future research are suggested which the authors consider significant and worthy of being explored in order to build on the results of this book.

19.3.1 TRENDS IN SOFTWARE ENGINEERING RESEARCH

Major trends in the research of software engineering in general, and of software engineering processes in particular, have been considered as follows.

19.3.1.1 Comparative Studies of Software Engineering and Other Engineering Disciplines

In tracing the history of software engineering, it has been found that many of the important concepts such as specification, requirement analysis, design, testing, process, and quality were borrowed or inspired by the methods and practices developed in other engineering disciplines. Therefore, comparative studies in the interdisciplinary areas of software engineering from a wide perspective of the engineering disciplines could be quite inspirational and useful for understanding how software engineering differs from other engineering disciplines, and how software engineering may be cross- fertilized from other disciplines.

For example, software design-review and inspection are popular techniques that were recently introduced into software quality assurance [Fagan, 1976/86; Gilb and Graham, 1993; Runeson and Wohlen, 1998], the personal software process (PSP) [Humphrey, 1997], and the team software process (TSP) [Humphrey, 1999]. These concepts are directly inspired by universal quality system practices and principles. It is reported that for ensuring the quality of a new model of a car there may be up to 10K inspection points in the checklists of the entire development process. If software inspection had identified the checking points and conducted inspections and tests at that magnitude, the quality of software would have reached levels of excellence.

Historically, the development of generic quality system technologies has evolved in three generations known as post, intermediate, and preventive quality assurance technologies:

- The first generation technology: **Post production quality check**

  There are no processes and intermediate quality checks. Quality control actions focus on inspection and test of the final products after defects have been injected.

- The second generation technology: **Intermediate quality check**

  A whole development or manufacturing procedure is divided into a series of processes so that intermediate quality checks are enabled and defects can be found earlier after they are injected.

- The third generation technology: **Defect prevention**

  This is a modern quality assurance technology that emphasizes actions that may prevent problems from happening via TQM and problem causal analysis. The former provides a precise process and quality assurance system; the latter identifies the causes of defect injection and pinpoints locations of the causes in processes in order to take measures that address the roots of the problems.

On the basis of the above classification of generic quality system principles, it is noteworthy that some of the current software engineering technologies are experiencing the early stage of generic quality system maturity.

Software engineering models and methodologies have very much adopted and followed mass manufacturing processes. Based on the improved understanding of the nature of software engineering as discussed in Chapter 1, researchers and practitioners may need to pay attention to innovative software composition and authoring processes rather than conventional mass production processes.

On the other hand, software engineering is probably the most complicated and mental-work-intensive engineering discipline. Its generic software process approach and inherent formal and rigorous methods have significantly influenced the other engineering disciplines. In recent years, a number of enterprise process models [Bignell et al., 1985], the workflow [Marshak, 1993; Schael, 1998], and business process reengineering methodologies [Johansson et al., 1993; Gruhn, 1994; Wastell et al., 1994] have been developed by using the software engineering process technologies.

19.3.1.2 Process-Based Software Engineering

In this book the software engineering process system has been presented as a fundamental infrastructure for software engineering. Process-based development has been proven a successful approach not only in software engineering, but also in other, long matured engineering disciplines.

A trend in software engineering process system modeling is to adopt an operating system technology known as "plug-ins." A plug-in is an extended process module that can be easily adapted to a host process system infrastructure. The plug-in process module usually has a conformant structure and identical syntax as those of the host process system model.

19.3.1.3 Process Reengineering

Process reengineering is a technology to adapt and reorganize an existing software engineering process system. Process reengineering has been found benefit-providing in the software industry.

For instance, in one of the pilot projects the authors advised a software organization to shift its test design process from postcoding to parallel with system specification and design processes. The simple reengineering of the processes has been proven beneficial. A large proportion of the requirement specification gaps and system design defects are found long before the software implementation processes begin. As a result, the postcoding defect rate has been reduced dramatically.

Further, and much more significantly, the project showed that the defects injected and revealed in different processes were not equivalent in terms of significance, scope of impact, and/or the costs to removal. Almost all of the defects found in the reengineered test design process were significant problems that would impact all following processes if they had not been removed at an early stage.

19.3.1.4 Software Engineering Process Model Integration and Innovation

As mentioned in Chapter 5, although the term "software engineering" has been introduced around 30 years since Bauer (1968), industrialized software engineering started from the widespread use of personal computers in the 1980s. Considering that the process models of other engineering disciplines such as electronic and mechanical engineering have developed and matured over several decades, or even centuries in the case of civil engineering, continuous improvement of current software process models themselves are the responsibility of both the model developers and the practitioners.

Software engineering process model integration and unification is a primary route toward software engineering process model excellence. Some practitioners may have thought that we have obtained enough process models with various orientations, therefore, the attempts at unification or integration would be natural. Both integration of existing processes and exploration of innovative processes are mutually complementary actions in process-based software engineering.

19.3.1.5 Software Engineering Process Data Mining

Data mining is a technology that seeks facts, trends, and regulations from a large-scale databank. In Appendix D we have documented a large set of survey data on attributes of industrial practices in software engineering. These data have been systematically analyzed in Chapter 10 using statistical techniques and benchmarking. Readers may find new facts and statistically significant regulations with this set of valuable data, or may use the same methods to gather, analyze, and measure their own data in order to find new results.

19.3.1.6 Internet-Based Software Engineering

With the Internet and Intranet as the backbone of an organization's information and software engineering environment, there is a trend that more and more software vendors and developers will become application service providers; and more and more software purchasers will become software renters.

As a result, current distributed computing and applications would become more or less centralized computing plus distributed applications. However, practitioners will not care where an application is implemented and run as long as they get a conventional system interface and the expected services and results. This trend will eventually influence the future software engineering process and deserves some prior thought and investigation.

19.3.2 TRENDS IN SOFTWARE PROCESS STANDARDIZATION

Major trends in software engineering process standardization have been considered to integrate the existing process-related standards and models, but standardization may also cover new process areas in software engineering.

19.3.2.1 Integration of Process-Related Standards

A number of process-related standards have been developed or are under development within the international and professional standardization organizations such as the ISO/IEC JTC1/SC7 software engineering subcommittee and the IEEE. Significant standards coming forward are, *inter alia:* ISO/IEC 12207 (1995) on software life cycle processes, ISO/IEC CD 15288 (1999) on system life cycle processes, and ISO/IEC TR 15504 (1998) on software process assessment and capability determination. The last has been extensively analyzed in this book; the structures of ISO/IEC 12207 and ISO/IEC CD 15288 are documented in Appendixes F and G.

A recent trend of ISO/IEC TR 15504 is to align its process dimension to ISO/IEC 12207. In addition, extension for ISO/IEC TR 15504 has been proposed to cover more of the system life cycle, such as the acquisition processes and broader system environment processes.

Part of a structural evolution of ISO/IEC TR 15504 is the shift from a self-contained software process and process assessment model to a standard software process assessment model with an open infrastructure for incorporating any existing or future process models with unified definitions and descriptions. This would mean that the future ISO/IEC 15504 might only provide a standard process assessment methodology and defined compliance requirements for any external software processes. Therefore, the existing and/or innovative software engineering processes compliant to the standard will be defined and developed by any process model providers who so wish.

19.3.2.2 Requirements for New Standards

The list of ISO/IEC JTC1/SC7 working groups is continuously expanding. As the evolution of software engineering theories, methodologies, and practices gets faster, more and more areas are expected be covered by efforts in software engineering standardization. Candidate examples, as the authors forecast, might be standards for system requirement definition, domain knowledge infrastructure, software architecture and frameworks, software engineering notations, reference software design samples, and so on.

19.3.2.3 Standardization of Software Engineering Notations

Almost all mature science and engineering disciplines have a common notation system. A requirement for establishing standard software engineering notations independent of languages and methodologies is beneficial to mainstream software development efforts.

Various software notations have been developed and adopted in software engineering, from graphical to symbolic notations, and from visual to mathematical (formal) notations. The existing software notations can be classified into five categories: the formal notations, state-machine-based notations, data-flow-based notations, object-oriented notations, and process notations.

The international standardization community is now investigating the feasibility of developing and unifying software engineering notations. The central concept of this effort is to develop a notation standard that is a primary independent entity built on a life cycle-based framework for the description of software archetypes. Archetypes may be described in different languages or meta-languages using the same core set of notations and a limited set of its extensions. The standard notation should be flexible enough to accommodate recent languages and implementations as well as those of the future.

19.3.3 TRENDS IN THE SOFTWARE INDUSTRY

Trends in the software industry are identified as being in the following areas: development of subdomain process models, benchmarking current process models, and software process diagnosis.

19.3.3.1 Subdomain Process Models

Chapter 1 explained that software engineering is a discipline requiring inter-disciplinary domain knowledge. A number of subdomain process models have been developed recently in order to provide a more detailed process methodology for a specific application and/or process area in software engineering. Examples of subdomain process models are the process models of requirement engineering processes [Sommerville and Sawyer, 1997], system engineering processes [Bate et al., 1993], software and IT acquisition processes [Dorling and Wang et al., 1999a/b], the Spiral software processes [Boehm and Bose, 1994], and the Rational software development processes [Jacobson et al., 1998]. For details, readers may wish to consult the references.

19.3.3.2 Benchmarking Current Process Models

The fundamental process benchmarks of SEPRM developed in Chapter 10 have enabled a new approach for benchmark-based process assessment and improvement. Periodical updating of the benchmarks is useful for finding new trends of software process performances and practices in software engineering and in the software industry.

Dutta and his colleagues (1998) reported a European benchmark on software management practices. IBM (1996) developed a European benchmark on software development practices. A benchmark database for the ISO/IEC TR 15504 (SPICE) process model is under construction which will derive worldwide software process benchmarks based on the three-phase trails of the ISO/IEC TR 15504 model and methodologies. Quantitative benchmarks for the other current process models are likely to be developed in order to provide more measurability.

19.3.3.3 Software Process Diagnosis and Software Process Analyst

Throughout this book key terms of software process modeling (SPM), analysis (SPAN), establishment (SPE), assessment (SPA), and improvement (SPI) have been used. In overviewing the discipline and its entire structure, it is predicted that a new practice, software process diagnosis (SPD), might be required in order to identify process problems, to provide causal analysis, and to recommend improvement opportunities and plans for an established software engineering process system.

SPD is a new concept that is different from SPA. The latter has been oriented to measure a current process system and to prove conformance of the system to a specific process model or standard. The former is aimed at finding problems, causes, and improvement opportunities in software process systems that may apply standard, tailored, integrated, external, or internal process models. SPD would be a flexible, practical and useful complement to current practices of SPA and SPI in process-based software engineering.

To conduct SPD, a new role is demanded, that of process system analyst. Process system analysts are those who are responsible for providing SPD services and to consult in process-based software engineering.

19.4 Concluding Remarks

The software process was recognized as a valid element of software engineering only a few years ago. This book has attempted to show that the software engineering process as a system is an ideal means and a powerful tool for infrastructuring the entire framework of software engineering. Therefore, developing from the structured, model-based, and object-oriented software engineering methodologies, process-based software engineering provides a new focus on overarching architectures of software engineering.

The reorientation from the software process to the software engineering process is quite similar to that of category theory in the history of mathematics. Before the 1970s, category theory was treated only as a branch of pure mathematics. However, mathematicians soon realized that category theory was an ideal means for organizing and describing the whole mathematical framework and for redescribing most other branches of mathematics. Even computer scientists have recently found that category theory is a powerful and expressive tool for computing.

This analogy can be extended to apply to the software engineering process. For the expanded domain of software engineering, the existing methodologies that cover individual subdomains are becoming inadequate. Therefore, an overarching approach has been sought for a suitable theoretical and practical infrastructure accommodating the full range of modern software engineering practices and requirements. An interesting approach, which is capable of accommodating most of these domains of software engineering, is the methodologies of process-based software engineering. Research into, and adoption of, the software engineering process approach may be made to encompass all the existing approaches to software engineering.

The software industry has grown rapidly to become one of the most important labor-intensive industries. It is quite encouraging to see that more and more software development organizations have adopted software process systems as the key architectural frameworks for implementing and improving software engineering. It is sure that we can expect more and more software development organizations and projects operating at higher capability levels in process-based software engineering.

The message is that as long as fast development of software engineering methodologies remaining viable, software engineering process models will need to evolve as quickly. However, what will be kept stable are the philosophies, principles, theories, and the unified framework behind these software engineering process models.

In concluding this book the authors would like to quote Richard Karp in his Turing Award interview in 1985 [Ashenhurst and Graham, 1987]:

> There are three levels of problems. There is the level of solving a very specific instance ... . That is the level closest to the practitioners. Then there is the level of studying the problem in general, with emphasis on methodology for solving it ... . That is one level up because you are not interested just in a specific instance. Then there is a metatheoretic level where you study the whole structure of a class of problems. This is the point of view that we have inherited from logic and computability theory.

Annotated References

Fifteen years ago, C.A.R. Hoare, a leading British theoretical computer scientist, made the following prediction: "I don't know what the programming language of the year 2000 will look like, but I know that it will be named FORTRAN [Hoare, 1989]." Here, "FORTRAN" meant "formula transformation" or implied the formal approach to programming.

Fuggetta and Wolf (1996) and Rubin (1997) provided useful resources and predictions for future trends in the software engineering process. Many good generic software engineering textbooks, such as Pressman (1992), Humphrey (1995), Sommerville (1996), and Pfleeger (1998), may help readers understand the entire domain of software engineering. In addition, readers may refer to some of the classical essays or books on software engineering, such as Hoare (1989), McDermid (1991), Brooks (1995), and Wasserman (1996).

Work on important individual or subdomain process models has been reported recently. The work covers specific process areas in software engineering, and would be useful references related to this book. Bate and his colleagues (1993) derived a system engineering process model based on CMM. Boehm and Bose (1994) extended the spiral software development model to a collaborative spiral software development process. Sommerville and Sawyer (1997) developed a requirement engineering process model based on a set of sixty-six "good practices." Humphrey (1996/97/98) developed a set of individual- and team-oriented software engineering processes known as the personal software process (PSP) and the team software process (TSP). Jacobson and his colleagues (1998) focused on the technical subsystem of the software engineering process system, and developed a unified software development process based on a use-case driven, architecture-centric, and incremental iterative approach. Zahran (1998) provided an informative and practical guidebook for software process improvement. Marshak (1993) and Schael (1998) proposed a workflow approach to generic process organization.

Jones (1999) and Bagchi (1999) reported the statistics of the numbers of software engineering professionals in the USA and India, respectively. These data provide a basis for estimating a global picture of the size of the software industry. Jones (1999) also classified a set of 29 roles in software engineering, while Noack and Schienmann (1999) identified 20 kinds of roles.

It is found that the process technologies have been cross-fertilized between software engineering and other engineering disciplines. Warboys et al (1999) adopted a process approach to business system development and showed an application of software engineering process system technology in the design of information systems. Gruhn (1994) reported software process applications in business process reengineering and organization on process modeling, analysis, simulation, enactment, measurement, assessment, and improvement. Johansson and McHugh (1993) explored business process reengineering and modeling.

For further repositories of research reports and industry experiences, readers may refer to the archives of *IEEE Software, IEEE Transactions on Software Engineering, ACM Transactions on Software Engineering and Methodologies,* the *International Journals of Empirical Software Engineering,* and *Annals of Software Engineering.* International conference series on software engineering and software process are documented by the *Proceedings of the International Conference on Software Engineering* (ICSE19, 1997; ICSE20, 1998; ICSE21, 1999), *Proceedings of the International Conference on the Software Process* (ICSP1, 1991 – ICSP5, 1998), *Proceedings of International Software Process Workshop* (ISPW5, 1989 – ISPW11, 1998), and *Proceedings of the European Workshop on Software Process Technology* (EWSPT1, 1992 – EWSPT6, 1998).

Bibliography

Agresti, W. W. (1986), *New Paradigms for Software Development*, IEEE Computer Society Press, Los Alamitos, CA.

Alberts, D. S. (1976), The Economics of Software Quality Assurance, *Proceedings of National Computer Conference*, Vol.45, AFIPS Press, Montvale, NJ, pp. 433-442.

Anthony, R. N. (1965*), Planning and Control Systems: A Framework for Analysis,* Harvard University Graduate School of Business Administration, Cambridge, MA.

Armenise, P., et al. (1992), Software Process Representation Languages: Survey and Assessment, *Proceedings of the 4th IEEE International Conference on Software Engineering and Knowledge Engineering*, Capri, Italy.

Aron, J, D. (1983), *The Program Development Process, Part 2 – The Programming Team*, Addison-Wesley, Reading, MA.

Ashenhurst, R.L. and Graham, S. (1987*), ACM Turing Award Lectures, The First Twenty Years: 1966 - 1985*, Anthology Series, ACM Press, Addison-Wesley Publishing Company, New York, pp. 458 - 466.

Aujla, S., Bryant, A. and Semmens, L. (1994), Applying Formal Methods within Structured Development, *IEEE Journal on Selected Areas in Communications,* February, IEEE.

Bagchi, S. (1999), India's Software Industry: The People Dimension, *IEEE Software*, Vol.16, No.3, May/June, pp.62-65.

Baker, F. T. (1972), Chief Programmer Team Management of Production Programming, *IBM Systems Journal*, Vol.11, No.1, pp.56-73.

Bandinelli, S., Fuggetta, A., and Ghezzi, C. (1992), Software Processes as Real-Time Systems: A Case Study using High-Level Petri Nets, *Proceedings of the International Phoenix Conference on Computers and Communications,* Arizona, April.

Bandinelli, S. et al. (1993), Computational Reflection in Software Process Modelling: the SLANG Approach, *Proceedings of the 15th International Conference on Software Engineering,* IEEE Computer Society Press, Los Alamitos, CA, pp.144-154.

Bandinelli, S., Fuggetta, A. and Ghezzi, C. (1993), Software Process Model Evolution in the SPADE Environment, Special Issue on Process Model Evolution, *IEEE Transactions on Software Engineering,* Dec., pp.1128-1144.

Barghouti, N.S. and Krishnamurthy, B. (1993), An Open Environment for Process Modeling and Enactment, *Proceedings of 8th International Software Process Workshop,* IEEE Computer Society Press, Los Alamitos, CA.

Bartlett, F. C. (1932), *Remembering,* Cambridge University Press, Cambridge, UK.

Basili, V. (1980*), Models and Metrics for Software Management and Engineering,* IEEE Computer Society Press, Los Alamitos, CA.

Basili, V. and Rombach, D. (1988), The TAME Project: Towards Improvement-Oriented Software Environments, *IEEE Transactions on Software Engineering,* Vol.14, No.6, June, pp.758-773.

Basili, V. (1993), The Experience Factory and Its Relationship to Other Improvement Paradigms, *Proceedings of 4th European Software Engineering Conference, LNCS 717,* Springer-Verlag, Berlin, pp. 68-83.

Basili, V.R., Caldiera, C., Rombach, H.D. (1994), Goal Question Metric Paradigm, *in Encyclopedia of Software Engineering (Marciniak, J.J. ed.),* Vol.1, John Wiley & Sons, New York.

Bate, R. et al. (1993), A System Engineering Capability Maturity Model, Version 1.1, *CMU/SEI-95-MM-03,* Software Engineering Institute, Pittsburgh, PA, 841993.

Bauer, F. L. (1976), Software Engineering, in Ralston, A. and Meek, C. L. (eds.), *Encyclopedia of Computer Science,* Petrocelli/Charter, New York.

Bell Canada (1992), *TRILLIUM - Telecom Software Product Development Capability Assessment Model,* Draft 2.1, July.

Bell Canada (1994), *TRILLIUM - Model for Telecom Product Development and Support Process Capability (Internet ed.)*, Release 3.0, December, pp. 1-118.

Benedicenti, L. et al. (1999), An Experience Report on Decoding, Monitoring and Controlling the Software Process, *Proceedings of International Conference on Product focused Software Process Improvement (Profes'99)*, VTT, Oulu, Finland, pp. 345-362.

Bignell, V.D. et al. (eds.) (1985), *Manufacturing Systems: Context, Applications and Techniques*, Basil Blackwell Ltd., Oxford, UK.

Boehm, B. W., Brown, J. R. and Lipow M. (1976), Quantitative Evaluation of Software Quality, *Proceedings of 2nd International Conference on Software Engineering, ACM, IEEE and National Bureau of Standards*, pp. 592-605.

Boehm, B. W., Brown, J. R., Lipow M., Macleod, G. J. and Merritt, M. J. (1978), *Characteristics of Software Quality*, North-Holland, NY.

Boehm, B. W. (1981), *Software Engineering Economics*, Prentice-Hall, Englewood Cliffs, NJ.

Boehm, B.W., Penedo, M.H. et al. (1986), A Software Development Environment for Improving Productivity, *IEEE Computer*, Vol. 17, No. 6, pp.30.

Boehm, B.W. (1987), Improving Software Productivity, *IEEE Computer*, Vol. 20, No. 9, pp.43.

Boehm, B. W. (1988), A Spiral Model for Software Development and Enhancement, *IEEE Computer*, Vol. 21, No. 5, May, pp.61-72.

Boehm, B.W. (1991), Software Risk Management: Principles and Practices, *IEEE Software*, Jan., pp.32-41.

Boehm, B. and Bose, P. (1994), A Collaborative Spiral Software process Moderl based on Theory W, *Proceedings of 3rd International Conference on the Software Process*, IEEE Computer Society Press, Reston, VA, October, pp.59-68.

Bollinger, T.B. and McGrowan, C. (1991), A Critical Look at Software Capability Evaluations, *IEEE Software*, July, pp. 25-41.

BOOTSTRAP Institute (1994), BOOTSTRAP Global Questionnaire, V.2.3, *Technical Report of BOOTSTRAP Project*, pp. 1- 28, Oulo, Finland.

BOOTSTRAP Team (1993), BOOTSTRAP: Europe's Assessment Method, *IEEE Software*, May, pp.93-95.

Bovet, D. P. and Crescenzi, P. (1994), Introduction to the Theory of Complexity, Prentice-Hall International, Englewood Cliffs, NJ.

Bowen, J.P., Fett, A. and Hinchey, M.G. (eds.) (1998), *Proceedings of the Z Formal Specification Notation,* Lecture Notes in Computer Science, Vol. 1493, Springer-Verlag, Berlin.

Brech, E. F. L. (1980), *The Principles and Practice of Management (2nd ed.),* Longman, London.

Brinch, H. P. (1973), *Operating System Principles,* Prentice-Hall, Englewood Cliffs, NJ.

Brodman J.G. and Johnson D.L. (1994), What Small Business and Small Organization Say about the CMM, *Proceedings of the 16th International Conference on Software Engineering (ICSE16),* pp.331-340.

Broadman, J. G. and Johnson, D. L (1995), *The LOGOS Tailored CMM[SM] for Small Businesses, Small Organizations and Small Projects (V.1.0),* LOGOS International Inc., August, USA, pp. 1-26.

Broadman, J.G. and Johnson, D.L. (1997), A Software Process Improvement Approach Tailored for Small Organizations and Small Projects, *Proceedings of 19th International Conference on Software Engineering,* ACM Press, Boston, pp.661-662.

Brooks, F. P. (1975), *The Mythical Man Month*, Addison-Wesley.

Brooks, F. P. (1987), *No Silver Bullet: Essence and Accidents of Software Engineering,* IEEE Computer, Vol.20, No.4.

Brooks, F.P. (1995*), The Mythical Man-Month: Essays on Software Engineering,* Addison Wesley Longman, Reading, MA.

Bruynooghe, R.F., Parker, J.M. and Rowles, J.S. (1991), PSS: A System for Process Enactment, *Proceedings of the first International Conference on the Software Process, Manufacturing Complex Systems*, IEEE Computer Society Press, Los Alamitos, CA.

Bryant, A. (1989), Better Professionals for the Tools, in G.X. Ritter (ed.), *Information Processing 89*, Proceedings of IFIP.

Bryant, A. (1992), A Framework for Methods Integration and Systems Quality, Introduction to *Proceedings of Leeds Workshop on Methods Integration,* Leeds, UK.

BSI (1987), *BS 5750: Quality Systems,* BSI, London.

Buckland, J.A. et al. (1991), *Total Quality Management in Information Systems,* QED Information Sciences, Wellesley, Dedham, MA.

CCITT (1988), Recommendation Z.100 – *Specification and Description Language SDL,* Blue Book, Volume VI.20 – Vol.24, ITU, Geneva.

Checkland and Peter (1981), *Systems Thinking and Systems Practice,* John Wiley, New York.

Corradini, A. et al. (1996), The Category of Typed Graph Grammars and Their Adjunction with Categories of Derivations, in *5th Int. Workshop on Graph Grammars and their Application to Computer Science, LCNS 1073,* pp. 56-74.

Cromer, T. and Horch, J. (1999), From the Many to the One – One Company's Path to Standardization, *Proceedings of 4th IEEE International Software Engineering Standards Symposium (IEEE ISESS'99),* IEEE CS Press, Brazil, May, pp.116-117.

Crosby, P. B. (1979), *Quality is Free,* McGraw Hill, New York.

Curtis, B. et al. (1987), On Building Software Process Models under the Lamppost, *Proceedings of the 9th International Conference on Software Engineering,* IEEE Computer Society Press, Monterey, CA., pp.96-103.

Curtis, B., Krasner, H. and Iscoe, N. (1988), A Field Study of the Software Design Process for Large Systems, *Communications of the ACM,* Vol.31, pp.1268-1287.

Curtis, B. (1992), Good Motivations for Process Improvement Programmers, *Software Process Improvement Seminar for Senior Executives,* Software Engineering Institute, Pittsburgh.

Curtis, B., Kellner, M.I., and Over, J. (1992), Process Modeling, *Communications of the ACM,* Vol.35, No.9, pp.75-90.

Cusumano, M. (1991), *Japan's Software Factories,* Oxford University Press, Oxford, UK.

Davis, A.M. (1994), Fifteen Principles of Software Engineering, *IEEE Software,* Nov., pp.94-96.

Dawes, J. (1991), *The VDM-SL Reference Guide*, Pitman, Marshfield, MA.

Deming, W. E. (1982a), *Methods for Management of Productivity and Quality,* George Washington University, Washington, D.C.

Deming, W. E. (1982b), *Quality, Productivity and Competitive Position*, Massachusetts Institute of technology Press, Center for Advanced Engineering Study, Cambridge, MA.

Deming, W. E. (1986), *Out of the Crisis*, Massachusetts Institute of Technology Press, Cambridge, MA.

Derniame, J.-C., Kaba, B.A. and Wastell, D. (ed.) (1999), *Software Process: Principles, Methodology, and Technology*, Lecture Notes in Computer Science, Vol. 1500, Springer-Verlag, Berlin.

Diaz, M. and Sligo, J. (1997), How Software Process Improvement Helped Motorola, *IEEE Software*, Sept/Oct., pp.89-96.

Dijkstra, E. W. (1965), Programming Considered as a Human Activity, in W. A. Kalenich (ed.), *Proceedings of IFIP Congress 65,* Spartan Books, Washington, D.C.

Dijkstra, E. W. (1968), The GOTO Statement Considered Harmful, *Communications of the ACM*, Vol.11, No.3, March, pp. 147-148.

Dijkstra, E. W. (1972), The Humble Programmer, *Communications of the ACM,* Vol.15, No. 10, Oct., pp. 895-866.

Dijkstra, E. W. (1976), *A Discipline of Programming*, Prentice-Hall, Englewood Cliffs, NJ.

Dion, R. (1992), Elements of a Process-Improvement Programme, *IEEE Software*, July, pp.83-85.

Donzelli, P. and Iazeolla, G. (1999), A Software Process Simulator for Software Product and Process Improvement, *Proceedings of International Conference on Product Focused Software Process Improvement (PROFES'99),* Oulu, Finland, June, pp.525-538.

Dorling, A. (1993), SPICE: Software Process Improvement and Capability Determination, *Information and Software Technology*, Vol.35, No.6/7, June/July.

Dorling, A. (1995), History of the SPICE Project, *Proceedings of the 2nd International SPICE Symposium,* Brisbane, Australia, pp. 1-7.

Doring, A., Wang, Y. and Steinmann, C. (1998), PULSE D.4.1 – 1998, IT Acquisition Process Assessment Tool, *European Commission SPRITE S2 Research Project 97/501155 PULSE Technical Report.*

Dorling, A., Wang, Y., Kirchhoff, U., Sundmaeker, H., Maupetit, C., Pitette, G., Pereira, J. and Hansen, S. (1999a), *ICT Acquisition Process Assessment Methodology,* The PULSE Consortium, March, pp.1-87.

Dorling, A., Wang, Y., et al. (1999b), Reference Model Extensions to ISO/IEC TR 15504-2 for Acquirer Processes, ISO/IEC JTC1/SC7/WG10, Curitiba, Brazil, May, pp. 1-34.

DTI (1987), *The TickIT Guide,* Department of Trade and Industry, London.

Dunn R. H. and Richard S. U. (1994*), TQM for Computer Software (2nd ed.),* McGraw-Hill, Inc., New York.

Dutta, S., Kulandaiswamy, S., and Wassenhove, L.V. (1998), Benchmarking European Software Management Best Practices, *Comm. ACM*, Vol. 41, No.6, June, pp.77-86.

Dutta, S., Lee, M., and Wassenhove, L.V. (1999), Software Engineering in Europe: A Study of Best Practices, *IEEE Software*, Vol. 16, No.3, May/June, pp.82-90.

EFQM (1993), *Total Quality Management - the European Model for Self-Appraisal 1993,* Guidelines for Identifying and Addressing Total Quality Issues, European Foundation for Quality Management, Brussels, Belgium.

El Eman, K., Madhavji, N.H. and Toubache, K. (1993), Empirically Driven Improvement of Generic Process Models, *Proceedings of 8th International Software Process Workshop (ISPW'8),* IEEE Computer Society Press, Los Alamitos, CA.

El Eman, Drouin, J.N. and Melo, W. (eds.) (1997*), SPICE: The Theory and Practice of Software Process Assessment and Capability Determination,* IEEE Computer Society Press, Los Alamitos, CA.

Ellis, D. O. and Fred, J. L. (1962), *Systems Philosophy*, Prentice-Hall, Englewood Cliffs, NJ.

ESA (1991), Software *Engineering Standard PSS-05-0, Issue 2*, European Space Agency (ESA), Paris, Feb.

Eskiciogla, H. and Davies, B. J. (1981), Interactive Process Planning System for Prismatic Parts (ICAPP), *International Journal of Machine Tool Design and Research,* Vol.21, No.19, pp. 193.

ESPRIT Programme (1991), Project 5441: BOOTSTRAP, SPU Assessment Report, Assessment Questionnaire, *BOOT/II-ETNO/RL-AR/3.91/ Questionnaire/IE*, European Commission, Brussels, Belgium, March.

ESSI Office (1996), *The Business Benefits of Software Best Practice: Case Studies*, pp. 1-40.

Evans M.W. and Marciniak J. J. (1987), *Software Quality Assurance and Management*, Wiley-Interscience, New York.

EWSPT'92 (1992), Derniame, J.-C. ed., *Proceedings of the First European workshop on Software Process Technology (EWSPT'92)*, Trondheim, Norway, September, LNCS 635, Springer-Verlag, Berlin.

EWSPT'94 (1994), Warboys ,B.C. ed., *Proceedings of the 3rd European workshop on Software Process Technology (EWSPT'94)*, Villard-de-Lans, France, Feb., LNCS 772, Springer-Verlag, Berlin.

EWSPT'95 (1995), Schafer, W. ed., *Proceedings of the 4th European Workshop on Software Process Technology (EWSPT'95)*, Noordwijkerhout, Netherlands, April, LNCS 913, Springer-Verlag, Berlin.

EWSPT'96 (1996), Montangero, C. ed., *Proceedings of the 5th European Workshop on Software Process Technology (EWSPT'96)*, Nancy, France, October, LNCS 1149, Springer-Verlag, Berlin.

EWSPT'98 (1998), Gruhn, V. ed., *Proceedings of the 6th European Workshop on Software Process Technology (EWSPT'98)*, Weybridge, UK, September, LNCS 1487, Springer-Verlag, Berlin.

Fabrycky, W. J., Ghare, M. and Torgersen, P. E. (1984), *Applied Operations Research and Management Science*, Prentice-Hall, NJ.

Fagan, M.E. (1976), Design and Code Inspections to Reduce errors in Program Development, *IBM Systems Journal*, Vol.15, No.3, pp.182-210.

Fagan, M.E. (1986), Advantages in Software Inspections, *IEEE Transactions on Software Engineering*, Vol.12, No.7, pp.744-751.

Fayad, M.E. (1997a), Software Development Process: the Necessary Evil? *Communications of the ACM*, Vol.40, No.9, Sept.

Fayad, M.E. and Laitinen, M. (1997b), Process Assessment: Considered Wasteful, *Communications of the ACM*, Vol.40, No.11, Nov.

Feigenbaum, A.V. (1991), *Total Quality Control*, 14th Anniversary edition, McGraw Hill, New York.

Feiler, P.H. and Humphrey, W.S. (1993), Software Process Development and Enactment, *Proceedings of 2nd International Conference on the Software Process*, IEEE Computer Society Press, Berlin, pp.28-40.

Fenton, N.E. (1991), *Software Metrics: A Rigorous Approach*, Chapman & Hall, London.

Fenton, N. E. and Pfleeger, S.L. (1997), *Software Metrics – A Rigorous and Practical Approach,* 2nd ed., PWS Publishing, London.

Finkelstein, A. et al. (eds.) (1994*), Software Process Modeling and Technology*, John Wiley & Sons Inc., New York.

Fitzgerald, B. and O'Kane, T. (1999), A Longitudinal Study of Software Process Improvement, *IEEE Software*, Vol. 16, No.3, May/June, pp.37 – 45.

Fuggetta, A. and Ghezzi, C. (1994), State of the Art and Open Issues in Process-Centered SEE, *Journal of Systems and Software*, Vol.26, No.1.

Garg, P.K. and Jazayeri, M. (eds.) (1995*), Process-Centered Software Engineering Environments*, IEEE Computer Society Press, Los Alamitos, CA.

Gersting, J. L (1982), *Mathematical Structures for Computer Science,* W. H. Freeman & Co., San Francisco.

Gilb, T. (1988), *Principles of Software Engineering Management,* Addison-Wesley, Reading, MA.

Gilb, T. and Graham, D. (1993), *Software Inspection*, Addison-Wesley, Reading, MA.

GMOD (1992), *V-Model: Software Lifecycle Process Model, General Report No. 250,* German Ministry of Defense.

Goldenson, D. and Herbsleb, J. (1995*),* After the Appraisal: A Systematic Survey of Process Improvement, its Benefits, and Factors that Influence Success, Software Engineering Institute, *CMU/SEI-95-TR-009*, 1995.

Grassman, W. and Tremblay, J. P. (1995*), Logic and Discrete Mathematics: A Computer Science Perspective*, Prentice-Hall International, Englewood Cliffs, NJ.

Grayson, C. J. (1973), *Management Science and Business Practice,* Harvard Business Review, Vol.51, No.4, July, pp.41-48.

Gries, D. (1981), *The Science of Programming*, Spinger-Verlag, Berlin.

Gruhn, V. (1994), Software Process Management and Business Process Re-Engineering, *Proceedings of the 3rd European workshop on Software Process Technology,* LNCS 772, Springer-Verlag, Villard-de-Lans, France, Feb., pp.250-253.

Gruhn, V. (ed.) (1998), *Proceedings on Software Process Technology*, Lecture Notes in Computer Science, Vol. 1487, Springer-Verlag, Berlin.

Gustavsson, A. (1989), Maintaining the Evaluation of Software Objects in an Integrated Environment, *Proceedings of 2nd International Workshop on Software Configuration Management*, ACM, Princeton, NJ, October, pp.114-117.

Haase, V., Messmarz, R., Koch, G., Kugler, H.J. and Decrinis, P. (1994), BOOTSTRAP Fine-Tuning Process Assessment, *IEEE Software*, July, pp.25-35.

Haeberer, A.M. (ed.) (1999), *Algebraic Methodology and Software Technology,* Lecture Notes in Computer Science, Vol. 1548, Springer-Verlag, Berlin.

Hall, A. D. (1967), *A Methodology for Systems Engineering*, Van Nostrand Reinhold, New York.

Hansen, G.A. (1996), Simulating Software Development Processes, *IEEE Computer,* January, pp. 73-77.

Hartnett, W. E. (1977), *Systems: Approaches, Theories and Applications*, D. Reidel Publishing Co., Dordrecht and Boston.

Harvey, R. L. (1994), *Neural Network Principles*, Prentice-Hall International, Englewood Cliffs, NJ.

Hayes, I.J. (ed.) (1987), *Specification Case Studies*, Prentice-Hall, London.

Hays, W. L. (1963), *Statistics,* Holt, Rinehart & Winston, New York.

Herbsleb, J. et al. (1994), Benefits of CMM-Based Software Process Improvement: Initial Results, Software Engineering Institute, *CMU/SEI-94-TR-13,* August.

Hoare, C. A. R. (1969), An Axiomatic Basis for Computer Programming, *CACM*, Vol. 12.

Hoare, C.A.R., E-W. Dijkstra and O-J. Dahl (1972), *Structured Programming,* Academic Press, New York.

Hoare, C.A.R. (1975), Software Engineering, *Computer Bulletin,* Dec., pp.6-7.

Hoare, C. A. R. (1985), *Communicating Sequential Processes,* Prentice-Hall International, Englewood Cliffs, NJ.

Hoare, C.A.R. (1986), *The Mathematics of Programming*, Clarendon Press, Oxford, UK.

Hoare, C.A.R. and Jones, C.B. (eds.) (1989), *Essays in Computing Science*, Prentice-Hall, Englewood Cliffs, NJ.

Hoare, C.A.R., (1995), Unified Theory of Computing Science, *OUCL Technical Monograph*, Oxford University Computing Laboratory.

Horowitz, E. (ed.) (1975), *Practical Strategies for Developing Large Software Systems,* Addison-Wesley, Reading, MA.

Huber, A. (1993), A Better Way to Represent BOOTSTRAP Data, *IEEE Software,* Sept., pp.10.

Huda, F. and Preston, D. (1992), KAIZEN: The Applicability of Japanese Techniques to IT, *Software Quality Journal,* No.1, pp.9-26, Chapman & Hall, Boca Raton.

Humphrey, W.S. and Sweet, W.L. (1987), A Method for Assessing the Software Engineering Capability of Contractors, *Technical Report CMU/SEI-87-TR-23,* Software Engineering Institute, Pittsburgh, PA.

Humphrey, W.S. (1988), Characterizing the Software Process: A Maturity Framework, *IEEE Software*, March, pp.73-79.

Humphrey, W.S. (1989), *Managing the Software Process*, Addison-Wesley Longman, Reading, MA.

Humphrey, W.S. and Curtis, B. (1991a), Comment on 'a Critical Look', *IEEE Software,* Vol.8, No.4, pp.42-47.

Humphrey, W.S., Snyder, T.R. and Willis, R.R. (1991b), Software Process Improvement at Hughes Aircraft, *IEEE Software*, July, pp.11-23.

Humphrey, W. S. (1995), *A Discipline for Software Engineering*, SEI Series in Software Engineering, Addison-Wesley, Reading, MA.

Humphrey, W. (1996), Using a defined and Measured Personal Software Process, *IEEE Software*, May, pp. 77-88.

Humphrey, W. (1997), *Introduction to the Personal Software Process*, Addison Wesley, Reading, MA.

Humphrey, W. (1999), *Introduction to the Team Software Process*, Addison Wesley, Reading, MA.

IBM (1996), Software Development Performance and Practices in Europe: A Benchmark of Software Development in Europe – Self Assessment Questionnaire, V.2.0, *IBM Eurocoordination*, pp.1-11.

ICSE19 (1997), *Proceedings of 19th International Conference on Software Engineering,* Boston, IEEE Computer Society Press, Los Alamitos, CA.

ICSE20 (1998), *Proceedings of 20th International Conference on Software Engineering,* Kyoto, IEEE Computer Society Press, Los Alamitos, CA.

ICSE21 (1999), *Proceedings of 21th International Conference on Software Engineering,* Los Angeles, IEEE Computer Society Press, Los Alamitos, CA.

ICSP1 (1991), *Proceedings of the First International Conference on the Software Process*, Redondo Beach, CA, IEEE Computer Society Press, Los Alamitos, CA..

ICSP2 (1993), *Proceedings of the 2nd International Conference on the Software Process,* Berlin, Germany, IEEE Computer Society Press, Los Alamitos, CA.

ICSP3 (1994), *Proceedings of the 3rd International Conference on the Software Process*, Reston, VA, IEEE Computer Society Press, Los Alamitos, CA.

ICSP4 (1996), *Proceedings of the 4th International Conference on the Software Process*, Brighton, UK, IEEE Computer Society Press, Los Alamitos, CA.

ICSP5 (1998), *Proceedings of the 5th International Conference on the Software Process,* IEEE Computer Society Press, Los Alamitos, CA.

IEEE (1983), *Software Engineering Standards, 1983 Collection*, IEEE Computer Society Press, Los Alamitos, CA.

IEEE (1988), *Software Engineering Standards, 1988 Collection*, IEEE Computer Society Press, Los Alamitos, CA.

Imai, M (1986), *KAIZEN: The Key to Japan's Competitive Success*, Random House, New York.

ISO 8258 (1991): *Shewhart Control Charts*, International Organization for Standardization, Geneva.

ISO 8807 (1988): *LOTOS – A Formal Description Technique Based on the Temporal Ordering of Observational Behavior*, Geneva.

ISO 9000-1 (1994): *Quality Management and Quality Assurance Standards (Part 1) - Guidelines for Selection and Use*, International Organization for Standardization, Geneva.

ISO 9000-2 (1994): *Quality Management and Quality Assurance Standards (Part 2) – Generic Guidelines for Application of ISO 9001, ISO 9002 and ISO 9003*, International Organization for Standardization, Geneva.

ISO 9000-3 (1991): *Quality Management and Quality Assurance Standards (Part 3) - Quality Management and Quality Assurance Standards (Part 3) - Guidelines to Apply ISO 9001 for Development, Supply and Maintenance of Software*, International Organization for Standardization, Geneva.

ISO 9000-4 (1993): *Quality Management and Quality System (Part 4) - Guidelines for Dependability Programme Management*, International Organization for Standardization, Geneva.

ISO 9001 (1989): *Quality Systems - Model for Quality Assurance in Design, Development, Production, Installation, and Servicing*, International Organization for Standardization, Geneva.

ISO 9001 (1994): *Quality Systems - Model for Quality Assurance in Design, Development, Production, Installation, and Servicing, Revised Edition*, International Organization for Standardization, Geneva.

ISO 9002 (1994): *Quality Systems - Model for Quality Assurance in Production, Installation and Servicing*, International Organization for Standardization, Geneva.

ISO 9003 (1994): *Quality Systems - Model for Quality Assurance in Final Inspection and Test*, International Organization for Standardization, Geneva.

ISO 9004-1 (1994): *Quality Management and Quality System Elements (Part 1) – Guidelines*, International Organization for Standardization, Geneva.

ISO 9004-2 (1991): *Quality Management and Quality System Elements (Part 4) - Guidelines for Quality Management and Quality Systems Elements for Services*, International Organization for Standardization, Geneva.

ISO 9004-4 (1993): *Quality Management and Quality System Elements (Part 2) - Guidelines for Quality Improvement,* International Organization for Standardization, Geneva.

ISO 9126 (1991): *Information Technology – Software Product Evaluation – Quality Characteristics and Guidelines for their Use*, International Organization for Standardization, Geneva.

ISO 10011 (1988): *Guidelines for Auditing Quality Systems*, International Organization for Standardization, Geneva.

ISO 10013 (1992): *Guidelines for Developing Quality Manuals*, International Organization for Standardization, Geneva.

ISO/IEC 12207 (1995): *Information Technology - Software Life Cycle Processes,* International Organization for Standardization, Geneva.

ISO/IEC (1991), Proposal for a Study Period on Process Management, *JTC1/SC7 N872,* International Organization for Standardization, Geneva.

ISO/IEC (1992), The Need and Requirements for a Software Process Assessment Standard, Study Report, Issue 2.0, *JTC1/SC7 N944R*, International Organization for Standardization, Geneva.

ISO/IEC (1993a), Requirements Specification for a Software Process Assessment Standard, Version 1.00, *JTC1/SC7/N017R*, International Organization for Standardization, Geneva.

ISO/IEC (1993b), Product Specification for a Software Process Assessment Standard, Version 1.00, *JTC1/SC7/N016R*, International Organization for Standardization, Geneva.

ISO/IEC CD 15288 (1999): *Information Technology – Life Cycle Management – System Life Cycle Processes*, ISO/IEC JTC1/SC7 N2184, Geneva, pp.1-42.

ISO/IEC DTR 15504-1 (1997): *Software Process Assessment - Part 1: Concept and Introduction Guide,* ISO/IEC JTC1/SC7/WG10, pp.1 - 16.

ISO/IEC DTR 15504-2 (1997): *Software Process Assessment - Part 2: A Reference Model for Processes and Process Capability,* ISO/IEC JTC1/SC7/WG10, pp. 1 - 38.

ISO/IEC DTR 15504-3 (1997): *Software Process Assessment - Part 3: Performing an Assessment,* ISO/IEC JTC1/SC7/WG10, pp. 1 - 7.

ISO/IEC DTR 15504-4 (1997): Software Process Assessment - Part 4: Guide to Performing Assessments, ISO/IEC JTC1/SC7/WG10, pp. 1 - 36.

ISO/IEC DTR 15504-5 (1997): *Software Process Assessment - Part 5: An Assessment Model and Indicator Guidance,* ISO/IEC JTC1/SC7/WG10, pp.1-138.

ISO/IEC DTR 15504-6 (1997): *Software Process Assessment - Part 6: Guide to Qualification of Assessors,* ISO/IEC JTC1/SC7/WG10, pp. 1 - 31.

ISO/IEC DTR 15504-7 (1997): *Software Process Assessment - Part 7: Guide for Use in Process Improvement,* ISO/IEC JTC1/SC7/WG10, pp. 1 - 47.

ISO/IEC DTR 15504-8 (1997): *Software Process Assessment - Part 8: Guide for Use in Determining Supplier Process Capability,* ISO/IEC JTC1/SC7/WG10, pp.1 - 25.

ISO/IEC DTR 15504-9 (1997*): Software Process Assessment - Part 9: Vocabulary,* ISO/IEC JTC1/SC7/WG10, pp.1 - 9.

ISO/IEC JTC1/SC7/WG10 (1997), *Software Process Assessment - Part 5: An Assessment Model and Indicator Guidance (V.2.0),* International Organization for Standardization, Geneva.

ISO/IEC JTC1/SC7/WG10 (1999), Reference Model Extension for Acquirer Processes, *WG10, N254*, May, Geneva, pp.1-4.

ISO/IEC SPICE Project (1998), SPICE Phase 2 Trial Report, V.1.1, *SPICE Project, ISO/IEC JTCI/SC7/WG10*, July, pp.40-41.

ISO/IEC TR 15271 (1998): *Information Technology – Guide for ISO/IEC 12207 (Software Life Cycle Processes),* International Organization for Standardization, Geneva.

ISO/IEC TR 15504-1 (1998): *Information Technology – Software Process Assessment – Part 1: Concept and Introduction Guide*, ISO/IEC, Geneva, pp.1 - 11.

ISO/IEC TR 15504-2 (1998): *Information Technology – Software Process Assessment – Part 2: A Reference Model for Processes and Process Capability,* ISO/IEC, Geneva, pp. 1 - 39.

ISO/IEC TR 15504-3 (1998): Information Technology – Software Process Assessment – Part 3: Performing an Assessment, ISO/IEC, Geneva, pp. 1 - 4.

ISO/IEC TR 15504-4 (1998*): Information Technology – Software Process Assessment – Part 4: Guide to Performing Assessments*, ISO/IEC, Geneva, pp. 1 - 18.

ISO/IEC TR 15504-5 (1998): *Information Technology – Software Process Assessment – Part 5: An Assessment Model and Indicator Guidance*, ISO/IEC, Geneva, pp.1-132.

ISO/IEC TR 15504-6 (1998): *Information Technology – Software Process Assessment – Part 6: Guide to Qualification of Assessors*, ISO/IEC, Geneva, pp. 1 - 23.

ISO/IEC TR 15504-7 (1998): *Information Technology – Software Process Assessment – Part 7: Guide for Use in Process Improvement*, ISO/IEC, Geneva, pp. 1 - 36.

ISO/IEC TR 15504-8 (1998): *Information Technology – Software Process Assessment – Part 8: Guide for Use in Determining Supplier Process Capability*, ISO/IEC, Geneva, pp.1 - 17.

ISO/IEC TR 15504-9 (1998): *Information Technology – Software Process Assessment – Part 9: Vocabulary,* ISO/IEC, Geneva, pp.1 - 11.

ISPW5 (1989), Perry, D. ed. *Proceedings of 5th International Software Process Workshop,* Kennebunkport, ME, October, IEEE Computer Society Press, Los Alamitos, CA.

ISPW6 (1990), Katayama, T. ed., *Proceedings of 6th International Software Process Workshop,* Hokkaido, Japan, IEEE Computer Society Press, Los Alamitos, CA.

ISPW7 (1991), Thomas, I. ed., *Proceedings of 7th International Software Process Workshop,* Yountville, CA., October, IEEE Computer Society Press, Los Alamitos, CA.

ISPW8 (1993), Schafer, W. ed., *Proceedings of 8th International Software Process Workshop,* IEEE Computer Society Press, Los Alamitos, CA.

ISPW9 (1994), Ghezzi, C. ed., *Proceedings of 9th International Software Process Workshop,* Airlie, VA, IEEE Computer Society Press, Los Alamitos, CA.

ISPW10 (1996), *Proceedings of 10th International Software Process Workshop,* Dijon, France, June, IEEE Computer Society Press, Los Alamitos, CA.

ISPW11 (1998), *Proceedings of 11th International Software Process Workshop,* Illinois, USA, June, IEEE Computer Society Press, Los Alamitos, CA.

Jacobson, I., Booch, G. and Rumbaugh, J. (1998), *The Unified Software Development Process*, Addison Wesley Longman, Reading, MA.

James, W.M. (1998), *Software Engineering Standards: A User's Road Map,* IEEE Computer Society Press, Los Alamitos, CA.

Jarvinen, J. (1994), On Comparing Process Assessment Results: BOOTSTRAP and CMM, *Software Quality Management*, pp.247-262.

Jenner, M.J. (1995), Software Quality Management and ISO 9001, John Wiley & Sons, Inc., New York.

Johansson, H. J. and Mchugh, P. et al. (1993), Business Process Reengineering, John Wiley & Sons Ltd., London.

Johnson, D. L and Broadman, J. G. (1992), Software Process Rigors Yield Stress, Efficiency, *Signal Magazine,* August.

Johnson, D. L and Broadman, J. G. (1997), Tailoring the CMM for Small Businesses, Small Organizations, and Small Projects, *Software Process Newsletter,* No.8, pp. 1-6.

Jones, C. (1996), The Pragmatics of Software Process Improvement, *IEEE Software Newsletter,* No.5, Winter, pp.1-4.

Jones, C. (1999), The Euro, Y2K, and the US Software Labor Shortage, *IEEE Software*, Vol.16, No.3, May/June, pp.55-61.

Juran, J. M., Seder, L. A. and Gryna, F. M. (eds.) (1962), *Quality Control Handbook (2nd ed.),* McGraw-Hill, New York.

Juran, J.M. and Gryna, F.M. (1980), *Quality Planning and Analysis*, McGraw-Hill, New York.

Juran, J. M. (1988), *Juran on Planning for Quality*, Macmillan, New York.

Juran, J. M. (1989), *Juran on Leadership for Quality,* The Free Press, New York.

Keen, P. G. and Morton, M. S. (1978), *Decision Support Systems: An Organizational Perspective,* Addison-Wesley, Reading, MA.

Khaden, R. and Schultzki, A. (1983), Planning and Forecasting Using a Corporate Model, *Managerial Planning*, Jan./Feb.

Khoshgoftaar, T.M. and Oman, P. (1994), Special Issues on Software Metrics, *IEEE Computer*, Vol.27, No.9, September, pp.13-81.

Kitson D.H. and Masters, S. (1992), An Analysis of SEI Software Process Assessment Results: 1987-1991, *Technical Report CMU/SEI-92-TR-24*, Software Engineering Institute, Pittsburgh.

Kitson, D.H. (1996), Relating the SPICE Framework and SEI Approach to Software Process Assessment, *Proceedings of International Conference on Software Quality Management (SQM'96)*, MEP Press, London, pp. 37-49.

Klir, G. J. (ed.) (1972), *Trends in General Systems Theory*, John Wiley, New York.

Knuth, D. E. (1974), Structured Programming with GOTO Statements, *ACM Computing Surveys*, Vol. 6, No. 4, December, pp. 261 - 302.

Koch, G.R. (1993), Process Assessment: The 'BOOTSTRAP' Approach, *Information and Software technology*, Vol.35, No.6/7, Butterworth-Heinemann Ltd., Oxford, June/July, pp.387-403.

Kolb, D. A. and Frohman, A. L. (1970), An Organization Development Approach to Consulting, *Sloan Management Review*, Vol.12, No.1, Fall, pp.51-65.

Kolmogorov, A. N. (1933), *Foundations of the Theory of Probability*, Chelsea Publishing Company, New York.

Krasner, H. et al. (1992), Lessons Learnt from a Software Process Modeling System, *Communications of the ACM*, Boston, Vol.35, Vol.9, September, pp.91-100.

Kugler, H.J. and Messnarz, R. (1994), From the Software Process to Software Quality: BOOTSTRAP and ISO 9000, *Proceedings of the First Asia-Pacific Software Engineering Conference*, Tokyo, Japan, IEEE Computer Society Press, pp. 174-182.

Kugler H.J. and Rementeria, S. (1995), Software Engineering Trends in Europe, *ESI Research Report*, Spain, pp.1-5.

Kuhn, T. (1970), *The Structure of Scientific Revolutions*, The Univ. of Chicago, Chicago, 1970.

Kuvaja, P., Simila, J., Kizanik, L., Bicego, A., Koch, G. and Saukkonen, S. (1994a), *Software Process Assessment and Improvement: The BOOTSTRAP Approach*, Blackwell Business Publishers, Oxford, UK.

Kuvaja, P. and Bicego, A. (1994b), BOOTSTRAP – A European Assessment Methodology, *Software Quality Journal*, June.

Kyburg, H. E. (1984), *Theory and Measurement*, Cambridge University Press, Cambridge, UK.

Leavitt, H. J. and Whisler, T. L. (1988), Management in the 1980s, *Harvard Business Review,* Vol.36, No.6, pp.41-48.

Lehman, M.M. (1985), *Program Evolution: Processes of Software Change*, Academic Press, London.

Lehman, M.M. (1991), Software Engineering, the Software Process and Their Support, *Software Engineering Journal*, September.

Lewis, H. R. and Papadimitriou, C. H. (1988), *Elements of the Theory of Computation*, Prentice-Hall International, Englewood Cliffs, NJ.

Lindsay, P. H. and Norman, D. A. (1972), *Human Information Processing*, Academic Press, New York.

Liskov, B. and Zilles, S (1974), Programming with Abstract Data Types, *ACM SIGPLAN Notices*, Vol.9, pp.50-59.

Liu, L. and Horowitz, E. (1989), A Formal Model for Software Project Management, *IEEE Transactions on Software Engineering,* Vol.15, No.10, October, pp.1280-1293.

Maclane, S. (1971), *Categories for the Working Mathematicians*, Springer-Verlag, New York.

MaCulloch, W. S. and Pitts, W. (1943), A Logic Calculus of the Ideas Imminent in Nervous Activity, *Bull. Math. Biophysics*, Vol. 5, pp.115-133.

Marshak, R.T. (1993), *Workflow White Paper – An Overview of Workflow Software*, International Workflow Coalition.

Marshall, A. (1938), *Principles of Economics*, The Macmillan Co., London.

Mathews, J. (1992), *Numerical Methods for Mathematics, Science and Engineering (2nd ed.)*, Prentice-Hall International, Englewood Cliffs, NJ.

Matsushita, M., Iida, H. and Inoue, K. (1999), Modeling Framework and Supporting System for Process Assessment Documents, *Proceedings of International Conference on Product Focused Software Process Improvement (PROFES'99)*, Oulu, Finland, June, pp.412-423.

Mazza, C. et al. (1994), *Software Engineering Standards*, Prentice-Hall, Englewood Cliffs, NJ.

McCabe, T.A. (1983), A Cyclomatic Complexity Measure, *IEEE Transactions on Software Engineering,* Vol.9.

McDermid, J. A., ed. (1991), *Software Engineer's Reference Book*, Butterworth-Heinemann Ltd., Oxford, UK.

Messnarz, R. and Tully, C. (eds.) (1999), *Better Software Practice for Business Benefit,* IEEE Computer Society Press, Tokyo.

Milenkovic, M. (1992), *Operating Systems: Concepts and Design* (2nd ed.), McGraw-Hill, New York.

Mills, H.D., O'Neill, D., Linger, R.C., Dyer, M. and Quinnan, R.E. (1980), The Management of Software Engineering, *IBM System Journal*, Vol.24, No.2, pp.414-477.

Mills, H.D., Dyer, M. and Linger, R.C. (1987), Cleanroom Software Engineering, *IEEE Software*, Vol.4, No.5, Sept., pp.19-25.

Milner, R. (1989), *Communication and Concurrency*, Prentice-Hall, Englewood Cliffs, NJ.

Mobil Europe Ltd. (1995), The Mobil Survey of ISO 9000 Certificates Awarded Worldwide (4th Cycle), *Quality System Update*, Vol.5, No.9.

Naur, P. and Randell, B. (eds.) (1969), *Software Engineering: A Report on a Conference Sponsored by the NATO Science Committee*, NATO.

Noack, J. and Schienmann, B. (1999), Introducing OO Development in a large Banking Organization, *IEEE Software*, Vol.16, No.3, May/June, pp.71-81.

Omto, N., Komiyama, T. and Fujino, K. (1995), Software Process Assessment Support System SPATS, *IPSJ Technical Journal*, 95-SE-102-28, pp. 159-164.

Osterweil, L.J. (1987), Software Processes are Software Too, *Proceedings of the 9th International Conference on Software Engineering,* March, pp.2-13.

Paulk, M.C., Curtis, B., Chrissis, M.B. et al. (1991), Capability Maturity Model for Software, Version 1.0, Software Engineering Institute, *CMU/SEI-91-TR-24,* August.

Paulk, M.C., Curtis, B., Chrissis, M.B. and Weber, C.V. (1993a), Capability Maturity Model for Software., Version 1.1, Software Engineering Institute, *CMU/SEI-93-TR-24*, February.

Paulk, M.C., Weber, C.V., Garcia, S., Chrissis, M.B. and Bush, M. (1993b), Key Practices of the Capacity Maturity Model, Version 1.1, *Technical Report CMU/SEI-93-TR-25*, Software Engineering Institute, Pittsburgh, PA.

Paulk, M.C., Curtis, B., Chrissis, M.B. and Weber, C.V. (1993c), Capability Maturity Model, Version 1.1, *IEEE Software*, Vol.10, No.4, July, pp.18-27.

Paulk, M.C., Konrad, M.D. and Garcia, S.M. (1994), CMM Versus SPICE Architectures, *Software Process Newsletters,* Spring , pp.7-11.

Paulk, M.C., Weber, C.V. and Curtis, B. (1995a), *The Capability Maturity Model: Guidelines for Improving the Software Process*, SEI Series in Software Engineering, Addison-Wesley.

Paulk, M.C. (1995b), How ISO 9001 Compares with the CMM, *IEEE Software*, January, pp.74-83.

Perry, D., Staudenmayer, N. and Votta, L. (1994), Finding Out What Goes on in a Software Development Organization, Special Issue on Measurement Based Process Improvement, *IEEE Software*, Vol.11, No.4, July.

Peterson, B. and Radice, R. (1994), IDEAL: An Integrated Approach to Software Process Improvement (SPI), *SEI Symposium*, Pittsburgh, August.

Pfleeger, S.L. and Rombach, H.D. (1994), Special Issue on Measurement Based Process Improvement, *IEEE Software*, Vol.11, No.4, July, pp. 8-11.

Pfleeger, S.L. (1998), *Software Engineering: Theory and Practice*, Prentice-Hall, Englewood Cliffs, NJ.

Pressman, R.S. (1988), *Making Software Engineering Happen*, Prentice-Hall, Englewood Cliffs, NJ.

Pressman, R. S. (1992), *Software Engineering: A Practitioner's Approach* (3rd ed.), McGraw-Hill International Editions, New York.

Pulford, K., Combelles, A.K. and Shirlaw S. (1996), *A Quantitative Approach to Software Management: The AMI Handbook,* Addison-Wesley, Reading, MA.

Radnor, M. et al. (1970), Implementation in Operations Research and R&D in Government and Business Organization, *Operations Research*, Vol.18, No.6, pp.976-991, Nov./Dec.

Reed, G.M. and Roscoe, A.W. (1986), A Timed model for Communicating Sequential Processes, *Proceedings of ICALP'86*, LNCS 226, Springer-Verlag, Berlin.

Richardson, A. R. (1966), *Business Economics*, Macdonald & Evans, Braintree, MA.

Roberts, F. S. (1979), Measurement Theory, *Encyclopedia of Mathematics and its Application*, Vol.7, Addison-Wesley, Reading. MA.

Rout, T. (1995), SPICE: A Framework for Software Process Assessment, *Software Processes: Improvement and Practice*, Vol.1, No.1.

Royce, W. W. (1970), Managing the Development of Large Software Systems: Concepts and Techniques, *Proceedings of WESCON*, August, USA.

Rubin, H.A. (1997), *Worldwide IT Trends and Benchmark Report*, META Group, Stamford, Conn., http://www.metagroup.com.

Rumbaugh, J. Jacobson, I, and Booch, G. (1998), *The Unified Modeling Language Reference Manual,* ACM Press, New York.

Runeson, P. and Wohlen, C. (1998), An Experimental Evaluation of an Experince-Based Capture-Recapture Method in Software Code Inspections, *Empirical Software Engineering*, Vol.3, pp.381-406.

Saeki, M., Kaneko, T. and Sakamoto, M. (1991), A Method for Software Process Modeling and Description using LOTUS, *in Proceedings of the 1st International Conference on the Software Process*, IEEE CS Press, pp. 90-104.

Saiedian, H. and Kuzara, R. (1995), SEI Capability Maturity Model's Impact on Contractors, *IEEE Computer*, Vol.28, No.1, pp.16-26.

Schael, T. (1998), Workflow Management Systems for Process Organizations, Second Edition, *Lecture Notes in Computer Science, Vol. 1096,* Springer-Verlag, Berlin.

Schafer, W. (1993), *Proceedings of 8th International Software Process Workshop*, IEEE Computer Society Press, Los Alamitos, CA.

Schein, E. H. (1961), Management Development as a Process at Influence, *Industrial Management Review*, Vol.2, No.2, Spring, pp.59-77.

Schneider, S.A. (1989), *Correctness and Communication in Real-Time Systems,* D. Phil. Thesis, Oxford University.

Seddon, J. (1997), *In Pursuit of Quality: The Cases Against ISO 9000*, Oak Tree Press, Oxford, UK.

SEI (1999), Process Maturity Profile of the Software Community 1999 Update, *SEI Technical Report SEMA 3.99*, Carnegie-Mellon University, Pittsburgh, March, pp. 1-33.

Shannon, C. E. (1948), A Mathematical Theory of Communication, *Bell System Technical Journal*, Vol. 27, p.379-423.

Shewhart, W.A. (1939), *Statistical Method from the Viewpoint of Quality Control,* The Graduate School, George Washington University, Washington, D.C.

Shooman, M. (1975), Software Reliability: Measurements and Models, *Proceedings of 1975 Annual Reliability and Maintainability Symposium,* IEEE Cat. No. 75CH0918-3RQC, pp.485-491.

Simon, H. A. (1960), *The New Science of Management Decision*, Harper & Row, New York.

Snyder, A. (1987), Inheritance and the Development of Encapsulated Software Components, *in Research Directions in Object-Oriented Programming,* (Shriver and Wagner, eds.), MIT Press, Cambridge, MA, pp.165-188.

Solingen, R.V. and Berghout, E. (1999), *The Goal/Question Metric Method – A Practical Guide for Quality Improvement of Software Development*, McGraw Hill, New York.

Sommerville, I. (1996), *Software Engineering* (5th edition), Addison-Wesley, Reading MA.

Sommerville, I. and Sawyer, P. (1997), *Requirements Engineering – A Good Practice Guide,* John Wiley & Sons, New York.

SPICE Project (1998), SPICE Phase II Trials Interim report, *ISO/IEC JTC1/SC7/WG10,* pp. 1-175.

SPIRE Project (1998), *The SPIRE Handbook: Better, Faster, Cheaper Software Development in Small Organizations*, The European Commission, Dublin, Ireland.

Spivey, J. M. (1988), *Understanding Z: A Specification Language and It Formal Semantics*, Cambridge University Press, Cambridge, UK.

Spivey, J. M. (1990), Specifying a Real-Time Kernel, *IEEE Software*, Vol.7, No.5, pp.21-28.

Spivey, J. M. (1992), *The Z Notation: A Reference Manual (2nd ed.)* Prentice-Hall, London.

SQPL (1990), *SQPA: Software Quality and Productivity Analysis at Hewlett Packard,* Hewlett Packard Software Quality and Productivity Laboratory, HP Report.

SSI (1950), *General Systems: Yearbook of the Society for General Systems Research*, Systems Science Institute, University of Louisville.

Steven, A. (1980), *Decision Support Systems: Current Practice and Continuing Challenges*, Addison-Wesley, Reading, MA.

Stoy, J. (1977), *Denotational Semantics*, MIT Press, Cambridge, MA.

Stroustrup, B. (1986), *The C++ Programming Language*, Addison-Wesley, Reading, MA.

Sutton, S. M. and Osterweil, L. J. (1997), The Design of a Next-Generation Process Language, in Jazayeri, M. and Schauer, H. (eds.), *LNCS 1301*, Springer-Verlag, Berlin, pp. 142-158.

Thomas, I. (1994), Software Processes and Business Processes, *Proceedings of 3rd International Conference on Software Processes (ICSP3),* Reston, VA, Oct.

TickIT Project Office (1987), *Guide to Software Quality Management System Construction and Certification using EN29001,* Issue 1.0, UK Department of Trade and Industry and BCS, UK.

TickIT Project Office (1992), *Guide to Software Quality Management System Construction and Certification using EN29001*, Issue 2.0, UK Department of Trade and Industry and BCS, UK.

Tully, C. (1995), The Software Process and the Modeling of Complex Systems, *Proceedings of the 4th European Workshop on Software Process*

Technology, Noordwijkerhout, Netherlands, April, LNCS 913, Springer-Verlag, Berlin.

Turing, A. M. (1936), On Computable Numbers with an Application to the Entscheidungs Problem, *Proceedings of London Math. Soc.,* Vol. 2, pp.230-265.

VASIE Project (1997), *VASIE Best Practice Repository,* The European Commission, Brussels, Belgium. http://www.esi.es/VASIE.

Waerden, B. L. (1969), *Mathematical Statistics,* George Allen & Unwin, London.

Wang, Y., Chouldury, I., Patel, D., Patel, S., Dorling, A., Wickberg, H. and King, G. (1999a), On the Foundations of Object-Oriented Information Systems, *The French Journal of the Object (L'Object: Logiciel Bases de Donnees Reseaux),* Vol.5, No.1, Feb., pp.9-27.

Wang, Y., King, G., Patel, D., Patel, S. and Dorling, A. (1999b), On Coping with Software Dynamic Inconsistency at Real-Time by the Built-in Tests, *International Journal of Annals of Software Engineering,* Vol.7, Baltzer Science Publishers, Oxford, UK, pp.283-296.

Wang Y., King, G., Dorling, A., Ross, M., Staples, G., and Court, I. (1999c), A Worldwide Survey on Best Practices Towards Software Engineering Process Excellence, *ASQ Journal of Software Quality Professional,* Vol.2, No.1, December, pp. 34-43.

Wang Y., King, G., Fayad, M., Patel, D., Court, I., Staples, G., and Ross, M. (1999d), On Built-in Tests Reuse in Object-Oriented Framework Design, *ACM Journal on Computing Surveys,* Vol.32, No.1, March, 2000, New York.

Wang Y., King, G., Doling, A. and Wickberg, H. (1999e), A Unified Framework of the Software Engineering Process System Standards and Models, *Proceedings of 4th IEEE International Software Engineering Standards Symposium (IEEE ISESS'99),* IEEE CS Press, Brazil, May, pp.132-141.

Wang Y., Wickberg, H. and Dorling, A. (1999f), Establishment of a National Benchmark of Software Engineering Practices, *Proceedings of 4th IEEE International Software Engineering Standards Symposium (IEEE ISESS'99),* IEEE CS Press, Brazil, May, pp.16-25.

Wang, Y., Dorling, A., Brodman, J, and Johnson, D. (1999g), Conformance Analysis of the Tailored CMM with ISO/IEC 15504, *Proceedings of*

International Conference on Product Focused Software Process Improvement (PROFES'99), Oulu, Finland, June, pp. 237-259.

Wang Y., Doling, A., Wickberg, H. and King, G. (1999h), Experience in Comparative Process Assessment with Multi-Process Models, *Proceedings of IEEE European Micro Conference (IEEE EuroMicro'99)*, Vol. II, IEEE CS Press, Milan, September, pp.268-273.

Wang Y., Wickberg, H. and King, G. (1999i), A Method for Built-in Tests in Component-based Software Maintenance, *Proceedings of 3rd IEEE International Conference on Software Maintenance and Reengineering (IEEE CSMR'99)*, IEEE CS Press, Amsterdam, March, pp.186-189.

Wang Y. and King, G. (1999j), Philosophies and Approaches to Software Process Improvement, *Proceedings of European Software Process Improvement (EuroSPI'99)*, ISBN 952-9607-29-6, Pori, Finland, October, pp.7.24 – 7.38.

Wang Y., King, G., Dorling, A., Patel, D., Court, I., Staples, G. and Ross, M. (1998a), A Worldwide Survey on Software Engineering Process Excellence, *Proceedings of IEEE 20th International Conference on Software Engineering (ICSE'98)*, Kyoto, April, IEEE Press, pp.439-442.

Wang Y., Bryant A. and Wickberg, H. (1998b), A Perspective on Education of the Foundations of Software Engineering, *Proceedings of 1st International Software Engineering Education Symposium (SEES'98)*, Scientific Publishers OWN, Poznan, pp.194-204.

Wang Y., King, G., Patel, D., Court, I., Staples, G., Ross, M. and Patel, S. (1998c), On Built-in Test and Reuse in Object-Oriented Programming, *ACM Software Engineering Notes*, Vol. 23, No.4, pp.60-64.

Wang, Y., Chouldury, I., Patel, D., Patel, S., Dorling, A. and Wickberg, H. (1998d), A Perspective on Foundations of Object-Oriented Information Systems, *Proceedings of International Conference on Object-Oriented Information Systems (OOIS'98)*, Springer-Verlag, Paris, 1998, pp.491-496.

Wang Y., Wickberg, H., Dorling, A. and King, G. (1998e), On Software Engineering Process Reuse in the Software Development Organizations, *Proceedings of 11th International Conference on Software Engineering and Its Applications (ICSEA'98)*, Vol. II, Paris, December, pp.S6.1-8.

Wang, Y. and Dorling, A. (1998f), PULSE D3.1 – IT Acquisition Process Assessment Method, *PULSE Project Technical Report,* Reviewed by European Commission SPRITE S2 Research Project 97/501155, pp.1-61.

Wang, Y., I. Court, M. Ross, G. Staples, G. King and A. Dorling (1997a), Quantitative Analysis of Compatibility and Correlation of the Current SPA Models, *Proceedings of The IEEE International Symposium on Software Engineering Standards (IEEE ISESS'97)*, USA, June, pp. 36-56.

Wang, Y., I. Court, M. Ross, G. Staples, G. King and A. Dorling (1997b), Quantitative Evaluation of the SPICE, CMM, ISO9000 and BOOTSTRAP, *Proceedings of the IEEE International Symposium on Software Engineering Standards (IEEE ISESS'97)*, USA, June, pp. 57-68.

Wang Y., King, G., Court, I., Ross, M. and Staples, G. (1997c), On Testable Object-Oriented Programming, *ACM Software Engineering Notes (SEN)*, July, Vol. 22, No.4, pp.84-90.

Wang, Y., I. Court, M. Ross, G. Staples and A. Dorling (1997d), Comparative Assessment of a Software Organization with the CMM and SPICE, *Proceedings of the BCS International Conference on Software Quality Management (SQM'97)*, Vol. II, Bath, UK, March, pp. S4 (1-11).

Wang, Y. and Ogawa, Y. (1997e), SUP.9 – Measurement Process, in *ISO/IEC DTR 15504-5*, Information Technology - Software Process Assessment Part 5: An Assessment Model and Indicator Guidance, 1998, pp.1-121.

Wang, Y. and Ogawa, Y. (1997f), SUP.10 – Reuse Process, *in ISO/IEC DTR 15504-5*, Information Technology - Software Process Assessment Part 5: An Assessment Model and Indicator Guidance, 1998, pp.1-121.

Wang, Y., I. Court, M. Ross and G. Staples (1996a), Towards a Software Process Reference Model (SPRM), *Proceedings of International Conference on Software Process Improvement (SPI'96)*, Brighton, UK, November, pp.145-166.

Wang, Y. (1996b), A New Sorting Algorithm: Self-Indexed Sort, *ACM SIGPLAN*, Vol.31, No.3, March, USA, pp. 28-36.

Wang, Y., Z. He, M. Ross, G. Staples and I. Court (1996c), Quantitative Analysis and Mutual Mapping between ISO 9001 and CMM, *Proceedings of the 1st International Conference on ISO 9000 and TQM (ICIT'96)*, Leicester, UK, April, pp.83-90.

Warboys, B.C. et al (1999), *Business Information Systems: A Process Approach*, McGraw-Hill, New York.

Wasserman, A. (1990), Tool Integration in Software Engineering Environments, in Long, F. (ed.), *Software Engineering Environments*, Springer-Verlag, Berlin, pp.138 – 150.

Wasserman, A. (1996), Towards a Discipline of Software Engineering, *IEEE Software*, Nov., pp.23-31.

Wastell, D.G., White, P. and Kawalek, P. (1994), A Methodology for Business Process Redesign: Experiences and Issues, *Journal of Strategic Information Systems*, Vol.3, No.1, pp.23-40.

Weinberg, G. M. (1971), *The Psychology of Computer Programming*, Van Nostrand Reinhold, New York.

Weinwurm, F. G. and Zagorski, H.J. (1965), Research into the Management of Computer Program: A Transition Analysis of Cost Estimation Techniques, *TM-27*, 1/100/00m, System Development Cop., Santa Monica, CA.

William, B. (1991), *Creating Value for Customers: Design and Implementing a Total Corporate Strategy*, John Wiley & Sons, New York.

Yasumoto, K., Higashino, T., and Taniguchi, K. (1994), Software Process Description using LOTOS and Its Enaction, *Proceedings of 16th International Conference on Software Engineering (ICSE'16)*, IEEE Computer Society Press, Sorrento, Italy, pp.169-178.

Zahran, S. (1998), *Software Process Improvement: Practical Guidelines for Business Success*, Addison-Wesley, London, UK.

Zubrow, D., Hayes, W., Siegel, J. and Goldenson, D. (1994), Maturity Questionnaire – Empirical Methods, V.1.1, Software Engineering Institute, *CMU/SEI-94-SR-7*, June.

Zubrow, D. (1997), The Software Community Process Maturity Profile, *Software Engineering Institute*, Pittsburgh.

APPENDIXES

Appendix A

MATHEMATICAL SYMBOLS AND NOTATIONS

Symbol	Description
#	Cardinal calculus, number of elements in a set
φ	Empty set
∃	Existential quantifier, there exists
∀	Universal qualifier, for all, or for every
∪	Union of sets
∩	Intersection of sets
∧	Logical and
∨	Logical or
¬	Logical negative
⇒	Implication
Σ	Summary calculus
⊃	Contained
∈	Is member of set
⌊ ⌋	Bottom of a decimal, nearest minimum integer
⌈ ⌉	Ceiling of a decimal, nearest largest integer
ρ	Relative correlation, ratio of correlation
r	Correlation
W	Mean weighted importance
r_w	Ratio of significance
r_p	Ratio of practice
r_c	Ratio of effectiveness
φ	Character value
O( )	Order of complexity

Appendix B

ABBREVIATIONS

Abbreviation	Description
1-D	One dimension(al)
2-D	Two dimension(al)
ACM	Association of Computing Machinery
ADT	Abstract Data Types
AI	Artificial Intelligence
ASQ	American Society of Quality
BCS	British Computer Society
BIT	Built-In Test
BP	Base Practice
BPA	Base Process Activity
CASE	Computer-Aided Software Engineering
CCITT	International Telegraph and Telephone Consulting Committee (now ITU)
CCS	The Calculus of Communicating Systems
CMM	Capability Maturity Model
COCOMO	Constructive Cost Model
COTS	Commercial Off-The-Shelf (software components)
CPM	Critical Path Method
CSCW	Computer-Supported Cooperative Work
CSP	Communicating Sequential Processes
DOS	Disk Operating System
DSS	Decision Support System
ESI	The European Software Institute
ESSI	European Systems and Software Initiative
IEC	The International Electrotechnical Commission
IEE	The Institute of Electrical Engineers
IEEE	The Institute of Electrical and Electronics Engineers
ISO	The International Organization for Standardization
IT	Information Technology
ITU	International Telecommunication Union

KP	Key Practice
KPA	Key Practice Area
MI	Management Issue
MIS	Management Information System
MTA	Main Topic Area
OOP	Object-Oriented Programming
OPRM	Organization's Process Reference Model
PC	Personal Computer
PCD	Process Capability Determination
PCL	Process Capability Level
PCM	Process Capability Model
PDCA	Plan-Do-Check-Act, the Deming circle
PERT	Program Evaluation and Review Technique
PIE	Process Improvement Experiment
PIM	Process Improvement Model
PSP	Personal Software Process
PTPM	Project's Tailored Process Model
QSA	Quality System Attribute
SDL	Specification and Description Language
SDO	Software Development Organization
SEI	The Software Engineering Institute at Carnegie-Mellon University
SESC	IEEE Software Engineering Standard Committee
SME	Small and Medium-sized Enterprises
SPA	Software Process Assessment
SPD	Software Process Diagnosis
SPE	Software Process Establishment
SPM	Software Process Modeling
SPI	Software Process Improvement
SPICE	Software Process Improvement and Capability dEtermination
SPIN	Software Process Improvement Network
SEPRM	Software Engineering Process Reference Model
SQA	Software Quality Assurance
TCSE	IEEE Technical Council on Software Engineering
TQM	Total Quality Management
TSP	Team Software Process
UML	Unified Modeling language

Appendix C

MAPPING BETWEEN CURRENT PROCESS MODELS

No.	Cat. No.	BPA (in SEPRM)	Rating	CMM	ISO 9001	Bootstrap	ISO 15504
	1	**Organization subsystem**					
	1.1	Organization structure processes					
	1.1.1	Organization definition					
1	1.1.1.1	Define organization structure	4		1.1.6	$2.2.1.4_2$	
2	1.1.1.2	Establish business strategy	4				5.1.1/2
3	1.1.1.3	Define management responsibilities	4		1.1.2/3	$1.1.1_2$	5.2.11
4	1.1.1.4	Establish organization's general quality policy	3				5.1.3
5	1.1.1.5	Assign project managers	4			$1.1.2_3$	
6	1.1.1.6	Define career plans	1				5.1.5/6
7	1.1.1.7	Review projects periodically	4			$1.1.14_2$	
	1.1.2	Project organization					
8	1.1.2.1	Define project teams	4				3.3.1/5.1.4
9	1.1.2.2	Define project management responsibilities	3				3.3.2
10	1.1.2.3	Assign SQA personnel or team	4		1.1.11	$1.1.5_2$	
11	1.1.2.4	Maintain project team interactions	2				3.3.3
12	1.1.2.5	Management commitment on quality	4		1.1.12	$1.1.10_3$	
13	1.1.2.6	Assign system analyst to management team	2			$2.3.1.8_3$	

1.2 Organization processes

1.2.1 Organization process definition

#	ID	Description					
14	1.2.1.1	Define process goals	3				5.2.1
15	1.2.1.2	Identify current activities/responsibilities	2				5.2.2
16	1.2.1.3	Identify inputs/outputs of process	3				5.2.3
17	1.2.1.4	Establish organization's standard process	4			$2.2.1.2_4$	
18	1.2.1.5	Document standard process	4	3.2.2/3	3.2.23	$2.1.1.1_3$	5.2.10
19	1.2.1.6	Report standard process	4	3.2.1			5.2.13
20	1.2.1.7	Define tailorability of standard process	3	3.2.4		$2.1.1.2_3$	
21	1.2.1.8	Organization level process coordination	3	3.1.3			
22	1.2.1.9	Define entry/exit criteria of processes	3				5.2.4
23	1.2.1.10	Define control points/milestones	3			$2.2.2.9_3$	5.2.5
24	1.2.1.11	Identify external interfaces	3			$2.2.1.11_3$	5.2.6
25	1.2.1.12	Identify internal interfaces	2				5.2.7
26	1.2.1.13	Define quality records	4				5.2.8
27	1.2.1.14	Define process measures	3				5.2.9
28	1.2.1.15	Establish performance expectations	1				5.2.12

1.2.2 Organization process improvement

#	ID	Description					
29	1.2.2.1	Plan process improvement	2	3.1.2/ 5.3.1/3			
30	1.2.2.2	Assess current process periodically	3	3.1.1		$2.1.3.14_4$	5.3.3
31	1.2.2.3	Identify improvement opportunities	4	5.3.5	3.3.10	$2.1.1.9_4$	5.3.1/4
32	1.2.2.4	Define scope of improvement activities	2				5.3.2
33	1.2.2.5	Prioritize improvement	3				5.3.5
34	1.2.2.6	Define measures of impact	1				5.3.6
35	1.2.2.7	Change process for improvement	2	5.3.2/4			5.3.7
36	1.2.2.8	Pilot trial of new process	2	5.3.7		$2.1.3.16_5$	
37	1.2.2.9	Assess new process	3	3.1.5			
38	1.2.2.10	Document improved process	4	3.1.7/ 5.3.8/9			5.3.8
39	1.2.2.11	Report/train new process	2	3.1.6/5 .3.6/ 5.3.10			5.3.9

1.3 Customer service processes

	1.3.1	Customer relations				
40	1.3.1.1.	Obtain customer requirements	4	2.3.8		1.3.1
41	1.3.1.2	Document customer requirements	3		$3.3.1.1_5/2_5$	
42	1.3.1.3	Define service procedures	4	2.4.8/3.8.1		
43	1.3.1.4	Understand customer expectation	3			1.3.2
44	1.3.1.5	Define customer responsibility	4	1.1.14		
45	1.3.1.6	Keep customers informed	4			1.3.3
46	1.3.1.7	Establish joint audits/reviews	1			1.4.1
47	1.3.1.8	Prepare for customer audits/reviews	1			1.4.2
48	1.3.1.9	Conduct joint management reviews	3			1.4.3
49	1.3.1.10	Conduct joint technical reviews	3			1.4.4
50	1.3.1.11	Support customer acceptance review	4	3.8.2		1.4.5
51	1.3.1.12	Perform joint process assessment	2			1.4.6
52	1.3.1.13	Regular interchange with customers	2		$2.2.4.11_2$	
	1.3.2	Customer support				
53	1.3.2.1	Identify operational risks	2			1.6.1
54	1.3.2.2	Support software installation	4			1.5.6
55	1.3.2.3	Perform operational testing	3			1.6.2
56	1.3.2.4	Demonstrate software operation	4			1.6.3
57	1.3.2.5	Resolve operational problems	4			1.6.4
58	1.3.2.6	Handle user requests	4			1.6.5
59	1.3.2.7	Document temporary workaround	2			1.6.6
60	1.3.2.8	Monitor system capacity and service	3			1.6.7
61	1.3.2.9	Train customer	3			1.7.1
62	1.3.2.10	Establish product support	2			1.7.2
63	1.3.2.11	Monitor performance	2			1.7.3
64	1.3.2.12	Install product upgrades	4			1.7.4
	1.3.3	Software/system delivery				
65	1.3.3.1	Define software replication procedure	3		$2.3.1.36_3$	
66	1.3.3.2	Define installation procedure	4		$2.3.1.37_2$ $/39_2$	
67	1.3.3.3	Define delivery procedure	4		$2.3.1.38_3$	
68	1.3.3.4	Identify installation requirements	3			1.5.1
69	1.3.3.5	Prepare site for installation	3			1.5.2
70	1.3.3.6	Pack software package	4			1.5.3
71	1.3.3.7	Deliver after conformance verified	4	2.4.2/		

No.	Code	Description				3.4.3/10	
72	1.3.3.8	Document acceptance of software	3				
73	1.3.3.9	Deliver software on time	4		2.4.7		1.5.4
74	1.3.3.10	Verify correct receipt	4		3.4.5		1.5.5
75	1.3.3.11	Provide handling and storage procedures	4		2.4.4-6		1.5.7
	1.3.4	**Service evaluation**					
76	1.3.4.1	SQA review with customers	4	2.5.8	1.6.7/3.4.6		
77	1.3.4.2	Feedback customer information	4		3.8.3		
78	1.3.4.3	Determine customer satisfaction level	4		1.6.3		1.8.1
79	1.3.4.4	Compare with competitors	2				1.8.2
80	1.3.4.5	Review customer satisfaction	3				1.8.3
81	1.3.4.6	Record customer failure reports	4		1.5.3	2.3.1.49$_4$	
	2	**Development subsystem**					
	2.1	**Software engineering methodology processes**					
	2.1.1	**Software engineering modeling**					
82	2.1.1.1	Aware of state-of-the-art in software engineering	4			3.1.1$_5$	
83	2.1.1.2	Survey methodologies/technologies adopted externally	2			3.1.2$_5$	
84	2.1.1.3	Evaluate life cycle model	3				
85	2.1.1.4	Evaluate prototype model	4				
86	2.1.1.5	Evaluate OOP model	4				
87	2.1.1.6	Evaluate combined model	2				
88	2.1.1.7	Evaluate CASE model	1				
89	2.1.1.8	Integrate methodologies and tools into process	3			3.3.2.1$_5$/2$_5$	
90	2.1.1.9	Distinguish development category: system prototype/new system/improved version	4			2.1.1.8$_2$	
	2.1.2	**Reuse methodologies**					
91	2.1.2.1	Determine organizational reuse strategy	3				5.5.1
92	2.1.2.2	Identify reusable components	4			2.3.1.48$_3$	5.5.2
93	2.1.2.3	Develop reusable components	2			2.3.1.28$_4$	5.5.3
94	2.1.2.4	Establish reuse library	2				5.5.4
95	2.1.2.5	Certify reusable components	1			2.3.1.27$_4$	5.5.5
96	2.1.2.6	Integrate reuse into life cycle	3				5.5.6

97	2.1.2.7	Propagate change carefully	4				5.5.7
	2.1.3	**Technology innovation**					
98	2.1.3.1	Plan technology change	3	5.2.1			
99	2.1.3.2	Identify processes needed in technology change	3	5.2.2/4			
100	2.1.3.3	Identify/replace obsolete technology/ process	2			$3.1.4_5$	
101	2.1.3.4	Select new technology	4	5.2.5			
102	2.1.3.5	Introduce new technology/metrics/process	2	5.2.3		$3.1.3_5$	
103	2.1.3.6	Pilot trial of new technology	2	5.2.6			
104	2.1.3.7	Incorporate trialed technology into current process	2	5.2.7/8			
	2.2	**Software development processes**					
	2.2.1	**Development process definition**					
105	2.2.1.1	Evaluate software development methodologies	4		3.2.17		3.1.1
106	2.2.1.2	Model software process	3	2.2.5		$2.3.1.1_3$	3.1.2
107	2.2.1.3	Describe activities and responsibilities	4		1.1.7/9 /3.3.6/7		3.1.3
108	2.2.1.4	Establish task sequences	4		1.1.5/1. 2.1/ 2.4.1		3.1.4
109	2.2.1.5	Identify process relationships	4		1.1.8		
110	2.2.1.6	Document process activities	4		1.2.2		3.1.5
111	2.2.1.7	Identify control point of project	4	2.2.8	3.3.17		
112	2.2.1.8	Maintain consistency across all processes	3	3.5.10			
113	2.2.1.9	Develop software according to defined process	4	3.5.1			
114	2.2.1.10	Derive project process by tailoring organization's standard process	4	3.4.1/3		$2.1.1.5_3$	
115	2.2.1.11	Approval of processes and equipment	4		3.2.16/1 9		
116	2.2.1.12	Identify special requirements in developing special system: real-time/safety-critical/etc	3			$2.3.1.2\text{-}7_3/$ $2.3.1.12_3$	
	2.2.2	**Requirement analysis**					
117	2.2.2.1	Analyze requirement according to defined process	3				
118	2.2.2.2	Specify formal requirements	4		3.3.1/3		
119	2.2.2.3	Define requirements	4		3.3.5		

		feasibility/testability					
120	2.2.2.4	Prevent ambiguities in specification	4		3.3.2		
121	2.2.2.5	Interpret/clarify requirements	4		3.3.12	$2.3.1.20_2$	3.4.4
122	2.2.2.6	Specify acceptance criteria	4		3.3.15/ 3.4.11/3 .6.3	$2.3.1.34_3$	
123	2.2.2.7	Allocate requirements for processes	3	3.5.2			
124	2.2.2.8	Adopt requirements acquisition tools	2			$3.3.2.3_5$	
	2.2.3	**Design**					
125	2.2.3.1	Design system according to defined process	4	3.5.3			
126	2.2.3.2	Design software architecture	4			$2.3.1.18_2/ 19_3$	2.3.1
127	2.2.3.3	Design module interfaces	3			$1.1.13_3$	2.3.2
128	2.2.3.4	Develop detailed design	3			$2.3.1.21_2$	2.3.3
129	2.2.3.5	Establish document traceability	4		3.3.13	$2.3.1.22_3$	2.3.4
130	2.2.3.6	Specify final design	4		3.3.14		
131	2.2.3.7	Define design change procedure	4		3.3.24		
132	2.2.3.8	Adopt architectural design tools	2			$3.3.3.1_5/2_5$	
133	2.2.3.9	Adopt module design tools	3			$3.3.4.1_5/6_5$	
	2.2.4	**Coding**					
134	2.2.4.1	Code according to defined process	4	3.5.4			
135	2.2.4.2	Choose proper programming language(s)	4			$3.3.4.2_5$	
136	2.2.4.3	Develop software modules	4				2.4.1
137	2.2.4.4	Develop unit verification procedures	3				2.4.2
138	2.2.4.5	Verify software modules	3				2.4.3
139	2.2.4.6	Document coding standards	4		3.3.25/ 30	$2.3.1.24_3/ 3.3.4.4_5$	
140	2.2.4.7	Define coding styles	4		3.3.29	$2.3.1.25_3 /26_2$	
141	2.2.4.8	Adopt coding support/auto-generation tools	2			$3.3.4.3_5$	
	2.2.5	**Module testing**					
142	2.2.5.1	Testing according to defined process	4	3.5.5		$2.3.1.31_3$	
143	2.2.5.2	Determine test strategy	3			$2.3.1.30_2$	2.5.1
144	2.2.5.3	Specify test methods	2			$2.3.1.29_2$	2.5.2/3
145	2.2.5.4	Generate test	3				2.5.5
146	2.2.5.5	Conduct testing	4				2.5.4

147	2.2.5.6	Adopt module testing tools	3		$3.3.5.1_5$	
	2.2.6	**Integration and system testing**				
148	2.2.6.1	Integration test according to defined process	4	3.5.6	$2.3.1.32_2/33_3$	2.6.1-3
149	2.2.6.2	Acceptance test according to defined process	4	3.5.7	$2.3.1.35_2$	
150	2.2.6.3	System tests generation	4			2.6.4
151	2.2.6.4	Test integrated system	4			2.5.6/2.6.5
152	2.2.6.5	Adopt software integration tools	2		$3.3.5.3_5 / 3.3.6.1_5/4_5$	
153	2.2.6.6	Adopt module cross-reference tools	2		$3.3.6.2_5$	
154	2.2.6.7	Adopt system acceptance testing tools	1		$3.3.7.1_5/3_5$	
	2.2.7	**Maintenance**				
155	2.2.7.1	Determine maintenance requirements	4			2.7.1
156	2.2.7.2	Analyze user problems and enhancements	3			2.7.2
157	2.2.7.3	Determine modifications for next upgrade	2			2.7.3
158	2.2.7.4	Implement/test modifications	3			2.7.4
159	2.2.7.5	Update user system	4			2.7.5
160	2.2.7.6	Maintenance consistency with specifications	4	3.8.4		
161	2.2.7.7	Maintain nonconforming products	4	2.5.3		
162	2.2.7.8	Record nonconformance treatment	4	2.5.5		
163	2.2.7.9	Adopt regression testing tools	2		$3.3.8.1_5/2_5$	
164	2.2.7.10	Conduct regression testing	2		$2.3.1.44_3$	
	2.3	**Software development environment processes**				
	2.3.1	**Environment**				
165	2.3.1.1	Identify environment requirements	4			5.6.1
166	2.3.1.2	Establish computer-supported cooperative work (CSCW) environment	2		$3.2.1.2_5$	
167	2.3.1.3	Provide software engineering environment	4	3.2.15	$3.4.5_5$	5.6.2
168	2.3.1.4	Provide development supporting tools	2		$3.3.8.4_5/3.4.2_5/4_5$	
169	2.3.1.5	Provide management supporting tools	2		$3.4.1_5$	5.6.3
170	2.3.1.6	Provide interactive communication	3		$3.2.1.1_5$	

		environment					
171	2.3.1.7	Maintain software engineering environment	4				5.6.4
	2.3.2	**Facilities**					
172	2.3.2.1	Plan required resources	4			$1.2.1.1_2$	
173	2.3.2.2	Identify specialized facilities	4				3.2.3
174	2.3.2.3	Acquire resources	4	1.1.10		$1.2.1.2_2$	3.7.1
175	2.3.2.4	Check resources availability	4	3.3.8			
176	2.3.2.5	Provide productive workspace	3			$1.2.1.3_2$	5.7.1
177	2.3.2.6	Provide data backup	4				5.7.3
178	2.3.2.7	Provide building facilities	3				5.7.4
179	2.3.2.8	Provide remote access facility	2				5.7.5
180	2.3.2.9	Adopt software design tools	3				
181	2.3.2.10	Adopt software testing tools	3			$3.4.3_5$	
182	2.3.2.11	Ensure data integrity	4				5.7.2
183	2.3.2.12	Register/maintain test equipment	4	3.6.1/5			
184	2.3.2.13	Control customer-supplied equipment	4	3.6.2			
185	2.3.2.14	Record equipment condition	4	3.6.4			
186	2.3.2.15	Ensure equipment availability	4	3.6.6-12			
	2.3.3	**Development support tools**					
187	2.3.3.1	CASE tools	2				
188	2.3.3.2	Software requirements acquisition tools	3				
189	2.3.3.3	Software design tools	4				
190	2.3.3.4	Software testing tools	4				
	2.3.4	**Management support tools**					
191	2.3.4.1	SQA management tools	2				
192	2.3.4.2	Software requirements review tools	1				
193	2.3.4.3	Software design review tools	2				
194	2.3.4.4	Software testing analysis tools	3				
195	2.3.4.5	Software configuration management tools	3				
196	2.3.4.6	Software documentation processing tools	4				
	3	**Management subsystem**					
	3.1	**Software quality assurance (SQA) processes**					
	3.1.1	SQA process definition					

197	3.1.1.1	Define SQA procedure	4		1.2.6		
198	3.1.1.2	Define project s/w engineering standards	4		1.2.3	$2.1.1.10_3$	4.3.1
199	3.1.1.3	Document SQA system	4		1.2.5/1.3.1	$2.1.1.6_3$	
200	3.1.1.4	Issue quality manual	4		1.1.1/1.2.4	$1.1.9_3/$ $2.2.2.1_3$	
201	3.1.1.5	Distribute quality policy	4		1.1.4		
202	3.1.1.6	Report SQA results	3	2.5.6		$1.1.4_3$	4.3.4
203	3.1.1.7	Assess process quality	3				3.5.5
204	3.1.1.8	Take correct actions	3	2.5.2			3.5.6
205	3.1.1.9	Assign independent reviewers	4		1.4.6/3.3.21		
206	3.1.1.10	Define extent of inspection	4		3.4.1		
207	3.1.1.11	Conduct SQA for each process	2			$2.1.1.7_4$	
208	3.1.1.12	Assign qualified person(s) to special process	4		3.2.22		
209	3.1.1.13	Document quality records	4		1.1.13/ 1.6.1/2		
210	3.1.1.14	Review SQA system suitability	4		1.1.15	$1.1.3_3/12_3$	
211	3.1.1.15	Decisional role of SQA in processes	3			$1.1.7_3$	
212	3.1.1.16	Decisional role of SQA in final products	4			$1.1.6_3$	
213	3.1.1.17	Adopt SQA tools	2			$3.2.3.2_5$	
	3.1.2	**Requirement review**					
214	3.1.2.1	Specification verification	4		3.3.23/3.4.2	$2.2.2.11_4$	
215	3.1.2.2	Formal review requirements	4		3.3.11		
216	3.1.2.3	Review statutory requirements	4		3.3.16		
217	3.1.2.4	Customer accepts specifications	4		2.5.4/3.3.4		
218	3.1.2.5	Adopt specification verification tools	2				
	3.1.3	**Design review**					
219	3.1.3.1	Define design review procedure	4		3.3.18/20/22	$2.2.2.2_3/3_4$	
220	3.1.3.2	Document design review	4		3.3.19		
221	3.1.3.3	Verify prototypes	2			$2.1.1.11_4$	
222	3.1.3.4	Measure design review coverage	2			$2.1.2.1_4/$ $2.1.3.4_4/5_4$	
	3.1.4	**Code review**					
223	3.1.4.1	Conduct code walk-through	4		3.3.27		

224	3.1.4.2	Conduct code review	4		3.3.28	2.2.2.4$_3$/5$_4$	
225	3.1.4.3	Measure code review coverage	2			2.1.2.2$_4$/ 2.1.3.6$_3$/7$_4$	
	3.1.5	**Module testing audit**					
226	3.1.5.1	Measure test coverage	4			2.1.2.3$_4$	
227	3.1.5.2	Estimate remaining error distribution	2			2.1.3.9$_4$	
228	3.1.5.3	Review test results	3			2.2.2.10$_3$	
229	3.1.5.4	Static/dynamic module test analysis	2			3.3.5.2$_5$	
	3.1.6	**Integration and system testing audit**					
230	3.1.6.1	Identify nonconforming software/functions	4		2.5.1-2/3.4.4	3.2.3.3$_5$	
231	3.1.6.2	Define inspection procedure	4		3.4.7/3.5.1		
232	3.1.6.3	Inspection against requirements	4		3.4.8		
233	3.1.6.4	Document inspection/test results	4		3.4.9/3.5.2	2.2.4.9$_2$/ 2.3.1.40$_3$	
234	3.1.6.5	Static/dynamic integration test analysis	2			3.3.6.3$_5$	
235	3.1.6.6	Static/dynamic acceptance test analysis	2			3.3.7.2$_5$	
	3.1.7	**Maintenance audit**					
236	3.1.7.1	Reinspect repaired products	4		2.5.6		
237	3.1.7.2	Audit nonconformance records	3				
238	3.1.7.3	Audit nonconformance treatment	3				
239	3.1.7.4	Audit consistency with specification	2				
240	3.1.7.5	Audit consistency of system documents	3			2.3.1.43$_3$	
241	3.1.7.6	Audit consistency of system configuration	4			2.3.1.46$_3$	
242	3.1.7.7	Audit user satisfaction with maintenance	3			2.3.1.47$_4$	
243	3.1.7.8	Review regression testing results	3			2.3.1.45$_3$	
	3.1.8	**Audit and inspection**					
244	3.1.8.1	Audit software development activities	4	2.5.4	3.2.21	2.1.3.3$_3$	4.3.2
245	3.1.8.2	Audit work products	4	2.5.5	3.2.20		4.3.3
246	3.1.8.3	Audit process quality	4		1.4.2		3.5.4
247	3.1.8.4	Audit on-site activities	4		1.4.3		
248	3.1.8.5	Document audit results	4		1.4.4/5		

249	3.1.8.6	Verify representativeness of examined samples	3			2.2.2.8$_3$	
	3.1.9	**Peer review**					
250	3.1.9.1	Plan peer review	4	3.7.1			
251	3.1.9.2	Select work products	3				4.5.1
252	3.1.9.3	Identify review standards	3				4.5.2
253	3.1.9.4	Establish completion criteria	4				4.5.3
254	3.1.9.5	Establish re-review criteria	2				4.5.4
255	3.1.9.6	Distribute review materials	3				4.5.5
256	3.1.9.7	Conduct peer review	4	3.7.2			4.5.6
257	3.1.9.8	Document review results	3	3.7.3			
258	3.1.9.9	Take actions for review results	3				4.5.7
259	3.1.9.10	Track actions for review results	2				4.5.8
	3.1.10	**Defect control**					
260	3.1.10.1	Plan defect prevention	2	5.1.1/2		2.1.3.17$_5$	
261	3.1.10.2	Defect reporting and record	4	3.5.9			4.4.1
262	3.1.10.3	Defect causal analysis	4	5.1.3	1.5.1/2	2.1.3.10$_4$/ 2.2.2.6$_2$/7$_4$	
263	3.1.10.4	Propose process change for defect prevention	4	5.1.6/7	1.5.6	2.1.3.15$_5$	
264	3.1.10.5	Track problem report	3				4.4.2
265	3.1.10.6	Prioritize problems	4		1.5.4		4.4.3
266	3.1.10.7	Determine resolutions	3				4.4.4
267	3.1.10.8	Correct defects	4			2.2.4.6$_3$	4.4.5
268	3.1.10.9	Review defect corrections	4	5.1.4/5	1.5.5		
269	3.1.10.10	Distribute correction results	2	5.1.8			4.4.6
	3.1.11	**Subcontractor's quality control**					
270	3.1.11.1	Subcontractor's quantitative quality goals	2	4.2.5			
271	3.1.11.2	Assess/test quality of subcontractor's product	4		2.4.3		3.8.7
272	3.1.11.3	Acceptance test for subcontractor's software	4	2.4.12			
273	3.1.11.4	Safeguard customer-supplied products	4		2.2.1-3	2.2.4.10$_2$	
274	3.1.11.5	Record customer-supplied products	4		2.2.4		
	3.2	**Project planning processes**					
	3.2.1	**Project plan**					
275	3.2.1.1	Assign project proposal team	3	2.2.1			

276	3.2.1.2	Design project process structure	4	2.2.2/3			3.2.1
277	3.2.1.3	Determine reuse strategy	2				3.2.4
278	3.2.1.4	Establish project schedule	4	2.2.12	3.2.9		3.2.8
279	3.2.1.5	Establish project commitments	3				3.2.9
280	3.2.1.6	Document project plans	4	2.2.6/7/15	3.2.1		3.2.10
281	3.2.1.7	Conduct progress management reviews	3				3.7.3
282	3.2.1.8	Conduct progress technical reviews	4				3.7.4
283	3.2.1.9	Management commitments in planning	3	2.2.4			3.7.5
284	3.2.1.10	Determine release strategy	2			$2.2.1.8_3$	2.1.4
285	3.2.1.11	Plan change control	1	2.3.2/3			
286	3.2.1.12	Define plan change procedure	1	2.3.4			
287	3.2.1.13	Plan development	4		3.2.4	$2.2.1.3_2$	
288	3.2.1.14	Plan testing	4		3.2.5		
289	3.2.1.15	Plan system integration	4		3.2.6/12		
290	3.2.1.16	Plan process management	4		3.2.7		
291	3.2.1.17	Plan maintenance	4		3.2.8	$2.2.1.5_2$	
292	3.2.1.18	Plan review and authorization	4		3.2.10/11		
293	3.2.1.19	Assign development task	3			$2.2.1.6_2$	
294	3.2.1.20	Adopt project/process planning tools	1			$3.2.2.1_5$	
	3.2.2	**Project estimation**					
295	3.2.2.1	Estimate project costs	4	2.2.10		$2.2.1.1_2$	3.2.5
296	3.2.2.2	Estimate project time	3				
297	3.2.2.3	Estimate resources requirement	4	2.2.14	3.2.13		
298	3.2.2.4	Estimate staff requirement	3				
299	3.2.2.5	Estimate software size	4	2.2.9		$3.3.8.5_5$	
300	3.2.2.6	Estimate software complexity	2			$3.3.8.6_5$	
301	3.2.2.7	Estimate critical resources	4	2.2.11			
	3.2.3	**Project risk avoidance**					
302	3.2.3.1	Identify project risks	3	2.2.13		$2.2.3.1_3$	3.2.6
303	3.2.3.2	Establish risk management scope	3				3.6.1
304	3.2.3.3	Identify unstable specification-related risks	4			$2.2.3.2_3/3_3$	3.6.2
305	3.2.3.4	Identify process change-related risks	2			$2.2.3.8_4$	
306	3.2.3.5	Identify market-related risks	2			$2.2.3.4_3$	
307	3.2.3.6	Analyze and prioritize risks	4				3.6.3
308	3.2.3.7	Develop mitigation strategies	3			$2.2.3.5_3$	3.6.4

#	Section	Description					
309	3.2.3.8	Define risk metrics for probability/impact	1			$2.2.3.6_4$	3.6.5
310	3.2.3.9	Implement mitigation strategies	2				3.6.6
311	3.2.3.10	Assess risk mitigation activities	2			$2.2.3.7_4$	3.6.7
312	3.2.3.11	Take corrective actions for identified risk	3				3.6.8
	3.2.4	**Project quality plan**					
313	3.2.4.1	Plan SQA	4	2.5.1/ 4.2.1/2	1.2.7/3. 2.3	$2.2.1.7_3$	
314	3.2.4.2	Establish quality goals	4				3.5.1
315	3.2.4.3	Define quality quantitative metrics	4	4.2.3	3.2.14/1 8		3.2.7/3.5 .2
316	3.2.4.4	Identify quality activities	3				3.5.3
317	3.2.4.5	Track project quality goals	4	4.2.4	1.4.1		3.2.2
318	3.2.4.6	SQA team participate in project planning	3	2.5.3			
319	3.2.4.7	Plan maintenance	3			$2.3.1.42_3$	
	3.3	**Process management processes**					
	3.3.1	**Process management**					
320	3.3.1.1	Plan quantitative process management	3	4.1.1			
321	3.3.1.2	Conduct quantitative process management	2	4.1.2			
322	3.3.1.3	Collect data for quantitative analysis	2	4.1.3/4			
323	3.3.1.4	Control defined process quantitatively	3	4.1.5			
324	3.3.1.5	Document quantitative analysis results	4	4.1.6			
325	3.3.1.6	Benchmark organization's baseline of process capability	1	4.1.7			
326	3.3.1.7	Manage project by defined process	4	3.4.4			
327	3.3.1.8	Adopt project/process management tools	2			$3.2.2.2_5$/ $3.2.3.4_5$	
	3.3.2	**Process tracking**					
328	3.3.2.1	Track project progress	4	2.3.1/1 2 /3.4.11		$2.1.3.1_3$	3.7.2
329	3.3.2.2	Track development schedule	4	2.3.8/9 /3.4.9		$2.2.4.8_2$	
330	3.3.2.3	Track process quality	4			$2.1.3.2_3$	
331	3.3.2.4	Track software size	4	2.3.5/			

				3.4.6			
332	3.3.2.5	Track project cost	4	2.3.6/3.4.7			
333	3.3.2.6	Track critical resources and performance	4	2.3.7/3.4.8		$2.3.1.23_3$	
334	3.3.2.7	Track project risks	3	2.3.10/3.4.10			
335	3.3.2.8	Track process productivity	4			$2.1.3.11_4$	
336	3.3.2.9	Track system memory utilization	3			$2.3.1.9_2$	
337	3.3.2.10	Track system throughput	2			$2.3.1.10_2$	
338	3.3.2.11	Track system I/O channel capabilities	3			$2.3.1.11_2$	
339	3.3.2.12	Track system networking	3				
340	3.3.2.13	Adopt process tracking tools	1			$3.2.3.1_5$	
341	3.3.2.14	Document project tracking data	4				
342	3.3.2.15	Identify and handle process deviation	3	2.5.7		$1.1.11_3$	4.3.5
	3.3.3	**Configuration management**					
343	3.3.3.1	Establish configuration management library	4	2.6.1/3	2.1.4	$1.1.8_2$	4.2.1
344	3.3.3.2	Adopt configuration management tools	4			$3.2.4.1_5/3_5$	
345	3.3.3.3	Identify product's configuration	4	2.6.4	2.1.1/3		4.2.2
346	3.3.3.4	Maintain configuration item descriptions	3				4.2.3
347	3.3.3.5	Control change requests	4	2.6.5	1.3.5	$2.3.1.41_3$	4.2.4
348	3.3.3.6	Release control	4	2.6.7	1.3.2		4.2.6
349	3.3.3.7	Maintain configuration item history	4	2.6.2/8	1.3.7/2.1.2		4.2.7
350	3.3.3.8	Report configuration status	3	2.6.9			4.2.8
	3.3.4	**Change control**					
351	3.3.4.1	Establish change requests/approval system	3				
352	3.3.4.2	Control requirement change	4			$2.2.4.2_3$	
353	3.3.4.3	Control design change	3			$2.2.4.3_3$	
354	3.3.4.4	Control code change	2			$2.2.4.4_2$	
355	3.3.4.5	Control test data change	2			$2.2.4.5_3$	
356	3.3.4.6	Control environment change	3				
357	3.3.4.7	Control schedule change	4				
358	3.3.4.8	Control configuration change	4	2.6.6/10	1.3.6		4.2.5
359	3.3.4.9	Adopt change control tools	1			$3.2.4.2_5$	

	3.3.5	Process review					
360	3.3.5.1	Review processes at milestones	4	2.3.13		$2.2.1.10_2$	
361	3.3.5.2	Document project review data	4	2.3.11			
362	3.3.5.3	Revise project process	2	3.4.2			
363	3.3.5.4	Conduct statistical analysis of process	4		3.7.1/2	$2.1.3.8_3$	
364	3.3.5.5	Gather process data	4				
365	3.3.5.6	Compare actual/forecast errors	3			$2.1.3.12_4$	
366	3.3.5.7	Compare actual/forecast schedule	2			$2.1.3.13_2$	
367	3.3.5.8	Compare actual/forecast resources	3				
	3.3.6	Intergroup coordination					
368	3.3.6.1	Define interface between project groups	4		3.3.9		
369	3.3.6.2	Plan intergroup activities	2	3.6.3			
370	3.3.6.3	Identify intergroup critical dependencies	3	3.6.4			
371	3.3.6.4	Handle intergroup issues	2	3.6.6			3.3.4
372	3.3.6.5	Technical/management representatives coordination	4	3.6.2	3.2.2		
373	3.3.6.6	Review last process output	3	3.6.5			
374	3.3.6.7	Conduct intergroup representatives review	1	3.6.7			
	3.4	**Contract and requirement management processes**					
	3.4.1	Requirement management					
375	3.4.1.1	Specify system requirements	4			$2.3.1.14_3$	2.1.1
376	3.4.1.2	Design system based on requirements	4	2.1.2			2.1.2
377	3.4.1.3	Allocate requirements	3	2.1.1			2.1.3
378	3.4.1.4	Determine operating environment impact	3			$2.3.1.17_3$	2.2.3
379	3.4.1.5	Determine software requirements	4			$2.3.1.15_2$	2.2.1
380	3.4.1.6	Analysis of software requirements	4				2.2.2
381	3.4.1.7	Evaluate requirements with customer	3	3.6.1		$2.3.1.13_2$	2.2.4
382	3.4.1.8	Update requirements for next iteration	3				2.2.5
383	3.4.1.9	Agree on requirements	4				3.4.1
384	3.4.1.10	Establish requirements standard	2			$2.3.1.16_3$	3.4.2
385	3.4.1.11	Manage requirements changes	3	2.1.3			3.4.3
386	3.4.1.12	Maintain requirements traceability	3				3.4.5

	3.4.2	Contract management					
387	3.4.2.1	Define contractual procedures	4		2.4.9		
388	3.4.2.2	Prepare contract proposal	4		3.1.1-3		
389	3.4.2.3	Review contract	4		3.1.4-6	$2.1.1.3_2/4_2$	1.2.1
390	3.4.2.4	Ensure agreement of terminology	4		3.1.8		1.2.2
391	3.4.2.5	Determine interfaces to independent agents	2				1.2.3
392	3.4.2.6	Assess contractor's capability	4		3.1.9		
393	3.4.2.7	Document contractor's capability	4		3.1.7		
	3.4.3	Subcontractor management					
394	3.4.3.1	Specify subcontracted development	3	2.4.1			
395	3.4.3.2	Assess capability of subcontractors	3			$2.2.5.3_3$	3.8.2
396	3.4.3.3	Record acceptable subcontractors	2			$2.2.5.1_3$	
397	3.4.3.4	Define scope of contracted work	4	2.4.3		$2.2.5.2_2$	3.8.1
398	3.4.3.5	Define interface of contracted work	4		2.3.2/5		
399	3.4.3.6	Select qualified subcontractor	3	2.4.2			3.8.3
400	3.4.3.7	Approve subcontractor's plan	2	2.4.4			3.8.4
401	3.4.3.8	Maintain interchanges with subcontractors	3	2.4.8			3.8.5
402	3.4.3.9	Track subcontractor's development activities	2	2.4.5/6			
403	3.4.3.10	Monitor subcontractor's SQA activities	4	2.4.10/ 11	2.3.4		
404	3.4.3.11	Review subcontractor's work	4	2.4.7/9 /13	2.3.3		
405	3.4.3.12	Assess compliance of contracted product	4				3.8.6
406	3.4.3.13	Determine interfaces to subcontractors	3				1.2.4
407	3.4.3.14	Document subcontractor's records	4		1.6.4		
	3.4.4	Purchasing management					
408	3.4.4.1	Identify need for purchasing	4				1.1.1
409	3.4.4.2	Define purchasing requirements	3			$2.2.5.5_3$	1.1.2
410	3.4.4.3	Prepare acquisition strategy	2				1.1.3
411	3.4.4.4	Prepare purchasing document	4		2.3.6		
412	3.4.4.5	Prepare request for proposal	2				1.1.4
413	3.4.4.6	Review purchasing document	4		2.3.7	$2.2.5.4_2$	
414	3.4.4.7	Select software product supplier	4		2.3.1		1.1.5
415	3.4.4.8	Verify purchased product	3			$2.2.5.6_3$	
416	3.4.4.9	Manage purchased tools configuration	3			$2.2.5.7_3$	

	3.5	Document management processes					
	3.5.1	Documentation					
417	3.5.1.1	Master list of project documents	4		1.3.8		
418	3.5.1.2	Determine documentation requirements	3				4.1.1
419	3.5.1.3	Develop document	4			$2.2.1.9_3$	4.1.2
420	3.5.1.4	Check document	3				4.1.3
421	3.5.1.5	Control document issue	4		1.3.3	$2.2.4.1_3$	4.1.4
422	3.5.1.6	Maintain document	4		1.3.4		4.1.5
423	3.5.1.7	Documentation according to defined process	4	3.5.8			
424	3.5.1.8	Establish documentation standards	4		1.6.5/3.3.26		
425	3.5.1.9	Safety document storage	4		1.6.6		
426	3.5.1.10	Identify current versions of documents	4			$2.2.4.7_3$	
427	3.5.1.11	Adopt interactive documentation tools	3			$3.3.4.5_5/$ $3.3.8.3_5$	
	3.5.2	Process database/library					
428	3.5.2.1	Establish organization's process library	2	3.2.6			
429	3.5.2.2	Establish organization's process database	3	3.1.4/ 3.2.5/ 3.4.5		$2.1.2.6_5$	
430	3.5.2.3	Establish software reuse library	3				
431	3.5.2.4	Establish organization's metrics database	2			$2.1.2.4_3/5_4$	
432	3.5.2.5	Establish operation manual library	3				
433	3.5.2.6	Establish practice benchmark database	1				
	3.6	Human resource management processes					
	3.6.1	Staff selection and allocation					
434	3.6.1.1	Define qualifications for positions	4				
435	3.6.1.2	Define experience for positions	4				
436	3.6.1.3	Assign personnel selection group	3				
437	3.6.1.4	Select staff by qualification / experience	4			$1.2.2.4_3$	
	3.6.2	Training					
438	3.6.2.1	Plan training	3	3.3.1		$1.2.2.3_3$	
439	3.6.2.2	Identify training needs	4	3.3.2/5	1.7.1		5.4.1

440	3.6.2.3	Develop training courses	3				5.4.2
441	3.6.2.4	Approval of training courses	2	3.3.4			
442	3.6.2.5	Conduct technical training	4	3.3.3	1.7.2	$1.2.2.2_3$	5.4.3
443	3.6.2.6	Conduct management training	3			$1.2.2.1_3$	
444	3.6.2.7	Document training records	4	3.3.6	1.7.3/4		5.4.4

Appendix D

BENCHMARKS OF THE SEPRM SOFTWARE ENGINEERING PROCESSES

No.	Cat. No.	BPA	W [0 .. 5]	r_w (%)	r_p (%)	r_e (%)	φ (%)
	1	**Organization subsystem**					
	1.1	**Organization structure**					
	1.1.1	Organization definition					
1	1.1.1.1	Define organization structure	3.8	82.6	92.6	95.2	72.4
2	1.1.1.2	Establish business strategy	4.0	95.7	78.3	85.0	63.6
3	1.1.1.3	Define management responsibilities	4.2	100	76.0	95.2	72.4
4	1.1.1.4	Establish organization's general quality policy	4.2	91.3	73.9	66.7	45.0
5	1.1.1.5	Assign project managers	4.1	95.7	95.5	90.9	83.0
6	1.1.1.6	Define career plans	2.6	50.0	47.6	47.4	11.3
7	1.1.1.7	Review projects periodically	3.8	82.6	73.9	77.3	47.2
	1.1.2	Project organization					
8	1.1.2.1	Define project teams	4.0	87.5	95.7	95.2	79.7
9	1.1.2.2	Define project management responsibilities	4.2	100	73.9	86.4	63.8
10	1.1.2.3	Assign SQA personnel or team	3.8	91.7	87.5	82.6	66.3
11	1.1.2.4	Maintain project team interactions	3.8	91.3	78.3	81.8	58.5
12	1.1.2.5	Management commitment on quality	4.5	100	83.3	91.7	76.5
13	1.1.2.6	Assign system analyst to management team	2.6	56.5	28.6	57.9	9.3

	1.2	**Organization processes**					
	1.2.1	Organization process definition					
14	1.2.1.1	Define process goals	3.9	90.9	72.2	85.0	55.8
15	1.2.1.2	Identify current activities/responsibilities	3.7	81.8	73.9	81.0	49.0
16	1.2.1.3	Identify inputs/outputs of process	3.9	90.9	90.9	77.3	63.9
17	1.2.1.4	Establish organization's standard process	3.8	90.9	85.7	85.0	66.2
18	1.2.1.5	Document standard process	3.9	87.5	87.5	73.9	56.6
19	1.2.1.6	Report standard process	3.4	89.5	66.7	70.6	42.1
20	1.2.1.7	Define tailorability of standard process	3.2	81.8	39.1	70.6	22.6
21	1.2.1.8	Organization level process coordination	3.3	82.6	50.0	66.7	27.5
22	1.2.1.9	Define entry/exit criteria of processes	3.6	83.3	68.4	72.7	41.5
23	1.2.1.10	Define control points/milestones	4.2	100	90.0	95.5	85.9
24	1.2.1.11	Identify external interfaces	3.8	90.9	69.6	81.0	51.2
25	1.2.1.12	Identify internal interfaces	3.5	81.8	71.4	84.2	49.2
26	1.2.1.13	Define quality records	3.3	81.0	68.2	68.8	37.9
27	1.2.1.14	Define process measures	3.8	86.4	42.1	70.0	25.5
28	1.2.1.15	Establish performance expectations	3.0	61.9	38.1	44.4	10.5
	1.2.2	Organization process improvement					
29	1.2.2.1	Plan process improvement	3.1	76.2	52.9	73.3	29.6
30	1.2.2.2	Assess current process periodically	3.8	91.3	68.2	73.7	45.9
31	1.2.2.3	Identify improvement opportunities	4.0	85.7	75.0	73.7	47.4
32	1.2.2.4	Define scope of improvement activities	3.5	76.2	42.9	60.0	19.6
33	1.2.2.5	Prioritize improvement	3.3	85.7	44.4	80.0	30.5
34	1.2.2.6	Define measures of impact	3.2	76.5	10.5	53.8	4.3
35	1.2.2.7	Change process for improvement	3.8	83.3	72.2	88.2	53.1
36	1.2.2.8	Pilot trial of new process	3.9	87.0	63.6	85.0	47.0
37	1.2.2.9	Assess new process	3.5	90.5	70.0	83.3	52.8
38	1.2.2.10	Document improved process	3.3	72.7	52.4	80.0	30.5
39	1.2.2.11	Report/train new process	3.7	78.3	69.6	76.2	41.5
	1.3	**Customer service**					
	1.3.1	Customer relations					
40	1.3.1.1.	Obtain customer requirements	4.2	89.5	100	83.3	74.6
41	1.3.1.2	Document customer requirements	3.4	73.7	72.2	72.2	38.4
42	1.3.1.3	Define service procedures	3.4	73.3	72.2	72.2	38.4
43	1.3.1.4	Understand customer expectation	4.3	100	90.0	85.0	76.5
44	1.3.1.5	Define customer responsibility	3.9	84.2	61.1	72.2	37.2
45	1.3.1.6	Keep customers informed	3.9	84.2	84.2	89.5	63.4
46	1.3.1.7	Establish joint audits/reviews	3.4	89.5	52.6	64.7	30.5
47	1.3.1.8	Prepare for customer audits/reviews	3.2	83.3	61.1	80.0	40.7
48	1.3.1.9	Conduct joint management reviews	3.3	78.9	63.2	70.6	35.2
49	1.3.1.10	Conduct joint technical reviews	3.4	83.3	61.1	76.5	38.9
50	1.3.1.11	Support customer acceptance review	3.8	85.7	75.0	100	64.3
51	1.3.1.12	Perform joint process assessment	2.1	44.4	29.4	50.0	6.5
52	1.3.1.13	Regular interchange with customers	3.9	90.0	75.0	89.5	60.4
	1.3.2	Customer support					

53	1.3.2.1	Identify operational risks	3.8	100	63.2	94.1	59.4
54	1.3.2.2	Support software installation	3.3	77.8	78.9	100	61.4
55	1.3.2.3	Perform operational testing	3.7	89.5	78.9	94.7	66.9
56	1.3.2.4	Demonstrate software operation	3.4	80.0	83.3	94.1	62.7
57	1.3.2.5	Resolve operational problems	3.9	89.5	100	94.4	84.5
58	1.3.2.6	Handle user requests	3.9	95.0	90.0	100	85.5
59	1.3.2.7	Document temporary workaround	2.7	41.2	33.3	61.5	8.4
60	1.3.2.8	Monitor system capacity and service	3.5	76.5	52.9	68.8	27.8
61	1.3.2.9	Train customer	3.7	94.4	94.1	94.1	83.7
62	1.3.2.10	Establish product support	3.9	78.9	87.5	100	69.1
63	1.3.2.11	Monitor performance	3.1	68.8	56.3	81.3	31.4
64	1.3.2.12	Install product upgrades	3.5	78.9	100	94.1	74.3
	1.3.3	**Software/system delivery**					
65	1.3.3.1	Define software replication procedure	3.1	58.8	50.0	78.6	23.1
66	1.3.3.2	Define installation procedure	3.8	88.2	87.5	87.5	67.6
67	1.3.3.3	Define delivery procedure	3.4	76.5	75.0	80.0	45.9
68	1.3.3.4	Identify installation requirements	3.7	100	93.3	93.3	87.1
69	1.3.3.5	Prepare site for installation	3.0	68.8	80.0	71.4	39.3
70	1.3.3.6	Pack software package	3.4	68.8	73.3	78.6	39.6
71	1.3.3.7	Deliver after conformance verified	3.8	93.8	93.3	92.9	81.3
72	1.3.3.8	Document acceptance of software	2.9	62.5	71.4	85.7	38.3
73	1.3.3.9	Deliver software on time	4.0	88.2	86.7	100	76.5
74	1.3.3.10	Verify correct receipt	3.3	73.3	73.3	76.9	41.4
75	1.3.3.11	Provide handling and storage procedures	3.0	64.7	62.5	83.3	33.7
	1.3.4	**Service evaluation**					
76	1.3.4.1	SQA review with customers	3.8	82.4	70.6	100	58.1
77	1.3.4.2	Feedback customer information	4.2	100	100	92.9	92.9
78	1.3.4.3	Determine customer satisfaction level	3.9	88.2	70.6	100	62.3
79	1.3.4.4	Compare with competitors	3.4	82.4	56.3	78.6	36.4
80	1.3.4.5	Review customer satisfaction	3.7	75.0	66.7	84.6	42.3
81	1.3.4.6	Record customer failure reports	4.3	94.7	94.4	100	89.5
	2	**Software development subsystem**					
	2.1	**Software engineering methodologies**					
	2.1.1	**Software engineering modeling**					
82	2.1.1.1	Aware of state-of-the-art in software engineering	3.4	81.3	81.3	80.0	52.8
83	2.1.1.2	Survey methodologies/technologies adopted externally	3.1	80.0	71.4	85.7	49.0
84	2.1.1.3	Evaluate life cycle model	3.4	100	71.4	92.3	65.9
85	2.1.1.4	Evaluate prototype model	3.4	93.3	73.3	84.6	57.9
86	2.1.1.5	Evaluate OOP model	3.2	85.7	53.8	75.0	34.6
87	2.1.1.6	Evaluate combined model	2.9	71.4	38.5	63.6	17.5
88	2.1.1.7	Evaluate CASE model	2.8	71.4	46.2	72.7	24.0
89	2.1.1.8	Integrate methodologies and tools into process	4.1	100	92.9	100	92.9

90	2.1.1.9	Distinguish development category: system prototype/new system/improved version	3.6	87.5	62.5	71.4 39.1
	2.1.2	**Reuse methodologies**				
91	2.1.2.1	Determine organizational reuse strategy	3.8	93.8	56.3	80.0 42.2
92	2.1.2.2	Identify reusable components	4.2	100	73.3	86.7 63.6
93	2.1.2.3	Develop reusable components	3.9	88.2	52.9	81.3 38.0
94	2.1.2.4	Establish reuse library	3.7	81.3	43.8	81.3 28.9
95	2.1.2.5	Certify reusable components	3.9	88.2	47.1	82.4 34.2
96	2.1.2.6	Integrate reuse into life cycle	3.9	86.7	60.0	78.6 40.9
97	2.1.2.7	Propagate change carefully	4.2	100	62.5	87.5 54.7
	2.1.3	**Technology innovation**				
98	2.1.3.1	Plan technology change	3.4	81.3	68.8	93.8 52.4
99	2.1.3.2	Identify processes needed in technology change	3.6	87.5	62.5	87.5 47.9
100	2.1.3.3	Identify/replace obsolete technology/process	3.4	76.5	68.8	93.8 49.3
101	2.1.3.4	Select new technology	3.9	100	87.5	100 87.5
102	2.1.3.5	Introduce new technology/metrics/process	3.8	94.1	88.2	87.5 72.7
103	2.1.3.6	Pilot trial of new technology	3.4	87.5	73.3	92.9 59.6
104	2.1.3.7	Incorporate trialed technology into current process	3.8	87.5	81.3	92.9 66.0
	2.2	**Software development**				
	2.2.1	**Development process definition**				
105	2.2.1.1	Evaluate s/w development methodologies	3.9	93.8	87.5	78.6 64.5
106	2.2.1.2	Model software process	3.8	94.1	81.3	100 76.5
107	2.2.1.3	Describe activities and responsibilities	4.3	100	87.5	100 87.5
108	2.2.1.4	Establish task sequences	3.8	81.3	93.3	93.3 70.8
109	2.2.1.5	Identify process relationships	3.7	93.3	92.9	92.9 80.5
110	2.2.1.6	Document process activities	3.9	87.5	92.9	86.7 70.4
111	2.2.1.7	Identify control point of project	3.8	93.8	71.4	84.6 56.7
112	2.2.1.8	Maintain consistency across all processes	3.6	80.0	57.1	76.9 35.2
113	2.2.1.9	Develop s/w according to defined process	4.3	100	78.6	92.9 73.0
114	2.2.1.10	Derive project process by tailoring organization's standard process	4.3	100	72.7	92.9 67.5
115	2.2.1.11	Approval of processes and equipment	3.5	85.7	71.4	76.9 47.1
116	2.2.1.12	Identify special requirements in developing special system: real-time /safety-critical/etc	4.3	100	85.7	93.3 80.0
	2.2.2	**Requirement analysis**				
117	2.2.2.1	Analyze requirement according to defined process	4.1	100	84.6	83.3 70.5
118	2.2.2.2	Specify formal requirements	3.0	73.3	53.3	76.9 30.1
119	2.2.2.3	Define requirements feasibility/testability	3.8	93.3	76.9	75.0 53.8
120	2.2.2.4	Prevent ambiguities in specification	3.9	93.3	78.6	84.6 62.1
121	2.2.2.5	Interpret/clarify requirements	3.7	94.1	68.8	84.6 54.8
122	2.2.2.6	Specify acceptance criteria	3.8	87.5	100	86.7 75.8
123	2.2.2.7	Allocate requirements for processes	3.1	90.9	44.4	87.5 35.4
124	2.2.2.8	Adopt requirements acquisition tools	2.1	28.6	7.7	80.0 1.8
	2.2.3	**Design**				

125	2.2.3.1	Design system according to defined process	3.9	93.8	78.6	84.6	62.3
126	2.2.3.2	Design software architecture	4.2	100	100	100	100
127	2.2.3.3	Design module interfaces	4.1	100	81.3	87.5	71.1
128	2.2.3.4	Develop detailed design	3.6	88.2	93.8	76.5	63.3
129	2.2.3.5	Establish document traceability	3.9	88.9	63.6	78.6	44.4
130	2.2.3.6	Specify final design	3.8	86.7	64.3	78.6	43.8
131	2.2.3.7	Define design change procedure	4.0	100	53.3	91.7	48.9
132	2.2.3.8	Adopt architectural design tools	2.9	56.3	43.8	80.0	19.7
133	2.2.3.9	Adopt module design tools	2.9	62.5	73.3	76.9	35.3
	2.2.4	**Coding**					
134	2.2.4.1	Code according to defined process	3.8	87.5	68.8	85.7	51.6
135	2.2.4.2	Choose proper programming language(s)	3.8	93.8	81.3	92.9	70.7
136	2.2.4.3	Develop software modules	4.0	93.3	100	92.3	86.2
137	2.2.4.4	Develop unit verification procedures	3.8	93.8	68.8	86.7	55.9
138	2.2.4.5	Verify software modules	4.1	100	80.0	92.9	74.3
139	2.2.4.6	Document coding standards	4.1	88.2	82.4	93.3	67.8
140	2.2.4.7	Define coding styles	3.6	82.4	56.3	66.7	30.9
141	2.2.4.8	Adopt coding support/auto-generation tools	2.9	60.0	28.6	50.0	8.6
	2.2.5	**Module testing**					
142	2.2.5.1	Testing according to defined process	4.5	100	82.4	93.8	77.2
143	2.2.5.2	Determine test strategy	4.4	100	76.5	93.8	71.7
144	2.2.5.3	Specify test methods	4.1	94.1	76.5	92.9	66.8
145	2.2.5.4	Generate test	3.8	93.8	75.0	84.6	59.5
146	2.2.5.5	Conduct testing	4.3	100	86.7	85.7	74.3
147	2.2.5.6	Adopt module testing tools	3.1	71.4	57.1	69.2	28.3
	2.2.6	**Integration and system testing**					
148	2.2.6.1	Integration test according to defined process	4.3	100	80.0	92.9	74.3
149	2.2.6.2	Acceptance test according to defined process	4.1	100	80.0	92.9	74.3
150	2.2.6.3	System tests generation	3.8	92.3	69.2	83.3	53.3
151	2.2.6.4	Test integrated system	4.1	100	84.6	91.7	77.6
152	2.2.6.5	Adopt software integration tools	2.8	53.8	16.7	63.6	5.7
153	2.2.6.6	Adopt module cross-reference tools	3.1	76.9	16.7	81.8	10.5
154	2.2.6.7	Adopt system acceptance testing tools	3.1	76.9	25.0	90.9	17.5
	2.2.7	**Maintenance**					
155	2.2.7.1	Determine maintenance requirements	4.0	92.9	78.6	92.3	67.3
156	2.2.7.2	Analyze user problems and enhancements	4.0	100	92.3	100	92.3
157	2.2.7.3	Determine modifications for next upgrade	3.7	83.3	75.0	90.9	56.8
158	2.2.7.4	Implement/test modifications	3.7	90.9	72.7	80.0	52.9
159	2.2.7.5	Update user system	3.9	90.9	50.0	77.8	35.4
160	2.2.7.6	Maintenance consistency with specifications	3.9	100	54.5	90.9	49.6
161	2.2.7.7	Maintain nonconforming products	3.5	76.9	58.3	80.0	35.9
162	2.2.7.8	Record nonconformance treatment	3.9	92.3	75.0	90.9	62.9
163	2.2.7.9	Adopt regression testing tools	3.5	84.6	33.3	81.8	23.1
164	2.2.7.10	Conduct regression testing	4.1	85.7	50.0	90.9	39.0
	2.3	**Software engineering infrastructure**					
	2.3.1	**Environment**					

165	2.3.1.1	Identify environment requirements	4.0	94.1	93.8	93.8	82.7
166	2.3.1.2	Establish computer-supported cooperative work (CSCW) environment	3.3	62.5	50.0	84.6	26.4
167	2.3.1.3	Provide software engineering environment	3.7	84.2	68.4	100	57.6
168	2.3.1.4	Provide development supporting tools	4.1	93.8	81.3	93.3	71.1
169	2.3.1.5	Provide management supporting tools	3.4	77.8	70.6	80.0	43.9
170	2.3.1.6	Provide interactive communication environment	3.5	75.0	56.3	84.6	35.7
171	2.3.1.7	Maintain software engineering environment	3.2	81.3	64.3	81.8	42.7
	2.3.2	**Facilities**					
172	2.3.2.1	Plan required resources	4.1	88.2	87.5	84.6	65.3
173	2.3.2.2	Identify specialized facilities	3.6	81.3	68.8	84.6	47.3
174	2.3.2.3	Acquire resources	3.7	78.9	88.9	88.2	61.9
175	2.3.2.4	Check resources availability	3.7	93.8	81.3	92.3	70.3
176	2.3.2.5	Provide productive workspace	3.6	76.5	87.5	100	66.9
177	2.3.2.6	Provide data backup	3.6	88.2	100	93.3	82.4
178	2.3.2.7	Provide building facilities	3.1	73.3	86.7	100	63.6
179	2.3.2.8	Provide remote access facility	2.7	58.8	68.8	100	40.4
180	2.3.2.9	Adopt software design tools	3.6	93.8	57.1	100	53.6
181	2.3.2.10	Adopt software testing tools	3.8	93.8	66.7	85.7	53.6
182	2.3.2.11	Ensure data integrity	3.6	82.4	66.7	100	54.9
183	2.3.2.12	Register/maintain test equipment	3.3	76.5	64.3	76.9	37.8
184	2.3.2.13	Control customer-supplied equipment	3.1	66.7	62.5	71.4	29.8
185	2.3.2.14	Record equipment condition	2.4	50.0	53.8	61.5	16.6
186	2.3.2.15	Ensure equipment availability	2.6	50.0	61.5	81.8	25.2
	2.3.3	**Development support tools**					
187	2.3.3.1	CASE tools	3.1	71.4	61.5	81.8	36.0
188	2.3.3.2	Software requirements acquisition tools	2.9	71.4	33.3	70.0	16.7
189	2.3.3.3	Software design tools	3.4	76.9	64.3	90.9	45.0
190	2.3.3.4	Software testing tools	3.6	85.7	75.0	81.8	52.6
	2.3.4	**Management support tools**					
191	2.3.4.1	SQA management tools	3.0	61.5	36.4	88.9	19.9
192	2.3.4.2	Software requirements review tools	2.5	46.2	18.2	77.8	6.5
193	2.3.4.3	Software design review tools	2.8	58.3	36.4	87.5	18.6
194	2.3.4.4	Software testing analysis tools	3.3	83.3	54.5	88.9	40.4
195	2.3.4.5	Software configuration management tools	3.7	91.7	75.0	100	68.8
196	2.3.4.6	Software documentation processing tools	3.5	92.3	66.7	81.8	50.3
	3	**Management subsystem**					
	3.1	**SQA**					
	3.1.1	**SQA process definition**					
197	3.1.1.1	Define SQA procedure	4.0	87.5	75.0	86.7	56.9
198	3.1.1.2	Define project s/w engineering standards	4.1	94.7	88.9	94.4	79.5
199	3.1.1.3	Document SQA system	4.0	88.9	83.3	87.5	64.8
200	3.1.1.4	Issue quality manual	3.9	83.3	70.6	85.7	50.4

201	3.1.1.5	Distribute quality policy	4.1	94.1	75.0	85.7	60.5
202	3.1.1.6	Report SQA results	4.1	100	72.2	100	72.2
203	3.1.1.7	Assess process quality	4.1	100	64.7	85.7	55.5
204	3.1.1.8	Take correct actions	4.4	100	88.2	87.5	77.2
205	3.1.1.9	Assign independent reviewers	3.8	88.2	70.6	80.0	49.8
206	3.1.1.10	Define extent of inspection	3.5	94.1	43.8	92.3	38.0
207	3.1.1.11	Conduct SQA for each process	3.6	82.4	58.8	78.6	38.1
208	3.1.1.12	Assign qualified person(s) to special process	3.5	82.4	68.8	80.0	45.3
209	3.1.1.13	Document quality records	3.7	81.3	75.0	80.0	48.8
210	3.1.1.14	Review SQA system suitability	4.0	94.4	62.5	84.6	49.9
211	3.1.1.15	Decisional role of SQA in processes	3.7	88.2	56.3	78.6	39.0
212	3.1.1.16	Decisional role of SQA in final products	3.8	94.1	62.5	84.6	49.8
213	3.1.1.17	Adopt SQA tools	2.8	56.3	50.0	75.0	21.1
	3.1.2	**Requirement review**					
214	3.1.2.1	Specification verification	4.2	94.1	64.7	93.3	56.8
215	3.1.2.2	Formal review requirements	4.0	93.8	81.3	92.9	70.7
216	3.1.2.3	Review statutory requirements	3.2	83.3	61.5	81.8	42.0
217	3.1.2.4	Customer accepts specifications	3.9	92.9	64.3	81.8	48.8
218	3.1.2.5	Adopt specification verification tools	2.5	66.7	13.3	80.0	7.1
	3.1.3	**Design review**					
219	3.1.3.1	Define design review procedure	3.9	94.1	86.7	78.6	64.1
220	3.1.3.2	Document design review	4.0	93.8	87.5	85.7	70.3
221	3.1.3.3	Verify prototypes	3.6	75.0	57.1	84.6	36.3
222	3.1.3.4	Measure design review coverage	3.1	64.3	21.4	80.0	11.0
	3.1.4	**Code review**					
223	3.1.4.1	Conduct code walk-through	4.1	93.3	73.3	78.6	53.8
224	3.1.4.2	Conduct code review	3.9	88.2	76.5	76.5	51.6
225	3.1.4.3	Measure code review coverage	3.0	73.3	6.7	63.6	3.1
	3.1.5	**Module testing audit**					
226	3.1.5.1	Measure test coverage	4.1	93.8	56.3	84.6	44.6
227	3.1.5.2	Estimate remaining error distribution	2.8	62.5	37.5	61.5	14.4
228	3.1.5.3	Review test results	3.9	93.8	80.0	84.6	63.5
229	3.1.5.4	Static/dynamic module test analysis	3.2	78.6	61.5	90.9	44.0
	3.1.6	**Integration/system testing audit**					
230	3.1.6.1	Identify nonconforming software/functions	4.2	100	93.3	100	93.3
231	3.1.6.2	Define inspection procedure	3.6	85.7	69.2	75.0	44.5
232	3.1.6.3	Inspection against requirements	4.3	100	76.9	100	76.9
233	3.1.6.4	Document inspection/test results	4.1	92.9	78.6	91.7	66.9
234	3.1.6.5	Static/dynamic integration test analysis	3.0	71.4	46.2	66.7	22.0
235	3.1.6.6	Static/dynamic acceptance test analysis	3.0	69.2	45.5	80.0	25.2
	3.1.7	**Maintenance audit**					
236	3.1.7.1	Reinspect repaired products	3.6	85.7	69.2	91.7	54.4
237	3.1.7.2	Audit nonconformance records	3.5	100	69.2	90.0	62.3
238	3.1.7.3	Audit nonconformance treatment	3.4	83.3	58.3	80.0	38.9
239	3.1.7.4	Audit consistency with specification	3.8	92.3	61.5	90.9	51.6
240	3.1.7.5	Audit consistency of system documents	3.5	92.9	64.3	91.7	54.7

241	3.1.7.6	Audit consistency of system configuration	3.4	78.6	46.2	63.6	23.1
242	3.1.7.7	Audit user satisfaction with maintenance	3.4	84.6	50.0	72.7	30.8
243	3.1.7.8	Review regression testing results	3.5	85.7	50.0	90.9	39.0
	3.1.8	**Audit and inspection**					
244	3.1.8.1	Audit software development activities	3.9	93.8	75.0	80.0	56.3
245	3.1.8.2	Audit work products	3.8	92.9	60.0	71.4	39.8
246	3.1.8.3	Audit process quality	3.7	93.3	66.7	71.4	44.4
247	3.1.8.4	Audit on-site activities	3.2	84.6	46.2	72.7	28.4
248	3.1.8.5	Document audit results	3.7	92.3	69.2	83.3	53.3
249	3.1.8.6	Verify representativeness of examined samples	3.2	83.3	41.7	72.7	25.3
	3.1.9	**Peer review**					
250	3.1.9.1	Plan peer review	3.7	88.2	64.7	85.7	48.9
251	3.1.9.2	Select work products	3.5	80.0	57.1	83.3	38.1
252	3.1.9.3	Identify review standards	3.9	100	70.6	84.6	59.7
253	3.1.9.4	Establish completion criteria	4.2	100	64.7	85.7	55.5
254	3.1.9.5	Establish re-review criteria	3.1	76.5	20.0	80.0	12.2
255	3.1.9.6	Distribute review materials	3.5	88.2	66.7	92.3	54.3
256	3.1.9.7	Conduct peer review	3.9	94.4	77.8	88.2	64.8
257	3.1.9.8	Document review results	3.6	87.5	81.3	82.4	58.5
258	3.1.9.9	Take actions for review results	4.0	94.1	75.0	86.7	61.2
259	3.1.9.10	Track actions for review results	3.8	88.2	52.9	81.3	38.0
	3.1.10	**Defect control**					
260	3.1.10.1	Plan defect prevention	3.8	83.3	52.9	78.6	34.7
261	3.1.10.2	Defect reporting and record	4.2	88.9	76.5	93.8	63.7
262	3.1.10.3	Defect causal analysis	4.1	95.0	80.0	94.7	72.0
263	3.1.10.4	Propose process change for defect prevention	4.2	89.5	61.1	80.0	43.7
264	3.1.10.5	Track problem report	4.3	100	86.7	100	86.7
265	3.1.10.6	Prioritize problems	3.9	83.3	76.5	93.8	59.7
266	3.1.10.7	Determine resolutions	3.8	88.2	81.3	93.3	66.9
267	3.1.10.8	Correct defects	4.4	100	100	100	100
268	3.1.10.9	Review defect corrections	3.6	77.8	62.5	78.6	38.2
269	3.1.10.10	Distribute correction results	3.6	82.4	76.5	82.4	51.9
	3.1.11	**Subcontractor's quality control**					
270	3.1.11.1	Subcontractor's quantitative quality goals	3.3	86.7	46.7	76.9	31.1
271	3.1.11.2	Assess/test quality of subcontractor's product	3.9	100	68.8	92.3	63.5
272	3.1.11.3	Acceptance test for subcontractor's software	4.1	100	73.3	100	73.3
273	3.1.11.4	Safeguard customer-supplied products	3.9	92.3	76.9	100	71.0
274	3.1.11.5	Record customer-supplied products	3.5	83.3	69.2	91.7	52.9
	3.2	**Project planning**					
	3.2.1	**Project plan**					
275	3.2.1.1	Assign project proposal team	3.7	100	92.9	92.3	85.7
276	3.2.1.2	Design project process structure	3.9	100	78.6	92.3	72.5
277	3.2.1.3	Determine reuse strategy	3.4	71.4	35.7	84.6	21.6
278	3.2.1.4	Establish project schedule	4.5	100	100	93.3	93.3

279	3.2.1.5	Establish project commitments	4.1	100	92.9	92.9	86.2
280	3.2.1.6	Document project plans	4.1	93.8	93.8	93.3	82.0
281	3.2.1.7	Conduct progress management reviews	3.9	100	92.9	92.3	85.7
282	3.2.1.8	Conduct progress technical reviews	3.6	92.9	76.9	84.6	60.4
283	3.2.1.9	Management commitments in planning	3.9	93.3	71.4	83.3	55.6
284	3.2.1.10	Determine release strategy	3.4	73.3	73.3	84.6	45.5
285	3.2.1.11	Plan change control	3.4	78.6	53.8	91.7	38.8
286	3.2.1.12	Define plan change procedure	3.1	71.4	53.8	91.7	35.3
287	3.2.1.13	Plan development	4.1	100	100	92.9	92.9
288	3.2.1.14	Plan testing	4.0	92.9	92.3	84.6	72.5
289	3.2.1.15	Plan system integration	3.9	92.9	83.3	100	77.4
290	3.2.1.16	Plan process management	3.6	85.7	91.7	91.7	72.0
291	3.2.1.17	Plan maintenance	3.6	93.3	78.6	85.7	62.9
292	3.2.1.18	Plan review and authorization	3.4	85.7	61.5	83.3	44.0
293	3.2.1.19	Assign development task	3.6	78.6	92.3	92.3	66.9
294	3.2.1.20	Adopt project/process planning tools	2.9	64.3	57.1	84.6	31.1
	3.2.2	**Project estimation**					
295	3.2.2.1	Estimate project costs	3.8	87.5	92.9	84.6	68.8
296	3.2.2.2	Estimate project time	4.4	100	100	92.9	92.9
297	3.2.2.3	Estimate resources requirement	4.5	100	100	73.3	73.3
298	3.2.2.4	Estimate staff requirement	4.3	92.9	100	83.3	77.4
299	3.2.2.5	Estimate software size	3.9	86.7	69.2	81.8	49.1
300	3.2.2.6	Estimate software complexity	3.4	78.6	41.7	90.9	29.8
301	3.2.2.7	Estimate critical resources	3.8	86.7	46.2	91.7	36.7
	3.2.3	**Project risk avoidance**					
302	3.2.3.1	Identify project risks	3.8	88.2	50.0	86.7	38.2
303	3.2.3.2	Establish risk management scope	3.3	78.6	30.8	66.7	16.1
304	3.2.3.3	Identify unstable specification-related risks	3.3	81.3	43.8	69.2	24.6
305	3.2.3.4	Identify process change-related risks	3.1	73.3	28.6	63.6	13.3
306	3.2.3.5	Identify market-related risks	3.8	93.3	64.3	83.3	50.0
307	3.2.3.6	Analyze and prioritize risks	3.4	73.3	40.0	71.4	21.0
308	3.2.3.7	Develop mitigation strategies	3.1	73.3	40.0	58.3	17.1
309	3.2.3.8	Define risk metrics for probability/impact	2.9	75.0	20.0	61.5	9.2
310	3.2.3.9	Implement mitigation strategies	3.1	78.6	28.6	63.6	14.3
311	3.2.3.10	Assess risk mitigation activities	2.9	68.6	33.3	58.3	13.4
312	3.2.3.11	Take corrective actions for identified risk	4.0	93.3	73.3	73.3	50.2
	3.2.4	**Project quality plan**					
313	3.2.4.1	Plan SQA	4.1	94.1	88.2	88.2	73.3
314	3.2.4.2	Establish quality goals	4.2	100	80.0	86.7	69.3
315	3.2.4.3	Define quality quantitative metrics	3.9	88.2	75.0	81.3	53.8
316	3.2.4.4	Identify quality activities	4.1	100	78.6	85.7	67.3
317	3.2.4.5	Track project quality goals	3.8	94.1	76.5	81.3	58.5
318	3.2.4.6	SQA team participate in project planning	3.6	86.7	57.1	84.6	41.9
319	3.2.4.7	Plan maintenance	3.3	73.3	71.4	85.7	44.9
	3.3	**Project management**					
	3.3.1	**Process management**					

320	3.3.1.1	Plan quantitative process management	3.6	94.7	37.5	76.9	27.3
321	3.3.1.2	Conduct quantitative process management	3.5	89.5	29.4	64.3	16.9
322	3.3.1.3	Collect data for quantitative analysis	3.5	94.7	43.8	71.4	29.6
323	3.3.1.4	Control defined process quantitatively	3.4	94.1	37.5	64.3	22.7
324	3.3.1.5	Document quantitative analysis results	3.3	78.9	41.2	80.0	26.0
325	3.3.1.6	Benchmark organization's baseline of process capability	2.8	57.9	37.5	71.4	15.5
326	3.3.1.7	Manage project by defined process	3.8	94.7	66.7	88.2	55.7
327	3.3.1.8	Adopt project/process management tools	3.2	78.9	47.1	70.6	26.2
	3.3.2	**Process tracking**					
328	3.3.2.1	Track project progress	4.3	100	100	100	100
329	3.3.2.2	Track development schedule	4.2	100	94.1	100	94.1
330	3.3.2.3	Track process quality	3.7	100	72.2	66.7	48.1
331	3.3.2.4	Track software size	2.9	63.2	68.8	86.7	37.6
332	3.3.2.5	Track project cost	3.8	94.4	80.0	93.3	70.5
333	3.3.2.6	Track critical resources and performance	3.3	80.0	70.6	94.1	53.1
334	3.3.2.7	Track project risks	3.2	84.2	52.9	68.8	30.7
335	3.3.2.8	Track process productivity	2.9	68.4	37.5	61.5	15.8
336	3.3.2.9	Track system memory utilization	2.4	44.4	31.3	53.3	7.4
337	3.3.2.10	Track system throughput	2.5	55.6	46.7	66.7	17.3
338	3.3.2.11	Track system I/O channel capabilities	2.4	58.8	37.5	60.0	13.2
339	3.3.2.12	Track system networking	2.5	58.8	33.3	66.7	13.1
340	3.3.2.13	Adopt process tracking tools	2.6	55.6	25.0	50.0	6.9
341	3.3.2.14	Document project tracking data	3.1	76.5	60.0	73.3	33.6
342	3.3.2.15	Identify and handle process deviation	3.7	95.2	78.9	83.3	62.7
	3.3.3	**Configuration management**					
343	3.3.3.1	Establish configuration management library	3.8	84.2	77.8	94.4	61.9
344	3.3.3.2	Adopt configuration management tools	3.8	93.3	53.3	84.6	42.1
345	3.3.3.3	Identify product's configuration	4.2	100	82.4	88.2	72.7
346	3.3.3.4	Maintain configuration item descriptions	3.9	93.3	71.4	78.6	52.4
347	3.3.3.5	Control change requests	4.4	100	88.2	100	88.2
348	3.3.3.6	Release control	4.3	100	81.3	87.5	71.1
349	3.3.3.7	Maintain configuration item history	3.9	94.1	68.8	80.0	51.8
350	3.3.3.8	Report configuration status	3.6	81.3	73.3	86.7	51.6
	3.3.4	**Change control**					
351	3.3.4.1	Establish change requests/approval system	4.0	100	76.9	100	76.9
352	3.3.4.2	Control requirement change	4.1	100	71.4	85.7	61.2
353	3.3.4.3	Control design change	3.9	100	71.4	92.9	66.3
354	3.3.4.4	Control code change	3.8	93.3	78.6	92.9	68.1
355	3.3.4.5	Control test data change	3.3	73.3	57.1	84.6	35.5
356	3.3.4.6	Control environment change	3.0	78.6	53.8	81.8	34.6
357	3.3.4.7	Control schedule change	3.6	84.6	66.7	100	56.4
358	3.3.4.8	Control configuration change	3.8	82.4	73.3	86.7	52.3
359	3.3.4.9	Adopt change control tools	2.9	60.0	35.7	76.9	16.5
	3.3.5	**Process review**					
360	3.3.5.1	Review processes at milestones	3.8	93.8	80.0	84.6	63.5

361	3.3.5.2	Document project review data	3.6	80.0	64.3	69.2	35.6
362	3.3.5.3	Revise project process	3.7	80.0	57.1	85.7	39.2
363	3.3.5.4	Conduct statistical analysis of process	3.1	68.8	42.9	61.5	18.1
364	3.3.5.5	Gather process data	3.2	71.4	61.5	66.7	29.3
365	3.3.5.6	Compare actual/forecast errors	3.5	86.7	57.1	76.9	38.1
366	3.3.5.7	Compare actual/forecast schedule	4.1	100	57.1	92.9	53.1
367	3.3.5.8	Compare actual/forecast resources	4.0	100	46.2	76.9	35.5
	3.3.6	**Intergroup coordination**					
368	3.3.6.1	Define interface between project groups	3.7	73.3	66.7	80.0	39.1
369	3.3.6.2	Plan intergroup activities	3.6	87.5	66.7	92.9	54.2
370	3.3.6.3	Identify intergroup critical dependencies	3.8	81.3	53.3	86.7	37.6
371	3.3.6.4	Handle intergroup issues	3.8	88.2	68.8	81.3	49.3
372	3.3.6.5	Technical/management representatives coordination	3.6	94.1	75.0	93.3	65.9
373	3.3.6.6	Review last process output	3.1	75.0	40.0	78.6	23.6
374	3.3.6.7	Conduct intergroup representatives review	3.5	86.7	64.3	85.7	47.8
	3.4	**Contract and requirement management**					
	3.4.1	**Requirement management**					
375	3.4.1.1	Specify system requirements	4.7	100	100	94.1	94.1
376	3.4.1.2	Design system based on requirements	4.4	100	100	86.7	86.7
377	3.4.1.3	Allocate requirements	3.8	86.7	85.7	85.7	63.7
378	3.4.1.4	Determine operating environment impact	3.6	94.1	68.8	86.7	56.1
379	3.4.1.5	Determine software requirements	4.5	100	100	93.8	93.8
380	3.4.1.6	Analysis of software requirements	4.3	100	93.8	87.5	82.1
381	3.4.1.7	Evaluate requirements with customer	4.2	100	100	100	100
382	3.4.1.8	Update requirements for next iteration	3.8	81.3	80.0	80.0	52.0
383	3.4.1.9	Agree on requirements	4.3	93.8	93.8	93.3	82.0
384	3.4.1.10	Establish requirements standard	3.7	76.5	68.8	73.3	38.6
385	3.4.1.11	Manage requirements changes	4.1	94.1	75.0	87.5	61.8
386	3.4.1.12	Maintain requirements traceability	3.8	93.8	62.5	80.0	46.9
	3.4.2	**Contract management**					
387	3.4.2.1	Define contractual procedures	3.9	93.8	87.5	100	82.0
388	3.4.2.2	Prepare contract proposal	3.6	87.5	93.3	100	81.7
389	3.4.2.3	Review contract	3.9	100	70.6	85.7	60.5
390	3.4.2.4	Ensure agreement of terminology	4.0	100	56.3	93.3	52.5
391	3.4.2.5	Determine interfaces to independent agents	3.3	80.0	46.7	85.7	32.0
392	3.4.2.6	Assess contractor's capability	3.7	87.5	50.0	92.3	40.4
393	3.4.2.7	Document contractor's capability	3.2	75.0	50.0	91.7	34.4
	3.4.3	**Subcontractor management**					
394	3.4.3.1	Specify subcontracted development	4.0	100	85.7	92.3	79.1
395	3.4.3.2	Assess capability of subcontractors	3.9	93.8	80.0	100	75.0
396	3.4.3.3	Record acceptable subcontractors	3.5	80.0	57.1	76.9	35.2
397	3.4.3.4	Define scope of contracted work	4.0	93.8	80.0	86.7	65.0
398	3.4.3.5	Define interface of contracted work	3.9	100	92.3	100	92.3
399	3.4.3.6	Select qualified subcontractor	3.9	100	73.3	93.3	68.4

400	3.4.3.7	Approve subcontractor's plan	3.5	80.0	50.0	84.6	33.8
401	3.4.3.8	Maintain interchanges with subcontractors	3.6	93.3	78.6	85.7	62.9
402	3.4.3.9	Track subcontractor's development activities	3.2	78.6	41.7	72.7	23.8
403	3.4.3.10	Monitor subcontractor's SQA activities	3.4	86.7	50.0	92.3	40.0
404	3.4.3.11	Review subcontractor's work	3.5	93.3	78.6	92.3	67.7
405	3.4.3.12	Assess compliance of contracted product	4.2	100	85.7	100	85.7
406	3.4.3.13	Determine interfaces to subcontractors	3.5	92.3	76.9	83.3	59.2
407	3.4.3.14	Document subcontractor's records	2.9	66.7	50.0	66.7	22.2
	3.4.4	**Purchasing management**					
408	3.4.4.1	Identify need for purchasing	3.7	93.3	92.9	92.9	80.5
409	3.4.4.2	Define purchasing requirements	3.7	87.5	93.3	93.3	76.2
410	3.4.4.3	Prepare acquisition strategy	3.0	61.5	53.8	72.7	24.1
411	3.4.4.4	Prepare purchasing document	2.9	64.3	71.4	84.6	38.9
412	3.4.4.5	Prepare request for proposal	3.1	76.9	69.2	90.0	47.9
413	3.4.4.6	Review purchasing document	3.3	73.3	66.7	84.6	41.4
414	3.4.4.7	Select software product supplier	3.8	92.9	85.7	92.3	73.5
415	3.4.4.8	Verify purchased product	4.1	100	71.4	100	71.4
416	3.4.4.9	Manage purchased tools configuration	3.0	71.4	50.0	75.0	26.8
	3.5	**Document management**					
	3.5.1	**Documentation**					
417	3.5.1.1	Master list of project documents	3.8	88.2	81.3	86.7	62.1
418	3.5.1.2	Determine documentation requirements	3.5	88.2	68.8	81.3	49.3
419	3.5.1.3	Develop document	4.2	100	86.7	93.3	80.9
420	3.5.1.4	Check document	3.9	100	78.6	85.7	67.3
421	3.5.1.5	Control document issue	3.8	89.5	66.7	82.4	49.1
422	3.5.1.6	Maintain document	3.8	94.4	87.5	82.4	68.1
423	3.5.1.7	Documentation according to defined process	3.5	76.5	81.3	82.4	51.2
424	3.5.1.8	Establish documentation standards	3.8	88.2	81.3	86.7	62.1
425	3.5.1.9	Safety document storage	3.0	62.5	60.0	66.7	25.0
426	3.5.1.10	Identify current versions of documents	4.0	94.1	86.7	87.5	71.4
427	3.5.1.11	Adopt interactive documentation tools	2.9	64.7	53.3	62.5	21.6
	3.5.2	**Process database/library**					
428	3.5.2.1	Establish organization's process library	3.1	68.8	40.0	78.6	21.6
429	3.5.2.2	Establish organization's process database	3.1	73.3	28.6	72.7	15.2
430	3.5.3.3	Establish software reuse library	3.3	60.0	33.3	80.0	16.0
431	3.5.4.4	Establish organization's metrics database	3.6	70.6	43.8	80.0	24.7
432	3.5.5.5	Establish operation manual library	3.1	73.3	61.5	92.3	41.7
433	3.5.6.6	Establish practice benchmark database	2.3	50.0	0	58.3	0
	3.6	**Human resource management**					
	3.6.1	**Staff selection and allocation**					
434	3.6.1.1	Define qualifications for positions	4.1	92.3	83.3	91.7	70.5
435	3.6.1.2	Define experience for positions	3.9	92.9	78.6	85.7	62.5
436	3.6.1.3	Assign personnel selection group	3.3	92.9	76.9	92.9	66.3
437	3.6.1.4	Select staff by qualification /experience	4.1	100	85.7	92.9	79.6
	3.6.2	**Training**					

438	3.6.2.1	Plan training	3.9	100	85.7	85.7	73.5
439	3.6.2.2	Identify training needs	4.1	100	93.8	93.8	87.9
440	3.6.2.3	Develop training courses	3.5	85.7	71.4	85.7	52.5
441	3.6.2.4	Approval of training courses	3.2	78.6	38.5	90.0	27.2
442	3.6.2.5	Conduct technical training	4.1	100	76.5	87.5	66.9
443	3.6.2.6	Conduct management training	3.7	92.9	50.0	78.6	36.5
444	3.6.2.7	Document training records	3.6	82.4	81.3	93.3	62.5

Appendix E

SEPRM PROCESS ASSESSMENT TEMPLATES

Template E.1 Assessment Purpose

ID#: _____   **Date:** _____

No.	Subject	Remarks
1	Organization to be assessed	Specify name of organization
2	Department to be assessed	Specify unit of organization
3	Project(s) to be assessed	Specify project name(s)
4	Sponsor of the assessment	Identify sponsor of the assessment
5	Aims of assessment	Specify aims of assessment
5.1	Process establishment	
5.2	Process capability assessment	
5.3	Process improvement	
5.4	Other (to be specified)	
6	Assessment classification	Specify type of assessment
6.1	Conformance of assessment to a certain model/standard	
6.2	Independent (third-party) assessment	

6.3	Second-party assessment	
6.4	Self-assessment	
6.5	Couched self-assessment	
6.6	Other (to be specified)	
7	Provisional date for assessment	Describe provisional date for the assessment
8	Special need(s) for assessment	Specify any special needs for the assessment

Template E.2 Assessment Scope

ID#: _____   **Date:** _____

No.	Subject	Remarks
1	Project to be assessed	
2	Processes to be assessed in SEPRM	Specify processes to be assessed
2.1	Organization process subsystem	
2.1.1	Organization structure process category	
2.1.1.1	Organization definition	
2.1.1.2	Project organization	
2.1.2	Organizational process category	
2.1.2.1	Organization process definition	
2.1.2.2	Organization process improvement	
2.1.3	Customer service process category	
2.1.3.1	Customer relations	
2.1.3.2	Customer support	
2.1.3.3	Software/system delivery	
2.1.3.4	Service evaluation	
2.2	Development process subsystem	
2.2.1	Software engineering methodology process category	
2.2.1.1	Software engineering modeling	
2.2.1.2	Reuse methodologies	
2.2.1.3	Technology innovation	
2.2.2	Software development process category	
2.2.2.1	Development process definition	
2.2.2.2	Requirement analysis	
2.2.2.3	Design	
2.2.2.4	Coding	
2.2.2.5	Module testing	
2.2.2.6	Integration and system testing	
2.2.2.7	Maintenance	
2.2.3	Software development environment process category	
2.2.3.1	Environment	
2.2.3.2	Facilities	
2.2.3.3	Development support tools	
2.2.3.4	Management support tools	
2.3	Management process subsystem	
2.3.1	Software quality assurance (SQA) process category	

2.3.1.1	SQA process definition	
2.3.1.2	Requirement review	
2.3.1.3	Design review	
2.3.1.4	Code review	
2.3.1.5	Module testing audit	
2.3.1.6	Integration and system testing audit	
2.3.1.7	Maintenance audit	
2.3.1.8	Audit and inspection	
2.3.1.9	Peer review	
2.3.1.10	Defect control	
2.3.1.11	Subcontractor's quality control	
2.3.2	Project planning process category	
2.3.2.1	Project plan	
2.3.2.2	Project estimation	
2.3.2.3	Project risk avoidance	
2.3.2.4	Project quality plan	
2.3.3	Project management process category	
2.3.3.1	Process management	
2.3.3.2	Process tracking	
2.3.3.3	Configuration management	
2.3.3.4	Change control	
2.3.3.5	Process review	
2.3.3.6	Intergroup coordination	
2.3.4	Contract and requirement management process category	
2.3.4.1	Requirement management	
2.3.4.2	Contract management	
2.3.4.3	Subcontractor management	
2.3.4.4	Purchasing management	
2.3.5	Document management process category	
2.3.5.1	Documentation	
2.3.5.2	Process database/library	
2.3.6	Human resource management process category	
2.3.6.1	Staff selection and allocation	
2.3.6.2	Training	
3	Constraints of assessment	For instance, resources, budget, and critical milestones
4	Assessment output requirements	Tick and describe additional output of assessment

4.1	Project process capability level	
4.2	Process capability profile	
4.3	Process strengths and weaknesses analysis report	
4.4	Potential process improvement opportunities	
4.5	Executive summary of assessment results	
5	Background factors which may affect performance	

Template E.3 Assessment Team and Responsibilities

ID#: _____   **Date:** _____

No.	Role [Name]	Responsibility
1	Sponsor	
		- prepare assessment agreement - select unit representative(s) - organize assessment supporting activities - review assessment report - report to higher management
2	Lead Assessor	
		- prepare assessment agreement with sponsor - select assessor(s) with sponsor - develop assessment brief - organize assessment activities - review assessment report - present assessment report
3	Assessors	
3.1	Assessor 1	
4	Others	
4.1	Project Management Representative	
4.2	Project Technical Representative	

Table E.4 Assessment Confidentiality Agreement

Assessment Confidentiality Agreement

ID#: _____   **Date:** _____

1. Scope and purpose of this document

This document has been agreed to provide mutual confidentiality to all parties involved in the assessment to be conducted at Organization X during <DD1/MM1/YY1> to <DD2/MM2/YY2>.

2. Parties to the agreement

The parties in this agreement will be Organization X (herein referred to as "Party A") and Organization Y (herein referred to as "Party B").

3. Confidentiality

Throughout the course of the assessment, and all times thereafter, the parties are hereby bound to observe complete confidentiality as to all matters concerning the affairs of each other; and all details relating to the assessment, now and in the future. None of the parties (including any associated companies or subsidiaries) will disclose information regarding the outcome of the assessment or engage in publicity pertaining to the other party without prior agreement from the other party.

All parties hereby confirm their acceptance.

Signed for and on behalf of Party A   Signed for and on behalf of Party B

Signature ....   Signature ....

Full name   Full name

(print) ....   (print) ....

Position	Project manager	Position	Lead assessor
Address	....	Address	....
	....		
....			
	....		
....			
Date		Date	
Place	....	Place	....

Table E.5 Assessment Schedule and Resources

ID#:   Date:

No.	Subject	Responsibility	Resource	Planed date	Completed date
1	Initiation of an assessment	Lead assessor/sponsor			
2	Sponsor commitment	Sponsor			
3	Define assessment purpose	Lead assessor/sponsor			
4	Define assessment scope	Lead assessor/sponsor			
5	Sponsor approval of assessment input	Lead assessor/sponsor			
6	Appoint assessment team	Lead assessor/sponsor			
7	Prepare assessment confidentiality agreement	Lead assessor/sponsor			
8	Plan schedule and Resources	Lead assessor/sponsor			
9	Determine assessment reference model, assessment model, and tool	Assessors			
10	Map customer's processes to SEPRM model	Assessors			
11	Define processes to be assessed and target capability levels	Assessors/ Sponsor			
12	Develop assessment brief	Lead assessor			
13	Organizational unit briefing	Lead assessor/sponsor			
14	Data collection	Assessors/ Assessees			
15	Data validation	Assessors/ Assessees			
16	Capability rating and analysis	Assessors/ Assessees			
17	Briefing initial assessment results	Assessors/ sponsor/ assessees			
18	Process strengths and weaknesses analysis	Assessors			
19	Process improvement opportunity analysis	Assessors			

20	Develop assessment report	Lead assessor/sponsor			
21	Review and presentation of assessment report	Lead assessor/sponsor/ assessees			
22	Action plan for process improvement	Sponsor/ competent assessor/ assessees			
23	Other (to be specified)				

Table E.6 Processes to be Assessed and Target Capability Levels

ID#:   Date:

No.	Process	Selection in Assessment	Target Capability Level	Corresponding Processes on Site
1	Organization subsystem			
1.1	Organization structure category			
1.1.1	Organization definition			
1.1.2	Project organization			
1.2	Organization process category			
1.2.1	Organization process definition			
1.2.2	Organization process improvement			
1.3	Customer service category			
1.3.1	Customer relations			
1.3.2	Customer support			
1.3.3	Software/system delivery			
1.3.4	Service evaluation			
2	Development			
2.1	Software engineering methodology category			
2.1.1	Software engineering modeling			
2.1.2	Reuse methodologies			
2.1.3	Technology innovation			
2.2	Software development category			
2.2.1	Development process definition			
2.2.2	Requirement analysis			
2.2.3	Design			
2.2.4	Coding			
2.2.5	Module testing			
2.2.6	Integration and system testing			
2.2.7	Maintenance			
2.3	Software development environment category			
2.3.1	Environment			
2.3.2	Facilities			
2.3.3	Development support tools			
2.3.4	Management support tools			
3	Management			
3.1	Software quality assurance category			
3.1.1	SQA process definition			
3.1.2	Requirement review			
3.1.3	Design review			
3.1.4	Code review			
3.1.5	Module testing audit			

3.1.6	Integration and system testing audit			
3.1.7	Maintenance audit			
3.1.8	Audit and inspection			
3.1.9	Peer review			
3.1.10	Defect control			
3.1.11	Subcontractor's quality control			
3.2	**Project planning category**			
3.2.1	Project plan			
3.2.2	Project estimation			
3.2.3	Project risk avoidance			
3.2.4	Project quality plan			
3.3	**Project management category**			
3.3.1	Process management			
3.3.2	Process tracking			
3.3.3	Configuration management			
3.3.4	Change control			
3.3.5	Process review			
3.3.6	Intergroup coordination			
3.4	**Contract and requirement management category**			
3.4.1	Requirement management			
3.4.2	Contract management			
3.4.3	Subcontractor management			
3.4.4	Purchasing management			
3.5	**Document management category**			
3.5.1	Documentation			
3.5.2	Process database/library			
3.6	**Human resource management category**			
3.6.1	Staff selection and allocation			
3.6.2	Training			

Table E.7 Assessment Brief

ID#: _____   Date: _____

No.	Item	Remark
1	Organization	Refer to Template E.1
2	Department to be assessed	Refer to Template E.1
3	Project(s)	Refer to Template E.1
4	Sponsor	Refer to Template E.1
5	Purpose of assessment	Refer to Template E.1
6	Scope of assessment	Refer to Template E.2
7	Constraints of assessment	Refer to Template E.2
8	Assessment team	Refer to Template E.3
9	Resources needed	Estimate amount of effort required and type of resources
10	Key milestones	Refer to Template E.5
11	Summary of process to be assessed and target capability level(s)	Refer to Template E.6

12	Assessment approach	Describe method and approach adopted for the assessment
13	Other	To be specified by assessors

Table E.8 Process Strengths and Weaknesses Analysis

ID#: _____   **Date:** _____

No.	Process	Assessed Level [AL]	Targeted Level [TL]	Strengths(+)/ Weaknesses (-) [AL-TL]
1	Organization			
1.1	Organization structure category			
1.1.1	Organization definition			
1.1.2	Project organization			
1.2	Organization process category			
1.2.1	Organization process definition			
1.2.2	Organization process improvement			
1.3	Customer service category			
1.3.1	Customer relations			
1.3.2	Customer support			
1.3.3	Software and system delivery			
1.3.4	Service evaluation			
2	Development			
2.1	Software engineering methodology category			
2.1.1	Software engineering modeling			
2.1.2	Reuse methodologies			
2.1.3	Technology innovation			
2.2	Software development category			
2.2.1	Development process definition			
2.2.2	Requirement analysis			
2.2.3	Design			
2.2.4	Coding			
2.2.5	Module testing			
2.2.6	Integration and system testing			
2.2.7	Maintenance			
2.3	Software development environment category			
2.3.1	Environment			
2.3.2	Facilities			
2.3.3	Development support tools			
2.3.4	Management support tools			
3	Management			
3.1	Software quality assurance category			
3.1.1	SQA process definition			
3.1.2	Requirement review			
3.1.3	Design review			
3.1.4	Code review			
3.1.5	Module testing audit			
3.1.6	Integration and system testing audit			

3.1.7	Maintenance audit			
3.1.8	Audit and inspection			
3.1.9	Peer review			
3.1.10	Defect control			
3.1.11	Subcontractor's quality control			
3.2	**Project planning category**			
3.2.1	Project plan			
3.2.2	Project estimation			
3.2.3	Project risk avoidance			
3.2.4	Project quality plan			
3.3	**Project management category**			
3.3.1	Process management			
3.3.2	Process tracking			
3.3.3	Configuration management			
3.3.4	Change control			
3.3.5	Process review			
3.3.6	Intergroup coordination			
3.4	**Contract and requirement management category**			
3.4.1	Requirement management			
3.4.2	Contract management			
3.4.3	Subcontractor management			
3.4.4	Purchasing management			
3.5	**Document management category**			
3.5.1	Documentation			
3.5.2	Process database/library			
3.6	**Human resource management category**			
3.6.1	Staff selection and allocation			
3.6.2	Training			

Table E.9 Process Improvement Opportunities Analysis

ID#:   Date:

No.	Process	Strengths(+)/ Weaknesses (-) [AL-TL]	Improvement Priority (IP)	Remarks and Risks
1	Organization			
1.1	Organization structure category			
1.1.1	Organization definition			
1.1.2	Project organization			
1.2	Organization process category			
1.2.1	Organization process definition			
1.2.2	Organization process improvement			
1.3	Customer service category			
1.3.1	Customer relations			
1.3.2	Customer support			
1.3.3	Software and system delivery			
1.3.4	Service evaluation			
2	Development			
2.1	Software engineering methodology category			
2.1.1	Software engineering modeling			
2.1.2	Reuse methodologies			
2.1.3	Technology innovation			
2.2	Software development category			
2.2.1	Development process definition			
2.2.2	Requirement analysis			
2.2.3	Design			
2.2.4	Coding			
2.2.5	Module testing			
2.2.6	Integration and system testing			
2.2.7	Maintenance			
2.3	Software engineering infrastructure category			
2.3.1	Environment			
2.3.2	Facilities			
2.3.3	Development support tools			
2.3.4	Management support tools			
3	Management			
3.1	Software quality assurance category			
3.1.1	SQA process definition			
3.1.2	Requirement review			
3.1.3	Design review			
3.1.4	Code review			
3.1.5	Module testing audit			

3.1.6	Integration and system testing audit			
3.1.7	Maintenance audit			
3.1.8	Audit and inspection			
3.1.9	Peer review			
3.1.10	Defect control			
3.1.11	Subcontractor's quality control			
3.2	Project planning category			
3.2.1	Project plan			
3.2.2	Project estimation			
3.2.3	Project risk avoidance			
3.2.4	Project quality plan			
3.3	Project management category			
3.3.1	Process management			
3.3.2	Process tracking			
3.3.3	Configuration management			
3.3.4	Change control			
3.3.5	Process review			
3.3.6	Intergroup coordination			
3.4	Contract and requirement management category			
3.4.1	Requirement management			
3.4.2	Contract management			
3.4.3	Subcontractor management			
3.4.4	Purchasing management			
3.5	Document management category			
3.5.1	Documentation			
3.5.2	Process database/library			
3.6	Human resource management category			
3.6.1	Staff selection and allocation			
3.6.2	Training			

Appendix F

ISO/IEC 12207 SOFTWARE LIFE CYCLE PROCESSES

No.	Group	Process	Process Activity (PA)	Process Task (PT)
1	Primary life cycle processes	5	35	135
1.1		Acquisition	5	23
1.1.1			Initiation	9
1.1.2			Request for proposal/tender preparation	4
1.1.3			Contract preparation and update	5
1.1.4			Supplier monitoring	2
1.1.5			Acceptance and completion	3
1.2		Supply	7	24
1.2.1			Initiation	2
1.2.2			Preparation of response	1
1.2.3			Contract	2
1.2.4			Planning	5
1.2.5			Execution and control	6
1.2.6			Review and evaluation	6
1.2.7			Delivery and completion	2
1.3		Development	13	55
1.3.1			Process implementation	5
1.3.2			System requirements analysis	2
1.3.3			System architecture design	2
1.3.4			Software requirements analysis	3
1.3.5			Software architectural design	7
1.3.6			Software detailed design	8
1.3.7			Software coding and testing	5

1.3.8		Software integration	6
1.3.9		Software qualification testing	5
1.3.10		System integration	3
1.3.11		System qualification testing	4
1.3.12		Software installation	2
1.3.13		Software acceptance support	3
1.4	Operation	4	9
1.4.1		Process implementation	3
1.4.2		Operational testing	2
1.4.3		System operation	1
1.4.4		User support	3
1.5	Maintenance	6	24
1.5.1		Process implementation	3
1.5.2		Problem and modification analysis	5
1.5.3		Modification implementation	2
1.5.4		Maintenance review/acceptance	2
1.5.5		Migration	7
1.5.6		Software retirement	5
2	Supporting life cycle processes	8	25	70
2.1	Documentation	4	7
2.1.1		Process implementation	1
2.1.2		Design and development	3
2.1.3		Production	2
2.1.4		Maintenance	1
2.2	Configuration management	6	6
2.2.1		Process implementation	1
2.2.2		Configuration identification	1
2.2.3		Configuration control	1
2.2.4		Configuration status accounting	1
2.2.5		Configuration evaluation	1
2.2.6		Release management and delivery	1
2.3	Quality assurance	4	16
2.3.1		Process implementation	6
2.3.2		Product assurance	3
2.3.3		Process assurance	6
2.3.4		Assurance of quality system	1
2.4	Verification	2	13
2.4.1		Process implementation	6
2.4.2		Verification	7
2.5	Validation	2	10
2.5.1		Process implementation	5
2.5.2		Validation	5
2.6	Joint review	3	8

2.6.1			Process implementation	6
2.6.2			Project management reviews	1
2.6.3			Technical reviews	1
2.7		**Audit**	**2**	**8**
2.7.1			Process implementation	7
2.7.2			Audit	1
2.8		**Problem resolution**	**2**	**2**
2.8.1			Process implementation	1
2.8.2			Problem resolution	1
3	**Organization life cycle processes**	**4**	**14**	**27**
3.1		**Management**	**5**	**12**
3.1.1			Initiation and scope definition	3
3.1.2			Planning	1
3.1.3			Execution and control	4
3.1.4			Review and evaluation	2
3.1.5			Closure	2
3.2		**Infrastructure**	**3**	**5**
3.2.1			Process implementation	2
3.2.2			Establishment of the infrastructure	2
3.2.3			Maintenance of the infrastructure	1
3.3		**Implement**	**3**	**6**
3.3.1			Process establishment	1
3.3.2			Process assessment	2
3.3.3			Process improvement	3
3.4		**Training**	**3**	**4**
3.4.1			Process implementation	1
3.4.2			Training material development	1
3.4.3			Training plan implementation	2
Total	**3**	**17**	**74**	**232**

Appendix G

ISO/IEC CD 15288 SYSTEM LIFE CYCLE PROCESSES

No.	Group	Process	Process Activity (PA)
1	Agreement processes	2	12
1.1		Acquisition	7
1.1.1			Plan the acquisition
1.1.2			Prepare the request for proposal
1.1.3			Solicit supplier proposals
1.1.4			Evaluate supplier proposals
1.1.5			Negotiate the agreement
1.1.6			Monitor the agreement
1.1.7			Conclude the agreement
1.2		Supply	5
1.2.1			Plan to respond to solicitation
1.2.2			Prepare the proposal
1.2.3			Negotiate the agreement
1.2.4			Execute the proposal
1.2.5			Monitor the agreement
2	Enterprise processes	4	32
2.1		Enterprise management	7
2.1.1			Strategic planning
2.1.2			Tactical planning
2.1.3			Set system life cycle policy
2.1.4			Define life cycle responsibility
2.1.5			Enterprise impact assessment
2.1.6			Assess life cycles
2.1.7			Enterprise change management

2.2		Investment management	7
2.2.1			Identify new business opportunities
2.2.2			Initiate new acquisition project
2.2.3			Initiate new supply project
2.2.4			Allocate resources for projects
2.2.5			Identify expected project outcomes
2.2.6			Identify interface between projects
2.2.7			Specify project milestones
2.2.8			Review ongoing projects
2.2.9			Project cancellation
2.3		System life cycle processes management	9
2.3.1			Establish standard system life cycle processes
2.3.2			Establish tailoring methods
2.3.3			Deploy standard processes in projects
2.3.4			Establish process performance metrics
2.3.5			Monitor process execution
2.3.6			Determine process improvement opportunities
2.3.7			Conduct process improvement
2.3.8			Provide project management aids
2.3.9			Control project management interfaces
2.4		Resource management	9
2.4.1			Maintain staff resources and quality
2.4.2			Define recruitment requirements
2.4.3			Provide project with competent staff
2.4.4			Provide training for technical and managerial personnel
2.4.5			Evaluate performance of staff
2.4.6			Establish reward mechanism
2.4.7			Define and maintain information systems
2.4.8			Provide resource infrastructure support
2.4.9			Provide working environment
3	Project management processes	7	44
3.1		Planning	8
3.1.1			Identify project objectives
3.1.2			Establish project scope and tasks
3.1.3			Establish project schedule
3.1.4			Establish project costs
3.1.5			Define project team
3.1.6			Define project infrastructure
3.1.7			Define project acquisitions
3.1.8			Define project communication

3.2		Assessment	7
3.2.1			Assess project scope and tasks
3.2.2			Assess project schedule
3.2.3			Assess project costs
3.2.4			Assess project team
3.2.5			Assess project infrastructure
3.2.6			Assess project acquisitions
3.2.7			Assess project communication
3.3		Control	8
3.3.1			Control project tasks
3.3.2			Control project schedule
3.3.3			Control project costs
3.3.4			Control project quality
3.3.5			Control project team
3.3.6			Control project infrastructure
3.3.7			Control project acquisitions
3.3.8			Control project communication
3.4		Decision management	5
3.4.1			Decision management planning
3.4.2			Problem and opportunity statement
3.4.3			Cause analysis
3.4.4			Decision resolution
3.4.5			Decision reporting
3.5		Risk management	7
3.5.1			Risk management plan
3.5.2			Define risk categories
3.5.3			Identify threats
3.5.4			Analyze risks
3.5.5			Control risk
3.5.6			Assess risk management effectiveness
3.5.7			Document risks
3.6		Configuration management	5
3.6.1			Configuration management planning
3.6.2			Configuration identification
3.6.3			Configuration documentation
3.6.4			Configuration change control
3.6.5			Configuration status accounting
3.7		Quality management	4
3.7.1			Establish quality management infrastructure
3.7.2			Establish quality management plans
3.7.3			Performance assessment
3.7.4			Corrective actions
4	Technical Processes	10	66
4.1		Stakeholder needs	10

		definition	
4.1.1			Recognize need or opportunity
4.1.2			Identify stakeholders
4.1.3			Needs elicitation
4.1.4			Context analysis
4.1.5			Human factors analysis
4.1.6			Safety factors analysis
4.1.7			Security factors analysis
4.1.8			Resolve stakeholder need conflict
4.1.9			Confirm stakeholder needs
4.1.10			Baseline the stakeholder needs
4.2		Requirements analysis	9
4.2.1			Define system functional boundaries
4.2.2			Functional analysis
4.2.3			Define performance measures
4.2.4			Human factors
4.2.5			Safety
4.2.6			Security
4.2.7			Analyze system requirements integrity
4.2.8			Requirements tracing
4.2.9			Establish requirements baseline
4.3		Architectural design	8
4.3.1			Partitioning
4.3.2			Procedure, acquire or reuse analysis
4.3.3			Component definition
4.3.4			Design trade-off
4.3.5			Interface definition
4.3.6			Review architectural design
4.3.7			Specify components
4.3.8			Baseline the architectural design
4.4		Implementation	5
4.4.1			Component specification
4.4.2			Component detailed design
4.4.3			Component fabrication
4.4.4			Component integration
4.4.5			Component verification
4.5		Integration	5
4.5.1			Integration planning
4.5.2			Receive components
4.5.3			Component acceptance
4.5.4			Integrate components
4.5.5			Document integration data
4.6		Verification	5
4.6.1			Define verification strategy
4.6.2			Plan verification
4.6.3			Detection of nonconformance and faults

4.6.4			Diagnosis of nonconformance and faults
4.6.5			Fault reporting and analysis
4.7		**Transition**	**7**
4.7.1			Plan transition
4.7.2			Prepare operating site
4.7.3			Deliver system product
4.7.4			Install system product
4.7.5			Accustom operators
4.7.6			Commission system
4.7.7			Record installation results
4.8		**Validation**	**5**
4.5.1			Define validation strategy
4.5.2			Plan validation
4.5.3			Detection of nonconformance
4.5.4			Diagnosis of nonconformance
4.5.5			Nonconformance reporting and analysis
4.9		**Operations**	**6**
4.9.1			System application
4.9.2			Staffing
4.9.3			Training
4.9.4			Operation management
4.9.5			Performance monitoring
4.9.6			Problem reporting and analysis
4.10		**Disposal**	**6**
4.10.1			Deactivation
4.10.2			Removal
4.10.3			Reuse
4.10.4			Storage
4.10.5			Destruction
4.10.6			Information archiving
Total	**4**	**23**	**154**

Index

699